(Continued on back endsheets)

Modern British Essayists, First Series

Dictionary of Literary Biography • Volume Ninety-eight

Modern British Essayists,
First Series

8346

Edited by
Robert Beum

A Bruccoli Clark Layman Book
Gale Research Inc.
Detroit, New York, London

Printed in the United States of America

Published simultaneously in the United Kingdom
by Gale Reseach International Limited
(An affiliated company of Gale Reseach Inc.)

The paper used in this publication meets the minimum requirements
of American National Standard for Information Sciences—Permanence
Paper for Printed Library Materials, ANSI Z39.48-1984. ∞™

Copyright © 1990
Gale Research Inc.
835 Penobscot Bldg.
Detroit, MI 48226-4094

ISBN 0-8103-4578-1
90-39010 CIP

For Marynel

Contents

Plan of the Series

. . . Almost the most prodigious asset of a country, and perhaps its most precious possession, is its native literary product—when that product is fine and noble and enduring.

Mark Twain*

The advisory board, the editors, and the publisher of the *Dictionary of Literary Biography* are joined in endorsing Mark Twain's declaration. The literature of a nation provides an inexhaustible resource of permanent worth. We intend to make literature and its creators better understood and more accessible to students and the reading public, while satisfying the standards of teachers and scholars.

To meet these requirements, *literary biography* has been construed in terms of the author's achievement. The most important thing about a writer is his writing. Accordingly, the entries in *DLB* are career biographies, tracing the development of the author's canon and the evolution of his reputation.

The purpose of *DLB* is not only to provide reliable information in a convenient format but also to place the figures in the larger perspective of literary history and to offer appraisals of their accomplishments by qualified scholars.

The publication plan for *DLB* resulted from two years of preparation. The project was proposed to Bruccoli Clark by Frederick G. Ruffner, president of the Gale Research Company, in November 1975. After specimen entries were prepared and typeset, an advisory board was formed to refine the entry format and develop the series rationale. In meetings held during 1976, the publisher, series editors, and advisory board approved the scheme for a comprehensive biographical dictionary of persons who contributed to North American literature. Editorial work on the first volume began in January 1977, and it was published in 1978. In order to make *DLB* more than a reference tool and to compile volumes that individually have claim to status as lit-

erary history, it was decided to organize volumes by topic, period, or genre. Each of these freestanding volumes provides a biographical-bibliographical guide and overview for a particular area of literature. We are convinced that this organization—as opposed to a single alphabet method—constitutes a valuable innovation in the presentation of reference material. The volume plan necessarily requires many decisions for the placement and treatment of authors who might properly be included in two or three volumes. In some instances a major figure will be included in separate volumes, but with different entries emphasizing the aspect of his career appropriate to each volume. Ernest Hemingway, for example, is represented in *American Writers in Paris, 1920-1939* by an entry focusing on his expatriate apprenticeship; he is also in *American Novelists, 1910-1945* with an entry surveying his entire career. Each volume includes a cumulative index of subject authors and articles. Comprehensive indexes to the entire series are planned.

With volume ten in 1982 it was decided to enlarge the scope of *DLB*. By the end of 1986 twenty-one volumes treating British literature had been published, and volumes for Commonwealth and Modern European literature were in progress. The series has been further augmented by the *DLB Yearbooks* (since 1981) which update published entries and add new entries to keep the *DLB* current with contemporary activity. There have also been *DLB Documentary Series* volumes which provide biographical and critical source materials for figures whose work is judged to have particular interest for students. One of these companion volumes is entirely devoted to Tennessee Williams.

We define literature as the *intellectual commerce of a nation:* not merely as belles lettres but as that ample and complex process by which ideas are generated, shaped, and transmitted. *DLB* entries are not limited to "creative writers" but extend to other figures who in their time and in their way influenced the mind of a people. Thus the series encompasses historians, journalists, publishers, and screenwriters. By this means readers of *DLB* may be aided to perceive litera-

*From an unpublished section of Mark Twain's autobiography, copyright © by the Mark Twain Company.

ture not as cult scripture in the keeping of intellectual high priests but firmly positioned at the center of a nation's life.

DLB includes the major writers appropriate to each volume and those standing in the ranks immediately behind them. Scholarly and critical counsel has been sought in deciding which minor figures to include and how full their entries should be. Wherever possible, useful references are made to figures who do not warrant separate entries.

Each *DLB* volume has a volume editor responsible for planning the volume, selecting the figures for inclusion, and assigning the entries. Volume editors are also responsible for preparing, where appropriate, appendices surveying the major periodicals and literary and intellectual movements for their volumes, as well as lists of further readings. Work on the series as a whole is coordinated at the Bruccoli Clark Layman editorial center in Columbia, South Carolina, where the editorial staff is responsible for accuracy of the published volumes.

One feature that distinguishes *DLB* is the illustration policy–its concern with the iconography of literature. Just as an author is influenced by his surroundings, so is the reader's understanding of the author enhanced by a knowledge of his environment. Therefore *DLB* volumes include not only drawings, paintings, and photographs of authors, often depicting them at various stages in their careers, but also illustrations of their families and places where they lived. Title pages are regularly reproduced in facsimile along with dust jackets for modern authors. The dust jackets are a special feature of *DLB* because they often document better than anything else the way in which an author's work was perceived in its own time. Specimens of the writers' manuscripts are included when feasible.

Samuel Johnson rightly decreed that "The chief glory of every people arises from its authors." The purpose of the *Dictionary of Literary Biography* is to compile literary history in the surest way available to us–by accurate and comprehensive treatment of the lives and work of those who contributed to it.

The *DLB* Advisory Board

Foreword

No pages in our English literature give it more glory than those written by its essayists.

—James Milne

The facts justify a further assertion, somewhat bolder than Milne's: the informal essay has flourished better in the British Isles than anywhere else. There are more great and good essays than one can read, and there are always essayists one has not yet discovered. Except for a brief period of enfeeblement in the closing decades of the eighteenth century, the form remained vital for well over two centuries. It became popular in the Enlightenment and more popular still—and considerably more diversified—in the nineteenth century. Hard as it is to imagine in the post-verbal era, from the time of Charles Lamb to the outbreak of World War II new essays of every sort, many of them of outstanding merit, were constantly on hand in the newspapers and popular magazines as well as in literary journals. As late as the 1950s, schoolchildren, even in the United States, read "classic" essays rather than simplistic accounts of current events.

It seems natural enough that the informal essay should have prospered in the British Isles. Nothing is more definitive of British life than the paradox of individualism balanced by a profound if unobtrusive sociableness that manifests itself particularly in the desire to communicate—to speak and write and to do so articulately but also familiarly. Such a penchant—essentially a romantic one because its individualism is inclined more toward reverie and particularism than toward combative logic or ideology—is immensely propitious for all the verbal arts and drama and most obviously for the personal essay. The essay's main motive forces are, in fact, individualism and sociability: wonder and intellectual curiosity centering around one's own impressions, and at the same time the balancing desire to bring this subjective material into the public sphere, that is, to invite readers to recognize, compare, discover, respond.

Francis Bacon (*Essays*, 1597) is not really the progenitor of the type, even in England. Though informal, his essays are not personal or "famil-iar." In fact he is wary of the first person singular and writes in a way that appealed to many of the Augustan essayists, who, as J. B. Priestley observes, "never saw life from the angle of the individual—vain, humble, ridiculous, tragic—but always merely from the angle of a committee of sensible, well-intentioned persons." Bacon's essays are oxymoronic: informal and impersonal. Laconic and aphoristic but always generalizing, they reveal the man of intellectual speculation, the philosopher of prudence and worldly success, the pragmatic moralist. Humor, fancy, and poetry are in abeyance. The very fact that Bacon's performance, though much lauded in its time and later, established little enthusiasm for the essay as a genre seems further evidence for the innate romanticism of the Britons.

To catch on in the British Isles, the essay had to wait for a practitioner who harked farther back—to the personalism of Michel Eyquem de Montaigne—and who was, if not as philosophical as Bacon, not only homier and more amiable but also more willing to dwell within his own responses to congenial, humorous, tender, or beautiful things. Doing no more than what must have seemed perfectly natural to him, Abraham Cowley (*Several Discourses by Way of Essays*, 1668), that immensely approachable and affectionate human being, created the flavor that was just right to the native taste. Even though he was an admirer of Bacon, Cowley could not bring himself to adopt the glacial manner of his illustrious predecessor.

Yet it was the thing given impetus by Bacon—the rationalistic and scientific temper—that came to dominate Cowley's era and place its stamp on the essay as on everything else. Though it profited to some extent from the Cowleian model of light touch, geniality, and personal reference, the Enlightenment essay, following the canon that the general is nobler and more interesting than the particular or individual, developed as a vehicle for witty, amiable, or caustic comment on manners and morals and retained much of the impersonal tone of Lord Verulam. Within a manner infinitely chattier or sprightlier than Bacon's, the presence of the author remained, nevertheless, almost unfelt. Priestley is right again when he says that most of the Augustans "denied the essay the quickening breath of personality."

It was not till Romanticism's fascination with the particular and the subjective that the essay could become an instrument that answered, as fully as any prose can, to all the needs of the human spirit. Complement of Romantic poetry, the Romantic essay helped bring intellectual respectability to the highly specific and personal, including sensations and tonalities difficult to convey with complete lucidity or success. It was Lamb, an admirer of Cowley, who gave the essay its final freedom and created a new enthusiasm for it that was to last for well over a century.

Volumes 98 and 100 of the *Dictionary of Literary Biography, Modern British Essayists,* first and second series, cover essayists who wrote and published mainly between 1880 and 1960. To do justice to those who will have been active between 1960 and 2040 will likely prove to be a less formidable task: the informal essay, for reasons some of which are cogently stated by Joseph Wood Krutch ("No Essays, Please!," *Saturday Review,* 10 March 1951), has been in decline throughout the past several decades and shows no signs of regaining its vitality. One might think that the cults of casualness and "self-expression," which have grown continually in the twentieth century, would favor the development of the personal essay. But the opposite has happened, and one suspects that the climate creating and created by "self-expression" is in fact inimical to the essay. In any event, the younger writers of the English-speaking world—as of all the other worlds, it seems—show only a limited interest in the genre. They write, in one form or another, autobiography and semi-autobiographical fantasy. Theirs is a freewheeling subjectivism based on unabashed self-absorption and self-projection. Some find clarities and demarcations actually abhorrent and write in such a way that no human face is indelibly drawn and no street's turnings are made a picture or a tale. The self becomes an all-devouring self-indulgence, and what constitutes, for most of us, the basis of reality—the "world . . . so full of a number of things"—is lost to view. The extreme example of such a writer is Jean Genet, who brings to radical development the subjectivism that was only a tendency in Jean-Jacques Rousseau. The accomplished essayists represented in these vol-

umes, on the other hand, put one in the presence of something somehow deeper, more permanent, more universal, and even in some sense more useful than aberration or phantasmagoric reverie. To Cowley, Joseph Addison, Lamb, Holbrook Jackson, or Richard Church, the sense of meaningfulness and of enhanced vitality created or at least initiated by something outside the self is so welcome that the writer pays that other the homage of keeping it in view, of trying to limn it so that others will locate it. Many an essay offers delineations every bit as exact, vivid, and "objective" as those cropping up in fiction.

Aside from its immediate personal value as literature—as something aesthetically interesting and eminently rereadable—the familiar essay has made a steady, massive, but quiet contribution to the spirit of peace and the principle of individual freedom. The contemplative spirit on which the personal essay thrives is at the opposite pole from any sort of combativeness or aggression. The truth of personal experience, which is the form's inspiration, argues implicitly for individual freedom and against the politics—whether right, left, or center—of mindlessness, conformity, collectivity, and regimentation.

The present volumes offer biography and commentary on sixty-three writers; the number could well be expanded to a hundred or more. Resources being, as usual, limited, something less than the ideal of completeness and full justice has undoubtedly obtained. On the other hand, several fine essayists never well known and today almost unknown have at last found their biographers and may in time escape neglect. Among these are Holbrook Jackson, Elizabeth Wordsworth, and Dixon Scott.

Many practioners of the familiar essay also wrote literary criticism of the traditional type, and sometimes the two modes perform simultaneously, as in many of the highly personal and intellectually ambient prose pieces of William Butler Yeats. Several of the writers represented in these two volumes are primarily literary critics but in every such case either the type of criticism they engage in or their extracritical pieces entitle them to representation. Essayists in "analytical" literary criticism have been excluded.

Finally, there seemed no good reason to exclude completely writers who favored the formal essay. In point of fact, a good many formal essays—even some purely scientific ones such as many of Max Planck's or Sir Humphry Davy's—have considerable literary merit and make their contribution to humanism because they can be read and re-read, just like the best pieces of William Hazlitt and Lamb, both for their largeness of vision and the charm of their performance. Nor are the lines always clearly drawn between the formal and the informal. In many of Michael Polanyi's essays, for example, a strong sense of personal involvement and even anecdotal and autobiographical elements accompany an analytical mode applied to a distinctly intellectual, sometimes even technical subject. There are further complica-tions. Chapters of books sometimes turn out to be self-contained essays. One discovers that there are book-length essays and that prefaces and introductions are often essays under other names. As usual, the empirical reality outstrips our desire for easy identifications and unexceptionable definitions and classifications. In doubtful or arguable cases I have opted for the principle that inclusion is usually healthier, fairer, and more useful than exclusion.

–Robert Beum

Acknowledgments

This book was produced by Bruccoli Clark Layman, Inc. Karen L. Rood is senior editor for the *Dictionary of Literary Biography* series. J. M. Brook was the in-house editor.

Production coordinator is James W. Hipp. Systems manager is Charles D. Brower. Photography editor is Susan Brennen Todd. Permissions editor is Jean W. Ross. Layout and graphics supervisor is Penney L. Haughton. Copyediting supervisor is Bill Adams. Typesetting supervisor is Kathleen M. Flanagan. Information systems analyst is George F. Dodge. Charles Lee Egleston is editorial associate. The production staff includes Rowena Betts, Anne L. M. Bowman, Polly Brown, Teresa Chaney, Patricia Coate, Marie Creed, Allison Deal, Holly L. Deal, Sarah A. Estes, Mary L. Goodwin, Cynthia Hallman, Susan C. Heath, David Marshall James, Kathy S. Merlette, Laura Garren Moore, John Myrick, Gina D. Peterman, Cathy J. Reese, Edward Scott, Laurrè Sinckler, Maxine K. Smalls, John C. Stone III, and Betsy L. Weinberg.

Walter W. Ross and Parris Boyd did the library research with the assistance of the following librarians at the Thomas Cooper Library of the University of South Carolina: Gwen Baxter, Daniel Boice, Faye Chadwell, Cathy Eckman, Gary Geer, Cathie Gottlieb, David L. Haggard, Jens Holley, Jackie Kinder, Thomas Marcil, Marcia Martin, Laurie Preston, Jean Rhyne, Carol Tobin, and Virginia Weathers.

Essential research facilities were made available to the editor by the library of the University of Saskatchewan, Love Memorial Library at the University of Nebraska at Lincoln, and by the Learning Research Center of Grande Prairie Regional College in Grande Prairie, Alberta.

Assistance in recruiting writers for these volumes came from William Blissett, University of Toronto; George Core, editor of the *Sewanee Review*; Samuel Macey, University of Victoria; Frank M. Tierney, University of Ottawa; and George Woodcock, professor emeritus, University of British Columbia. From the outset of the project Mr. Woodcock gave constant encouragement and offered many helpful suggestions. Dr. R. D. Schell of Laurentian University provided valuable assistance in the completion of the project.

The editor's wife, Marynel, gave her support in many ways, including typing, proofing of manuscript, and discussion of substance and points of style.

Dictionary of Literary Biography • Volume Ninety-eight

Modern British Essayists, First Series

Dictionary of Literary Biography

Sir John Adamson

(11 January 1867 - 25 April 1950)

David Rampton
University of Ottawa

BOOKS: *The Teacher's Logic* (London: Charles & Dible, 1898);
The Theory of Education in Plato's "Republic" (London: Sonnenschein, 1903);
Songs from the South (London: Longmans, Green, 1915);
The Individual and the Environment: Some Aspects of the Theory of Education as Adjustment (London & New York: Longmans, Green, 1921);
Externals and Essentials (London: Longmans, Green, 1932; London & New York: Longmans, Green, 1933).

OTHER: "The University in South Africa," *Proceedings of the Forum on Higher Education* (N.p., 1936), pp. 137-162.

Sir John Adamson was a distinguished man of letters whose writings reflect his lifelong dedication to the improvement of educational theory and practice. He also wrote poetry and popularizing accounts of philosophy; he was a patriot who studied the history of his adopted country, South Africa, and wrote moving descriptions of its natural beauty; he was well versed in and made frequent reference to English literature; and he kept abreast of the rapid advances made in science during the first decades of the twentieth century. But Adamson's first love was education, and his other interests were all subsumed in his desire to improve the teaching of the young and the administration of the school system. He was not a prolific writer, but his themes are diverse: nature, science, society, politics, religion, economics,

Sir John Adamson (courtesy of the University of South Africa, Pretoria)

logic, language and literature, morality. His style

3

is readable and clear, tending at times to the aphoristic. Whatever his subject, he creates the impression of an enthusiastic teacher intent on effectively communicating his material.

John Ernest Adamson was born at Westgate Common, Wakefield, on 11 January 1867. After attending public school, he performed his teacher training at St. Mark's College, Chelsea, and received a B.A. from London University in 1894. He worked as master of method at the South Wales Training College from 1895 until 1902. Adamson married a Welsh girl, Gwendolyn Thomas, in 1897. They had no children and she predeceased him.

In 1898 he published *The Teacher's Logic*, a handbook for teachers that serves as an introduction to the general principles of logic, and attempts to demonstrate how closely connected this particular branch of philosophy is to the theory and practice of teaching. Admirably organized and lucidly written, this book contains in embryo all the major concerns that were to preoccupy Adamson in his later work. To make accessible without oversimplifying what many find abstruse, to improve teaching by instructing teachers in the methods and matter of their discipline, to advance the cause of the intellectual life by conveying his love for it–these are the principles that guided Adamson throughout his career. In addition, his interest in animating his subject with vivid examples makes even this early and relatively unambitious work a delight to read.

Adamson left Wales in 1902 to become principal of the Normal College in Pretoria. From this point he devoted most of his life to the administration and improvement of the educational system in South Africa. In 1903 he published a study of Plato's views on education, *The Theory of Education in Plato's "Republic."* The book is much more than a collection of essays about a crucial aspect of Plato's philosophy: it is in effect a comprehensive account of Adamson's own views on the relation between the individual and society, the ideal and material ends of education, the theory and practice of creating a harmonious society.

According to Plato individual education cannot be considered in isolation. The virtues of any society, Adamson insists, "must have their ultimate origin and basis in the virtues of the individuals of which it is composed." If there is a "key" to all of Adamson's thought, it is this notion of "individualism." Pupils who do nothing but imitate others' modes of thought are as unpopular in Adamson's ideal republic as are artists who only imitate reality in Plato's. Discovery, the new pedagogical method, will replace the dull round of continuous exposition by the teacher and mechanical regurgitation by the students. As in thought so too in feeling and conduct: the student must discover his own enthusiasms, and impose his duty on himself, for his own sake. Adamson agrees with Plato that an understanding of what constitutes good and evil is necessary for moral development and advocates training students to appreciate the beauty of good conduct. Aesthetic culture should imply moral culture. Although he refuses to endorse John Ruskin's view that taste is "the *only* morality," Adamson insists that it is a part and index of morality, that rhythm and harmony refine the moral being of man.

Aware that such large generalizations might be of relatively little use to his readers, Adamson usually documents his case with supporting examples. Here he adduces the teaching of math, grammar, literature, and music as evidence that Plato's precepts about "the seemliness of the good" still have relevance. With Plato's claim that physical education trains character Adamson also agrees, particularly if one views physical education as "sense training." The accuracy with which something is seen and described braces the cognitive power, enriches and refines the life of feeling, and translates into truthfulness, which in turn becomes more of an unconscious habit than a conscious striving for an ideal.

The Theory of Education in Plato's "Republic" provides the perfect forum for a display of Adamson's special talents. He conveys the essence of Plato's thought in language a layman can understand; he defends, criticizes, and extends Plato's views. The book's reputation and Adamson's skills as an administrator led to his appointment in 1905 as director of education for the Transvaal. Two years later, when it became a self-governing colony, he worked closely with Jan Smuts, the colonial secretary, on the Transvaal Education Act of 1907. At this time two groups–an Afrikaner majority and an English minority–accounted for just over one-fifth of the country's six million inhabitants. The Education Act, based on the European system, sought to unite these groups and entrench their rights in a redesigned system of schools and universities. Education was (with various limitations) to be bilingual; school boards were to be locally controlled. Adamson's skills as a conciliator were in large part responsible for reconciling the Afrikaners, who had set up their own schools, to the government system.

THE INDIVIDUAL AND THE ENVIRONMENT

SOME ASPECTS OF THE THEORY OF EDUCATION AS ADJUSTMENT

BY

J. E. ADAMSON

M.A., D.LIT.

DIRECTOR OF EDUCATION, TRANSVAAL PROVINCE

LONGMANS, GREEN AND CO.
39 PATERNOSTER ROW, LONDON
FOURTH AVENUE & 30TH STREET, NEW YORK
BOMBAY, CALCUTTA, AND MADRAS
1921

Title page for the published version of Adamson's dissertation. He received his doctorate in education from London University in 1920.

His desire for a more centralized control of education led him to advocate a system by which thirteen regional authorities would carry out policy set by the central government; in the end, however, those in favor of local autonomy prevailed.

During World War I Adamson enrolled in the graduate program at London University; he received his doctorate in education in 1920. His dissertation was published the next year as *The Individual and the Environment: Some Aspects of the Theory of Education as Adjustment*. It covers some of the same material as the book on Plato, but ranges more widely and offers new and interesting practical applications as well as a detailed theoretical apparatus for teaching. The book consists of a substantial introduction, followed by three main sections that constitute separate essays in themselves: "Nature," "The World of Civilisation," and "The World of Morality."

The introduction is an overview of metaphysics that enables Adamson to establish a context for his argument. John Locke's atomistic theory of experience and his mechanical conception of consciousness are now outmoded, says Adamson. He follows Immanuel Kant in assuming that the phenomenal world owes its ordering in space to the a priori constitution of the mind of man, and that things acquire unity as a projection of the unity of the self. Because Adamson defines education as an adjustment of the individual to his environment, he naturally concentrates on those philosophers who offer analogues to such a process. William James's "stream of consciousness" concept and Henri Bergson's philosophy of creative evolution both figure prominently in his argument, since both James and Bergson discuss the individual as an active, acquisitive, contributory subject, constantly in the process of creating his world.

"Nature" for the educator means science and how to teach it. The child must travel along the track that leads to classification, instead of simply being presented with a series of tables and species and laws, because classification is the late product of rational thought; and material should be selected with this aim in mind. The teacher assists the process already started by life. Again, the practical is emphasized. There are twenty pages on the teaching of geography, a three-page syllabus for organic chemistry, and another equally detailed for health education.

The chapters gathered under the heading "Civilization" discuss the spiritual nature of the social order; political, national, religious, and economic strands in the social fabric; vocational education; and the teaching of history and literature. The last item in this series serves as an impressive example of Adamson's ability to range widely and confidently over a vast array of material. He thinks history should pay more attention to the process of life as a whole and less to its spectacular events. The history of trade unions deserves at least as much attention as the events of the French Revolution. If social evolution is a process revealed by the experience of the individual then it must be studied as such. The section on literature conveys all the Edwardian scholar's typical love of his subject, and the lists of recommended readings are fascinating documents in the history of literary taste. Charles Reade, Sir Henry John Newbolt, Richard Doddridge Blackmore, and Edward Bulwer-Lytton do not find their way onto many reading lists these days.

In the third section, "The World of Morality," Adamson argues that the moral world is a continuum, like its physical and social counterparts, because all thoughts and acts have a moral value. It differs from nature and society in that it only begins to exist when the individual commits himself to it, by trying to realize his best self, the rational and social self. The school is an important part of the moral order the student inhabits, and as a depository of tradition it reproduces itself in its members and is recreated by them. It channels congenital instincts and emotional dispositions toward the ideals the school embodies; it "reinforces habitual action by means of moral purpose definitely willed as an end for the self." The teacher's role in all of this is paramount. His strivings toward a goal must be conveyed to his students, not by precept but by example. And only the struggle to improve matters: better avowed shortcoming as a moral guide than ostentatious achievement. Religious instruction must form a part of this process of moral education, and it is in this area that Adamson sets limits to the skeptical and questing intelligence whose independence he celebrates in much of his work. The question of the historical truth of any part of the biblical narrative cannot arise for the teacher, he claims. Conscientious schoolmasters do not sow the seeds of doubt. Adamson borrows a phrase from Bergson, "the reality which is God," to explain how religion is inextricably bound up with the individual's adjustment to the natural, social, and moral orders, because "the work of the Divine Architect is visible in the fabric of experience which the individual inherits." One would have expected the author of a textbook on logic to handle the argument from design rather differently.

Adamson was made vice-chancellor of the University of South Africa in 1922. For his services to education he was appointed C.M.G. in 1923 and knighted in 1924. The same year he left his government post and became master of Rhodes University College, Grahamstown, and professor of education. He retired in 1930.

In 1932 Adamson published *Externals and Essentials,* a book of essays that includes the best of the shorter pieces he wrote for the public press in South Africa and England. The most interesting aspect of these essays is the lucid, compassionate, sincere, informed Adamson voice, topical and learned, amusing and serious, colloquial and literary, detached and committed by turns. He is as comfortable talking about Bobby Jones's golf swing as he is summarizing John Dewey's philoso-

Sir John Adamson (courtesy of the University of South Africa, Pretoria)

phy; he even brings the two together in an essay called "Concentration." His wit often subtly undercuts his own soaring cadences: after suggesting that civilization is man-made and "forever becoming," he notes that "much of it is unbecoming" too. Sir James Jeans's *The Mysterious Universe* (1930) seems to have had a great influence on both the substance and style of these essays, and scientific analogies inform a great deal of Adamson's thought. As dynamic mass must be added to static mass so too, Adamson states, must value be added to everyday experience. Adamson even takes a stab at an equation for human development, suggesting that if B = the evolutionary adjustment of the individual and V = the value, then E (Education) = BV. And, in general, Adamson likes to illustrate ideas with metaphors. A word is an iceberg, a comet, an electrical charge, all within the same paragraph in an essay on language. The "self is at the wheel with the instincts and emotions providing the petrol," he suggests in another. Adamson quotes approvingly Desmond MacCarthy's remark that when language divides itself too clearly into prosaic and poetic diction, "life fades out of eloquence and poetry, while serviceable prose becomes colourless and dry." At the same time he thinks the cardinal weakness of poor writing is insincerity, which he equates with an excessively mannered prose style (for example, that of Algernon Charles Swinburne).

The content of these essays features an adventurous conservatism in attitude. Adamson can speak glowingly of the hope offered by scientific advance and then, as he is musing about why the perfect car (capable of traveling at a smooth seventy-five miles per hour) should precede the perfect road (he had recently been subjected to a very bumpy one), he casually but presciently warns against the potential destructiveness of atomic science unleashed. Adamson revels in human variety and wants everyone to be educated so that they can learn how different they are. Adult education opens doors to culture, and culture makes man's daily lot easier to bear. But social services and unemployment insurance, he warns, sap self-reliance and initiative. The happy menial worker should be allowed to stay that way, since there must be leaders and followers. Compassionate capitalism, traditional humanism, and common decency will provide for the latter.

Adamson was a self-defined South African patriot, and in an essay called "South Africa First" he explains what he understands the word patriot to mean. Just as an individual has a will to live, so has a group pride in an individuality that is shaped by heredity and environment. Patriotism requires a material or geographic unity as well as a spiritual one, and "Nationality is ultimately oneness of thought, emotion and will." No true South African citizen thinks in terms of Briton, Boer, and Kaffir. Rather, these form a spiritual trinity with a common destiny. The long trek still to be made will end when that ideal is realized. In this sense, true patriotism, devoid of fanatical suspicion and xenophobia, is something to be

praised. Adamson is short on specifics about how his ideal union might be achieved; but, on the basis of this essay at least, it does not seem likely that he would have thought apartheid much of a solution.

In 1936 Adamson published his last essay of note, "The University in South Africa." It briefly recounts the historical reasons for the dual nature of South Africa's universities, explains their current status, and offers some predictions about their future. Adamson discusses the first colleges for nineteenth-century English and Dutch pioneers, Cecil Rhodes's failed attempt to establish one national university, and the eventual founding of universities in Cape Town, Stellenbosch, Johannesburg, and Pretoria. He goes on to defend the system against the charge of excessive duplication, applauds its vocational component as a solid fusion of the academic and the utilitarian, and explains how the system is financed primarily by corporate and government grants. Adamson ends with a discussion of current attempts to unify the system and of race relations in general. He supports "the sacred right of the opportunity for culture for all who are ready for it," but admits that the whites should "remain in a position of leadership and trusteeship for generations to come." It is only fair to say that this was the view of most enlightened South Africans in 1936.

There is not much likelihood of a dramatic change in Adamson's reputation. He was an educational theorist and popularizer who wrote lucidly and cared passionately about every aspect of culture. He is remembered in South Africa for the cool intelligence and warm sympathy with which he approached the problem of accommodating the desires of Afrikaners for full linguistic and cultural rights in the educational system of the new union. Adamson helped solve that problem because he knew their language, their history, their church, and their leaders and teachers. The problems that were to rend the social fabric of the nation he helped to build are much greater now than the ones he faced but their solution requires men of his compassion, intelligence, sensitivity, and broad culture.

Arnold Bennett

(27 May 1867 - 27 March 1931)

James Hepburn

See also the Bennett entries in *DLB 10: Modern British Dramatists, 1900-1945* and *DLB 34: British Novelists, 1894-1929: Traditionalists.*

BOOKS: *A Man from the North* (London & New York: John Lane / Bodley Head, 1898);

Journalism for Women: A Practical Guide (London: John Lane / Bodley Head, 1898);

Polite Farces for the Drawing Room (London: Lamley, 1900 [i.e. 1899]);

Fame and Fiction: An Enquiry into Certain Popularities (London: Richards, 1901; New York: Dutton, 1901);

The Grand Babylon Hotel: A Fantasia on Modern Themes (London: Chatto & Windus, 1902); republished as *T. Racksole and Daughter: Or, the Result of an American Millionaire Ordering Steak and a Bottle of Bass at the Grand Babylon Hotel, London* (New York: New Amsterdam Book Company, 1902);

Anna of the Five Towns (London: Chatto & Windus, 1902; New York: McClure, Phillips, 1903);

The Gates of Wrath: A Melodrama (London: Chatto & Windus, 1903);

The Truth About an Author, anonymous (London: Constable, 1903; New York: Doran, 1911);

How to Become an Author: A Practical Guide (London: Pearson, 1903);

Leonora: A Novel (London: Chatto & Windus, 1903; New York: Doran, 1910);

A Great Man: A Frolic (London: Chatto & Windus, 1904; New York: Doran, 1911);

Teresa of Watling Street: A Fantasia on Modern Themes (London: Chatto & Windus, 1904);

Tales of the Five Towns (London: Chatto & Windus, 1905);

The Loot of Cities: Being Adventures of a Millionaire in Search of Joy (A Fantasia) (London: Rivers, 1905); enlarged as *The Loot of Cities: Being the Adventures of a Millionaire in Search of Joy (A Fantasia) and Other Stories* (London: Nelson, 1917);

Arnold Bennett (photograph by Howard Coster)

Sacred and Profane Love: A Novel in Three Episodes (London: Chatto & Windus, 1905); republished as *The Book of Carlotta: Being a Revised Edition (With New Preface) of Sacred and Profane Love . . .* (New York: Doran, 1911);

Hugo: A Fantasia on Modern Themes (London: Chatto & Windus, 1906; New York: Buckles, 1906);

Whom God Hath Joined (London: Nutt, 1906; New York: Doran, 1911);

The Sinews of War: A Romance of London and the Sea, by Bennett and Eden Phillpotts (London: Laurie, 1906); republished as *Doubloons* (New York: McClure, Phillips, 1906);

Things That Interested Me: Being Leaves from a Journal (Burslem: Privately printed, 1906);

The Ghost: A Fantasia on Modern Themes (London: Chatto & Windus, 1907; Boston: Turner, 1907);

The Reasonable Life: Being Hints for Men and Women (London: Fifield, 1907); revised as *Mental Efficiency, and Other Hints to Men and Women* (New York: Doran, 1911; London: Hodder & Stoughton, 1912);

The Grim Smile of the Five Towns (London: Chapman & Hall, 1907);

The City of Pleasure: A Fantasia on Modern Themes (London: Chatto & Windus, 1907; New York: Doran, 1915);

Things Which Have Interested Me: Being Leaves from a Journal, Second Series (Burslem: Privately printed, 1907);

The Statue, by Bennett and Phillpotts (London: Cassell, 1908; New York: Moffat Yard, 1908);

Buried Alive: A Tale of These Days (London: Chapman & Hall, 1908; New York: Brentano's, 1910);

How to Live on 24 Hours a Day (London: New Age Press, 1908; New York: Doran, 1910);

The Old Wives' Tale: A Novel (London: Chapman & Hall, 1908; New York: Doran, 1911);

The Human Machine (London: New Age Press, 1908; New York: Doran, 1911);

Things Which Have Interested Me, Third Series (Burslem: Privately printed, 1908);

Literary Taste: How to Form It, with Detailed Instructions for Collecting a Complete Library of English Literature (London: New Age Press, 1909; New York: Doran, 1911; revised, with an American book list by John Farrar, New York: Doran, 1927; revised, edition, with additional lists by Frank Swinnerton, London: Hodder & Stoughton, 1937; revised, London: Hodder & Stoughton, 1912; New York: Doran, 1927);

Cupid and Commonsense: A Play in Four Acts (London: New Age Press, 1909);

What the Public Wants: (A Play in Four Acts) (London: Duckworth, 1909; New York: Doran, 1911);

The Glimpse: An Adventure of the Soul (London: Chapman & Hall, 1909; New York: Appleton, 1909);

The Present Crisis (Burslem: Privately printed, 1910);

Helen with the High Hand: An Idyllic Diversion (London: Chapman & Hall, 1910; New York: Doran, 1910);

Photograph inscribed by Bennett "to Henry" (his nickname for Frank Swinnerton), which Swinnerton published in his Arnold Bennett: A Last Word, *1978*

Clayhanger (London: Methuen, 1910; New York: Dutton, 1910);

The Card: A Story of Adventure in the Five Towns (London: Methuen, 1911); republished as *Denry the Audacious* (New York: Dutton, 1911);

Hilda Lessways (London: Methuen, 1911; New York: Dutton, 1911);

The Honeymoon: A Comedy in Three Acts (London: Methuen, 1911; New York: Doran, 1912);

The Feast of St. Friend (London: Hodder & Stoughton, 1911; New York: Doran, 1911); republished as *Friendship and Happiness: A Plea for the Feast of St. Friend* (London: Hodder & Stoughton, 1914);

The Matador of the Five Towns, and Other Stories (London: Methuen, 1912; with somewhat different contents, New York: Doran, 1912);

Milestones: A Play in Three Acts, by Bennett and Edward Knoblock (London: Methuen, 1912; New York: Doran, 1912);

Those United States (London: Secker, 1912); republished as *Your United States: Impressions of a*

First Visit (New York & London: Harper, 1912);

The Regent: A Five Towns Story of Adventure in London (London: Methuen, 1913); republished as *The Old Adam: A Story of Adventure* (New York: Doran, 1913);

The Great Adventure: A Play of Fancy in Four Acts (London: Methuen, 1913; New York: Doran, 1913);

The Plain Man and His Wife (London: Hodder & Stoughton, 1913); republished as *Married Life: The Plain Man and His Wife* (New York: Doran, 1913); republished as *Marriage (The Plain Man and His Wife)* (London: Hodder & Stoughton, 1916);

Paris Nights and Other Impressions of Places and People (London: Hodder & Stoughton, 1913; New York: Doran, 1913);

The Author's Craft (New York: Doran, 1914; London, New York & Toronto: Hodder & Stoughton, 1915 [i.e. 1914]);

The Price of Love: A Tale (London: Methuen, 1914; New York & London: Harper, 1914);

Liberty! A Statement of the British Case (London: Hodder & Stoughton, 1914; New York: Doran, 1914);

From the Log of the Velsa (New York: Century, 1914; London: Chatto & Windus, 1920);

Over There: War Scenes on the Western Front (London: Methuen, 1915; New York: Doran, 1915);

These Twain (New York: Doran, 1915; London: Methuen, 1916);

The Lion's Share (London: Cassell, 1916; New York: Doran, 1916);

Books and Persons: Being Comments on a Past Epoch, 1908-1911 (London: Chatto & Windus, 1917; New York: Doran, 1917);

The Pretty Lady: A Novel (London: Cassell, 1918; New York: Doran, 1918);

The Title: A Comedy in Three Acts (London: Chatto & Windus, 1918; New York: Doran, 1918);

Self and Self-Management: Essays About Existing (London: Hodder & Stoughton, 1918; New York: Doran, 1918);

The Roll-Call (London: Hutchinson, 1919; New York: Doran, 1919);

Judith: A Play in Three Acts, Founded on the Apocryphal Book of "Judith" (London: Chatto & Windus, 1919; New York: Doran, 1919);

Sacred and Profane Love: A Play in Four Acts Founded Upon the Novel of the Same Name (London: Chatto & Windus, 1919; New York: Doran, 1920);

Our Women: Chapters on the Sex-Discord (London: Cassell, 1920; New York: Doran, 1920);

Things That Have Interested Me (London: Chatto & Windus, 1921; New York: Doran, 1921);

Body and Soul: A Play in Four Acts (New York: Doran, 1921; London: Chatto & Windus, 1922);

The Love Match: A Play in Five Scenes (London: Chatto & Windus, 1922; New York: Doran, 1922);

Mr. Prohack (London: Methuen, 1922; New York: Doran, 1922);

Lilian (London: Cassell, 1922; New York: Doran, 1922);

Things That Have Interested Me, Second Series (London: Chatto & Windus, 1923; New York: Doran, 1923);

How to Make the Best of Life (London: Hodder & Stoughton, 1923; New York: Doran, 1923);

Don Juan de Marana: A Play in Four Acts (London: Laurie, 1923);

Riceyman Steps: A Novel (London: Cassell, 1923; New York: Doran, 1923);

London Life: A Play in Three Acts and Nine Scenes, by Bennett and Knoblock (London: Chatto & Windus, 1924; New York: Doran, 1924);

The Bright Island (London: Golden Cockerel Press, 1924; New York: Doran, 1925);

Elsie and the Child: A Tale of Riceyman Steps and Other Stories (London: Cassell, 1924); republished as *Elsie and the Child, and Other Stories* (New York: Doran, 1924);

The Clayhanger Family. I. Clayhanger. II. Hilda Lessways. III. These Twain. (London: Methuen, 1925);

Things That Have Interested Me, Third Series (London: Chatto & Windus, 1926; New York: Doran, 1926);

Lord Raingo (London: Cassell, 1926; New York: Doran, 1926);

The Woman Who Stole Everything and Other Stories (London: Cassell, 1927; New York: Doran, 1927);

Mr. Prohack: A Comedy in Three Acts, by Bennett and Knoblock (London: Chatto & Windus, 1927; Garden City, N.Y.: Doubleday, Doran, 1928);

The Vanguard: A Fantasia (New York: Doran, 1927); republished as *The Strange Vanguard: A Fantasia* (London: Cassell, 1928);

The Savour of Life: Essays in Gusto (London: Cassell, 1928; Garden City, N.Y.: Doubleday, Doran, 1928);

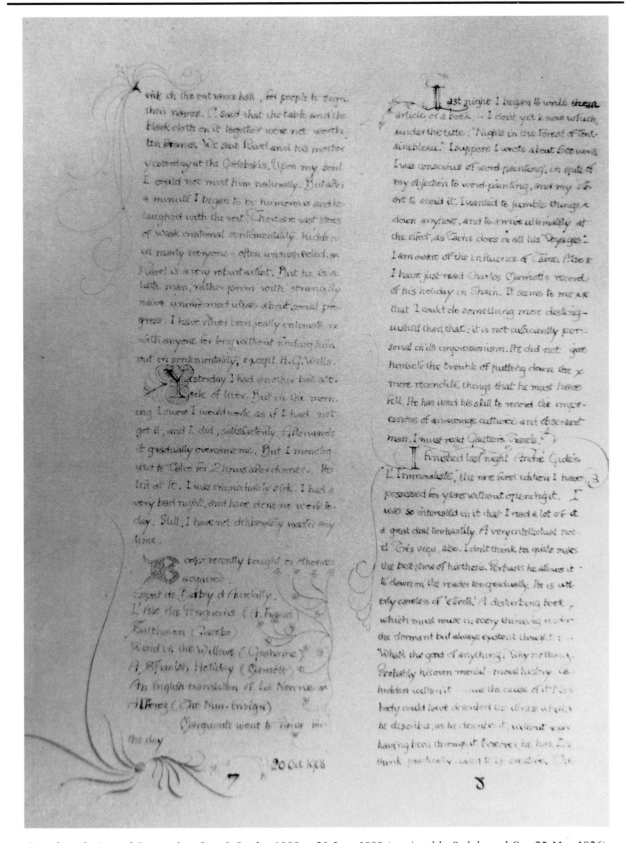

Page from the journal Bennett kept from 9 October 1908 to 29 June 1909 (auctioned by Sotheby and Co., 25 May 1936)

Mediterranean Scenes: Rome–Greece–Constantinople (London: Cassell, 1928);

Accident (Garden City, N.Y.: Doubleday, Doran, 1928; London: Cassell, 1929);

The Religious Interregnum (London: Benn, 1929);

"Piccadilly": The Story of the Film (London: Readers Library, 1929);

Journal 1929 (London: Cassell, 1930); republished as *Journal of Things New and Old* (Garden City, N.Y.: Doubleday, Doran, 1930);

Imperial Palace (London: Cassell, 1930; Garden City, N.Y.: Doubleday, Doran, 1930);

Venus Rising from the Sea (London: Cassell, 1931);

The Night Visitor and Other Stories (London: Cassell, 1931; Garden City, N.Y.: Doubleday, Doran, 1931);

Dream of Destiny: An Unfinished Novel and Venus Rising from the Sea (London: Cassell, 1932); republished as *Stroke of Luck and Dream of Destiny: An Unfinished Novel* (Garden City, N.Y.: Doubleday, Doran, 1932);

The Journals of Arnold Bennett, 1896-1928, 3 volumes, edited by Newman Flower (London: Cassell, 1932-1933; revised edition, New York: Viking, 1932-1933); republished with additions from the years 1906-1907 and with the *Florentine Journal* (London: Penguin, 1971);

Florentine Journal, 1st April-25 May 1910, edited by Dorothy Cheston Bennett (London: Chatto & Windus, 1967);

The Author's Craft and Other Critical Writings of Arnold Bennett, edited by Samuel Hynes (Lincoln: University of Nebraska Press, 1968);

Arnold Bennett: The Evening Standard Years. Books & Persons, 1926-1931, edited by Andrew Mylett (London: Chatto & Windus, 1974; Hamden, Conn.: Shoe String Press, 1974);

Sketches for Autobiography, edited by James Hepburn (London & Boston: Allen & Unwin, 1980).

Arnold Bennett was born at 90 Hope Street in Hanley, one of the six towns that make up Stoke-on-Trent, now as then the chief English home for the manufacture of pottery and china. The scene in Bennett's day was dominated by great bottle-shaped brick kilns and by the smoke that issued from them. In 1897, eight years after leaving the district, Bennett made a brief return, and recorded a romantic impression in his journal: "during this week. . . , when I have been traversing the district after dark, the grim and original beauty of certain aspects of the Potteries . . . has

fully revealed itself for the first time." But though Bennett used the six towns (changing them to five) for much of his fiction of the next seventeen years, he rarely alluded to such beauty, and gave negligible attention to the pottery industry. The characteristic emphasis in the novels is that in *Clayhanger* (1910): "narrow uneven alleys leading to higgledy-piggledy workshops and kilns; cottages transformed into factories and factories into cottages; clumsily, hastily, because nothing matters so long as 'it will do'; everywhere something forced to fulfil, badly, the function of something else; in brief, the reign of the slovenly makeshift, shameless, filthy, and picturesque." In 1927 Bennett passed through the Potteries on the train from Manchester to London, and he recorded in his journal that "the sight of this district gave me a shudder."

Bennett's family on his father's side traces back uncertainly to the 1600s in the Potteries. His grandfather was a potter's thrower. His father, Enoch, born in 1843, began working life in the pottery trade, but with the failure of his firm moved into the drapery trade and pawnbroking. Presently he trained to become a solicitor. In "The Making of Me," written for the *Daily Express* in 1929, Bennett says: "Beyond doubt my father's influence was the main factor in making a home in which the 'humanities' flourished more brightly than in any other home of my acquaintance. Entering the houses of his friends, wealthier or poorer, I always felt that I was going into something inferior, intellectually more confined and stuffy, places where the outlook was less wide and the dominant mentalities less vigorous, original, and free."

On his mother's side, Bennett's family were Derbyshire people. His maternal grandfather, Robert Longson, came from there to the Potteries to set up the drapery shop that became the model for the shop in *The Old Wives' Tale: A Novel* (1908). In "The Making of Me" Bennett describes Longson as "the biggest individuality in my early experience"; he "confirmed me in Radicalism for life." Longson's elder daughter, Sarah Ann, born in 1840, married Enoch. Bennett describes her as an affectionate woman, with a great curiosity about people and with a total lack of a sense of humor.

Bennett left the Potteries at age twenty-one to go to London to be a shorthand clerk in a law office. Although he had been head boy at school, he had failed his law examinations twice, and the four years he spent at the law office offered little prospect for him. In 1894, with money from his father, he became assistant editor of a weekly magazine, *Woman,* and in another three years he became editor. In all of these years, indeed from well before he left the Potteries, he was engaged in the process of making a writer of himself, and presently–to his own surprise–he discovered the fluency that eventually produced more than a hundred books. In 1900 he quit his editorship to become a full-time writer. The venture was precarious financially for several years, but he had early successes of several sorts–with popular fiction such as *The Grand Babylon Hotel: A Fantasia on Modern Themes* (1902), with serious fiction such as *Anna of the Five Towns* (1902), and with the "Savoir-Faire Papers" in *T. P.'s Weekly* (1902-1930). By 1911 he was a well-known author in Great Britain, Europe, and America.

Bennett married twice. His first wife was Marguerite Soulié, whom he met and married in 1907 in Paris, where he had gone to live after the death of his father in 1902. He and Marguerite made their home in the French countryside near Fontainebleau and then in Paris for several years. In 1912 they went to live in Thorpe-le-Soken, Essex. They had no children, and separated without divorce in 1921. After the separation, and for the rest of his life, Bennett lived in London. In 1922 he met Dorothy Cheston, who presently took the name of Bennett by deed poll. A daughter, Virginia, was born to them in 1926. The fourth volume of *Letters of Arnold Bennett* (1986) is largely devoted to letters to Marguerite and Dorothy, and shows his complex relationships with them.

Reviewing his literary career late in life, Bennett said, "I began to write novels because my friends said I could. The same for plays. But I always had a strong feeling for journalism, which feeling is as strong as ever it was." He began his formal literary career as an unpaid writer of weekly chat for the *Staffordshire Knot* when he was nineteen years old, and the last thing he wrote in the weeks before his death was a weekly article for the *Evening Standard.* In between came nearly three thousand other items of journalism, many of which were drawn into more than thirty published volumes. Much of the material is so slight and ephemeral as hardly to deserve the name of essay, and much of it will never be read again. An unknown quantity, published anonymously in his early London years, is irretrievably lost.

Yet Bennett the journalist is a lively writer, usually amusing, often wise, always readable. His interests range widely across worldly affairs, his observations are realistic and shrewd, his judgments detached and compassionate. Many of the essays that emerge from the journalism deserve the attention of a later age. But in the general eclipse of his reputation since his death, no aspect of his work has suffered more than the journalism. A dozen of his novels are still highly esteemed; he retains historical importance as a dramatist; his journals are admired. But aside from a gathering of literary essays designed for the academic market (*The Author's Craft and Other Critical Writings of Arnold Bennett,* 1968), only one book of his journalism remains in print today (*How to Live on 24 Hours a Day,* 1908). Other occasional reminders of his journalistic career (*Arnold Bennett: The Evening Standard Years,* 1974, and *Sketches for Autobiography,* 1980) have drawn little attention.

It was very much otherwise during his lifetime. In the years 1908-1911 his "Books and Persons" articles in the *New Age* were the envy and admiration of his fellow journalists. In the years 1914-1918 his columns in the *Daily News,* the *New Statesman,* and other places had observable influence upon the social-political conduct of the war. And in the years 1926-1931 his articles in the *Evening Standard* were required reading for anyone in London who was interested in books. Andrew Mylett's introduction to *Arnold Bennett: The Evening Standard Years* gives a good glimpse of Bennett's reputation then, and the 1952 biography by journalist Reginald Pound a more extended one. Regrettably almost nothing remains of the thousands of letters Bennett received (and answered) from the public who read him. In the first years of his success as a journalist, when *T. P.'s Weekly* was publishing his anonymous "Savoir-Faire Papers" and "A Novelist's Log-Book," he wrote in a letter to his literary agent, J. B. Pinker: "Anyone who wants to know what sort of effect these things have had on a solid regular public of 150,000 a week has only got to enquire at the editorial department of *T. P.'s W.*" Years later he remarked of his second "pocket philosophy," *How to Live on 24 Hours a Day:* "It has brought me more letters of appreciation than all my other books put together."

The best of Bennett's journalism is autobiographical–though in a loose sense all his journalism is autobiographical. Whether he is writing about games or doctors, sailboats or authorship, religion or women, politics or music, the basis is "things that have interested me." His

*Bennett on the Riviera in 1911 with his literary agent, J. B. Pinker (left), and Edgar Selwyn, an American theater manager
(Committee of the City Museum, Stoke-on-Trent)*

pocket philosophies dealt with parts of his life (living alone in London, dealing with the opposite sex), and his little book *Journalism for Women* (published in 1898, three weeks after his first book, the novel *A Man from the North*) came straight from his editorial desk on *Woman*. This strong personal element helped to give the journalism its popularity, for his readers saw the sensible, compassionate man in his words.

The writing that is explicitly autobiographical begins with *The Truth About an Author*, published anonymously in 1903 and acknowledged as Bennett's own work in 1905. The book is a series of essays on his early literary life: his first reading at home and then at school, his first efforts at writing, his first journalism in the Five Towns and then in London, his first novel, his editorial life, his first play. The frankness of discussion of the material aspect of a writer's life annoyed people, just as Anthony Trollope's *Autobiography* (1883) had, and they cast doubt upon its truthfulness; but at no point where disguise has been penetrated has the book proved to be untruthful except in a few slips of memory. Especially in its earlier parts it is full of delights.

Bennett never undertook any subsequent formal autobiographical writing of great length. The longest piece of this type is a set of four

brief sketches entitled "My Reminiscences," published serially in 1913 and republished in *Things That Have Interested Me* (1921). Bennett seems to have begun these sketches with a larger aim in mind, but he limited them to some entertaining glimpses of his life in Paris in the first decade of the century. His other autobiographical pieces were written at scattered times. An early one, "A Tale of Tyranny," concerns his relationship with a waitress in the French restaurant where he conceived *The Old Wives' Tale: A Novel*. It first appeared anonymously in *T. P.'s Weekly* in the series "A Novelist's Log-Book" and was republished in 1908 in *Things Which Have Interested Me, Third Series* which consists of essays, unlike its two predecessors, which are composed of journal entries. Other pieces bear such titles as "The Making of Me," "School-Days in the Five Towns," "The Greatest Moment," and "My Religious Experience." *The Truth About an Author* aside, all of these explicitly autobiographical essays and sketches are gathered into the collection *Sketches for Autobiography*.

The Truth About an Author led to other more detached essays about authorship and literature: *How to Become an Author: A Practical Guide* (1903), *Literary Taste: How to Form It* (1909), and *The Author's Craft* (1914). The first of these books was of a sort common at the time and was a popular example. It covers some of the same ground as *The Truth About an Author*, abstracting from it such advice as might be useful to more ordinarily gifted people. *Literary Taste*, a guide to the formation thereof, was a similar distillation of the development of Bennett's own taste in his omnivorous reading. The book was often republished, and after Bennett's death an edition appeared with supplementary reading lists by Bennett's good friend Frank Swinnerton. *The Author's Craft*, consisting of four essays, was Bennett's most elaborate statement about his own writing and his general views on the relationship of an author to his material and to his public. The whole of the book is reprinted in *The Author's Craft and Other Critical Writings of Arnold Bennett*. In *Literary Taste* and *The Author's Craft* appear views that might startle anyone who thinks of Bennett the novelist as a workaday realist:

> The book is nothing but the man trying to talk to you, trying to impart to you some of his feelings.
>
> ***
>
> When the real intimate work of creation has to be done—and it has to be done on every page—the novelist can only look within for effective aid.
>
> ***
>
> In considering the equipment of the novelist there are two attributes which may always be taken for granted. The first is the sense of beauty . . . ; the other . . . is passionate intensity of vision.

In his first years in London, Bennett moved only slowly into a literary career, and even by the middle 1890s he was rather more an editor, reviewer, and essayist than a writer of serious fiction. As reviewer he read and skimmed an enormous quantity of books, and he had a lot of ideas about what he read. For several years he contemplated writing a literary history of England, but the actual significant fruit of his early reflections was a series of essays gathered under the title *Fame and Fiction* in 1901. The subtitle of the book is *An Enquiry into Certain Popularities*, and the aim of most of the essays is, without condescension, to account for the popular appeal of several authors of the day, now nearly forgotten figures such as Mary Elizabeth Braddon, Silas Hocking, and James Lane Allen. It is an interesting book, written with unusual knowledge of the authors and of the audiences they wrote for. But the ephemeral fame of the authors seems to have meant ephemeral fame for the book. Except for photographic reproduction for library sales in the 1970s, it has not been republished. One or another of its chapters is occasionally anthologized, notably the three substantial essays on less popular authors of the day: George Gissing, Ivan Turgenev, and George Moore. These three and a couple of other pieces appear in *The Author's Craft and Other Critical Writings of Arnold Bennett*.

In the year following *Fame and Fiction* Bennett established himself as a popular author with *The Grand Babylon Hotel: A Fantasia on Modern Themes*, and by and large he gave up writing long essays on other authors. Henceforth his characteristic form was the causerie. His two extended series of literary causeries were those done under the pseudonym Jacob Tonson for the *New Age* in 1908-1911, one-third of them gathered into the collection *Books and Persons: Being Comments on a Past Epoch* in 1917, and those done for the *Evening Standard* in 1926-1931, all except one gathered in Andrew Mylett's collection. The titles of the first pieces in *Books and Persons* give a good indication of the range of all these discussions, most of which vary in length from long paragraphs to twelve hundred words: "Wilfred Whitten's Prose," "Ugliness in Fiction," "Letters by Queen Victoria," "French Publishers," "Wordsworth's Single Lines." All of the pieces in the *New Age* were contributed gratis or for a token fee. A few of the pieces in both series appear in *The Author's Craft and Other Critical Writings of Arnold Bennett*, along with a few larger pieces that Bennett wrote over the years, including essays on his friends H. G. Wells and Eden Phillpotts and "The Progress of the Novel," which he wrote for the short-lived highbrow magazine the *Realist* in 1929.

In the six years 1894-1899 Bennett published more than seven hundred periodical pieces. By far the greatest number were book reviews, followed in order by theater reviews, music reviews, and his own light fiction. His book reviewing came to nearly the rate of one book a day during these six years. But along with this attention to the arts came wider interests. His first journalism in the Five Towns concerned steam tramways and football clubs, and when he first came to London he made use of his experience as a law clerk to write items on legal matters. His reviews themselves characteristically kept literature, theater, and music close to life, and his short stories—with titles such as "The Advanced Woman" and "In a Hospital"—were often

Letter from Bennett to Pinker in which Bennett discusses his plan for the composition of Our Women: Chapters on the Sex-Discord *(1920) and his desire for Pinker to arrange serial publication of the work in the United States (C. K. Ogden Library, University College, London)* social comment. It is hardly surprising, then, that he was soon publishing articles on broader social-political matters. In 1894 he described a Salvation Army shelter and discussed the education of men. In 1899 he discussed the walking craze and the inadequacy of London teashops, and he wrote a series of "Household Notes" from a bachelor's point of view. With the turn of the century he took up a "Diary of the War" (the Boer War) in thirteen parts in *Woman* and followed that with "The Week's War" in twenty-one parts. By 1902, with the first of fifty-two "Savoir-Faire Papers" in *T. P.'s Weekly*, he was ready to talk about any subject that struck his fancy, from "The Importance of Going to Belgium" to "The Nobility of the Horse" to "The City Lunch" (titles of the first three lighthearted items). Politically he was a Socialist, and presently his sympathies got expressed. In 1909 he published a violent attack on Toryism in the *New Age*. It was published as a pamphlet, *The Present Crisis*, in 1910.

The most trenchant of such social-political writing came with World War I. Bennett was by this time one of the most famous authors of the day in England, and his views were sought, and they were given in profusion. He had friends in government, he served on voluntary and official war committees and eventually in the government itself, in the ministry of information. Occasionally he wrote at the request of the government, as with the small book that followed from his official tour of the front (*Over There: War Scenes on the Western Front*, 1915), and in articles on the Irish uprising in 1916.

The war articles began with the chance that he was "in Calais Harbour during mobilisation" (he published a piece with that title on 8 August 1914). Later that month he wrote the first of what proved to be a long series of articles for the *Daily News*. With interruptions, these articles continued throughout the war, numbering more than one hundred thirty pieces. They were often severely critical of government policy. In America the *Saturday Evening Post* wanted "a statement of the British case" from him, and he obliged with *Liberty!*, which appeared in the *Post* in October 1914 and was published in pamphlet form in America and England the same month. Two years later, at a time when the *Daily News* articles were in abeyance, he began a weekly causerie on war matters in the *New Statesman*, of which he was a director. These pieces, written gratis under the pseudonym Sardonyx, numbered more than one hundred by the end of the war. Much information on all of Bennett's wartime journalism is contained in Kinley Roby's *A Writer at War* (1972).

With the end of the war, the things that interested Bennett resumed their wide range. Four collections of such material, some of it from before the war, appeared in later years: *Things That Have Interested Me* in three volumes (1921, 1923, and 1926), and *The Savour of Life: Essays in Gusto* (1928). In his introduction to the last book, he wrote: "Life for me has many savours, which I relish keenly. Therefore many subjects interest me. I never write on a subject that does not interest me, and I always write as well as heaven permits."

One special category of things that interested him was travel. He was an inveterate traveler, taking in early years excursions to the Continent and to North Africa, in middle years a visit to America, in later years trips through the Mediterranean and to Russia. He lived in France for nine years. He loved boats all his life and spent much time sailing ("I like nothing extremely, except a yacht," he wrote in later life), and he was able to work as fully and efficiently on his yacht as at home. The chief literary results of his travels are four books: *Those United States* (1912), concerning his visit to America in 1911; *Paris Nights and Other Impressions of Places and People* (1913), which gathers essays of several years on travels in France, Italy, Switzerland, and England; *From the Log of the Velsa* (which was published in America in 1914, though publication in England was delayed for six years on account of the war), a description of his travels along the coasts of England and the Continent in his first large boat; and *Mediterranean Scenes: Rome–Greece–Constantinople* (1928), which describes sights on a trip with the American financier Otto Kahn. By all odds the finest of these books is *Paris Nights*, which mingles observation with considerable autobiographical detail. Some of the best essays in it are republished in *Sketches for Autobiography*: "Evening with Exiles" (in Paris with other expatriates), "Monte" (gambling in Monte Carlo), "First Journey into the Forest" (Fontainebleau, near his country home), "In Watling Street" (at his country home in Bedfordshire at the turn of the century).

Much of the travel writing remains uncollected, and much of it is part and parcel of that compendium of things that interested Bennett-his journals. One brief travel sketch, "Railway Accident at Mantes," published in the *Cambridge Review* in 1920 and reprinted in *Things That Have*

"The Business Man of Letters," a caricature of Bennett by Owl that appeared in the 2 April 1913 issue of Vanity Fair

1929 (1930) is an assortment of entries distinct from the regular journal he kept for that year. Some of the entries do not concern 1929. *The Journals of Arnold Bennett* (1932-1933) reproduce about one-third of the whole of the journals. They include nothing from the years 1929, 1930, and 1931, and omit a journal kept in 1906-1907 (it was unavailable at the time the published journals were assembled). The manuscript volume for 1931 was probably willfully destroyed in the 1970s. The Penguin edition of the *Journals* in 1971 includes material from the 1906-1907 volume and also the *Florentine Journal.* The introduction to the fourth volume of *Letters of Arnold Bennett* (1986) shows that there was systematic omission of sexual material by all editors, at least for the years through 1907.

In 1904, a year in which he wrote three novels along with weekly journalism, Bennett had to try to allay the fears of his literary agent that he was writing more books of more sorts than the market would bear. He asked Pinker to name an author who had "spoiled his reputation by too rapid production of good work." He himself was not even working rapidly: "You would be under a false impression if you imagined that I am working at pressure. I am not. I could do lots more. I have vast leisure." It was true. But Pinker's concern was in part the rapid production of bad work, and he thought that publication of the "Savoir-Faire Papers" and "A Novelist's Log-Book" in book form would damage Bennett's more serious reputation. He won on them, but not on the subsequent similar pocket philosophies. In the introduction to *The Savour of Life: Essays in Gusto* Bennett wrote about *How to Live on 24 Hours a Day:*

> Many years ago I wrote a series of articles on the daily organization of time for the *Evening News.* They excited considerable interest. When I proposed to republish them in book form I was most strongly urged not to do so, and terrible prophecies were made to me of the sinister consequences to my reputation if I did. I republished them. . . . I followed it up with a dozen or more books in a similar vein. And I do not suppose that my reputation would have been any less dreadful than it is if I had never published a line for plain people about the management of daily existence.

Interested Me the following year, was lifted with only the slightest addition from a journal entry of 8 July 1911. The much longer "Evening with Exiles," which first appeared in the *English Review* in 1910, was drawn from journal entries of 28 September 1903, 26 April 1904, 6 May 1904, and 24 May 1904. No doubt other essays were similarly composed. An illustrated journal that he kept on a trip to Florence was published in part in the *Criterion* in 1927, and the whole was published as a little book, *Florentine Journal,* forty years later.

Bennett himself published brief selections from his early journals as Christmas gifts: *Things That Interested Me* (1906) and *Things Which Have Interested Me . . . , Second Series* (1907). His *Journal*

There is no doubt, though, that in highbrow quarters the existence of the pocket philosophies has usually been a mark against Bennett, and it may be of no effect to say that the two most popular ones–*How to Live on 24 Hours a Day* and *The Human Machine*–were written in the same months that Bennett was planning and writing what is generally regarded as his finest novel, *The Old Wives' Tale.* He wrote in a letter to his friend George Sturt in November 1907, when he had finished *The Human Machine* and was writing the first section of *The Old Wives' Tale,* "At the end of this year I shall have jolly near written 365,000 words in the year–much of which is nothing but Marcus Aurelius & Christ assimilated & excreted by me in suitable form." A few months later he wrote to Pinker to say that the installments of *The Human Machine* in *T. P.'s Weekly* were causing an immense sensation.

The first of the pocket philosophies, *The Reasonable Life: Being Hints for Men and Women* (1907), came from the anonymous series of "Savoir-Vivre Papers" in *T. P.'s Weekly,* including such titles as "Settling Down in Life," "Marriage," "Books," "Success." The flavor of the little book and of the other pocket philosophies can be had from the opening passage in the first of these chapters.

The other day a well-known English novelist asked me how old I thought she was, *really.* "Well," I say to myself, "since she has asked for it, she shall have it; I will be as true to life as her novels." So I replied audaciously: "Thirty-eight." I fancied I was erring, if at all, on the side of "really," and I trembled. She laughed triumphantly. "I am forty-three," she said. The incident might have passed off to my satisfaction had she not proceeded: "And now tell me how old *you* are." That was like a woman. Women imagine that men have no reticences, no pretty little vanities. What an error! Of course I could not be beaten in candour by a woman. I had to offer myself a burnt sacrifice to her curiosity, and I did it, bravely but not unflinchingly. And then afterwards the fact of my age remained with me, worried me, obsessed me. I saw more clearly than ever before that age was telling on me. I could not be blind to the deliberation of my movements in climbing stairs and in dressing. Once upon a time the majority of persons I met in the street seemed much older than myself. It is different now. The change has come unperceived. There is a generation younger than mine that smokes cigars and falls in love. Astounding! Once I could play left-wing forward for an hour and a half without dropping down dead. Once I could swim a hundred and fifty feet submerged at the bottom of a swimming-bath. Incredible!

Simply incredible! . . . Can it be that I have already lived? [Ellipsis Bennett's.]

The chapter is concerned with living in the present and living to the full. The final chapter of the book, "The Secret of Content," is republished in *Sketches for Autobiography.*

How to Live on 24 Hours a Day and *The Human Machine* followed in 1908. In 1911 came *The Feast of St. Friend,* which recommends an agnostic celebration of Christmas. In 1913 Bennett published *The Plain Man and His Wife,* which largely concerns relations between the sexes. *Self and Self-Management: Essays About Existing* appeared in 1918. Bennett described it as "a book of moral essays for the young of both sexes." The last of such books was *How to Make the Best of Life,* published in 1923. Bennett said to his nephew Richard Bennett that it was "a subject as to which I know 1/2 nothing, but a good subject."

Two other books are related to the pocket philosophies. *Our Women: Chapters on the Sex-Discord* (1920) is concerned to define the character of women and their changing status in society. Among other things, Bennett sees that female economic independence will transform relations between the sexes. He advises on relations and draws considerably upon his quarrels with his first wife. *The Religious Interregnum* (1929) was commissioned by the Bishop of Liverpool in consequence of reading an article by Bennett entitled "What I Believe," which appeared in the *Daily Express* in 1925. While working on the book, Bennett wrote to his nephew, "I know nothing about God or the Holy Ghost or anything. This gives me a marked advantage over religious writers and experts." The book aims to describe a natural faith to replace supernaturalism.

Bennett's motto for his life was "strive for perfection," and his mature view of religion was given in the final words of his 1925 *Evening Standard* essay "My Religious Experience" (collected in *Things That Have Interested Me, Third Series*): "For many years I was full of hatred, resentment, and scorn for the fierce upholders of the cult (Wesleyan Methodism) which clouded my youth. Now I am humbler. Those religionists had terrific ideals, even though kindliness in thought and broad tolerance were not among them. And if they arrogated to themselves the authority of God they were unconsciously demonstrating the divinity of man." The motto and the belief in the divinity of man give special meaning to Bennett's assertion that "I always write as well as heaven permits."

Letters:

Arnold Bennett's Letters to His Nephew, edited by Richard Bennett (New York & London: Harper, 1935; London & Toronto: Heinemann, 1936);

Dorothy Cheston Bennett, *Arnold Bennett: A Portrait Done at Home, together with 170 Letters from A. B.* (London: Jonathan Cape, 1935; New York: Kendall & Sharp, 1935);

Arnold Bennett and H. G. Wells: A Record of a Personal and a Literary Friendship, edited by Harris Wilson (London: Hart-Davis, 1960; Urbana: University of Illinois Press, 1960);

Correspondance André Gide–Arnold Bennett: Vingt Ans D'Amitié Littéraire (1911–1931), edited by Linette F. Brugmans (Geneva: Librarie Droz, 1964);

Letters of Arnold Bennett, 4 volumes, edited by James Hepburn (London & New York: Oxford University Press, 1966-1986);

Arnold Bennett in Love, edited and translated by George and Jean Beardmore (London: Bruce & Watson, 1972).

Bibliography:

Norman Emery, *Arnold Bennett: A Bibliography* (Stoke-on-Trent: Central Library, Hanley, 1967);

Anita Miller, *Arnold Bennett: An Annotated Bibliography, 1887-1932* (New York: Garland, 1977).

Biographies:

Reginald Pound, *Arnold Bennett* (London: Heinemann, 1952; New York: Harcourt, Brace, 1953);

Margaret Drabble, *Arnold Bennett: A Biography* (London: Weidenfeld & Nicolson, 1974).

References:

James Hepburn, *The Art of Arnold Bennett* (Bloomington: Indiana University Press, 1963);

Hepburn, ed., *Arnold Bennett, the Critical Heritage* (London & Boston: Routledge, 1981);

Georges Lafourcade, *Arnold Bennett: A Study* (London: Muller, 1939);

Kinley Roby, *A Writer at War* (Baton Rouge: Louisiana State University Press, 1972).

Papers:

Major collections of Bennett's papers are located at the University of Arkansas, Bibliothèque Littéraire Jacques Doucet in Paris, Cambridge University, University of Illinois in Urbana, Keele University, Berg Collection in the New York Public Library, City Museum of Stoke-on-Trent, University of Texas in Austin, and University College in London.

A. C. Benson

(24 April 1862 - 17 June 1925)

Keith Wilson
University of Ottawa

BOOKS: *Memoirs of Arthur Hamilton, B. A., of Trinity College, Cambridge, Extracted from His Letters and Diaries, with Reminiscences of His Conversation, by His Friend, Christopher Carr of the Same College* (London: Kegan Paul, Trench, 1886; New York: Holt, 1886);

William Laud, Sometime Archbishop of Canterbury: A Study (London: Kegan Paul, Trench, 1887);

Le Cahier Jaune: Poems (Eton: Printed by George New, 1892);

Poems (London: Elkin Matthews & John Lane, 1893);

Babylonica (Eton: New, 1895);

Genealogy of the Family of Benson, of Bangor House and Northwoods in the Parish of Ripon and Chapelry of Pately Bridge (Eton: New, 1895);

Lyrics (London: John Lane / New York: Macmillan, 1895);

The Professor (Eton: New [privately printed], 1895);

Thomas Gray (Eton: Drake [privately printed], 1895);

Essays (London: Heinemann, 1896; New York: Macmillan, 1896);

Monnow: An ode (Eton: Drake, 1896);

Lord Vyet, and Other Poems (London & New York: John Lane, 1897);

Ode in Memory of the Rt. Honble. William Ewart Gladstone (Eton: Drake [privately printed], 1898);

Fasti Etonenses: A Biographical History of Eton, Selected from the Lives of Celebrated Etonians (Eton: Drake, 1899; London: Simpkin, Marshall, 1899);

The Life of Edward White Benson, Sometime Archbishop of Canterbury, 2 volumes (London: Macmillan, 1899);

The Professor, and Other Poems (London & New York: John Lane, 1900);

Coronation Ode, Set to Music by Edward Elgar: Book of Words, with Analytical Notes by Joseph Bennett (London: Boosey, 1902);

photograph by J. Palmer Clarke

Ode to Japan (London: Chiswick Press [privately printed], 1902);

The Schoolmaster: A Commentary upon the Aims and Methods of an Assistant-Master in a Public School (London: Murray, 1902; New York: Putnam's, 1908);

The Hill of Trouble and Other Stories (London: Isbister, 1903);

The Myrtle Bough: A Vale (Eton: Spottiswoode, 1903);

21

Alfred Tennyson (London: Methuen, 1904; New York: Dutton, 1904);

The House of Quiet: An Autobiography, edited by J. T. (London: Murray, 1904; New York: Dutton, 1904);

The Isles of Sunset, and Other Stories (London: Isbister, 1904);

The Olive Bough (Eton: Spottiswoode, 1904);

Rossetti (London: Macmillan, 1904; New York & London: Macmillan, 1904);

Edward Fitzgerald (New York & London: Macmillan, 1905);

Peace, and Other Poems (London & New York: John Lane, 1905);

The Thread of Gold (London: Murray, 1905; New York: Dutton, 1905);

The Upton Letters, by T. B. (London: Smith, Elder, 1905; New York & London: Putnam's, 1905);

From a College Window (London: Smith, Elder, 1906; New York & London: Putnam's, 1906);

The Gate of Death: A Diary (London: Smith, Elder, 1906; New York & London: Putnam's, 1906);

Walter Pater (London: Macmillan, 1906; New York & London: Macmillan, 1906);

The Altar Fire (London: Smith, Elder, 1907; New York & London: Putnam's, 1907);

Beside Still Waters (London: Smith, Elder, 1907; New York & London: Putnam's, 1907);

Hymns and Carols (Eton: Spottiswoode [privately printed], 1907);

The Letters of One: A Study in Limitations, by Charles Hare Plunkett (London: Smith, Elder, 1907; New York & London: Putnam's, 1907);

At Large (New York: Putnam's, 1908; London: Smith, Elder, 1908);

The Church and Literature (London: Society for Promoting Christian Knowledge, 1908);

The Personality of the Teacher: The Presidential Address to the Teachers' Guild (London: Hodgson, [1908]);

The Poems of A. C. Benson (London & New York: John Lane, 1909);

The Silent Isle (London: Smith, Elder, 1910; New York & London: Putnam's, 1910);

The Leaves of the Tree: Studies in Biography (London: Smith, Elder, 1911; New York & London: Putnam's, 1911);

Paul the Minstrel, and Other Stories—comprises *The Hill of Trouble* and *The Isles of Sunset* (London: Smith, Elder, 1911; New York: Putnam's, 1912);

Ruskin: A Study in Personality (London: Smith, Elder, 1911; New York & London: Putnam's, 1911);

The Child of the Dawn (London: Smith, Elder, 1912; New York & London: Putnam's, 1912);

Thy Rod and Thy Staff (London: Smith, Elder, 1912; New York & London: Putnam's, 1912);

Along the Road (London: Nisbet, 1913; New York & London: Putnam's, 1913);

Joyous Gard (London: Murray, 1913; New York & London: Putnam's, 1913);

Watersprings (London: Smith, Elder, 1913; New York & London: Putnam's, 1913);

The Orchard Pavilion (London: Smith, Elder, 1914; New York & London: Putnam's, 1914);

Where No Fear Was: A Book About Fear (London: Smith, Elder, 1914; New York & London: Putnam's, 1914);

Escape, and Other Essays (London: Smith, Elder, 1915; New York: Century, 1915);

Father Payne (London: Smith, Elder, 1915; New York & London: Putnam's, 1916);

Hugh: Memoirs of a Brother (London: Smith, Elder, 1915; New York: Longmans, Green, 1915);

Meanwhile: A Packet of War Letters by "H. L. G." (London: Murray, 1916; New York: Dutton, 1916);

The Happy Warrior: A Sight of General Smuts at Cambridge, May 1917 (Cambridge: University Press, 1917);

The Life and Letters of Maggie Benson (London: Murray, 1917; New York & London: Longmans, Green, 1917);

Magdalene College, Cambridge: A Little View of its Buildings and History (Cambridge: Bowes & Bowes, 1923);

The Trefoil: Wellington College, Lincoln, and Truro (London: Murray, 1923; New York: Putnam's, 1924);

Chris Gascoyne: An Experiment in Solitude, From the Diaries of John Trevor (London: Murray, 1924; New York: Dutton, 1924);

Memories and Friends (London: Murray, 1924; New York & London: Putnam's, 1924);

Selected Poems (London: John Lane, 1924);

The House of Menerdue (London: Heinemann, 1925; Garden City, N.Y.: Doubleday, Page, 1925);

The Canon (London: Heinemann, 1926);

Rambles and Reflections, compiled by E. F. Benson (London: Murray, 1926; New York: Putnam's, 1926);

Basil Netherby (London: Hutchinson, 1927);

Cressage (London: Heinemann, 1927).

OTHER: "Eton of To-day: By a Modern," in *Eton of Old; or, Eighty Years Since, 1811-1822, By an Old Colleger*, by William Hill Tucker (London: Farran, 1892), pp. 229-240;

Men of Might: Studies of Great Characters, compiled by Benson and H. F. W. Tatham (London: Arnold, 1892; New York: Longmans, Green, 1921);

"Dr. Samuel Parr," in *Essays by Divers Hands, Second Series* (London: Royal Society of Literature, 1893), pp. 131-147;

Edward White Benson, *Cyprian: His Life, His Times, His Work*, edited by Benson (London: Macmillan, 1897);

Matthew Arnold, *Collected Poems*, introduction by Benson (London: John Lane, 1900 [i.e., 1899]);

John Greenleaf Whittier, *Poems*, selected, with an introduction by Benson (Edinburgh: Jack, [1906]);

The Letters of Queen Victoria: A Selection from Her Majesty's Correspondence Between the Years 1837 and 1861, edited by Benson and Viscount Esher, 3 volumes (London: Murray, 1907);

The Little Flowers of St. Francis of Assisi, introduction by Benson (London: Blackie, 1909);

H. F. W. Tatham, *The Footprints in the Snow and Other Tales*, memoir by Benson (London: Macmillan, 1910);

George Acorn, *One of the Multitude*, introduction by Benson (London: Heinemann, 1911; New York: Dodd, Mead, 1912);

Edward Fitzgerald, *Rubaiyat of Omar Khayyam*, introduction by Benson (London: Siegle, Hill, [1911]);

Brooke F. Westcott, *Daily Readings from the Works of Bishop Westcott*, introduction by Benson (London: Mowbray, 1911);

Charles Dickens, *The Adventures of Oliver Twist*, introduction by Benson (London: Waverley, [1913]);

Brontë Poems: Selections from the Poetry of Charlotte, Emily, Anne and Branwell Brontë, edited, with an introduction by Benson (London: Smith, Elder, 1915; New York & London: Putnam's, 1915);

Robert Keable, *A City of the Dawn*, introduction by Benson (London: Nisbet, 1915; New York: Dutton, 1915);

"The Training of the Imagination," in *Cambridge Essays on Education*, edited by Benson (Cambridge: University Press, 1917), pp. 34-52;

The Reed of Pan: English Renderings of Greek Epigrams and Lyrics, translated by Benson (London: Murray, 1922);

Selections from Ruskin, edited by Benson (Cambridge: University Press, 1923; New York: Macmillan, 1923);

The Book of the Queen's Doll's House, 2 volumes, volume 1 edited by Benson and Sir Lawrence Weaver (London: Methuen, 1924);

"The Art of the Biographer," in *Essays by Divers Hands, Third Series* (London: Royal Society of Literature, 1926), pp. 139-164.

Arthur Christopher Benson was one of the most prolific and popular essayists of the Edwardian period. Son of an archbishop of Canterbury, editor of the selected letters of Queen Victoria, and author of "Land of Hope and Glory," he was an unofficial poet laureate at a time of little competition from the official one, Alfred Austin. While he dabbled in various genres, including poetry, the short story, the novel, and biography, it was the meditative essay, written from the standpoint of a liberal and somewhat sentimental Christian, that he made most distinctively, and lucratively, his own. He had a wide following throughout the English-speaking world, maintained a daunting correspondence, and for the last twenty-eight years of his life kept a diary that amounted at his death to 180 volumes comprising over four million words. He published more than seventy books, most of which have disappeared into an obscurity that is as much a function of changing fashion as of inflated reputation.

Benson was born on 24 April 1862, the second of the six children of Mary Sidgwick and Edward White Benson, headmaster of Wellington College and later archbishop of Canterbury. Educated initially at Temple Grove School at Mortlake, under O. C. Waterfield, of whom he was later to write warmly in *Memories and Friends* (1924), he entered Eton as a King's scholar in 1874 and was elected to a scholarship at King's College, Cambridge, in 1881. He gained a first in the classical tripos in 1884 and in January 1885 returned to Eton as a member of staff, which he was to remain until 1903. His time at Cambridge had been marred by crises both personal and theological, crises which are in part fictionalized in his first, pseudonymously published book, *Memoirs of Arthur Hamilton* (1886) and in *The House of Quiet* (1904). The depression that shadowed his undergraduate years at Cambridge was to return more severely in later life; and his failure to gain a fellowship at King's, for a book on Archbishop William Laud (published in 1887) that was excoriated by G. W. Prothero–the King's tutor–for its scholarly shortcomings, was a disappointment that distanced him emotionally from Cambridge for some years.

It was poetry that occupied Benson during the first years back at Eton, much of it published privately before eventual appearance in volumes published by John Lane in 1893, 1895, and 1897. His first volume of essays (entitled simply *Essays*) was published in 1896, although all but one of the thirteen had already appeared in periodicals. "Henry Bradshaw," "The Late Master of Trinity," "The Ever-Memorable John Hales," "Thomas Gray," "Elizabeth Barrett Browning," "A Minute Philosopher [John Earles]," "Andrew Marvell," and "Vincent Bourne" had all appeared in *Macmillan's Magazine* between April 1886 and April 1895. "Henry More, the Platonist" and "The Poetry of Keble" had appeared in the *Contemporary Review* in 1888 and 1895 respectively, "Christina Rossetti" in the *National Review* in 1895, and "The Poetry of Edmund Gosse" in the *New Review* in 1894. The new essay was on William Blake. The earliest of these, the essays on Bradshaw, the King's fellow and university librarian, and on W. H. Thompson, late master of Trinity, display the anecdotal whimsy, its good humor kept subservient to the eulogizing of greatness, that would come to characterize all of Benson's biographical work. (It is of passing interest to note in the Bradshaw piece an interpretive disagreement with Prothero that may already signal the split that was to widen during Benson's attempt at the King's fellowship.) The literary subjects are addressed with the belletristic confidence that would in turn distinguish the critical work. The essay on Marvell declines into elegiac sonority: "And the singer of an April mood, who might have bloomed year after year in young and ardent hearts, is buried in the dust of politics, in the valley of dead bones." That on Gosse's poetry, praised for its virility, absence of mannerism, and good taste, concludes "to have made some exquisite mood your own, and to have presented it with passionate accuracy, is no light

achievement." Responsiveness to the exquisite is high on the list of Benson's literary virtues–"Mr Austin Dobson is the soul of exquisite *finesse*" while Blake's poetry is "childish" with "the fresh simplicity, but also the vapid deficiences [*sic*] of its quality"–and is inevitably productive of a critically fastidious taste that eschews the fashion for realism and admires idealistic literature as "the anodyne of the spirit, the mother of faith, the nurse of hope!"

This earliest collection provides in its epilogue an indication of the terms within which Benson's biographical and meditative work will consistently shape itself. He declares that "the only true consolation is our faith in the incompleteness of the world as we see it, and in the ultimate completeness of the Divine plan," a position of enduring deference to contingency and divine inscrutability that becomes the repeated refrain of his most popular work. And as a biographer, he takes pride in not pursuing his subjects beyond the bounds of dignity: "They are not sliced into sections and bottled, but sketched with what would fain be a careful and affectionate hand." These twin articles of faith, declared early and adhered to scrupulously, would become both the foundation of Benson's appeal and the limit that circumscribed his talent.

The Eton years, much as the workaday responsibilities of the schoolmaster (and, after 1892, housemaster) came to chafe Benson, provided a stability and emotional center for his young maturity. His closest friendships were all, to some degree, Eton based. Herbert Tatham, with whom he collaborated on *Men of Might* (1892), a book for boys that provided "studies of great characters," had been a friend since their days as pupils at Eton. Both Tatham and A. C. Ainger, nearly twenty years Benson's senior, were fellow masters at Eton. It was through Ainger that Benson met Howard Sturgis, the Eton-educated art patron and literary dabbler. Ainger and Sturgis held the lease of Tan-yr-allt, a house in North Wales that became a bachelor holiday home for Benson and sympathetic Eton colleagues between 1887 and 1899. Francis Warre Cornish and H. E. Luxmoore, both, like Ainger, Eton masters of considerable seniority to Benson, became close friends. Thus Eton was for Benson a home and a social center as well as a workplace, a connection reflected in the substantial (536-page) biographical history of Eton, entitled *Fasti Etonenses*, that Benson published in 1899. The book is a compendium of material "selected

Bishop Benson, his wife Mary Sidgwick Benson (seated to his right) and their children (clockwise from top): Arthur, Maggie, Fred, Hugh, and Nelli. The eldest son, Martin, died in 1878, at age seventeen. (Two Victorian Families, *by Betty Askwith, 1971*)

from the lives of celebrated Etonians" and joined the essay "Eton of To-day: By a Modern," included in William Hill Tucker's *Eton of Old* (1892), as Benson's tribute to an institution from which he was eventually to feel the need to extricate himself but which provided for his younger years the home that Magdalene College, Cambridge would provide for his later ones.

The need for such a center became more pressing as mortality took its toll of Benson's immediate family. His older brother Martin had died in 1878 while still a schoolboy at Winchester, and his sister Eleanor died in 1890. Both deaths, one from meningitis, the other from diphtheria, had been sudden and unexpected. The death of his father in October 1896 was similarly sudden, occurring in Hawarden Church during a visit to the Gladstones. The effect on Benson was devastating, coming close to triggering a breakdown and resignation from Eton. Work on the two-volume life, *Edward White Benson* (1899-1900),

which not only became a public memorial to his father but also provided a route to personal reconciliation with the memory of a man who had often seemed an austere paternal presence, was to prove therapeutic. By the end of the century, Benson had achieved a degree of personal security and public reputation that would prepare him for the more widespread renown that was shortly to be his.

It came almost by accident and somewhat circuitously, generated by service both to the old monarch and the new. The Duke of Albany, son of Leopold and grandson of Victoria, was in Benson's house at Eton for a year, a connection which in the late 1890s placed Benson on cordial terms both with the boy and his mother, the widowed Duchess. Benson was known to Victoria because of his father and was presented to her three times in 1899, on the last occasion being invited to dine at Windsor Castle after having given the Queen a presentation copy of the life of his father. Various commissions for hymns to mark royal occasions culminated in the *Coronation Ode* (1902), set to Edward Elgar's *Pomp and Circumstance March No. 1* and including, as the words to the trio melody, the verse "Land of Hope and Glory." Authorship of what rapidly became a surrogate national anthem was followed, in July 1903, by an invitation to coedit with Reginald, Viscount Esher, the selected correspondence of Queen Victoria. Benson readily accepted, and equally readily wrote a letter of resignation to the headmaster of Eton.

Some of the professional reasons for his resignation are implicit in the sixteen essays that comprise *The Schoolmaster: A Commentary upon the Aims and Methods of an Assistant-Master in a Public School* (1902). In a book that is essentially sympathetic to the profession and convinced of its vocational importance, Benson is forthright in detailing its limitations and inadequacies, many of which are presented as failures of imagination in its practitioners: "It must be frankly admitted that the intellectual standard maintained at the English public schools is low; and, what is more serious, I do not see any evidence that it is tending to become higher." Part of the blame is assigned to a society that privileges action over contemplation, and therefore prizes for its youth an education that emphasizes collective and competitive effort, epitomized in the unhealthy worship of athletics over quieter and more individual achievements. The intellectual counterpart to the dominance of compulsory sport is the emphasis on a classical curricu-

Arthur Christopher Benson, age twenty-one, with his brothers, Edward Frederic, age fifteen, and Robert Hugh, age eleven (photograph by Elliott & Fry)

lum for all boys: "a very small percentage of the boys who do Greek ever get within measurable distance of appreciating it as literature. . . . how we dare to exclude enjoyment so rigorously from our system of education is one of those mysteries that it is difficult to fathom." The ultimate indictment of the existing system for Benson is "that we send out from our public schools year after year many boys who hate knowledge and think books dreary, who are perfectly self-satisfied and entirely ignorant . . . not only satisfied to be so, but thinking it ridiculous and almost unmanly that a young man should be anything else." Benson was to return to these themes in later works, with attacks on slavish submission to classics in the classroom and competitive sports outside it as discursive hobbyhorses that would always afford a quick canter when other invention failed.

Upon leaving Eton, Benson moved to the Old Granary in Cambridge, where he was to live for the next two years before experimenting with rural solitude in a move to Hinton Hall at Haddenham, further within the fen country, in March 1906. He was elected fellow of Magdalene in October 1904, an honor that occurred simultaneously with some months of speculation about whether he would be offered, and whether he would accept, the headmastership at Eton. In the event, he let it be known that he would not accept, and the offer was not made. Thus by 1905, the ties to Eton had been decisively loosed as those to Magdalene became tighter.

Benson's publication during this period was becoming ever more prolific. As work on the royal letters progressed, he produced also three volumes–*Rossetti* (1904), *Edward Fitzgerald* (1905), and *Walter Pater* (1906)–for Macmillan's English Men of Letters series. These biographies had been preceded in 1904 by a life of Tennyson for Methuen. At the same time Benson was compiling two volumes of short stories, *The Hill of Trouble* (1903) and *The Isles of Sunset* (1904), which were based on medieval fantasy tales that he had created to tell boys at Eton; they were later republished in a single volume entitled *Paul the Minstrel* (1911). There was also a book that returned to the format of *Memoirs of Arthur Hamilton*, offering the supposed life story of an editor's cousin under the title *The House of Quiet: An Autobiography*. The nature of the reflections is familiar from the earlier volume, although here the central protagonist is unnamed and tells his own story through the pages of a diary. Benson's preface to the third edition–it was to go through four editions and twelve reprintings in seven years–reveals the possible reason for its popularity and indicates the market to which Benson's meditative work, whether fictionalized or in essay form, would increasingly appeal: *The House of Quiet* "was written for all whose life, by some stroke of God, seemed dashed into fragments, and who might feel so listless, so dismayed, that they could not summon up courage even to try and save something from the desolate wreck." The protagonist, whose musings on education echo those in *The Schoolmaster* and whose thoughts on religion and life presage those in later essays, faces death in the knowledge "that there is nothing worth fretting over or being heavy-hearted about; that the Father's arm is strong, and that His heart is very wide."

In 1905, in addition to *Edward Fitzgerald* and *The Isles of Sunset*, Benson published a volume of poetry, *Peace, and Other Poems*; a volume of essays, *The Thread of Gold*; and another volume of thinly fictionalized musings, *The Upton Letters*, this time masquerading as a collection of letters sent by a schoolmaster, known only as T. B., to an ailing friend who has taken up residence in Madeira for health reasons. In April 1904 Benson had taken a holiday in the Cotswolds with Herbert Tatham, and it was the experience and landscape of that trip that formed the associative background to both *The Thread of Gold* and *The Upton Letters*–indeed, *The Upton Letters* received its name because of the proximity of Broadway, the idyllic village where Benson and Tatham were based, to the town of Upton-on-Severn. *The Upton Letters* was undoubtedly the best of Benson's books published under a semifictionalized format and achieved a following indicated commercially by the thirteen impressions it enjoyed in its first three years. Its subject matter is wide-ranging but predictable to readers of the earlier volumes, and Benson takes the opportunity not only to launch another attack on the classical curriculum but also to offer an alternative program in which Latin is retained but loses centrality to French and shares secondary position with history, modern geography, a little mathematics, and elementary science. Speculation on educational matters also allows suggestions for reforming school religious services by reducing emphasis on dogma and liturgical tradition and encouraging spiritual vitality and a sense "that there is indeed a golden clue that leads through the darkness of the labyrinth"–a motif that is picked up in the title of *The Thread of Gold*. The assumption of a "golden clue" lies behind the two things in which T. B. places his hope: faith in God and faith in love, "not . . . the more vehement and selfish forms of love, the desire of youth for beauty, the consuming love of the mother for the infant. . . . But the tranquil and purer manifestations of the spirit, the love of a father for a son, of a friend for a friend." The emphasis here reflects Benson's world, that of Eton and Magdalene and romanticized, if not overtly romantic, male friendship, as much as T. B.'s. T. B. also speculates about the modern novel, biography, autumnal pleasures, egotism, failing friendships, and the ultimate mystery of death, about which he arrives at confident conclusions: "either the spirit that we knew has lost the individuality that we knew and is merged again in the great vital force . . . or else . . . the identity remains, free from the dreary material conditions, free to be what it desired to be."

The Upton Letters is one of Benson's most controlled ruminative works, primarily because of the center that the device of T. B. provides it.

Benson in 1896 (photograph by Kissack)

The Thread of Gold covers much the same ground but, lacking the need to keep in touch with a narrative core, it rapidly becomes indulgently discursive, trite homily never more than a ubiquitous first-person pronoun away. It is divided into forty-two sections, and after section twenty-seven, which describes a trip to Canterbury, sentimentalized theological speculation dominates: "And then all these anxious visions left me; and I felt for awhile like a tiny spray of sea-weed floating on an infinite sea, with the brightness of the morning overhead." The basic idea of the book–"that there is a certain golden thread of hope and love interwoven with all our lives, running consistently through the coarsest and darkest fabric"– reveals in its phrasing the capacity for metaphor to become distractingly incarnate, and the coy implication of the reader in the writer's joys and sorrows does not disguise the preciousness of the authorial sensibility. The problem is with the basic conception. "I have for a great part of my life desired . . . to make a beautiful book. . . . I mean to put into my book only the things that appear to me deep and strange and beautiful; and I can happily say that things seem to me to be more and more beautiful every day." The adjectival approximateness and panglossian sentiment indicate the element of strain in the emotional and spiritual satisfactions that the book celebrates.

The appointment to Magdalene bore titular fruit in Benson's work in the publication of *From a College Window* (1906), a collection of eighteen essays, twelve of which originally appeared in *Cornhill Magazine* between May 1905 and April 1906. This was the first collection of general speculative essays, offering musings both pragmatic and theoretical on a range of matters whose nature is indicated by the twelve original *Cornhill* subjects: "The Point of View," "On Growing Older," "Books," "Sociabilities," "Conversation," "Beauty," "Art," "Egotism," "Education," "Authorship," "The Criticism of Others," and "Religion." The six additions were "Priests," "Ambition," "The Simple Life," "Games," "Spiritualism," and "Habits." The opening essay, "The Point of View," may indicate something of the source of the addictive appeal that Benson's rhetorical stance seems to have held for his public: "My desire is but to converse with my readers, to speak as in a comfortable *tête-à-tête*, of experience, and hope, and patience." The essay "Conversation" reveals that comfort is increased in a context of "simple openness" and "equal comradeship" that is more feasible between men: "with women there is a whole range of experience and emotions that one does not share, so that there is an invisible and intangible barrier erected between the two minds." Such gender distinctions are invoked also in the essay "Art": women rarely achieve prominence in art because "they seldom or never have that calm, strong egotism . . . which . . . seems almost a condition of attaining the highest success in art." By contrast, the essay "Priests" not only claims that the qualities of a priest are more commonly encountered in women than in men but also sees "the conception of God as masculine" as "in itself a limitation of His infinite perfection." The corollary to this is that "if we could divest ourselves of a thought which possibly has no reality in it, we should perhaps grow to feel that the true priesthood of life could be exercised as well by women as by men, or even better."

When such thematic lines are drawn between discrete essays, not merely within a single volume but throughout the prose volumes, it is possible to identify in Benson's observations an unusual compound of conventional opinion and originality. At their best, Benson's essays can be assertive and challenging—hence his uncompromising

attacks, repeated in *From a College Window*, on contemporary education and games—however predictable their clubman approach: "I was staying the other day in the house of an old friend, a public man" begins "The Criticism of Others" or "I was sitting the other day in a vicarage garden with my friend the vicar" begins "Spiritualism." The artifice of the conversational gambit, which helps to obscure the distinction between essays proper, biographical fiction, and autobiography, may pall, but the familiarity of the speaking voice reflects a sincerity that has the capacity to beguile as frequently as it bores.

The year 1907 was a momentous one for Benson. The selection from Queen Victoria's letters was published in three volumes, and four other books appeared, one a slim collection of hymns and carols published privately at Eton. Of the others, *The Letters of One: A Study in Limitations*, published under the pseudonym Charles Hare Plunkett, is similar in vein to a 1906 volume, *The Gate of Death: A Diary*. Both use the same device of discovered letters, letters which muse upon the pains of love and death. The two other 1907 volumes, *The Altar Fire* and *Beside Still Waters*, are variations on similar themes. *The Altar Fire* comprises the spiritual diary of an imagined friend who endures the loss of his son, his wife, and his daughter, himself surviving long enough to face the horrors of both life and death with joyful equanimity: "The secret was to bear, to endure, not stoically nor stolidly, but with a quiet inclination of the will to sorrow and pain, that were not so bitter after all, when one abode faithfully in them." In a preface, Benson summarizes the purpose that inspires this group of books as a whole, a purpose that was shortly to be uncomfortably relevant to his own life: "the motive of this book is to show that . . . [suffering] is at once curative and curable, a very tender part of a wholly loving and Fatherly design." The most directly autobiographical of the group is *Beside Still Waters*, whose hero, Hugh Neville, reflects on a life closer to Benson's than that of any of the other thinly veiled autobiographical protagonists who author diaries and letters for the "posthumous" benefit of sympathetic editors.

Benson's actual life at this time was beginning to pass through dangerous extremes of joy and pain. His friendship with George Mallory, who had arrived at Magdalene from Winchester as an exhibitioner in October 1905, was a source both of companionship and niggling jealousies. The young Magdalene men to whom he became

A. C., R. H., and E. F. Benson at Tremans, Horsted Keynes, in December 1913 (photograph by H. Abbott, Lindfield)

close were as much a reminder of generational differences as of emotional sympathies. The health of his sister Maggie, who in May 1907 suffered a mental breakdown that necessitated her confinement under a committal order that Benson was called upon to sign, gave cause for both personal and familial concern. By November 1907, Benson himself was in a state of nervous collapse that resulted in his departure temporarily from Magdalene and specialist care at a London nursing home. Thus began the first of the two lasting bouts of depression that troubled Benson's mature life. The illness was to last until the autumn of 1909, and to run concurrently with a degree of financial success and public honor that were to be given respective embodiment in the check for forty-six-hundred pounds that he received as his profits from the popular edition of the Victoria letters and his being made a commander of the Royal Victorian Order. After his illness had run

its course, Benson returned to Magdalene with renewed vigor, a return to community concerns from introspective brooding that was signaled in his resignation of the tenancy of the isolated Hinton Hall. From this point on, Magdalene was to occupy ever more of his energies and to benefit ever more from his generosity.

During his illness, Benson published another substantial collection of eighteen essays entitled *At Large* (1908), repeating the format that had been so successful in *From a College Window*. The group's eclecticism is again indicated in the oblique relationship between the component parts of the contents page: "The Scene," "Contentment," "Friendship," "Humour," "Travel," "Specialism," "Our Lack of Great Men," "Shyness," "Equality," "The Dramatic Sense," "Kelmscott and William Morris," "A Speech Day," "Literary Finish," "A Midsummer Day's Dream," "Symbols," "Optimism," "Joy," and "The Love of God." The opening essay speculates about the Hinton Hall experiment and is couched as a defense of the quiet contemplative life by "a reluctant bachelor" who invites chosen friends to a secluded country house. The emphasis throughout the collection is on the gentler pleasures that are independent of money and success, written very much with the oracular confidence of someone who has both. Even those essays that would seem to concern themselves with more muscular subjects, such as "Travel," tend to return to the virtues of contemplation: "what good comes from the multiplication of unnecessary activity. . . . I do not feel any doubt that we are not sent into the world to be in a fuss." The essay "Specialism" laments the decline of the amateur, and the spirit of the amateur, defined by Benson as "a leisurely lover of fine things," dominates. The closer that Benson gets to palpable social questions, the clearer the limits of his imagination become. Thus while he can declare himself in "Equality" to be "a sincere believer in socialism," he remains convinced that "radical inequality of character" and the demands of the family system must remain inconsistent with grandiose schemes for social equality. Besides, "Such property as I possess has . . . been entirely acquired by my own exertions. I have never inherited a penny, or received any money except what I have earned." Such confidence in the possibility of total self-determination in one who was the son of an archbishop of Canterbury, educated at Eton and Cambridge, and on visiting terms with royalty suggests an almost impertinent failure of perspective and is not alleviated by the courtesies of condescension: "I am democratic enough to maintain that I have no sense whatever of personal superiority.... I do not think my social traditions are. better than the social traditions of any other stratum of society ... all I would say is that they are different from the social traditions of other strata, and I much prefer to live without having to consider such matters at all." It is difficult to reconcile such self-deception with the satirical freshness of "A Speech Day," in which even old positions are argued with verve and wit: "to persist in regarding the classics as the high-water mark of the human intellect seems to me to argue a melancholy want of faith in the progress of the race." The overall impression of the collection is that Benson is working through, with fluctuating attention, a familiar formula and to an inevitable conclusion: "we can never wander beyond the range of the Will that has made us, and bidden us to be what we are."

Benson's output in 1909 was limited, as a result of his extended illness, to a republication by John Lane of poems selected from earlier volumes, and his single book of 1910, *The Silent Isle*, was very much in the vein of the earlier *Beside Still Waters* but without the interceding presence of a fictionalized narrative voice. This time Benson muses on life in his own person and from the perspective of his solitude in the fen country. The book comprises fifty-nine sections, with an introduction and epilogue, and the only unity of mood that Benson claimed for it derives from his decision to retire from the restlessness of public responsibilities into a life of seclusion. The book is thus a kind of spiritual autobiography, lauding again the contemplative virtues as a partial justification of the decision to retreat.

The next collection of essays, *The Leaves of the Tree*, is a group of biographical cameos of people known to Benson, written at a time when questions about individual identity were increasingly interesting him, as evidenced in the title of his other new work of 1911, *Ruskin: A Study in Personality*. There are eleven sketches in all, providing personal impressions of Bishop Westcott, Henry Sidgwick, J. K. Stephen, Bishop Wilkinson, Professor Newton, Frederic Myers, Bishop Lightfoot, Henry Bradshaw, Charles Kingsley, Bishop Wordsworth, and Matthew Arnold. While the emphasis in the essays is on individual idiosyncrasy and, in the broadest sense, the spiritual qualities that inspired it, an epilogue both explains the metaphor of the book's title ("The sap that to-day flows through one leaf may to-morrow flow in another. Just so I hold it to be with men") and elaborates on the primary idea that provoked its use. The conclusion reached is "that there is some central collective force, some ultimate source of life and light, of which our lesser wills are but manifestations and emanations." The path to "fulness of life" is through disinterested love and "the highest and noblest of all human qualities–the quality of faith," a quality displayed in their very different ways by the collection's subjects. Thus even in a biographical volume, the often repeated philosophizing of the reflective works nudges its way into prominence and individual portraits are subsumed under its incandescence.

The two volumes published in 1912 complement *Beside Still Waters*. *Thy Rod and Thy Staff* centers on the return to the world of action after the retreat imaged in the earlier volume and includes the experience of Benson's nervous breakdown. *The Child of the Dawn* is a fantasy work in which Benson dies, is taken into heaven, and returns to earth, an odyssey perhaps owing something to the work of George MacDonald, whose *Phantastes* (1858) Benson frequently praised. There was to be another volume that logically belongs to this group–*Where No Fear Was: A Book About Fear* (1914) –which again uses the experience of Benson's mental illness. As a group these provide, in extended and more personally applied form, essentially the same consolatory ruminations offered in the meditative essays, two more volumes of which were published in 1913.

These two volumes show graphically both the strengths and limitations of Benson's essay writing. The titles, *Along the Road* and *Joyous Gard*, grow out of the recurrent tendency to view life as spiritual quest and literature as homily. The essays in *Along the Road* had originally appeared as weekly contributions to the *Church Family Newspaper* and had two declared aims: to indicate "the supreme worth of conciliation, appreciation, tolerance, and brotherly love" and "to awaken the interest ... in common and ordinary things." There are sixty-two essays in all, ranging from evocations of English history and landscape to biographical sketches (William Ewart Gladstone, Robert Browning, John Henry Newman, John Keats, and "Roddy," the Benson family dog), to discussions of moral, literary, or personality matters ("Sympathy," "Jealousy," "Gossip," "Tactfulness," "Liveliness," "Pride," "Art and Life," "The Use of Poetry," "Reading"). Whatever the subject, the essays tend to move toward vaguely uplifting cur-

ARTHUR CHRISTOPHER BENSON

Memories and Friends

By
Arthur Christopher Benson
Master of Magdalene College, Cambridge

*" Thou turnest man to destruction; again Thou
sayest, Come again, ye children of men."*

G. P. Putnam's Sons
New York & London
The Knickerbocker Press
1924

Frontispiece and title page for the American edition of the last volume of Benson's essays to be published in his lifetime

tain lines ("what matters is that we should fill up with wise patience the little gaps of hope, as we walk together, quietly and cheerfully, along the heavenward road"). The more that the speculations are rooted in anecdotal specifics, such as the discussion of service that rests on Beth, the Benson family nurse, or the discussion of death in an essay about Benson's nearly fatal climbing accident in the Alps in 1896, the stronger the individual essay tends to be. The essays that begin in abstraction tend to decline into portentousness. The *Joyous Gard* volume is similar in manner, although less set in the particular, and with a greater tendency to use somewhat automatic evocation of natural imagery to bolster facile notions of spiritual fulfillment at an essay's end. This is encouraged by the image that defines the collection: "I have called this book . . . *Joyous Gard*, because it speaks of a stronghold that we can win with our own hands, where we can abide in great

content, so long as we are careful not to linger there in sloth and idleness, but are ready to ride abroad at the call for help." There are twenty-seven essays in all, and their disparate subjects (some by now looking a little tired—"Poetry and Life," "Art," "Art and Morality," "Education," "Thought," "Sympathy," "Hope," "The Sense of Beauty," "The Principle of Beauty," "Life") are loosely linked into a homiletic chain by the Joyous Gard motif. Since the whole book was completed in two weeks its predictability is not surprising. Nor was Benson's decision to try variations in genre if not in theme: his other work published in 1913 and 1914 was fiction, two novels—*Watersprings* and *The Orchard Pavilion*—which received short shrift from critics and enjoyed little success, even with Benson devotees.

In the years since his illness Benson's life had become increasingly centered on Magdalene and Cambridge, his emotional sympathies focused on various young undergraduates, of whom the most congenial were George Mallory and, by 1914, Geoffrey Madan. As older friends were removed from his immediate circle, either by geographical circumstance or death, as in the case of Herbert Tatham, Benson became more reliant on friendships with undergraduates, particularly those with an Eton connection. These quasi-romantic interludes always seem to have been kept in check by Benson's own fastidiousness and integrity (the section on "purity" in *The Schoolmaster* had been unequivocal in its morality) and by the innate heterosexuality of the recipients of Benson's attentions. His need was for emotional companionship and, in some degree, respect. As with the question of the Eton headmastership, Benson's inclination was to demur at suggestions he might aspire to public office and then bridle a little when it was not offered. He was hurt at not being offered in 1910 the newly created chair of English literature at Cambridge, and delighted at being made president of Magdalene in 1912, moving easily into the role of acting master while Stuart Donaldson was ill for a term in 1913. Thus Magdalene gave him both emotional support and respect, while he gave Magdalene faithful service and much needed financial assistance.

The war years were to be hard on Benson as he witnessed the final fragmentation of his family. The much-loved family nurse, Beth, had died in 1911, but much more shattering and unexpected was the death of his brother Hugh in 1914. This was followed by the deaths of his sister Maggie in May 1916 and of his mother in June 1918, the latter occurring when he was already in the grip of another major depression that had plagued him intermittently since August 1917. When compounded by the carnage of the war, particularly traumatic for a sensibility so shaped by a romanticized notion of male companionship, these personal griefs precipitated Benson into a series of mental crises from which he did not fully emerge until 1922.

Despite the war, Benson maintained until 1918 a regular output of new works, two of them a final act of devotion to his brother and sister: *Hugh: Memoirs of a Brother* (1915) and *The Life and Letters of Maggie Benson* (1917). Fictionalized philosophizing continued in *Meanwhile: A Packet of War Letters by "H. L. G."* (1916) and *Father Payne* (1915), in which a talkative and paternalistic patron of the arts echoes the sentiments of Benson's many essays on art and life. One of these, "Literature and Life," is the second of fif-

teen compositions published as *Escape, and Other Essays* (1915), the only collection of actual essays Benson published during the war. Echoing Dr. Johnson, the essay concludes that a book's function is to show "how to enjoy life or how to endure it," an end that Benson's own work always kept well in view. An essay entitled "Authorship" ascribes three motives to the act of writing: the expression of beauty, the desire to communicate, and the desire for applause, and again the personal application is clear. Benson's observations on literary matters inevitably reflect his own practice, just as his observations on life reflect his own Christian resignation, and those on the English countryside his own topographical allegiances, particularly to the villages around Cambridge. Benson's perennial chafing under a sense of his own cautiousness, responsible for the unusual mixture of convention and originality in his musings, is caught in one of the most interesting pieces, a reminiscence of his time at Eton: "the spirit of the place was potent, and taught me to acquiesce in an ideal of decorum, of subordination, of regular, courteous, unenthusiastic life." Never far beneath the surface confidence of his judgments lurks a self-doubt that owes much to the personal power of a kindly but authoritarian father and the institutional power of a school that Benson could neither fully admire nor fully escape. It is difficult to resist the temptation to read his various mental illnesses as at least in part a result of the conflict between the public life to which he was born and aspired and the life of the anonymous contemplative to which he seemed constitutionally suited. The mastership of the smallest, most familial, and most impecunious Cambridge college was an ideal public position for an essentially private man, just as the chatty, ruminative essay was the ideal literary form.

The mastership finally came to him in November 1915, and he enjoyed the influence and status the position carried. When his depression recurred in 1917, he left Cambridge for a nursing home and did not return for more than two years. In all this time he produced no books, and it is fitting that the first thing he published after his illness was a slim volume entitled *Magdalene College, Cambridge: A Little View of its Buildings and History* (1923). But he had also been working on two more volumes of reminiscences, one a family history recalling the years before his father had been made archbishop of Canterbury (*The Trefoil*, 1923), the other a final collection of biographical sketches, *Memories and Friends*. There were eighteen in all, and together they comprise an affectionate memorial to people he had known and, in the main, liked: Thomas Hare, John Ruskin, O. C. Waterfield, Lady Ponsonby, Margaret Oliphant, J. L. Joynes, Dr. Edmond Warre, Oscar Browning, Edward Compton, Austen Leigh, Blanche Warre-Cornish, Henry James, Charles Fairfax Murray, Stuart Donaldson, J. D. Bourchier, Howard Sturgis, Reginald John Smith, Cecil Spring-Rice, and Rupert Brooke. It was to be the last volume of essays published in Benson's lifetime.

The end came fast, signaled by the periodic chest pains that troubled Benson from the summer of 1924. The symptoms gradually worsened until, on 10 June 1925, he suffered a severe heart attack in his study at Magdalene. He died a week later, very genuinely mourned by the college for which he had done so much. There was to be one final collection of essays, compiled by his surviving, and now more famous brother, E. F. Benson. Entitled *Rambles and Reflections* (1926) and totaling forty essays, it is vintage Benson, ranging over evocations of favorite English locations, elegant literary opinionativeness, biographical and critical sketches, the anatomizing of social graces (including four essays on the art of conversation or public speaking), and optimistic judgments on contemporary social morality. The final essay, "Identity," closes with what might have been an epitaph for its author: "that is the heart of the mystery, that we cannot know whether we can change ourselves or mould our hearts into the pattern which we dimly discern, and sorrowfully desire."

Despite the popularity of his essays with a contemporary audience, Benson's posthumous reputation suffered a rapid decline as both his beliefs and the genre in which he most successfully expressed them became unfashionable. Indeed, they were already becoming unfashionable by the end of the war in which Benson lost many of his younger friends. His greatest successes were enjoyed during the reign of Edward VII, a reign which Benson welcomed with an ode whose title is now largely unknown but which includes words as familiar in Britain as those of the national anthem. It is ironic that "Land of Hope and Glory" should be a secular hymn to expansionist imperial virtues that Benson in more meditative and more representative moods would have found repugnant, just as he came to find the public school orthodoxies that fostered them unconducive to individuality, creativity, and intellectual speculation. It was his misfortune that he and his closest friends should have been shaped so finally by the terms of that world, especially in their dealings with the opposite sex, and his salvation that he should ultimately have found a secure and respected niche in a contemplative corner of it.

Letters and Diaries:

The Diary of Arthur Christopher Benson, edited by Percy Lubbock (London: Hutchinson, 1926; New York: Longmans, Green, 1926);

Extracts from the Letters of Dr. A. C. Benson to M. E. A. (London: Jarrolds, 1926?);

Edwardian Excursions: From the Diaries of A. C. Benson 1898-1904, edited by David Newsome (London: Murray, 1981).

References:

E. F. Benson, *As We Were: A Victorian Peep-Show* (London: Longmans, 1930);

Benson, *Final Edition: Informal Autobiography* (London: Longmans, Green, 1940);

Benson, *Mother* (London: Hodder & Stoughton, 1925);

Benson, *Our Family Affairs* (London: Cassell, 1920);

T. E. B. Howarth, *Cambridge Between Two Wars* (London: Collins, 1978);

M. R. James, *Eton and King's: Recollections, Mostly Trivial, 1875-1925* (London: Williams & Norgate, 1926);

C. C. Martindale, *The Life of Monsignor Robert Hugh Benson* (London: Longmans, 1916);

David Newsome, *Godliness and Good Learning: Four Studies on a Victorian Ideal* (London: Murray, 1961);

Newsome, *On the Edge of Paradise. A. C. Benson: The Diarist* (London: Murray, 1980; Chicago: University of Chicago Press, 1980);

E. H. Ryle, ed., *Arthur Christopher Benson, as Seen by Some Friends* (London: Bell, 1925).

Papers:

The Benson diaries are held at Magdalene College, Cambridge.

Augustine Birrell
(19 January 1850 - 20 November 1933)

Christopher Kent
University of Saskatchewan

BOOKS: *Obiter Dicta* (London: Stock, 1884; New York: Scribners, 1885);

Obiter Dicta: Second Series (London: Stock, 1887; New York: Scribners, 1888);

Life of Charlotte Brontë (London: Scott, 1887);

Res Judicatae: Papers and Essays (London: Stock, 1892; New York: Scribners, 1892);

Essays about Men, Women, and Books (London: Stock, 1894; Scribners, 1894);

The Duties and Liabilities of Trustees: Six Lectures (London: Macmillan, 1896; New York: Macmillan, 1897);

Four Lectures on the Law of Employers' Liability at Home and Abroad (London & New York: Macmillan, 1897);

Sir Frank Lockwood: A Biographical Sketch (London: Smith, Elder, 1898);

Collected Essays, 2 volumes (London: Stock, 1899);

Seven Lectures on the Law and History of Copyright in Books (London & New York: Cassell, 1899);

Essays and Addresses (New York: Scribners, 1901);

Miscellanies (London: Stock, 1901);

William Hazlitt (London & New York: Macmillan, 1902);

Emerson: A Lecture (London: Green, 1903);

Andrew Marvell (London & New York: Macmillan, 1905);

In the Name of the Bodleian and Other Essays (London: Stock, 1905; New York: Scribners, 1905)

Frederick Locker-Lampson: A Character Sketch (London: Constable, 1920; New York: Scribners, 1920);

The Collected Essays and Addresses of the Rt. Hon. Augustine Birrell, 1880-1920, 3 volumes (London & Toronto: Dent, 1922; New York: Scribners, 1923);

More Obiter Dicta (London: Heinemann, 1924; New York: Scribners, 1924);

Augustine Birrell, edited by Francis Henry Pritchard (London: Harrap, 1926);

Et Cetera: A Collection (London: Chatto & Windus, 1930);

Augustine Birrell

Things Past Redress (London: Faber & Faber, 1937).

Augustine Birrell was born in Liverpool on 19 January 1850 to Charles Morton Birrell, a highly respected Baptist minister of Scottish birth, and Harriet Jane Grey Birrell. At sixteen, after a sound education at Dissenting schools, he was articled to a local solicitor. He was an avid reader, and took full advantage of the local resources for self-improvement, the Liverpool Lyceum and the Law Clerk's society. An unexpected legacy enabled him at nineteen to go to Cambridge where he read quietly and took a modest degree in law and modern history while concurrently taking an L.L.B. by correspondence from the University of London. He then settled back into law, to become a barrister in London and soon to achieve a reasonable income from routine litigation. Once established, in 1878 he duly married his boyhood love, Margaret Mirrlees, only to see her die in miscarriage a year later. He thereupon took in his spinster sister as his housekeeper, and resumed sober bachelorhood. All the while, beneath this dull suburban respectability, there twitched an embryonic man of letters. Birrell states that he wrote his first essay at Cambridge, on the Congress of Vienna for the Regius Professor of history, J. R. Seeley. His first published essay, "A Curious Product," which first appeared in *Macmillan's Magazine* in July 1874, was an anonymous outburst of unrequited love for his future wife. Neither was characteristic of his later style, which matured among his lawyer friends and old schoolfellows in the Sons of Ishmael debating society. In 1884 Birrell published, anonymously and at his own expense, six of his own essays and one by a friend, George Radford, under the precociously overripe title *Obiter Dicta*. Their success was startling: six editions were called for in a year. Birrell obliged his suddenly discovered public with five more volumes of essays over the next twenty years, three volumes of literary biography, a memoir of a friend, and some legal writings.

Simultaneous with the rise of his literary career was that of his political career. After two unsuccessful tries in 1885 and 1886, Birrell entered Parliament in 1889 as a Liberal M.P. for the Scottish constituency of West Fife. To complete his transformation into a personage he married in 1888 Eleanor Locker Tennyson, widow of the poet laureate's second son, daughter of Frederick Locker-Lampson, the poet-dilettante, and granddaughter of the earl of Elgin. This marriage produced two sons. With it, said Birrell, began the eleven "happiest years of my life." Without being hedonistic Birrell's was an enjoying nature. He enjoyed the law, even the dull reaches of business law. He enjoyed reading about religion and theology although he was an agnostic. He enjoyed old books, generally, reading them and collecting them. He enjoyed good conversation, being himself a witty conversationalist, and he moved genially in political and literary circles.

Birrell took great interest in the ordinary traffic of life, for which the law affords an excellent vantage point. He did not have great financial success at the bar, though he became a King's Counsel in 1894. He was not a pushing man, but he had a reputation for knowing the law and might have made an excellent judge. He was appropriately made professor of comparative law at University College in 1896, a position that he held until 1899. His published lectures on trusteeship (1896), employer liability (1897), and copyright (1899) are models of lucidity. Solicitors in fact complained that making the law so intelligible jeopardized their profession. Directorships of a leading bank and insurance company testified to Birrell's own soundness as a man of business while providing further grist to this connoisseur of the mundane.

Birrell quietly made his mark in Parliament and the Liberal party, where tact was a much-needed quality during the 1890s. He was able to act as a cultural mediator between the world of provincial nonconformity into which he had been born, a world which gave the Liberal party its core of support, and the Establishment to which he had ties by virtue of his Cambridge education, his profession, and his marriage, and from which the party drew its leadership. That Birrell also considered himself a Scot perhaps added to his detachment and reinforced his cultural self-confidence. His *locus standi* as a politician and as an essayist coincided to a remarkable degree. In 1900 he yielded his safe constituency at his party leader's request to contest a virtually unwinnable one in Manchester, but he returned to Parliament in the Liberal landslide of 1906 as member for North Bristol. Under Henry Campbell-Bannerman's prime ministership he entered the cabinet as education minister, but in 1907 was appointed chief secretary for Ireland (the cabinet minister responsible for Irish affairs). This difficult and onerous post, traditionally a graveyard of political reputations (or worse—one chief secretary was assassinated in 1882), was to be avoided at all costs by ambitious politicians. Birrell was more obliging than ambitious.

The received view has long been that he was a failure as a politician, an archetypal man of the library out of his element in the hard world of politics. However, recent reassessments of his career by Leon Ó Broin and Patricia Jalland argue persuasively that he was in fact a remarkably successful chief secretary during his first six years (the average tenure being two years) and had he resigned in 1912 as he wished, instead of loyally acceding to his prime minister (and very close friend) Herbert Henry Asquith's pressing request that he stay on, he would be remembered far differently. His talent for conciliation, his

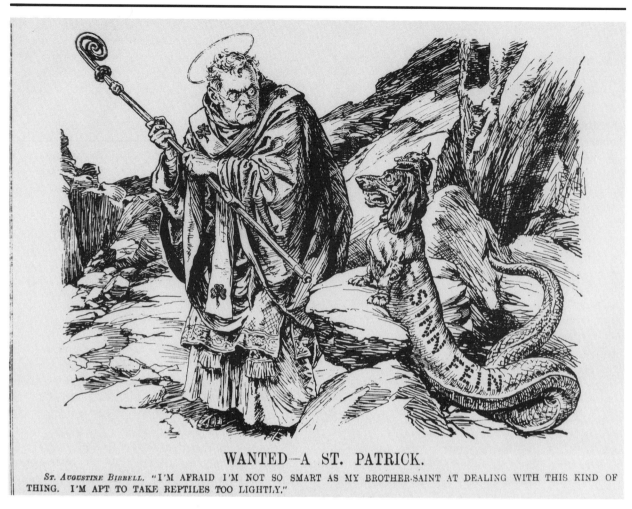

WANTED—A ST. PATRICK.

St. Augustine Birrell. "I'M AFRAID I'M NOT SO SMART AS MY BROTHER-SAINT AT DEALING WITH THIS KIND OF THING. I'M APT TO TAKE REPTILES TOO LIGHTLY."

Political cartoon that appeared in Punch *on 3 May 1916, soon after the Irish Easter Rebellion. Birrell, who in 1907 was appointed chief secretary for Ireland, was severely criticized in England for his inability to prevent the Home Rule Crisis, aggravated by the outbreak of World War I, from erupting in violence.*

deep sympathy with Ireland and total commitment to Home Rule, his understanding and ability to make allowance for the pressures that beset the Irish Home Rule party, perhaps too his non-ruling class manner—all these combined with a businesslike administrative style made him very effective. Unfortunately, his last three years in office were overshadowed by the Home Rule crisis in Ulster and then World War I. Birrell finally was released from his office in 1916, a scapegoat for the Easter Rebellion. Yet, by the testimony of rebels his policy came closer than any other to succeeding in the perhaps impossible task of keeping Ireland loyal to Britain. His last years in office were further blighted by the agonizing illness of his wife, who developed an inoperable brain tumor in 1911 and finally died, insane, in 1915.

Birrell retired pensionless from Parliament in 1918 to a modest literary life. He earned only four thousand pounds over his whole life from his books. He lived to play the part, which he seems to have enjoyed, of one of the last surviving Victorians. With certain exceptions the literary smart set succumbed to his charm. Lytton Strachey found him entertaining, charming but "Underneath, there really seems to be nothing." Birrell reviewed Strachey's *Eminent Victorians* (1918), gracefully praising its elegance and wit, and then quietly pointing out that many of Strachey's criticisms of Thomas Arnold had been made by Arnold's own contemporaries, thus reminding us that there were no more severe critics of the Victorians than the Victorians themselves. Birrell's death on 20 November 1933 drew obituaries generally disparaging of his political career. He was a victim of that double standard by which intellectuals in politics tend to be judged more severely than nonintellectuals, and middle-class politicians more severely than their upper-class counterparts, who might adopt a casual, genial, somewhat skeptical political style and yet be credited with nicely concealed ability and energy. However, when the son of a Liverpool Baptist minister acted thus, it could only be laziness and indecision.

Posterity has not treated Birrell's literary career much more kindly. He is now remembered, somewhat dismissively, chiefly for his essays. He lived to see his work fall sharply in public estimation, but staunchly maintained that he could reread all his essays with pleasure, and that they were at least as good as William Shenstone's. His style gave rise to the eponym "Birrelling," which one editor described as writing "all about nothing and then off at a tangent." Genial rambling over a light subject was no invention of his. Birrell was a great admirer of Charles Lamb, and he might have been defending himself when he wrote of Lamb in *Obiter Dicta: Second Series* (1887), "he was not a fisherman but an angler in the lake of letters, an author by chance and on the sly. He had the right to disport himself on paper, to play and frolic with his own fancies, to give the decalogue the slip, whose life was made up of the sternest stuff, of self-sacrifice, devotion, honesty and good sense."

Birrell's authorial persona was very much that of the literary amateur, the man of the world at ease in his library, gossiping about his beloved books. Many of his slighter essays, with such titles as "Bookworms" or "Old Booksellers" (from *In the Name of the Bodleian and Other Essays*, 1905), were on the pleasures of book collecting, but in no snobbish vein. Books were for reading, not investment, and Birrell deplored the nouveau riche collectors, many of them Americans, who were driving up prices with their acquisitiveness. Why this "odd craze for reading new books" he asked. He was dismayed by the mounting flood of new books which critics failed to stem because they were too generous in their criticism—too reluctant to stigmatize the bad. His attitude to literature was somewhat that of a common-law judge with a full docket. Time being short, one relied on precedent. Cling to the tried and true; the classics provide the touchstones of excellence.

Most of Birrell's essays are about individual authors, somewhat in the spirit of Charles-Augustin Saint-Beuve. Books are an avenue to the author's personality, and this was what interested Birrell most. Not surprisingly, therefore, he was interested less in novelists and poets than in essayists or prose writers, who reveal themselves

Birrell, circa 1922

most directly. He did write book length studies of Charlotte Brontë and Andrew Marvell, but they were primarily biographies ("No criticism of Miss Brontë's novels is possible apart from the story of her life" he declared) as was his book on William Hazlitt, the best of the three. These Brontë and Hazlitt books appeared in the "English Men of Letters" series edited by his good friend John Morley—another distinguished liberal intellectual in politics. This series was the crutch of generations of civil service exam candidates, and reminds one of the prolonged amateur status of English literary criticism before it finally won a place in the English universities. However unfashionable it may seem to many academic professionals today, the notion that literature is chiefly a means of moral education in the broadest sense was an assumption that Birrell reasonably felt he could take for granted. But there was also perhaps an even more utilitarian appeal to his work. The essay was a favorite Victorian examination device, a test of the candidate's fluency, nerve, and ingenuity, and one suspects that many examinees read him not just for literary history, but to learn the useful art of Birrelling. Another practical feature of Birrell's essays is his extensive and often extremely apt use of quotation. In an age when the commonplace book was still a short-cut to wisdom for those of limited education, an author who was liberal with "gems" was much appreciated. But Birrell did not condescend either. He tended to avoid classical allusions, the traditional hallmark of the Establishment: as a Dissenter his classical background was slight. His chosen authors were British–Benvenuto Cellini and Sainte-Beuve being virtually the sole exceptions, for he had no cosmopolitan pretensions. Birrell's essays do not make the intelligent reader uncomfortable about the limitations of his education.

Birrell's best essays number about a dozen and are considerably longer than average. Most were written before 1902, many considerably earlier. They deal mostly with his favorite authors: Samuel Johnson, Thomas Carlyle, Ralph Waldo Emerson, John Henry Newman, Robert Browning, Walter Bagehot, Matthew Arnold, and James Anthony Froude, though one might include a few on religion and history, such as "Truth-Hunting" (*Obiter Dicta*) and "The Muse of History" (*Obiter Dicta: Second Series*). Here one finds little Birrelling, but rather shrewd appreciations of the personalities of figures whom, with the exception of Froude and, perhaps, Emerson, he found sympathetic. "The temper of the man" is the richly Victorian phrase that conveys Birrell's interest. He was fascinated by spiritual temper. A reverent agnostic like many late-Victorian liberal intellectuals, he devoured dry theological works–rather as Leslie Stephen did, though he lacked Stephen's masochistic edge. (His short essay on Stephen, "Anti-Humbug," in *More Obiter Dicta* [1929], is also worthwhile: it shrewdly notes his mortal fear of "speaking humbug.") Yet Birrell deplored what he called "truth-hunting"–overindulgence in vain intellectual speculation, a practice he felt Samuel Taylor Coleridge exemplified: "The real wants of the age are not . . . discussions as to whether 'Person' or 'Stream of Tendency' are apter words to describe God by; but a steady supply of honest, plain sailing men who can be safely trusted with small sums. . . ." There are varieties of anti-intellectualism in Birrell's essays. Thus he was greatly impressed by the power of Newman's writings, by the no-nonsense dogmatism conveyed with immense fertility of style for the single purpose of convincing the reader. The lawyer in Birrell appreciated this. Emersonian transcendentalism, on the other hand, was insipid. In that vein he much preferred the worldly pessimism of Carlyle to Emerson's naive optimism even if he doubted that Carlyle was the puritan he liked to think himself.

Another facet of Birrell's anti-intellectualism emerges in his views on history. Birrell disagreed with his old professor J. R. Seeley, who was one of the chief advocates of introducing professionalism and scientific methodology into the study of history, of taking it out of the hands of the men of letters who were content to keep it a branch of "mere literature." Much of Birrell's appeal to his readers must have lain in his persistent advocacy of cultural amateurism and populism, and the reassurance they conveyed that plain thinking is all that is really needed, that artistic, intellectual, and religious complexities are largely spurious, mystifications generated by people without enough to do, without sufficient contact with the real world. Birrell had an endless supply of anecdotes and epigrams illustrating this theme, such as how Lord Byron hated an author who was "all author and nothing else." Two of his best essays deal with men whose lives exemplify the point. Walter Bagehot did so supremely. Banker, lawyer, economist, and editor–"the hum of affairs sounds through all his writings." Not surprisingly Birrell does full justice to the meaty worldliness of Bagehot, the sense of reality, of how things are actually done in politics, business, or the law, that pervades his writings. But he also captures their subtle spiritual flavor, persuasively attributing it to the influence of William Wordsworth and Newman with the help of two well-chosen passages. But Birrell, although he is rarely negative in his essays (practically his only really hostile essay is on Hannah More), is not unremittingly celebratory. Thus Bagehot is found wanting by one of Birrell's favorite touchstones, admiration of Laurence Sterne's *Tristram Shandy* (1759-1767), which Bagehot found "indecent." This opinion is indicative in Birrell's eyes of a spirit "too much alive to the risks of the social structure, far too anxious lest any convention on which it seems to rest should be impaired in the handling." This comment nicely identifies a certain political valetudinarianism in Bagehot, as well as Birrell's easier confidence in the way of the world.

Somewhat less expected is Birrell's warm admiration of Matthew Arnold, arch-Oxonian, classic, Establishmentarian, scourge of middle-class and particularly dissenting culture. One might expect Arnold to grate particularly on the ears of a man who told how his father, attending a rare ecumenical social event, was mistaken for the Establishment representative on account of his cultured manner and handsome appearance by a bystander who referred to his vulgar-looking Anglican counterpart by the Arnoldian sobriquet "Stiggins." "My father replied in his iciest tones: 'You are mistaken. I am Stiggins'" (*Things Past Redress*, 1937). But in his essay on Arnold, Birrell praised him as a man who had made it one of his chief missions to close the great divide between Establishment and Dissenting culture. Although he admired Arnold the poet, and Arnold the theologian, he regretted that Arnold the man of the world was not better appreciated. "There is a pleasant ripple of life through Mr. Arnold's prose writings." Arnold was not just a literary man, he was a school inspector, and it is very high praise coming from Birrell when he says that if Arnold did not know everything about Dissenters, "he did know a great deal, and used his knowledge with great cunning and effect, and a fine instinctive sense of the whereabouts of the weakest points." Of Arnold's *Essays in Criticism* (first series, 1865; second series, 1888) he says what he would surely wish to be said of his own essays: "They were not written for specialists, or even for students, but for ordinary men and women. . . ."

In one particular Birrell was virtually unique among Victorian essayists. Most of his best essays were published first in book form. He did not publish them first in the reviews as did Bagehot, Morley, Stephen, and the rest. He did write for the review magazines and newspapers, recycling a good deal of this slighter work, though not all, in his later volumes of essays. But his best work appeared first in hard covers. Birrell probably denied himself some significant earnings by this practice. But then Birrell was not a professional man of letters. That was the whole point.

References:
A. G. Gardiner, "Augustine Birrell, K.C.," in *Prophets, Priests and Kings* (London: Dent, 1914);

John Gross, *The Rise and Fall of the Man of Letters* (London: Weidenfeld & Nicolson, 1969);

Patricia Jalland, "A Liberal Chief Secretary and the Irish Question: Augustine Birrell, 1907-1914," *Historical Journal*, 19 (June 1976): 421-452;

Raymond Mortimer, "Augustine Birrell," in *Channel Packet* (London: Hogarth, 1942);

Leon Ó Broin, *The Chief Secretary: Augustine Birrell in Ireland* (London: Chatto & Windus, 1969);

Sir Charles Tennyson, *Stars and Markets* (London: Chatto & Windus, 1957).

Papers:
A collection of Birrell's personal correspondence is at the University of Liverpool; the Birrell papers at the Bodleian Library, Oxford University, include mainly material pertaining to the chief secretaryship.

Robert Bridges

(23 October 1844 - 21 April 1930)

Donald E. Stanford
Louisiana State University

See also the Bridges entry in *DLB 19: British Poets, 1880-1914.*

SELECTED BOOKS: *Poems* (London: Pickering, 1873);

The Growth of Love, anonymous (London: Bumpus, 1876; revised and enlarged edition, Oxford: Daniel, 1889);

An Account of the Casualty Department (London: St. Bartholomew's Hospital, 1878);

Poems (London: Bumpus, 1879);

Poems (London: Bumpus, 1880);

Prometheus the Firegiver (Oxford: Printed at the private press of H. Daniel, 1883);

Poems (Oxford: Printed at the private press of H. Daniel, 1884);

Nero Part I (London: Bell & Bumpus, 1885);

Eros & Psyche (London: Bell, 1885; revised, 1894);

On the Elements of Milton's Blank Verse in Paradise Lost (Oxford: Clarendon Press, 1887); revised and republished in *Milton's Prosody* (1893);

The Feast of Bacchus (Oxford: Privately printed by H. Daniel, 1889);

On the Prosody of Paradise Regained and Sampson Agonistes (Oxford: Blackwell / London: Simpkin, Marshall, 1889); revised and republished in *Milton's Prosody* (1893);

Palicio (London: Bumpus, 1890);

The Return of Ulysses (London: Bumpus, 1890);

The Christian Captives (London: Bumpus, 1890);

Achilles in Scyros (London: Bumpus, 1890);

The Shorter Poems (London: Bell, 1890);

Eden: An Oratorio, words by Bridges, music by C. V. Stanford (London: Bell / London & New York: Novello, Ewer, 1891);

The Humours of the Court (London: Bell & Bumpus, 1893; New York: Macmillan, 1893);

Shorter Poems Book V (Oxford: Printed by H. Daniel, 1893);

Milton's Prosody (Oxford: Clarendon Press, 1893); revised and enlarged edition, with an addi-

Robert Bridges

tional chapter by William Johnson Stone (Oxford: Oxford University Press, 1901; revised and enlarged again, 1921);

Nero Part 2 (London: Bell & Bumpus, 1894);

John Keats: A Critical Essay (Oxford: Privately printed, 1895);

Invocation to Music: An Ode (In Honour of Henry Purcell) (London: Novello, Ewer, 1895);

Poetical Works, 6 volumes (London: Smith, Elder, 1898-1905);

Now in Wintry Delights (Oxford: Daniel Press, 1903);

Demeter (Oxford: Clarendon Press, 1905);

Poetical Works (London, New York, Toronto & Melbourne: Oxford University Press, 1912);

An Address to the Swindon Branch of the Workers' Educational Association (Oxford: Clarendon Press, 1916);

The Necessity of Poetry (Oxford: Clarendon Press, 1918);

October and Other Poems (London: Heinemann, 1920; New York: Knopf, 1920);

The Tapestry (London: Privately printed, 1925);

New Verse (Oxford: Clarendon Press, 1925);

Henry Bradley (Oxford: Clarendon Press, 1926); republished in *Three Friends* (1932);

The Influence of the Audience: Considerations Preliminary to the Psychological Analysis of Shakespeare's Characters (Garden City, N.Y.: Doubleday, Page, 1926);

Collected Essays, Papers, &c., 10 volumes, volumes 4-10 edited by Monica Bridges (London: Oxford University Press, 1927-1936);

The Testament of Beauty (Oxford: Clarendon Press, 1929; New York: Oxford University Press, 1929);

Poetry (London: British Broadcasting Corporation, 1929);

Three Friends: Memoirs of Digby Mackworth Dolben, Richard Watson Dixon, Henry Bradley (London: Oxford University Press, 1932).

OTHER: *Hymns: The Yattendon Hymnal*, edited by Bridges and H. Ellis Wooldridge, four parts (Oxford: Oxford University Press, 1895-1899);

The Influence of the Audience, in *The Works of William Shakespeare*, volume 10 (Stratford-on-Avon: Shakespeare Head Press, 1907);

Poems by the Late Rev. Dr. Richard Watson Dixon, edited, with a memoir, by Bridges (London: Smith, Elder, 1909);

The Poems of Digby Mackworth Dolben, edited, with a memoir, by Bridges (London, New York, Toronto & Melbourne: Oxford University Press, 1911);

Ibant Obscuri, an experiment in the classical hexameter, paraphrases of *Aeneid*, VI: 267-751, 893-898, and *Iliad*, XXIV: 339-660 (Oxford: Clarendon Press, 1916);

The Spirit of Man, edited by Bridges (London, New York, Bombay, Calcutta & Madras: Longmans, Green, 1916);

Gerard Manley Hopkins, *Poems*, edited, with a preface and notes, by Bridges (London: Milford, 1918).

Bridges, circa 1862 (by permission of Robert Bridges, the poet's grandson)

Robert Seymour Bridges is known primarily as a lyric poet and as the author of the long philosophical poem *The Testament of Beauty* (1929). His major concern, poetry, dominates his essays, thirty of which he began editing·in 1927, according to his own rules of phonetic spelling, for his *Collected Essays* (1927-1936), which was printed in a phonetic typeface designed by Bridges and Stanley Morison. (All quotations below taken from this collection have been put into conventional spelling and type.) Bridges's wife, Monica, completed the collected edition after the poet's death in 1930. Of Bridges's literary criticism the American critic and poet Yvor Winters has written, "Any civilized reader will find the critical essays of Bridges to be profitable reading."

His wide-ranging interests also included medicine, secular music, church music and hymns, the pictorial arts, prosody, calligraphy, the correct pronunciation of Greek and Latin, the drama (especially verse drama, including that of the Greeks and Romans), typography, and the problems of textual editing. He wrote well on these subjects in occasional essays and in his letters, which are available in a two-volume edition. He founded the Society for Pure English (S.P.E.) in 1913, supervised its publications, and wrote several tracts published by the society. He wrote memoirs of three friends, the poets Digby Mackworth Dolben and Richard Watson Dixon and the philologist Henry Bradley, which were published separately and then collected under the title *Three Friends* in 1932. He edited the wartime anthology *The Spirit of Man* (1916), and he was the first editor of the poems of his friend Gerard Manley Hopkins and the author of the first serious critique of Hopkins's poems.

Bridges was born on 23 October 1844 in Walmer, Kent, the son of John Thomas Bridges (who died in 1853) and Harriett Elizabeth Affleck. He was educated at Eton (1854-1863), at Corpus Christi College, Oxford (1863-1867), and at St. Bartholomew's Hospital, London (1869-1874). During his brief medical career, which ended with his retirement in 1881, he was a physician at St. Bartholomew's Hospital, the Hospital for Sick Children, and the Great Northern Hospital, all in London. His experiences at St. Bartholomew's gave rise to his first published essay, *An Account of the Casualty Department* (1878), in which he severely criticized the heavy work load imposed on him and fellow physicians.

In 1882 Bridges moved into the Manor House in the Berkshire village of Yattendon, where he met Monica Waterhouse, the daughter of the architect Alfred Waterhouse. They were married in 1884 and had two daughters, Elizabeth and Margaret, and a son, Edward. In 1907 the family made its final home in Chilswell on Boar's Hill overlooking Oxford. In July 1913 Bridges was appointed poet laureate. In 1924 he was a guest for several months of the University of Michigan at Ann Arbor. In this same year he received honorary doctor's degrees from the University of Michigan, Columbia University, and Harvard University. He was awarded the Order of Merit in June 1929. He died at Chilswell on 21 April 1930.

Bridges wrote to his brother-in-law Samuel Butler on 16 February 1900, "I should like you to read my 'Essay on Keats.' Art is what I most care for, and that tract expresses or at least implies my attitude toward it." Bridges's most substantial and important essay, "A Critical Introduction to Keats," was commissioned by A. H. Bullen in the

Bridges's wife, Monica Waterhouse Bridges, in 1888 (by permission of the estate of Robert Bridges)

spring of 1894 for the Muses Library edition of the poems of Keats (1896). It was first published separately (as *John Keats: A Critical Essay*) in Oxford in 1895 and republished as volume 3 of *Collected Essays, Papers, &c.* (1929). Because Bridges considered Keats "one of the highest gifted poets that was ever born into the world," he undertook his commission with care and deliberation. As was his custom when composing his most important works, Bridges asked for advice from friends whose literary judgment he respected. He sent drafts of his essay to the novelist and poet Margaret L. Woods, the poet Canon Richard Dixon, and the music historian Harry Ellis Wooldridge. In his letters to Woods he discussed in detail the major problems to be overcome in achieving his aim—a just evaluation of all the poetry of Keats. There were difficulties of interpretation and questions of style. Specifically, how could the argument in "Ode to a Nightingale" that the bird was immortal and man was not be maintained when in fact both were equally mortal or "immortal" in the terms of the poem? And what were the proper explanations of the obscure allegorical matter in *Endymion* and *Hyperion*? As to style, Bridges mentioned blemishes in diction and imagery found in "Ode to Autumn," "Ode to Indolence," and "Bacchic Ode to Sorrow." All of these subjects discussed in the correspondence found their way into the final version of the essay, which was completed in October 1894. Bridges's overall judgment was positive: Keats had "the highest gift of all poetry . . . the power of concentrating all the far-reaching resources of language on one point, so that a single and apparently effortless expression rejoices the aesthetic imagination at the moment when it is most expectant and exacting and at the same time astonishes the intellect with a new aspect of truth."

In the summer of 1905 Bridges took his family to Switzerland for their health, and by winter he had begun writing an essay on William Shakespeare's plays that had been commissioned by A. H. Bullen as an introduction to volume 10 of the Stratford Town edition of Shakespeare's works. He wrote to Bullen from St. Moritz on 15 January 1906, offering to withdraw the essay (not yet completed) for fear that Bullen and his readers would not like it. He said that his attempt to "solve the problem which his [Shakespeare's] extraordinary mixture of brutality with extreme, even celestial gentleness offers" would "be unpleasant to most readers." Bullen persisted and Bridges finished the article in time for publication in 1907. Entitled "The Influence of the Audience on Shakespeare's Drama" it soon became Bridges's most notorious essay. (It was republished as volume 1 of *Collected Essays*, 1927.) Bridges examines Shakespeare's offenses against propriety and common sense and explains the mixture of "brutality" and "celestial gentleness" by blaming Shakespeare's desire to please a heterogeneous theater audience that for the most part held aesthetic ideals far below Shakespeare's. Shakespeare's offenses indicate that the dramatist "had to reckon with an audience far blunter in feeling than he would find today." The chief offenses are unnecessary and irrelevant obscenities to please the pit; unmitigated horror such as the blinding of Gloucester; unnecessary rudeness of manners and speech; incredible changes in behavior such as the sudden repentance of Angelo in *Measure for Measure* followed by his pardoning; incredible actions such as Macbeth, a man of "magnificent qualities of mind," stooping to the mur-

der of Duncan, and of Othello being so quickly and completely duped by Iago. According to Bridges, these last offenses reveal a weakness of motivation in many of Shakespeare's plots. That is, the characters, even the most noble, are made to act *surprisingly* without proper cause for the sake of dramatic effect, and indeed the effects are often so intense that even a modern audience will overlook them in the theater, but not if they read the plays deliberately and carefully as literature, as Bridges was doing when he wrote this essay.

The essay was controversial, as Bridges intended it to be, coming after a century of Shakespeare idolatry. It drew sharp responses from Alfred Harbage, who in his book *Shakespeare's Audience* (1941) called it a "frivolous assault"; from Augustus Ralli; and from other Shakespearean scholars. However, from the viewpoint of the literary critic (in contrast to the theatergoer) Bridges's objections to Shakespeare's improprieties are not wide of the mark.

When Bridges's friend Mary Elizabeth Coleridge, the great-grandniece of Samuel Taylor Coleridge, died unexpectedly in the summer of 1907, Bridges set to work immediately on a generous tribute to her that appeared in the *Cornhill Magazine* in November of that same year under the title "The Poems of Mary Coleridge" (republished in volume 5 of *Collected Essays*, 1931). Bridges praises Coleridge's verses for their intimacy, spontaneity, beauty, and originality, finding in them "Imagination of a very rare kind, conveyed by the identical expression of true feeling, and artistic insight." Her imagination, which Bridges describes as "intellectual" and "tyrannous," coexisted with "a wide, light hearted active enjoyment of life." From this tension came her best poetry. The obscurity of some of her imagery reminds him of her favorite poet, William Blake; the ethereal tone of her verse owes something to her good friend Richard Watson Dixon. Bridges concludes that she resembles the German poet Heinrich Heine in the masterful ease of her style, but she is more successful than he in approaching the Greek attainment (form) and the Christian Ideal (spirituality), for Heine's verse is not spiritual and is cheapened by cynicism.

An examination of Bridges's other favorite woman poet, "The Poems of Emily Brontë" was first published in the London *Times Literary Supplement*, 12 January 1911, as a review of *The Complete Poems of Emily Brontë*, edited by Clement Shorter. (It was republished in volume 6 of *Col-*

Portrait of Bridges by Roger Fry, painted in 1923 at Chilswell, Boar's Hill, Oxford (by permission of Lord Bridges; photograph by Mrs. Frances Spalding)

lected Essays, 1932.) However, Bridges finds that Brontë is "not delicately conscious" of her rhythm or her rhyme, that her diction is sometimes stereotyped, her imagery sometimes ambiguous. She has not "a perfected style." On the other hand, her simplicity of diction is in her successful poems "the best means of verbal touch with felt reality." She has "a wide intellectual grasp" and "a concentrated fire of native passion." The essay is a judicious evaluation, with faults carefully weighed against virtues. Bridges reveals more enthusiasm for her work in his poem "Emily Brontë" (collected in *New Verse*, 1925), which begins, "Thou hadst all Passion's splendour."

There are several other essays on individual poets that deserve mention. In "Dryden on Milton" (*Speaker*, 24 October 1903; republished in volume 6 of *Collected Essays*) Bridges vents his lifelong contempt for John Dryden, whose verses in praise of John Milton and other poets are quoted only to be attacked. Of Dryden's verse in general he says: "He sinks to dulness of metre, dulness of rhythm, dulness of rhyme (of which he was most

proud), dulness of matter; a dulness as gross as his ruinous self conceit." Of Dryden's attempt to "improve" certain poems such as Geoffrey Chaucer's *The Knight's Tale*, he wrote: "How could Dryden imagine that he was 'improving' Chaucer when he was stuffing in all that stodgy padding?" And at the conclusion of the essay, Dryden's entire career is dismissed with "if all poetry had been like Dryden's, I should never have felt any inclination towards it."

In "Lord de Tabley's Poems" (*Speaker*, 12 December 1903; republished in volume 5 of *Collected Essays*, 1931) Bridges pays tribute to a well-liked friend whose social position he respected. Lord de Tabley was fairly well known in the Victorian period for his verse play *Philoctetes* (1866) and for several volumes of poems. Bridges, in reviewing in this essay a definitive selection of de Tabley's verse, finds much to praise, especially "Ode to Pan," written under the influence of Keats, and also those poems dealing with Lord de Tabley's favorite science, botany.

The essay "George Darley," published in 1930 in volume 4 of the *Collected Essays*, is a composite of an article published in the *Academy* (4 August 1906) and a review (*Times Literary Supplement*, 6 March 1908). Time has not dealt kindly with the reputation of the Romantic poet George Darley. Bridges criticized much of his poetry for weakness of sentiment and looseness of form, but he liked the blank verse of the historical play *Ethelstan* (1841) and the two completed cantos of the allegory *Nepenthe* (1835).

"Dante in English Literature" (*Times Literary Supplement*, 24 June 1909; republished in volume 6 of *Collected Essays*), a review of Paget Toynbee's *Dante in English Literature from Chaucer to Cary*, points to the Italian poet's influence on Chaucer, Milton, Thomas Gray, Percy Bysshe Shelley, Samuel Taylor Coleridge, William Wordsworth, Walter Savage Landor, and George Gordon, Lord Byron. In "The Springs of Helicon" (1909; republished in volume 7 of *Collected Essays*, 1933), a review of J. W. Mackail's book of the same title, Bridges discusses the faults and virtues of Chaucer, Edmund Spenser, and Milton. In "Wordsworth and Kipling" (1912; republished in volume 7 of *Collected Essays*) Bridges argues that in their use in poetry of the speech of the common man Wordsworth and Rudyard Kipling allow their styles to be flawed by the mannerisms resulting from the attempted "dialectic regeneration" of decaying speech forms. Bridges goes on to argue that the needed reforms in poetic style should be

KEATS

Among Keats' poems, too, a quantity of indifferent and bad verse is nau printed, not only from a reverence for his first volume, which he never revis'd, and which is very properly reprinted as he issued it, but also from a feeling which editors hav had, that since enything miht be of value, everything was; so that eny scrap of his which coud be recover'd has gon into the collections. Concerning which poor stuff we my be consol'd to know that Keats himself would hav had no care; for, not to speak of what was plainly never intended for poetry at all, he seems to hav regarded at least his earlier work as a mere product of himself and the circumstances, nau good nau bad, its quality depending on influences beyond his control and often adverse, under which he alwys did his best. On one point only was he sensitiv, and that was his belief that he sometymes did well, and would do better. The failures he left as they were, having too much pride to be asham'd of them, and, as he felt, too strong a conviction of an everflowing, and, an increasing and bettering inspiration, to think it worth while to spend fresh tyme in revising what a younger moment had cast off.

The purpos of this essay is to examin Keats' more important poems by the highest standard of excellence as works of art, in such a manner as my be both useful and

78

CRITICAL INTRODUCTION

interesting; to investigate their construction, and by naming the faults to distinguish their beauties, and set them in an approximat order of merit; also, by exhibiting his method, to vindicate both the form and meaning of some poems from the assumption of even his reasonable admirers that they hav neither one nor other. Within the limits of an introductory chapter this cannot be done, even imperfectly, without omitting much which the reader my look for in an account of Keats' poetry, but such omissions can be easily supply'd: a knowledg, too, of the circumstances of Keats' life will be assumed,¹ and some acquaintance with his letters to his friends; and since these make of themselves a most charming book, and one that can never be superseded as a commentary on his work in its personal aspect, this view of the subject will here be disregarded except when required to eid the criticism or interpretation of a poem.

I shall take the poems in what seems the most convenient order for my purpos, and shall not trouble the reader with eny other artificial connection, reserving general remarks till the end. The worser pieces I shall not notice at al.

¹Mr. Sidney Colvin's Life of Keats, in the English Men of Letters series, supplies all these desiderata most satisfactorily.

79

M

Opening pages of the revised version of Bridges's essay "A Critical Introduction to Keats" included in Collected Essays, Papers, &c. *(1927-1936). This collection, which consists of thirty essays edited according to Bridges's own rules of phonetic spelling, is printed in a phonetic typeface designed by Bridges and Stanley Morison (Ewelme Collection of Robert Bridges, Special Collections, Thomas Cooper Library, University of South Carolina).*

achieved by new prosodies but not necessarily by new poetic diction.

The most interesting passage in "The Glamour of Grammar" (1912; republished in volume 8 of *Collected Essays*, 1934), a review of Logan Pearsall Smith's *The English Language* and of Ernest Weekley's *The Romance of Words*, occurs when Bridges expresses his love of archaic locutions, those "exiled aristocrats," as he calls them, which, now banished, may eventually be welcomed, together with certain lowborn expressions, once again to the language: "there are many patiently awaiting their opportunity, like the democratic and oligarchical parties in the cities of ancient Greece; those whom one revolution drives out the next will bring back; and they have plenty of old friends at home ready to welcome them." Bridges not only welcomed them but frequently used them in his own poetry. Among the words he wants back are old vocalized inflections of plurals such as *frostës, postës,* and *flamës,* which he prefers to "the unpronounceable mono-syllables that, having taken their place, strew their cacophonies broadcast over our best literature."

In *An Address to the Swindon Branch of the Workers' Educational Association,* delivered on 28 October 1916 and published as a book by the Clarendon Press the same year (it was republished in volume 10 of *Collected Essays,* 1936), Bridges's topic is the "improvement of the educational condition of the working classes," which he says is important if democracy is to be preserved and stabilized after the war. Legislation necessary to give the workers leisure to educate themselves must be passed, but leisure alone is not enough, especially in the cities, where so many workers spend their free time in cheap, sensation-seeking amusements such as the cinema. "This trifling with the emotions is the most soul-destroying habit that can be indulged." The chief purpose of education is to awaken and train the inborn love of Beauty and Good. Proper environment for this would be provided if hostels and colleges could be established that would teach the workers to make proper use of the city's theaters, concert halls, and art galleries or to respond to the beauties of nature in the country. Thus the working man may escape "wrong-loving," which leads to "vulgarity . . . our national blemish and sin."

Bridges's famous critique of his friend Hopkins was written not as an independent essay but as a "Preface to Notes" for the *Poems of Gerard Manley Hopkins* (1918). Hopkins died on 8 June 1889, and by August of that year Bridges had written to Canon Dixon that he planned an edition of Hopkins's poems with a memoir. The following August, Bridges wrote to Hopkins's mother that the edition had not yet been completed and that it should contain a memoir or at least a preface that would "put the poems out of the reach of criticism." Bridges then decided that the time was not yet right for the publishing of his friend's highly experimental verse, and he delayed further work on the edition and preface until 1917. On 7 September of that year Bridges wrote to Hopkins's mother that the selection of her son's poems that he had published in *The Spirit of Man* the previous year had been well received and that the Oxford Press would probably be willing to publish a complete edition of the poems. By February 1918 Bridges was working up to seven or eight hours a day at his task. The edition was published in December 1918 with Bridges's preface.

In putting "the poems out of the reach of criticism" the editor attempted to foresee the faults that the critics might find in Hopkins's verse, to define them, and to point to the virtues of the poetry that he felt were in danger of being obscured by the faults. As to the faults—those of taste include affectation and exaggeration of metaphor. Bridges defined Hopkins's chief errors in style as those oddities deriving from his doctrine of inscapes, the frequent obscurities caused by the omission of the relative pronoun to make space for more "poetical" words, and the deliberate use of words (including homophones) that are ambiguous in meaning and in grammatical function. Clarity was always one of Bridges's criteria. Hopkins frequently preferred multiplicity of meaning to lucidity. Other faults are undue harshness in sound effect and freakish and repellant rhymes. The reader, warns Bridges, must learn to tolerate these flaws and not allow them to obscure the power of the "terrible posthumous sonnets" nor "the rare masterly beauties that distinguish Hopkins' work."

In "George Santayana" (*London Mercury,* August 1920; republished in volume 8 of the *Collected Essays*), a review of *Little Essays, Drawn from the Writings of George Santayana* (1920) by Logan Pearsall Smith, Bridges, in praising Santayana's style, achieved a beautifully written essay on Santayana, the man and his thought. Bridges was reading Santayana's work by the turn of the century, when he also began a correspondence with him. They met for the first time at Oxford during World War I and continued a friendly relationship until Bridges's death. In interpreting those concepts of Santayana's philosophy that had special meaning for him, Bridges wrote: "The philosophy as I understand it is very consonant with my own thought." A few years later when Bridges was writing *The Testament of Beauty* (1929) these ideas he shared with Santayana and which he discusses in this essay were very much in his mind, especially what he defines as the "building up of idealism–that is, the supremacy of the imagination–on a naturalistic or materialistic basis," and the function of reason, which "harmonizes the various instincts and impulses, and establishes an ideal good." He also agrees with Santayana about the importance of Beauty, which Santayana states "gives men the best hint of ultimate good which their experience as yet can offer," and of which Bridges writes in the *Testament of Beauty*:

> Beauty is the highest of all these occult influences,
> the quality of appearances that thru' the sense
> wakeneth spiritual emotion in the mind of man.

Furthermore, he shares Santayana's notion that "Morals . . . requires only the harmony of each life," an idea which Bridges fully develops in book 4 ("Ethick") of the *Testament*. And by writing his long poem, Bridges put into practice Santayana's opinion that "it is the function of poetry to emotionalize philosophy." Bridges's essay is a valuable introduction to Santayana's work and also to *The Testament of Beauty*.

    Milton's Prosody, published in its final version in 1921, was the culmination of a long interest in the intricacies of prosody, ancient and modern, a subject that Bridges approached from a theoretical as well as a practical point of view. The rules of prosody that he formulated were consistently applied in the composition of his own verse, which included two thousand lines of experimental poetry written according to the rules of classical (quantitative) prosody as laid down by his young friend William Johnson Stone in the tract "Classical Metres in English Verse," which was privately printed in 1898 and republished in the 1901 edition of Bridges's *Milton's Prosody*.

    Bridge's first analysis of Milton's verse appeared as a pamphlet in 1887 entitled *On the Elements of Milton's Blank Verse in Paradise Lost*. Subsequent versions and expansions appeared in 1889, 1893, and 1901. Included in the 1921 edition is the final version of a tract entitled "On the Prosody of Accentual Verse." It has a history even

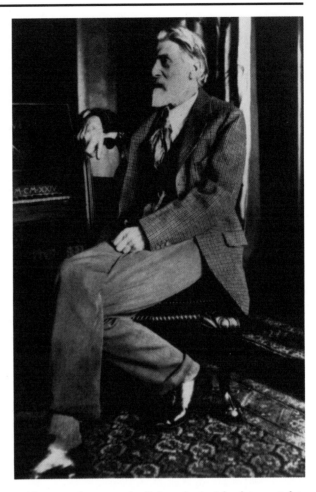

Bridges seated next to the Dolmetsch clavichord presented to him by friends on his eightieth birthday (by permission of Lord Bridges)

longer than the work on Milton. Bridges's interest in accentual verse probably began about 1877 when Hopkins sent him a copy of "The Wreck of the Deutschland" (1875), written in what Hopkins called "sprung rhythm" and what Bridges usually referred to as accentual verse or the "new prosody." It was designed to invigorate poetic rhythms and bring them closer to speech rhythms. Bridges's formulation of the rules of accentual verse first appeared in 1901. There are elements of his system repeated in "A Letter to a Musician on English Prosody" (*Musical Antiquary*, October 1909), in which he examines the proposition that poetic rhythms derive their beauty from a conflict between metrical and speech rhythms.

    In "Humdrum and Harum-Scarum: A Lecture on Free Verse," first published in the *London Mercury* (November 1922; republished in volume 2 of *Collected Essays*, 1928), Bridges confronts the free-verse movement begun by the French and continued in England by Ezra Pound and others.

He sets out "to discover the meaning of the term Free Verse, and then to show some of the results that must follow from writing in the new or free manner." He comes to the conclusion that the poets of the future will find "a wide field for exploration in the metrical prosody." A complete rejection of all prosody will result in chaos.

Bridges's last comments on prosodic matters are in the form of a note rather than an essay. " 'New Verse:' Explanations of the Prosody of My Late Syllabic 'Free Verse' " was written in 1923 and first published in 1933 in volume 7 of the *Collected Essays*. The essays on prosody discussed above are written in a precise, analytical style appropriate for the subject and are not designed for easy or popular reading. To those who would object, Bridges, in his 1921 study of Milton, makes this statement: "people . . . think that prosody is pedantic rubbish, which can only hamper the natural expressions of free thought and so on. But in all arts the part that can be taught is the dry detail of the material which has to be conquered; and it is no honour to an art to despise its grammar."

In "Humdrum and Harum-Scarum" Bridges was concerned with revolt against prosody. In "Poetic Diction in English" (*Forum*, May 1923; republished in volume 2 of *Collected Essays*) he turned his attention to the simultaneous revolt against what he called "the old diction" as it appears in the "poets of today," whom he does not name. He probably had in mind Pound and his fellow imagists who eschewed archaisms and poeticism (though Pound himself used many of them in his earliest poetry) and insisted on the vocabulary of common speech. He admits that the general attitude of these rebels is rational as was a similar movement the preceding century begun by Wordsworth and other Lake Poets. However, with quotations from Milton's "Lycidas," with its heightened and inspired poetic diction, from Shelley's "Adonais," with its extravagant yet beautiful expressions, and from Matthew Arnold's "Thyrsis," with its simplified diction, he attempts to demonstrate that Milton's and Shelley's poems are powerful and convincing whereas Arnold's poem is lacking in passion and is unconvincing. A diction elevated above the colloquial may be employed in our greatest poems and should not be rejected. He also defends the use of archaic language and poeticisms when they are appropriate for the texture of the verse, as he did in his essay "The Glamour of Grammar," discussed above.

Of Bridges's "capacity for friendship" R. K. R. Thornton has said that it "manifests itself in a variety of ways; and this is not the friendship which insists on the friend's perfections but a generous friendship which loves at the same time as perceiving faults." Nowhere is this capacity for loving friendship more evident than in the memoirs of Digby Mackworth Dolben, Richard Watson Dixon, and Henry Bradley. The first of these was published as an introduction to Bridges's edition of *The Poems of Digby Mackworth Dolben* (1911) and was republished after revisions in 1915 and again in *Three Friends* (1932). Bridges met Dolben at Eton in 1862 and quickly took the younger boy under his guidance. Dolben was always in delicate health, pale and sensitive with a strong interest in religion that became almost obsessive and that led him from High Church views toward Roman Catholicism. He was suspended from Eton in 1863 under suspicion of being a Catholic. Bridges describes their brief days at Eton and Dolben's religious and psychological problems there with tact and eloquence. In commenting on a picture of Dolben in the Eton Gallery he remarks, "You can see the saint, the soul rapt in contemplation, the habit of a stainless life, of devotion, of enthusiasm for high ideals." Henry James, on completing his reading of the volume sent him by Logan Pearsall Smith, was moved to write: "The disclosure and picture of the wondrous young Dolben have made the liveliest impression on me, and I find his personal report of him very beautifully and tenderly, in fact just perfectly, done. . . . Bridges seems to me right that no *equally* young case has ever given us ground for so much wonder (in the personal and aesthetic connection)."

Bridges's memoir includes a critique of Dolben's poetry that is chiefly about his religious experiences and that abounds in Pre-Raphaelite imagery and diction. Bridges's evaluation is generous, perhaps too generous. In the course of comparing Dolben's poetic methods with his own, Bridges makes a statement about personal and impersonal poetry that has become famous: "Our instinctive attitudes toward poetry were very dissimilar, he regarded it from the emotional, and I from the artistic side. . . . What had led me to poetry was the inexhaustible satisfaction of form, the magic of speech, lying as it seemed to me in the masterly control of the material. . . . Dolben imagined poetic forms to be the naive outcome of peculiar personal emotion."

Bridges with Aldous Huxley at Garsington, 1928 (by permission of Alfred A. Knopf, Inc.)

ers of the Willow," his finest poem according to Bridges.

In 1928, five years after the death of the philologist Henry Bradley, Bridges wrote to his widow in response to her praise of his memoir of Bradley that he was "among the few men with whom I have had full friendship without any intellectual or moral reserve." They met about the turn of the century at Oxford, and Bradley made his first visit to Bridges's home at Yattendon in September 1901. Their fast-developing friendship is described in Bridges's memoir, first published in 1926 and republished in *Three Friends*. Bradley's major contribution to scholarship was the part he played in the editing of the *Oxford English Dictionary*, to which he devoted forty years of his life. Beginning work on it in 1883, he became senior editor in 1915, a position he maintained until his death in 1923. Bridges loved the man and respected his learning and literary judgment. He consulted Bradley when he was compiling *The Spirit of Man* and when he was experimenting with his neo-Miltonic syllabics from about 1913 on, and also on such diverse matters as Chaucer's prosody and Bridges's own system of phonetic spelling and phonetic script. He chose Bradley in 1913 to be one of the founders of the Society for Pure English.

Two essays written a dozen years apart may be considered a defense of the importance of poetry in the scientifically oriented twentieth century. *The Necessity of Poetry* (1918; republished in volume 10 of *Collected Essays*) was delivered as an address to an audience of workingmen on 22 November 1917. It is an attempt to "justify the claim of poetry to that high place which is and always has been granted it." The poet, Bridges goes on to say, like the scientist, uses words, but he uses them as an artist, connotatively, with all their suggestive meanings, whereas the scientist uses them denotatively, in their single meanings. Yet the poet has truths to impart about the human condition just as important as those communicated by the scientist. Furthermore, the poet has the advantage of working in metered, that is, precisely rhythmic, language, which adds an extra emotional dimension to his compositions. This emotional power of poetry is identical with "those universal primary emotions of man's spirit which give rise also to morals and religion and which lead us naturally toward Beauty and Truth."

Bridges's final essay, *Poetry* (1929; republished in volume 10 of *Collected Essays*), was delivered as the first of the National Lectures on the

The memoir of Richard Watson Dixon was published in 1909 as an introduction to a selection of Dixon's poems edited by Bridges, who had first heard about Dixon from Dixon's former student Hopkins in 1878. The next year he traveled to Hayton for a visit with the Canon, who was rector there (they corresponded until Dixon's death in 1900), and when Dixon went to London to engage in research on his six-volume history of the Church of England, he stayed in Bridges's apartment. As with Dolben, the memoir is a tribute to the man as well as the poet. Bridges was much taken with the Canon's personality. In the course of a long description he wrote, "his eyes did their angelic service to the soul without distraction." Bridges and Dixon liked to take long walks together in the woods, walks commemorated in Bridges's poem "Eclogue I: The Months." In his critique of Dixon's poetry Bridges commented on its mysticism, its medieval and Pre-Raphaelite sources, and on Dixon's response to the beauties of nature, especially as it appears in "The Feath-

Robert Bridges (by permission of Lord Bridges)

B.B.C. on 28 February 1929, when he was still at work on *The Testament of Beauty*. In his lecture as in his poem Bridges sees human life as a progression from material origins (the atom) to a vision of God, a vision motivated in some elect souls by a consciousness of Beauty to which the art of poetry contributes.

A few other essays deserve mention. The publication of volume 1 of *The Works of Sir Thomas Browne*, edited by Charles Sayle, gave Bridges the opportunity to attack this much-admired stylist of the seventeenth century. In his review-essay "Sir Thomas Browne" (*Speaker*, 14 May 1904; republished in volume 8 of *Collected Essays*) he argues that Browne "was a mass of superstition" and that his *Pseudodoxia Epidemica* (1646) contains "gems of fatuity." "I have never found it readable except piecemeal." Bridges is again on the attack in "Bunyan's *Pilgrim's Progress*" (*Speaker*, 8 April 1905; republished in volume 8 of *Collected Essays*), a review of a new edition of *Pilgrim's Progress* illustrated by George Cruickshank. It is a severe analysis of the aesthetic and ethical weaknesses of Bunyan's work. "The story being bad in itself, is not excused or sustained by the allegory." Bridges finds the style crude, the theology narrow, and Pilgrim's abandonment of wife and

children morally inexcusable. "Studies in Poetry" (1907; republished in volume 7 of *Collected Essays*), a review of Stopford Brooke's volume of the same name, praises Brooke for his "fine tastes" and "true instincts" but condemns him for faulty methods in evaluating and explaining poetry. Brooke overestimates the influence of such historical movements as the French Revolution on individual poets; he mistakenly thinks a poem can be explained by an account of its genesis; and he is not severe enough in his critical evaluations. Of Brooke's statement "When criticism seeks to find out faults, I never think it worth much," Bridges ironically observes, "It would have been delightful if Aristotle had said this when lecturing on Homer." Bridges also condemns Brooke's facile acceptance of the notion that the complicated structure of Shelley's "Ode to the West Wind" was the result of spontaneous, unconscious, unpremeditated inspiration; and of Brooke's statement that "there is a logic of emotion as well as of thought," Bridges observes that it would have been useful if Brooke had demonstrated "what some of the laws of this logic are."

In "Word-Books" (1910; republished in volume 7 of *Collected Essays*), a review of *A New Shakespearean Dictionary* by Richard John Cunliffe and a new edition of W. W. Skeat's *An Etymological Dictionary of the English Language*, Bridges argues the importance of sound dictionaries for the understanding, appreciation, and writing of literature; and to illustrate his point he mentions that Robert Browning "when he determined to devote himself to poetry . . . read the whole of Johnson's dictionary through." "The Bible" (first published in 1911; enlarged and republished the same year; enlarged version republished in volume 8 of *Collected Essays*) is one of the most positive essays that Bridges wrote. It gives high praise to the Miles Coverdale / William Tyndale bible of the sixteenth century. It is "an early and inimitable masterpiece of abounding grace," and its coming into existence "we must recognize to be a piece of extravagant good fortune . . . it was Tyndale and Coverdale who raised the plant; the revisers of 1611 only pruned and trained it." An account of the composition of the Coverdale / Tyndale bible and an analysis of the style are given to support Bridges's high estimate of its worth and of its influence on English-speaking peoples.

Of interest chiefly to specialists are "On the Musical Setting of Poetry" (1896), first published as a preface to Bridges's "ode" for the bicentenary of the death of Henry Purcell, which was set to music by Sir Hubert Parry and sung at the Leeds Festival and at the Purcell Commemoration in London in 1895, and three essays on church music: "A Practical Discourse on Some Principles of Hymn-Singing" (*Journal of Theological Studies*, October 1899), "English Chanting" (*Musical Antiquary*, April 1911), and "Anglican Chanting" (*Musical Antiquary*, January 1912). These four essays were republished in 1935 in volume 9 of *Collected Essays* (with some repetitious parts of "Anglican Chanting" omitted) together with a few separate notes on church music too brief to be considered essays. Bridges published two essays entitled "The Proper Pronunciation of Latin" (*Oxford Point of View*, May 1902 and November 1903), and later two more entitled "The Pronunciation of Latin" (*Speaker*, 30 July 1904; *Times Educational Supplement*, 1 October 1912), and he also wrote a brief letter in 1912 on the subject to the London *Times* (20 September). His essay "On the Pronunciation of English" appeared in the 23 July 1904 issue of the *Speaker*. To the tracts of the Society for Pure English from 1919 to 1928 he contributed the following essays: "On English Homophones," "On the Dialectical Words in Edmund Blunden's Poems," "What is Pure French?" (written under the pseudonym Matthew Barnes in collaboration with Monica Bridges), "On the Terms Briton, British, Britisher" (in collaboration with Henry Bradley), "Pictorial, Romantic, Grotesque, Classical," "Poetry in Schools," and "Words from the French, E–EE" (as Matthew Barnes in collaboration with Monica Bridges.) Also, in 1927 he edited for S. P. E. *English Handwriting* (*Tract No. XXVIII*), with thirty-one calligraphic plates and eleven pages by Bridges of "General Remarks."

As an essayist Bridges will be remembered chiefly for his critiques of the poetry of Keats and the plays of Shakespeare and his memoirs of Dolben, Dixon, and Bradley. His highly theoretical but valuable articles on prosody will not be forgotten by specialists in the field. Nor will serious readers of poetry forget the high standards of lucidity, precision, and decorum he expected to be maintained in the art of poetry.

Photograph of Bridges used as the frontispiece for The Testament of Beauty *(1929), his last volume of poetry*

Donald E. Stanford, *The Selected Letters of Robert Bridges with the Correspondence of Robert Bridges and Lionel Muirhead*, 2 volumes (Newark: University of Delaware Press, 1983-1984).

Bibliography

George L. McKay, *A Bibliography of Robert Bridges* (New York: Columbia University Press / London: Oxford University Press, 1932);

Lee Hamilton, *Robert Bridges: An Annotated Bibliography* (Newark: University of Delaware Press, forthcoming).

References:

Nicolas Barker, *The Printer and the Poet* (Cambridge: University Printing House, 1970);

Sister Mary Gretchen Berg, *The Prosodic Structure of Robert Bridges' "Neo-Miltonic Syllabics"*

Letters:

The Correspondence of Robert Bridges and Henry Bradley 1900-1923 (Oxford: Clarendon Press, 1940);

Richard J. Finneran, ed., *The Correspondence of Robert Bridges and W. B. Yeats* (London: Macmillan, 1977);

(Washington: Catholic University of America Press, 1962);

Roy Fuller, "The Case for Bridges," *Times Literary Supplement*, 30 November 1970, p. 54;

Fuller, "Untroubled Waters," *London Magazine*, 24 (December 1984-January 1985): 133-137;

Albert Guerard, *Robert Bridges: A Study of Traditionalism in Poetry* (Cambridge, Mass.: Harvard University Press, 1942);

William G. Holzberger, "Remembering the Bard of Boar's Hill," *Michigan Quarterly Review*, 19 (Winter 1980): 117-127;

George L. Lensing, "Bridges Redivivus," *Hudson Review*, 32 (Summer 1979): 308-312;

Catherine Phillips, "Robert Bridges and the English Musical Renaissance," in *Order in Variety: Essays and Poems in Honor of Donald E. Stanford* (Newark: University of Delaware Press, forthcoming);

Jean-Georges Ritz, *Robert Bridges and Gerard Hopkins 1863-1889: A Literary Friendship* (London: Oxford University Press, 1960);

John Sparrow, *Robert Bridges* (London: Oxford University Press, 1955);

Lindon Stall, "Robert Bridges and the Laws of English Stressed Verse," *Agenda*, 2 (Spring-Summer 1973): 96-108;

Donald E. Stanford, *In the Classic Mode: The Achievement of Robert Bridges* (Newark: University of Delaware Press, 1978);

Stanford, "Robert Bridges and the Free Verse Rebellion," *Journal of Modern Literature*, 1 (September 1971): 19-31;

Edward Thompson, *Robert Bridges* (London: Oxford University Press, 1944);

R. K. R. Thornton, Review of *The Selected Letters of Robert Bridges*, *Hopkins Quarterly*, 11 (Spring / Summer 1984): 48-55;

Yvor Winters, "Robert Bridges and Elizabeth Daryush," *American Review*, 8 (January 1937): 353-367;

Winters, "The Shorter Poems of Robert Bridges," *Hound & Horn*, 5 (January-March 1932): 321-327;

Elizabeth Cox Wright, *Metaphor Sound and Meaning in Bridges' Testament of Beauty* (Philadelphia: University of Pennsylvania Press, 1951);

F. E. Brett Young, *Robert Bridges: A Critical Study* (London: Secker, 1914).

Papers:
Most of Bridges's papers are in the Bodleian Library, Oxford. There are letters in the British Library, London; the University of Reading Library; and in the archives of the Royal College of Physicians, London; and letters and manuscripts in the Cooper Library, University of South Carolina, Columbia, South Carolina.

G. K. Chesterton

(29 May 1874 - 14 June 1936)

Peter Hunt

See also the Chesterton entries in *DLB 10: Modern British Dramatists, 1900-1945*; *DLB 19: British Poets, 1880-1914*; *DLB 34: British Novelists, 1890-1929: Traditionalists*; and *DLB 70: British Mystery Writers, 1860-1919*.

BOOKS: *Greybeards at Play: Literature and Art for Old Gentlemen. Rhymes and Sketches* (London: Johnson, 1900);

The Wild Knight and Other Poems (London: Richards, 1900; revised edition, London: Dent / New York: Dutton, 1914);

The Defendant (London: Johnson, 1901; New York: Dodd, Mead, 1902; enlarged edition, London: Dent, 1903);

Twelve Types (London: Humphreys, 1902); enlarged as *Varied Types* (New York: Dodd, Mead, 1903); abridged as *Five Types* (London: Humphreys, 1910; New York: Holt, 1911); also abridged as *Simplicity and Tolstoy* (London: Humphreys, 1912);

Robert Browning (New York & London: Macmillan, 1903);

G. F. Watts (London: Duckworth / New York: Dutton, 1904);

The Napoleon of Notting Hill (London & New York: Lane, 1904);

The Club of Queer Trades (London & New York: Harper, 1905);

Heretics (London & New York: Lane, 1905);

Charles Dickens (London: Methuen, 1906; New York: Dodd, Mead, 1906);

The Man Who Was Thursday (Bristol: Arrowsmith / London: Simkin, Marshall, Hamilton, Kent, 1908; New York: Dodd, Mead, 1908);

Orthodoxy (New York: Lane, 1908);

All Things Considered (London: Methuen, 1908; New York: Lane, 1908);

The Ball and the Cross (New York: Lane, 1909; London: Gardner, Darton, 1910);

Tremendous Trifles (London: Methuen, 1909; New York: Dodd, Mead, 1909);

G. K. Chesterton (photograph by Howard Coster)

George Bernard Shaw (London: Lane, Bodley Head / New York: Lane, 1910; enlarged edition, 1935);

What's Wrong With the World (London & New York: Cassell, 1910);

Alarms and Discursions (London: Methuen, 1910; enlarged edition, New York: Dodd, Mead, 1911);

William Blake (London: Duckworth / New York: Dutton, 1910);

Appreciations and Criticisms of the Works of Charles Dickens (London: Dent / New York: Dutton, 1911);

The Innocence of Father Brown (London & New York: Cassell, 1911);

The Ballad of the White Horse (London: Methuen, 1911; New York: Lane, 1911);

Manalive (London & New York: Nelson, 1912);

A Miscellany of Men (London: Methuen, 1912; enlarged edition, New York: Dodd, Mead, 1912);

The Victorian Age in Literature (London: Williams & Norgate, 1913; New York: Holt, 1913);

Magic: A Fantastic Comedy (London: Secker, 1913; New York & London: Putnam's, 1913);

The Flying Inn (London: Methuen, 1914; New York: Lane, 1914); enlarged as *Wine, Water and Song* (London: Methuen, 1915);

The Wisdom of Father Brown (London & New York: Cassell, 1914);

The Barbarism of Berlin (London & New York: Cassell, 1914); republished in *The Appetite of Tyranny, Including Letters to an Old Garibaldian* (New York: Dodd, Mead, 1915);

Letters to an Old Garibaldian (London: Methuen, 1915); republished in *The Appetite of Tyranny, Including Letters to an Old Garibaldian* (New York: Dodd, Mead, 1915);

Poems (London: Burns & Oates, 1915; New York: Lane, 1915);

The Crimes of England (London: Palmer & Hayward, 1915; New York: Lane, 1916);

A Short History of England (London: Chatto & Windus, 1917; New York: Lane, 1917);

Utopia of Usurers (New York: Boni & Liveright, 1917);

Irish Impressions (London: Collins, 1919; New York: Lane, 1920);

The Superstition of Divorce (London: Chatto & Windus, 1920; New York: Lane, 1920);

The Uses of Diversity (London: Methuen, 1920; New York: Dodd, Mead, 1921);

The New Jerusalem (London: Hodder & Stoughton, 1920; New York: Doran, 1921);

Eugenics and Other Evils (London & New York: Cassell, 1922);

What I Saw in America (London: Hodder & Stoughton, 1922; New York: Dodd, Mead, 1922);

The Ballad of St. Barbara and Other Verses (London: Palmer, 1922; New York & London: Putnam's, 1923);

The Man Who Knew Too Much and Other Stories (London & New York: Cassell, 1922; abridged edition, New York & London: Harper, 1922);

Fancies Versus Fads (London: Methuen, 1923; New York: Dodd, Mead, 1923);

St. Francis of Assisi (London: Hodder & Stoughton, 1923; New York: Doran, 1924);

The End of the Roman Road (London: Classic, 1924);

Tales of the Long Bow (London & New York: Cassell, 1925);

The Everlasting Man (London: Hodder & Stoughton, 1925; New York: Dodd, Mead, 1925);

William Cobbett (London: Hodder & Stoughton, 1925; New York: Dodd, Mead, 1926);

The Incredulity of Father Brown (London & New York: Cassell, 1926);

The Outline of Sanity (London: Methuen, 1926; New York: Dodd, Mead, 1927);

The Queen of Seven Swords (London: Sheed & Ward, 1926; London & New York: Sheed & Ward, 1933);

The Catholic Church and Conversion (New York: Macmillan, 1926; London: Burns, Oates & Washbourne, 1926 [i.e., 1927]);

The Return of Don Quixote (London: Chatto & Windus, 1927; New York: Dodd, Mead, 1927);

The Collected Poems of G. K. Chesterton (London: Palmer, 1927; New York: Dodd, Mead, 1932);

The Secret of Father Brown (London: Cassell, 1927; New York & London: Harper, 1927);

The Judgement of Dr. Johnson; A Comedy in Three Acts (London: Sheed & Ward, 1927; New York & London: Putnam's, 1928);

Robert Louis Stevenson (London: Hodder & Stoughton, 1927; New York: Dodd, Mead, 1928);

Generally Speaking: A Book of Essays (London: Methuen, 1928; New York: Dodd, Mead, 1929);

The Moderate Murderer, and The Honest Quack (New York: Dodd, Mead, 1929);

The Poet and the Lunatics: Episodes in the Life of Gabriel Gale (London: Cassell, 1929; New York: Dodd, Mead, 1929);

The Thing (London: Sheed & Ward, 1929); republished as *The Thing; Why I Am a Catholic* (New York: Dodd, Mead, 1930);

G. K. C. as M. C., edited by J. P. de Fonseka (London: Methuen, 1929);

Four Faultless Felons (London & Toronto: Cassell, 1930; New York: Dodd, Mead, 1930);

The Resurrection of Rome (London: Hodder & Stoughton, 1930; New York: Dodd, Mead, 1930);

Come to Think of It . . . (London: Methuen, 1930; New York: Dodd, Mead, 1931);

The Ecstatic Thief (New York: Dodd, Mead, 1930);

Caricature of Chesterton and Hilaire Belloc by Max Beerbohm, 1907 (from A Book of Caricatures, *by Max Beerbohm, 1907).*

All Is Grist: A Book of Essays (London: Methuen, 1931; New York: Dodd, Mead, 1932);

Chaucer (London: Faber & Faber, 1932; New York: Farrar & Rinehart, 1932);

Christendom in Dublin (London: Sheed & Ward, 1932; London & New York: Sheed & Ward, 1933);

Sidelights on New London and Newer York and Other Essays (London: Sheed & Ward, 1932; New York: Dodd, Mead, 1932);

All I Survey: A Book of Essays (London: Methuen, 1933; New York: Dodd, Mead, 1933);

St. Thomas Aquinas (London: Hodder & Stoughton, 1933; New York: Sheed & Ward, 1933);

Avowals and Denials: A Book of Essays (London: Methuen, 1934; New York: Dodd, Mead, 1935);

The Scandal of Father Brown (London: Cassell, 1935; New York: Dodd, Mead, 1935);

The Well and the Shallows (London: Sheed & Ward, 1935; New York: Sheed & Ward, 1935);

As I Was Saying (London: Methuen, 1936; New York: Dodd, Mead, 1936);

Autobiography (London: Methuen, 1936; New York: Sheed & Ward, 1936);

The Paradoxes of Mr. Pond (London: Cassell, 1937; New York: Dodd, Mead, 1937);

The Coloured Lands (London: Sheed & Ward, 1938; New York: Sheed & Ward, 1938);

The End of the Armistice (London: Sheed & Ward, 1940; New York: Sheed & Ward, 1940);

The Common Man (London: Sheed & Ward, 1950; New York: Sheed & Ward, 1950);

The Surprise (London & New York: Sheed & Ward, 1952);

A Handful of Authors, edited by Dorothy Collins (London & New York: Sheed & Ward, 1953);

The Glass Walking-Stick and Other Essays, from the Illustrated London News, 1905-1936, edited by Collins (London: Methuen, 1955);

Lunacy and Letters, edited by Collins (London & New York: Sheed & Ward, 1958);

Where All Roads Lead (London: Catholic Truth Society, 1961);

*The Man Who Was Orthodox: A Selection from the Un-
collected Writings of G. K. Chesterton*, edited by
A. L. Maycock (London: Dobson, 1963);

The Spice of Life and Other Essays, edited by Collins
(Beaconsfield, U.K.: Finlayson, 1964; Philadelphia: Dufour, 1966);

Chesterton on Shakespeare, edited by Collins (Henley on Thames, Oxfordshire & Chester
Springs, Pa.: Dufour, 1971);

The Apostle and the Wild Ducks, and Other Essays, edited by Collins (London: Elek, 1975);

GK's Weekly: A Sampler, edited by Lyle W. Dorsett
(Chicago: Loyola University Press, 1986).

Collection: *The Collected Works of G. K. Chesterton*,
15 volumes to date (San Francisco: Ignatius
Press, 1986-   ).

Best known for his Father Brown detective
stories, and most admired as a thinker for his full-
length books, of which he wrote almost fifty,
G. K. Chesterton is numbered among the great essayists of the English language. His essays so far
collected total almost forty volumes, and although most of them were newspaper or magazine articles, they have established Chesterton in
the tradition of the fine art of the essay, which
runs from Francis Bacon through Joseph Addison, Samuel Johnson, William Hazlitt, Charles
Lamb, Leigh Hunt, Robert Louis Stevenson, Augustine Birrell, E. V. Lucas, Max Beerbohm, Robert Lynd, and H. L. Mencken. Most anthologies
of the essay contain samples of his work, and as
Ifor Evans puts it in his *A Short History of English
Literature* (1940), Chesterton is regarded as "outstanding in the essay's final phase."

Evans's use of the term "final phase" indicates the notion of a change (related to the sort
of decline summed up in the title of John Gross's
book, *The Rise and Decline of the Man of Letters*,
1969) away from belles lettres, and a splendid versatility by which literary journalists were also
poets, essayists, critics, debaters, and participants
in the great conversation that spans the centuries. Academic professionalism and the triumph
of the specialist have greatly reduced the role of
the gifted generalist, and with exceptions such as
Malcolm Muggeridge, P. J. Kavanagh, or a few
writers for such journals as the *Spectator* or the *Listener*, the essay as a practiced literary art has almost disappeared. The newspaper or even journal article is often no longer seen as, and rarely
is, a literary work. And past classics in the genre
are mainly embalmed in collections, nowadays

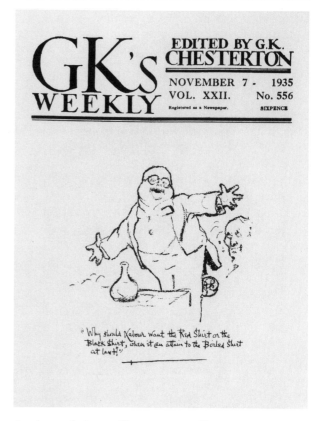

*An issue of the weekly newspaper Chesterton founded in
1925 with the aim of promoting Distributism (based upon the
principle that workers should own or control the means of
production) and Roman Catholicism*

not usually studied in universities, though valued
as a source of literary history, and, in the case of
a few luminaries, admired as models of "personal" style.

Chesterton himself, never claiming to be
more than a journalist, but nonetheless a prolific
writer of essays (most of them written to meet
deadlines in newspapers and journals), expressed
misgivings about the essay. Admitting that he
took perhaps his "greatest literary pleasure" in
reading essays, Chesterton, in a late *Illustrated London News* "Notebook" piece ("On the Essay,"
1929), described the essay as "wavering and wandering" like a serpent, and lacking a definite
form. It dealt, he said, "with theoretical matters
without the responsibility of propounding a theory," unlike the thesis of the medievals, and he
cites Hazlitt as a writer who fell into inconsis-
tency through not having to set forth his
thoughts more methodically. It is also quite clear
that Chesterton felt that to be dogmatic, even provocative, like George Bernard Shaw, for instance,
was not a sign of egotism. This self-focus lies

rather in the writing of essays in which often the assumption is that the reader is interested in "anything whatever that is connected with" the writer. He did not accuse any essayist of being an egotist; he claimed only that the tendency of the personal essay is more toward egotism than is the stance of a missionary writer such as Shaw, who puts things into popular language and is a sort of buffoon for the sake of what he sees as truth. In the course of his disquisition, Chesterton says: "I am perfectly well aware that all my articles are articles, and that none of my articles are essays." But he also identifies the amusing writer who entertains and instructs with the man who "has something to say," and the "perfect and polished stylist" (whose work he parodies) with someone who, though not flippant, is also not serious. It should be noted how consonant this view is with his statement in *Orthodoxy* (1908) that, in modern times, modesty had moved from the organ of ambition where it belonged to the organ of conviction where it should not be. Although himself accused of frivolity and insincerity, Chesterton always claimed to be serious, but stated that no man "can be merry unless he is serious." For him humor and truth were inseparable.

The first point to note from his view of the essay and of his own work is that Chesterton, although placed among the great essayists by such literary men as J. C. Squire, Birrell, Lucas, Bonamy Dobrée, and others, did not take his work seriously as literature, though he was ardent to share his insights with others. Yet, despite the journalistic haste, the day-to-day dealing with the topical, he often struck from his pen sparks of divine fire, as he did in the conversations (in pub or hall or street) for which he was almost as noted as Dr. Johnson had been. The fact is that Chesterton was–at least in his younger days, when the best of his short pieces were published– one of those whom T. S. Eliot described as being temperamentally in need of deadlines. This does not mean that he did not ponder and meditate. The evidence of his writing is that, although he often wrote quickly, he had the habit of much thinking and dreaming. Journalism was for Chesterton in some ways detrimental to fine writing, but it was also the occasion for sharing (to use his own phrase about Charles Dickens) some of "the mixed and flowing substance" of his visionary mind. It may even be said that the wandering, ruminative quality that runs through all his work reflects his whole speculative temperament, his awareness of multitudinous angles of vision and

perspectives intrinsic to man's finite condition and the nature of existence, and, ironically, given his suspicion of the genre, makes him a gifted practitioner of the discursive, conversational essay.

Because he mainly wrote for causes (orthodox Christianity and wide distribution of property) and not for a place in literature, it is somewhat artificial to regard his short essays on their own. Books such as *St. Thomas Aquinas* (1933), *The Everlasting Man* (1925), and *St. Francis of Assisi* (1923) are often like extensions of his essays. His writing is all of a piece, with a central thread of appreciation of existence, an essentially poetic view of the universe. His short essays are, even in the case of the lighter, more entertaining ones, like microcosms of his entire philosophy and vision. And his novels and short stories, even when as intriguing and captivating as the best Father Brown stories, are written with parable and allegory in mind. Some books, such as *Orthodoxy*, *Charles Dickens* (1906), or *The Victorian Age in Literature* (1913), have chapters like essays in their own right: there is an organic unity including "recurrent melodies" rather than an ordered structure. Moreover, even his most serious prose works, though much more careful and methodical, often have a wit and buoyancy similar to that of his essays.

Though never eclipsed, Chesterton's work is well to the fore today, and books about him are being added to the many written over the past fifty years. Although the books of his most read today are the full-length ones, a strong revival, reflected in the pages of the vigorous journal the *Chesterton Review* (which attracts writers from all over the world), has overflowed into a fresh appreciation of his periodical essays. Collections such as the *Bodley Head Chesterton* by P. J. Kavanagh also give more stimulus to enjoyment of his prose, and the massive projects of a Complete Works undertaken in Canada and the publishing of his sixteen hundred *Illustrated London News* essays indicate the way in which his journalism as well as his books are accorded an attention rare among his contemporaries.

Gilbert Keith Chesterton, born on 29 May 1874 into the family of Edward Chesterton, an estate agent in Kensington, and to a mother (Marie Louise Grosjean Chesterton) whose own mother was French, was blessed in his home life. His father, as Chesterton says in his *Autobiography* (1936), was a man of many hobbies who loved reading and had many books, and who was

Caricature by Chesterton of Edgar Allan Poe, captioned "When Prose comes in at the door, Poetry flies out the window"
(Reproduced from the original held by the Department of Special Collections of the University Libraries of Notre Dame)

blessed with a whimsical sense of humor. He entertained his children with, among other things, a toy theater that became a symbol to Chesterton of the wonder and drama of life itself. After late but marked growth as a literary and intellectual leader at St. Paul's School, in contrast to many of his friends, Chesterton went to art school rather than to university. The choice of art school is significant. Chesterton had an unusually strong gift for the pictorial (despite his poor eyesight), and he retained throughout his life a sense of celebration of the color of life. At the Slade School of Art he underwent a period of spiritual darkness in which, as he notes in his *Autobiography*, he was made acutely aware of the attractive power and reality of absolute evil and, reacting against the emptiness of ultimate doubt, emerged with fresh appreciation of existence. Some of this experience was no doubt a reflection of the despair and decadence of the fin de siècle period in which Chesterton grew up. His optimism was associated with a lifelong rejection of the "art-for-art's-sake" cult that he saw as leading to the dead end of a "sick-cloud on the mind of men" as he calls it in his prologue to one of his early novels, *The Man Who Was Thursday* (1908). In this resistance to the intellectual atmosphere associated with Walter Pater, Algernon Swinburne, Oscar Wilde, and Ernest Dowson (some of whom nevertheless influenced his literary style), Chesterton found sustenance in the robust and vitally positive outlook of Dickens–whose gusto was a tradition of Chesterton's family–and of Stevenson. And he never forgot that, as he said, he also "was born a Victorian" and frequently returned to appreciations or critiques of writers of that era.

Reviewing for a publisher in London gave Chesterton his first outlet for literary talent. Having left art school, he became a publisher's reader, then reviewer, and amusingly says that having failed to learn how to draw or paint, "I tossed off easily enough some criticisms of the weaker points of Rubens or the misdirected talents of Tintoretto." When a few years later he contributed a series of articles to the *Speaker*, a liberal journal formed by some of his friends, he had found his vocation as a journalist. It was during this period, too, that he came to know Hilaire Belloc–a powerful and lifelong influence on Chesterton–and Shaw, an affectionate antagonist

Chesterton and his wife, Frances Blogg Chesterton

in witty, even uproarious debates. Meanwhile, Chesterton, in 1900, produced two books of poetry: *Greybeards at Play*, which he himself regarded as simply an amusement but which was subsequently highly valued by W. H. Auden as an excellent sample of light verse; and *The Wild Knight and Other Poems*, a book that won high praise for its lyrical quality from most critics.

By the time his first collection of essays came out in 1901 as *The Defendant* (defending nonsense, detective stories, skeletons, farce, ugly things, and so on), Chesterton was already recognized as a rising star of literary London through his poetry, his *Speaker* and *Daily News* articles, and his *Bookman* essays and reviews. From the first he was quite a controversial figure. One reviewer of the *Defendant* essays anticipated many later opinions when he said (in the *Academy*, 30 November 1901) that Chesterton had great "prowess as a mental gymnast" and great energy but overdid the paradoxical method, which is a "good device . . . sparingly used," but which Chesterton adopted as a means of setting a "train of epigrammatic gunpowder with time fuses carefully adjusted." Another reviewer of this first book of

essays, C. F. G. Masterman, in a review titled "The Blasphemy of Optimism" (*Speaker*, 26 April 1902), was full of tributes to Chesterton's "agile brilliancy . . . the flashing paradox, the bold metaphor, the statement that leaves one doubled up and speechless, the divine lunacy of the intoxicated inspiration" but went on at much length to quarrel with his optimism, seeing it as missing the element of tragedy in human lives and "attempting a short-cut to Paradise." Significantly in a later essay, "G. K. Chesterton, an Appreciation" (*Bookman*, February 1903), the same reviewer eulogized Chesterton's "appreciation" of "the astonishing and delightful mystery" of being, seeing him as the poet of "things as they really are." And to the charge of some of Chesterton's friends that he was writing too much, Masterman replied that it is doubtful "if any man with ideas can write too much—the ephemeral perishes, the permanent survives." Reviewers of his second book of essays, *Twelve Types* (1902)–a collection on various writers and thinkers and historical figures such as St. Francis, Leo Tolstoy, Thomas Carlyle, Alexander Pope, Charlotte Brontë, and others–all agreed on the brilliance of the work, but differed widely in their estimates. While stating that Chesterton's paradoxes are mostly sound and rightly based, that the pages bristled with wit, and praising the criticism as intelligent, one reviewer took umbrage with the familiarity with which the young Chesterton clapped these great figures on the back, and criticized what he called "a hungry devil of rhetoric." He also said that to praise Chesterton as a writer-critic is not to praise him as an essayist, for "No man is a good essayist who has no repose, no interludes, and who is always at high pressure" (*Academy and Literature*, November 1902). On the other hand, another (in *New Age*, November 1902) stated that Chesterton "occupies today a position in English letters which any writer might be proud of" and is "an essayist who preserves the best traditions of a fast-vanishing art" along with the "minute and precious band" of those who "remain almost the sole exponents of the literary essay in England": Pater, Andrew Lang, Edmund Gosse, Birrell, William Henley, G. S. Street, Charles Whibley, Sidney Lee, and Alice Meynell.

Once established, with a moderate income, Chesterton married Frances Blogg in 1901, a woman who proved to be a good manager and "tidied up" the absentminded, careless Chesterton, eventually persuading him to leave Fleet Street and move out into Beaconsfield, near London. The move away from his beloved Fleet Street, where he lived a life of conviviality amidst the pressures of daily journalism, enabled him to concentrate sufficiently on books to produce the sort of later works for which he is most admired, including *St. Thomas Aquinas* and *The Everlasting Man*; but books of essays continued to appear up to and after his death. The Chestertons, to their regret, had no children but entertained many people in their picturesque home.

A measure of Chesterton's reputation early in his career is the offer to him to write the Robert Browning book (1903) in the English Men of Letters series, a book that—despite a neglect of dates, many factual inaccuracies, and several misquotations—has from the first been regarded as a classic of biographical criticism. James Douglas, who reviewed it for the *Bookman* (July 1903), said the book represented "a delicate feat of imaginative wit on the part of Mr. John Morley to choose [Chesterton] for this task, not only because he brings out the best in Browning, but also because Browning brings out the best in him."

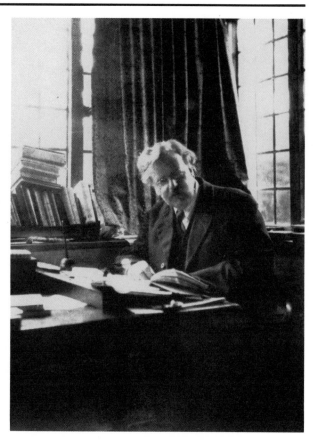

Chesterton in his study at Top Meadow, the house he built in Beaconsfield, near London (by permission of the Estate of G. K. Chesterton)

There followed in quick succession a 1904 book on G. F. Watts, the Victorian painter (with Chesterton's appreciative responses to the Victorian age as well as to Watts); Chesterton's first novel, *The Napoleon of Notting Hill* (also 1904); some stories; and from 1905 to 1908, three of his most celebrated nonfiction works: *Heretics* (1905), *Charles Dickens*, and *Orthodoxy*; a second novel, *The Man Who Was Thursday*; and a third book of essays, *All Things Considered* (1908). The last was a sample of his *Illustrated London News* "Notebook" essays begun in 1905–to the delight of the editor, who paid him seven pounds per essay, an amount Chesterton later refused to have increased because of his gratitude to the journal for the opportunity it offered when he badly needed regular income. He continued to write the "Notebook" essays until his death in 1936 (when Arthur Bryant took over), and of a total of sixteen hundred only a fraction have been collected, though a complete edition of them is underway.

Of all of the books mentioned so far, *Orthodoxy* is the most influential and highly regarded today, but opinions have been divided on it since its publication. However, for those who appreciate his paradoxes and his fresh way of looking at commonplaces or conventional notions this book is his classic. It has been attacked as defending the indefensible and praised for its profundity. Whatever the judgments (and a great deal depends on how the reader reacts to Chesterton's defense of Christianity, summed up in the Apostles' Creed–and to his associated critique of scientism), it does contain the greatest fund of the imagery, parallelism, and wit for which his prose has been celebrated. It seems a distillation of all his essays in one essay. In his introduction to this book Chesterton, significantly responding to previous criticism, writes, "I do not see how this book can avoid being egotistical; and I do not quite see (to tell the truth) how it can avoid being dull. Dullness will, however, free me from the charge which I most lament; the charge of being flippant. Mere light sophistry is the thing that I happen to despise most of all things, and it is perhaps a wholesome fact that this is the thing of which I am generally accused. I know nothing so contemptible as a mere paradox; a mere ingenious defence of the indefensible." Some critics failed to see a core of truth in such statements as "The madman is the man who has lost everything except his reason," in which Chesterton put forth startlingly the idea that mere logic (the confines of a narrower reason, without the larger, healthy, imaginative intellect at work) often is the morbid cage that imprisons the lunatic mind. They accused him of denying intellect for the sake of emotion, yet Chesterton always upheld reason in the sense of man's capacity to know certainty and reality. Such criticism has been leveled at Chesterton since the beginning.

Chesterton wrote a good deal of literary criticism, though that term does not suffice to describe his writings on other writers, for he followed few rules and usually empathized with the poets, novelists, and others he discussed. Of all his books and essays on writers his *Charles Dickens* has been the most influential and is quoted and echoed everywhere in Dickens criticism. Yet it has been the subject of extreme differences of judgment, too. Of the early reviews the most virulent, that by Whibley, said that Chesterton acted the buffoon, or clown at the fair, used antithesis and paradox for the sake of mere effect, and exaggerated wildly. Some, such as James Douglas, saw the close affinity of Chesterton with Dickens and

praised his exuberant swimming in "the sea of Dickens with shouts of gleeful epigram."

Alongside full-length books, such as *What's Wrong With the World* (1910), *The Victorian Age in Literature* (one of the best loved and most quoted in literary circles today), and the first two collections of the Father Brown stories, four collections of Chesterton's magazine and newspaper articles appeared between 1909 and 1916, the year in which he almost died during a long illness. These collections were *Tremendous Trifles* (1909), *Alarms and Discursions* (1910), *A Miscellany of Men* (1912), and *The Barbarism of Berlin* (1914). They reflect and in some instances anticipate the themes of his other books–for example, his growing concern for social justice and his belief in the sanity of ordinary people as opposed to the bureaucrats, themes powerfully presented in *What's Wrong With the World*. Of these collections, the best example of a blend of wit and humor and of a serious message with the lightest touch is probably *Tremendous Trifles*, a volume from which anthologists usually glean their samples. Essays such as "A Piece of Chalk," "What I Found in My Pocket," "On Lying in Bed," and "The Little Birds Who Won't Sing" are typical of Chesterton at his most genially entertaining. Yet they also include serious convictions.

It is often taken for granted that Chesterton's work before World War I was his best and that, although he later wrote some important books and produced essays with gems of insight, there was a postwar decline in his overall powers as a writer. However, one must distinguish between his later full-length books and his essays. Of the former, several are widely regarded as his most profound. Because their challenge to his talent as a stylist is greater, in that their themes require the utmost care in thought and, for a teacher like Chesterton, a constant attempt to make the abstract and esoteric crystalline to a wide audience, they may be the best exemplars of his powers as a prose writer. Among them are his *St. Thomas Aquinas*, which so astounded the eminent philosopher Etienne Gilson by its effective treatment of central problems that he declared Chesterton to be one of the deepest thinkers who ever lived, and *The Everlasting Man*, written mainly to answer the view of history propounded in *An Outline of History* (1920) by H. G. Wells.

Of his later collections of essays, all produced by an indefatigable journalist who also edited a journal–*G. K.'s Weekly*, devoted to the cause

Chesterton in 1925, when he launched an unsuccessful campaign for election to the Lord Rectorship at Glasgow University

more recent vintage, *Chesterton on Shakespeare* (1971), shows, even if only in the too-typical Chestertonian fragments, his insight into the Bard. In 1975, another volume of his essays, *The Apostle and the Wild Ducks*, was published, and more are on the way. Indeed, the full bibliography has not yet emerged, for he wrote for many U.S. journals, and only recently have these been listed.

Perhaps the most illuminating book about Chesterton, and one of his most genial long essays–youthful in tone, interestingly anecdotal, and rich in that blend of whimsicality and seriousness that distinguishes his best short essays–is his own *Autobiography*, published not long after his death in 1936. It is one further evidence that he had not lost his magical touch even in his closing months. The book is worth reading both as a key to Chesterton's own life and work and for the light it sheds on his times and on other authors.

As made clear already, Chesterton the essayist cannot be properly appreciated through his short essays alone, because there is a sense in which all his nonfiction prose consisted of essays of various lengths. It is true that, as Auden says in the introduction to his anthology of Chesterton's writings, *G. K. Chesterton* (1970), the essays are sometimes "repetitious and self-indulgent" while his full-length books are far superior to any collections. But the short pieces also offer some of his finest "light" work, as well as his more eloquent, and often contain in seed form the best insights of his major books. Moreover, the faults of Chesterton's writing are more evident in full-length books, where an excess of rhetoric, a boundless flow of epigrammatical paradox, is given more room, though the sound matter and deeply engaging style are far more common than some critics have allowed. It seems that, though more brilliant, the early, full-length books, such as *Heretics*, *Orthodoxy*, and *What's Wrong With the World*, are often less quiet and urbane in tone than early collections of essays and have become the epitome of qualities for which Chesterton is most loved but also most detested. These books are nevertheless full of amazing originality of thought, with paradox shown to be at the heart of that puzzle of "appearance versus reality," a main theme of *Orthodoxy*. However, though the larger works exhibit Chesterton's "metaphysical jesting" at its height, they also tend to magnify those fissures (some would say abysses) of wilder rhetoric that divide his readership. Of course, his later full-length books tend to be grav-

of distributism with a passionate zeal–*The Uses of Diversity* (1920), *Fancies Versus Fads* (1923), *Come to Think of It . . .* (1930), *All Is Grist* (1931), *All I Survey* (1933), *Avowals and Denials* (1934), *The Well and the Shallows* (1935), and *As I Was Saying* (1936) are the most representative of his work in the essay as such. On the whole, they are not as sparkling and fresh or, for the most part, even as well structured as his earlier ones, but still contain many good individual essays, and rarely is any essay without some arresting passage.

Most of the *G. K.'s Weekly* articles and columns do not share the high quality of other pieces, but after Chesterton's death further collections, usually taken from periodical writing, have appeared. Of these *The Common Man* (1950), *A Handful of Authors* (1953), and *The Glass Walking-Stick* (1955; from *Illustrated London News* essays) are the best-known. A remarkable collection of er (though not without humor) and more carefully considered, some would say more mature. All the same, it is a strange truth that his "reflective" essays, criticized by Auden as too-hasty pieces by a busy journalist, appear to have, in common with his best later, mainly religious books, a more moderate style.

Significantly, there is almost always a serious, even deep core amidst all the divine nonsense and lightly narrative approach of his best-loved early essays. Even in those pieces, essays such as "On Lying in Bed" or "A Piece of Chalk" in *Tremendous Trifles*, or "Fairy Tales" and "On Running After One's Hat" in *All Things Considered*, one can see the elements of longer "theses." In "On Lying in Bed," for instance, Chesterton moves from lighthearted joking about ceiling painting, wallpapers, and Michelangelo to the theme that "If there is one thing worse than the modern weakening of major morals it is the modern strengthening of minor morals." And quite smoothly, but with trenchant antitheses, he goes on to one of his favorite themes in such social works as *What's Wrong With the World* and *The Outline of Sanity* (drawn from *G. K.'s Weekly*), that of modern relativism in values associated with mechanical routine in everyday life: "it is the great peril of our society that all its mechanism may grow more fixed while its spirit grows more fickle. A man's minor actions and arrangements ought to be free, flexible, creative; the things that should be unchangeable are his principles, his ideals. But with us the reverse is true; our views change constantly; but our lunch does not change." The notion of change that largely prevails is one of constantly evolving change in moral values and in religious doctrines, while change in the big units of organized life is seen as almost impossible. Similarly, even in so humorous a piece as "On Running After One's Hat" (with its echoes of Pickwick), Chesterton brings out the importance of wonder and "an inconvenience as only an adventure wrongly considered," bound up with his mainspring of seeing the world with appreciative surprise. In "A Piece of Chalk," one of his most amusing "trifles," superb in its discursive, anecdotal treatment of serious themes, one sees the main Chestertonian theme of virtue as positive and dazzling, and a touch of the patriotic English vision which informs his "Ballad of the White Horse." The little essay "Fairy Tales" expresses one of the central themes of *Orthodoxy*, that "all positive joy" depends on the presence of ethical vetoes and vows, "the great mysti-

cal basis for all commandments."

These are examples only from essays regarded as light because of their entertaining style and personally reflective tone. But one could take hundreds of others, early and late, and show how they share thematic concerns with full-length books: marriage and divorce, business and success, race theories, the power of evil, the spirit of the Middle Ages, and so on. Because many essays are written with a desire to entertain and to be topical does not mean that they are ephemeral or shallow. And it should be noted that, though many were done in haste, few of the many essays Chesterton wrote lack a real shape, for no matter how discursive, seminarrative, wandering, or uneven in structure they may seem to be, they show a capacity for bringing the reader back to an underlying theme with accumulated force through the associations of ideas that appear to come to Chesterton's mind as he writes, clarified by concrete instances and analogies. Often the essays open rather than close a topic, leaving the reader wondering, and wandering about the field of a topic to see more in it, thus fulfilling Chesterton's purpose.

As Chesterton is one of the most quoted of authors, and as Auden has said, one of the finest aphorists in the language, it may be well to offer a few examples, especially as these illustrate chief qualities of his prose, whether in books or in everyday journalism: "Tradition may be defined as an extension of the franchise. Tradition means giving votes to the most obscure of all classes, our ancestors. It is the democracy of the dead" (*Orthodoxy*); "My country right or wrong is a thing that no patriot would think of saying except in a desperate case. It is like saying my mother drunk or sober" (*The Defendant*); "Democracy means government by the uneducated while aristocracy means government by the badly educated" (*New York Times*, February 1931); "There is no such thing on earth as an uninteresting subject; the only thing that can exist is an uninterested person" (*Heretics*); "Do not be proud of the fact that your grandmother was shocked at something which you are accustomed to seeing or hearing without being shocked ... It may be that your grandmother was an extremely lively and vital animal, and that you are a paralytic" (*As I Was Saying*); "The most sentimental thing in the world is to hide your feelings; it is making too much of them" (*Alarms and Discursions*).

Chesterton was always concerned with bringing out central truths or neglected dimensions of

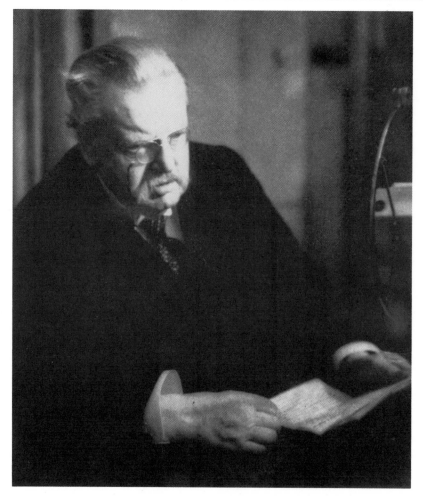

Chesterton delivering a radio broadcast in 1935. He began a regular B.B.C. series in 1932
(by permission of the Estate of G. K. Chesterton).

common experience. And one glimpses even in such brief excerpts the Chestertonian use of antitheses, the illuminating and often amusing use of analogy, and the capacity for showing the weakness of certain attitudes through the method of reductio ad absurdum. Moreover, a rich and broad humor, punning, and the use of alliteration are so blended with the terseness of the core truth that the word "wit" does not suffice to describe the overall effect.

As far as wit is concerned, Wilde, Shaw, and Chesterton were probably the most gifted in the period in which Chesterton came to maturity and began as a London writer. All three provoked laughter and thought simultaneously, though Chesterton appears to have a more Dickensian dimension to his fun, as is seen in novels such as *Manalive* (1912), *The Man Who Was Thursday*, or *The Napoleon of Notting Hill*, which, like many small essays, share in the picaresque tradition.

Wilde was, in some respects, one of Chesterton's masters (as were Dickens, Swinburne, John Ruskin, and William Morris).

For richer and fuller examples of Chestertonian humor in his essays the reader is referred to such extended examples of his reductio ad absurdum method as the delightful little essay "The Little Birds Who Won't Sing," in which he suggests songs for modern work, the passage in *The Everlasting Man* in which he looks at the caveman "myth" of Wells, or the discussion of "The Maniac" in *Orthodoxy*. There, and in many other places, the "argument" is even more devastating in its effect than the wittiest epigrams, for it is charged with the humorous irony associated with that gift of parallelism for which Belloc praised his work.

It ought to be more widely realized that Chesterton's prose in general and his little essays in particular had much more variety of tone than is sug-

Chesterton in May 1936 at his last public engagement, a festival at St. Joseph's Nursing Home (by permission of the Estate of G. K. Chesterton)

gested by many of the references to his "exuberance." Chesterton's essays offer plenty of examples of serene, contemplative writing, magisterial exposition, and poetic vision. As far as the second of these qualities is concerned, the most outstanding examples are in his full-length books, and his early *G. F. Watts* and *Robert Browning* show, almost as much as do the later *St. Thomas Aquinas* and *The Everlasting Man*, the quiet mastery of a discriminating and literary prose as effective as most work of his times. However, in any of these books the wit and humor, the wordplay and antitheses are also present, and this mingling of tones, of the more polished with the more journalistic, is the main reason why so many have said that he produced no masterpiece. The real question for those who share much or all of Chesterton's vision (as it was for Chesterton) is whether his books taught readers better because of the mixture.

Sometimes individual essays, both early and late, cover the range of these tones and prose

skills; and again some see this as spoiling what might have been perfect specimens of the essay genre. It can be argued that the blend makes his main theme and its expression all the more convincing and piercing. For example, in "The Architect of Spears" (in *A Miscellany of Men*) Chesterton compares Oriental and Gothic architecture, using an abundance of imagery of the most mixed kind, classical and Cockney; argues for the gaiety and "vulgarity" of the medieval buildings; and after relating the anecdote of furniture vans moving in front of a cathedral giving him the secret of the Gothic, leads into a passage that is visionary and eloquent. Here one sees journalistic chatting with the reader, a broad sweep over periods of history, a mixture of the most mundane articles of everyday life (though Chesterton thought nothing mundane), and a climax that somehow is reached effectively. The emotive and rhythmical language begins about halfway through, and finally takes over altogether as Chesterton is caught up in the fresh realization of Lincoln Cathedral as the Church on the march: "All its spires are spears at rest; and all its stones are stones asleep in a catapult. In that instant of illusion, I could hear the arches clash like swords as they crossed each other. The mighty and numberless columns seemed to go swinging by like the huge feet of imperial elephants. The graven foliage wreathed and blew like banners going into battle; the silence was deafening with all the mingled noises of a military march; the great bell shook down, as the organ shook up its thunder. The thirsty-throated gargoyles shouted like trumpets from all the roofs and pinnacles as they passed, and from the lectern in the core of the cathedral the eagle of the awful evangelist clashed his wings of brass. . . . And the fiercely-coloured saints marching eternally in the flamboyant windows would have carried their glorioles like torches across dark lands and distant seas; till the whole mountain of music and darkness and lights descended on the lonely Lincoln hill. So for some hundred and sixty seconds I saw the battle-beauty of the Gothic; then the last furniture-van shifted itself away; and I saw only a church tower in a quiet English town, round which the English birds were floating." There may be a little too much clamor here, similar to some of the more obvious effects of his "Battle of Lepanto," and some emphases are overdone. But the exaggerations are akin to speeches in *King Lear* or *A Midsummer Night's Dream*, and the riot of imagery gives it the sense of a child's wonderment. Above all, Chesterton's poetic prose had the power of expressing and evoking a sense of an overarching vision that is a height reached through a sort of ecstasy, as the imaginative intellect sees, if only momentarily, and after much contemplation and thought, a truth to which all things point. One sees this quality of Chesterton the mystical thinker in many passages from such books as *St. Francis of Assisi* or *The Everlasting Man*.

It is true that sometimes Chesterton's resources of paradox and wit, of a dazzling gift of rhetoric, actually mar his message, when he is carried away by a delight in the ambiguities and punning nature of language, faults that most essayists of his day rarely if ever displayed. This is apart from the sometimes slack language and tired sentences, which, though noticeable (beginning sentences with "anyhow" or "as a fact" too often, or wasting space on needless repetition), are really only frayed edges of a vast output of high quality. The sort of fault that irritates most is that of using terms in a loaded or exaggerated way, as

for instance in the treatment of "law" in *Orthodoxy*, or the sort of excess shown in the essay "Cockneys and Their Jokes" in *All Things Considered*. Here, to answer the charge that he was not even a Cockney humorist, Chesterton says that he is a Cockney—like Chaucer, Dickens, Lamb, and others. The definition of a Cockney is, to say the least, stretched too conveniently. Similarly, when he says, as he does in "An Essay on Two Cities," that "the chief object of education is not to learn things; nay, the chief object is to unlearn things," one feels slackness in the language, but more seriously a sense of wearisomeness in the paradox, which is made worse by his going on to declare that he would ask teachers not "how much knowledge they had imparted," but "how much splendid and scornful ignorance they had erected like some royal tower in arms." His real point is, of course, that students should *unlearn* "all the weariness and wickedness of the world" that prevents a fresh exhilaration at its "dumb alphabet of signs and symbols." But why not simply say that the chief object of education is to learn wonder, delight, and the metaphors all around us in everyday life itself? The obvious answer is that he wants to surprise the reader into seeing the matter afresh. But in instances like this, the habit of rhetorical exaggeration allied with paradox actually obscures or weakens that main idea through statements that offer, on first reading, nonsense deliberately designed to shock. The rhetoric is too rhetorical and appears to be a mere imitation of Chesterton, a sort of formula overused. Such faults occur often enough to make some readers overcritical of his prose.

If real faults tend to obscure the positive merits of Chesterton's essays for some readers, especially for those who simply reject the ideas on religion and politics he expounded, his own view of his journalism is probably even more detrimental. In a later book of essays, *All I Survey*, Chesterton writes, "The re-issue of a series of essays so ephemeral and even superfluous may seem at first glance to require some excuse." This is only a repetition of earlier statements; for instance, in the introductory essay to *All Things Considered*, he calls the pieces "a collection of crude and shapeless papers upon current or flying subjects . . . written as a rule, at the last moment." Unfortunately his own words about his work are echoed by those who have not caught up to the revival and who appear not to know of his earlier reputation or his persistently large readership. For example, Margaret Drabble in her entry on Chesterton in the 1985 edition of *The Oxford Companion to English Literature* makes the perfunctory remark that "he also wrote literary criticism" and says that "much of his vast output has proved ephemeral." So, too, Malcolm Muggeridge, who has often quoted or drawn on Chesterton's fund of wit and wisdom, says in *Of Things Past* that Chesterton's own view of his work was juster than that of Frank Swinnerton, who said that "It will be at least a hundred years before Chesterton's greatness is fully recognised." Muggeridge wrote this in 1963. Since then, Chesterton's influence and reputation have grown enormously. It is significant that Auden, who came to admire Chesterton's writing, says he had "imagined him to be what he himself claimed, just a 'jolly journalist,' a writer of weekly essays on amusing themes." Auden knew the qualities of Chesterton's books but had underestimated his weekly essays.

T. S. Eliot stated that the commentator's task is to "find the topical excuse for the permanent." This is an apt description of what Chesterton did in his periodical essays. And the topics he wrote about only *appear* to be less relevant today than they did in his own time, for he did show quite often in his shorter essays the tremendous significance of "trifles." In going far beyond the usual expectations of the literary essay, which at least in his own time, and to some extent in earlier periods, so concentrated on personal style and the impressions of its authors as to tend toward the condition of "art for art's sake," Chesterton's articles lived on to be widely read and quoted today. Some of the attention they now receive is an overflow from the revival of interest in his more substantial works, but not all of it; the brief Chestertonian gems are durable in their own right.

How odd but massive a joke it is that the hasty journalist managed so much in the province of the genre he doubted. Yet the key to this achievement lies in the fact that he transcended that genre. More than anyone else he made the essay the vehicle of both a vision and an art of populist communication, with some of the seriousness of Johnson and, though not usually with the uniformly polished style of Hazlitt, often with the virtues, for his own day, of a "familiar style." And though he did not write with the quieter whimsicality and urbane resonance of Lamb's engaging fireside manner, his reflections are mostly deeper, and at times the words in which they are expressed are just as limpid and fresh. His contemporaries Birrell, Lucas, Lynd, and Beerbohm

G. K. and Frances Chesterton's tombstone, designed by Eric Gill

were also usually more urbane than he, but though they could touch the chord of common daily experience, Chesterton's best essays strike a new chord of common experience felt or seen afresh, while being just as conversationally mellow, but with more consequence, more permanent substance than most of theirs. Ironically it is Chesterton's less smooth and polished discourse, with its vital toughness like that of William Cobbett, its springiness and aphoristic richness, and its disregard for the merely sonorous (though hardly ever lacking in a "good ear") that has lived on to be felt as a tonic, a surprise, when the writings of Pater, the father of "art for art's sake," admirable though they are, are for the wider readership of today almost soporific.

If the art of the essay suffers an even more radical decline, that will be a real loss; but Chesterton's writing has not, and is not likely to decline. His shorter essays are often fragments, mostly shining, sometimes merely glittering, sometimes glowing with the inner life of an interior sun, but they are all fragments of a larger whole.

And they are all reminders of the milieu in which his talent was nurtured, in a Victorian setting that was heir to the inspired humor of Chaucer, Shakespeare, and Dickens, and in the golden era of literary journalism, in Chesterton's beloved Fleet Street.

Bibliographies:

John Sullivan, *G. K. Chesterton: A Bibliography* (London: University of London Press, 1958);

Sullivan, *Chesterton Continued: A Bibliographical Supplement* (London: University of London Press, 1968).

Biographies:

W. R. Titterton, *G. K. Chesterton: A Portrait* (London: Organ, 1936);

Maisie Ward, *Gilbert Keith Chesterton* (New York: Sheed & Ward, 1943);

Dudley Barker, *G. K. Chesterton: A Biography* (New York: Stein & Day, 1973);

Alzina Stone Dale, *The Outline of Sanity: A Life of G. K. Chesterton* (Grand Rapids, Mich.: Eerdmans, 1982).

References:

W. H. Auden, ed., Introduction to *G. K. Chesterton: A Selection from His Non-fictional Prose* (London: Faber & Faber, 1970);

Ian Boyd, *The Novels of G. K. Chesterton: A Study in Art and Propaganda* (New York: Barnes & Noble, 1975);

Emile Cammaerts, *The Laughing Prophet* (London: Methuen, 1937);

Margaret Canovan, *G. K. Chesterton, Radical Populist* (New York & London: Harcourt Brace Jovanovich, 1977);

D. J. Conlon, ed., *G. K. Chesterton: The Critical Judgments, Part 1: 1900-1937* (Antwerp: Antwerp Studies in English Literature, 1976);

T. S. Eliot, Obituary for Chesterton, *Tablet*, 20 June 1936, p. 785;

Maurice Evans, *G. K. Chesterton* (Cambridge: Cambridge University Press, 1939);

Jeffrey Hart, "In Praise of Chesterton," *Yale Review*, 53 (1963): 49-60;

Lynette Hunter, *G. K. Chesterton: Explorations in Allegory* (London: Macmillan, 1979);

Hugh Kenner, *Paradox in Chesterton* (London: Sheed & Ward, 1948);

Elizabeth Sewell, "G. K. Chesterton: the Giant Upside-Down," *Thought*, 30 (1955-1956): 555-576;

Maisie Ward, *Return to Chesterton* (London & New York: Sheed & Ward, 1952);

Gary Wills, *Chesterton: Man and Mask* (New York: Sheed & Ward, 1961).

Papers:

The largest collection of Chesterton's papers is held in the Robert John Bayer Memorial Chesterton Collection at the John Carroll University Library, Cleveland, Ohio. Other materials are held at Columbia University, Marquette University, and the British Library.

Arthur Clutton-Brock

(23 March 1868 - 8 January 1924)

G. K. Blank
University of Victoria

BOOKS: *The Cathedral Church of York: A Description of its Fabric and Brief History of the Archi-Episcopal See* (London: Bell, 1899; revised edition, 1899; revised and enlarged by F. Harrison, 1931);

Eton (London: Bell, 1900);

Shelley, the Man and the Poet (New York: Putnam's, 1909; London: Methuen, 1910; revised edition, London: Methuen, 1923; New York: Dutton, 1923);

Thoughts on the War (London: Methuen, 1914);

William Morris: His Work and Influence (New York: Holt, 1914; London: Williams & Norgate, 1914);

More Thoughts on the War (London: Methuen, 1915);

The Cure for War, Papers for War Time, no. 18 (London: Oxford University Press, 1915);

Bernhardism in England, Papers for War Time, no. 26 (London: Oxford University Press, 1915);

Are We to Punish Germany, if We Can?, Papers for War Time, no. 32 (London: Oxford University Press, 1915);

Simpson's Choice: An Essay on the Future Life (London: Omega Workshops, 1915);

Socialism and the Arts of Use, Fabian tract, no. 177 (London: Fabian Society, 1915);

The Philosophy of Socialism, Fabian tract, no. 180 (London: Fabian Society, 1916);

Studies in Gardening (New York: Scribners, 1916);

The Ultimate Belief (London: Constable, 1916; New York: Dutton, 1916);

A Modern Creed of Work, Pamphlet no. 4 (London: Design and Industries Association, 1917);

Studies in Christianity (London: Constable, 1918; New York: Dutton, 1918);

What Is the Kingdom of Heaven? (London: Methuen, 1919; New York: Scribners, 1920);

Essays on Art (London: Methuen, 1919; New York: Scribners, 1920);

Essays on Books (London: Methuen, 1920; New York: Dutton, 1920);

Sketch of Arthur Clutton-Brock by William Rothenstein that appeared in the February 1922 issue of Arts and Decoration

More Essays on Books (London: Methuen, 1920; New York: Dutton, 1921);

Shakespeare's "Hamlet" (London: Methuen, 1922; New York: Dutton, 1922);

Essays on Life (London: Methuen, 1925; New York: Dutton, 1925);

Essays on Literature & Life (London: Methuen, 1926; New York: Dutton, 1926);

Essays on Religion (London: Methuen, 1926; New York: Dutton, 1926);

The Miracle of Love and Other Poems (London: Benn, 1926);

More Essays on Religion (London: Methuen, 1927; New York: Dutton, 1927).

OTHER: "The Fantastic School of English Poetry," in *The Cambridge Modern History*, volume 4, edited by A. W. Ward, G. W. Prothero, and Stanley Leathes (Cambridge: University Press, 1906), pp. 760-775;

"Description in Poetry," in *Essays and Studies by Members of the English Association*, volume 2 (Oxford, 1911), pp. 91-103;

C. D. Locock, ed., *The Poems of Percy Bysshe Shelley*, introduction by Clutton-Brock (London: Methuen, 1911);

"England at War: An Essay," in *The Question of the Mind*, by Henry James (London: Central Committee for National Patriotic Organizations, 1915), pp. 13-20;

"Progress in Art," in *Progress and History*, edited by F. S. Marvin (London & New York: Milford/Oxford University Press, 1916), pp. 224-247;

"A Dream of Heaven," in *Immortality: An Essay in Discovery, Co-ordinating Scientific, Psychical, and Biblical Research*, edited by B. H. Streeter (London & New York: Macmillan, 1917), pp. 219-240;

Eugene Emmanuel Lemercier, *Letters of a French Soldier, 1914-1915*, introduction by Clutton-Brock (London: Constable, 1917);

Kenneth Richmond, *The Permanent Values in Education*, introduction by Clutton-Brock (London: Constable, 1917);

"Spirit and Matter," in *The Spirit*, edited by Streeter (New York: Macmillan, 1919), pp. 307-342;

"Spiritual Experience," in *The Spirit*, edited by Streeter (New York: Macmillan, 1919), pp. 275-305;

"Art," in *Recent Developments in European Thought*, edited by Marvin (London: Oxford University Press, 1920), pp. 247-261;

"Literature as a Vocation," in *Essays on Vocation, Second Series*, edited by Basil Mathews (London & New York: Milford/Oxford University Press, 1921), pp. 18-25;

"Dead Metaphors," in *Metaphor*, edited by Clutton-Brock, E. B., and H. W. Fowler (Oxford: Clarendon Press, 1922), pp. 305-326;

"How Shall We Think of the Kingdom of God?," in *Religious Foundations*, edited by Rufus Matthew Jones (New York: Macmillan, 1923), pp. 73-86;

"Art and the Escape from Banality," in *The Necessity of Art*, edited by Clutton-Brock and others (London: Student Christian Movement, 1924), pp 1-27;

"The English Bible," in *The English Bible*, edited by Vernon F. Storr (London: Methuen, 1938).

Arthur Clutton-Brock's reputation as an essayist rests on the numerous essays on literature and art he wrote mainly for the *Times Literary Supplement* (*TLS*), many of which were collected during his lifetime. In 1922 Ernest Rhys said of him that he had "shown again how to give the periodical essay the savour of permanent things." His lively and demanding approach to a variety of subjects created a wide readership during the first two decades of the twentieth century. Besides literature and art, his two other concerns as an essayist were socialism and Christianity; he was active and innovative as a practitioner, reformer, and theorist for both causes. The most important influences on his thought are William Morris's blend of socialism and aestheticism and Benedetto Croce's unpretentious and unclouded pursuit of spirit and truth in art. Today Clutton-Brock is best remembered for his studies of Percy Bysshe Shelley (1909) and Morris (1914). His essays on World War I also have some significance as documents representing a less militant and more cautious attitude in England toward the war and the feelings it evoked. The criticism most often leveled against Clutton-Brock's work in general is that it too frequently displays unrehearsed thoughts and rapidity of composition.

Clutton-Brock was born at Weybridge, Surrey, on 23 March 1868. His father, John Alan Clutton-Brock, was a banker, and his mother, Mary Alice Hill Clutton-Brock, was the daughter of a clergyman. He attended school at Summerfields, Oxford. In 1882 he won a scholarship to Eton, then went on to New College, Oxford, where he studied classics and philosophy. After university he trained as a lawyer and practiced law for almost ten years. He married Evelyn Vernon-Harcourt in 1903 and thereafter devoted most of his life to writing. For two years (1904-1906) he was literary editor for the *Speaker* (later retitled the *Nation*), while contributing work to various journals, including *Burlington Magazine*. He also had short stints with the *Morning Post* and the *Tribune*. In 1908 he became an art critic and general essayist for the *Times Educational* and *Literary* supplements. Clutton-Brock was among the first regular contributors to the *TLS*, and certainly one of the most influential. The following year he joined the socialist Fabian Society, for which he wrote several tracts. After the war, and because of its impact upon his views, he became interested in contemporary Christian ethics and morality. Many of his essays on religion were published posthumously, but Clutton-Brock did enjoy a reputation as an occasional lecturer on the topic. Clutton-Brock's association with the *Times* newspapers continued until, at the age of fifty-five, he died at Godalming, Surrey, on 8 January 1924, leaving behind his wife and three sons.

The kind of essay that Clutton-Brock established in the *TLS* is characterized as much by its style as by its content. His book reviews are more than reviews: they do not address the particular book so much as they do its general topic. They inform at least as much as they criticize. For Clutton-Brock the moral and ethical values expressed by a writer are secondary to the aesthetic qualities of the work. For example, in reviewing Edward Garnett's study of Russian novelist Ivan Turgenev, Clutton-Brock utterly condemns Turgenev's pessimism, or "negative unreason," as pathological, yet admits that "it is foolish to be hindered by this intellectual difference from the aesthetic enjoyment of him" ("Turgenev," *TLS*, 25 October 1917; collected in *Essays on Books*, 1920). And although he flatly calls François Villon, Paul Verlaine, and Edgar Allan Poe "disreputable," he can say that even with this mark against them their art is transcendent and approaches the "absolute" ("Pure Literature," *TLS*, 26 May 1921; collected in *Essays on Literature & Life*, 1926).

Despite this seemingly objective approach to art emphasizing aesthetic qualities, Clutton-Brock was fond of reading authors from their works— his essays often simultaneously discuss the writer's character and intention beyond the qualities, values, and structures of the work. For the most part his essays are the better for this, adding human interest and general speculation of a more personal nature to the subject. He could say that *Hamlet* ought to be studied as a work on its own terms ("The Razor of Croce," collected in *Essays on Literature & Life*), yet he thought it necessary to add that Shakespeare was a man of the world and that "Hamlet has all Shakespeare's genius of expression" ("Shakespeare," collected in *Essays on Books*).

"The Artist and His Audience" in Clutton-Brock's first volume of literary essays, *Essays on Art* (1919), is representative of both his mode of working and his views on art. The ostensible aim of the essay is to reconcile James McNeill Whistler's theory of art with that of Leo Tolstoy. His

Fabian Tract No. 180.

THE PHILOSOPHY OF SOCIALISM - -

By A. CLUTTON BROCK.

Published and sold by the Fabian Society at the Fabian Bookshop, 25 Tothill Street, Westminster, S.W.   Sept. 1916.   Price 1d.

Title page for one of the tracts Clutton-Brock wrote for the Fabian Society, which he joined in 1909. The society was founded in 1883 by a group of socialist intellectuals including George Bernard Shaw

strategy is to give an account of Whistler's theory, noting that it is "historically untrue as well as unintelligible," and then to paraphrase Tolstoy's views. The piece is typical of Clutton-Brock's tone and common sense approach: "Now, if we find ourselves intimidated by one or other of these views, if we seem forced to accept one of them against our will, it is a relief and liberation from the tyranny of Whistler's or Tolstoy's logic to ask ourselves simply what does actually happen to us in our own experience and enjoyment of a work of art." The key terms in this passage are not just "enjoyment" and "experience" (although the latter was certainly a favorite word); "we," "ourselves," and "us" are also important, for it is in these words that the argument develops by the irresistible participation of a reader who, like Clutton-Brock, only wants a level-headed answer. And of course the answer is something we already "know": "The fact of our enjoyment and experience makes art for us a social activity; we know that our enjoyment of it is good; we know also that the artist likes us to enjoy it; and we do not believe that either the primitive artist or the primitive man was different from us in this respect." What Clutton-Brock introduced into his essays was an honest and eloquent authority. That authority was called "we," and he was master of this mode of rhetorical persuasion. This "we" could pass judgments, debunk, examine, and explain. At its best it was intended to signify the public's voice of common sense and consent.

Because he took the duty of art criticism very seriously, the tone of his writing at times becomes preacherly and, more often, didactic. The "we" becomes just a little pushy. Even his obituary in the London *Times* (9 January 1924) admitted that his prose could be "dogmatic without loss of urbanity." But his intention remained the same: to promote common sense for the common good, and to disclaim the banal. He believed in cultivating good taste, and that with effort this goal is necessarily within the grasp of every viewer of art and every reader of literature: "Art is made for men as surely as boots are made for them." Because art is ultimately public, it must have a direct relationship with its audience. Again, note the rhetorical logic of common sense: "A story is a story because it is told, and told to some one not the teller. A picture is a picture because it is painted to be seen." Clutton-Brock states everything as if it is both obvious and important. Inevitably, the effect is sometimes overemphatic and lacking in subtlety.

One other essay in *Essays on Art* is central to understanding Clutton-Brock's attitude toward his vocation. In "A Defence of Criticism" he counters the view of an artist (Sir Thomas Jackson) who holds that "art criticism is harmful to the public," that art criticism prevents art lovers from appreciating art and thinking for themselves, and that the only worthy or instructive art criticism is that of artists. Through a critique, Clutton-Brock expresses his own views on the job of art criticism. First of all, he says, the critic is to be judged as a writer—moreover, as a writer who is writing as an interested member of the public. The opinions of the critic are important, but more so is the "process" by which the opinions evolve. Second, art criticism "ought to provoke

thought rather than to suppress it; and if it does not provoke thought it is worthless." And finally, art expresses the "common interests of mankind" and therefore its value is for people, not just for artists. The job of the art critic is to enrich the experience of his readers by expressing his own experience of the art. Clutton-Brock's conclusions are, as is too often the case, rather glib: "Either art is of value to us all, and our own experience of it is of value to us; or art has no value whatever to anyone, but is the meaningless activity of a few oddities who would be better employed in agriculture." And to this end, the art critic is "simply one of the public with a natural and human interest in art" (preface to *Essays on Art*). The art critic is a specialist in one thing only: clear expression.

Being a member of society, the art critic should write in such a way as to be understood by the public. Clutton-Brock's notion of what prose writing should be like corresponds to his own mode of expression: "In the best prose," he says, "we are so led on as we read, that we do not stop to applaud the writer: nor do we stop to question him" ("The Defects of English Prose," collected in *More Essays on Books*, 1921). Because the beauty comes from the clear expression of the idea rather than the qualities of the language, prose should not attempt to be poetic. Thus the best prose writers "described without a laboured eagerness or momentum, and without vivid words, just what they have seen and felt." Clutton-Brock would of course consider himself to be included with these writers: his prose leads the unquestioning reader to the desired conclusions.

Clutton-Brock's apparently casual observations often appear at the same time to be definitive judgments. This is especially true of his literary opinions. For example, he could write of John Keats that he "is the first modern art student known to us" ("The Promise of Keats," collected in *Essays on Books*) or of Dostoevsky that "No modern writer has been so well acquainted with evil and misery as he was" ("Dostoevsky," collected in *Essays on Books*). These kinds of generalizations are for the most part as haphazard as they are challenging, but they nonetheless succeed in drawing the attention of his readers.

For some of his contemporaries, Clutton-Brock was seen as "an artist whom the war has turned into a prophet and a preacher" (*TLS*, 22 May 1919); but for those who followed his version of theology where the individual can only achieve conversion on a socially and morally responsible basis, his views were considered highly significant. His obituaries acknowledged his qualities and importance. The London *Mercury* called him "one of the sanest and most humane critics of his day" (February 1924). The *TLS* said he was "a writer without a trace of affectation" (17 January 1924). "In the main," wrote the *Times* obituarist, "his criticism of literature and of art not only revealed his intense, direct enjoyment, but was backed by clear and resolute thinking, im-

patient of convention and of pretence." Moreover, it was noted in the *Saturday Review* that he "was a godsend to The *Times* and *Times Literary Supplement*" (19 January 1924). It was reported that his final act was to direct his physician's attention to the beauty of an iris.

Reference:
Frank Swinnerton, *A London Bookman* (London: Secker, 1930), pp. 118-122.

Mary Coleridge

(23 September 1861 - 25 August 1907)

Warren Stevenson
University of British Columbia

See also the Coleridge entry in *DLB 19: British Poets, 1880-1914*.

BOOKS: *The Seven Sleepers of Ephesus* (London: Chatto & Windus, 1893);
Fancy's Following, as Anodos (Oxford: Daniel, 1896; Portland, Maine: Mosher, 1900);
The King With Two Faces (London & New York: Arnold, 1897);
Fancy's Guerdon, as Anodos (London: Mathews, 1897);
Non Sequitur (London: Nisbet, 1900);
The Fiery Dawn (London: Arnold, 1901; New York: Longmans, Green, 1901);
The Shadow on the Wall (London: Arnold, 1904);
The Lady on the Drawingroom Floor (London: Arnold, 1906; New York: Longmans, Green, 1906);
Poems by Mary E. Coleridge, edited by Henry Newbolt (London: Mathews, 1908 [i.e., 1907]);
Holman Hunt, edited by T. L. Hare (London: Jack / New York: Stokes, 1908);
Gathered Leaves from the Prose of Mary E. Coleridge, edited by Edith Sichel (London: Constable, 1910; New York: Dutton, 1910);

The Collected Poems of Mary Coleridge, edited by Theresa Whistler (London: Hart-Davis, 1954).

"Strong as a man, and gentle as a maid," in the words of Bernard Holland (as quoted by Edith Sichel in *Gathered Leaves*, 1910), Mary Elizabeth Coleridge was best known in her lifetime as a novelist and essayist, but she is now mostly remembered as a poet. A great-grandniece of Samuel Taylor Coleridge, she belonged to a family that had achieved eminence in literature and law. Music was also important to her family. Her mother, Mary Ann Jameson Coleridge, was musically talented, and her father, Arthur Duke Coleridge, was an amateur singer, as well as a lawyer and a staunch member of the Church of England. Among the Coleridges' family friends were Alfred, Lord Tennyson, John Everett Millais, Anthony Trollope, Holman Hunt, John Ruskin, and Fanny Kemble. Most memorable to Mary Coleridge were the occasional visits of a still more august personage: as she wrote toward the end of her life, in "The Drawing-Room" (collected in *Non Sequitur*, 1900), "I should like to think of another girl–as gay, as full of bold ambition and not so shy–acting and dancing where I danced and acted. I hope she will see the greatest man in the world come in as I saw Robert Browning come through the door one evening, his hat under his arm."

From her childhood on, Coleridge read widely and traveled regularly to the Continent, mastering an assortment of modern languages as well as Greek and Latin. At the age of twenty she was publishing essays in the *Monthly Packet* and other periodicals. She never married, staying with her family throughout her short life. In typically Victorian fashion, her life was deeply involved with family and friends. Coleridge was merry, but she was also spiritual, like Christina Rossetti, and shy until her brief sunset period of literary success. As a poet she also has affinities with her famous ancestor, with William Blake, whom she secretly admired, and with Emily Brontë and Emily Dickinson. Her poetry is haunted by a sense of loss and change, reminding one in this respect of that of some of her more famous contemporaries. Her Christian faith was steady but not dogmatic, and she preferred Percy Bysshe Shelley to John Keats, doubtless responding to the elder poet's greater sense of evanescence, which so closely resembles her own.

As an essayist, Mary Coleridge's style is pithy and imaginative, thrusting and sometimes enigmatic, and full of wise humor. In her essay on John Webster's *The Duchess of Malfi* (1614), entitled "Her Grace, the Duchess" (in *Gathered Leaves*), Coleridge remarks: "It is one of the most ungrateful tasks in the world to depict a woman making the first advances to a man; even Shakespeare achieved a very doubtful triumph with such a character as Helena in *All's Well That Ends Well*. There is something absolutely repugnant to good taste about the leap-year lady. All the more wonderful for its refinement is the scene in which the Duchess of Malfi declares her love."

In "On Noises" (in *Gathered Leaves*), Coleridge comes out (unlike Arthur Schopenhauer) in favor of noise: "Let us make noises, and be happy. It is such a nice, human thing–noise!" In "More Worlds Than One" (also in *Gathered Leaves*), she considers the influence of one's surroundings: "Live in a Cathedral town for a week and you will come to feel that the Dean is the most important person in England, and that the one object of life is not to be late for Evensong at the Minster." In "Cologne" (in *Non Sequitur*), she writes: "It is strange that a Cathedral, which is built to hold great multitudes of the faithful,

Mary Coleridge, age twenty-two

should never, in the moments when it is truly an ideal church, hold more than one."

In "The Making of Heroines" (in *Gathered Leaves*), she reveals her essential femininity: "Woman is, as a rule, quicker to take advantage of her life than man; she is less passive. Man at a crisis–unless it be a crisis of war–is a stupid thing. He either makes a fool of himself, or allows the world to make a fool of him, from which fate woman is preserved by her innate self-respect, and by a certain capacity which she possesses for making the most of emotion. A bridegroom is either the silliest or the most miserable of mortals, but marriage can always make a heroine out of the least heroic of women." Coleridge's own ability to make the most of emotion (and humor) may be seen in the following passage from her diary, written after viewing Piero di Cosimo's painting of the battle of the Centaurs and the Lapithae out of Ovid: "I never knew there were lady Centaurs.... How much more agreeable sporting ladies would be if they were only half horse in body as well as in mind! The rollicking fun of part of the picture is most remarkable–and the terrific enjoyment of the struggle" (Gathered Leaves).

Of the early work of William Butler Yeats she wrote perceptively: "About the poems of a true Irishman there is a curious remote charm. Here is a fellow-creature speaking the same language as ourselves–and yet his voice, his way of thought, his music, are as different from anything Saxon as though he were an inhabitant of Yokahama" (Non Sequitur). But to convey a truer impression of Coleridge's wonderful sense of prose rhythm and timing, it is necessary to quote her at some length. The following passage from "Fountains and Flowers" (also in Non Sequitur) is representative: "The squirrels got up late. One carried the finest, bushiest red tail that a squirrel could boast. He took an impish pleasure in making the slender boughs crackle under him, as he raced to and fro among them; he was consumed with vanity. There is a recklessness, combined with thrift, which makes the squirrel character peculiarly attractive; and they are even more human than other little beasts–than the mouse for instance, or the white rat; I think the first squirrel must have heard primeval woman angrily chattering to primeval man in the first forest. No doubt he is a common sight to those who live in the country, ... but to those who spend their days (according to those who frequent the country, they cannot be said to live) in a great city, he is strange. It makes a date to me to see him; I remember it, as I should the day that I saw [Algernon Charles] Swinburne." The poetic sensuousness of her nature, attracted alike by the squirrel's red tail and Swinburne's red hair, is also seen in her fascination with fire: "There's one desire I never can resist–a longing to break the great black root, a lump of coal, and free the golden flower within. What if people do call it prosaically, 'poking the fire from the top'?" And again, writing of people who burn letters (in "On Paper Matches" from Non Sequitur), she says: "There would seem to be a secret affinity between flowers and flames. Our fires are made of trees that have known, long ago, blossoms upon their boughs. There must be somewhere a garden of fire. And in that Eden, it may be, the poor heretics of letters flower brightly in flame."

There are several travel pieces in Non Sequitur, and though some of these are a bit dated, it is interesting to see her criticizing Prussian militarism and the anti-Semitism formerly associated with the Judengasse in Frankfurt (in her "Frankfurt-on-Main"). She can also sound a prophetic note when writing on Darwinism: "The ancients did not trouble themselves to think about evolution in theory; in practice they had a convenient evolution that went backwards. The monkeys did not turn into men, the men turned into monkeys. It is a pity that we have lost the art; science was dearly gained at the expense of it. Man is become a more conceited animal since then" ("Among the Foxgloves").

Coleridge's stories, as seen in Gathered Leaves, are stylistically and structurally akin to her essays, being short and pithy. Of the title character in "The Conscientious Secretary" Coleridge remarks: "He is one of those who are obliged to tell the truth because they have no imagination." And in "Cats in Council," which T. S. Eliot would have appreciated, her feline protagonist sets out to prove with relentless logic and a dazzling array of quotations that "Shakespeare ... was a cat himself."

On a more serious note, in the same book, she can compare Elizabeth Cleghorn Gaskell to Leo Tolstoy: "In her unending compassion, in her love of the gentleness of the frail and the old, in her clear condemnation of violence as a remedy, her scorn of military prowess, she resembles the great Russian more closely than any of her countrymen." With a glance further ahead into the twentieth century (and perhaps a hit at Thomas Carlyle), she remarks of Mrs. Gaskell, "She held a brief for the heroism of everybody as against the heroism of a favoured few." One is reminded of Mary Coleridge's efforts to teach literature and composition to working women in evening classes, a practical application of her Christian and democratic instincts, although she found it difficult to love the poor en masse. Her essential humanism is seen in "The Will to Die," wherein she shrewdly observes: "Grand as the death of a man 'drunken with God' must be, we are more moved as we grow older by the quiet jests and courtesies of the balanced mind that refuses to make either a fast or a feast of the occasion."

Although Mary Coleridge's poetry will always have readers, perhaps it is time to turn again to her essays, which in addition to their poetic qualities have something of the "downright cut-and-thrust manliness" of style that she admired in William Hazlitt, as contrasted to the "airy-fairy" manner of some of her contemporaries, including Matthew Arnold and Andrew Lang.

References:

Robert Bridges, *Collected Essays, Papers, &c.*, volume 5 (London: Oxford University Press, 1931), pp. 205-229;

Edith Sichel, "Memoir," in *Gathered Leaves from the Prose of Mary E. Coleridge*, edited by Sichel (London: Constable, 1910; New York: Dutton, 1910);

T. E. Welby, "Mary Coleridge," in his *Back Numbers* (London: Constable, 1929);

Beatrice White, "Mary Coleridge: An Appreciation," in *Essays and Studies by Members of the English Association*, 31 (1945).

Cyril Connolly

(10 September 1903 - 26 November 1974)

Averil Gardner
Memorial University of Newfoundland

BOOKS: *The Rock Pool* (Paris: Obelisk, 1936; New York: Scribners, 1936; revised edition, London: Hamilton, 1947; Norfolk, Conn.: New Directions, 1948);

Enemies of Promise (London: Routledge, 1938; Boston: Little, Brown, 1939; revised edition, London: Routledge & Kegan Paul, 1948; New York: Macmillan, 1948);

The Unquiet Grave: A Word Cycle, as Palinurus (London: Curwen, 1944; revised and enlarged edition, New York & London: Harper, 1945);

The Condemned Playground: Essays: 1927-1944 (London: Routledge, 1945; New York: Macmillan, 1946);

Ideas and Places (London: Weidenfeld & Nicolson, 1953; New York: Harper, 1953);

Les Pavillons: French Pavilions of the Eighteenth Century, by Connolly and Jerome Zerbe (London: Hamilton, 1962; New York: Macmillan, 1962);

Previous Convictions (London: Hamilton, 1963; New York: Harper & Row, 1963);

The Modern Movement: 100 Key Books from England, France and America, 1880-1950 (London: Deutsch / Hamilton, 1965; New York: Atheneum, 1966);

The Evening Colonnade (London: Bruce & Watson, 1973; New York: Harcourt Brace Jovanovich, 1975);

Cyril Connolly: Journal and Memoir, edited by David Pryce-Jones (London: Collins, 1983);

The Selected Essays of Cyril Connolly, edited by Peter Quennell (New York: Moss/Persea, 1984).

OTHER: *Horizon Stories*, edited by Connolly (London: Faber & Faber, 1943; New York: Vanguard, 1946);

Great English Short Novels, edited by Connolly (New York: Dial, 1953).

"If I have a gift," Cyril Connolly stated in his introduction to *Previous Convictions* (1963), "it is that of being able to communicate my enthusiasm for literature and throw a little light on my favourite authors." *Previous Convictions* was

Connolly's third collection of essays and reviews; the first two, he complained, were "both out of print: I really don't know why one goes on." The self-mocking, histrionic petulance of that remark, characteristic of the individuality and flair of Connolly's style, suggests why his earlier description, though accurately conveying the intention behind much of his work, is too modest an index of the high quality of its execution.

Connolly was, in fact, one of the finest British essayists and reviewers—and one of the sharpest parodists—of this century. Indeed, through his friendships with other writers and his ten-year editorship of the literary magazine *Horizon* (1940-1950), he stood at the center of British literary and aesthetic life. His literary contemporaries' sense of his importance was conveyed clearly in 1972, when on the recommendation of the Royal Society of Literature of Great Britain he was made a Companion of Literature. In the same year he was also made a Companion of the Order of the British Empire.

Nevertheless, Connolly often viewed himself as a failed creative writer, the result either of native indolence or of the high standards with which, formidably well-read in classical and later Western European literature, he approached the writing of his own time. His exacting approach is summed up at the beginning of the second of his "creative" works, his "word cycle" *The Unquiet Grave* (1944): "The more books we read, the sooner we perceive that the true function of a writer is to produce a masterpiece and that no other task is of any consequence." Connolly did not see his journalism as fulfilling that requirement, though it contains many phrases that have entered the permanent collection of twentieth-century literary memory. The most haunting occurs in the editorial he wrote for the last issue of *Horizon* (November-December 1949), reprinted in *Ideas and Places* (1953): "It is closing time in the gardens of the West." Connolly's own closing time as a writer did not come for another two decades, during which he produced the nearly two hundred pieces reprinted in *Previous Convictions* and *The Evening Colonnade* (1973). All of these were journalism, most were reviews, and their predominant characteristics—as with their prewar and wartime predecessors—are quickness of perception, generosity of response, and an eloquence and crispness of expression that belie the label "unsure in my judgements" hung by Connolly on himself in chapter 11 of *Enemies of Promise* (1938), his partly autobiographical survey

of the prewar literary situation. Discerning in his tastes and possessed of enormous natural talent, Connolly was almost incapable of writing badly. If, as he said in his essay "First Edition Fever" (*Previous Convictions*), "the test of our devotion to an author is whether we are prepared to collect his journalism," the test is one Connolly passes with distinction. But even though he managed to arrange matters so that the journalism he wrote would bear reprinting and rereading, Connolly could never quite bring himself to see journalism, per se, as other than a second best: "The test of an author's devotion to his collectors is not to provide us with any." Given his daunting notion of the "masterpiece," Connolly's career as an essayist may thus be seen as the unwilling triumph of the urge to write over a high-minded but unrealistic hankering for silence.

Cyril Vernon Connolly, an only child, was born on 10 September 1903 at Whitley, three miles southeast of Coventry in the English Midlands. A more unlikely spot than the center of British bicycle manufacturing could hardly have been devised as the birthplace for a writer as "aesthetic" and cosmopolitan as Connolly: he referred to himself at the end of *Enemies of Promise* as one "whom ill-famed Coventry bore," and his birth there implied no local associations or allegiances. Three years older, and he would have been born in Ireland; three years younger, in South Africa. His father, Matthew Connolly, was an army officer who at this time happened to be stationed outside Coventry, as adjutant to the Second Volunteer Battalion of the Royal Warwickshire Regiment, himself the son of an admiral, who died at the age of eighty-five, two years before his grandson was born; further back in the family were other army and navy officers. This military descent was to be amusingly conflated in "What Will *He* Do Next?," a spoof on the "military appreciation" paper Cyril Connolly wrote in August 1940 (reprinted in *The Condemned Playground*, 1945), giving himself the title "Rear-Colonel Connolly." His exact Oxford contemporary and friend, Evelyn Waugh, also made use of Connolly's background for farcical purposes in *Black Mischief* (1932) by calling the commander of the black emperor Seth's forces "General Connolly." In his memoir of Connolly (1983), David Pryce-Jones notes another aspect of Connolly's inheritance: "On all branches of his family tree were large houses and private incomes." Admiral Connolly had married Harriet Kemble, whose father, the rich rector of Bath,

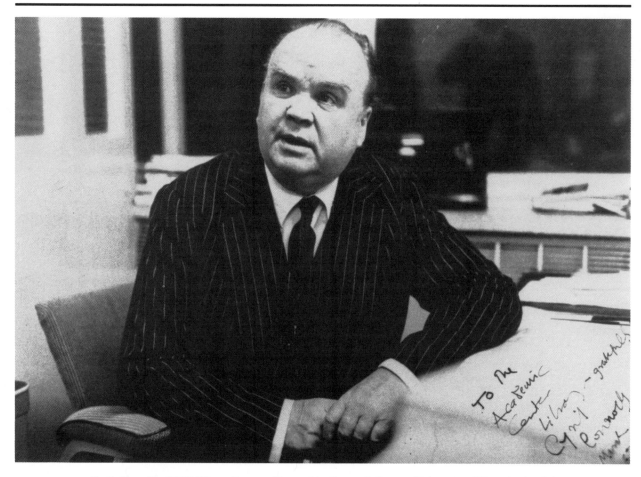

Cyril Connolly, 1967 (Harry Ransom Humanities Research Center, University of Texas at Austin)

had once donated the then vast sum of fifty thousand pounds to restore Bath Abbey; the Kemble family money derived from tea planting. Cyril Connolly's mother, Muriel Maud Connolly, née Vernon, came of the Anglo-Irish "ascendancy": her father, a member of the exclusive Kildare Street Club in Dublin, had been high sheriff of Ireland. Thus, in both England and Ireland, Connolly was able as a boy to stay with affluent relatives–his maternal great-aunt, the countess of Kingston, lived in a huge eighteenth-century Gothic castle, Mitchelstown, near Cork–although his parents could not themselves be described as rich.

After a brief posting in 1906 to Gibraltar, Connolly's father was transferred the same year to Pretoria in South Africa. Here the young Connolly spent one year, returning in October 1908, after a short interlude in England, to South Africa's Cape Colony, where his father, now stationed at Wynberg, was district signaling officer. Connolly lived at Wynberg until 1910, and there formed his earliest memories: of ani-

mals, the smells of flowers and fruit, and the arid subtropical scenery, all of which he loved and which gave him a lifelong taste, reflected in many of his essays, for a Mediterranean type of landscape that stood in warm and welcome contrast to that of England. His fine late essay, "The Flawed Diamond" (1964; collected in *The Evening Colonnade*), written after a visit to his mother, who had returned to live in South Africa, conveys in its mature description of the area around Cape Town something of the beauty that affected him as a child of seven and did much to shape his hedonistic temperament: "strange flowers and trees bloom in abundance, the unique silver-tree, the proteas and lilies, the dapper yet languorous frangipani; while the ubiquitous Norfolk Island pine and Canary palm proclaim that this is a completely Mediterranean climate with winter rainfall and no frost." In later life Connolly's father gained a considerable reputation as a conchologist, producing a substantial study of the non-marine mollusks of South Africa; in addition, some snails in the collection of the London Natu-

Sketch of Connolly by Augustus John (Collection of Romilly John)

ral History Museum were named after him. This exact absorption in the natural world has its counterpart in some of his son's later essays, which transmit not only love for the animate world but a respect amounting to reverence for its distinct and independent existence. This is memorably expressed in his response to the Serengeti in "Tanzanian Sketch Book" (1968; in *The Evening Colonnade*): "The light is dazzling, the air delectable: *kopjes* rise out of the grass at far intervals, some wooded; the magic of the unraped American prairie here blends with the other magic of the animals as they existed before man. There is a lightening of the spirit, a sense of atonement, of being able to compound at last for the endless cycle of vanity and greed to which they have been subjected."

In 1910 Connolly's father, promoted from captain to major, was posted to Hong Kong, whose humid climate was thought less likely to suit a child. Cyril Connolly, feeling rejected by his parents, was sent back to England, which, however, he reached by way of Corsica, where relatives had taken a house, thus providing him with

his first encounter with the true Mediterranean (and a side trip to Tangier into the bargain). Reaching Great Britain at last, Connolly stayed in Ireland with well-to-do relatives of his mother, then with his Connolly grandmother in Bath, where he attended his first school, St. Christopher's, as a day boy.

In 1914, when his father retired from the army and returned to England, Connolly was sent as a boarder to St. Cyprian's, an ambitious and efficient preparatory school at Eastbourne, on the Channel coast south of London. Here he became particularly friendly with two boys who, like himself, were to make a substantial mark on English cultural life: the future photographer and stage designer Cecil Beaton, and the future novelist and essayist George Orwell, many of whose best essays Connolly later published in *Horizon*. The strict yet capricious regime of St. Cyprian's was made notorious by Orwell's long essay "Such, Such Were the Joys," first published in *Partisan Review* in 1952. Connolly, who described his years there in chapter 19 ("White Samite") of *Enemies of Promise*, resented the school far less, though he too responded poorly to its orthodox molding of "character." But St. Cyprian's also valued academic achievement, and here Connolly did especially well, in 1916 winning the Harrow History Prize, competed for by preparatory-school boys all over England, and in 1917 obtaining a King's Scholarship to Eton College, possibly the most prestigious public school in the country.

Connolly went up to Eton in the summer of 1918. His brief portrait of himself in the early stages of his Eton career, given in chapter 20 of *Enemies of Promise*, is extremely unflattering: "dirty, inky, miserable, untidy, a bad fag, a coward at games, lazy at work, unpopular with my masters and superiors, anxious to curry favour and yet to bully whom I dared." Nevertheless, he acquired there a knowledge, and an abiding love, of Latin poetry–particularly that of Juvenal, Catullus, Martial, and Propertius–which is evidenced in many of his essays; and his classics tutor described him, glowingly and perceptively, as "an extraordinary boy of great individuality and a way of looking at things at once quaint and amusing and unexpected." In fact, Connolly gained at Eton an awareness of literature that was both formidable ("by the time I had left . . . I knew by heart something of the literature of five civilizations") and idiosyncratic, in that "the only literature which appealed to me was pessimistic"–a note frequently struck by his own work later, especially in *The Un-*

quiet Grave. His last two years at Eton were academically concentrated on modern history, in which he distinguished himself first by winning the school's Rosebery History Prize (whose honorarium he was allowed to spend on Medici Society prints of paintings) and then by gaining the Brackenbury History Scholarship to Balliol College, Oxford, where he went in the fall of 1922.

By that time he had further extended his knowledge of the world by some trips to Europe: first to Paris and the Great War battlefields with his parents; then to Switzerland, where he saw the Eiger and the Jungfrau; and at Easter 1922 to Paris again, on his first unsupervised trip abroad. In the aesthetic way of the 1920s, he hastened to the Folies Bergères, thrilling himself by drinking with two "thin, dark prostitutes" in the interval. More deeply fulfilling was his arrival the following day in Avignon, and thus his first momentous encounter with Provence, returned to many times and frequently celebrated in his essays. In *Enemies of Promise* he indicated the area's supreme importance to him, combining as it did the beauty of southern landscape and the riches of Western European history and culture: "I know only that they are sacred places, that the country between Mont Ventoux and the Canigou, from Avignon and Vaucluse to Figueras and Puigcerdá, is the expression of the complete south, the cradle of my civilization."

"There was now nothing which could happen to me," was Connolly's comment, made sixteen years later, on his state of mind when leaving Eton. His last weeks there were spent in reading his favorite Latin poets, the aesthetic and decadent poetry of nineteenth-century France, the prose of Walter Pater and Joris-Karl Huysmans; and in sitting through "the lime-flowered summer evenings" wearing "grey flannel trousers, a black dinner-jacket, and a panama hat." Out of this fin-de-siècle, nineteen-year-old flaccidity came one of his most famous dicta, summed up as "The Theory of Permanent Adolescence"– "the theory that the experiences undergone by boys at the great public schools, their glories and disappointments, are so intense as to dominate their lives and arrest their development." Oxford, certainly, seems to have been an anticlimax for Connolly. He wrote nothing about it until his very short essay of 1973, "Oxford in the Twenties" (*The Evening Colonnade*), which crisply reduced any lurking nostalgia to a recital of names and fashions, punctuated by a Wildean witticism: "the only exercise we took was running up bills."

He worked little, obtaining only a Third Class history degree in 1925. Nevertheless, his Oxford friend and contemporary, the art historian Kenneth Clark, described him fifty years later in his autobiography as "without doubt the most gifted undergraduate of his generation," adding that Connolly's letters to him of that period were, unlike anyone else's, "brilliant, erudite, original, observant and so perfectly phrased that they could have been published as they stood."

Unfortunately these letters perished not long after in a fire, though a batch of Connolly's Oxford letters to another friend, Noel Blakiston (published with later ones in *A Romantic Friendship* in 1975), show something of the quality referred to by Clark. But it was a couple of years before Connolly broke into print (a review in 1927), nine more before his first book, *The Rock Pool*, appeared in Paris, and two more again before *Enemies of Promise*, his first book to be published in England, revealed not only the beauty of his achieved literary style but also some of the obstacles, temperamental and circumstantial, that stood in the way of the would-be author. Compared to his contemporary Evelyn Waugh, who by 1938 had published some half-dozen books, Connolly was a notable late developer.

At the end of *Enemies of Promise*, Connolly speaks of having "drifted into [being a critic] through unemployability." There is an element of literal truth in the statement but a larger element of affectation, since it ignores the positive keys to such a career that Connolly possessed: wide reading, verbal talent, and a privileged access to useful contacts. Some middle-class careers might have been closed to him by his mediocre degree in history, but they were also uncongenial; moreover, Connolly's apparent access to at least modest financial means obviated the necessity for him to be a square peg in a round hole. In retrospect, his drifting can be seen rather as a semiconscious purposefulness that procured for him what he was best fitted for: the self-contained "literary life" (not quite synonymous with being a "man of letters") of which his career furnishes one of the best twentieth-century examples.

Connolly's entry into that life, after a six-month period pleasantly spent as a private tutor in Jamaica, came in the summer of 1926, when at the suggestion of Clark he applied for the vacant post of secretary/assistant to the sixty-year-old writer Logan Pearsall Smith. Smith, a rich expatriate American, lived in Chelsea and had taken British citizenship in 1917. He had become a minor ce-

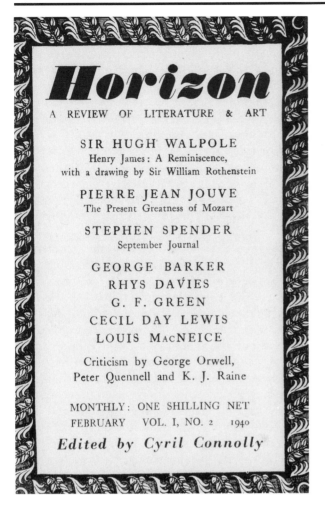

Horizon
A REVIEW OF LITERATURE & ART

SIR HUGH WALPOLE
Henry James: A Reminiscence,
with a drawing by Sir William Rothenstein

PIERRE JEAN JOUVE
The Present Greatness of Mozart

STEPHEN SPENDER
September Journal

GEORGE BARKER
RHYS DAVIES
G. F. GREEN
CECIL DAY LEWIS
LOUIS MacNEICE

Criticism by George Orwell,
Peter Quennell and K. J. Raine

MONTHLY: ONE SHILLING NET
FEBRUARY   VOL. I, NO. 2   1940

Edited by Cyril Connolly

Cover for the journal founded by Connolly and Peter Watson

lebrity in literary circles in 1918 when he published *Trivia*, a collection of aphorisms that was translated into French in 1921; it was followed by *More Trivia* in 1922. Civilized and learned—and rather old-fashioned in their privileged and sensitive approach to life—both works clearly influenced Connolly's writing: not long after beginning his association with Smith, Connolly began work on a book of aphorisms himself, which flowered finally in 1944 as *The Unquiet Grave*. It hardly seems too much to say that, in literary terms as well as in financial patronage, Smith was a kind of father to Connolly: Connolly was his secretary and helper only until September 1927, but they remained friends for some years after, and it was to Smith that Connolly dedicated *Enemies of Promise*. Connolly also wrote warmly of Smith on his death in 1946, and the last essay in *The Evening Colonnade* represents him as a still-powerful, haunting presence, a telephoner from the land of the unforgotten dead.

Through Smith, Connolly significantly extended the range of his acquaintance in the literary and artistic world, visiting the well-known art historian Bernard Berenson (whose wife was Smith's sister) in Italy, and in London forming a friendship with Desmond MacCarthy, literary editor of the *New Statesman*, who published Connolly's first signed essay in July 1927 and invited him to contribute a fiction review each fortnight to that journal at the generous salary of ten pounds per week. Through MacCarthy, who incidentally shared with Connolly both high standards and comparatively small "creative" production, Connolly grazed the fringes of "Bloomsbury," though that literary enclave, both liberal and priggish, viewed the "Chelsea" milieu of Smith as unduly worldly. Hence, by the age of about twenty-five, Connolly was well placed to make a career in literary London.

Connolly contributed reviews of novels (which he called "the white man's grave of journalism") to the *New Statesman* only until August 1929, when he signed off with an essay ironically entitled "Ninety Years of Novel Reviewing." Besides this parting comment, he reprinted only three of his earliest pieces in *The Condemned Playground* in 1945: his very first review (1927), on the Oxford edition of Laurence Sterne; a 1928 review of André Gide's *Les Faux-Monnayeurs* (1925; translated as *The Counterfeiters*, 1927); and an interim assessment of James Joyce, published in 1929. These three essays can, however, stand for the general range of literary topics on which, as an experienced reviewer free to choose his own areas of interest, Connolly later preferred to concentrate: the literature of the eighteenth century (English and French), and the lives and works of the twentieth-century modernists (British and American), who were for him the living literary environment in which he grew up from Eton onward. To these areas of interest adumbrated in *The Condemned Playground* and returned to faithfully until the end of his life, one more needs to be added. From the early 1950s, when he began regularly contributing to the *Sunday Times* of London, he expressed his fascination for the British and French writers of the nineteenth and early twentieth centuries, with special emphasis on the work of decadents and aesthetes, such as Charles Baudelaire, Oscar Wilde, and Marcel Proust.

Connolly's range of literary interests, all of them underpinned by his early and never-slackened love for Latin poetry, was thus exceptionally wide, a blend of the classical and romantic past and his own experimental present, and above all else cosmopolitan. As one reads Connolly in the final years of the twentieth century, this last aspect of his outlook combines with his sharply relished nostalgia to give his literary essays the air of valedictory addresses to a civilization well past its zenith. It is remarkable that only a minority of those about whom Connolly wrote (at least in the essays he chose to reprint) were still alive when he wrote about them, and also remarkable–allowing him great scope for the magisterial urbanity at which he excelled–how many of the books he reviewed in his later years were biographies of writers and collections of their letters, rather than novels or volumes of poetry. Connolly was no less a historian and archivist of literature, and of the life and culture that produced it, than he was a critic of literary works. Though always clear and cogent in its expression of his critical judgments, Connolly's work has a particular value when he deals with writers with whom he was contemporary and whom he survived, since he is so often able to illuminate them and their books by means of a personal anecdote or a corrective factual detail–something the critic in academe is rarely able to do. Connolly's range, style, and temperament are encapsulated in this well-turned sentence from the introduction to his first retrospective collection, *The Condemned Playground*: "The authors I most enjoy writing about are first those great, lonely, formal artists who spit in the eye of their century, and after them the wild and exquisitely gifted young writers who came to an untimely end through passion, and lastly those wise epicureans who combine taste with the gossiping good sense of the world, and whose graceful books are but the shadow of their intimate communion with their friends or with nature."

Peter Quennell, to whom Connolly dedicated his only novel, *The Rock Pool*, in 1936, returned the compliment in 1984 by selecting and reprinting thirty of Connolly's essays–only a small portion (yet running to three hundred pages) of the ones Connolly had himself chosen to reprint in his four volumes published between 1945 and 1973. Like Connolly himself, Quennell sensibly makes no distinction between the rather theoretical term "essay" and any of the subtypes into which the writer's need to earn a living has in practice divided it. Any such distinction, applied to Connolly, would be either too stringently reductive–since few of his pieces were generated solely by the wish to express ideas and responses–

or largely meaningless, since he brought to all his writing the same care for stylistic polish and vitality, whether in literary reviews (from which Quennell selects only a handful, dealing with Joyce and Wilde), general articles, or the many editorials Connolly wrote for *Horizon*, which make up the bulk of his second collection, *Ideas and Places*.

Quennell included none of these editorials in his selection. More than any other of Connolly's writings they reflect the preoccupations of a particular era: the war years of the 1940s, in which so much of what Connolly valued from the past seemed doomed to vanish, and the years of uncertain postwar reconstruction, which seemed to offer less and less of a future for the writer. In his novel *Unconditional Surrender* (1961), Evelyn Waugh alluded to *Horizon* under the apt name of *Survival*. In Connolly's selection of material for his magazine (underwritten by money supplied by a friend), he exerted his energy to combat the barbarism of the times by including the best writing by others that he could find. One representative issue, that for December 1948, eclectically joined the civilized past with hope for the future by including essays by George Santayana and E. M. Forster alongside work by writers just emerging, such as Norman Nicholson and Alan Ross. Many of Connolly's editorials, however (when they did not display a rather "busy," committed air that he later came to dislike), took on a more and more pessimistic tone for which he apologized in his introduction to *Ideas and Places*, even wondering whether "I was imagining the predicament." Whether or not he was, his mode of expressing it still remains rhetorically persuasive, especially the last words of his last editorial, partly quoted earlier: " 'Nothing dreadful is ever done with, no bad thing gets any better, you can't be too serious.' This is the message of the Forties from which, alas, there seems no escape, for it is closing time in the gardens of the West and from now on an artist will be judged only by the resonance of his solitude or the quality of his despair." Connolly's farewell as editor of *Horizon* was made in a slightly earlier editorial and couched in language that shows the self-mocking resilience that was always Connolly's other face: "An editor frays away his true personality in the banalities of good mixing, he washes his mind in other people's bath-water, he sacrifices his inner voice to his engagement book. Those of us who wish to survive middle-age must all walk the plank."

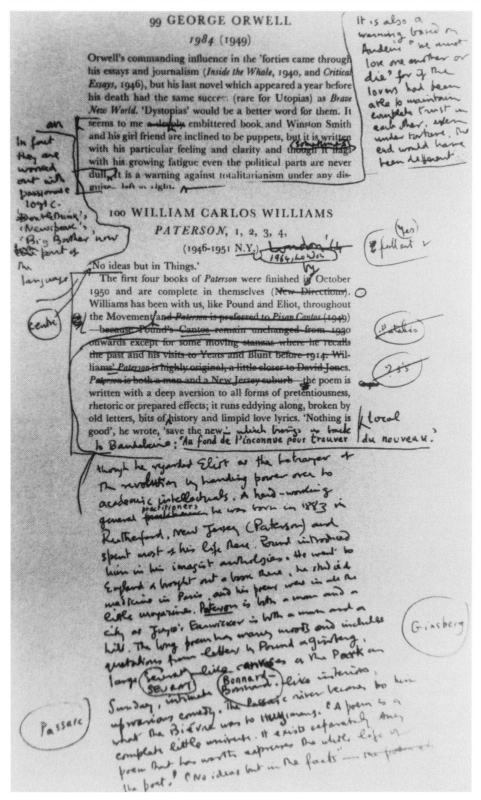

Galley proof, with Connolly's corrections and additions, for The Modern Movement: 100 Key Books from England,
France and America, 1880-1950 *(Harry Ransom Humanities Research Center, University of Texas at Austin)*

Both self-mockery and mockery of others are displayed in Connolly's satirical pieces and parodies, five of which Quennell reprinted in his selection. Two of them, "Felicity" and "Felicity Entertains," though still amusing, have by now lost the inter-war-years topicality that gave them much of their point: they are a kind of self-defensive spin-off from Connolly's experience as a reviewer of fifth-rate novels of a sort no longer in vogue, though they also glance at a world of wine-and-food snobbery that is far from extinct. "Where Engels Fears to Tread" has worn distinctly better, being a kind of spoof autobiography, in which the Eton and Oxford "aesthetic" Connolly, under the guise of "Christian de Clavering," gradually mutates into the comically threatening Party comrade ("no–COMMISSAR") "Cris Clay." The names of real friends–Evelyn Waugh, John Betjeman, Robert Byron, and Peter Quennell–rub shoulders with imaginary and increasingly fantastic others: "Alvanley, Gleneagles, Prince Harmatviz, Graf Slivovitz, the Ballygalley of Ballygalley, the Duc de Dingy, the Conde de Coca y Cola." The names vividly illustrate Connolly's gift for the evocative travesty of periods and styles, a gift that placed him, as a parodist, on a level with Max Beerbohm. This particular talent is most brilliantly in evidence in "Told in Gath," whose characters' names–Mr. Encolpius, Giles Pentateuch, Roland Narthex–and recondite conversational allusions evoke the world of early Aldous Huxley, in *Crome Yellow* (1921) and *Antic Hay* (1923), with uncanny accuracy. All these pieces date from before 1940, and convey nostalgia as well as mockery. After the war Connolly showed his ability to move with the times in his parody of Ian Fleming, "Bond Strikes Camp" (1962). Here James Bond's boss, the aloof and enigmatic "M," is shown as having a homosexual passion for his subordinate, whom he sends on a trumped-up mission *en travesti* in order, himself disguised as a Russian general, to seduce him. Connolly's subversive distortion of Fleming's plots and ethos–partly a comment on the recent defection of Guy Burgess–is combined, as in the parody of Huxley, with a wickedly insidious rendering of the style and stage properties of Connolly's target.

Cyril Connolly died in 1974. One of the last things he wrote was the introduction (itself an essay, on the search he always went through for appropriate titles for his books) to his final collection, resonantly entitled *The Evening Colonnade*. In it he spoke of wanting to spend the rest of his life less "in terms of the library and reflections on the past" than in seeing "a great many more elephants in the wild." Connolly saw his life, by that point, as a juxtaposition of interests, which he summed up as "love of nature, love of books." (It is noteworthy that in the long wartime piece, entitled "Writers and Society," which he included at the end of *The Condemned Playground*, he described writers as an endangered species, comparable to the "hunted" sea otter and the "despoiled" egret.) In 1939 he had written what was his own favorite prewar essay, "The Ant-Lion" (reprinted in *The Condemned Playground*) which evocatively, though a trifle obscurely, brings together three lifelong predilections–art, Mediterranean landscapes, and the fascinating ways of animals. Beautiful, subtle, and truly an essay rather than a review or an article, "The Ant-Lion" represented for Connolly an "advance in sensibility," which he attributed to "shedding possessions and living in the South of France." Postwar relaxations on travel enabled him not only to renew his contact with France, memorably described in "Bordeaux-Dordogne" (*Ideas and Places*) and "Farewell to Provence" (1971, *Evening Colonnade*), but to go farther afield: to Egypt ("Impressions of Egypt," 1955, *Previous Convictions*); to Senegal and the Canary Islands ("Destination Atlantis," 1972); and, in between, to southern Africa–South Africa itself ("The Flawed Diamond," 1964), then Uganda ("On Safari," 1967) and Tanzania ("Tanzanian Sketch Book," 1968). These last four essays were printed in the *Evening Colonnade*.

The freshness, excitement, and openness of response evinced in these essays on places, people, and animals are at least as impressive as the critical acumen and aesthetic appreciation conveyed by Connolly's essays on literary subjects. They also reveal a progressive movement toward an innocent hedonism free of the melancholy self-absorption one finds in many of Connolly's sophisticated essays on literature. The same simplicity is found in Connolly's postwar reviews of books about wild animals, reprinted in *Previous Convictions* (1963), and in his delightful and quite unsentimental essay, also printed there, "Living with Lemurs" (many of these animals, together with ferrets, Connolly had kept as pets over the years).

"Art is the conscious apprehension of the unconscious ecstasy of all created things," Connolly wrote in his essay "Beyond Believing," printed last in *Previous Convictions*. In his essays and reviews concerned with the natural world, one may feel that Connolly the literary aesthete had found expression for a side of himself that Eton and Oxford had done little to foster but which sprang from his earliest years. One of the best-known dicta of Connolly the stylist is from *The Unquiet Grave*, the most haunting distillation he ever made of the literary works in which his education and his love of books had steeped him: "Imprisoned in every fat man a thin one is wildly signalling to be let out." That "thin" man inside the bulky and celebrated writer, who in 1967 stated that he "had never possessed anything larger than a bookcase" ("Confessions of a House Hunter," *Evening Colonnade*), found his final release in death, which, Connolly said in the introduction to *The Evening Colonnade*, "colours my every thought." Before death, however, his release was into the ever-adjacent world of the non-human, as is suggested by the conclusion to his review of a book by Peter Dance called *Shell Collecting* (1966). Reading that book returned Connolly to his childhood in the landscape of South Africa and to memories of his father's work as a conchologist. The last sentences of his "Shell Collecting" serve well to round out this essay on Connolly, which began by presenting him, also in his own words, as a lover of litera-

ture: "Mountain sunshine of Montagu; a child of six turning over the stones by the river; the waters of science as yet unmuddied by literature, the heart unclouded, the conscience clear. I'm glad Mr. Dance has kept to sea-shells. The Precious Wentletrap and Gloria Maris every time."

Letters:
Noel Blakiston, *A Romantic Friendship: The Letters of Cyril Connolly to Noel Blakiston* (London: Constable, 1975).

Biography:
David Pryce-Jones, "Memoir," in *Cyril Connolly: Journal and Memoir* (London: Collins, 1983).

References:
Eric Bentley, ed., *The Importance of "Scrutiny"* (New York: Stewart, 1948), pp. 255-261;
Evelyn Waugh, "Present Discontents" and "Palinurus in Never-Never Land," in *A Little Order*, edited by Donat Gallagher (London: Methuen, 1977), pp. 123-131;
Edmund Wilson, *Classics and Commercials: A Literary Chronicle of the Fifties* (New York: Farrar, Strauss, 1950), pp. 280-285.

Joseph Conrad

(3 December 1857 - 3 August 1924)

J. H. Stape
Université de Limoges

See also the Conrad entries in *DLB 10: Modern British Dramatists, 1900-1945* and *DLB 34: British Novelists, 1890-1929: Traditionalists.*

BOOKS: *Almayer's Folly: A Story of an Eastern River* (London: Unwin, 1895; New York & London: Macmillan, 1895);

An Outcast of the Islands (London: Unwin, 1896; New York: Appleton, 1896);

The Children of the Sea: A Tale of the Forecastle (New York: Dodd, Mead, 1897); republished as *The Nigger of the "Narcissus": A Tale of the Sea* (London: Heinemann, 1898 [i.e., 1897]);

Tales of Unrest (London: Unwin, 1898; New York: Scribners, 1898);

Lord Jim (Edinburgh & London: Blackwood, 1900; New York: Doubleday & McClure, 1900);

The Inheritors: An Extravagant Story, by Conrad and Ford Madox Hueffer [Ford] (New York: McClure, Phillips, 1901; London: Heinemann, 1901);

Youth: A Narrative, and Two Other Stories (Edinburgh & London: Blackwood, 1902; New York: McClure, Phillips, 1903);

Typhoon (New York & London: Putnam's, 1902);

Typhoon and Other Stories (London: Heinemann, 1903); published without "Typhoon" as *Falk; Amy Foster; To-morrow: Three Stories* (New York: McClure, Phillips, 1903);

Romance: A Novel, by Conrad and Ford (London: Smith, Elder, 1903; New York: McClure, Phillips, 1904);

Nostromo: A Tale of the Seaboard (London & New York: Harper, 1904);

The Mirror of the Sea: Memories and Impressions (London: Methuen, 1906; New York & London: Harper, 1906);

The Secret Agent: A Simple Tale (London: Methuen, 1907; New York & London: Harper, 1907);

A Set of Six (London: Methuen, 1908; Garden City, N.Y.: Doubleday, Page, 1915);

Under Western Eyes (London: Methuen, 1911; New York: Harper, 1911);

Joseph Conrad, 1919 (photograph by Arbuthnot)

Some Reminiscences (London: Nash, 1912); republished as *A Personal Record* (New York & London: Harper, 1912);

'Twixt Land and Sea (London: Dent, 1912; New York: Hodder & Stoughton/Doran, 1912);

Chance: A Tale in Two Parts (London: Methuen, 1913; Garden City, N.Y.: Doubleday, Page, 1913);

Within the Tides (London, N.Y.: Dent, 1915; Garden City, N.Y.: Doubleday, Page, 1916);

Victory: An Island Tale (Garden City, N.Y.: Doubleday, Page, 1915; London: Methuen, 1915);

One Day More: A Play in One Act (London: Privately printed by C. Shorter, 1917; Garden City, N.Y.: Doubleday, Page, 1920);

The Shadow-Line: A Confession (London & Toronto: Dent, 1917; Garden City, N.Y.: Doubleday, Page, 1917);

The Arrow of Gold: A Story Between Two Notes (Garden City, N.Y.: Doubleday, Page, 1919; London: Unwin, 1919);

The Rescue: A Romance of the Shallows (Garden City, N.Y.: Doubleday, Page, 1920; London & Toronto: Dent, 1920);

Notes on My Books (Garden City, N.Y., & Toronto: Doubleday, Page, 1921; London: Heinemann, 1921); republished as *Conrad's Prefaces to His Works* (London: Dent, 1937);

Notes on Life and Letters (London & Toronto: Dent, 1921; Garden City, N.Y., & Toronto: Doubleday, Page, 1921);

The Secret Agent: Drama in Four Acts (Canterbury: Printed for the author by H. J. Goulden, 1921);

The Rover (Garden City, N.Y.: Doubleday, Page, 1923; London: Unwin, 1923);

Laughing Anne: A Play (London: Bookman's Journal, 1923);

The Nature of a Crime, by Conrad and Ford (London: Duckworth, 1924; Garden City, N.Y.: Doubleday, Page, 1924);

Suspense: A Napoleonic Novel (Garden City, N.Y.: Doubleday, Page, 1925; London & Toronto: Dent, 1925);

Tales of Hearsay (London: Unwin, 1925; Garden City, N.Y.: Doubleday, Page, 1925);

Last Essays, edited by Richard Curle (London & Toronto: Dent, 1926; Garden City, N.Y.: Doubleday, Page, 1926);

The Sisters (New York: Gaige, 1928);

Joseph Conrad on Fiction, edited by Walter F. Wright (Lincoln: University of Nebraska Press, 1964);

Congo Diary and Other Uncollected Pieces by Joseph Conrad, edited by Zdzislaw Najder (Garden City: Doubleday, 1978).

Collections: *The Works of Joseph Conrad*, Uniform Edition, 22 volumes (London: Dent, 1923-1928); reprinted and enlarged, 26 volumes (London: Dent, 1946-1955);

Complete Works, Canterbury Edition, 24 volumes (Garden City, N.Y.: Doubleday, Page, 1924);

The Complete Short Stories of Joseph Conrad (London: Hutchinson, 1933);

The Portable Conrad, edited by Morton Dauwen Zabel (New York: Viking, 1947).

Joseph Conrad's reputation as a major modern writer rests almost exclusively on his novels and short fiction. But even if his five volumes of occasional writings only infrequently achieve the high distinction of his creative work, they deserve attention for the considerable light they throw on the mind, character, and art of such a significant author.

Conrad was born Teodor Józef Konrad Korzeniowski in the Polish Ukraine, the son of Apollo Korzeniowski, a translator, poet, dramatist and political activist. Exiled for their involvement in anti-Russian activities, his parents, their health undermined, died when he was still a boy—his mother, Ewa Bobrowska Korzeniowski, in 1865 and his father in 1869. The dream of going to sea, unusual in a Pole, brought him to Marseilles in 1874 and then in 1878 to England, at that time the world's greatest maritime power. His deep water voyages to the Far East and Australia are re-created and idealized in his fiction, an activity that began to engage him even as he progressed through the ranks of the British Merchant Service. In 1890, carrying with him some chapters of a first novel, he went to the Congo to command a river steamer. By the time this novel, *Almayer's Folly,* appeared in 1895, his life as a seaman lay behind him. His early novels and short stories earned the admiration of critics and fellow writers, but popular and commercial success proved elusive until the publication of *Chance* in 1913. On the whole, however, popularity seems to have had a negative influence, and his later work, affected as well by declining health and weakening imaginative powers, is generally considered inferior to his early and middle-period writings.

Although disdainful of journalism and its commercialism, Conrad, particularly in the early part of his career, nonetheless found himself obliged to supplement his earnings by writing for newspapers and periodicals. But however uncongenial, this journalism publicized his name and strengthened literary friendships. Edward Garnett, an early friend, well connected in literary circles, actively sought out commissions for him, while another friend, fellow novelist Ford Madox Ford, solicited a series of reminiscences for the *English Review*. Lord Northcliffe, an acquaintance who owned the *Daily Mail*, often requested contributions, and in 1910 Conrad even undertook—but only for three issues—a review column. Still later, the activities of friends and his own growing fame demanded more occasional writing, in-

Conrad and his wife, Jessie (standing in doorway), at Stephen Crane's home at Ravensbrook in 1898. Crane is standing at left; Cora Crane is seated at right, holding the Conrads' son Borys (by permission of the Harry Ransom Humanities Research Center, University of Texas at Austin).

nature of the seaman's craft, life at sea, and concepts such as duty, tradition, and fidelity. Anecdotes culled from Conrad's sea years enliven the more general reflections, but rather than accurate reminiscence, these form and shape a personal mythology; recent biographers have cast doubt on some of their claims. Nonetheless, the book's personal "recollections"–whatever their basis in fact–often display Conrad at his best: the scenes are vivid and convincing, the various sea captains and shipmates come to life. Throughout *The Mirror of the Sea* the novelistic imagination at work on scene and character almost always succeeds, but for the most part the volume reveals Conrad's defects as a writer and thinker. The failure of the general topics to engage either his emotions or his imagination results in conventional and at times even platitudinous reflections. The prose is consequently weakened, and glittering generalities and commonplace philosophizing are often embodied in a style marred by idiomatic problems and overwriting.

The volume is further weakened by a lack of coherence and the absence of a sustained conception. The final piece, "The Heroic Age" (written to celebrate Adm. Horatio Nelson's centenary), was obviously tacked on only to bring the book to usual length. Some readers have been misled by Conrad's characterization of the volume as "a very intimate revelation," a claim unjustified by the collection itself, which shares the formal posture of most of his autobiographical writing. Despite its flaws, *The Mirror of the Sea* contains two fine essays–"Initiation" and "The *Tremolino*"– that shed considerable light on significant transitional moments in Conrad's life.

Serialized in Ford's *English Review* from December 1908 to January 1909, *Some Reminiscences* (1912; also published as *A Personal Record*), Conrad's most important nonfiction work, treats the discovery of his two vocations–the call to the sea and the call to art. Unlike most autobiographies, however, but like his own fiction, the work abandons chronology and relies on temporal dislocation to illuminate the relationships between the seemingly disparate and disconnected strands of a single life. The narrative ranges widely and selectively in time and place, opening in 1894 with Conrad aboard his last ship in Rouen and closing with his first glimpse of a British merchant vessel. The book includes memories of his last visit to his uncle and guardian, Tadeusz Brobowski, in the Polish Ukraine and then moves further back in time to relate events

cluding prefaces, reviews, polemical essays, and introductions to his own work. As he became better known, journalism proved lucrative as editors vied for contributions: the *Daily Mail* paid 250 guineas for "Well Done!" (1918), and the *London Mercury* paid ten pounds for a thousand-word essay on Stephen Crane (1919). As he once wrote of journalism to a cousin, "If you begin writing, try to do it. It always pays." Yet it would be inaccurate and unfair to see all of Conrad's occasional writing in this light, for in it he expressed artistic and personal commitments and reflected upon his art and life.

Originally published in the *Daily Mail* and in such well-established periodicals as *Blackwood's*, *Harper's Weekly*, and *Pall Mall Magazine*, the fifteen "sea sketches" that make up *The Mirror of the Sea* (1906) form an uneven collection. Written in 1904 and 1905, partly at Ford's prompting and with his occasional assistance, the essays treat the in the life of Conrad's great-uncle Nicholas Bro-bowski, a soldier in Napoleon's army during the retreat from Moscow in 1812 and a patriot in the Polish insurrection of 1863. The account of the London morning in 1889 when Conrad embarked on his career as writer dissolves into his meeting in Dutch East Borneo with Charles William Olmeijer, the original of the hero of his first novel (*Almayer's Folly*). And the dramatization of his three examinations for his certificates in the British Merchant Service forms the prelude to an account of youthful adventures in Marseilles in the late 1870s, the segment that closes the book. As in *Lord Jim* (1900) or *Nostromo* (1904) the meaning of experience is revealed only gradually, in juxtaposition with similar or contrasting incidents, hence family history in Poland is intermingled with his life as a writer aboard ship or in London and his experiences as a seaman in the Far East. The book, however, is not motivated by a desire to "explain" the transformation from Pole to seaman to English writer, nor does a simplistic causality link the apparently disjointed and unrelated existences. Just as Conrad's life lacked linear patterning, so his chosen method of portraying it faithfully reflects the complex skeins of his development and demonstrates the depth of his personal understanding of it.

The central thematic tensions in *Some Reminiscences* are between fact and reality and idealism and the imagination, a conflict delineated in the volume's three worlds: Conrad's family background, including the life of his parents, and, more particularly, that of his great-uncle Brobowski, soldier and patriot; Conrad's personal experience, in which his early idealization of the seaman's life confronted its banal, routine reality; and Conrad's life as an artist, in which words transformed actual people and events into characters and scenes. His explicit identification with Don Quixote throughout the volume establishes his shared fate with Cervantes's hero in lacking a choice between the opposed worlds of reality and imagination. For the artist, as for the seaman and the patriot, these are linked and conflated, and grounding and giving shape and significance to this vision is a code of conduct expressed by three key words: restraint, fidelity, and solidarity. Thus, allegiance and commitment—the word "duty" is another key Conradian term—reflect a moral imperative and transcend, even make irrelevant, considerations of chronology. Fidelity to one's inner world—to one's "personal record"—creates and defines (as does art) one's reality.

Some Reminiscences, then, eschews documentation and fact to reveal, more importantly, the structure of Conrad's mind and imagination and in so doing becomes a major statement about the nature of his art.

While some of Conrad's prefaces collectively form another statement of his artistic intentions, many—written at the urging of his various publishers—evidence a problematic relationship with his audience. The first of Conrad's prefaces, that to *Almayer's Folly,* attempts to justify, even domesticate, the novel's exotic setting and characters. For his American readers Conrad wrote author's notes to *The Nigger of the "Narcissus"* (1897) and *A Set of Six* (1908); he provided a preface to *Victory* (1915) and added introductions to *Youth* (1902), *Lord Jim,* and *Nostromo,* on the occasion of their reissue in 1917. Most of his prefaces, however, were composed in 1919 and 1920, at the request of F. N. Doubleday, who saw them as a means of further stimulating collector interest in the Limited Collected Edition of Conrad's works, then in preparation, issued jointly by Doubleday and Heinemann in England in 1921. Taking advantage of this collector interest, Doubleday and Heinemann gathered together Conrad's prefaces and published them in a limited edition under the title *Notes on My Books* (1921).

The prefaces produced on demand rarely illuminate Conrad's aesthetic intentions and only occasionally reflect on his methods. For the greater part they chattily—and at times inaccurately—focus on the genesis of a given work and on the relationship between events in his own life and their reworking in fiction, frequently watering down and simplifying a complex tension and interaction in the interests of popularization. The method and approach in the prefaces, then, tend to be that of a successful author commenting on his work for a popular audience, an audience that Conrad had finally won by the end of his creative career. And although his popularity and financial success were largely based upon a misconception of his intentions and a misreading of his work, they nonetheless gratified him. Thus some of the prefaces purposefully de-emphasize the subtlety and complexity of his vision and aims and evade the discussion of theoretical matters and technique that motivated Henry James's prefaces to the famous New York edition of his works (1907-1909)—no doubt an edition whose success inspired Doubleday to elicit introductions from Conrad.

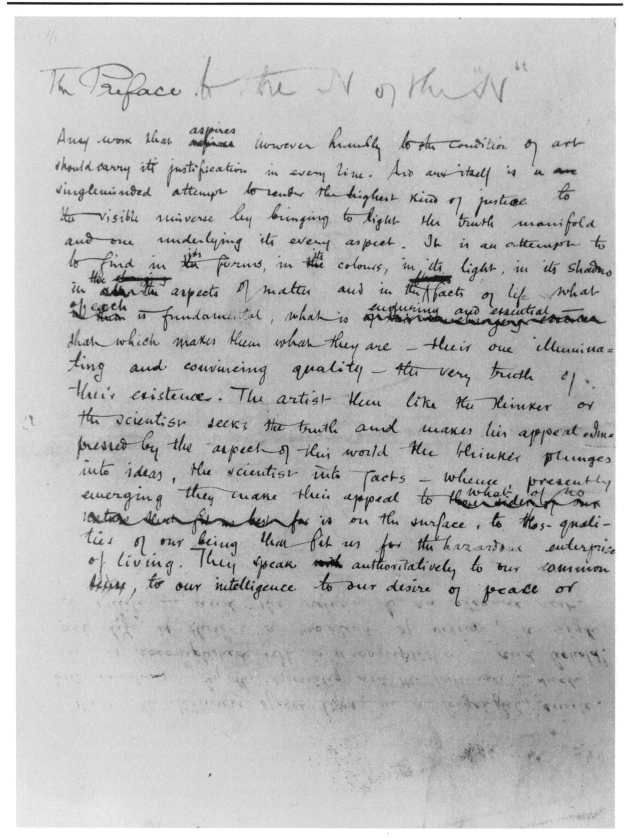

Opening pages of the manuscript for Conrad's preface to The Nigger of the "Narcissus." *In the preface, which is not directly linked to the novel, Conrad focuses on the craft of fiction and the role of the artist (Board of Trustees of the Philip H. and A.S.W. Rosenbach Foundation).*

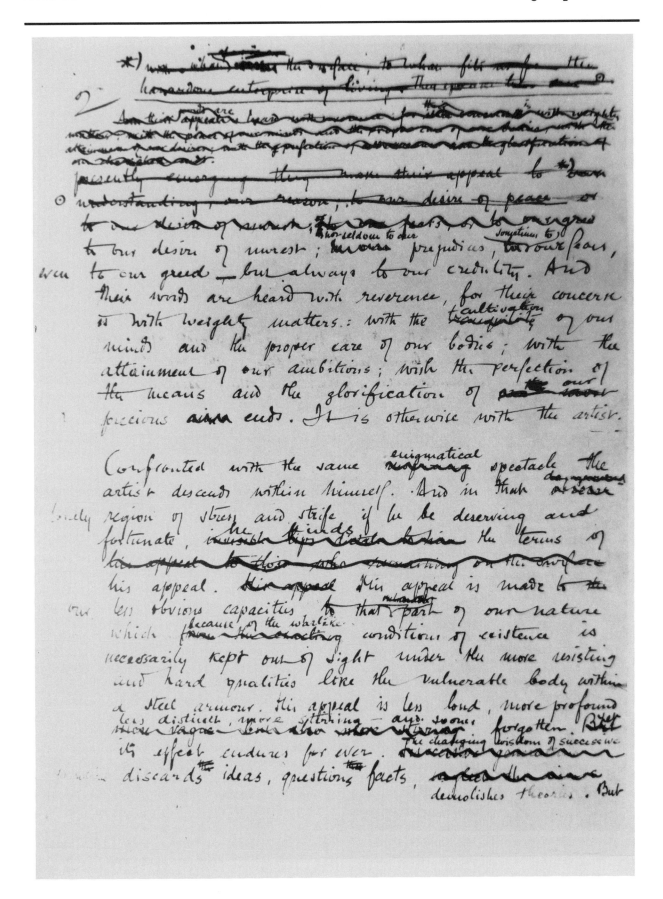

Joseph and Jessie Conrad with Jane Anderson, an aspiring American novelist whom the Conrads befriended in 1916, and the Conrads' son John. This photograph was probably taken at Capel House, in Orlestone, near Ashford, which Conrad rented from June 1910 until March 1919 (Collection of John Conrad).

The introductions occasioned by Conrad's own desire to state his aesthetic intentions and comment upon his vision–the justly famous preface to *The Nigger of the "Narcissus"* and "A Familiar Preface" to *Some Reminiscences*–are distinguished from those written for his publishers in subject and manner. The preface to *The Nigger*, originally printed with the final installment of that tale in the *New Review* of December 1897, is linked not to that specific work but instead focuses on Conrad's views of art and the role of the artist. Eschewing ready-made formulae and "schools," Conrad claims for the artist the exacting task of giving permanence to the ephemeral by the relentless exploration of a personal vision, a solitary act that, nonetheless, links him to the human community, for whom he functions as a "voice." Although the ideas are sometimes marred by a tortured prose style and at moments are unclearly elaborated, the preface to *The Nigger* has been justly considered Conrad's classic statement on the art of fiction. Less abstract and less rhetorically strained, "A Familiar Preface" also stands apart from the bulk of Conrad's introductions. A statement in part about his conception of himself and the autobiographical methods imposed upon an existence so evidently lacking continuity, the preface also subtly explores the basis of Conrad's art in his system of values.

As early as 1904 Conrad, characteristically pressed by financial need, had prematurely considered publishing a volume of his occasional writings, supplemented by some yet-to-be-written critical essays. His agent, J. B. Pinker, appears to have discouraged this idea, and it was dropped. And when the publication of a volume of collected essays was proposed from time to time in his later career, Conrad himself was disinclined to pursue it. But in 1919, partly inspired by the limited-edition pamphlet printing of some of his miscellaneous pieces for collectors, he asked his friend Richard Curle to gather together the texts of his scattered writings "in view of a vol. by and bye." With Curle's advice and assistance *Notes on Life and Letters* (1921) took a more definite shape, and in September 1920, while on holiday at Deal, Conrad revised the essays that appear in it. As he indicated in the preface to *Notes on Life and Letters*, the volume covers the range of his interests as artist and as public man, presenting "Conrad literary, Conrad political, Conrad reminiscent, Conrad controversial."

Written from 1898 to 1919 and published in various monthlies, in newspapers, and in the books of friends, the essays in *Notes on Life and Letters* are indeed a heterogeneous collection. Essays on Anatole France and Alphonse Daudet, introductions to Ada Galsworthy's translations of Guy de Maupassant and to Edward Garnett's book on Ivan Turgenev, and pieces on Henry James, Stephen Crane, and the sea novels of James Fenimore Cooper and Capt. Frederick Marryat, as well as reviews from the *Academy* and the *Daily Mail*, represent "Conrad literary." His most important political statement, "Autocracy and War" (1905), is reprinted here along with "The Crime of Partition," an essay on the newly emerging Polish state, and a note written on Poland for presentation at the Foreign Office. One of his finest autobiographical essays, "Poland Revisited" (1915), recalls a visit to Poland at the time of the outbreak of World War I, while minor pieces treat such subjects as the London Sailors' Home and Conrad's wartime flight in a biplane. "Tradition," " 'Well Done!,' " and "Confidence," also written during the war, comment on the character and values of the Merchant Service, while an attack on the censorship of plays (1907) and two essays on the sinking of the *Titanic* (1912), as well as another on the sinking of the *Empress of Ireland* (1914), represent "Conrad controversial." Contemporary reviewers expressed dissatisfaction with the book's failure to reveal Conrad intimately–an aim he specifically disavowed in the volume's "Author's Note"–but the publisher of his later works, J. M. Dent, rightly commented when *Notes on Life and Letters* was in preparation that it would be "a most interesting volume for those who care for the psychology of the man." Whatever their various occasions, the essays are linked together by the force of Conrad's character and his highly individual vision and style. And although some of the pieces are decidedly minor, the collection as a whole illuminates the depth of his commitment to the brotherhood of letters as well as to that of the sea, and, importantly, to the concept of national identity.

While the essays on literary topics reveal the range of Conrad's interests–the emphasis falls on Continental and American writers–no claims can be made for them as penetrating critical evaluations. Impressionistic and informal, the "notes" on letters largely fail to extend a reader's insights, however well they represent Conrad's own sympathetic reading of his mentors–James, Maupassant, Turgenev–and his contemporaries.

The political essays are more dense and rhetorically more complex statements, of interest partly for the light they shed on the "political" novels–*Nostromo*, *The Secret Agent* (1907) and *Under Western Eyes* (1911)–but also as demonstrations of a temperament profoundly skeptical of ready-made formulae and anxiously conscious of modern man's alienation and duality. Although valuing national identity and the heritage of the past, Conrad posits his primary allegiance in the individual, seeing all political conflicts as essentially moral problems. Thus, "Autocracy and War," written during the Russo-Japanese War, transcends its specific occasion as an analysis of the decline of czarist autocracy to become a demonstration of how both autocracy and democracy, the latter a system grounded in "material interests," tend toward anarchy, a moral position abhorrent to Conrad. While Conrad's political orientation was, on the one hand, traditionalist–the epithet "conservative" frequently applied to his viewpoint is less appropriate and considerably too circumscribed–he was also highly critical of prevailing economic and social structures and institutions, as "Autocracy and War" and "The Crime of Partition" establish. This criticism is also elaborated in his two essays on the sinking of the *Titanic*, miniature masterpieces of irony, in which materialism is seen to undermine a sense of community and responsibility, necessary conditions for civilization's very existence.

The posthumous collection *Last Essays* (1926) brings together Conrad's miscellaneous writings published after the appearance of *Notes on Life and Letters* and also contains a few essays located after the earlier book's publication. Edited and arranged by Curle, *Last Essays* is a witness to Conrad's status and popularity (unlike *Notes on Life and Letters*, it contains little significant work) and to the friendship between author and editor, a particularly important one to Conrad in his later years and for Curle, a journalist, an association that was also professionally valuable.

The volume necessarily lacks the unity Conrad was able to give to *Notes on Life and Letters*, but Curle's workmanlike arrangement of the nineteen pieces included in the collection reveals familiar patterns and relationships–the past, the sea, literature–and like the volume that preceded it, *Last Essays* touches upon numerous interests, loyalties, and allegiances. The works collected in the volume were composed throughout Conrad's career and range from his "Congo Diary," written from June to August 1890, to "Legends," the

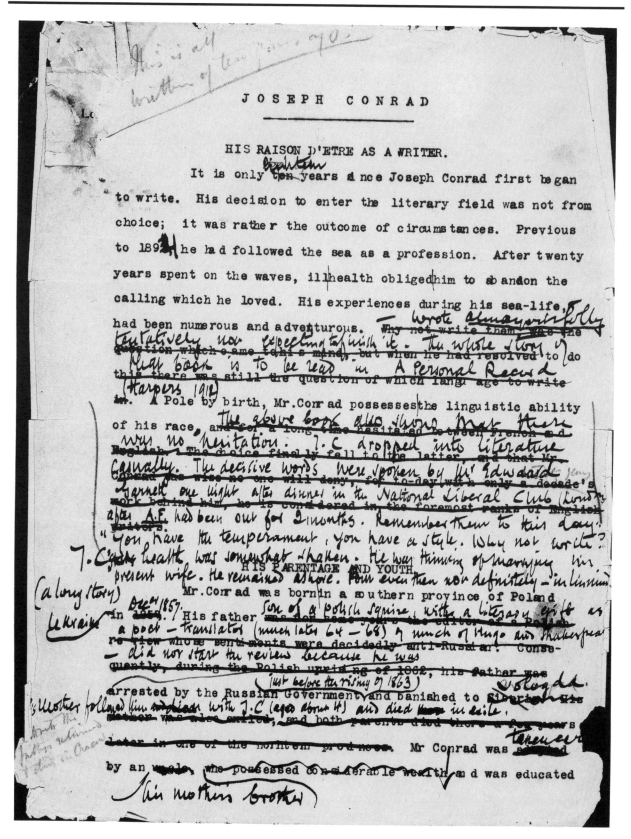

First page of a biographical sketch by an unknown writer, with Conrad's corrections and revisions (HM 33795; by permission of the Henry E. Huntington Library and Art Gallery)

essay left unfinished at his death. The scope is equally wide: letters about the future of Constantinople written in 1912 at the time of the Balkan crisis, a memorandum about the proper outfitting of a training ship, and a preface to his wife's cookery book appear alongside a reminiscence of his childhood reading of travel literature, reviews of John Galsworthy's *The Island Pharisees* (1904) and *The Man of Property* (1906), and introductions to a book on Stephen Crane and to his *Red Badge of Courage* (1895). The essays on the sea range widely in time, and include a tribute to the *Torrens,* the famous clipper on which Conrad served as first mate from 1891 to 1893, a propaganda piece written (but not published) for the admiralty during the war, and a reflection on modern ocean travel written during Conrad's voyage to New York in 1923.

The essays of personal reminiscence are the volume's most important, but as in Conrad's other autobiographical writings fact often mingles with and collides against slightly idealized self-portraiture. Some of these pieces also betray characteristic "problems" with chronology: the account dramatized in "Christmas Day at Sea," for example, which purports to recall events of Christmas 1879 in the Southern Ocean, is contradicted by Conrad's being in the Mediterranean in that year. On the other hand, the diary of his trip up the Congo, an entirely factual record, brightly illuminates *Heart of Darkness* (*Blackwood's*, 1899; published with *Youth* in 1902) and provides insights into the transformation of his experiences in Africa into fiction. The essay on his voyage to America, "Ocean Travel," and the affectionate recollection of the *Torrens* expose his fundamental traditionalism in his preference for the days of sail to those of steam. The volume's two most finely crafted pieces—"Geography and Some Explorers," an essay about travel writing, and his reminiscence of his friendship with Crane—display a characteristic sympathy with solitary men exploring the actual globe as well as the landscape of the imagination. On the whole, however, the collection's principal value lies in its further revelation of Conrad's temperament and personality through the discussion of characteristic concerns and interests.

Much of Conrad's occasional writing, produced on demand and written in response to specific events and circumstances, lacks the creative dynamism and polish of his fiction, yet even the most casual efforts bear the unmistakable accent of his character, and, collectively, the volumes of

Conrad, circa 1922

nonfiction he produced may be seen as an attempt to give coherence and pattern to his life and art, an explanation for their diversity and "exoticism." Conrad's essays function, then, as a catalogue of his personal tastes and interests, as a revelation of temperament, and despite their formal manner and aloof pose, as his most complete and revealing self-portrait. The writing is for the most part professionally crafted, and some of the essays reach a higher level of distinction and may justly stand independent of Conrad's major achievement in the novel.

Letters:

Letters to Conrad, edited by Georges Jean-Aubry (London: First Edition Club, 1926);

Joseph Conrad's Letters to His Wife (London: Privately printed, 1927);

Letters: Joseph Conrad to Richard Curle, edited by Curle (New York: Gaige, 1928); republished as *Conrad to a Friend: 150 Selected Letters from Joseph Conrad to Richard Curle* (Garden City, N.Y.: Doubleday, Doran, 1928; London: Low, Marston, 1928);

Letters from Joseph Conrad, 1895-1924, edited by Edward Garnett (London: Nonesuch, 1928; Indianapolis: Bobbs-Merrill, 1928);

Letters of Joseph Conrad to Marguerite Poradowska, 1890-1920, translated and edited by John A. Gee and Paul J. Sturm (New Haven: Yale University Press / London: Milford, Oxford University Press, 1940);

Joseph Conrad: Letters to William Blackward and David S. Meldrum, edited by William Blackburn (Durham, N.C.: Duke University Press, 1958);

Conrad's Polish Background: Letters to and from Polish Friends, edited by Zdzislaw Najder (London & New York: Oxford University Press, 1964);

Joseph Conrad and Warrington Dawson: The Record of a Friendship, edited by D. B. J. Randall (Durham, N.C.: Duke University Press, 1968);

Joseph Conrad's Letters to Cunninghame-Graham, edited by C. T. Watts (Cambridge: Cambridge University Press, 1969);

The Collected Letters of Joseph Conrad, volume 1, 23 May 1861-31 December 1897, edited by Frederick R. Karl and Laurence Davies (Cambridge: Cambridge University Press, 1983).

Bibliographies:

Thomas J. Wise, *A Bibliography of the Writings of Joseph Conrad (1895-1921)* (London: Privately printed, 1921; revised and enlarged edition, London: Dawsons, 1964);

Kenneth A. Lohf and Eugene P. Streehy, *Joseph Conrad at Mid-Century: Editions and Studies, 1895-1955* (Minneapolis: University of Minnesota Press, 1957);

Theodore G. Ehrsam, *A Bibliography of Joseph Conrad* (Metuchen, N.J.: Scarecrow, 1969);

Bruce E. Teets and Helmut E. Gerber, *Joseph Conrad, An Annotated Bibliography of Writings About Him* (DeKalb: Northern Illinois University Press, 1971).

Biographies:

Ford Madox Ford, *Joseph Conrad: A Personal Remembrance* (Boston: Little, Brown, 1924);

Georges Jean-Aubry, *Joseph Conrad: Life and Letters,* 2 volumes (Garden City, N.Y.: Doubleday, Page, 1927; London: Heinemann, 1927);

Jessie Conrad, *Joseph Conrad and His Circle* (New York: Dutton, 1935);

Joselyn Baines, *Joseph Conrad: A Critical Biography* (London: Weidenfeld & Nicolson, 1960; New York: McGraw-Hill, 1960);

Bernard Meyer, *Joseph Conrad: A Psychoanalytic Biography* (Princeton: Princeton University Press, 1967);

Gustave Morf, *The Polish Shades and Ghosts of Joseph Conrad* (New York: Astra, 1976);

Frederick R. Karl, *Joseph Conrad, The Three Lives* (New York: Farrar, Straus & Giroux, 1979);

Zdzislaw Najder, *Joseph Conrad,* translated by Halina Carroll-Najder (New Brunswick, N.J.: Rutgers University Press, 1983).

References:

Jacques Berthoud, "*A Personal Record,*" in his *Joseph Conrad: The Major Phase* (Cambridge: Cambridge University Press, 1978), pp. 1-22;

Berthoud, "The Preface to *The Nigger of the 'Narcissus,*'" in *The Nigger of the 'Narcissus': A Tale of the Sea,* edited by Berthoud (Oxford: Oxford University Press, 1984), pp. 175-182;

A. Busza, "The Rhetoric of Conrad's Non-Fictional Political Discourse," *Annales de la Faculté des Lettres et Sciences humaines de Nice,* 34 (1978): 159-170;

Richard Curle, introduction to *Last Essays* (London & Toronto: Dent, 1926; Garden City, N.Y.: Doubleday, Page, 1926);

Avrom Fleishman, *Conrad's Politics: Community and Anarchy in the Fiction of Joseph Conrad* (Baltimore: Johns Hopkins University Press, 1967);

Fleishman, "*The Mirror of the Sea:* Fragments of a Great Confession," *L'Epoque Conradienne* (1979): 136-151;

J. M. Kertzer, "Conrad's Personal Record," *University of Toronto Quarterly,* 44, no. 4 (1974-1975): 290-303;

Juliet McLauchlan, "'Piety' in Joseph Conrad's *A Personal Record,*" *Polish Review,* 29, no. 3 (1984): 11-23;

David R. Smith, ed., *Conrad's Manifesto: Preface to a Career—The History of the Preface to "The Nigger of the 'Narcissus'"* (Philadelphia: Rosenbach, 1966);

J. H. Stape, "'The Crime of Partition': Conrad's Sources," *Conradiana,* 15 (1983): 219-226;

Stape, "Establishing Identities: Exile and Commitment in Conrad's Non-Fiction Prose," *English Literature in Transition, 1880-1920,* 31, no. 1 (1988): 53-63;

Stape, "The Writing and Publication of Conrad's 'Poland Revisited,'" *Conradiana*, 16 (1984): 155-159;

David Thorburn, "The Autobiographies," in his *Conrad's Romanticism* (New Haven: Yale University Press, 1974), pp. 61-99;

Ian Watt, "*The Nigger of the 'Narcissus'* ii. The Preface," in his *Conrad in the Nineteenth Century* (Berkeley: University of California Press; London: Chatto & Windus, 1979), pp. 76-88;

Cedric Watts, *A Preface to Conrad* (London & New York: Longman, 1982).

Papers:
The following institutions hold collections of Conrad's papers related to his occasional writings: Boston Public Library, British Library, Bryn Mawr College, Colgate University, Dartmouth College, Free Library of Philadelphia, Indiana University (Lilly Library), New York Public Library (Berg Collection), New York University (Fales Library), Pierpont Morgan Library, Public Records Office (London), Rosenbach Museum and Library, Stanford University, Syracuse University, Texas Tech University, University of Texas, University of Virginia, and Yale University.

Ford Madox Ford
(17 December 1873 - 26 June 1939)

Edward Krickel
University of Georgia

See also the Ford entry in *DLB 34: British Novelists, 1890-1929: Traditionalists.*

BOOKS: *The Brown Owl: A Fairy Story* (London: Unwin, 1892 [i.e., 1891]; New York: Stokes, 1891);

The Feather (London: Unwin, 1892; New York: Cassell, 1892);

The Shifting of the Fire (London: Unwin, 1892; New York: Putnam's, 1892);

The Questions at the Well, with Sundry Other Verses for Notes of Music, as Fenil Haig (London: Digby, Long, 1893);

The Queen Who Flew (London: Bliss, Sands & Foster, 1894);

Ford Madox Brown: A Record of His Life and Work (London, New York & Bombay: Longmans, Green, 1896);

Poems for Pictures and for Notes of Music (London: MacQueen, 1900);

The Cinque Ports: A Historical and Descriptive Record (Edinburgh & London: Blackwood, 1900);

The Inheritors: An Extravagant Story, by Ford and Joseph Conrad (New York: McClure, Phillips, 1901; London: Heinemann, 1901);

Rossetti: A Critical Essay on His Art (London: Duckworth / New York: Dutton, 1902);

Romance: A Novel, by Ford and Conrad (London: Smith, Elder, 1903; New York: McClure, Phillips, 1904);

The Face of the Night: A Second Series of Poems for Pictures (London: MacQueen, 1904);

The Soul of London: A Survey of a Modern City (London: Rivers, 1905);

The Benefactor: A Tale of a Small Circle (London: Brown, Langham, 1905);

Hans Holbein the Younger: A Critical Monograph (London: Duckworth / New York: Dutton, 1905);

The Fifth Queen: And How She Came to Court (London: Rivers, 1906);

The Heart of the Country: A Survey of a Modern Land (London: Rivers, 1906);

Christina's Fairy Book (London: Rivers, 1906);

Privy Seal: His Last Venture (London: Rivers, 1907);

From Inland and Other Poems (London: Rivers, 1907);

An English Girl: A Romance (London: Methuen, 1907);

Ford Madox Ford (by permission of Princeton
University Library)

The Pre-Raphaelite Brotherhood: A Critical Monograph (London: Duckworth / New York:
Dutton, 1907);

The Spirit of the People: An Analysis of the English
Mind (London: Rivers, 1907);

The Fifth Queen Crowned: A Romance (London:
Nash, 1908);

Mr. Apollo: A Just Possible Story (London: Methuen, 1908);

The "Half Moon": A Romance of the Old World and
the New (London: Nash, 1909; New York:
Doubleday, Page, 1909);

A Call: The Tale of Two Passions (London: Chatto
& Windus, 1910);

Songs from London (London: Mathews, 1910);

The Portrait (London: Methuen, 1910);

The Simple Life Limited, as Daniel Chaucer (London: Lane, Bodley Head / New York: Lane,
1911);

Ancient Lights and Certain New Reflections, Being the
Memories of a Young Man (London: Chapman
& Hall, 1911); republished as Memories and

Impressions: A Study in Atmospheres (New
York: Harper, 1911);

Ladies Whose Bright Eyes: A Romance (London: Constable, 1911; revised edition, Philadelphia:
Lippincott, 1935);

The Critical Attitude (London: Duckworth, 1911);

High Germany: Eleven Sets of Verse (London:
Duckworth, 1912);

The Panel: A Sheer Comedy (London: Constable,
1912); revised and enlarged as Ring for
Nancy: A Sheer Comedy (Indianapolis: Bobbs-
Merrill, 1913);

The New Humpty-Dumpty, as Chaucer (London:
Lane, Bodley Head / New York: Lane,
1912);

This Monstrous Regiment of Women (London: Mi-
nerva, 1913);

Mr. Fleight (London: Latimer, 1913);

The Young Lovell: A Romance (London: Chatto &
Windus, 1913);

Collected Poems (London: Goschen, 1913);

Henry James: A Critical Study (London: Secker,
1914; New York: Boni, 1915);

Antwerp (London: Poetry Bookshop, 1915);

The Good Soldier: A Tale of Passion (London: Lane,
Bodley Head / New York: Lane, 1915);

When Blood Is Their Argument: An Analysis of Prussian Culture (London & New York: Hodder
& Stoughton, 1915);

Between St. Dennis and St. George: A Sketch of Three
Civilisations (London, New York & Toronto:
Hodder & Stoughton, 1915);

Zeppelin Nights: A London Entertainment, by Ford
and Violet Hunt (London: Lane, Bodley
Head / New York: Lane, 1915);

On Heaven and Poems Written on Active Service (London: Lane, Bodley Head / New York: Lane,
1918);

A House (Modern Morality Play) (London: Poetry
Bookshop, 1921);

Thus to Revisit: Some Reminiscences (London: Chapman & Hall, 1921);

The Marsden Case: A Romance (London:
Duckworth, 1923);

Women & Men (Paris: Three Mountains, 1923);

Mister Bosphorus and the Muses, or A Short History of
Poetry in Britain: Variety Entertainment in Four
Acts (London: Duckworth, 1923);

Some Do Not . . . : A Novel (London: Duckworth,
1924; New York: Seltzer, 1924);

The Nature of a Crime, by Ford and Conrad (London: Duckworth, 1924; Garden City, N.Y.:
Doubleday, Page, 1924);

Joseph Conrad: A Personal Remembrance (London: Duckworth, 1924; Boston: Little, Brown, 1924);

No More Parades: A Novel (London: Duckworth, 1925; New York: Boni, 1925);

A Mirror to France (London: Duckworth, 1926; New York: Boni, 1926);

A Man Could Stand Up–: A Novel (London: Duckworth, 1926; New York: Boni, 1926);

New Poems (New York: Rudge, 1927);

New York Is Not America (London: Duckworth, 1927; New York: Boni, 1927);

New York Essays (New York: Rudge, 1927);

The Last Post: A Novel (New York: Literary Guild, 1928); republished as *Last Post* (London: Duckworth, 1928);

A Little Less Than Gods: A Romance (London: Duckworth, 1928; New York: Viking, 1928);

The English Novel from the Earliest Days to the Death of Joseph Conrad (Philadelphia: Lippincott, 1929; London: Constable, 1930);

No Enemy: A Tale of Reconstruction (New York: Macaulay, 1929);

Return to Yesterday (London: Gollancz, 1931; New York: Liveright, 1932);

When the Wicked Man (New York: Liveright, 1931; London: Cape, 1932);

The Rash Act: A Novel (New York: Long & Smith, 1933; London: Cape, 1933);

It Was the Nightingale (Philadelphia: Lippincott, 1933; London: Heinemann, 1934);

Henry for Hugh: A Novel (Philadelphia: Lippincott, 1934);

Provence: From Minstrels to the Machine (Philadelphia: Lippincott, 1935; London: Allen & Unwin, 1938);

Vive Le Roy: A Novel (Philadelphia: Lippincott, 1936; London: Allen & Unwin, 1937);

Collected Poems (New York: Oxford University Press, 1936);

Great Trade Route (New York: Oxford University Press, 1937; London: Allen & Unwin, 1937);

Portraits from Life: Memories and Criticisms (Boston: Houghton Mifflin / New York: Riverside, 1937); republished as *Mightier than the Sword: Memories and Criticisms* (London: Allen & Unwin, 1938);

The March of Literature from Confucius' Day to Our Own (New York: Dial, 1938); republished as *The March of Literature from Confucius to Modern Times* (London: Allen & Unwin, 1939);

Buckshee (Cambridge: Pym-Randall, 1966);

A History of Our Own Times, edited by Solon Beinfeld and Stang (Bloomington & Indianapolis: Indiana University Press, 1988; Manchester: Carcanet, 1989).

Collections: *England and the English: An Interpretation* (New York: McClure, Phillips, 1907)– comprises *The Soul of London*, *The Heart of the Country*, and *The Spirit of the People*;

Parade's End (New York: Knopf, 1950)–comprises *Some Do Not*, *No More Parades*, *A Man Could Stand Up*, and *The Last Post*;

The Bodley Head Ford Madox Ford, 4 volumes (London: Bodley Head, 1962-1971);

The Fifth Queen (New York: Vanguard, 1963)– comprises *The Fifth Queen*, *Privy Seal*, and *The Fifth Queen Crowned*;

Critical Writings of Ford Madox Ford, edited by Frank MacShane (Lincoln: University of Nebraska Press, 1964);

Selected Poems (Cambridge: Pym-Randall, 1971);

Your Mirror to My Times: The Selected Autobiographies and Impressions of Ford Madox Ford, edited by Michael Killigrew (New York: Holt, 1971);

The Ford Madox Ford Reader, edited by Sondra J. Stang (Manchester: Carcanet, 1986; New York: Ecco, 1986).

Ford Madox Ford is one of the important novelists of the century and one of the creators of modern literature. *The Good Soldier* (1915) is one of the indisputable classics in the modern idiom. The tetralogy *Parade's End* (1950) looms increasingly large as perhaps the finest English novelistic treatment of World War I. Ford's *Fifth Queen* trilogy (1963) will stand comparison with the best of the historical fiction of the past. Ezra Pound gave Ford credit as an important influence in taking poetry away from the high and artificial rhetoric of the Victorians and into the more natural and conversational style of modern poetry. Ford is acknowledged as having created and edited for a year the finest literary journal England ever had: the *English Review*. In the Paris of 1924 the *Transatlantic Review* under his editorship served the cause of avant-garde literature (as did a good many other short-lived journals), but did it without losing sight of the great tradition of literature and civilization the journal both derived from and served. Few journals of that or of any time served the latter cause as clear-sightedly and as well. A fair percentage of the works Ford printed in both journals have joined

Ford with his wife, Elsie, and their daughters, Katherine and Christina, 1900 (Collection of Mr. Jocelyn Baines)

the ranks of the permanent literary possessions of our time.

The great novels apart, nearly every other book Ford wrote remains controversial. He has the qualities we expect of a major writer, yet according to Arthur Mizener, who builds his comprehensive biography around the idea that the writer's "achievement was not what his gifts would lead us to expect," Ford's is "the saddest story." This contention may or may not be true; Janice Biala, who lived with Ford the last decade of his life, believes Mizener's portrait misrepresents its subject. But one thing is certain–every one of his many books offers special pleasures to the reader. As he said of himself, "If I had not written so many books, I might have written better." Most of Ford's work has been out of print and unavailable for years, even in otherwise well-stocked libraries. The problem has been alleviated in the last few years by the republications of Ford's books by the Carcanet Press of England and the Ecco Press of America, but it remains

hard for an individual reader to form an opinion of Ford's worth.

If Ford is one of the important novelists, is he also one of the important essayists? Are his friends Pound, Henry James, Stephen Crane, Joseph Conrad, Ernest Hemingway, James Joyce, and Gertrude Stein important essayists? It would not deny any of them their qualities if the questions were answered "probably not." However, it seems unlikely that writers of genius would write inferior essays even if their main interests were with other forms. Mizener says of Ford, "It is almost literally true that he could, in the words Conrad ascribed to their agent, J. B. Pinker, write anything and write it well." A third of Ford's books are essays or nonfiction prose. His books, Mizener says, were "the purpose of his existence, the one commitment of his life that nothing–disaster, illness, despair–was allowed to interfere with. They are the meaning of his life, and its most valuable product."

In addition, since he was a professional

Ford, circa 1915, when he enlisted in the British army. He served in France as a company officer.

writer, Ford published a great amount of literary journalism that has not been collected. David Dow Harvey identifies fourteen "literary portraits" in the *Daily Mail (Books Supp.)* in 1907 as "most probably by Ford, though none of them are signed." There is a weekly series of twenty-seven literary portraits in the *Tribune* (1907-1908), these signed and "a bit more serious critically" than the *Daily Mail* group, and still another such group in *Outlook* (London) from 1913 until 1915, the year Ford entered the military service; there are literally dozens of other pieces. Their flavor may be sampled in the excerpts Harvey gives; also, Sondra Stang reprints seven of the *Outlook* pieces in *The Ford Madox Ford Reader* (1986). Thomas C. Moser has identified a series of "weekly causeries" in *Bystander* (1911-1912) overlooked by Harvey. Ford wrote editorials and miscellaneous pieces in the *English Review* and the *Transatlantic Review* under more than one name; the best of the former with a few others are collected in *The Critical Attitude* (1911). Ford also wrote prefaces and book reviews and left at his death, among manuscripts never published in

any form, "A History of Our Own Times," one volume completed of three projected. Mizener tallies up 419 periodical pieces by Ford and 57 miscellaneous contributions to the books of others, and other work has since been identified. Frank MacShane collected some in his *Critical Writings of Ford Madox Ford* (1964).

Ford was born Ford Hermann Hueffer on 17 December 1873 in Merton, Surrey, the son of Francis and Catherine Brown Hueffer. His maternal grandfather was the artist Ford Madox Brown. An early marriage to Elsie Martindale took place on 17 May 1894. Ford had personal and professional contacts with most of the important artistic and literary figures of late-Victorian and Edwardian England, Paris in the twenties, and America in the twenties and thirties. If, as Paul L. Wiley says, he is the "novelist of three worlds," he is equally the essayist of the three: England, France, and the United States, during the sixty years in which modernism in the arts was unquestionably born. In anything pertaining to the arts, Ford was extraordinarily generous with his time, help, and encouragement, especially to young artists, of whom only a few responded with gratitude.

Women were important in Ford's life and work. In addition to his marriage, which was never legally terminated, he had liaisons or affairs with his sister-in-law Mary Martindale, Violet Hunt, Brigit Patmore, Stella Bowen, Jean Rhys, René Wright, and Janice Biala. Three of them wrote books about or based on the relationship: the reminiscences by Hunt and Bowen, *I Have This To Say* (1926) and *Drawn from Life* (1941), respectively; and the novels by Rhys, *Quartet* (1929) and *After Leaving Mr. MacKenzie* (1931). Also, some of Ford's best fictional creations are women–Anne Jeal, Katharine Howard, Florence, Leonora, Sylvia, Valentine, Eudoxie, and others.

He came early to the position that the arts served civilization indispensably, and that he would serve the arts with every resource he had. Two experiences that marked his life and work were agriculture and military service during World War I, but first, last, and always he was a writer–"an old man mad about writing," he eventually put it (in *Thus to Revisit*, 1921). The evidence is overwhelming that there was never a time in his life of which this was not equally true.

One of Ford's early books, *Ford Madox Brown: A Record of His Life and Work* (1896), though still the standard work on its subject, is an "official" Victorian biography in conception and execution, distinguished more for its slow-moving factual compilation than for its interpretation. Ford had the disadvantage of lack of access to interesting letters his grandfather had written to Dante Gabriel Rossetti because the poet's brother, William Michael, who was also Brown's son-in-law, had reserved them for his own reminiscences. Ford's style is dignified to the point of woodenness; the diction is formal, yet, given the young man's reverence for his grandfather, the work must have been a labor of love as well as a solemn duty. The volume follows chronologically the testimonies, diaries, and letters Ford did have, and it includes catalogs of artworks that are allowed to speak for themselves at length. Ford shows himself sufficiently the master of the materials and aims of painting that he can write informed art criticism. However, the fabulous old man of Ford's later reminiscences does not appear; evidently, he had not been created in his grandson's transforming imagination. Nor for that matter had the grandson himself.

The Cinque Ports (1900), Ford's next nonfiction book, is a four-hundred-page account of the old Kent and Sussex port towns of Hastings, Winchelsea, Rye, Romney, Hythe, Dover, Sandwich, and their environs. The essay on each town ranges from its Roman and Saxon beginnings to the present. Ford knew the area well, in fact had loved it since he went there to boarding school as a boy of eight. This is where he lived and farmed with his wife, Elsie, where their two daughters were born, where he collaborated with Conrad, where he knew James, and where he later lived with Stella Bowen. He did an immense amount of research for the book, according to MacShane (*The Life and Works*, 1965), "examining the ancient charters of the towns, reading local history and consulting the records of archaeological societies." From this background he also drew material for *Romance* (1903), *The Heart of the Country* (1906), *The "Half Moon"* (1909), *Women & Men* (1923), his book on Conrad (1924), and most of his volumes of reminiscences.

Robert Green has called *The Cinque Ports* "a curious mixture of travelogue and jeremiad," the latter because Ford "had bemoaned the passing of old traditions and their replacement by a bustling materialism." In 1905 James saw similar changes in his native America when he returned after twenty years. The book ends with the kind of passage Green objects to: "I have sometimes thought that, in the end, a time will come when the brain of man—of humanity all the world over—

will suddenly grow unable to bear with the hurry and turmoil that itself has created. Then it will no longer seem worth while to set in motion all these wheels, all this machinery; the fascination of the slow, creaking waggons of the past will grow overpowering, the claims of the simple will be rediscovered, will be deemed something new, strange, and enthralling. Then, the naive and the human will reign again, the Makeshift even will have its principality. In that new Golden Age the Five Ports might again flourish, might again find their account." One sees a certain languor of the 1890s in the manner, but insofar as there is a respect for old ways and simplicities, for tradition, the theme is a permanent one in Ford's writing.

A criticism not based on ideology might be that the book is loosely structured; it ends with appendices of material that did not fit in elsewhere. Still, the form, if loose, was to become a characteristic one for its author. It is able to hold together history, geography, anecdotes, and personal responses of all kinds. The unity of each work may be precarious, but it is real. The books are recognizably akin in form, but each is a distinct entity that offers to the reader pleasures not found in the others. Ford's remarkable sense of place made its first appearance in *The Cinque Ports*. Continuing through the trilogy *England and the English* (1907) and *No Enemy* (1929), the same kind of mixture appears in *Provence* (1935) and *Great Trade Route* (1937) more than thirty years later.

If Ford's future direction was not predictable, *The Cinque Ports* is nevertheless, in Mizener's words, a "modest, informative, and entertaining book, a remarkable achievement for a young man of twenty-six." It was this time in Ford's career that H. G. Wells later remembered: "His brain is an exceptionally good one and when first he came along, he had cast himself for the role of a very gifted scion of the Pre-Raphaelite stem, given over to scientific purposes and a little undecided between music, poetry, criticism, The Novel, Thoreau-istic horticulture and the simple appreciation of life" (*Experiment in Autobiography*, 1934). It may not be true that James modeled his character Merton Densher of *The Wings of the Dove* (1902) on Ford, but the impression is the same: a young man who looked like Ford, with seemingly incompatible parts to his nature.

The Cinque Ports, a massive work, was the real beginning of Ford's career as a writer. It is the first appearance of views that culminated in *The March of Literature* (1938), a work appraising and reappraising the accomplishments of the

First page of a letter from Ford (written in the war zone) to Joseph Conrad (by permission of Princeton University Library) past, done on the eve of a war that came near to destroying the civilized values he had served in all his work. The concern for local history and tradition in *The Cinque Ports* is only the beginning of Ford's concern for the nature of civilization and the human qualities that best make it up. For example, in chivalry, manners, and altruism, Ford saw values that are more than historical.

Rossetti (1902), *Hans Holbein the Younger* (1905), and *The Pre-Raphaelite Brotherhood* (1907) are Ford's three books in Duckworth's Popular Library of Art, in the last of which his grandfather Brown figures as mentor and friend. The requirements of the series were that the artists be seen as "exemplifying the dominant ideals and assumptions" of their age. All three seem less necessary books in Ford's development than something he could do and get paid for doing. They do show the young writer coming up with an aesthetic of his own and working out its pertinence to the literary and plastic arts on the one side and the connection with society and civilization on the other. Ford was always interested in the technical details of the arts or how artists "get their effects," a phrase he used many times, once putting it in Conrad's mouth. In all of these books, he writes convincingly of the technical details of painting, and by no means uninterestingly.

In *Rossetti* he declined to pursue Edward Garnett's suggestions for a more lurid book, telling Garnett in a letter, "I cannot enter into the pathological details. . . . Because how can I distinguish between the symptoms, on canvas, of chloral, uraemia, gout in the wrist and incipient blindness, all of which (not to mention chronic delusions) had a share." Such details of Rossetti's life and work are present but sketched very lightly. If there is an overall interpretation, it is that, despite great personal charm and natural ability, Rossetti failed because of a lack of self-discipline. He never mastered the technical tools of his art but took the easy way of natural genius and chose self-indulgence rather than a harder course that might have made him a greater artist. In *Ancient Lights* (1911) Ford generalized this deficiency beyond art: "Rossetti was a man without any principles at all, who earnestly desired to find some means of salvation along the lines of least resistance."

When Ford wrote *Holbein* in 1903, he was suffering one of his bouts of ill health and went to Germany and Switzerland seeking a cure. He also did the research for his book. His symptoms were a neurasthenic languor and agoraphobia.

The consensus among biographers is that the ill health was directly related to the fact that his marriage to Elsie was breaking up and that he had begun an affair with her sister Mary.

One of the most fruitful themes in Ford's fiction is that of the man or woman who is misplaced in time, who holds a set of values from an earlier and usually better time, and who must live in a time inimical to those values. Witness Edward Ashburnham and Christopher Tietjens of *The Good Soldier* and *Parade's End*. The pattern also holds for women—for example, Valentine Wannop of the latter novel, Katharine Howard of the *Fifth Queen* trilogy, and others. They are versions of Ford's "alien protagonist," a theme set forth by H. Robert Huntley. But if there are people out of phase with their times, there must be people who are not. While the former get the more sympathetic treatment from Ford, probably in some way corresponding to a view of himself, Hans Holbein, the German painter who painted Tudor eminences from 1525 to 1540, including Henry VIII, was the right artist to capture the qualities people had in the age in which the modern began. Ford's heart may have lain with an idealized, chivalric Middle Ages, but he gives a good account of an artist who was able to depict the new because he was by temperament and talent suited to it. Holbein was also a favorite of Brown's.

Holbein is an admirable book, the interest more than just implicit in the subject. With few details known for certain about the painter's life, the novelist's imagination is allowed to function and flesh out the skeleton of facts. The book is much superior to *Rossetti*, in which the author's problem was holding back things he knew very well. Ford shows the ability to reason convincingly from a few scatterings of historical facts. If his best fiction were not so good, one might regret his loss to the field of history. In fact, the loss was not total. Ford actually did write a formal history in the 1930s and left it unpublished, the first volume of a projected trilogy to be called "A History of Our Own Times." Beginning in about 1880, the series was to have included World War I. The completed part appeared in 1988 under the editorship of Sondra Stang and Solon Beinfeld.

The Pre-Raphaelite Brotherhood is Ford's third foray through the fields of his own youth and his grandfather's past. Most of the issues illustrate aspects of Victorian moral aesthetic; this side of modernism they seem merely quaint. Though

Ford at work (Collection of Edward Naumburg, Jr.)

Ford shows his usual competence, his usual intelligence, when he deals with a Victorian subject he seems to regress to a Victorian style, stiff and formal, which in his other books he had mostly worked his way out of.

Ford prefers the term "Pre-Raphaelism" in the face of Holman Hunt, whom he quotes as insisting that the original members "were disciples *not* of the painters who painted before Raphael, but of the painters who painted before the painters who imitated Raphael ... Raphael himself being a Pre-Raphaelite." Using the same logic, Ford suggests that Hunt should be called a "Pre-Raphaeliteite." By whatever term, the movement, Ford claimed, was "a return to Nature–it was nothing more and nothing less." Here "Nature" seems to mean the eschewal of certain artificialities and conventions rather than the God-filled mystery

of William Wordsworth and other Romantics.

In *The Pre-Raphaelite Brotherhood* Ford sees his grandfather Brown in a way that anticipates what biographers were eventually to say about himself. He was "a singularly luckless man, whether as an artist or an individual. It seems likely that he never did justice to the remarkable powers that were his; it is certain that he never received any material reward at all commensurate with his diligence, his sincerity, or his very considerable achievement." Strictly speaking, "he was not, either officially or in spirit, ever a Pre-Raphaelite," but Ford uses his example as something to measure the others by, since Brown was briefly Rossetti's teacher and in later life was a friend and associate of the group. What he did that they did not do was to "initiate modern art."

Ford cites a portrait entitled *Modern Holbein* as proof. In a painting "not otherwise very remarkable," Brown was "the first man in modern days to see or to put into practice the theory that aesthetic salvation was to be found not in changing the painter's subject, but in changing his method of looking at and rendering the visible world. He began trying to paint what he saw." This is an inchoate definition of what Ford would soon call Impressionism.

What Ford most admired about the painters was their sense of brotherhood as artists. Their unselfish support of each other with patrons and purchasers was "a fine record of generosity." Another part of their appeal was that "the Brotherhood attacked an accepted idea, and to do that has always been to show oneself an enemy of the people." Finally, the painters came "as near to being a union for the furtherance of the mechanical qualities of any art–as near to such a union as seems to be possible in this country where social conditions make it almost impossible for any man to take a whole-hearted interest in the practices of his art and in nothing else." Perhaps already forming in Ford's mind was the idea for the *English Review*, along the lines of his own idealism and new ideas. (When Ford did institute the *Review* with the intention of sharing profits among the contributors, they turned out to be dancers around a calf of gold rather than brothers in the service of the arts.) Also, he gave another concise definition of Impressionism when he said that the secret of a given artist's "particular charm–of all charm in works of art–was to be attained to only by observation filtered through personality." Ford had finished his apprenticeship in the school of ideas, one feels, and was ready to add whatever light he was vouchsafed to the dawning of the new day in the arts.

When Ford brought out *The Soul of London* (1905), it was a relative success in England and was widely reviewed. The author had been suffering from nervous depression for at least a year and was elated to the point of recovery. The book and its two sequels, *The Heart of the Country* (1906) and *The Spirit of the People* (1907), were collected in a slightly altered form in America under the title *England and the English* before the last volume of the trilogy appeared in England. Of *The Soul of London*, Garnett said (as quoted by Mizener), "It *is* very good, you know," in fact, "the best thing he's done."

Ford in these books is not yet the master he was to become, but even the unsympathetic

Mizener calls them "the best of his early nonfiction. . . . They have an easiness and an insight Ford had not before shown." The limitations Mizener does see are the result of the author's "commitment to impressionism," that much-vexed problem of Ford studies. In a preface to the American collection, Ford calls his work "these analyses of feeling": "For what I offer is not a statement of facts: it is precisely a set of analyses of feelings." Almost certainly, such ideas derive from his association with Conrad; another possible influence is the so-called travel writings of James, only some of which, however, had been collected at this time. Mizener sees only "a random selection of subjects" in regard to which Ford "allows his thoughts to drift from vignettes of London life to random personal feelings." Although Ford's kind of Impressionism needs for its reality a personality for the impression to register upon and to be refracted through, he shows a convincing grasp of the experiences of others. Even Mizener praises Ford's rendering of one of the London poor, a woman who by making matchboxes ekes out a living for a crippled husband ("or perhaps she was not married" to him) and four children under the age of nine. The author seems astonished himself: "What was appalling was not the poverty. It was not the wretchedness, because, on the whole, neither the man nor the woman were anything other than contented. . . . You could not pity her because she was so obviously and wonderfully equipped for her particular struggle. . . . It was like interviewing the bedrock of human existence in a cavern deep in the earth."

Ideas and values that Ford merely touches on in *The Heart of the Country* have a profounder import after his experiences in World War I. By undergoing the privations of the war and coming to terms with its horrors, he gained a new perspective on the necessities by which ordinary people live their lives. He saw new worth in poverty, self-sufficiency, stoicism, frugality, individualism, courage, and cheerfulness in the face of adversity. The extravagant squandering of lives and property in the war gave him a "change of heart" whereby he joined in imaginative sympathy those who did their jobs as best they could for the sake of the job well done rather than for its monetary rewards. By the multiplication and practical application of values as simple as these, he came to believe that the civilization he loved could be saved from the destructive ferocities of another world war. In the 1920s and 1930s he doffed his Pre-

Ford (at right) with James Joyce, Ezra Pound, and John Quinn, an American lawyer and book collector, in Paris, 1923

Raphaelite cape (he had actually worn one that belonged to Rossetti) and donned a prophet's mantle in Cassandra-like efforts to turn the world away from materialism, power worship, and technology. He sought by means of his art to point the people of the world in a better direction–in fact, back to values he had perceived near the turn of the century, though at that time he had not seen their full significance.

A half dozen or so of Ford's nonfiction books are reminiscences. He says in a late one, *It Was the Nightingale* (1933), that he has never tried autobiography "mainly for fear of the charge of vanity," but instead has "written reminiscences of which the main features were found in the lives of other people" and in which, as well as he could, he obscured himself. It is fair to ask what Ford's qualities are in this vein. A reader's first response might be to the tone, which is amiable, genial, wise, a little patronizing, all borne by a style that is conversational yet learned, that reveals the man, or all of the man the author chooses to reveal. For–and this is curious–all of these volumes are strangely reticent about personal details. The English gentlemanly code (which English literati seem intent to deny him any natural right or

claim to) perhaps forbade such information being dwelt on. His relations with women, with his children, his mother, brother, sister, and grandmother appear sketchily or not at all, though his grandfather Brown is a perpetual reference, and his father is a less frequent but still recurrent one. World War I, which broke his life in two, does not appear except remotely in any of the volumes, unless the sui generis *No Enemy* counts. Strangely, Ford has often been depicted in other people's impressions as a monster of vanity.

What one sees in the reminiscences is a parade of the various great men he encountered, mostly artists of some kind, depicted in terms of their work, their public significance, but also their vanity, the last presented indirectly, gently, so that a too-relaxed reader might miss it. True, Ford himself is shown as on intimate terms with them, and this is what has irritated some critics. Yet, although numerous small corrections have been made in Ford's statements, many unlikely ones have been confirmed, such as his writing an installment of *Nostromo*, which is still part of the text, when Conrad was ill. Despite denials by Conrad's widow, Jessie, Ford did supply plots to

Conrad, and he also wrote the larger part of the collaborative *Romance*.

A certain amount of vanity colors Ford's impressions, but the personal claims are usually modest and undercut by himself before he finishes. Of course, he did not need to undercut tall tales such as the one he told Richard Aldington's father about meeting Lord Byron. All genres to Ford require the methods of fiction for their fulfillment; all is art, which is his way of approaching fact. As Stang has observed, "The dividing line between fiction and autobiography was never a clear one for Ford" (*Ford Madox Ford*, 1977). There is nothing of malice or spite. One is left with an impression of a kind man who misses little of what went on around him and who is devoted to the best of a civilized tradition through the arts. The viciousness of the world is acknowledged but little resented. Ford was well regarded by Stephen Crane, Pound, Conrad, D. H. Lawrence, William Carlos Williams, and others, none of whom denied his faults. That is high praise, indeed honor. Ford's air of lordly superiority provoked many people, but Crane wrote: "You must not mind Hueffer: that is his way. He patronises me; he patronises Mr. Conrad; he patronises Mr. James. When he goes to Heaven he will patronise God Almighty. But God Almighty will get used to it, for Hueffer is all right!" (quoted in *Return to Yesterday*, 1931).

Ancient Lights, published in the United States as *Memories and Impressions* (1911), is one of Ford's most engaging books. He is fully matured as a writer, the master of a style, tone, and subject, and shows carefully defined attitudes. Mizener says he "practically invented a form of fictional reminiscence." At the same time, the book is one of his most controversial because of the distinction he makes between impression and fact, even though he had made the same distinction several times before, if less blatantly: "This book," he states in the preface, "is full of inaccuracies as to facts, but its accuracy as to impressions is absolute." Further, "I don't really deal in facts; I have for facts a most profound contempt. I try to give you what I see to be the spirit of an age, of a town, of a movement. This cannot be done with facts." Ford had the advantage of the previous periodical publication of the book (*Harper's*, 1910), which elicited a rather pompous public correction of some of his facts, and in the book he answered it. He presented his early "pretty and romantic impression" that he had heard Thomas Carlyle "tell how at Weimar he borrowed an apron from a waiter and served tea to Goethe and Schiller, who were sitting in eighteenth-century court dress beneath a tree." As an adult he was admittedly aware that Carlyle "never was in Weimar, and that Schiller died when Carlyle was aged five" and other facts. He "intended to show the state of mind of a child of seven brought into contact with a Victorian great figure," who appeared "monumental, loud-voiced, and distressing."

Many things mentioned in *Ancient Lights* become lifelong motifs for Ford. He told most of the stories again and again, with many variations. An example is his father's regarding him as "the patient but extremely stupid donkey" (he also suffers a nearly identical denomination from the poet Mathilde Blind). At the same time, genius was enjoined upon him, and a life in the arts was the only allowable one. The same kind of contradictions colored his view of Victorianism, a sort of pro and con rather than a resolution.

A theme that was to be pervasive in Ford's work, seen in *Ancient Lights*, is the growing materialism of modern life that by the end of the century had affected literature. The new commercial standards for writing, price per thousand words or "price per thou," came to be "the sole literary God in England." This is not to say that the painters of Brown's group and the writers who surrounded them had any contempt for money as such. They wanted it, but it was not the end and aim of their existence. And "price per thou" not having been invented in those days, they did "not become agonized, thrilled, or driven mad at the thought of this deity." Ford, the professional writer, remained true to the ideals of his upbringing by his objection to letting money determine the nature of the writing or any of the arts. The arts could not fulfill their offices by this false standard. Not only is the more idealistic position made explicit in Ford's books, but it is exemplified in his life, Though the author of acknowledged masterpieces, he died penniless, in actual need. In 1966 Robert Lowell, in his preface to *Buckshee* (1966), citing Pound's firsthand knowledge of Ford, said that Ford "actually lived the heroic artistic life" that W. B. Yeats only talked about.

"Ford's bringing together the French nineteenth-century tradition of fiction with the twentieth-century English novel was part of his effort to remove English intellectual life from its insularity and bring it into what he considered to be the mainstream of European culture"–thus

Ford with Violet Hunt, Rebecca West, and West's child by H. G. Wells, Anthony West

Stang sums up Ford's efforts as a critic. *The Critical Attitude* is the place to read much of the best of his early criticism. Six of the eight chapters appeared as editorials in the *English Review* from December 1908 through December 1909, the other two in journals in 1909 and 1910. Presumably, the essays reflect the editorial policies of the *Review*. Ford's effort was in general to appraise the state of the arts in his own time in England and, on the basis of the superior French practice, point to better directions. This, with Victorian amateurism, moralizing, black-and-white characterization, structureless rambling, digressions, and inexact use of language, was to be a recurrent theme all the way through Ford's *English Novel* essays of 1929. In opposition Ford posed the artist who knew how he got his effects, the self-conscious artist, and a reader who could appreciate the efforts. This, in short, is what Ford means by "the critical attitude." Literature leads people to self-understanding, to the understanding of one's fellow humans, and to more informed actions. For "the chief value of the arts to the State is that they are concerned with Truth." Truth is

what a proper critic serves, also. Ford quotes Gustave Flaubert, who said that if his countrymen had read and understood *L'Education Sentimentale* (1874) they could have been spared the Franco-Prussian humiliation. (Ford claimed to have read the novel fourteen times.)

The best essay in *The Critical Attitude* is "On the Objection to the Critical Attitude." It expresses Ford's bitterness at the failure of the *English Review* under his editorship and has a vehemence and bite that are unusual with Ford. More typical of him is to ring the changes in the bell tower of irony: "the end of the ass is to draw carts, the end of the respectable journal is to limit thought within the bounds of respectability; the end of the hyena is to disinter from graveyards the great bones which with its powerful jaws it crushes, extracting no doubt succulent marrow. So the *English Review* had its purposes and its ends. . . . Its purposes were several, chief amongst these being the furthering of a certain school of literature and of a certain school of thought." As far as making an Englishman think, "he is just God's Englishman." It follows that an

English Review is a "contradiction in terms," not to mention "a splendid forlorn hope": "But no sane man would set out to make the ass play upon a musical instrument, the respectable journal to take broad views, or the hyena to distil eau-de-cologne. For these things upon the face of them would be insane enterprises. So with the *English Review*, which set out to enjoin upon the Englishman a critical attitude." Ford is at his best when he talks about the arts in their essential nature, in their broad social function, in a historical pattern–any of the arts, all of the arts. Though his views were modified somewhat as times changed, his essential principles remained intact. The same themes and illustrations show up again and again in Ford's criticism, but they never received a more vigorous statement than in *The Critical Attitude*.

Ford's book on Henry James (1914) has the distinction of being the first full-length study of that author. Ford regarded James as "the greatest of living writers and in consequence . . . the greatest of living men." James's greatness lies in his value to the world, which is "that of the historian–the historian of one, of two, and possibly three or more, civilizations." As historian he is objective and impartial: he gives the material upon which the reader must make his own judgment that may affect his life in the future. The typical English novel, by contrast, is filled with special pleading, the author indulging himself by writing his own views because it pleases him. James "has remained an observer, passionless and pitiless. . . . As a writer, he has had no more sympathy for chivalrous feelings than for the starving poor." Like Baudelaire, and like Flaubert whom he disliked, James "has looked at life with its treacheries, its banalities, its shirkings and its charlatanries, all of them founded on the essential dirtiness of human nature . . . and, if the world read him to any great extent, the world might well be a pleasanter place."

When Blood Is Their Argument and *Between St. Dennis and St. George*, published respectively in March and September 1915, were doubtless written at the instigation of Ford's friend C. F. G. Masterman, a member of Herbert Henry Asquith's cabinet. Ford began to write the books in September 1914, got a commission in the army in late July 1915, and was in uniform by the middle of August at age forty-one. The project was highly secret and was known only by the name of the building where Masterman's office was, Wellington House; Masterman had been put in charge of countering German propaganda in the United States. Copies of the books were sent to influential Americans nominally as the gift of this or that distinguished British professor. Richard Aldington and Alec Randall did research for Ford, and Aldington recalled taking down Ford's dictation in longhand. The English were more apt to be pro-German than pro-French at the time, and the effort of the books was to turn these and similar American opinions around. The South Germany of Ford's family, of Holbein, and home of whatever important art Germany possessed, had fallen to Bismarck's Prussia, which, in *When Blood Is Their Argument*, stands for "commercialism, applied science, philology, and war, instead of idealism, pure science, human learning, and peace." Mizener credits Ford with intelligence and restraint and sees the effort as fair to "the merits of Wagner and Nietzsche and Bismarck, a rare thing in such works." Ford claims that from his father and grandfather Brown he acquired in childhood "a deep hatred of Prussianism, of materialism, of academicism, of pedagogism, and of purely economic views of the values of life." At the same time and from the same source, he was "inspired with a deep love and veneration for French learning, arts, habits of mind, lucidity, and for that form of imagination which implies a sympathetic comprehension of the hopes, fears, and ideals of one's fellow-men." He also sees his work as "in essence, a reassertion of the claims of, or of the necessity for, altruism, whether Christian or Hellenic. . . . " He stresses this idea by repeating it; the problem before humanity is "whether the culture of the future, the very life and heart of the future, shall be materialist or altruist." Such ideas appear from start to finish in Ford's work, giving it a unity that is not sufficiently appreciated. Both of these books are personal: their anecdotes and reminiscences are the best parts, certainly the parts that are least dated.

Perhaps avowed propaganda should be allowed to sleep with the war dead, but the question of Ford as historian is also involved. Anne Barr Snitow finds that "the tone of Ford's essays is authoritative, bold, but their imaginative leaps are in fact quite precarious. . . . His logic often disintegrates under any sort of scrutiny." L. L. Farrar (in *The Presence of Ford Madox Ford*, edited by Stang, 1981) notes that the essays "reveal a good deal about the wartime attitudes of the English ruling class." Reading as a historian, he is "struck by both Ford's grasp of the issues and the limitations of his approach." Ford has "relied on the pop-

Ford with Ezra Pound at Rapallo (by permission of the Cornell University Library)

ularizer's gift, the use of metaphor, symbol, anecdote, and interpolations from fiction" in order to appeal to the general reader. It is only fair to point out, as Farrar does, that "the circumstances–those of England in World War I–determined not only the spirit in which the books were written but also the spirit in which they were read: the books insist on their context." Ford received no pay for this work.

It is easy to suppose that Ford's evident appeal to women is perceptible in his essays. For lack of a better term, one might call it masculine charm. It is compounded of a very great intelligence, learned in history, literature, music, painting, and accompanied by amusing stories about them all, but at the same time playful, sympathetic and kind, ironic without becoming cynical, subtle, intuitive, wise (in everything that did not pertain to his own affairs, Stella Bowen said), and possessed of a sense of humor. These qualities are in every one of Ford's nonfiction books, including the relatively slight *Thus to Revisit*. The

book contains one of the ideas never far from the author's work: "Creative Literature–Poetry–is the sole panacea for the ills of harassed humanity." If this seems fatuous, the reason is not: "For Creative Literature is the only thing that can explain to man the nature of his fellow men"–an article of Ford's faith in the worth of the arts. All artists are heroes to him, and war's folly is indicated by the loss of Henri Gaudier-Brzeska, the young French sculptor Pound also wrote about. A negative concomitant of this faith in the arts is that, as Mizener says, "all scholars, critics, and reviewers are unmitigated fools, busy proving from a study of poets' laundry bills what is not of the slightest significance," something Ford says several times in other ways.

He is surprisingly modern enough to offend moralists of every stripe, with statements such as "I am interested only in how to write, and . . . I care nothing–but nothing in the world!–what a man writes about." This kind of remark is offensive to Robert Green sixty years later, especially when he discovers a similar one in *The March of Literature*. The critic does not share Ford's faith in the utility to the world of unfettered artists and their work. Flaubert had made such a remark long before. However, Ford was never a detached aesthete, as Green seems to imply, but always a believer in the responsibilities of art. With James, he thought that art must be true to *something*; both were wise enough not to confine it to a particular subject.

The four essays collected in *Women and Men* marked Ford's first appearance in print in Paris (in April 1923), where he and Stella Bowen and their infant daughter, Julie, had moved from rural England in November 1922. The book was printed at William Bird's Three Mountains Press on the Ile Saint-Louis; in 1924 the building was to house the editorial office of the *Transatlantic Review* in a minute balcony overlooking the printing press. The essays had been published in the *Little Review* in 1918 at Pound's insistence and had been written at a still earlier date. As early as January 1911 Ford had projected the book as "a sort of philosophical discussion on the relations and the differences between the sexes." These relations are the heart of his fiction but do not find their best exemplification in his essays. He intended fourteen chapters of five thousand words apiece as a kind of counterpart to the great and famous personages of *Ancient Lights*. These new essays would be "reminiscences of undistinguished people" he had met. It is hard to tell how serious known him to shew.

The anecdote was this: Turgenev had a peasant girl for mistress. One day he was going   to St. Petersburg and he asked the girl what he should bring her back from town. She begged him to bring her back some cakes of scented soap. He asked her why she wanted scented soap and she answered:"So that it may be proper for you to kiss my hand as you do those of the great ladies, your friends."

I never liked the anecdote much,myself. But Galsworthy, telling it in the sunlit breakfast room of my cottage at Winchelsea , found it so touching that he appeared to be illuminated, and really had tears in his eyes. I daresay the reflection of the sunlight from the table-cloth may have had something to do with the effect of illumination, but it comes back to me as if,still, I saw him in a sort of aura that emanated from his features. And from that day he was never quite the same.... The morning is also made memorable for me by the ghost of the odour of a very strong embrocation that hung about us both. He was, at the moment,suffering from severe sciatica and I had spent the last half-hour of the night before and the first half-hour of that morning in rubbing him in his bed with that fluid which consisted of turpentine, mustard,and the white of egg o   And suddenly I had of him a concept-ion of a sort of frailty,as if he needed protection from the hard truths of the world. It was a conception that remained to me till the very end/... till the last time/but one when I came upon him accidental-ly watching one of his own plays in New York, all alone and, seemingly, very perturbed. I don't know by what .

Page from the typescript, corrected by Ford, for his essay "Galsworthy," first published in the April 1936 issue of the American Mer-cury *and included in* Portraits from Life *(MA 1417, gift of Mr. H. Bradley Martin; by permission of the Pierpont Morgan Library)*

Ford was when he said, with two of the pieces completed, that "whilst it is deeply serious it is also wildly amusing and it will be bought in large quantities by my large following of suffragettes" (quoted by Harvey). Ford had written favorably on women's rights and related issues in several short pieces that were put together in *The Critical Attitude*, and sympathetically also in the pamphlet *This Monstrous Regiment of Women* (1913). Twenty years later in *Return to Yesterday* he was still proud that the suffragette leader Emmeline Pankhurst had approved of his work.

When Margaret Anderson edited the *Little Review Anthology* in 1953, she found Ford's group of pieces "so uninteresting, as I reread it, that I will include only episodes V and VI, under the sub-title of 'Average People.'" The part she reprinted, however, bears out Pound's positive judgment rather than her derogation. It is the memorable account of the illiterate old country woman, Meary Walker, whose story Ford had told as early as *The Heart of the Country* and would tell again in *Return to Yesterday*. Meary is one of the "brown men and women of Kent," as he characterized them in the later volumes, peasants who, leading an almost immemorial life, caused him to retain a deep love for England. Of Meary he said (in *Return to Yesterday*), "This was the wisest and upon the whole the most estimable human being that I ever knew at all well." Her qualities were courage and endurance. She lived by a practical philosophy that enabled her to accept her hard lot in life without self-pity, yet keep a sense of humor. Meary, like Ford Madox Brown, embodies many of the values Ford held all his adult life. Anderson was right in her appraisal to the extent that the essays in *Women and Men* have a distinct tone of the time in which they were written. Despite the perennial interest of their subject, they were in manner more than ten years away from the bright modernism she favored.

When his old friend and collaborator Conrad died on 3 August 1924, Ford was living in Paris and editing the *Transatlantic Review*, a journal only slightly less distinguished than the *English Review*. He tried on short notice to put together a Conrad supplement. Several of the young writers he asked for contributions showed their youthful bumptiousness and lack of civility, none more so than Ernest Hemingway, who in his piece gratuitously insulted T. S. Eliot without praising Conrad and went so far as to imply he would prefer his benefactor Ford dead rather than Conrad. Ford himself began to write a book

on Conrad and finished it in two months; it was published in November. The first five sections of part 1 ran in the review from September through December 1924, the last issue. As he said in 1926, "I wrote this book at fever heat–in an extraordinarily short time. . . . Nevertheless, I see very little that I want to change in it and I think it remains a very accurate account of our relationship–Conrad's and mine." In his preface Ford characterized the book: "This then is a novel, not a monograph; a portrait, not a narration . . . a work of art, not a compilation. It is conducted exactly along the lines laid down by us, both for the novel which is biography and for the biography which is a novel. It is the rendering of an affair intended first of all to make you see the subject in his scenery." Ford used all of the novelist's methods of selection and heightening to bring his subject to life. In dozens of short sections, some no more than a sentence, Ford portrays the man he knew, admitting to this or that distortion of this or that fact, but always in an effort to make the reader see the essential truth. The result is a kind of pointillistic portrait: with the right perspective and distance, the pieces fall into place. Still, the book includes the old problem of Ford's kind of Impressionism, which maddened many philistines, including Conrad's widow, Jessie. There is no question, however, of Ford's devotion to Conrad, even though they had long been estranged.

Initial reviews were favorable, but Mrs. Conrad, writing in a *TLS* letter dated 4 December 1924, refers to Ford's book as "merely an attempt to glorify himself at his late friend's expense," thus precipitating "a literary controversy that was damaging to Ford's reputation" to the end of his life (MacShane, *Life and Works*). To many he appeared as a crass opportunist using the death as an occasion to write a book he could not have dared to write had Conrad been alive. Mrs. Conrad's view has not prevailed, though her hatred was unrelenting. Ford did know a side of her husband that she neither knew nor comprehended. Mizener speaks up for Ford: "There is an aspect of Conrad's nature, and an important one, that no one has ever represented so convincingly as Ford does." But he does find objectionable the "far too much irrelevant information" about Ford himself, much of it "grossly flattering" and giving an "effect of silly vanity" that damaged him badly even in the eyes of sympathetic critics. Still, the book is "a remarkable achievement."

Most of the negative remarks are based on the idea that Conrad is a great writer and Ford a negligible one. In the relationship, Ford may or may not have given as good as he got, but he gave enough that the relationship was not one-sided. There were many instances, too, of Ford's help and advice to younger artists, but none on the part of Conrad. Ford supplied money and housing to Conrad and his family. (When Conrad's son Borys went to prison in 1928 for a year as the result of a fraud concerned with his father's manuscripts, Ford offered to support Borys's wife and child, though nothing came of it.) Most of Ford's claims as to what he contributed to the other's work are now substantiated, including plots, passages that remain in the works, intelligent criticism, moral support and encouragement, taking down Conrad's dictation, and more. Each writer would have been different but for the other. Their ten years of close contact and collaboration came at a crucial time in the career of each. In the present view, Ford's stature is acknowledged to the point that one may validly prefer his best to his friend's best. Also, Ford's temperament seems more attuned to the modern age than does that of Conrad, sixteen years older.

There is another aspect to the book on Conrad. While the first part is devoted to reminiscences, the second part deals largely with the technique, the theories, and the devices he and Conrad developed together. Because of the frequency with which it is quoted by novelists and critics, MacShane feels that it is "one of the most cogent and intelligent summaries ever written on the subject of the novel." The substance is "still important for the craft of fiction." The topics in part 2 are General Effect, Impressionism, Selection, Speeches, Conversations, Surprise, Style, Cadence, Structure, Philosophy, Progression d'Effet, and Language. Ford is wise enough to say that he and his friend were aware of "other methods" for writing novels. The writers were not rigid even in their own methods and knew that "compromise is at all times necessary to the execution of a work of art." Even though on the negative side this book may have helped to foster the erroneous view that Ford was a master technician who had nothing to say, it is not too large a claim to say that portions of it are as significant as James's prefaces and "Art of Fiction."

In *A Mirror to France* (1926), Ford reprinted some twenty pages from *Between St. Dennis and St. George*, the rest being composed between 1 March 1923 and 18 January 1926, by his own reckoning. One may ask why he wrote so many "portraits of places." James had done the same, and his are both more aesthetic and personal than Ford's, more pictorial, more the personal adventures of a discriminating tourist. By contrast, Ford's are, as Stang puts it in *Ford Madox Ford*, "discussions of culture," which "express a way of looking at human culture that is consistent and coherent and that suggests possible directions now—perhaps even more compellingly than when Ford first offered them." She adds that he had "an abiding belief in the wholeness of human life and in the possibility of restoring life to wholeness in spite of the disintegrative forces of modern life." France figured prominently in Ford's remedy, an artist's France, a France become symbol, but also the France of his grandfather Brown's birth and the land the writer himself lived in for most of his last two decades. On the personal level, he wrote about the places of his heart, especially Provence and Paris. "Prussianism" was his early name for what he disliked in the modern world—too much materialism, technology, force, and reliance on conscious intellectualism at the expense of a fullness of human resources. Obviously, Ford has much in common with Lawrence in his diagnosis if not his cure. France and especially Provence stood for what Ford approved of, civilization at its finest, the best of the human achieved by a long history and tradition of unaggressive individualism and tolerance.

Ford's social values may have distant roots in the ideas of John Ruskin, William Morris, and Pyotr Kropotkin, and perhaps should be classed among the varieties of philosophical anarchism. Alternative social views were rife in the nineteenth and early twentieth centuries, brought on as industrialism and commercialism with unprecedented force worked dislocations in old traditions and patterns. If Ford's social ideas seem out of touch with social reality, they are at least in the company of Henry David Thoreau, Leo Tolstoy, Mahatma Gandhi, the Vanderbilt Agrarians, and others who cannot be dismissed as inconsequential. In his "From the Grey Stone," an essay published by Eliot in his *Criterion* in 1923, Ford is perched on a rock overlooking the Mediterranean, rejecting technological dogmas and faith in progress. In *The American Scene* (1907) James prefers walking up steps to the "sempiternal lift," and misses the small parks of European cities in which one could withdraw for a few moments of repose and thought. In *I'll Take My Stand* (1930) John Crowe Ransom gave as one mark of a high

Ford and Janice Biala (foreground) with Caroline Gordon and Allen Tate, in Clarksville, Tennessee, circa 1935

civilization the amount of leisure it allowed its people. Ford is far from solitary in his values.

The *chose donnée* of *A Mirror to France* is that "chivalric generosity, frugality, pure thought and the arts are the first requisites of a Civilization—and the only requisites of a Civilization." Originating in Provence, these are doomed by Mass Production, here symbolized by a white-tiled bathroom with glass and chrome. He sets out to make this book "reflections in a perfectly impersonal mirror," by which he means he has derived nothing "from other people's works on France." He claims as result "the purest, the most will-less impressionism." At the same time, "try how he will, an Impressionist's book about an actual place or an actual man is bound to assume a rather reminiscential air." Here is the paradox that lies at the heart of Ford's Impressionism. The narrator is an objective reflector of the truth of times, places, events, and people, but nevertheless is sufficiently subjective to engage in reminiscence. It is a big order, to which Ford had best not be held strictly accountable. Anyone who finds his manner acceptable will find *A Mirror to*

France an enjoyable tour of one of the perennial places in Ford's heart that supplied material for some of his poems in *On Heaven* (1918) and *Buckshee*, which are among his best. Already trying on the prophets' mantles he would wear in the 1930s, Ford the Francophile tells how to be happy by giving the example of "people intensely individualistic who intend to remain intensely individualistic; of small shopkeepers who intend to remain and only to deal with small shopkeepers; of people with adequate means of living who intend to retain adequate means of living but to leave it at that; of a people of some culture who get enough pleasure out of their culture to remain a people of some culture; of a people whose peasant families work immensely hard in order that one member of the family may practise an art or indulge in abstract thought; and of a people less represented by its governments than any other people that ever was."

Also in *A Mirror to France*, Ford picks up his old quarrel with the England that let the *English Review* pass out of his hands: "Of Thought we are usually incapable; frugality we despise; we believe before all things in the doctrine of Something for Nothing, so we have nearly forgotten the impulses of chivalric generosity that once, rudimentarily, raised us above brute creation. Of the Arts we know nothing; we are as nearly as possible illiterate. Wherever we go in any numbers the civilisation, the thought, the arts, the simplicities and the gentlenesses of the native races die. . . ." Had he not specified England, one would have thought his diatribe was directed at the United States. Ford says many of these same things in *No Enemy* (written in 1919, published in 1929 in America only), there putting them into the mouth of a fictionalized version of himself called Gringoire.

When French virtues are listed, they sound like those of the critic in *The Critical Attitude*: the French "keep themselves singularly in contact with the realities of life. They know, extraordinarily and beyond the knowledge of most people, which things are real and which illusions." Small people go about their jobs, putting their "hopes of glory in that curious, vague and very definite thing they call *l'honneur*." In Ford's use the term means pride in one's work derived from a living tradition that includes personal discipline. The idea is different from conceptions called by the same name in England in that "it can subsist side by side with avarice, with meanness, with personal dilapidation and with want of cleanliness. It can endure the oppressions of very bad forms of government. . . ." In this tradition each person is "sober, hard-working, without many illusions as to life, tenacious of the honour of his craftsmanship, of his village, of his *arrondissement*, of his Midi, or of his Nord. . . ."

A Mirror to France goes as a kind of prolegomenon to *Provence* and *Great Trade Route*. At the same time, it picks up ideas from *No Enemy* and *The Heart of the Country*, which drew upon his experiences from 1894 on. World War I had given them a new intensity. Time now seemed important if certain values were to be preserved, certain follies to be avoided. The 1930s intensified the issues still more while the follies of the past, like sown dragon teeth, erupted in bellicose forms.

Some of the ideas from the French book reappear in *New York Is Not America* and *New York Essays* (both 1927). The first is his most diffuse, full of opinions about America based on inadequate experience. His wit gets lost in a cloud of words so that the final impression is of a voluble talker more than of the things talked about. Ford had

had critical and popular successes in the States and may have seen a possible future for himself there, his English reputation having declined to its nadir. Four of the essays from the first book make up four of the eight in the second, which was published in a limited signed edition of 750 copies. The books are essentially a tribute; there is a genuine sympathy and affection for New York City, which he had known as far back as 1906. But there is also an air of omnipotence that leads to what may be unintentional patronizing of Americans. Ford's future was uncertain. His relation with Stella was essentially ended; René Wright would not live with him outside of marriage; and Elsie would not divorce him, though he asked one more time. However, the persona of a sophisticated Englishman, worldly and especially literary-wise, conversant with literary greats for most of fifty years, was not entirely a defensive mask for the veteran author to put on; after all, in Ford's case, it was quite literally true.

New York Essays includes prefaces for and reviews of books by William Makepeace Thackeray and Anthony Trollope; an essay on Chicago in which Ford expresses a preference for New York City; and reviews of the Knopf edition of Crane's works and of Pound's *Personae* (1926). As part of the miscellany of these two books the author writes knowingly of American cooking and French wines but rarely strays far from literature. He defends the expatriation of American writers and insists that work rather than debauchery is their aim in Paris. And he criticizes the way writing and literature are taught in American colleges, with no thought that in another decade he would be asked to put his ideas to the test as a professor of comparative literature at Olivet College in Michigan (1937-1938).

Ford's next work of nonfiction, *The English Novel*, is a short book in "The One Hour Series," published in March 1929 from essays that had appeared serially in the *Bookman* from December 1928 through March 1929. The first American reviews were favorable, some noting that it was aimed at an American audience, but the reviewers seemed not to realize that Ford had been saying most of these things for thirty years. The special value Ford claims for his critical and historical views of his favorite genre is that he looks "at the matter with the eyes of a craftsman surveying his own particular job," as he was to say when he surveyed world writing in *The March of Literature* ten years later. What he finds lacking in the English novel is a sense of tradition. The En-

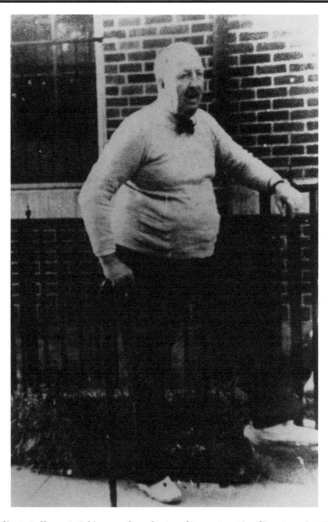

Ford at Olivet College, Michigan, where he taught comparative literature in 1937-1938

glish writer without thought or training sits down and "writes any sort of story in any sort of method–or in any sort of mixture of any half dozen methods." If such a writer has any of the requisites of artistry, he may, like Trollope, Henry Fielding, Samuel Butler, or George Meredith, rise as a "separate peak but each absolutely without inter-relation with any other." Ford is obviously playing off the English tradition of noncommunicative solitariness against the European one in which Flaubert, Guy de Maupassant, Ivan Turgenev, the Goncourt brothers (Edmond and Jules), Théophile Gautier, and Alphonse Daudet "all met frequently, dining together almost weekly [and] discussed words, cadences, forms, progressions of effect–or the cannon-strokes with which one concludes short-stories." Nothing else mattered, not "fame, wealth, the course of public affairs, ruin, death." There existed "only one en-

during Kingdom–that of the Arts–and only one Republic that shall be everlasting: the Republic of Letters."

Ford's criticism is increasingly tinged with the moral. In his view "the novel has become indispensable to the understanding of life," by which he means that modern life has become so diffuse, so various, that one can know little of it firsthand. Essentially he charged English writers with preferring to be popular entertainers rather than serious artists, with preferring to be English gentlemen who could not take their or any art seriously. (Charles Dickens had accused Thackeray of this.) Ford praises Trollope and Jane Austen. It is their unpretentiousness he likes, the responsibility to their craft rather than to their egos. Thus they have no passages of "super genius" such as occur in Dickens and which seem ends in themselves, or at least are something other than purely functional.

Return to Yesterday is the successor to *Ancient Lights* which dealt with Ford's childhood among the great Victorian figures and Pre-Raphaelites. This book, as MacShane notes in *The Life and Works*, "covers the years from 1894 to 1914 and treats of the various forces of Edwardian England which combined to move England towards the World War." Ford gives one more version of his collaboration with Conrad and of his time with the *English Review*. Every time he tells these stories, he adds details somewhat different from those in other versions, as seems called for by the Impressionist response of the moment. In a dedication, he sets forth an amiable defense of such methods: "being a novelist," he says, "it is possible that I romance." His "true intent" is only to delight his readers. He admits in advance the charge against him and tries to turn it into a virtue: "Where it has seemed expedient to me I have altered episodes that I have witnessed but I have been careful never to distort the character of the episode." Why? Of course, because "the accuracies I deal in are the accuracies of my impressions." *Return to Yesterday* is a happy, confident book, which biographers attribute to his new liaison with the gifted painter Janice Biala—beautiful, loyal, stimulating, and tough-minded. The affair lasted until his death.

In Ford's own terms *Return to Yesterday* is a splendid success, a bouillabaisse of Fordian entertainment, with the chef himself as fallible narrator/hero—far more fallible than he admits to, as reviewers, critics, and writers of their own remembrances were quick to point out. One of the most vicious was Archibald Marshall in *Out and About* (1933), who claimed Ford had never really been close to Conrad and James, certainly not as close as Marshall was. Actually Ford had been friends with both older writers and had been especially close to Conrad. With every personal book by Ford, critics have rushed to show the fictional departures from fact, as with his novels they have urged the factual basis of every fiction. The books are of such quality as to deserve better.

Two years after *Return to Yesterday*, Ford published *It Was the Nightingale*. The book is a technical tour de force in that much of it takes place in the author's memory while he pauses before raising the second foot to join his first on a curb in Campden Hill, London. By now (1933) Ford was incomparably the master of an ease of manner, a style, a form; his Impressionism is consummated here as it has not been before. Thomas Moser, a psychological critic, sees in the book a bleakness

and austerity of vision, but the time it covers–the decade of the 1920s–began with a self-appraisal and a stocktaking followed by a rededication to the best of Ford's earlier values. He originally intended to call the book "Towards Tomorrow." It seems the most personal of the reminiscences. His allegiance is clear to "the only perfect republic and the only permanent kingdom," the Republic of Letters and the Kingdom of the Arts. He still takes the idealist position that one cannot write motivated by money but only by the dictates of the work itself. He has not capitulated to the "price per thou" rationale.

It Was the Nightingale opens on the happiest of notes–"There was never a day so gay for the Arts as any twenty-four hours of the early 'twenties in Paris"–then turns immediately back to the day of Ford's army discharge in 1919 (1 January, to be exact). He was illusionless in a new world of personal and financial disaster, forgotten as a writer by the public, convinced that he could no longer write, but at the end of the book he is turning to write the volumes that make up *Parade's End*. Among other things, we get an account of his founding and losing the *Transatlantic Review* that includes his association with Pound, Hemingway, Basil Bunting, James Joyce, and Gertrude Stein. Like his hero Christopher Tietjens, Ford comes to reject the ideal of the English gentleman as inadequate in the postwar world. Details he did not give were that his liaison with Violet Hunt, though long ended, was still having unpleasant repercussions in 1919 and that his health, never robust, had suffered lasting impairment because of military service in the war. The time called for beginning anew–or giving up entirely. Recently returned from active service in France, he was refused a passport for France by some governmental blunder or malice for four years. He returned to the English countryside and sought the fundamental experiences of agriculture for his "reconstruction." He was soon joined by the young Australian painter Stella Bowen, whom he had met through Pound. The day she came he changed his name legally to Ford Madox Ford–a dramatic way to signal the beginning of a new life. Stella bore his third child, Esther Julia, in 1920.

In *No Enemy* Ford had given a fictionalized and highly selective version of his war experiences and efforts at putting himself back together in a rural setting. It is a brilliant, neglected book that goes over some of the same material as *Nightingale*. In it he dramatizes the

Portrait of Ford by Georg Hartmann (by permission of the New York Public Library)

principles that inform the books of his postwar life: the necessity for a universal change of heart from hatred to benevolence and responsibility; doing a job well for its own sake; the avoidance of waste, including the eschewal of personal great wealth; relative self-sufficiency by growing part of one's own food–in short, the responsible cultivation of one's own garden, literally and metaphorically. These became his guidelines for saving the civilization he loved and, since the war, feared was doomed and damned by technology and business. These ideas are the very warp and woof of *Provence* and *Great Trade Route*. Varieties of them were common between the wars as others saw looming the disaster called World War II, which began only a few weeks after Ford's death.

Ford intended *Provence* and *Great Trade Route* as parts of "a trilogy in which I project–for what it is worth–my message to the world." A third volume, despite details given in a letter of

what it would contain, was never written, though most of the things enumerated are in *Great Trade Route*. The "message," which also structures *The March of Literature*, is his version of peace and civilization, represented by "the great prehistoric Trade Route" that began in legendary Cathay, traveled westward for purposes of trade but also served cultural interchange. In Provence it turned north and moved up the Rhone, taking in Paris, and after jumping the English Channel took in London and the Cinque Ports area. In fact, it touched all the places dear to Ford. In the second volume, when the route leaped the Atlantic by way of the Azores, it took in New York City before it ended in Memphis, Tennessee. Obviously, there is nothing objective to bear out such a notion. As historical metaphor, the route stands for cultural pluralism, temperateness, and moderation; it is small and local at any point yet part of a grand design, self-serving but concerned for others, else self could not be served. It is on the order of the system of historical change Karl Marx called "Dialectical Materialism," or the cycles of history Yeats devised out of astrology and the like. It has the truth that metaphor and symbol have; it has the untruth that metaphor and symbol have. It shows the same faith in the value of art that Yeats's great poem "Lapis Lazuli" does.

As a "depressed optimist" Ford offers the conclusions of a lifetime of thought in an effort to save a dying world for human beings. Provence had been his longtime personal image of such salvation. The desire to retire from a technology-dominated world to the fundamentals of a small farm in Provence had been a recurrent grace note for Ford since early in the century. Clearly "a state of mind as well as a real place," Provence was equally a place in the heart of his German father, who had written about its poets, and of his French-born grandfather, who had lived and painted there. It supplied the physical details for the "workable heaven" in his poem "On Heaven"; it was the "corner in France" that was the ultimate earthly reward in boyhood games, the substance of which he describes in the *Buckshee* poems. Stang, in *Ford Madox Ford*, compares it to Yeats's Byzantium as a "region where the soul can live . . . his image of the golden age . . . not of pre-civilization but of civilization at its best." It is, says Ford in *Provence*, a "blessed oasis in the insupportable madhouse for apes that is our civilization." It embodies the "gladness" and "loveliness that in the end civilization should be." Provence stands for the blessings that come after power is rejected in all forms, including great wealth.

A harsh view of Ford's late works is held by Robert Green. He may take the author's metaphors too literally. Green feels that "reality is trivialized" because of Ford's frequent remarks on diet. He sees a "retreat from significance" into a private world "hermetically sealed from any contact with a living reality of exertion and disappointment," as if Ford wrote in a cocoon. Almost certainly, Ford himself did not see his last decade in that way, but rather the effort of an artist to use the resources of his art in a public cause. Fifty years later people are concerned more and more about the importance of diet and redistributing food resources, thus confirming Ford's interests as legitimate.

Reluctantly (because he had covered the material many times before), Ford agreed to do a series of magazine pieces for the *American Mercury* on "the history of the great in letters" as he had known them. He is very much present in the essays, which were published in book form as *Portraits from Life* (1937). Usually, he portrays his man as he first saw him, then gives an anecdote in a kind of benevolent pastiche that captures the qualities of the man and his conversational style. Theodore Dreiser, for example, "hurls gigantic trains of polyphonic, linked insults" in which for the moment Ford becomes "a Nazi Jew-baiter; a perfidious Briton; an American financier; the proprietor of brothels in Paris; an unpractical poet; a mere unit floating in and indistinguishable from eleven hundred million similar units; a Jewish proprietor of chain-goods stores; a hereditary aristocrat; an incapable and reactionary small farmer; a Washington hanger-on. . . . " After an explanation by Dreiser that he is "emphatic by nature," the insults resume.

The book has chapters on W. H. Hudson, Thomas Hardy, H. G. Wells, John Galsworthy, Ivan Turgenev, Theodore Dreiser, Algernon Charles Swinburne, Crane, Conrad, Lawrence, and James. All the old stories told long ago are told again. Ford's capability as a critic is startlingly illustrated in his essay on Lawrence by an anecdote from his days as editor of the *English Review*. He accepted for publication on the strength of the first paragraph the unknown author's "Odor of Chrysanthemums" and concluded that he had discovered "another genius . . . a big one this time." Later in the essay, he analyzes that first paragraph with authority and brilliance. What Ford said of Lawrence could as easily be said of himself: "Because this man knows. He knows how to pen a story with a sentence of the right cadence for holding the attention. He knows how to construct a paragraph. He knows the life he is writing about in a landscape just sufficiently constructed with a casual word here and there. You can trust him for the rest." In short, here is an artist who knows how he gets his effects.

Ford is still harsh in *Portraits from Life* on "the mid-Victorian Great Figure," even seeing World War I as "the logical corollary of the bitter-hating age" that produced the great figures. "Wouldn't," he asks, "Poison Gas be just the sort of thing that, could they have invented it, the Ruskins and Carlyles and Wilberforces and Holman Hunts would have employed on their enemies or their blood-brothers become rivals?" There is, too, the faith in the worth of true art that results from "an essential honesty–of writing, of purpose, of selection, of presentation." Ford no doubt hopes he has those indispensable literary qualities that will cause readers to "rediscover him among the shards of ruined Empires." Perhaps the preliminary excavation is Moser's response to this as "a wonderful book."

The March of Literature, written in deteriorating health and published in 1938, was Ford's last service to literature in his life, and his longest book. It grew out of his experiences as a teacher at Olivet College. His effort is nominally to instruct American students in the great tradition of literature, in the service of which he had spent his life. MacShane calls it "his literary testimonial, the outgrowth of all his reading and writing and the fullest statement of his literary credo." Ford insists that the only way he can cause more people to undergo the advantages literature confers is, "contrary to the habits of the learned," to write only about the books he has found attractive. He regards all good writers as contemporary and ranges freely between present and past. The result is "extraordinarily vivid and readable," as MacShane says. The breadth of Ford's knowledge is astonishing. He responds to dozens of writers and works, one by one. Which man of his or any other generation could have written such a book in such readable prose? MacShane is right when he calls Ford "the last really rounded man of letters our century has known." *The March of Literature* is a vindication, if one is needed, of "the old man mad about writing."

Eight months after the book was published, on 26 June 1939, Ford died and was buried in Deauville, his last "corner in France." Three people attended his funeral. "A true man of letters," MacShane says, "he died with a contract for a new book on his desk and with some two hundred manuscripts by young writers in his hotel room." World War II began in September.

Ford's original title for *The Good Soldier* was "The Saddest Story," which Mizener took as the title and theme of his biography, but perhaps the real "saddest story" is, as Stang puts it in *Ford Madox Ford*, "the simple fact that except for a handful of his books, Ford is largely unread today." The signs are now strong that such will not always be the case.

Letters:

Letters of Ford Madox Ford, edited by Richard M. Ludwig (Princeton: Princeton University Press, 1962);

Pound / Ford, the Story of a Literary Friendship: The Correspondence between Ezra Pound and Ford Madox Ford and Their Writings about Each Other, edited by Brita Lindberg-Seyersted (New York: New Directions, 1982);

The Ford Madox Ford Reader, edited by Sondra Stang, includes sixty previously unpublished Ford letters (Manchester: Carcanet, 1986; New York: Ecco, 1986).

Bibliographies:

David Dow Harvey, *Ford Madox Ford, 1873-1939: A Bibliography of Works and Criticism* (Princeton: Princeton University Press, 1962);

Linda Tamkin, "A Secondary Source Bibliography on Ford Madox Ford, 1962-1979," *Antaeus* (Spring 1986): 219-230;

Rita Malenczyk, "A Secondary Source Bibliography on Ford Madox Ford, 1979-1985," *Antaeus* (Spring 1986): 231-244.

Biographies:

Douglas Goldring, *The Last Pre-Raphaelite: The Life and Writings of Ford Madox Ford* (London: Macdonald, 1948); republished as *Trained for Genius: The Life and Writings of Ford Madox Ford* (New York: Dutton, 1949);

Frank MacShane, *The Life and Works of Ford Madox Ford* (New York: Horizon, 1965);

Arthur Mizener, *The Saddest Story: A Biography of Ford Madox Ford* (Cleveland: World, 1971);

Thomas C. Moser, *The Life in the Fiction of Ford Madox Ford* (Princeton: Princeton University Press, 1980);

Nicholas Delbanco, *Group Portrait: Joseph Conrad, Stephen Crane, Ford Madox Ford, Henry James, and H. G. Wells* (New York: Morrow, 1982).

References:

Robert J. Andreach, *The Slain and Resurrected God: Conrad, Ford, and the Christian Myth* (New York: New York University Press, 1970);

Stella Bowen, *Drawn from Life: Reminiscences* (London: Collins, 1941);

Richard A. Cassell, *Ford Madox Ford: A Study of His Novels* (Baltimore: Johns Hopkins University Press, 1961);

Cassell, ed., *Ford Madox Ford: Modern Judgments* (London: Macmillan, 1972);

Douglas Goldring, *South Lodge: Reminiscences of Violet Hunt, Ford Madox Ford and the English Review Circle* (London: Constable, 1943);

Ambrose Gordon, Jr., *The Invisible Tent: The War Novels of Ford Madox Ford* (Austin: University of Texas Press, 1964);

Caroline Gordon, *A Good Soldier: A Key to the Novels of Ford Madox Ford* (Davis: University of California Library, 1963);

Robert Green, *Ford Madox Ford: Prose and Politics* (Cambridge: Cambridge University Press, 1981);

Charles G. Hoffman, *Ford Madox Ford* (New York: Twayne, 1967);

Violet Hunt, *I Have This To Say* (New York: Boni & Liveright, 1926);

H. Robert Huntley, *The Alien Protagonist of Ford Madox Ford* (Chapel Hill: University of North Carolina Press, 1970);

Norman Leer, *The Limited Hero in the Novels of Ford Madox Ford* (East Lansing: Michigan State University Press, 1966);

R. W. Lid, *Ford Madox Ford: The Essence of His Art* (Berkeley: University of California Press, 1964);

Frank MacShane, ed., *Ford Madox Ford: The Critical Heritage* (London: Routledge & Kegan Paul, 1972);

John A. Meixner, *Ford Madox Ford's Novels* (Minneapolis: University of Minnesota Press, 1962);

Carol Ohmann, *Ford Madox Ford: From Apprentice to Craftsman* (Middletown, Conn.: Wesleyan University Press, 1964);

Bernard J. Poli, *Ford Madox Ford and the Transatlantic Review* (Syracuse, N.Y.: Syracuse University Press, 1967);

C. Ruth Sabol and Todd K. Bender, *A Concordance to Ford Madox Ford's The Good Soldier* (New York: Garland, 1981);

Grover Smith, *Ford Madox Ford* (New York: Columbia University Press, 1972);

Anne Barr Snitow, *Ford Madox Ford and the Voice of Uncertainty* (Baton Rouge: Louisiana State University Press, 1984);

Sondra J. Stang, *Ford Madox Ford* (New York: Ungar, 1977);

Stang, ed., *The Presence of Ford Madox Ford: A Memorial Volume of Essays, Poems, and Memoirs* (Philadelphia: University of Pennsylvania Press, 1981);

Stang and Daniel Halpern, eds., Special Ford Madox Ford Issue, *Antaeus*, no. 56 (Spring 1986);

Timothy Weiss, *Fairy Tale and Romance in Works of Ford Madox Ford* (New York: University Press of America, 1984);

Paul L. Wiley, *Novelist of Three Worlds: Ford Madox Ford* (Syracuse, N.Y.: Syracuse University Press, 1962);

Kenneth Young, *Ford Madox Ford* (London: Longmans, 1956).

Papers:

The following libraries hold significant collections of Ford materials: Cornell, Huntington, New York Public Library, Princeton, University of Texas (Austin), and Yale.

E. M. Forster

(1 January 1879 - 8 June 1970)

Philip Gardner
Memorial University of Newfoundland

See also the Forster entry in *DLB 34, British Novelists, 1890-1929: Traditionalists.*

BOOKS: *Where Angels Fear to Tread* (Edinburgh & London: Blackwood, 1905; New York: Knopf, 1920);

The Longest Journey (Edinburgh & London: Blackwood, 1907; New York: Knopf, 1922);

A Room with a View (London: Arnold, 1908; New York & London: Putnam's, 1911);

Howards End (London: Arnold, 1910; New York & London: Putnam's, 1910);

The Celestial Omnibus and other Stories (London: Sidgwick & Jackson, 1911; New York: Knopf, 1923);

The Story of the Siren (Richmond: Leonard & Virginia Woolf at the Hogarth Press, 1920);

The Government of Egypt, Recommendations by a Committee of the International Section of the Labour Research Department, with Notes on Egypt by E. M. Forster (London: Labour Research Department, 1920);

Alexandria: A History and a Guide (Alexandria: Whitehead Morris, 1922; Garden City, N.Y.: Doubleday, 1961; London: Michael Haag, 1982);

Pharos and Pharillon (Richmond: Leonard & Virginia Woolf at the Hogarth Press, 1923; New York: Knopf, 1923);

A Passage to India (London: Arnold, 1924; New York: Harcourt, Brace, 1924);

Anonymity: An Enquiry (London: Leonard & Virginia Woolf at the Hogarth Press, 1925);

Aspects of the Novel (London: Arnold, 1927; New York: Harcourt, Brace, 1927);

The Eternal Moment and other Stories (London: Sidgwick & Jackson, 1928; New York: Harcourt, Brace, 1928);

A Letter to Madan Blanchard (London: Leonard & Virginia Woolf at the Hogarth Press, 1931; New York: Harcourt, Brace, 1932);

Sinclair Lewis Interprets America (Cambridge, Mass.: Harvard Press, 1932);

Goldsworthy Lowes Dickinson (London: Arnold, 1934; New York: Harcourt, Brace, 1934);

Pageant of Abinger, in Aid of the Parish Church Preservation Fund (Dorking: Printed by A. A. Tanner & Son, 1934);

Abinger Harvest (London: Arnold, 1936; New York: Harcourt, Brace, 1936);

What I Believe (London: Hogarth Press, 1939);

England's Pleasant Land, a Pageant Play (London: Hogarth Press, 1940);

Nordic Twilight, Macmillan War Pamphlet, no. 3 (London: Macmillan, 1940);

Virginia Woolf: The Rede Lecture (Cambridge: Cambridge University Press, 1942; New York: Harcourt, Brace, 1942);

The Development of English Prose between 1918 and 1939 (Glasgow: Jackson, Son, 1945);

The Collected Tales of E. M. Forster (New York: Knopf, 1947); republished as *Collected Short Stories of E. M. Forster* (London: Sidgwick & Jackson, 1948);

Two Cheers for Democracy (London: Arnold, 1951; New York: Harcourt, Brace, 1951);

Billy Budd: an Opera in Four Acts. Libretto by E. M. Forster and Eric Crozier, Adapted from the Story by Herman Melville (London, New York, Toronto, Sydney, Capetown, Buenos Aires, Paris & Bonn: Boosey & Hawkes, 1951);

The Hill of Devi (London: Arnold, 1953; New York: Harcourt, Brace, 1953);

Marianne Thornton (1797-1887): A Domestic Biography (London: Arnold, 1956; New York: Harcourt, Brace, 1956);

Maurice (London: Arnold, 1971; New York: Norton, 1971);

Albergo Empedocle and other Writings by E. M. Forster, edited by George H. Thomson (New York: Liveright, 1971);

The Life to Come and other Stories (London: Arnold, 1972); republished as *The Life to Come and Other Short Stories* (New York: Norton, 1972);

E. M. Forster, 1950 (by permission of Mrs. May Buckingham)

The Manuscripts of "Howards End," edited by Oliver Stallybrass (London: Arnold, 1973; New York: Holmes & Meier, 1978);

Goldsworthy Lowes Dickinson and Related Writings, edited by Stallybrass (London: Arnold, 1973; New York: Holmes & Meier, 1978);

Aspects of the Novel and related Writings, edited by Stallybrass (London: Arnold, 1974; New York: Holmes & Meier, 1978);

The Lucy Novels: Early Sketches for "A Room with a View," edited by Stallybrass (London: Arnold, 1977; New York: Holmes & Meier, 1978);

The Manuscripts of "A Passage to India," edited by Stallybrass (London: Arnold, 1978; New York: Holmes & Meier, 1979);

Commonplace Book, facsimile edition (London: Scolar Press, 1978);

Arctic Summer and other Fiction, edited by Elizabeth Heine and Stallybrass (London: Arnold, 1980; New York: Holmes & Meier, 1981);

The Hill of Devi and Other Indian Writings, edited by Heine (London: Arnold, 1983; New York: Holmes & Meier, 1983);

Commonplace Book, edited by Philip Gardner (London: Scolar Press, 1985; Stanford: Stanford University Press, 1985).

Collection: *The Abinger Edition of E. M. Forster*, 14 volumes, edited by Oliver Stallybrass and Elizabeth Heine (London: Arnold, 1972-1984; New York: Holmes & Meier, 1972-1984).

E. M. Forster's reputation as a writer may justly be said to rest, essentially, on his novels. His output as a novelist was not large: only six novels were completed, of which the fifth, *Maurice* (finished in 1914), became available to readers only after his death in 1970. Nevertheless Forster belongs, with D. H. Lawrence and Virginia Woolf, in the front rank of twentieth-century English novelists, and his last novel, the undisputed masterpiece *A Passage to India*, not only continues to attract the educated general reader but figures in the curricula of university departments of English all over the world.

The writing of novels, however, occupied Forster only from about 1900 (the composition date of his first, unfinished attempt at one, published in 1980 under the title *Nottingham Lace*) to

1924, when *A Passage to India* appeared. He had also written short stories from the very beginning of his career, and a few late examples of these, at ever-widening intervals, prolonged his activity in fiction until the early 1960s. But what engaged Forster throughout a far longer period of his ninety-one-year life was the writing of various forms of nonfiction, beginning with short essays published when he was a student and ending with longer essays and reviews published as late as the mid 1960s, by which time he had become the Grand Old Man of English letters.

This status in his lifetime owed at least as much to the alert and sensitive intelligence, the human commitment, and the accessible yet subtle style of his many essays (particularly those collected in *Abinger Harvest* of 1936 and in *Two Cheers for Democracy* of 1951) as it did to his fiction, where a gift for shrewd social observation was unusually blended with a deeper poetic response to life. For various personal and external reasons Forster's fictional imagination ceased to operate at full power after his fifth decade; but as an essayist, a reviewer, and what may conveniently be termed a historian, he continued to function to within only a few years of his death, producing his last sizable work, the "domestic biography" *Marianne Thornton* (1956), at the age of seventy-five, and making the last of many entries in his *Commonplace Book* when he was eighty-eight. Though at times it not unnaturally flagged, Forster never lost (and never lost the ability to express) his interest in three predominant things: people, places, and books. When one examines Forster's nonfictional writings, this range of responsiveness is found to leave little out of account, and to be transmitted with a freshness which enables the personality of Forster himself to survive the frequent dating of his subject matter. What that "personality" was, and what it remains through Forster's many essays and longer pieces, is accidentally caught in a description of André Gide which Forster gave in "Gide and George," first published as "Humanist and Authoritarian" (*Listener*, 26 August 1943): "He is a humanist. The humanist has four leading characteristics–curiosity, a free mind, belief in good taste, and a belief in the human race." In "Voltaire and Frederick the Great," (first published as "But . . . ," *Listener*, 23 January 1941), describing the not quite identical characteristics of Voltaire, Forster explicitly claimed them as his: "Voltaire cared for the truth, he believed in tolerance, he pitied the oppressed, and since he was a

forceful character he was able to drive his ideas home. They happen to be my own ideas."

Of well-to-do professional antecedents on his father's side and poorer, artistic ones on his mother's, Edward Morgan Forster was born at 6 Melcombe Place, in the Marylebone district of central London, on 1 January 1879. An earlier sibling having died at birth, Forster was destined to remain an only child, since his father, Edward Morgan Llewellyn Forster, an architect, died of consumption in October 1880. Forster's upbringing thus passed entirely into the hands of his mother, Alice Clara Forster, to whom he very soon became devoted, and of various female relatives on both sides of the family: his maternal grandmother Louisa Graham Whichelo (later the model for Mrs. Honeychurch in *A Room with a View*, 1908); his father's cousin by marriage Maimie Synnot; and his paternal great-aunt, the dominating but benevolent Marianne Thornton, who died in 1887 and left Forster the sum of £8,000. This money from "Aunt Monie" paid for his school and university education, between 1890 and 1900, and enabled him first to travel and then to concentrate, without the need to find other employment, on becoming a writer. Nearly seventy years after his great-aunt's death, returning with a characteristic mixture of objective curiosity and family piety to his own past and what had led up to it, Forster devoted his last full-scale energies as a writer to the biography of her, which both proclaimed his debt ("she and no one else made my career as a writer possible") and repaid it.

Marianne Thornton, published in 1956, bore the simple dedication "To My Mother"; not "To the Memory of My Mother," although Forster's mother had died eleven years previously. This sense of her as still living and accessible (or declaration of the wish to keep her so) is of a piece with Forster's general view of "the past," so many aspects of which provide the material of numerous published essays, from the earliest of this type, "Macolnia Shops" (1903; republished in *Abinger Harvest*), to perhaps the latest, "Recollections of Nassenheide," which appeared in the *Listener* on Forster's eightieth birthday in 1959. Toward the end of *Marianne Thornton*, Forster devoted a chapter to his early childhood spent with his mother in rural Hertfordshire–all the year round from 1883 to 1890, and from 1890 to 1893 on his vacations from Kent House preparatory school in Eastbourne. Forster's years at Rooksnest, the house near Stevenage which his

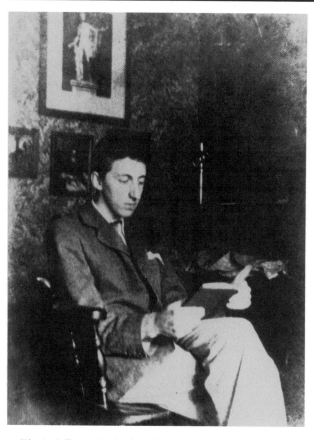

Forster at King's College, Cambridge, circa 1901 (by permission of the Provost and Scholars of King's College, Cambridge)

mother rented in order to give her son the benefit of country air, and which became the model for the Wilcox house in *Howards End* (1910), were the most idyllic of his life. Rooksnest itself, with its surrounding garden and panoramic view to the north and northeast, was the subject of Forster's first piece of extended nonfictional prose, a twelve-page descriptive memoir (complete with detailed map) which he wrote in 1894 and which was eventually appended to the Abinger Edition (1973) of *Howards End*. There is nothing stylistically remarkable about this performance of a fifteen-year-old schoolboy, but the impulse behind it–the wish to preserve the value of the past from oblivion–was to recur throughout Forster's life as a writer.

Forster's Rooksnest memoir was the work of an exile uprooted from Eden and dropped down into the uncongenial world of the English public school. Forster spent the years 1893 to 1897 at Tonbridge School in Kent, his mother having moved to Tonbridge (and later to nearby Tunbridge Wells) so that he could attend as a day boy. His dislike of the school itself surfaced in

the "Sawston" section of *The Longest Journey* (1907); that name, applied to the school, had already been used in *Where Angels Fear to Tread* (1905) to describe the conformist, philistine provinciality of its small-town setting. In Forster's later life, dissatisfaction with his school days still rankled. Contributing a "Letter from the College" to the December 1961 issue of *Fleur-de-Lys*, the magazine of King's College School, Cambridge, he wrote apropos of his preparatory school in Eastbourne that "we were just told that 'school is the world in miniature' and as far as my experience goes it isn't." Asked to contribute to a collection of pieces by "Old Boys" of Tonbridge, Forster subversively offered an essay to be called "How I got out of playing games at Tonbridge." The editor's refusal to accept such an approach suggests that little had changed since the pomposity embodied in Forster's fictional housemaster Herbert Pembroke. Nevertheless, B. J. Kirkpatrick records as the earliest items in her Soho bibliography of Forster two pieces written by him at Tonbridge and published in *Prolusiones Praemiis Annuis Dignatae, in Scola*

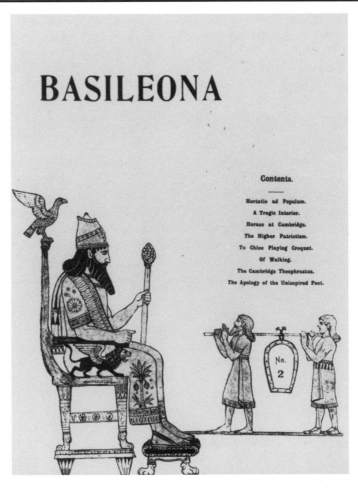

Cover for the 21 November 1900 issue of the King's College to which Forster contributed some of his earliest essays.
In addition to "A Tragic Interior" and "The Cambridge Theophrastus," both listed above, Forster also wrote
"The Pack of Anchises" for this issue.

Tonbrigiensi, a Tonbridge School prize compilation, in 1897. The first, a Latin poem titled "Trafalgar," may have originated as much in family piety (perhaps a wish to please his mother) as in history-book patriotism (an impulse of which his far later essay *What I Believe*, [1939] is famously suspicious): his maternal ancestor Richard Mayle Whichelo had been fleet paymaster aboard H.M.S. *Victory* and had painted a highly regarded portrait of Admiral Horatio Nelson. The second piece was an English essay which, though in style a pastiche of John Ruskin (to be treated less reverently in *Howards End*), in its subject matter adumbrated interests which recurred in various forms in Forster's later writing: it was dryly titled "The Influence of Climate and Physical Conditions upon National Character."

In the autumn of 1897 Forster entered King's College, Cambridge, for whose liberating atmosphere–a total contrast to Tonbridge–he remained grateful all his life. His academic performance was respectable rather than brilliant. In his first subject, classics, he reached the same level as he facetiously attributed, perhaps recalling himself, to the Italian Renaissance physician whose story he told in an early essay: accused of atheism, Girolamo Cardano "was placed in the first division of the second class." In his second subject, history, Forster attained only a lower second. His love of ancient Greece, however, took a more personal form in his essay of 1904, "Cnidus" (written after a visit to its ruins in Asia Minor); and history in general provided him with the material for many essays from "Cardan" (1905) onward. Forster's response to the English novel, elegantly demonstrated in 1927 in *Aspects of the Novel*, and more summarily in many shrewd entries made about that time in his *Commonplace Book*, was first revealed in an essay he wrote in 1899 for a King's College prize. Though uninspiringly titled "The Novelists of the 18th Century and their influence on those of the

19th," it won a half-share. While a student Forster submitted for another prize an essay, of forty pages, on "The Relation of Dryden to Milton and Pope." The outcome of this competition is not recorded, and except for a few *Commonplace Book* entries the area was not one to which he returned in later life. However, the poetic pseudonym with which Forster signed his essay, "Peer Gynt," clearly indicates the widening out of his undergraduate literary awareness to the significant writers of his own time.

Forster's earliest contributions to that literature were essays written at Cambridge and published while he was still there, in 1900 and 1901. For two of these, which appeared in the long-established *Cambridge Review*, he used his "Peer Gynt" pseudonym; the rest (some half dozen) appeared unsigned in the first issues of the jokingly named King's College magazine *Basileona (basileus* is Greek for "king," as practically every public schoolboy then knew). None of these early essays, intended essentially for university consumption, were republished by Forster himself. They did not reappear until 1971, when George Thomson included them in *Albergo Empedocle and other Writings*, an edited collection of pieces which Forster wrote (and separately published) between 1900 and 1915.

Thomson performed a valuable historical service in resurrecting Forster's undergraduate essays; but considered simply as literature they now have a rather faded air, though they brought Forster some local notice when they first came out. A few are parodic: his two descriptions of Cambridge "characters" ("The Stall-Holder" and "The Early Father") in the manner of Theophrastus; his more lively debunking versions ("A Tragic Interior 1 and 2," *Basileona*, 21 November 1900 and 21 February 1901) of Aeschylus's *Agamemnon* and *The Choephori*; and his brief, four-part "Strivings after Historical Style" (*Basileona*, June 1901). Others, such as "A Long Day" (*Basileona*, 1 June 1900), a description of a visit to Cambridge by two of Forster's relatives in 1899, and "A Brisk Walk" (*Basileona*, 21 February 1901) are a blend of the pedantic and the whimsical. A further essay, "On Grinds" (*Cambridge Review*, 1 February 1900), a comparison of the various standard walks in the environs of Cambridge, is unlikely to involve present-day readers in the niceties of deciding the relative merits of "those who walk by Trumpington to Grantchester" and "those who walk by Grantchester to Trumpington." They may, however, remember-

ing *The Longest Journey*, be struck by its passing reference to "the little chalk pit this side of the village" (Madingley) where "the happy few . . . may wander among the firs and undergrowth, folded off from the outer world." In a word, the interest of Forster's Cambridge essays lies less in what they achieve than in their suggestion of a versatile talent in the process of "trying out."

With two fellows of King's, Forster formed particularly important friendships: his tutor in classics, Nathaniel Wedd, and the political scientist Goldsworthy Lowes Dickinson, whose biography Forster wrote in 1933, a year after Dickinson's death. These two friends, and another from Trinity College, the historian G. M. Trevelyan, became members in 1903 of the editorial board of the *Independent Review*, a newly founded Liberal journal. Forster was invited to contribute, and it was in the earliest issues of this influential, forward-looking magazine (whose general style Forster's biographer P. N. Furbank has, however, characterized as "leather-and-horsehair") that Forster published, between 1903 and 1906, the earliest of his essays which he chose to republish in *Abinger Harvest*. (A further essay, which appeared in the June 1906 issue of the *Independent Review*, was left for George Thomson to disinter in 1971. Titled "Rostock and Wismar," it is a rather mocking sketch–mostly architectural–of two eminently bourgeois Hanseatic towns which Forster visited in 1905 while serving as tutor to the children of Elizabeth, Countess von Arnim, at her estate at Nassenheide, north of Berlin.)

The four essays which Forster chose to republish in *Abinger Harvest* sprang from visits, and interests, far more important to him. In late 1901 and early 1902 he visited Italy and Sicily for the first time, and his experiences there, in addition to sparking off short stories and planting the seeds of two novels, prompted him to write what he called "sentimental articles." The thrust behind these is indicated in one (unpublished) concerning Syracuse: "Those who cannot understand the past with the knowledge of the archaeologist or recreate it with the genius of the poet, must perforce call in sentiment and dream inaccurately of its greatness." In "Macolnia Shops" (*Independent Review*, November 1903) Forster exercised his recreating imagination on a bronze toilet case he encountered in the Kirchner Museum in Rome. While not underrating the historical import ("Praise of Water! Praise of Friendship!") of the mythological figures engraved on it, Forster

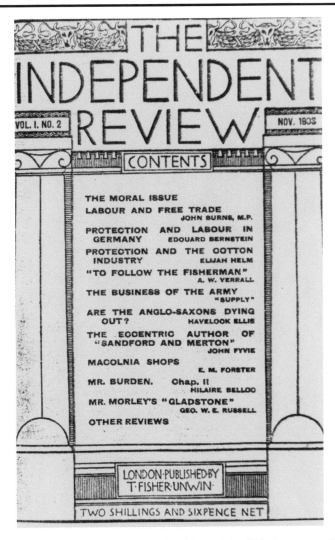

THE
INDEPENDENT
REVIEW
VOL. I. NO. 2   NOV. 1903
CONTENTS

THE MORAL ISSUE
LABOUR AND FREE TRADE
        JOHN BURNS, M.P.

PROTECTION AND LABOUR IN
GERMANY   EDOUARD BERNSTEIN
PROTECTION AND THE COTTON
INDUSTRY   ELIJAH HELM
"TO FOLLOW THE FISHERMAN"
        A. W. VERRALL
THE BUSINESS OF THE ARMY
        "SUPPLY"
ARE THE ANGLO-SAXONS DYING
OUT?   HAVELOCK ELLIS
THE ECCENTRIC AUTHOR OF
"SANDFORD AND MERTON"
        JOHN FYVIE
MACOLNIA SHOPS
        E. M. FORSTER
MR. BURDEN.   Chap. II
        HILAIRE BELLOC
MR. MORLEY'S "GLADSTONE"
        GEO. W. E. RUSSELL
OTHER REVIEWS

LONDON·PUBLISHED·BY
T·FISHER·UNWIN·
TWO SHILLINGS AND SIXPENCE NET

Cover, designed by Roger Fry, for an issue of the Liberal journal to which Forster contributed the earliest of the essays that he chose to collect in Abinger Harvest *(1936)*

placed his final emphasis on the aesthetic attractiveness it possessed in its own age, which surely was what made a real Roman matron buy it as a present for her daughter. And when, at Easter 1903, Forster took an educational cruise from Italy to Greece and landed near the ruins of Cnidus in dusk and rain, what he came away with, and "fixed" in his essay "Cnidus" (*Independent Review*, March 1904), was not a list of facts and buildings (which he treats ironically), but a sense of the livingness of ancient Greece, embodied in a ghostly "extra person" who "melted away in the darkness" and whose identity is left for the reader to explicate.

The other two essays, "Cardan" and "Gemistus Pletho" (*Independent Review*, April, October 1905), are longer and more straightforwardly historical, drawing a great many facts from

Forster's reading and linking them together in an expository style of great crispness and clarity. Nevertheless, the impulse behind them is the same as for "Cnidus" and "Macolnia Shops": to reinvigorate history by humanizing it. Both are the stories of men whom Forster found fascinating, partly as individuals, partly because of the civilizations and periods to which they belonged: Cardan the doctor to Italy of the late Renaissance and the Counter-Reformation, Gemistus the Neoplatonist (hence his appellation "Pletho") to the later days of the Byzantine Empire. "Gemistus Pletho" is also, however, in part a response to landscape: to the plains of Sparta and the great Frankish fortress town of Mistra, rising out of them, which was the home of Gemistus before he went to Florence and cofounded its Neoplatonic Academy, and which (before he turned

Forster (second from right) in Rhodes during his Easter 1903 cruise from Italy to Greece (by permission of the Provost and Scholars of King's College, Cambridge)

to his essay) inspired Forster to begin a short story, "The Tomb of Pletone," which he was unable to complete.

For Gemistus Forster felt the gratitude of a modern agnostic humanist for one who, in a Christian age, had tried to recapture–like Forster in contemporary short stories such as "The Story of a Panic" (*Independent Review*, August 1904)–the spirit of ancient Greece and pass it on. Gemistus had put part of this effort into a work he called *The Laws*, an abstract revamping of ancient Greek religion. Forster found this work frigid and overdogmatic; and yet his final comment on Gemistus presents him as a type of human aspiration, however misguided, and thus worthy of tribute: "If he is absurd, it is in a very touching way; his dream of antiquity is grotesque and incongruous, but it has a dream's intensity, and something of a dream's imperishable value." Cardan also dreamed, but fitfully and often inconsequentially; once famous as a doctor and a mathematician, he fell foul of Catholic orthodoxy in later life (though not fatally), but always believed in "the other world" and hoped for immortality.

This, in a sense, he attained through his candid and quirky autobiography, since Forster's lively, sympathetic essay is based on it. The precise nature of Forster's response is made clear in his brief final paragraph, which jumps the gap of time between commentator and subject to present Cardan as a real person, faults and virtues blended, not as a bottled specimen from an extinct past: "To raise up a skeleton, and make it dance, brings indeed little credit either to the skeleton or to us. But those ghosts who are still clothed with passion or thought are profitable companions. If we are to remember Cardan today, let us not remember him as an oddity."

Between 1905 and World War I, Forster's preoccupation with fiction, from *The Longest Journey* to *Maurice* (1971), largely displaced essays from his output. In 1907 and 1908 his part-time teaching for the Working Men's College in London resulted in two lectures, "Pessimism in Literature" and "Dante," which were printed in its journal (January-February 1907 and February-April 1908); but no nonfiction is recorded by Kirkpatrick for 1909 and 1910, when Forster was writing *Howards End*. A few more lectures appeared later, notably "The Function of Literature in War-Time" (*Working Men's College Journal*, March 1915); but Forster chose to republish neither earlier nor later ones in his collections. Forster's first visit to India (six months that straddled 1912 and 1913) added fuel to the interest in India already kindled by his friendship, dating from 1906, with Syed Ross Masood (later vice-chancellor of Aligarh Muslim University); but, here again, few of the nonfictional writings which it stimulated (among them various reviews, printed in 1914, of books on Indian topics by Indians) ever saw republication in Forster's lifetime.

Forster spent the years 1915 to 1919 in Egypt, working in Alexandria as a "Searcher" for the Red Cross, an interviewer of the wounded in hospitals for information about missing soldiers. Here, in 1917, during the temporary absence of Mohammed el Adl, a young tram conductor with whom he had fallen in love, Forster began to contribute articles to the *Egyptian Mail*. Only one of these was republished by Forster in *Abinger Harvest*: dealing with a wartime concert party called "The Scallies" (18 November 1917), it employs the facetious tone which made his contributions popular with fellow Britishers temporarily in foreign parts (another, published in the 16 December 1917 issue, was called "Gippo English"). Forster was, however, more seriously drawn to Alexandria, partly because of its history as a melting pot and meeting point of East and West, partly because his own love affair–a contemporary instance of this–had cast over the city the kind of glamour of which, for many readers, Lawrence Durrell's *Alexandria Quartet* (1957-1960) has been the most haunting embodiment. Forster's pieces for the *Egyptian Mail* were signed with a new pen name, Pharos, the name of the ancient lighthouse at Alexandria which had been one of the Seven Wonders of the World. Gradually he formed the notion of writing a history of, and guidebook to, the city.

Published in 1922, but only in Alexandria, *Alexandria: A History and a Guide* was for decades the most difficult of Forster's books to obtain: it was not published in the United States until 1961, or in England until 1982. It is exactly what it purports to be (the "Guide" section is as comprehensive as the Baedekers carried by Forster's fictional tourists in Italy); but mention must be made of Forster's other book in Alexandria, first published in England in May 1923–exactly a year after Mohammed el Adl's death from consump-

tion. Titled *Pharos and Pharillon* (Pharillon was a smaller and later lighthouse), this book was intended by Forster as a tribute to his dead Egyptian friend as well as to his city, and it consists of two sets of essays (eight and six respectively, some already published in Alexandria during the war) framed by a short introduction and a shorter conclusion. Unlike Forster's two large collections of essays (though both *Abinger Harvest* and *Two Cheers for Democracy*, [1951] were arranged and assembled with some care), *Pharos and Pharillon* is a deliberately constructed miniature, in all senses a gem of a book. Its two sections, concerned with the ancient past (pagan to early Christian) and Forster's own present, create a multifaceted and multitonal city of both the mind and the senses. The aspect of the book perhaps most commented on is its introduction to English-speaking readers of the Alexandrian Greek poet C. P. Cavafy, whom Forster had met in 1917: the first section ends appropriately with Cavafy's poem "The God Abandons Antony," the second with a short essay on his work–Forster's tribute to a friendship about which he could be more open. But the whole book is of great charm and often great beauty; especially (in the first section) Forster's essay on one of the milder Church Fathers, Clement of Alexandria, who lived for a brief and precious time in a city which seemed able to reconcile "the graciousness of Greece" with "the Grace of God"; and (in the second section) Forster's lyrical description, titled "The Solitary Place" (first published in the 10 March 1918 issue of the *Egyptian Mail*), of the short-lived and delicate landscape of spring flowers to the west of Lake Mariout or Mareotis.

Forster's Clark Lectures at Cambridge, given in 1927 and published that year as *Aspects of the Novel*, are a witty, elegant, and lucid commentary on the literary form in which he achieved his greatest distinction, a distinction on which his *A Passage to India* (1924) had set the seal. But the lectures were also, as it turned out, his farewell to that form: his concluding remarks, in which he relates the term "the development of the novel" to the more tentative notion "the development of humanity," can now be seen to carry a hint that, without what he called "a new coat of quicksilver," the novel, at least for him, no longer held up a viable mirror to life. There is no evidence that he ever attempted a novel again, though a 1943 entry in his *Commonplace Book* makes it clear that he could still, just, entertain the possibility when a close friend put it to him.

Forster in Alexandria, circa 1916 (by permission of the Provost and Scholars of King's College, Cambridge)

In fact (except for a few short stories and his late revisions to *Maurice*), all Forster's work after 1924 was in nonfiction: two biographies, *Goldsworthy Lowes Dickinson* (1934) and *Marianne Thornton* (1956); *The Hill of Devi* (1953), which is a fascinating combination of biography and autobiography based on, and extensively quoting from, the letters he wrote home from the Native State of Dewas Senior in 1912-1913 and 1921; a handful of essays and lectures published as individual books (between 1925 and 1947); and the two sizable compilations of essays, *Abinger Harvest* (1936) and *Two Cheers for Democracy*, in which (as this writer put it a decade ago) "Forster most clearly appears as a liberal humanist, concerned for the life of the individual, and of the spirit, against philistinism, intolerance, and any kind of political totalitarianism."

This view of both books is true as far as it goes. *Abinger Harvest* begins with "Notes on the En-

glish Character" (first published in the *Atlantic Monthly*, January 1926), a plea for international understanding and tolerance as much as a survey of the strengths and limitations of Englishness ("the undeveloped heart" being Forster's prime example of the latter). The second section of *Two Cheers for Democracy* begins with and takes its subtitle from *What I Believe* (published as a pamphlet in 1939), Forster's assertion of "an aristocracy of the sensitive, the considerate and the plucky" against the overriding claims of the monolithic state. These two are probably Forster's best-known essays, and in both collections there are others which display the same explicit concern for the survival of humane values and individual freedom, notably (in the earlier book) "Liberty in England," the text of Forster's speech in 1935 to the International Congress of Writers in Paris (first published in the *London Mercury*, August 1935); and (in the later) "The Duty of Society to the Art-

Forster during his second visit to India, 1921 (by permission of the Provost and Scholars of King's College, Cambridge)

ist," a radio talk delivered in 1942 and first published in the *Listener* (30 April 1942), which defends the right of the artist, as part of his duty to humanity, not to "fit in," and yet his right, also, to expect the state's tolerance, and even its support.

This concern for humanity, however, is only one aspect of Forster; as, indeed, the essays included in the two books are themselves only a selection from a larger body of previously published prose pieces. *Abinger Harvest*, though reaching back to 1903 for its earliest essay, predominantly consists of some fifty pieces which first appeared between 1919 and 1935; yet in 1919-1920 alone Forster had contributed double that number to the *Nation*, the *Daily News*, the *Daily Herald* (of which he was briefly literary editor), and the *Athenæum*. The sense that, for practical purposes, so many of Forster's prose pieces remain out of sight makes it all the more invidious, and misleading, to select for detailed treatment, as if they were "typical," individual essays from the quite considerable number (there are a further sixty-eight in *Two Cheers for Democracy*) which

Forster did choose to republish. There are not only variations of tone and approach from essay to essay (Forster referred to some as "allusive," to others as "expository"); there are also differences in kind between them. Some, especially in *Two Cheers for Democracy*, are reviews; others (which are essays proper) are free of external motivation, pursuing ideas or celebrating places, people, or incidents, solely. as a result of Forster's own wish to get something clear or give it a degree of permanence. Of this type *Anonymity* (1925) and *A Letter to Madan Blanchard* (1931), both originally published as Hogarth Press pamphlets, are particularly memorable examples; yet each is distinct in tone and atmosphere, *Anonymity* being a logical progression of ideas, *Madan Blanchard* the evocation of an odd episode from the eighteenth century which haunted Forster's imagination. Other essays were originally speeches or invited lectures in which Forster, rather against the grain, adopted a public persona, as for instance in "The Raison d'Être of Criticism in the Arts," delivered at Harvard in 1947. Others again were broadcasts, in which Forster's ability to simplify his material without falsifying it made him very effective and produced a tone at once authoritative and intimate. (It is a pity, in this connection, that Forster never chose to republish, except in the *Listener* [30 April 1930], the generous broadcast he made in 1930 about D. H. Lawrence, with whom as a novelist he had important affinities.)

Forster's own arrangement of the material in *Abinger Harvest* (he speaks in his prefatory note of "eighty" pieces, but in fact there are sixty) is neither chronological nor generic, but in four sections according to subject. (The fifth and last section consists simply of the text of the "Abinger Pageant," put on in aid of Forster's village church. Forster's affection for this part of Surrey, where he lived from 1925 to 1946 with his mother in a house designed by his father, is given public emphasis both by the inclusion of this local item and by the collection's title. He expressed it again, with retrospective sadness, by printing at the end of *Two Cheers for Democracy* some entries relating to the area made in his *Commonplace Book* between 1930 and 1946.) The four sections, each of approximately the same length, are titled "The Present" (glossed by Forster as "a commentary on passing events"), "Books," "The Past," and "The East" (from Egypt to India). The range of matters covered, both across the four sections and within each one, is extraordinarily wide, as is the variation of tone, pace, angle of vision, and scope—whether the baffled close-up of "The Doll Souse" (first published as "The Bad Fairies," *Nation & Athenæum*, 2 August 1924), a kind of nonevent, or the synoptic approach, livened by anecdote, adopted in "The Mind of the Indian Native State" (*Nation & Athenæum*, 29 April and 13 May 1922).

Through all the essays, however, one registers Forster as a man with an alert eye for the telling detail, who responds to what he sees, reads, and hears with emotions ranging from delight to indignation, but always with intelligence and personal concern. His voice is never that of a detached academic observer, but that of a human being reaching out to other human beings, on the one hand his readers, on the other the individuals, dead as well as living, about whom he writes. His essays on authors living or recently dead, such as T. S. Eliot, Marcel Proust, Joseph Conrad, Ronald Firbank, and his friend the Ulster novelist Forrest Reid, are as much reactions to the personalities revealed in their writing as they are comments on the literary value of their work, a point oddly unappreciated by Lionel Trill-

ing, who in 1945 stated that "the quaint, the facetious and the chatty sink [Forster's] literary criticism below its proper level."

The "proper" (in another sense) was something of which Forster was deeply suspicious, as is shown in his satirical essay "Mrs. Grundy at the Parkers" (*New Statesman & Nation*, 10 September 1932), and in his essay (*Listener*, 31 July 1935) on T. E. Lawrence, a personal friend, with its splendidly irreverent first sentence: "The little man who is labelled for posterity as Lawrence of Arabia detested the title." That debunking, but not therefore destructive, approach is most wittily displayed at the start of Forster's long and appreciative essay "Salute to the Orient!" (*London Mercury*, July 1921): "Salute to the Orient! Given at Port Said presumably, where the statue of M. de Lesseps points to the Suez Canal with one hand and waves in the other a heavy bunch of large stone sausages. 'Me voici!' he gesticulates, adding 'Le voilà' as an afterthought." Such an opening, however quaint, irresistibly draws the reader in, as does the first sentence of Forster's essay on Edward Gibbon, one of his three favorite authors (the others being Shakespeare and Jane Austen, on whom there are three essays in *Abinger Harvest*). Forster enjoys the indirect approach, preceding seriousness with a quirky briskness or a fanciful whimsicality which is by no means without point. Beginning his essay on "The Early Novels of Virginia Woolf" (first published as "The Novels of Virginia Woolf," *New Criterion*, April 1926), he loses the fountain pen with which he is to write it; beginning "Captain Edward Gibbon" (first published as "Incongruities: Captain Gibbon," *New York Herald Tribune*, 16 August 1931), he looks out from his garden at West Hackhurst and almost recaptures the living past: "The garden where I am writing slopes down to a field, the field to a road, and along that road exactly a hundred and seventy years ago passed a young officer with a rather large head." By the end of the essay that "rather large head" is seen to contain within it *The Decline and Fall of the Roman Empire* (1776-1788). A similar technique (the mark of a writer in full control of his style and form) is used to astonishingly moving effect in "Me, Them and You" (*New Leader*, 22 January 1926), in which an ironic view of the ruling class (among whom Forster includes himself) gives place to compassion for the working class which it betrays, most recently in World War I. Forster begins, as if inconsequentially: "I have a suit of clothes. It does not fit, but is of stylish cut. I can

Forster and Ulster novelist Forrest Reid

go anywhere in it and I have been to see the Sargent pictures at the Royal Academy." Clothes, however, turn out to be a metaphor for what falsifies. They hide real humanity, just as does John Singer Sargent's battlefield painting *Gassed*, in which "no one complained, no one looked lousy or over-tired." Forster's conclusion, though credibly reached from his opening, is poles apart from it—a reminder, in an essay, of the visionary element found in his novels: "The misery goes on, the feeble impulses of good return to the sender, and far away, in some other category, far away from the snobbery and glitter in which our souls and bodies have been entangled, is forged the instrument of the new dawn."

Oliver Stallybrass, editing it for the Abinger Edition of Forster's works in 1972, felt that *Two Cheers for Democracy* "established" Forster as "an outstanding essayist." He did not mean by this remark to denigrate *Abinger Harvest*, but to suggest that Forster's second collection of essays, published in 1951, set the seal on the mastery demonstrated by the first. This view of the relationship between the two books is probably a just one.

Given that, in addition to republishing pieces mostly produced after *Abinger Harvest, Two Cheers for Democracy* also includes three essays written before 1936, and given that two of these, *Anonymity* and *A Letter to Madan Blanchard*, are in their different ways among the best essays Forster ever wrote, it would be a pointless exercise to attempt a distinction between the two collections on the grounds of merit. But because *Two Cheers for Democracy* contains Forster's most self-defining "public" essay, *What I Believe* (which may, Forster said in his prefatory note, "be regarded as the key to the book"), and because its first section, "The Second Darkness," represents his response to the narrowing historical perspectives of the late 1930s, the volume had the particular effect of presenting Forster to post-World War II readers as the voice of humanity and wisdom, both defending individual freedom against the dangers of state control (in prewar Hitlerian Germany and in postwar socialist Britain) and, in his essays on literature and "Places" (the title of the book's last subsection), exemplifying the operations of a free and sensitive intelligence.

This intelligence, as in *Abinger Harvest*, plays over a wide variety of subjects. "Jew-Consciousness" (*New Statesman & Nation*, 7 January 1939) mocks the "silliness" of anti-Semitism in an attempt to avert the "insanity" into which it might turn; "Racial Exercise" (first published as "Notes on the Way," *Time and Tide*, 18 March 1939) goes beyond Forster's more characteristic ironic mockery to treat the "doctrine" of racial purity with head-on contempt as "pompous and pernicious rubbish." The onset of war, bringing with it all the diminutions of individuality which Forster most detested and feared, notably altered his tone, not only in antitotalitarian essays but also, on occasion, when he wrote about personal experiences. This change is strikingly apparent in "Ferney," his account of a visit he had made with his French translator and friend Charles Mauron, in June 1939, to the house built by Voltaire near the border between Switzerland and France. First published as "Happy Ending" (*New Statesman & Nation*, 2 November 1940), it begins in self-deprecation and slangy wit: "Cultivated monkeys, Charles and I clung to the iron palings of the park. Froggy as well as monkey, he appreciated better than I did what we saw, but even to me the sight was an exciting one." It goes on to celebrate Voltaire—one of Forster's personal heroes—as an advancer of the boundaries of knowledge as well as the creator of a house and a planter of trees. It ends, however, in somberness and dry melancholy, as Forster and Mauron are presented not only as onlookers beyond the physical pale of Voltaire's park, but also as exiles from a past enlightenment. Locked out of that, they are locked into the diminishing world of Hitler's war: " 'I am content to have seen Ferney,' remarked Charles, as he dusted his paws. I popped the object into my pouch for future use. One never knows, and I had no idea how precious it would become to me in a year's time, nor how I should take it out, and discover that it had turned faintly radioactive. We caught the tram back to Geneva all right, crossed the almost unguarded frontier, and then we departed to our respective cages, which were closed and locked not long after we entered them."

Forster's life span, looked back on from that low point, might have seemed to him similar to the history of the London Library, which he summed up at the beginning of an essay on it for the 10 May 1941 issue of the *New Statesman & Nation*: "In May 1841 the London Library was launched on the swelling tides of Victorian pros-

perity. It celebrates its centenary among the rocks." Even the end of the war brought Forster a world which, though it offered increased possibilities to "the poor" and to the "backward races" (who were "kicking—and more power to their boots"), was less rewarding to one like himself, an "individualist" who belonged to "the fag-end of Victorian liberalism." Those references occur in his essay "The Challenge of Our Time" (*Listener*, 11 April 1946), in which he mentioned, as an example of "a collision of loyalties," his difficulty in equating the necessary postwar creation of "New Towns" with the likely ruin which one of them, Stevenage, would bring to the area of Hertfordshire ("which I still think the loveliest in England") in which he had spent his happiest childhood years: "I cannot free myself from the conviction that something irreplaceable has been destroyed, and that a little piece of England had died as surely as if a bomb had hit it. I wonder what compensation there is in the world of the spirit, for the destruction of the life there, the life of tradition." Given that Forster was seventy-two when it was published, much of *Two Cheers for Democracy* has an inevitable flavor of sadness and retrospection: its happiest essay, the delightfully inconsequential "Luncheon at Pretoria" (*Abinger Chronicle*, January 1940), describes an experience twenty years in the past, and two of its postwar essays, on Gide (*Listener*, 1 March 1951) and Forrest Reid (*Listener*, 16 January 1947), are concerned with writers whom Forster had long admired and who had recently died. Nevertheless, a degree of self-renewal and pleasure in the visible world came to Forster after the war and emerges in two of the later pieces in *Two Cheers for Democracy*. Forster's essay "The United States," written after his first visit there in 1947 and first published as "Impressions of the United States" (*Listener*, 4 September 1947), ends with a lyrical description of high summer in the Berkshires, where the flowers, birds, and butterflies of day gave place at night to fireflies "sparkling in the warm rain and the thunder." And in India, which he revisited in the autumn of 1945 for a P.E.N. conference at Jaipur, he felt that though he could "contribute no solution" to the country's problems, he had been able to do what was always, in his view, within the grasp of an individual: "And did I do any good? Yes, I did. I wanted to be with Indians, and was, and that is a very little step in the right direction" ("India Again," first published as "India after Twenty-five Years," *Listener*, 31 January and 6 February 1946).

it, I want to keep them in proportion. No one can spend his or
her life entirely in the creation or the appreciation of masterpieces.   Man lives, and ought to live, in a complex world, full
of conflicting claims, and if we simplified them down into the
aesthetic he would be sterilized.   Art for art's sake does not
mean that only art matters, *and I would also like to retract such phrases as "The life of Art," "Living for Art," and even "Art is human." They confuse and mislead.*
What does it mean?   Instead of generalising let us take a   (space)
specific instance - Shakespeare's _Macbeth_, for example, and
pronounce the words "Macbeth for Macbeth's sake."   What does that
mean?   Well, the play has several aspects $\frac{1}{m}$ it is educational, it
teaches us something about legendary Scotland, something about
Jacobean England, and a good deal about human nature and its perils.
We can study its origins, and study and enjoy its dramatic technique
and the music of its diction, as Edith Sitwell has.   ~~That is all~~ *All that is*
true.   But _Macbeth_ is furthermore a world of its own, created by
Shakespeare and existing in virtue of its own poetry.   It is in
this aspect Macbeth for Macbeth's sake, and that is what I ~~mean~~ *intend* by
the phrase "Art for Art's sake."   A work of art $\frac{1}{m}$ whatever else it
may be $\frac{1}{m}$ is a self-contained entity, with a life of its own imposed
on it by its creator. *(It has internal order. It may have external form. That is how we recognize it.)*   Take for another ~~instance~~ *example: La Grande Jatte* that picture of
Seurat's, which I saw two years ago *in* ~~at~~ Chicago $\frac{1}{m}$ ~~Les Grandes Jattes~~.
Here again there is much to study and to enjoy: the pointillisme,
~~the rendering of sunlight~~, the charming face of the seated girl,
(the nineteenth-century Parisian Sunday sunlight)
~~the composition~~, the sense of motion in immobility.   But here again
there is something more; ∧ *Les Grandes Jattes* the ~~picture~~ forms a world of its own,

La Grande Jatte

Page from the revised typescript for "Art for Art's Sake," an address delivered to the American Academy of Arts and Letters in May 1949 and published in the August 1949 issue of Harper's Magazine *before it was included in his 1951 collection,* Two Cheers for Democracy *(MA 1248, Gift of Mr. Russell Lynes; by permission of the Pierpont Morgan Library)*

For about a decade after the appearance of *Two Cheers for Democracy* Forster continued to publish essays and to review, often in the *Listener*, whose literary editor, J. R. Ackerley, had for many years been one of his closest friends. In an interview he gave in 1965, Ackerley indicated in passing the key element that lay behind most of Forster's reviews: "He always did for *The Listener* whatever I asked him to do, if he was interested. 'Send the book along,' he'd say, 'and I'll see if I like it.'" Liking was the impulse behind the greater part of Forster's nonfictional pieces, "essays proper" as well as reviews: what he admired and loved was what he wished to pass on to others, often out of a personal as well as a literary response—unlike many academic writers, he had little wish to denigrate, undermine, or "place" in an abstract pecking order. The more substantial of his later essays—"Revolution at Bayreuth" (*Listener*, 4 November 1954), concerned with the staging of Wagner's music dramas; "Recollections of Nassenheide" (*Listener*, 1 January 1959), about his time as a tutor in Pomerania; and "Fog Over Ferney: A Fantasy" (*Listener*, 18 December 1958), which wryly imagines the small impact a polymath like Voltaire could have on the vastly more specialized fields of modern science and the complex problems of modern politics—are various forms of recollected tribute to writers and musicians whose work had uplifted him and to experiences which he wished to commemorate.

One can fairly say of Forster what he himself said of Voltaire in his essay "Voltaire and Frederick the Great" (1941): he "kept faith with the human spirit." In 1934 he became the first president of the National Council for Civil Liberties, an organization to which he belonged for several years. Having returned after the war to Cambridge, to an honorary fellowship of his old college, he became in 1959 president of the Cambridge Humanists. One of the last of his essays was the printed form of his presidential address, which appeared in the *Bulletin of the University Humanist Federation* in spring 1963. At the end of it, speculating on the approach of death and on whether, at that juncture, his agnostic humanism would help him, he effectively reasserted his lifelong sense of the importance of the individual and, with it, the importance of the individual's response to as wide a range of available experience as possible. "I should be glad," he concluded, "if it did. I do not want to recant and muddle people. But I do not take the hour of death too seriously. It may scare, it may hurt, it probably ends

the individual, but in comparison to the hours when a man is alive, the hour of death is almost negligible." Forster's essays, with their unique blend of elusive charm, clarity of utterance, and authoritative moral concern, combine with his fiction not only to offer a lasting record of one man's "aliveness," but to reach out toward his readers and continually reinvolve them in it.

Letters:
Selected Letters of E. M. Forster, 2 volumes, edited by Mary Lago and P. N. Furbank (London: Collins, 1983, 1985; Cambridge, Mass.: Harvard University Press, 1983, 1985).

Bibliography:
B. J. Kirkpatrick, *A Bibliography of E. M. Forster*, second edition (Oxford: Clarendon Press, 1985).

Biographies:
P. N. Furbank, *E. M. Forster: A Life, Volume One: The Growth of a Novelist (1870-1914)* (London: Secker & Warburg, 1977); *E. M. Forster: A Life, Volume Two: Polycrates' Ring (1914-1970)* (London: Secker & Warburg, 1978); republished as *E. M. Forster: A Life*, 1 volume (New York: Harcourt Brace Jovanovich, 1978);

Francis King, *E. M. Forster and His World* (London: Thames & Hudson, 1978; New York: Scribners, 1978).

References:
Laurence Brander, *E. M. Forster: A Critical Study* (London: Hart-Davis, 1968; Lewisburg: Bucknell University Press, 1970);

John Colmer, *E. M. Forster: The Personal Voice* (London & Boston: Routledge & Kegan Paul, 1975);

Phillip Gardner, *E. M. Forster* (London: Longman, 1977);

Judith Scherer Herz, *The Short Narratives of E. M. Forster* (Basingstoke: Macmillan, 1982);

Rose Macanlay, *The Writings of E. M. Forster* (London: Hogarth Press, 1938);

Frederick P. W. McDowell, *E. M. Forster* (New York: Twayne, 1969);

Wilfred Stone, *The Care and the Mountain: A Study of E. M. Forster* (London: Oxford University Press, 1966; Stanford: Stanford University Press, 1966);

Claude J. Sumners, *E. M. Forster* (New York: Ungar, 1983);

Lionel Trilling, *E. M. Forster: A Study* (Norfolk, Conn: New Directions, 1943; London: Hogarth Press, 1944).

Papers:

The E. M. Forster Archive is at King's College Library, King's College, Cambridge.

John Galsworthy

(14 August 1867 - 31 January 1933)

Thomas A. Kuhlman
Creighton University

See also the Galsworthy entries in *DLB 10: Modern British Dramatists, 1900-1945*, and *DLB 34: British Novelists, 1890-1929: Traditionalists*.

BOOKS: *From the Four Winds*, as John Sinjohn (London: Unwin, 1897);

Jocelyn, as Sinjohn (London: Duckworth, 1898); as Galsworthy (St. Clair Shores, Mich.: Scholarly Press, 1972);

Villa Rubein: A Novel, as Sinjohn (London: Duckworth, 1900; New York & London: Putnam's, 1908);

A Man of Devon, as Sinjohn (Edinburgh & London: Blackwood, 1901);

The Island Pharisees (London: Heinemann, 1904; New York: Putnam's, 1904; revised edition, London: Heinemann, 1908);

The Man of Property (London: Heinemann, 1906; New York & London: Putnam's, 1906);

The Country House (London: Heinemann, 1907; New York & London: Putnam's, 1907);

A Commentary (London: Richards, 1908; New York & London: Putnam's, 1908);

Fraternity (London: Heinemann, 1909; New York & London: Putnam's, 1909);

Plays: The Silver Box; Joy; Strife (London: Duckworth, 1909; New York & London: Putnam's, 1909);

Justice: A Tragedy in Four Acts (London: Duckworth, 1910; New York: Scribners, 1910);

A Motley (London: Heinemann, 1910; New York: Scribners, 1910);

John Galsworthy (photograph by Riess)

The Patrician (London: Heinemann, 1911; New York: Scribners, 1911);

The Little Dream: An Allegory in Six Scenes (London: Duckworth, 1911; New York: Scribners, 1911);

The Pigeon: A Fantasy in Three Acts (London: Duckworth, 1912; New York: Scribners, 1912);

Moods, Songs, and Doggerels (New York: Scribners, 1912; London: Heinemann, 1912);

The Inn of Tranquillity: Studies and Essays (London: Heinemann, 1912; New York: Scribners, 1912);

The Eldest Son: A Domestic Drama in Three Acts (London: Duckworth, 1912; New York: Scribners, 1912);

The Fugitive: A Play in Four Acts (London: Duckworth, 1913; New York: Scribners, 1914);

The Dark Flower (London: Heinemann, 1913; New York: Scribners, 1913);

The Mob: A Play in Four Acts (London: Duckworth, 1914; New York: Scribners, 1914);

The Little Man and Other Satires (New York: Scribners, 1915; London: Heinemann, 1915);

A Bit o' Love: A Play in Three Acts (London: Duckworth, 1915; New York: Scribners, 1915); also published as *The Full Moon: A Play in Three Acts* (London: Duckworth, 1915);

The Freelands (London: Heinemann, 1915; New York: Scribners, 1915);

A Sheaf (New York: Scribners, 1916; London: Heinemann, 1916);

Beyond (New York: Scribners, 1917; London: Heinemann, 1917);

Five Tales (New York: Scribners, 1918; London: Heinemann, 1918);

Another Sheaf (London: Heinemann, 1919; New York: Scribners, 1919);

The Burning Spear, Being the Experiences of Mr. John Lavender in Time of War, as A. R. P–M (London: Chatto & Windus, 1919); as Galsworthy (New York: Scribners, 1923);

Addresses in America (New York: Scribners, 1919; London: Heinemann, 1919);

Saint's Progress (New York: Scribners, 1919; London: Heinemann, 1919);

Tatterdemalion (London: Heinemann, 1920; New York: Scribners, 1920);

The Foundations: An Extravagant Play in Three Acts (London: Duckworth, 1920; New York: Scribners, 1920);

The Skin Game: A Tragi-comedy in Three Acts (London: Duckworth, 1920; New York: Scribners, 1920);

In Chancery (London: Heinemann, 1920; New York: Scribners, 1920);

Awakening (New York: Scribners, 1920; London: Heinemann, 1920);

The First and the Last (London: Heinemann, 1920; enlarged edition, New York: Scribners, 1925);

To Let (New York: Scribners, 1921; London: Heinemann, 1921);

Six Short Plays (London: Duckworth, 1921; New York: Scribners, 1921);

The Forsyte Saga (New York: Scribners, 1922; London: Heinemann, 1922);

A Family Man, in Three Acts (London: Duckworth, 1922; New York: Scribners, 1922);

Loyalties: A Drama in Three Acts (London: Duckworth, 1922; New York: Scribners, 1923);

Windows: A Comedy in Three Acts for Idealists and Others (London: Duckworth, 1922; New York: Scribners, 1923);

Captures (London: Heinemann, 1923; New York: Scribners, 1923);

The Forest: A Drama in Four Acts (London: Duckworth, 1924; New York: Scribners, 1924);

The White Monkey (New York: Scribners, 1924; London: Heinemann, 1924);

Abracadabra & Other Satires (London: Heinemann, 1924);

Old English: A Play in Three Acts (London: Duckworth, 1924; New York: Scribners, 1925);

Caravan: The Assembled Tales of John Galsworthy (London: Heinemann, 1925; New York: Scribners, 1925);

The Show: A Drama in Three Acts (London: Duckworth, 1925; New York: Scribners, 1925);

The Silver Spoon (London: Heinemann, 1926; New York: Scribners, 1926);

Escape: An Episodic Play in a Prologue and Two Parts (London: Duckworth, 1926; New York: Scribners, 1927);

Verses New and Old (London: Heinemann, 1926; New York: Scribners, 1926);

Castles in Spain, & Other Screeds (London: Heinemann, 1927; New York: Scribners, 1927);

Two Forsyte Interludes: A Silent Wooing; Passers By (London: Heinemann, 1927; New York: Scribners, 1928);

Swan Song (New York: Scribners, 1928; London: Heinemann, 1928);

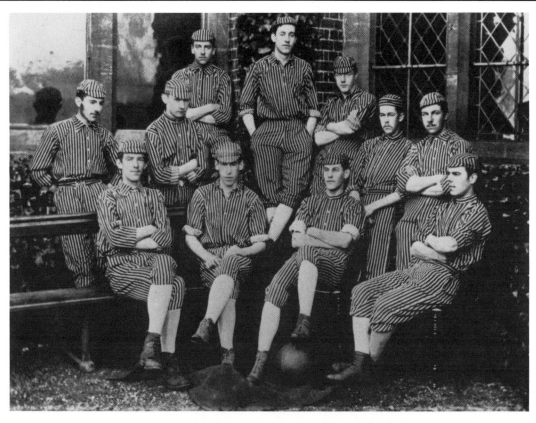

Galsworthy (with foot on ball) and the Harrow football team

Galsworthy (right) and his roommate, Claude Douglas Pennant, at breakfast in their Oxford rooms

Exiled: An Evolutionary Comedy (London: Duckworth, 1929; New York: Scribners, 1930);

Four Forsyte Stories (New York: Fountain / London: Heinemann, 1929);

A Modern Comedy (London: Heinemann, 1929; New York: Scribners, 1920);

The Roof: A Play in Seven Scenes (London: Duckworth, 1929; New York: Scribners, 1931);

On Forsyte 'Change (London: Heinemann, 1930; New York: Scribners, 1930);

Soames and The Flag (London: Heinemann, 1930; New York: Scribners, 1930);

The Creation of Character in Literature (Oxford: Clarendon Press, 1931);

Maid in Waiting (London: Heinemann, 1931; New York: Scribners, 1931);

Flowering Wilderness (London: Heinemann, 1932; New York: Scribners, 1932);

Author and Critic (New York: House of Books, 1933);

Over the River (London: Heinemann, 1933); republished as *One More River* (New York: Scribners, 1933);

End of the Chapter (New York: Scribners, 1934; London & Toronto: Heinemann, 1935);

The Collected Poems of John Galsworthy (New York: Scribners, 1934; London: Heinemann, 1934);

Forsytes, Pendyces, and Others (London: Heinemann, 1935; New York: Scribners, 1935);

The Winter Garden: Four Dramatic Pieces (London: Duckworth, 1935);

Glimpses and Reflections (London & Toronto: Heinemann, 1937).

Collections: *The Works of John Galsworthy*, 18 volumes (London: Heinemann, 1921-1925 [i.e., 1923-1924]);

The Works of John Galsworthy, Manaton Edition, 25 volumes (New York: Scribners, 1922-1929; London: Heinemann, 1923-1929);

The Novels, Tales and Plays of John Galsworthy, Devon Edition, 22 volumes (New York: Scribners, 1926-1929);

Plays, by John Galsworthy (New York & London: Scribners, 1928);

The Plays of John Galsworthy (London: Duckworth, 1929);

Candelabra: Selected Essays and Addresses (London: Heinemann, 1932; New York: Scribners, 1933);

Ex Libris John Galsworthy [quotations from his writings], compiled by John and Ada Galsworthy (London: Heinemann, 1933);

Galsworthy in His Humour (London: Duckworth, 1935).

Television has revived interest in many a once popular but then forgotten author. Perhaps the most striking example of this occurred from 1967 to 1974, when a multipart black-and-white dramatization of John Galsworthy's *The Forsyte Saga* (1922) enthralled millions of viewers on both sides of the Atlantic. Having been dismissed by critics for several decades as a middlebrow writer who failed to participate in the significant innovations of modern drama and fiction, Galsworthy was at least granted an audience not only vastly larger than that of his highbrow rivals but actually larger than that which had eagerly awaited his books during his lifetime. This audience was described demographically as cutting across age groups and social classes, but the popularity of the series was greatest, both in Britain and in the United States, among the very people the novelist of manners was satirizing, the upper middle class. "The Forsytes," as the television series was called, dissected the structure and mores of society from the viewpoint of individuals who were, if not elite, certainly genteel. The palatable moderation of this social criticism perfectly caught the spirit of Galsworthy the novelist, playwright, and essayist of several decades before.

While the Forsyte stories were not point-by-point autobiographical, they nevertheless recapitulated Galsworthy's heritage and experience, and many characters can be identified with members of his family, just as the comfortable settings of Kensington, Hyde Park, Surrey, and Devon are integral to his life and fiction. He was born on 14 August 1867 in Kingston Hill, Surrey, the son of John and Blanche Bartleet Galsworthy. The father, a solicitor and director of several large companies, who served as the model for "Old Jolyon" in *The Forsyte Saga*, so enlarged the fortune the novelist's Devonshire-born grandfather had amassed that the younger John Galsworthy was exposed from birth to a considerable amount of material luxury. His childhood memories of Coome Warren, the family country house, contributed to the picture of Robin Hill, the home of Soames Forsyte. After attending the Sangcen Preparatory School in Bournemouth, Galsworthy went to Harrow, where he enjoyed considerable success at athletics. At New College, Oxford, however, he put aside his interest in sports and became known primarily as a mediocre student and a dandy. He read law and was admitted to the bar in London,

Photograph of Galsworthy taken by H. G. Wells in 1898

but when it became clear that he had neither the need nor the desire to work hard as a solicitor, his father sent him on an extended tour of Canada, supposedly to inspect coal mines of which the senior Galsworthy was a director. The tour eventually encircled the globe, and in the South Pacific he formed what would become a lifelong friendship with Joseph Conrad, who then was still a ship's first mate.

Galsworthy began his literary career with a Kiplingesque short-story collection entitled *From the Four Winds* published in 1897. For this and three succeeding books he used the pseudonym John Sinjohn. While collecting rents on London slum housing owned by his father, his social conscience was awakened, and he conceived the plot of *The Island Pharisees* (1904), the first edition of which he suppressed. It was not until 1906 with *The Man of Property* that he tasted real success as a novelist; this first book of the Forsyte series was based on the unhappy marriage of Ada Cooper to Galsworthy's cousin, Maj. Arthur Forsyte, and

on her divorce and subsequent marriage to the author. In the same year, Galsworthy wrote his first play, *The Silver Box* (collected in *Plays*, 1909), while on holiday in Devon. Soon he was known internationally for his use of contemporary social problems as material for fiction and the stage. Twenty-five plays, such as *Strife* (in *Plays*, 1909), *Justice* (1910), and *Loyalties* (1922), and the continuation of the Forsyte narrative led to the awarding of honorary doctorates from Manchester, Dublin, Cambridge, Oxford, Sheffield, and Princeton. Although he declined a knighthood in 1918, he accepted the Order of Merit in 1929, and the Nobel Prize for Literature in 1932. The check he received with the latter award he endorsed to the P.E.N. club; he had served as its first president in 1921. His last years were spent at Grove Lodge in Hampstead. After his death on 31 January 1933, his ashes were scattered on Bury Hill in Sussex.

As an essayist, Galsworthy is above all a man of good will: his pieces on literature, which comprise roughly half of his nonfiction prose, and those on various social problems are utterly devoid of malice, pugnacious brilliance for its own sake, or abstruse intellectuality for the sake of matching wits with the greatest minds, past or contemporary. Rather, the impression given is always that of the kind friend who has pondered much on issues that concern him because they concern all of humanity, and who sincerely offers his opinions, facts, and analogies because he believes that they will assist in the answering of questions and in the meeting of moral challenges. From the early collections published before World War I to those that appeared near the end of his life, the tone varies little, despite the enormous impact of war and the rush of events in the 1920s and early 1930s. A stoic, avuncular blend of warning and hopefulness characterizes the voice of a quiet, gentlemanly critic of life and of letters.

This two-part division gives order to *The Inn of Tranquillity* (1912): part 1, "Concerning Life," consists of short stories; part 2, "Concerning Letters," displays Galsworthy the essayist on literature. In "A Novelist's Allegory," for example, Galsworthy subtly defends the realistic and naturalistic modes of storytelling without specifically identifying them. He imagines a city long in darkness, in which the citizens claim to have no troubles because no troubles are easily visible. An old man, an "illuminator," comes to brighten the *Via Publica*, and he is immediately blamed for the troubles seen by the light of his lantern. He is put on trial and defended by a young man who obviously symbolizes the latest generation of British writers. The old man is exonerated and, when he dies, is succeeded by another, younger illuminator. The theme is that novelists have a mission to tell truths about human weakness and social injustice and that their mission will be carried on.

In "Some Platitudes Concerning Drama," written in 1909, Galsworthy for the first time expresses his admiration for John Millington Synge's *Playboy of the Western World* (1907) as perhaps the greatest artistic success on the stage in the new century. It would not be the last time he praised the Anglo-Irish playwright so highly. But here he does so to express his conviction–related to the theme of the essay–that Synge's comedy-drama was a fluke, an exception to the nearly universal principle that naturalism and poetic-prose drama are opposites impossible of combination. There can be no "crude unions," he asserts; "We want no more bastard drama." Not surprisingly,

given the substance of his own work for the theater, Galsworthy devotes most of this essay to a positive evaluation of the naturalistic mode. Finding three courses open to the serious dramatist, he rejects the first two: presenting material immediately acceptable to the audience or mixing one's views with those of the audience like medicinal powder in a sweet-tasting drink. The true course, he enjoins, is to let a story speak for itself. Matters change, morals change, but men remain, and the true seer blinks at nothing. This seer will have one of two roles in society: scientist or artist.

In the next essay in this collection, "Meditation of Finality," written in 1912, Galsworthy again praises Synge, this time for being a splendid combination of the "man of facts" and the "man of feeling." The controlling metaphor in this essay is America's Grand Canyon. Too often tourists respond to such a work of nature as though its essence could be equated with its measurements. But they deceive themselves; those who react to natural wonders solely in the mode of men of fact will never grasp the infinite. Art, then–and here Galsworthy means literature–is not to be measured by the limits of the world it depicts and must not be expected to be a source for mere facts. How does this opinion fit with that suggestion in "The Novelist's Allegory" that the writer's function is to illuminate problems? A reconciliation of opposites for Galsworthy exists in the rejection of simple quantification when dealing with facts and in an appreciation of a primacy of the things of the spirit. This last does not mean submission to any theological doctrine, but rather an acknowledgment that human consciousness and personal relationships, even to the naturalist, are objects for wonder.

The next two essays in *The Inn of Tranquillity* develop this idea by stressing the seriousness of the writer's obligation to confront hard truth. In "Wanted: Schooling" Galsworthy declares that there is a large audience for "bad and false fiction" because too many writers have knowingly created the demand for it. Writers should instead discipline themselves and write only what they can justify as psychologically true and morally valuable. The essay "Reflections on Our Dislike of Things As They Are" expresses this idea more specifically, especially in regard to sex. "We English are too civilized and look on nature as indecent," he says, citing as faulty or insufficient two national ideals: "the Will to Health" and "the Will to Material Efficiency." Deploring "Beards-

John Galsworthy, his wife, Ada, Hugh Walpole, and Arnold Bennett on the terrace at Grove Lodge, Galsworthy's home in Hampstead

leyism," he nevertheless declares that until authors and the public at large place equal emphasis on the "Will to Sensibility," British writers will never equal European ones in their treatment of sex, and the English people will never be psychologically comfortable.

The next essay, though, cautions that, for the writer, there really is no such thing as "the public." In "The Windlestraw" Galsworthy urges that there be no writing aimed at any "hypothetical average human being." There exists as the ultimate audience only the conscience, ever demanding the truth as the writer sees it. This statement leads naturally to the final essay in the collection, "About Censorship." Here he coolly analyzes the various elements of British culture that at the time (unlike the theater) were free from any government censorship—art, fiction, religion, science, and politics—and carefully shows how each of them is capable of provoking major instances of civil injury or discord. These might well be the objects of censorship by those who would protect the common good, but they are not. For the same reasons that they are not, he concludes, the censorship of the British stage should be abolished. Liberalism for one should be liberalism for all. This theme Galsworthy was to repeat often in

the succeeding volumes of his essays.

The essays in *A Sheaf* (1916) turned for their subjects to the problems of society with which Galsworthy had been identified in his successful novels and plays. The volume appeared in the middle of the war years, but many of the essays had been written prior to the beginning of the conflict. Because these usually had little to do with what wartime readers had foremost on their minds, Galsworthy found it necessary to explain his selections in a preface defending the urgency of his topics of reform and humanitarianism: "the war will not last forever, and in the peace that follows, life will be rougher, the need for these pleas more insistent than it ever was." Upon looking at the first few essays on the humane treatment of animals, one might question the accuracy of the author's prescience: his protests against the use of horses in mines or the docking of their tails suggest a lack of awareness that the postwar world would be radically more mechanized, and two pleas for the abolition of performing-animal shows seem almost (given the human carnage of 1916) the ravings of a sentimental crank. This impression is balanced, at least, by reasoned arguments against the vivisection of dogs. The prewar essays on the issues of prisons

Galsworthy in his study at Bury House, his country retreat in Sussex (photograph by London General Press)

and feminism are no less emotional. Galsworthy denounces solitary confinement and the revenge motivation behind penal facilities; it is practical, he maintains, to make reformation of the criminal the sole or at least primary goal of such institutions. In "Gentles, Let Us Rest!," written in 1910, he offers a summary of his views on the emancipation of women, making as his chief point a dictum of John Stuart Mill's, that society ought not to add to nature's evils by jealousy and prejudice.

The remainder of *A Sheaf* deals with matters of peace and war. In his 1909 essay "The Will to Peace" Galsworthy had concluded with a comment on a poster he had seen, which said, "Where there is a will to peace there is a way." "War between two countries," Galsworthy had written, "two trustees of civilization, need not be inevitable. To believe that is to blaspheme, to belittle human nature, to deny the Earth." In a 1916 foot-

note to that essay, he insists he has not changed his belief that wars occasioned by trade rivalry are *not* inevitable; he confesses, nevertheless, that he had been wrong on a different point. He says that England's will to peace was not enough to guarantee peace, because the ruling classes of Germany did not want it. His own countrymen, having rejected war for commercial reasons alone, finally accepted it for "a better, an inspiring cause." Galsworthy developed this idea through the rest of *A Sheaf*, and indeed, through the rest of his career, confidently insisting that the "inspiring cause" was the triumph of democracy over autocracy. The essays written after the declaration of war show Galsworthy as an idealistic patriot. "England went to war for honour, for democracy, for the future of mankind," he writes in "Credo." In "First Thoughts on the War" he excitedly proclaims, "It is the death of dogmatic Christianity! Let us will that it be the birth of a God within us, and an ethic Christianity that men really practice!" Other, more specific hopes for postwar Britain are identified in the essays "And After?" and "Freedom and Privilege," in which, respectively, he advises the design of a constitution for a League of Peace and the transformation of the British Empire into a confederacy characterized by such reforms as woman suffrage and training schools for all boys from fourteen to eighteen.

After the war *Addresses in America* was published (1919). Galsworthy had presented to audiences in the United States just what might be expected from one renowned as the quintessential novelist-playwright of the humane wing of the British upper middle class. Speaking at the celebration of the centenary of the birth of James Russell Lowell, Galsworthy indulged in hyperbole, ranking the American poet with Marcus Aurelius, Dante, Saint Francis, Miguel de Cervantes–the list goes on to include half a dozen more of the greatest writers of all ages. His central point was subtly chauvinistic: that Great Britain and the United States shared, in the English language, the greatest possible instrument of truth, which could and should be used for purposes of national propaganda, both nations having the obligation to communicate their goodness to the rest of the world. Optimism and tempered pride characterize the next address in the collection, "American and Briton." The bulk of the essay concerns the Briton, and although Galsworthy includes English traits of which he disapproves, such as the tendency of the public schools to "crush individuality, spontaneity and engaging frankness," he emphasizes the benevolent effects of the sea, the climate, the vigorous town life, democracy, freedom of speech and press, and freedom from compulsory military service except in time of war. He concludes on a high and hortatory note: "We do know that Earth is yet on the upgrade of existence, the mountain top of man's life not reached, that many centuries of growth are yet in front of us.... We shall not fail–neither ourselves, nor each other. Our comradeship will endure."

Galsworthy's addresses in America, however lacking in the irreverent, debunking, disillusioned anger of a younger generation of writers on either side of the Atlantic, nevertheless demonstrate a sharper awareness of the near future than he had seemed to possess earlier. He cautions that beauty and simplicity must be "the natural antidotes to the feverish industrialism of our age" and tells the Society of Arts and Sciences in New York that "we have seen Science work miracles of late; now let Art work her miracles in return." At Columbia University he states: "America is yet on the threshold. Is she to step out in the sight of the world as a great leader? That is to be worked out not so much in her Senate and her Congress as in her homes and schools. On America . . . the destiny of civilization may hang for the next century...." He then asks the younger nation to avoid provincialism, and to solve problems of labor and capital, of the distribution of wealth, of national health, and of the mastery of inventions and machinery. Not to do so will result in anarchy, disruptions, and even dictatorship. Another of these American lectures, one to the League of Political Education in New York, especially expresses Galsworthy's hostility to corrupting materialism and also delineates his model for an ideal society. "The great modern fallacy," he says, "is the identification of the word wealth with the word welfare.... We ought to produce wealth only in such ways and to such an extent as shall make us all good, clean, healthy, intelligent and beautiful to look at.... The most important need of the world today is to learn . . . the love of quality."

The volume *Castles in Spain, & Other Screeds* (1927), bringing together the most significant of Galsworthy's essays of the postwar decade, again treats both social questions and literature. The title essay, "Castles in Spain," was written in 1920; in it, Galsworthy contrasts the values of science, industry, and trade with those of beauty. It is only according to aesthetic norms, he insists, that human progress is real, and this demands a farsightedness tragically rare in contemporary western democracy. Progress ought to mean leveling up the decencies of life, "gradually diminishing the distance between the manor and the hovel. Are we not unfortunate in letting civic life be run by those who were born seeing two inches before their nose? . . . Only the love and cult of beauty will save us . . . a higher and wider conception of the dignity of human life." Another essay written in 1920, "Where We Stand," explicitly calls for a rejection of industrialism. The primary lesson of World War I was that humankind must "substitute health and happiness for wealth as a world-ideal; translate that new ideal into action by *education from babyhood up*."

This desire to turn idealism into action may have suggested to some contemporary readers

John and Ada Galsworthy, circa 1930 (Collection of Rudolf Sauter)

that here was proof of a weak sentimentality on Galsworthy's part, and as if to answer such a charge with careful logic, he wrote "A Note on Sentiment" in 1922. Here he precisely distinguishes between "sentimentalism, when the feeling is not genuine," and 'sentiment'–the verbal expression of true feeling, of which he approves. He admits to having been guilty of the less admirable quality on some occasions and considers the failing universal. But, his argument proceeds, "as often as not the charge 'sentimentalist' is a mere partisan form of abuse, unfounded in fact." Galsworthy the essayist here perhaps more than in any other short piece merges with Galsworthy the novelist and playwright, as he draws examples from what he calls practical life to demonstrate the relativism of moral and social judgments. Anyone familiar with *The Forsyte Saga*, with his works for the theater, or with the writer's personal life can surely guess at the emotions that lie behind the following passage from this essay: "A judge, out of a sentimental regard for marriage, will rebuke counsel for using the expression 'this poor woman' of one who, having run away with her husband's brother, tries to atone by committing suicide. 'She is a married woman,' he says, 'and to pity her is sentimental.' " There are probably readers who find fault with Galsworthy's ironic logic here, but the passage is significant as an example of his conviction that sensitivity to individual feelings is more important in judging behavior than any abstract system of moral absolutes. The final social essay of the *Castles in Spain* collection, "International Thought," first published in 1923, is equally idealistic, accusing science, finance, and the press of unjustified acceptance of destructive technology.

The essays on literature in this volume casually rather than dogmatically set forth Galsworthy's philosophy of fiction and drama. Although he is open to the overtures of talented newcomers, his enthusiasms are, with rare exceptions, not for the avant-garde. In "On Expression" (1924) he praises Katherine Mansfield and Anton Chekhov; he finds the "Americanese" or slang in Sinclair Lewis's *Babbitt* (1922) and in the for modern man—perhaps—the only possible faith." In "Faith of a Novelist" (1926), after discussing some of his favorite heroes and villains in literature, and distinguishing between valid and invalid novelistic presentations of sex, Galsworthy concludes with his own quietly agnostic perception of the ultimate: "The novelist will confess: that human realization of a First Cause is to him inconceivable. He is left to acceptance of what is. Out of Mystery we came, into Mystery return. Life and death, ebb and flow, day and night, world beginning and without end is all that he can grasp. But in such little certainty he sees no cause for gloom. Life for those who still have vital instinct in them is good enough, even if it lead to nothing further.... Courage and kindness ... make human life worthwhile and bring an inner happiness."

On 21 May 1931 Galsworthy delivered the annual Romances Lecture in the Sheldonian Theater at Oxford, *The Creation of Character in Literature*, which was published in a small volume later that year. Now near the end of his life, with dry humor he professes agnosticism about the act of literary creation as well as about the Deity. Philosophies, he states, "Are like the fashion of ladies' clothes, which appear absolute until by a new dash of the Parisian intellect they are shown to be relative." Galsworthy calls his opinions "suspicions" rather than conclusions. Without mentioning Sigmund Freud or any other psychologist by name, he places the creative act within the influence of the subconscious, which he describes as "a sort of lava of experience, over which the conscious mind has formed in a crust more or less thin, and more or less perforated by holes through which the lava bubbles.... Creative genius [is] a much more than normal perforation." He then discusses straight biography as a first level of presenting a character through the medium of language. Next he moves to the subject of the personae in drama and finally to characters in novels. His literary agnosticism comes through in his confession that, "speaking as one who has been trying to write novels of character over a period of more than thirty years, the lecturer can make no contribution to precision. To this day he knows not how he begins, or why, or how he goes on; he is only sure that there is no rule, and that the process of character creation varies not only from novelist to novelist, but even in himself." Galsworthy ends the address by naming a few of his favorite characters from Cervantes, Shakespeare, and Dickens. The continuing exis-

Galsworthy in New York, 1931 (photograph by S. Dreier)

plays of Eugene O'Neill interesting, but clearly he most admires the same writers his close friend Conrad preferred: Henry James, Gustave Flaubert, Anthony Trollope, Charles Dickens, and Ivan Turgenev. These last two are included with Conrad, Guy de Maupassant, Leo Tolstoy, and Anatole France in the 1924 essay "Six Novelists in Profile." An earlier essay collected in this volume, the 1915 foreword to an edition of W. H. Hudson's *Green Mansions* (1904), expresses an intense sympathy with that novelist's "spirit of revolt against our new enslavement by towns and machinery." "Six Novelists" concludes with a suggestion that meaning can be found in or through humanism, which is defined as "the creed of those who believe that men's fate is in their own hands ... a faith which is becoming tence of these characters in the public imagination gives him the single certainty in the lecture—"One thing is sure: The enduring characters in literature are ever such as have kicked free of swaddling clothes and their creators. Theirs is a sublime unconsciousness of the authors of their being."

After Galsworthy's death three hundred copies of a pamphlet entitled *Author and Critic* were published (1933). Scarcely a thousand words in length, it pays tribute to critics he had admired, foremost among them Matthew Arnold and his own longtime friend Edward Garnett. Their work, he says, "illuminated men's minds by their interpretations, and kept the flag of a fine calling flying very high." He concludes with a practical and characteristically generous suggestion: "Would it not be well for critics to select from the books of unknown or little known authors only those of which they can say something encouraging?"

In 1935 an anthology entitled *Forsytes, Pendyces, and Others* was published, with a brief foreword by his widow, Ada Galsworthy. The volume consists mostly of fiction and fragments from plays; the few essays included, most of which had been published before, discuss his typical literary enthusiasms: Anatole France, Conrad, Mansfield, Hudson, Dickens, and Tolstoy.

Glimpses and Reflections (1937) tantalizingly lacks a table of contents and is arranged in a novel way—alphabetically by subject, with material dating from as early as 1906 to as late as the end of August 1932. Included are letters from the author in whole or in part, generally to unidentified correspondents from the general public, as well as whole essays that appeared in newspapers and magazines. The topics are the familiar ones of literature and designs for social amelioration. As always, the voice is gentlemanly, never so harsh as to give offense, and rarely is it comic or even terse.

An assessment of Galsworthy's essays can be made with few qualifications or hesitant submissions of paradox or caution. Galsworthy never attempted to dazzle readers and made no pretense of possessing an extraordinary intellect. The range of topics is quite limited: it is surprising, considering the importance of architecture and painting in the Forsyte novels and his regular urgings that modern society pay more attention to the aesthetic, that the essays never deal in a specific way with those arts. Furthermore, for all his attention to the moral imperatives facing leaders in sci-ence, industry, and government, he addresses issues, whether general or particular, without including accounts of the actions of individual men and women—odd for a writer so successful in portraying character types in novels and plays. That Galsworthy never deigned to stoop to vulgar, ad hominem arguments, however, is unquestionably consistent with his principles and methods. Essentially he was the Edwardian humanitarian who continued his efforts for justice and liberty into the postwar era, aware of the great wrongs of imperialism and racial and ethnic prejudice but terribly proud that, as an Englishman, he belonged to a people dedicated to a rather simple sense of fair play.

Letters:

Autobiographical Letters of John Galsworthy (New York: English Book Shop, 1933);

Letters from John Galsworthy, 1900-1932, edited by Edward Garnett (London: Cape / New York: Scribners, 1934);

Margaret Morris, *My Galsworthy Story Including 67 Hitherto Unpublished Letters* (London: Owen, 1967);

John Galsworthy's Letters to Leon Lion, edited by Asher Boldon Wilson (The Hague: Mouton, 1968).

Bibliographies:

H. V. Marrott, *A Bibliography of the Works of John Galsworthy* (London: Mathews & Marrott / New York: Scribners, 1928);

Earl E. Stevens and H. Ray Stevens, *John Galsworthy: An Annotated Bibliography of Writings about Him* (DeKalb: Northern Illinois University Press, 1980).

Biographies:

H. V. Marrott, *The Life and Letters of John Galsworthy* (London: Heinemann, 1935; New York: Scribners, 1936);

M. E. Reynolds, *Memories of John Galsworthy by His Sister* (London: Hale, 1936; New York: Stokes, 1937);

R. H. Mottram, *For Some We Loved: An Intimate Portrait of John and Ada Galsworthy* (London: Hutchinson, 1956);

Dudley Barker, *The Man of Principle: A View of John Galsworthy* (London: Heinemann, 1963; New York: Stein & Day, 1963);

Rudolf Sauter, *Galsworthy the Man: An Intimate Portrait by His Nephew* (London: Owen, 1967);

Catherine Dupré, *John Galsworthy: A Biography* (London: Collins, 1976; New York: Coward, McCann & Geoghegan, 1976);

James Gindin, *The English Climate: An Excursion into a Biography of John Galsworthy* (Ann Arbor: University of Michigan Press, 1979).

References:

Natalie Croman, *John Galsworthy: A Study in Continuity and Contrast* (Cambridge, Mass.: Harvard University Press, 1933);

John Fisher, *The World of the Forsytes* (New York: Universe, 1976);

Ford Madox Ford, "Galsworthy," *American Mercury*, 37 (April 1936): 448-459;

Alex Fréchet, *John Galsworthy: A Reassessment*, translated by Denis Mahaffey (Totowa, N.J.: Barnes & Noble, 1982);

Richard Gill, *Happy Rural Seat: The English Country House and the Literary Imagination* (New Haven & London: Yale University Press, 1972);

David Holloway, *John Galsworthy* (London: Morgan-Grampion, 1968);

Richard M. Kain, "Galsworthy, the Last Victorian Liberal," *Madison Quarterly*, 4 (1944): 84-94;

Sheila Kaye-Smith, *John Galsworthy* (New York: Holt, 1916);

Kathryne S. McDorman, "Imperialism Debit and Credit–Some Edwardian Authors' Views," *Illinois Quarterly*, 43 (Summer 1981): 41-50;

Peter McQuitty, "The Forsyte Chronicles: A Nineteenth Century Liberal View of History," *English Literature in Transition*, 23 (1980): 99-114;

R. H. Mottram, *John Galsworthy* (London: Longmans, Green, 1953);

Herman Ould, *John Galsworthy* (London: Chapman & Hall, 1934);

Joseph John Reilly, "John Galsworthy–An Appraisal," *Bookman*, 74 (January-February 1932): 483-493;

Leon Schalit, *John Galsworthy: A Survey* (New York: Scribners, 1928; London: Heinemann, 1929);

William J. Scheick, "Chance and Impartiality: A Study Based on the Manuscript of Galsworthy's *Loyalties*," *Texas Studies in Language and Literature*, 17 (1975): 653-672;

Harold Ray Stevens, "Galsworthy's *Fraternity*: The Closed Door and the Paralyzed Society," *English Literature in Transition*, 19 (1976): 283-298;

Walter H. R. Trumbauer, *Gerhart Hauptmann and John Galsworthy: A Parallel* (Philadelphia: University of Pennsylvania Press, 1917).

Papers:

Some of John Galsworthy's manuscripts and letters are held by the Bodleian Library, Oxford University; the Houghton Library, Harvard University; and the Firestone Library, Princeton University.

Eric Gill
(22 February 1882 - 17 November 1940)

Carl Rapp
University of Georgia

BOOKS: *Songs to Our Lady of Silence* (Ditchling, U.K.: St. Dominic's, 1920);

Art-Nonsense and Other Essays (London: Cassell, 1929);

Clothes: An Essay upon the Nature and Significance of the Natural and Artificial Integuments Worn by Men and Women (London: Cape, 1931);

An Essay on Typography (London: Sheed & Ward, 1931; enlarged edition, 1936);

Beauty Looks After Herself (London & New York: Sheed & Ward, 1933);

Money & Morals (London: Faber & Faber, 1934; enlarged edition, 1937);

Art and a Changing Civilisation (London: Lane, 1934);

Work and Leisure (London: Faber & Faber, 1935);

The Necessity of Belief (London: Faber & Faber, 1936);

Work & Property &c (London: Dent, 1937);

Trousers & the Most Precious Ornament (London: Faber & Faber, 1937);

Sacred & Secular &c (London: Dent, Hague & Gill, 1940);

Christianity and the Machine Age (London: Sheldon, 1940; New York: Macmillan, 1940);

Autobiography (London: Cape, 1940; New York: Devin-Adair, 1941);

Last Essays (London: Cape, 1942);

In a Strange Land (London: Cape, 1944);

From the Palestine Diary (London: Harvill, 1949); enlarged as *Palestine Diary* (London: Harvill, 1951).

OTHER: Jacques Maritain, *The Philosophy of Art*, translated by Gill and John O'Connor, with an introduction by Gill (Ditchling, U.K.: St. Dominic's, 1923).

Eric Gill was not primarily a writer, and he certainly never thought of himself as a man of letters. He was, as he says in the epitaph he prepared for his own tombstone, a stone carver. He made his living carving inscriptions and bas-reliefs, and he achieved both fame and success as an engraver, sculptor, and typographic designer. But Gill was also a thinker, and after his conversion to Catholicism was completed in 1913, he began to reflect with an ever-increasing intensity on the social and economic conditions that affect the production of art in the modern world and the relationship between those conditions and the teachings of the Catholic faith. As a result of his reflections, Gill produced a series of essays and lectures, mainly in the 1920s and 1930s, which constitute a powerful critique of modern culture in the tradition of John Ruskin and William Morris. Among his own contemporaries, Gill bears comparison with such important culture critics as Ezra Pound and D. H. Lawrence, though he owes his distinctive approach to the prominence in his writing of his Catholic principles.

Arthur Eric Rowton Gill was born on 22 February 1882 at Brighton in Sussex, the son of Rev. Arthur Tidman Gill and Rose King Gill, his father a Congregationalist minister who eventually joined the Church of England. At the age of fifteen, Gill was sent by his father as a whole-day student to the Chichester Technical and Art School. There he developed an interest in the church music associated with Chichester Cathedral, and he became equally interested in calligraphy. In 1899, however, Gill left Chichester in order to work for W. H. Caroe, who was then architect to the Ecclesiastical Commissioners in London. During Gill's apprenticeship, he became attracted to Fabian socialism and was gradually weaned away from religion by reading the sixpenny tracts of the Rationalist Press Association and the books of authors such as H. G. Wells. Thomas Carlyle and John Ruskin were also among his favorites at this time. Gill decided that he would rather not become an architect, because he did not want to be too far divorced from the work of actually constructing something. Preferring the role of the honest workman to that of the somewhat aloof designer, he enrolled in the Westminster Technical Institute to learn about masonry and attended

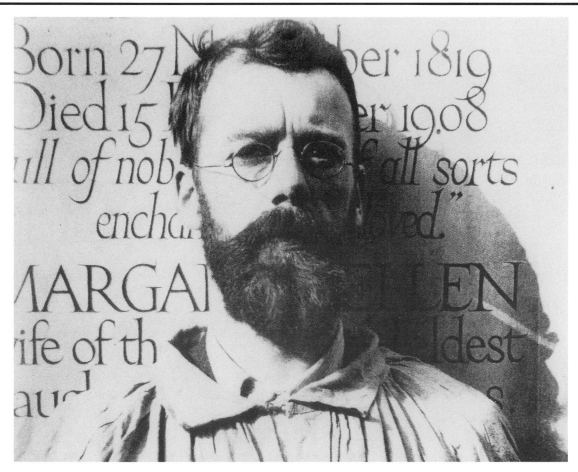

Eric Gill (photograph by Adam Tegetmeier; by permission of the Harry Ransom Humanities Research Center, University of Texas at Austin)

the LCC Central School of Arts and Crafts to learn about lettering. At the Central School he came under the strong influence of Edward Johnston, who approached the art of lettering with an intensity and a wholeness of vision that fascinated Gill. It was Johnston's example that caused Gill to realize that a work of art is, above all, an expression of the intellectual and emotional integrity of a free and responsible artist. And this led, in turn, to a consideration of the conditions that foster or frustrate such expressions, which became the main preoccupation of Gill's later writing.

In 1904, having left his apprenticeship with Caroe and begun his career as a stone carver, Gill married Ethel Mary Moore, who was the daughter of the beadle of Chichester Cathedral. Over the next ten years, as his family grew, Gill himself continued to grow both artistically and intellectually. In 1906 he took on his own apprentice, Joseph Cribb, and in 1907 Gill moved from his home in Hammersmith, taking his wife, his ap-

prentice, and his two small daughters, Elizabeth and Petra (another daughter, Joan, and an adopted son, Gordian, would complete the family), to Ditchling in Sussex, where he eventually gathered around him a community of fellow artists and kindred spirits who shared his distaste for the methods and products of the industrial factory system. While he was still at Hammersmith, he had attended meetings of the Fabian Society and listened with enthusiasm to the speeches of Wells and George Bernard Shaw. He had read Nietzsche with equal enthusiasm and even embarked, very briefly, on an extramarital affair with a young lady whom he met at a Fabian meeting. As Gill's reputation grew, his circle of friends and acquaintances began to include such men as A. R. Orage, editor of *The New Age*; Ananda Coomeraswamy, the Hindu scholar of Ceylonese and Indian art; the classicist Francis Cornford; and such luminaries of the art world as William Rothenstein, Jacob Epstein, and Roger Fry. Gradually Gill's freethinking began to abate.

Gill (center, beneath his Mulier *carving), his wife, Mary (holding their adopted son, Gordian) and (left to right) Desmond Chute, the Gills' daughter Joan, niece Cicely, and daughters, Petra and Betty, at Ditchling Common. The carving is now at the University of California, Los Angeles (photograph by Peter Hill; collection of Angela Lowery)*

He began to consider the spiritual origins of the Indian art Coomeraswamy had shown him and of such monuments of Western art as Chartres Cathedral, which he saw for the first time in 1907 during Easter. By early 1912 he was attending Mass at St. George's Retreat on Ditchling Common and seeking the advice of such Catholic friends as Everard and Wilfred Meynell. Finally, on his birthday in 1913, both Gill and his wife were received into the Catholic Church by Canon Connelly.

Gill's conversion was probably the most important event in his intellectual life, for it gave him the focus and the orientation he needed not only for his own graphic work but also for his mature criticism of modern culture. In 1914 he completed his designs for the Stations of the Cross in Westminster Cathedral, the carving of which he finished in 1918. Meanwhile, in 1917 the project of forming a religious order of artists at Ditchling was conceived. In 1918 Gill, his wife, and two friends, Desmond Chute and Hilary Pepler, were received as novices of the Third Order of St. Dominic. Later in 1918, Gill received the habit of a Dominican tertiary from Father Vincent McNabb and was professed on 1 January 1920. Gill was further influenced by the neo-Thomism of Jacques Maritain, whose *Art et Scholastique* (1919) he helped to translate with Father John O'Connor as *The Philosophy of Art*, published in 1923 with an introduction by Gill. Although his views were sometimes alarming to those in authority, it is clear that Gill's Catholicism was deep and unwavering and strongly affected all of his activities.

In 1923 Gill also produced a highly controversial carving for the Leeds University War Memorial. He depicted Christ driving the money-changers out of the Temple, alluding both to the fact that World War I had been caused by the commercial rivalries–the Mammon worship–of nations involved in it and also to the fact that Christ himself gave his sanction to the making of war on such worship. Many of those who saw the memorial found it distasteful, because it seemed to suggest that all commercial interests might be tainted, which, of course, was precisely Gill's intention. Gill was, in fact, insisting that a fundamental critique of contemporary culture was the logical consequence of an adherence to Catholicism, it being clear (to Gill, at least) that the Germans were not alone responsible for the disaster of the war.

As the result of an argument with his Ditchling colleague Pepler concerning the community's financial management, Gill struck out on his own in the summer of 1924, removing his home and workshop to the rather remote Capel-y-ffin in South Wales. However, the inaccessibility of Capel-y-ffin made it necessary for Gill to spend much of his time traveling in connection with his work, and so in 1928 he moved back to England to a place called Pigotts, near High Wycombe. There he found just the right conditions for his work and his home life, and there he remained until his death. It was at about this time–1928–that Gill designed two new printing types called Felicity and Perpetua. The latter was used the following year in the printing of Gill's first major collection of essays. This collection, entitled *Art-Nonsense and Other Essays* (1929), gathered together in one volume almost all the pieces Gill had published separately during the preceding twelve years, beginning with "Slavery and Freedom," which had appeared in 1917.

In the 1930s Gill continued to meditate on what he took to be the artistic and social implications of the religion to which he had attached himself. Indeed, his essays during this decade denounce the ill effects of capitalism with an increasing stridency that began to alarm his fellow Catholics, who feared that he might be leaning in the direction of communism. These fears took the form of open criticism when, in 1934, Gill ventured to exhibit a woodcut with Artists International and allowed his name to appear on the cover of *Left Review*. It is clear from his own pronouncements, however, that he was never seriously inclined to become a communist, even in the 1930s. In fact, the most authoritative Catholic estimate of the orthodoxy of Gill's political views seems to have come from Pope Pius XII himself, who is reported to have said on the basis of a perusal of one of Gill's books: "This man has understood our Encyclicals."

During the last ten years of his life Gill's professional work as a carver included two major commissions. The first came at the end of 1930 from the governors of the BBC and involved the carving of two figures–Prospero and Ariel–over the main entrance of Broadcasting House in London. The second commission came in 1935 for a sculptured panel for the assembly hall of the new League of Nations in Geneva. Gill chose for his subject the creation of Adam, although the point of his representation, as he explained in a memorandum, was to suggest "the *re*-creation of man, which the League of Nations is assisting." Among his other commissions was the monument for G. K. Chesterton, who died in 1936.

Gill's last years were crowded with honors. He was elected an honorary associate of the Institute of British Architects in 1935, and in 1937 he was made an associate of the Royal Academy. The following year he was elected an honorary associate of the Royal Society of British Sculptors and was included among the first eleven appointments to the distinction of Designer for Industry conferred by the Royal Society of Arts. In the same year (1938) he was even given an honorary Doctorate of Laws by the University of Edinburgh. Perhaps the best indication of Gill's attitude toward these honors is to be found in a remark he made to his brother Cecil regarding those who had commissioned him to do the League of Nations panel: "They think I'm prophet & seer & at the same time don't believe in my prophecies." In October 1940, having just finished writing his *Autobiography* (published later that year), Gill was informed that he was suffering from lung cancer. In spite of a modified operation, which was carried out successfully on 11 November, his condition rapidly worsened, and he died six days later in Harefield House hospital in Middlesex.

Gill had great strengths as an essayist, which were due primarily to his singleness of purpose and to the directness–the forthrightness–of his arguments and expression. Almost invariably his essays begin with a statement of first principles in which the basic terms of his exposition are set forth and defined. In effect, this means that what-

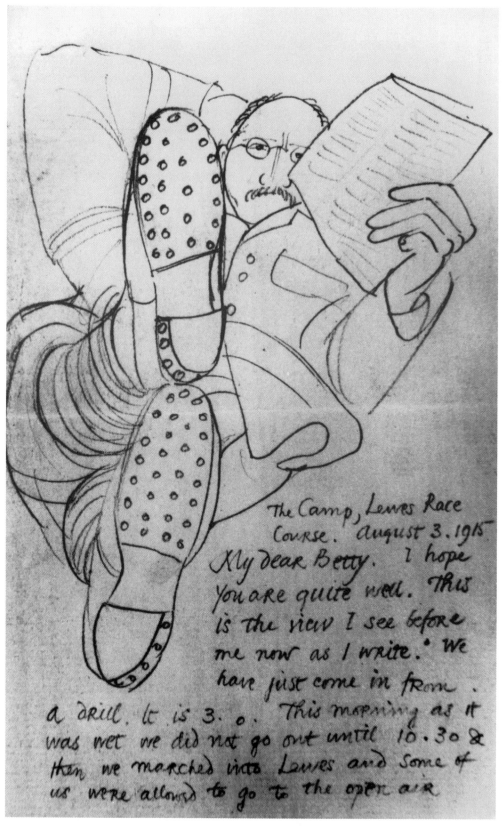

The Camp, Lewes Race Course. August 3. 1915 My dear Betty. I hope you are quite well. This is the view I see before me now as I write.° We have just come in from. a drill. It is 3. o. This morning as it was wet we did not go out until 10.30 & then we marched into Lewes and some of us were allowed to go to the open air

Letter from Gill to his daughter Betty, written at a Home Defence Brigade training camp (Clark Library, University of California, Los Angeles)

ever his particular subject happens to be–styles of clothing, the nature of wood engraving, the Song of Songs, or the analogy between slavery and capitalism–he always begins by considering his subject in relation to his most basic beliefs concerning the nature of man and man's relationship to God. Starting from these fundamental beliefs, he arrives by a process of deduction at their implications for the particular subject at hand. The unmistakable impression is that one is looking at the whole of Gill's philosophy in terms of the light it sheds on a particular, concrete aspect of human experience. The gist of Gill's approach, in essay after essay, is to insist that both bad thinking and bad practice in the various areas of human experience are attributable to the fact that people have lost sight of first principles. If only one would start with some sort of coherent vision of what human beings are, such as Catholicism provides, then the solutions to social and economic problems, as well as to artistic problems, would naturally fall into place. Instead of trying to solve problems piecemeal, one could see how all the departments of human activity and expression fit in relation to each other harmoniously. Whatever disharmony, confusion, or tension seems to plague the world can be attributed directly to a refusal to entertain just this kind of vision.

The most striking expression of Gill's conception of human nature is to be found, perhaps, in the following passage at the very end of his *Autobiography* (1940): "The thing about Christianity, the thing about the Cross, about Calvary, is that it is true to man. Man, not that creature, that biped, known to Science–measured as to his dimensions, his comparative dimensions, for there are no others; dissected as to his physiology; analysed as to his psyche–but man, the person known to himself and to God, the creature who knows and wills and loves, master of his acts (however much he be hindered by and subject to heredity and circumstance), therefore responsible. That is the creature who desires happiness and by the very nature of things, by his own nature, cannot find it except in God." Everything in Gill's writing, from beginning to end, follows from this particular conception of human nature in its relation to God. It is this idea that explains his objection to what he calls slavery in his first considerable essay, "Slavery and Freedom." There he writes: "A man is a slave when between him and God who is the *final* cause is interposed another man as an *efficient* cause." From this it follows that the

factory system, which depends entirely on the direction of labor and which lies at the heart of all modern industrial modes of production, is a great evil, because it thwarts the relation between God and man that both requires and permits man to be free and responsible. Gill's social writings recur constantly to this particular argument, and that is why his socialism has so little to do with the goal of achieving the most equitable distribution of goods and services.

Gill's conception of human nature is also the source of his views about art. Every man, according to Gill, is an artist, because every man takes a natural delight in doing well or making well something that needs doing or needs making. In such doing and making, he praises his Creator and expresses his love of God. In modern society, however, most men are wage slaves who have no control over what they are doing or making. Since they take no delight in, because they have no control over, the products of their own labor, those products are inferior and the men themselves dehumanized. Those few men who refuse to conform and insist on expressing themselves freely and directly all too often become estranged from the process of doing that which needs doing or making that which needs making. As a result, they tend to produce an increasingly self-indulgent, rarefied "fine" art, which is culturally rootless and spiritually barren. The mystique of such art in a world otherwise devoted to spiritual and material ugliness represents for Gill a fatal disfigurement of human nature. Thus Gill's objection to both the banalities of commercial art and the pretensions of "high" art or "fine" art is rooted in a consistent analysis of human need and human nature. Indeed, it is the consistency of his viewpoint and the relentlessness with which he works out its implications in particular instances that impress the reader of his essays.

For all the fervency of his appeal to first principles, Gill speaks in his essays not as a cloistered monk or as a professional theologian but as a practicing artist situated firmly in the world. He never seeks to divorce spirituality from the concreteness of actual life, and therefore he tends to regard every activity, every human function, no matter how trivial or apparently gross, as a significant expression of the total spiritual ethos of the culture that produced it. Cheap, machine-made goods, like the mindless reproduction of Gothic ornamentation in church architecture, are, for him, the symptoms of a pervasive spiritual sickness; hence the need to take a prophetic stance after

Gill and W. I. Burch, managing director of the Monotype Corporation, in 1929. Gill designed three typefaces for Monotype: Perpetua, Gill Sans-serif, and Solus.

the manner of Blake or Ruskin. No wonder, then, that a *Sunday Times* critic once described Gill's style as a cross between Euclid's axioms and the Athanasian Creed.

In the preface to his second large collection of essays, *Beauty Looks After Herself* (1933), Gill admits that his basic theme is always the same and that his key points are often repeated from essay to essay. This in no way diminishes the pleasure to be derived from Gill's usually strong style with its characteristic passages of fierce indignation. Frequently enough, the reader will find such stylistic gems as the following passage from *The Necessity of Belief* (1936) in which Gill says, to capitalists and communists alike, a plague on both your

houses. The communists, he avers, have "thrown away the god whom capitalists profess to worship and do not, and have accepted the servitude which capitalism has developed and perfected but whose existence capitalists deny. Thus they have not emptied out the baby with the bath water. They have retained that bath water while emptying out the baby. They have emptied out the Baby of Bethlehem only to swallow the foul and befouling bath water of London and Manchester."

A year later, in his tour de force called *Trousers & the Most Precious Ornament* (1937), the affinity between Gill's attack on modern society and Lawrence's attack (from a different point of

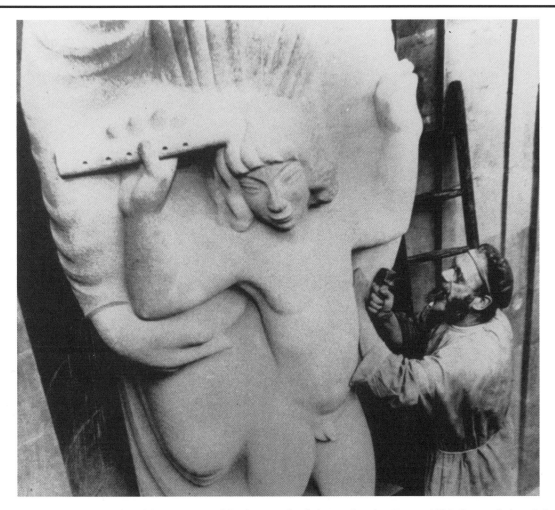

Gill working on Prospero and Ariel, *commissioned by the BBC for their Broadcasting House, 1931 (by permission of the BBC)*

view) can be felt in passages like this one, which is typical in its intensity: "Hence it is that in a world devoted to commerce, trading, shop-keeping, money-making, the male creature is under eclipse. He is not wanted, and a premium is put upon the rabbit type, the kind that sees nothing wrong in travelling in a tube to and from the city where, cooped up in burrows, they scuffle and scoop and nibble and grab for little profits and 'quick returns,' where the highest ambition is to make lots of money, by means proper to tricksters & card sharpers (always remembering that 'honesty is the best policy' and that the only sin is being found out), and thus gain the extraordinarily not-worth-having power of being able to buy large quantities of things, food, clothing, houses, cars & amusements provided by people who regard such things as the rabbit man himself does, simply as so many means of making money to be spent in similar ways–all men more or less cheating and scrounging and wangling and grabbing and grasping in order to get enough money to buy the products of the same cheating and scrounging and wangling and grabbing and grasping as performed by others–the baker baking inferior commercial bread in order to make money to buy the inferior bread of other commercial bakers. No wonder they dress him in trousers and tie up his maleness all crushed and sideways and tell him it's dirty." Because of Gill's ability to produce passages like these, his essays will continue to appeal to a small but dedicated audience of kindred minds.

Letters:

Letters of Eric Gill, edited by Walter Shewring (London: Cape, 1947; New York: Devon-Adair, 1948).

Bibliography:

Evan R. Gill, *Bibliography of Eric Gill* (London: Cassell, 1953).

Biographies:

Robert Speaight, *The Life of Eric Gill* (New York: Kenedy, 1966);

Donald Attwater, *A Cell of Good Living: The Life, Works and Opinions of Eric Gill* (London: Chapman, 1969).

References:

Donald Attwater, *Modern Christian Revolutionaries* (New York: Devin-Adair, 1947);

Peter Faulkner, *William Morris and Eric Gill* (Salisbury, U.K.: William Morris Society, 1975);

Cecil Gill, and others, *The Life and Works of Eric Gill: Papers Read at a Clark Library Symposium, 22 April 1967* (Los Angeles: William Andrews Clark Memorial Library, 1968);

Rayner Heppenstall, *Four Absentees* (London: Barrie & Rockliff, 1960);

David Kindersley, *Eric Gill: Further Thoughts by an Apprentice* (New York: Sandstone, 1982).

Papers and Art Collections:

The largest collection of engravings, drawings, sculpture, and other works by Gill is in the Iconography Collection of the Humanities Research Center at the University of Texas at Austin. This collection is based on the Liverpool collection of Mr. and Mrs. S. Samuels, which was acquired by the Humanities Research center in 1963. A catalogue of the Austin collection was compiled in 1982 by Robert N. Taylor. Yet another American collection of Gill's work, including inscriptions, sculpture, drawings, illustrations, and type design, as well as books and articles, is in the William Andrews Clark Memorial Library at the University of California, Los Angeles. An important collection of Gill's engravings is in the Victoria and Albert Museum in London, the catalogue for which, by J. F. Physick, was published in 1963.

R. B. Cunninghame Graham

(24 May 1852 - 20 March 1936)

Rita Malenczyk
New York University

BOOKS: *The Nail and Chainmakers,* by Graham, J. L. Mahon, and C. A. V. Conybeare (London: London Press, n.d.);

Economic Evolution (Aberdeen: Leatham / London: Reeves, 1891);

Notes on the District of Menteith, for Tourists and Others (London: Black, 1895);

Father Archangel of Scotland, and Other Essays, by Graham and Gabriela Marie Cunninghame Graham (London: Black, 1896);

Aurora La Cujiñi: A Realistic Sketch in Seville (London: Smithers, 1898);

Mogreb-el-Acksa: A Journey in Morocco (London: Heinemann, 1898; revised edition, London: Duckworth, 1921; New York: Viking, 1930);

The Ipané (London: Unwin, 1899; New York: Boni, 1925);

Thirteen Stories (London: Heinemann, 1900);

A Vanished Arcadia: Being Some Account of the Jesuits in Paraguay, 1607-1767 (London: Heinemann / New York: Macmillan, 1901);

Success (London: Duckworth, 1902);

Hernando de Soto: Together with an Account of One of His Captains, Gonçalo Silvestre (London: Heinemann, 1903; New York: Dial, 1924);

Progress and Other Sketches (London: Duckworth, 1905);

His People (London: Duckworth, 1906);

Faith (London: Duckworth, 1909);

Hope (London: Duckworth, 1910);

Charity (London: Duckworth, 1912);

A Hatchment (London: Duckworth, 1913);

Scottish Stories (London: Duckworth, 1914);

Bernal Diaz del Castillo: Being Some Account of Him, Taken from His True History of the Conquest of New Spain (London: Nash, 1915; New York: Dodd, Mead, 1915);

Brought Forward (London: Duckworth, 1916; New York: Stokes, 1916);

A Brazilian Mystic: Being the Life and Miracles of Antonio Conselheiro (London: Heinemann, 1920; New York: Dodd, Mead, 1920);

Cartagena and the Banks of the Sinú (London:

R. B. Cunninghame Graham

Heinemann, 1920; New York: Doran, 1921);

The Conquest of New Granada: Being the Life of Gonzalo Jimenez de Quesada (London: Heinemann, 1922; Boston: Houghton Mifflin, 1922);

The Dream of the Magi (London: Heinemann, 1923);

The Conquest of the River Plate (London: Heinemann, 1924; Garden City, N. Y.: Doubleday, Page, 1924);

Doughty Deeds: An Account of the Life of Robert Graham of Gartmore, Poet and Politician,

1735-1797 (London: Heinemann, 1925; New York: MacVeagh, 1925);

Pedro de Valdivia, Conqueror of Chile (London: Heinemann, 1926; New York & London: Harper, 1927);

Redeemed, and Other Sketches (London: Heinemann, 1927);

José Antonio and Páez (London: Heinemann, 1929; Philadelphia: Macrae-Smith, 1929);

Bibi (London: Heinemann, 1929);

The Horses of the Conquest (London: Heinemann, 1930; Norman: University of Oklahoma Press, 1949);

Writ in Sand (London: Heinemann, 1932);

Portrait of a Dictator, Francisco Solano Lopez (Paraguay, 1865-1870) (London: Heinemann, 1933);

Mirages (London: Heinemann, 1936);

Three Fugitive Pieces (Hanover, N.H.: Westholm, 1960).

Collections: *Thirty Tales and Sketches,* edited by Edward Garnett (London: Duckworth, 1929; New York: Viking, 1929);

Rodeo: A Collection of the Tales and Sketches of R. B. Cunninghame Graham, edited by A. F. Tschiffely (London: Heinemann, 1936; Garden City, N.Y.: Doubleday, Doran, 1936);

The Essential R. B. Cunninghame Graham, edited by Paul Bloomfield (London: Cape, 1952);

Selected Short Stories, edited by Clover Pertiñez (Madrid: Alhambra, 1959);

The South American Sketches of R. B. Cunninghame Graham, edited by John Walker (Norman: University of Oklahoma Press, 1978);

Beattock for Moffat: and the Best of R. B. Cunninghame Graham (Edinburgh: Harris, 1979); republished as *Reincarnation: the Best Short Stories of R. B. Cunninghame Graham* (New Haven: Ticknor & Fields, 1980);

Selected Writings of Cunninghame Graham, edited by Cedric T. Watts (East Brunswick, N.J.: Fairleigh Dickinson University Press, 1981);

Tales of Horsemen (Edinburgh: Canongate, 1981);

Scottish Sketches, edited by John Walker (Edinburgh: Scottish Academic Press, 1982).

Discussions of the life and works of R. B. Cunninghame Graham have typically given less attention to the works than to the life. George Bernard Shaw, for example, while acknowledging his debt to Graham's *Mogreb-el-Acksa* (1898) in his notes to *Captain Brassbound's Conversion* (in *Three Plays for Puritans*, 1906), discusses Graham's book briefly at the beginning of the notes and then de-

Graham, age seventeen

votes far more space to a sketch of Graham the man: "He is, I understand, a Spanish hidalgo. . . . He is, I know, a Scotch laird. How he contrives to be authentically the two things at the same time is no more intelligible to me than the fact that everything that has ever happened to him seems to have happened in Paraguay or Texas instead of in Spain or Scotland. He is, I regret to add, an impenitent and unashamed dandy: such boots, such a hat, would have dazzled D'Orsay himself." Though Graham was a prolific essayist as well as a translator, historian, and biographer, and though Ford Madox Ford later called him "the most brilliant writer of that or of our present day" (*Return to Yesterday,* 1931), most contemporary observers seemed to agree with the painter John Lavery's comment that Graham's masterpiece was himself. As Socialist member of Parliament, world traveler, pamphleteer, horseman, and friend of the literati, he captured the imagination of his generation. It is not, perhaps, surprising that in the years immediately following Graham's death his writings, left without the help of his living, breathing presence, passed into obscurity and took second place to the work of his friends and acquaintances: Joseph Conrad, Ford, and Shaw. Today, however, a new generation of scholars is examining Graham's literary as well as personal influence on the work of Conrad and others, evaluating his importance as an anti-imperialist writer.

Robert Bontine Cunninghame Graham was born at 5 Cadogan Place, London, on 24 May 1852, the first of three sons of Maj. William Cunninghame Bontine, a cavalry officer in the Scots Greys, and Anne Elizabeth Fleeming Bontine. His background was both aristocratic and cosmopolitan. From his father, one of the Cunninghame Grahams of Menteith (Bontine was an alternating surname), he inherited claims to the Scottish earldoms of Menteith, Glencairn, Strathearn, and Airth, as well as an ancestry that could be traced back to King Robert I of Scotland. From his mother came Hispanic blood and a history of involvement in Latin America: his maternal grandfather, Adm. Charles Elphinstone Fleeming, had married a Spanish heiress and served as a mediator between José Antonio Páez and Simon Bolívar during the South American wars of liberation. As a boy Graham received private tutoring, and in 1865 he entered Harrow, an institution at which he excelled in athletics but proved less proficient in academic skills. Two years later, possibly because family funds were scarce, he withdrew and continued his education privately in London and Brussels. In 1870, having learned Spanish while in school and uninspired by the thought of the military future his family envisioned for him, Graham sailed for South America to learn cattle ranching on the Argentine estate of James Ogilvy. He remained in Central and South America for the better part of the next eight years, working as rancher, horse trader, surveyor in the Paraguayan tea trade, and—unofficially—as interpreter for non-Spanish speakers, and observer of the life of the pampas. Dressed in the gaucho *chiripá*, he learned the arts of horsemanship and fighting and grew excited by the prospect of recording the customs of the country.

Graham in 1886, when he was elected Liberal M.P. for North-West Lanarkshire

During a return to Europe in 1878 he met and married the writer and painter Gabrielle Marie de la Balmondière, called Gabriela, reputedly the orphaned nineteen-year-old daughter of a Chilean merchant. The couple spent the first two years of their marriage in Texas and Mexico, ostensibly breeding mules but in reality traveling from place to place on Graham's family funds to avoid the violence perpetuated by racism and civil war. In 1881, due largely to the failure of several money-making ventures and to Graham's ill health—he had inflamed kidneys and had, at one point, contracted malaria—they returned to Europe, living for a time at Vigo, Spain, and then on a farm in Hampshire.

In 1883 Major Bontine, who had suffered for twenty years from periods of insanity brought on by a head wound, died and left the family estates to Graham, his eldest son. For a time Graham concerned himself with the management of his inheritance, particularly the main estate of Gartmore in Perthshire, which was encumbered by debts totaling more than sixty thousand pounds. Soon, however, he proved to have inherited the family political tendencies: Bontine, a Radical, had once stood unsuccessfully for Parliament, and in the summer of 1886 Graham, after two tries, was elected Liberal M.P. for North-West Lanarkshire. He soon created a sensation among the electorate by becoming "the only member of Parliament who can really be called a Socialist" (*People's Press*, 26 April 1890). Though other politicians in England supported Socialist causes– the eight-hour workday, nationalization of industry, free education, and an end to child labor– Graham distinguished himself by behaving, in deliberate contrast to the Lib-Labs and the Fabians, as a man of action.

In 1888, with Keir Hardie, Graham founded the Scottish Labour Party and was an original member of the Scottish Home Rule Association; in the summer of 1889 he campaigned with Ben Tillett, Tom Mann, and John Burns for increased wages for the London dockers; on the literary scene, he served on the board of directors of the *People's Press* and on the committee of management for the *Labour Elector*, contributing articles to these and other periodicals and producing two pamphlets, *The Nail and Chainmakers* (circa 1889, with J. L. Mahon and C. A. V. Conybeare) and *Economic Evolution* (1891). On Bloody Sunday, 13 November 1887, in his most notorious political exploit, he and Burns were beaten, arrested, and jailed after marching into a line of police during the free-speech riots in Trafalgar Square. They were subsequently charged with assaulting the police, causing a riot, and illegal assembly. Despite Graham's claims of innocence–"all the arms collected from that vast crowd," he wrote in a 10 November 1888 letter to *Commonweal*, "amounted to three pokers, one piece of wood, and an oyster-knife"–he and Burns were found guilty of illegal assembly and sentenced to six weeks in Pentonville Jail. The incident, together with the fact that Graham had been suspended from Parliament several times for making inflammatory remarks (including the "I never withdraw" speech immortalized by Shaw in *Arms and the Man*, 1913), caused certain Londoners to admire his idealistic, Quixotic windmill charging but led others to say he was crazy.

Graham began his literary career in the 1880s with the writing of political polemics and continued it in later years by branching out into other genres. By the time of his death he had written more than four hundred essays and sketches, many of which were subsequently collected in book form, as well as a guidebook, two travel

Graham in prison garb at Pentonville Gaol, after being arrested during the Bloody Sunday riots of November 1887 (engraving based on a sketch by Tom Merry; published in the 28 January 1888 issue of St. Stephen's Review)

books, seven histories of the Spanish conquest, four biographies, and numerous prefaces, pamphlets, and translations. Though Graham continued to write political pieces throughout his life, he is best known for his other works. His essays and sketches, which are often difficult to classify, show a preoccupation with the desirability of apparent failure instead of worldly success; a preference for "uncultivated" societies over the civilization of England; and a contempt for white imperialism. Stylistically they are marked by a habit of apparently random and unplanned digression from the description or narrative at hand, which often leads to reflections on human– specifically, British–morality. Though Graham's method was often criticized as haphazard, his work, though admittedly less disciplined than that of most impressionists–Conrad and Ford come to mind–shares with theirs the presence of accumulated detail designed to lead the reader to discerning traces of the personal preoccupations and moral issues behind the writing.

In 1891, in what some regarded as yet another high-minded but ultimately futile political gesture, Graham participated in a May Day march with workers in France and subsequently delivered a speech condemning the shooting of striking miners at Fourmies. The tone of the speech caused the French authorities to expel him from the country and the *Times* to chastise him for not minding his own business while a guest in another nation. With his reputation as a "wild man" thus firmly established among the more staid portions of the electorate, Graham contested and lost the parliamentary seat for the Camlachie district of Glasgow in 1892. His parliamentary obligations finished, he proceeded to divide his time between managing Gartmore–which was falling dangerously into disrepair–and traveling, sometimes alone and sometimes with Gabriela, in Spain and Morocco. His ventures in Spain ranged from research into the history of South America to an unsuccessful attempt to prospect for gold, based on a description of the mines of Lusitania in Pliny's *Historia Naturalis*. He also continued to read in Spanish, becoming so well versed in the literature and language that he was soon acknowledged by the Hispanist James Fitzmaurice-Kelly to be one of the most capable translators in the world.

During this time Graham continued to write political polemics; in the pages of *Justice*, the *Social-Democrat*, the *Saturday Review*, and other periodicals he condemned the Jameson Raid, the Boer War, and U.S. intervention in Latin America, and took the side of Spain in the Spanish-American War. He had, however, been encouraged by his friend William Henry Hudson–who had also spent his youth in Latin America–to record his South American experiences in print. It was partly at Hudson's suggestion, partly as a relief from political polemics, that Graham began to compose essays and sketches on Latin America and Scotland. The sketches first appeared as "middles" (fillers) in the *Saturday Review* and, along with some other articles, were subsequently published in two collections by A. and C. Black: *Notes on the District of Menteith* (1895) and *Father Archangel of Scotland, and Other Essays* (1896). The two books reveal Graham's concern with the impending disappearance of certain non-English cultures and illustrate his habit of not keeping strictly to one particular form or tone. In the first, which Cedric T. Watts and Laurence Davies call a "lament for mutability" occasioned by the decay of Gartmore, Graham provides portraits of some of

Graham, circa 1890

his famous ancestors as well as descriptions of the Menteith region of Scotland. Alternately wry (it is dedicated to a poacher) and florid, the volume serves both as a guidebook and as a commentary on the passage of time: "Could we but see a shadow of the future, and compare it with the shadows of the past, why, then, we might know something of Menteith and other districts where the shadows play, coming, like life, from nowhere, and returning into nothing."

The second book, *Father Archangel of Scotland,* is a collection of essays, sketches, and tales based on Graham's experiences in Morocco, South America, and Scotland, and partly written by his wife. Unlike *Notes on the District of Menteith,* in which Graham provides the controlling image of shadows passing over the hills and valleys of Scotland, *Father Archangel of Scotland* has no apparent organizing principle: Graham claims in the preface that the pieces in the book will probably "resemble a crowd of people at a railway junction, all rushing to and fro, without connection save only of the labels on their luggage." What connects them is Graham's concern, indirectly expressed, for vanishing civilizations. In "The Horses of the Pampas," written while he was in Parliament, Graham explains that he has been asked (by *Times* editor Belfort Bax) to write an essay on the Eight Hours Bill but that his thoughts keep straying into other areas: "my friend's letter brought back to me the broad plains, the countless herds of horses, the wild life, the camp fire. . . . " He proceeds to discuss what he remembers of "horses who have been to me what horses can never be to a man who surveys them through the eyes of his stud groom." Anticipating the preconceived notions of British readers, he writes that the gaucho's horse "appears the most indolent of the equine race" until "the owner of the horse approach[es] with his waving poncho, his ringing spurs, his heavy hide and silver-mounted whip, and his long, flying black hair; let him by that mysterious process, seemingly an action of the will, and known only to the Gaucho, transfer himself to their backs, without apparent physical exertion, and all is changed. The dull, blinking animal wakes into life, and in a few minutes his slow gallop, regular as clockwork, has made him and his half-savage rider a mere speck upon the horizon." By providing a vivid description of the gaucho's relationship to his horse, Graham allows the reader to contrast Argentine society–in which horse and man are one–with British society, in which horses are often regarded as mere property. Though occasionally unsubtle and excessively wistful, Graham succeeds in providing a critique of industrial civilization.

Graham's first two collections received mixed reviews: the *Times, Guardian,* and *Atheneum* generally praised *Notes on the District of Menteith,* the *Times* critic commenting that readers would find "not a little to entertain" in the book even though it was "often wayward and whimsical" (6

Graham's wife, Gabriela, in 1900 (by permission of the Baker Library, Dartmouth College)

September 1895). Reviewers of *Father Archangel of Scotland* were more irritated by what they considered Graham's tendency to go off on tangents: the *Bookman* (April 1896), for instance, while acknowledging the exceptional interest of many of the pieces, implied that the successful passages were too few and far between to sustain the book as a whole: it was, said the reviewer, marked by "passages of great liveliness, useless angry outbursts, and foolish jokes." Neither book was reprinted in its entirety, though individual pieces have been included in later collections.

While the critics' responses to Graham's work was less than effusive, the late 1890s saw Graham establishing a loyal readership among other writers and many friendships in the literary, political, and artistic world. A partial list of Graham's friends and acquaintances reads like a roll call of famous names of the period: Shaw, Conrad, Ford, Hudson, Oscar Wilde, W. B. Yeats, Edward Garnett, Ezra Pound, H. G. Wells, John Galsworthy, William Morris, Charles Stewart Parnell, Prince Pyotr Kropotkin, Friedrich Engels. To the painters William Rothenstein, John Lavery, and

William Strang, Graham served not only as a friend but as a model, allowing his gracefully up-turned moustaches and dashing figure to adorn several portraits and sculptures, notably Strang's series of etchings illustrating *Don Quixote*; Graham also wrote prefaces to catalogues of art exhibitions. Perhaps his most important friendship, however, was with Conrad, to whom he introduced himself in an 1897 letter praising Conrad's story "An Outpost of Progress," which had appeared in *Cosmopolis*. The letter began a correspondence and close friendship that lasted until Conrad's death in 1924. Graham took it upon himself to lend Conrad money and praise the up-and-coming writer's works in conversation and print. In a letter of 9 August 1897, Conrad wrote: "I am both touched and frightened by what you say about being the prophet of my inarticulate and wandering shadow. I can not help thinking with alarm of the day when you shall find me out or rather find out that there is nothing there. How soon will you regret your magnificent imprudence?" (*Joseph Conrad's Letters to R. B. Cunninghame Graham*, edited by Cedric T. Watts, 1969). Conrad, in his turn, proved to be a faithful reader of Graham's own work and occasionally offered to correct Graham's proofs, a labor Graham often neglected. Though Conrad decried Graham's idealism, the two shared a love of the sea and travel and a hatred of imperialism. Some commentators have suggested that Conrad's friendship with Graham was the source of his concept of the secret sharer, and that Graham's work and ideas were a strong influence on Conrad's writings during the years up to 1907.

Shortly after his meeting with Conrad, Graham embarked on the most notorious exploit of his nonpolitical career. He had for some time been attracted by the idea of traveling to the Forbidden City of Tarudant in the Sus region of Morocco, partly because of the "forbiddenness" of the whole enterprise—only a few Christians had been to Tarudant in the previous hundred years—and partly out of love of the Moroccan landscape and a desire to see the city. The year 1897, however, was particularly dangerous for political as well as religious reasons: a British major, A. G. Spilsbury, had set out with the Globe Venture Syndicate to sell arms to the sheikhs of the Sus, thereby incurring the wrath of the Sultan of Morocco, who technically ruled the region. In England, Graham had been advised by a friend that the journey through Morocco was not unusually

hazardous; yet when he arrived in Mogador in October 1897, the situation was more tense than he thought. Not only was the Sultan hostile to Europeans, but the Howara tribe was in rebellion in the Sus, blocking a relatively easy approach to Tarudant; to reach the city Graham would have to cross the Atlas Mountains, a formidable undertaking in itself. Graham decided that the best course to take was to attempt the journey disguised as a Moslem. With three fellow travelers—a Moor, a Christian, and a Berber muleteer—to act as guides and interpreters, Graham became Sheikh Mohammed el Fasi, an Arab with skill in medicine, and set out to reach the Forbidden City. On the way he and his party were captured, detained for a period of time, and ultimately forced to turn back. On his return to England, Graham submitted his chronicle of this journey to Heinemann for publication; it was accepted and published in December 1898 as *Mogreb-el-Acksa* ("the Far West"). The wealth of local description in the book, as well as the fact that Graham makes his journey disguised as a Moslem, has prompted some critics to place it in the company of Richard Burton's *Pilgrimage to El-Medinah and Meccah* (1855-1856).

Yet *Mogreb-el-Acksa* refuses to be classified a simple book of travel literature. Interspersed with lively descriptions of the North African countryside and customs are reflections on the differences between Moroccan and British culture, enlivened by Graham's anti-imperialist views and his awareness of himself as an outsider. Clad as Sheikh Mohammed el Fasi, Graham undergoes an unusual reversal of roles: he is not a white man who is attempting to impose his own form of civilization on another culture, but an escapee from a "wilderness of broadcloth" who sees the Arab way of life as just as appealing as his own. This ability to empathize, left over from Graham's days in the pampas, distinguishes Graham from Burton and places *Mogreb-el-Acksa*, somewhat tentatively, in the category of political polemic, though Graham blunts the force of his political opinions through humor.

Mogreb-el-Acksa was admired by Graham's friends and fellow writers for its artistic achievements as well as for its political stance. Edward Garnett (in *Academy*, 4 February 1899) called it "a delicious commentary on our Anglo-Saxon civilisation; a malicious and ironic comparison of the British commercialised world with the feudal world of Morocco; a subtle, witty commentary that must rejoice all who are rejoiced by *Candide*."

Graham in 1897 disguised as an Arab sheikh in order to gain safe passage through Morocco (Collection of John Conrad)

Conrad, more effusive, wrote to his friend: "No thirsty men drank water as we have been drinking in, swallowing, tasting, blessing, enjoying gurgling, choking over, absorbing, your thought, your phrases, your irony. . . . The individuality of the book is amazing, even to me who know you or pretend to." In the notes to *Captain Brassbound's Conversion* Shaw wrote that he had "been intelligent enough to steal its scenery, its geography, its knowledge of the east . . . from an excellent book of philosophic travel and vivid adventure entitled *Mogreb-el-Acksa*" and had asked Graham, in a long questionnaire, to provide additional details. Reviewers and critics were also enthusiastic about the book, which Richard Haymaker has since termed a masterpiece.

While awaiting the publication of *Mogreb-el-Acksa*, Graham had published *Aurora La Cujiñi: A Realistic Sketch in Seville*, a word portrait of a dancer based on a lithograph he and Rothenstein had seen while traveling in Spain. The booklet was brought out in 1898 by Leonard Smithers after rejection by several other publishers, all of whom were put off by the excessive realism of

the piece (Graham had included some vivid details, among them a mention of the hair under the dancer's armpits). The little volume was well-received by Graham's peers, earning praise from Conrad and Arthur Symons. Also in 1898 Graham made the acquaintance of Edward Garnett, then an editor for T. Fisher Unwin, who had just convinced his employers to undertake the Overseas Library, a projected series of books about English people overseas. Having admired Graham's work in the *Saturday Review* for years, Garnett approached Graham by letter with the suggestion of anthologizing certain of his pieces for the first book of the series. The result of their correspondence was *The Ipané*, published in 1899; the book is notable for a burlesque of Rudyard Kipling–whose politics Graham detested–entitled "Bristol Fashion." The business dealings between Graham and Garnett also started a close friendship and prolific correspondence that lasted through both men's lives.

In 1900 Graham was finally forced to sell his ancestral home of Gartmore. Debts and other obligations had made the estate more of a respon-

Graham in England (Collection of John Conrad)

sibility than he could afford, and consequently it was put up for auction and sold to the shipping magnate Charles Cayser for £126,000. After the sale, the Grahams moved to 7 Sloane Street in London. Soon, however, Graham began to feel the pull of Scotland, and he and Gabriela bought back a cottage at Ardoch, another Graham estate that had been sold; they refurbished it and moved in during the fall of 1904. Easier to manage than Gartmore, the cottage served from that time on as Graham's base in Scotland.

The years between 1900 and 1913 were busy ones for Graham. He continued to be politically active, writing polemics and taking part in demonstrations and campaigns for woman's and laborer's rights. In the pages of the *Glasgow Herald,* he protested the proposed French annexation of Morocco, as well as the subsequent "compromise" by which Spain and France were both authorized to police Morocco. The period included great sorrow: Gabriela died in 1906. Still, Graham was prolific, producing ten volumes, which included *Thirteen Stories* (1900), *Success* (1902), *Progress* (1905), *His People* (1906), *Faith*

(1909), *Hope* (1910), *Charity* (1912), and *A Hatchment* (1913). Two of the best-known stories of the period, "A Gold Fish" (*Thirteen Stories*) and "Beattock for Moffat" (*Success*), illustrate Graham's preoccupation at this time with failed endeavors and transience. In "A Gold Fish" an Arab messenger is entrusted with carrying a bowl of goldfish to the Sultan, with instructions to keep the bowl intact; he follows the instructions but, ironically, dies of thirst along the way. In "Beattock for Moffat," a dying Scotsman makes his final train journey but dies just as the train arrives at his destination. Ford, in *Return to Yesterday,* numbered "Beattock for Moffat" among "pieces of writing that can never die." In addition to books of sketches and essays, Graham published during this period a history of the Jesuits in Paraguay entitled *A Vanished Arcadia* (1901) as well as a biography, *Hernando de Soto* (1903).

In 1914 Graham, who had initially written and spoken against the entry of Britain into World War I, paradoxically applied for service as a Rough Rider. Though he was rejected because of his advanced age–he was then sixty-two, well

Graham speaking in Scotland (the Duke of Montrose is seated at left)

above the acceptable limit–he persisted in trying to obtain employment at the War Office and by November of that year was on the payroll of the government, working in Uruguay to procure horses for the war effort. He returned to England in 1915. In 1918 he made his last attempt to win a parliamentary seat, this time standing as Liberal candidate for West Stirling; he came in last in the election. From that time on he devoted the bulk of his political energy to the cause of Scottish home rule. In 1920 he became president of the Scottish Home Rule Association and, except for one temporary breach, was active in that organization until his death, working in association with Hugh MacDiarmid, Eric Linklater, and Compton Mackenzie. In 1928 he stood as the Scottish Nationalist candidate for the lord rectorship

of Glasgow University and was narrowly beaten by Stanley Baldwin.

Graham's writings after 1915 include five histories, four biographies, a travel book, and four books of essays and sketches: *Brought Forward* (1916), *Redeemed* (1927), *Writ in Sand* (1932), and *Mirages* (1936). The final collections of essays show an aging Graham coming to terms with the vicissitudes of life. In the preface to *Writ in Sand* Graham writes: "Nature has so contrived it, and I admit it is annoying of her, that even genius must eat and sleep, endure the pangs of tooth and belly ache, fall into and out of love, and fulfill all the functions of any ordinary man. . . . " Though his ironic power is still evident ("I admit it is annoying of her"), Graham seems to be admitting his status as an "ordinary man": he pokes fun at himself, rather than at his readers, something he would not have done in the preface to *Father Archangel of Scotland,* where he referred with disdain to "the grinning faces of the respectable public."

In January 1936, in the process of working on a preface to the works of Hudson, Graham made a final visit to South America in the company of a friend, Elizabeth Dummett; he remained until March, but became ill with bronchitis and subsequently contracted pneumonia. He died in Buenos Aires on 20 March and was buried at the family seat of the Clan Graham, on the island of Inchmahome in the Scottish lake of Menteith. Malcolm Muggeridge wrote of him after his death, "In contrast to this calculating, capitalist world he set another, an heroic world, full of richness and colour, with proud values, partly imagining it, partly hoping for its coming to pass. . . . He liked to think of men as fearless and unpusillanimous, sensual, unafraid of their appetites, satiating themselves and so grudging neither their own youth nor youth in others. Since they were not so, he had to comfort himself with dreams, and self-dramatization, and heroic episodes. It gave a flavour of unreality to his writing and of fantasy to his character, even appearance." (*Time and Tide,* 28 March 1936).

It may have been Graham's late-Victorian chivalric ethic, coupled with his tendency to take unpopular political stands, that kept him, in his time, from finding a substantial readership among anyone other than his fellow writers. In a letter to Graham dated 20 December 1897, Conrad wrote: "You want from men faith, honour, fidelity to truth in themselves and others. . . . The respectable classes which suspect you of such pernicious longings lock you up and would just as soon have you shot–because your personality counts and you can not deny that you are a dangerous man. What makes you dangerous is your unwarrantable belief that your desire may be realized. This is the only point of difference between us. I do not believe. . . . Consequently I am not likely to be locked up or shot." With the danger past, however, scholars have begun to reassess Graham's place in the history of twentieth-century literature. Though two biographies were written during Graham's lifetime and though articles on his work appeared occasionally after his death, the first book-length study of his works did not appear until 1952 (MacDiarmid's *Cunninghame Graham: A Centenary Study*). Since then, critics such as Cedric T. Watts, Laurence Davies,

and John Walker have been studying Graham's literary relationship to Conrad as well as to Latin American and Scottish writers; a critical biography was published by Watts and Davies in 1979. Scholarship may yet find a way to correct the imbalance between appreciation for Graham's writings and admiration for and interest in his life.

Letters:
Two Letters on an Albatross, by Graham and William Henry Hudson, edited by Herbert Faulkner West (Hanover, N.H.: Westholm, 1955).

Bibliographies:
Leslie Chaundy, *A Bibliography of the First Editions of the Works of Robert Bontine Cunninghame Graham* (London: Dulau, 1934);

C. T. Watts, "R. B. Cunninghame Graham (1852-1936): A List of His Contributions to Periodicals," *Bibliotheck,* 4 (1965): 186-199;

John Walker, "A Chronological Bibliography of Works on R. B. Cunninghame Graham (1852-1936)," *Bibliotheck,* 9 (1978): 47-64;

Walker, "R. B. Cunninghame Graham: An Annotated Bibliography of Writings about Him," *English Literature in Transition,* 22 (1979): 78-156;

Walker, *Cunninghame Graham and Scotland: An Annotated Bibliography* (Dollar, Scotland: Mack, 1980).

Biographies:
Herbert Faulkner West, *A Modern Conquistador: Robert Bontine Cunninghame Graham: His Life and Works* (London: Cranley & Day, 1932);

A. F. Tschiffely, *Don Roberto* (London: Heinemann, 1937); abridged as *Tornado Cavalier* (London: Harrap, 1955);

Cedric T. Watts and Laurence Davies, *Cunninghame Graham: A Critical Biography* (London: Cambridge University Press, 1979).

References:
Anonymous [Edward Garnett], "An Ironist's Outlook," *Academy and Literature,* 63 (25 October 1902): 436-437;

Richard Curle, *Caravansery and Conversation* (London: Cape, 1937);

Laurence Davies, "Cunninghame Graham's South American Sketches," *Comparative Literature Studies,* 9 (September 1972): 253-265;

Davies, "R. B. Cunninghame Graham: The Kailyard and After," *Studies in Scottish Literature,* 11 (January 1974): 156-157;

Ford Madox Ford, *Return to Yesterday* (London: Gollancz, 1931);

John Galsworthy, "Note on R. B. Cunninghame Graham," in his *Forsytes, Pendyces and Others* (London: Heinemann, 1935; New York: Scribners, 1935), pp. 192-194;

Edward Garnett, Introduction to *Thirty Tales and Sketches,* edited by Garnett (London: Duckworth, 1929; New York: Viking, 1929), pp. v-ix;

Stephen Graham, "Laird and Caballero: Cunninghame Graham," in his *The Death of Yesterday* (London: Benn, 1930), pp. 36-52;

Frank Harris, "Cunninghame Graham," in his *Contemporary Portraits* (New York: Harris, 1920), pp. 45-60;

Eloise Knapp Hay and Cedric T. Watts, "To Conrad from Cunninghame Graham: Reflections on Two Letters," *Conradiana,* 5, no. 2 (1973): 5-19;

Richard E. Haymaker, *Prince-Errant and Evocator of Horizons* (Kingsport, Tenn.: Privately printed, 1967);

C. Lewis Hind, "R. B. Cunninghame Graham," in his *More Authors and I* (London: Lane, Bodley Head, 1922): 71-76;

W. H. Hudson, *Letters to R. B. Cunninghame Graham,* edited by Richard Curle (London: Golden Cockerel, 1941);

John Lavery, *The Life of a Painter* (London: Cassell, 1940);

D. H. Lawrence, "*Pedro de Valdivia* by R. B. Cunninghame Graham," *Calendar,* 3 (January 1927): 322-336;

Robie Macauley, "Stranger, Tread Light," *Kenyon Review,* 16 (Spring 1955): 280-290;

Hugh MacDiarmid, *Cunninghame Graham: A Centenary Study* (Glasgow: Caledonian, 1952);

MacDiarmid, "The Significance of Cunninghame Graham," in *Selected Essays of Hugh MacDiarmid,* edited by Duncan Glen (London: Cape, 1969), pp. 121-128;

Frank MacShane, "R. B. Cunninghame Graham," *South Atlantic Quarterly,* 68 (Spring 1969): 198-207;

Malcolm Muggeridge, "Cunninghame Graham," *Time and Tide,* 17 (28 March 1936): 440-441;

William Rothenstein, "A Journey to Morocco," in his *Men and Memories* (London: Faber and Faber, 1931; New York: Coward-McCann, 1935), pp. 215-225;

George Bernard Shaw, "Notes to *Captain Brassbound's Conversion,*" in his *Three Plays for Puritans* (London: Richards, 1901; New York: Brentano's, 1906), pp. 295-301;

James Steel Smith, "R. B. Cunningham Graham as a Writer of Short Fiction," *English Literature in Transition,* 12 (1969): 61-75;

R. W. Stallman, "Robert Cunninghame Graham's South American Sketches," *Hispania,* 28 (1945): 69-75;

A. F. Tschiffely, *Bohemia Junction* (London: Hodder & Stoughton, 1950);

John Walker, "R. B. Cunninghame Graham and the *Labour Elector,*" *Bibliotheck,* 7 (1974): 72-75;

Walker, "R. B. Cunninghame Graham: Gaucho Apologist and Costumbrist of the Pampa," *Hispania,* 53 (March 1970): 102-106;

Cedric T. Watts, "Conrad and Cunninghame Graham: A Discussion with Addenda to Their Correspondence," *Yearbook of English Studies,* 7 (1977): 157-165;

Watts, *R. B. Cunninghame Graham* (Boston: Twayne, 1983);

Watts, ed., *Joseph Conrad's Letters to R. B. Cunninghame Graham* (Cambridge: Cambridge University Press, 1969).

Papers:

Some of Graham's papers are in the Scottish Record Office; the National Library of Scotland; Dartmouth College; the Academic Center Library, University of Texas at Austin; the Bodleian, Oxford; the British Library; the Berg Collection, New York Public Library; the Brotherton Collection, University of Leeds; the British Library of Political Science; the Fawcett Library; the University of Michigan; Yale; and Harvard.

W. H. Hudson

(4 August 1841 - 18 August 1922)

Alan Thomas
University of Toronto

BOOKS: *The Purple Land that England Lost*, 2 volumes (London: Low, Marston, Searle & Rivington, 1885); revised as *The Purple Land* (London: Duckworth, 1904; New York: Illustrated Editions, 1904);

A Crystal Age (London: Unwin, 1887; revised edition, London: Unwin, 1906; New York: Dutton, 1906);

Argentine Ornithology, by Hudson and P. L. Sclater, 2 volumes (London: Porter, 1888, 1889); revised as *Birds of La Plata*, by Hudson alone, 2 volumes (London: Dent/New York: Dutton, 1920);

The Naturalist in La Plata (London: Chapman & Hall, 1892; New York: Appleton, 1892);

Fan: the Story of a Young Girl's Life, as Henry Harford, 3 volumes (London: Chapman & Hall, 1892; republished in 1 volume under Hudson's name, London: Dent/New York: Dutton, 1923);

Idle Days in Patagonia (London: Chapman & Hall, 1893; New York: Appleton, n.d.);

Birds in a Village (London: Chapman & Hall, 1893; Philadelphia: Lippincott, 1893); revised and enlarged as *Birds in Town and Village* (London: Dent/New York: Dutton, 1919);

Lost British Birds (London: Chapman & Hall, 1894); enlarged as *Rare, Vanishing & Lost British Birds*, compiled by Linda Gardiner (London: Dent/New York: Dutton, 1923);

British Birds (London & New York: Longmans, Green, 1895);

Birds in London (London & New York: Longmans, Green, 1898);

Nature in Downland (London & New York: Longmans, Green, 1900);

Birds and Man (London & New York: Longmans, Green, 1901; revised edition, London: Duckworth, 1915; New York: Knopf, 1916);

El Ombú (London: Duckworth, 1902; enlarged edition, London & Toronto: Dent/New York: Dutton, 1923); republished as *South American Sketches* (London: Duckworth,

photograph by Marie Leon

1909); revised as *Tales of the Pampas* (New York: Knopf, 1916);

Hampshire Days (London & New York: Longmans, Green, 1903);

Green Mansions (London: Duckworth, 1904; New York: Putnam's, 1904);

A Little Boy Lost (London: Duckworth, 1905; New York: Knopf, 1918);

The Land's End (London: Hutchinson, 1908; New York: Appleton, 1908);

Afoot in England (London: Hutchinson, 1909; New York: Knopf, 1922);

A Shepherd's Life (London: Methuen, 1910; New York: Dutton, 1910);

Adventures Among Birds (London: Hutchinson, 1913; New York: Kennerly, 1915);

Far Away and Long Ago (London: Dent/New York: Dutton, 1918);

The Book of a Naturalist (London & New York: Hodder & Stoughton, 1919);

Dead Man's Plack and An Old Thorn (London: Dent/New York: Dutton, 1920);

A Traveller in Little Things (London: Dent, 1921; New York: Dutton, 1921);

A Hind in Richmond Park (London: Dent, 1922; New York: Dutton, 1923);

Ralph Herne (New York: Knopf, 1923);

Collections: *The Collected Works of W. H. Hudson*, 24 volumes (London: Dent/New York: Dutton, 1922-1923);

A Hudson Anthology, edited by Edward Garnett (London & Toronto: Dent/New York: Dutton, 1924);

Tales of the Gauchos, edited by Elizabeth Coatsworth (New York: Knopf, 1946);

The Best of W. H. Hudson, edited by Odell Shepard (New York: Dutton, 1949).

Hudson, circa 1868 (Smithsonian Institution, Washington, D.C.)

Born in the Argentine, far from England's countryside and literary life, and only beginning to gain attention in his forties with *The Purple Land that England Lost* (1885), William Henry Hudson achieved at the last such prominence that the *Times* described him, on his death in 1922, as being "unsurpassed as an English writer on Nature." Some of the best-known figures of the Georgian literary world were among his admirers: the novelist John Galsworthy wrote the preface to Hudson's autobiographical *Far Away and Long Ago* (1918), and the publisher's reader Edward Garnett, a legendary discoverer of talent and an important figure in Hudson's later career, provided the preface to his last completed book of essays, *A Traveller in Little Things* (1921). Hudson's reputation at that time rested on two kinds of writing: his South American romances and his books of outdoor essays, mainly on English subjects, though begun in *Argentine Ornithology* (1888, 1889). The romances developed quite a following on both sides of the Atlantic. *Green Mansions* (1904) sold vigorously in the United States on its publication there, and Penguin published popular editions of *The Purple Land* and *Green Mansions* in the 1930s. However, the romances have receded somewhat from view since World War II, while the naturalist writing has shown considerable vitality. In particular, *A Shepherd's Life* (1910) has appeared in several new editions over the past half century and has become established as a classic record of English country life.

The feeling for nature Hudson was to develop into his subject as a professional writer came early to him as a child born on a ranching *estancia* at Quilmes, on the broad plains, the pampas, near Buenos Aires. His parents, Daniel and Caroline Kimble Hudson, were New Englanders, active people but of thoughtful and gentle disposition. For their children, four boys and two girls, they attempted to provide some formal education through tutors, but it was sporadic and of uncertain quality. The ranching life offered freedom and excitement to a young boy. Hudson says in his autobiography that he rode his own pony freely across the pampas from the age of six. The plain was a feeding ground for birds of passage both from the subtropic regions and from Patagonia and Antarctica to the south; the young Hudson delighted in the variety and activity. Interposed with this natural world was a human society also strongly colored and dramatic in its behavior. Decades of hard, isolated ranching life had created among the descendants of the Spanish colonists a gaucho culture that Hudson refers to often, particularly in *Far Away and Long Ago*, in terms of its simplicity and also its brutal ferocity. His mother, a Quaker, provided what comfort she could to the sensitive boy, who was sharply responsive both to the beauty and the cruelty of the world around him and troubled from an early age by an awareness of death.

Hudson's capacity for private reflection, essential to his later success as an essayist on out-of-the-way subjects, was strengthened during periods of forced inactivity. The first was a lengthy convalescence from typhus, contracted on a visit to Buenos Aires when he was fourteen. This provided the occasion for a self-prescribed course of education through reading and was followed by more reading a year later while he was recovering from rheumatic fever, which damaged his heart. The sequence of intense activity, followed by rest and reflection can be seen as establishing a pattern in his life and became the initiating idea of one of his books, *Idle Days in Patagonia* (1893), the idleness of the title being an enforced period of recovery from an accidental gunshot wound, during which he lay contemplating the dance of the flies above his bed and thinking "on a variety of subjects" beyond the specific reason for his visit to the area, a study of migratory birds.

This study had the professional support of the Smithsonian Institute, Washington, which had commissioned Hudson in his mid twenties to collect bird skins. The director of the Natural History Museum in Buenos Aires had recommended Hudson to the American ornithologist, Spencer Baird, who was then engaged in expanding the Smithsonian collection. Through Baird, Hudson was brought into correspondence with the Zoological Society of London, where some of his skins were sent, and his letters on South American birds, particularly those of Buenos Aires Province, were published in the *Proceedings* of the Society from 1869 onward, his first words in print.

They were packed with accurate, informed observations, and the society made him a corresponding member. The sojourn in Patagonia was one episode in some years of journeying through the Argentine and Uruguay (the Banda Oriental of *The Purple Land*) that provided Hudson with experiences used later for his romances.

Hudson's father died in 1868, and the family of six brothers and sisters, so close in childhood, spread out. Only one sister was living with Hudson at a small ranch, which was all that remained to the family of their estates, when in 1874, evidently encouraged by the publication of his bird observations, Hudson took ship for London. He was twenty-eight years old, had little money and few connections, and his written English needed improvement.

On his own in London, Hudson engaged in writing a large romantic epic on a fictional family, the Lambs, an English-speaking family who lived in South America; from this manuscript, Hudson took a section that was published as *The Purple Land that England Lost*, a picaresque romance in which a young English adventurer travels through a land of proud, dangerous men and beautiful women. The book received one encouraging review, but Hudson destroyed the remainder of the material and often declared himself, later, as weak in narrative skills.

In 1876, not long after his arrival in England, Hudson married his landlady, a singer, music teacher, and boardinghouse keeper named Emily Wingrave. This gave him some personal stability and companionship through years of penury; the inheritance by his wife of a large house in Westbourne Park provided the couple, in 1886, with an established home. They lived in an upper flat, and rented the remainder of the house. Over a dozen or so years he lived thus, in a nether world of genteel poverty, picking up some occasional employment and writing romances and articles. Advice and encouragement came from Morley Roberts, a traveler and journalist, who met Hudson in 1880 and directed him toward the magazine market. *Country Life, Contemporary Review, Cornhill Magazaine, Field, Fortnightly Review, Longman's Magazine, Macmillan's Magazine, Nation, National Review, New Statesman,* and *Nineteenth Century* were some of the many periodicals that were to publish nature articles and romance stories by Hudson, though rejections, in the early years, were frequent. Following common practice, Hudson subsequently gathered these articles into books.

Hudson, circa 1875

Hudson's friends during these years were principally Roberts, George Gissing, the realist novelist, and the illustrator Alfred Hartley; they formed a bohemian group he could be comfortable with. He also developed a stimulating acquaintance with the M.P. and adventurer R. B. Cunninghame Graham, who knew the Argentine pampas and, like Hudson, spoke Spanish. In the 1880s Hudson began to interest himself in the work of the Society for the Preservation of Birds. As the society grew and moved its headquarters from Manchester to London in 1891, he involved himself more closely, writing pamphlets for them and being elected to the society's council. His work with the S.P.B. brought Hudson influential and close personal friends. Late in his life he authorized republication of some of his early books, including the pseudonymously published novel, *Fan* (1892; by "Henry Harford"), in order to increase the value of the estate that would go to the society on his death.

The publication of *Fan,* a realist novel imitative of George Gissing, and of *A Crystal Age* (1887), a utopian novel, in addition to his ro-

mances, indicates that Hudson seriously sought a career as a writer of fiction and explored different modes. But it was his writing on nature that finally proved most fruitful. After years of fitful publication and bare living, Hudson gained an unqualified success with the publication of *The Naturalist in La Plata* (1892), and a steady flow of books followed. The field work in the Argentine and the literary apprenticeship in London had given him his voice as writer-naturalist. But financial security was not yet achieved; in 1900 Hudson became a British citizen, a necessary step to his acceptance in the following year of a civil list pension of £150 a year, awarded in recognition of the originality of his writings on Natural History. This came through the good offices of influential friends including Edward Grey, a landowner, nature lover, and member of the government. Hudson gave up the pension in 1920, when his romances were selling well. His name had become a byword in Britain, at that date, as an observer of nature and protector of birds.

Those letters Hudson wrote in his twenties to the Zoological Society, and which were published, to his surprise and pleasure, in the *Proceedings,* show the features that invigorated his later essays on natural history. First comes presentation of information through close, accurate recording, then comes speculation. Hudson, reflective in youth as he was later in age, always sought to apply his observations to general theories of natural existence. In one of these letters the young man displays the temerity to challenge a statement by Charles Darwin in the *Origin of the Species* (1859) that the South American woodpecker, the *carpinteros,* had so completely adapted to life on the plain that it never climbed trees. Hudson's attention to detail is apparent in the passage in which he notes that the favorite nesting place of the bird in his district was actually a tree, the *ombu* tree. "This tree attains considerable size; there is one within fifty paces of the room I am writing in, that has a trunk measuring, three feet above the ground, thirty feet in circumference. This very tree was for many years a breeding place for carpinteros, and still exhibits on its trunk and larger branches scars of the wounds inflicted by their bills. The wood of the ombu is very soft and the carpinteros invariably bores for breeding where it is green and sound: the hole it forms runs horizontally about nine inches, then slants upward a few inches more, and at the end of the passage a round chamber is excavated to receive the eggs." Darwin replied with a calm and qualified acknowledgment of his error; Hudson's broad hint that Darwin might have "wrested" his observations around to fit his theory was, however, firmly rejected.

This first and somewhat brash challenge to Darwin was not an isolated incident but an expression of a deep-seated aversion to some aspects of the theory of evolution. Hudson recognized Darwin's greatness and was intellectually stimulated by the idea of a common descent for all living things. He came to express himself as an evolutionist in some areas, but he disliked what he regarded as the reductive quality of Darwinian selection. Toward the end of his life Hudson wrote that he could never be "wholly satisfied with natural selection as the only and sufficient explanation of the change in the forms of life" (*Far Away and Long Ago*). Though he has been associated with a Lamarckian belief in the transmission of learned attributes, such ideas are not argued by Hudson but expressed as fantasies in which, for instance, humans take bird shape, or vice versa. The most popular of Hudson's romances, *Green Mansions*, is built upon a young adventurer's encounter, in the wilds of Guyana, with an elusive girl, Rima, who signals her presence with birdlike melodies as she passes through the forest. A memorial bird pool and sanctuary in Hyde Park, London, created by Hudson's admirers in 1925, features a stylized bas-relief carving of Rima, symbol of wild nature.

As a natural philosopher Hudson might properly be distinguished by the stress he placed on the continuity of all forms of life. Humans are kin to animals and birds; the natural world is our world, he asserted, though we might unwisely separate ourselves from it. Hudson insisted on the presence of an aesthetic and pleasure-loving side to bird and animal life; all activities need not be understood, he thought, as functions of Darwinian survival. In the chapter "Music and Dancing in Nature" in *The Naturalist in La Plata*, Hudson describes many different kinds of display and song in South American birds, including the black tyrant bird he was first to observe, the *Cnipolegus Hudsoni*. He follows these particular descriptions with the general assertion that "conscious sexual selection on the part of the female is not the cause of music and dancing performances in birds, nor of the brighter colours and ornaments that distinguish the male." Instead, Hudson observed, in a vast majority of species "the male takes the female he finds or is able to win from competition," and in butterflies "the female gives herself up to the embrace of the first male that appears." Finally, he extends the meaning of dancing and singing beyond mating behavior to expressions of pleasure: "the joyous instinct is expressed by duet-like performances between male and female.... [T]he inferior animals, when the conditions of life are favourable, are subject to periodical fits of gladness."

In addition to attributing human psychological states to animals and birds, Hudson also argued for animal intelligence and ultimately for an "intelligence like our own but more powerful in all visible things." His reverent approach to nature reaches its fullest expression and explanation in *Far Away and Long Ago*, the story of his boyhood on the pampas, a book that is at some points suggestive of another autobiographical account of a boy's awakening to the power of the natural world, William Wordsworth's *Prelude* (1850). Such an awareness Hudson terms "animism." The concept is first expressed and developed in *Idle Days in Patagonia*. In the chapter "The Plains of Patagonia" Hudson describes his solitary daily rides across the plateau, pondering the relationship between sensory response, abstract thinking, and natural existence. The monotony of the landscape reduced his intellectual activity, he noted, while leaving his instinctive capacities free to respond to any changes registered by sensory perception. Such was the mental state of man living in nature and of animals and birds, too. Similar operations of the mind linked all living things. Further, the mind's projection of itself onto nature provided that "primitive universal faculty on which the animistic philosophy of the savage is founded." To accept that "the earth and all nature is alive and intelligent and feels as we feel" (*Far Away and Long Ago*) was basic to human perception. Hudson insisted that "animism" could not be extinguished by human ratiocination and remained latent in all people. Expression of this feeling by poets was not metaphor, and Wordsworth, for one, wrote as if "convinced that the flower enjoys the air it breathes." Hudson's admiring and respectful attitude to the animated universe finds its logical issue in his close, patient description of natural phenomena.

Despite the eccentricity of these ideas, the distinguished naturalist Alfred Russel Wallace wrote a long and enthusiastic review in *Nature* of *The Naturalist in La Plata*, commending it for facts and observations of great value to other naturalists, for its "ingenious speculations," and for its appeal to the general reader. *Idle Days in Patagonia* was also

Hudson, circa 1900 (Glasgow Art Gallery and Museum)

a success, though it struck a different tone, more reflective and essaylike; it, too, was favorably reviewed by Wallace, though regarded as a minor work. Having gained his foothold as a nature writer with his South American material, Hudson now began to show how he could apply his knowledge and habits of observation to his new country, the land of his ancestors as he called it. His first thoroughly English work was *Birds in a Village* (1893), a record of a springtime passed in the Berkshire village of Cookham Dean. This slender book, made up of a lengthy title essay and a miscellany of shorter essays on birds, shows Hudson's sensitivity to locale. He writes with fascination of the bird life to be found in the minutely varied, gardenlike settings of the Thames valley, so different from the wastes of Patagonia. His observations of greenfinches, blue tits, warblers, and kingfishers were made with the help

of field glasses, a new possession for Hudson, who also at this time became interested in nature photography. The essays in *Birds of a Village* characteristically move from particular observation to general idea. The melodious song of a nightingale, uttered as Hudson approached the agitated bird's nest, leads him to speculate on why birds may continue to utter pleasant calls while in distress. He also allows himself some whimsical fantasy, in his romantic manner, in an account of his search for the elusive wryneck, a bird with a strange, penetrating call like a dry, human laugh. Hudson imagines that a village boy, alarmed by a too-early awareness of death, adopts as a stay against mortality a diet of ants, and lives on to become a lean, gray little man with a dark cap and pair of round, brilliant eyes; in short, a wryneck. It is the animistic vision again, though expressed in this story as imagination. Such passages of play-

The Cornhill Magazine.

OCTOBER, 1883.

PELINO VIERA'S CONFESSION.

WILL be necessary to inform the reader—in all probability unacquainted with the political events of ~~the year~~ 1829 in Buenos Ayres—that the close of that year was more memorable for tumults of a revolutionary character than usual. During these disturbances the prisoners confined in the city gaol, taking advantage of the outside agitation and of the weakness of their guard, made an attempt to recover their liberty. They were not acting without precedent, and had things taken their usual course they would, no doubt, have succeeded in placing themselves beyond the oppressive tyranny of the criminal laws. Unfortunately for them they were discovered in time and fired on by the guard;

VOL. I.—NO. 4, N. S.   16

First page from the magazine version of one of Hudson's South American romances, with his revisions for his 1916 collection, Tales of the Pampas *(RB 136406; by permission of the Henry E. Huntington Library and Art Gallery)*

ful mythologizing led reviewers to comment on Hudson's poetic strain.

Practical confirmation that Hudson had managed to naturalize himself to British life came with the publisher Longman's commission for Hudson to write *British Birds,* a descriptive compilation of 375 species, which appeared in 1895. It was followed by *Birds in London* (1898), which evidently arose from *force majeure* in 1896 and 1897, when Hudson and his wife, through ill health or lack of funds, were unable to leave London in the summers. Some light essays on dogs, the only mammals to be observed in the city, were also written by Hudson in this period for magazines (and were collected years later in *The Book of a Naturalist,* 1919). They show Hudson using a conversational and humorous tone in handling readers who might not enjoy his iconoclastic views on dogs. Though this work of the mid 1890s has not been highly regarded, it shows Hudson established as a writer, turning his hand to what subjects were available, and developing his skills as a

The great period of Hudson's career as a writer on country life opened with *Nature in Downland* (1900), a collection of essays drawn from rambles on the Sussex Downs. The book opens with a brilliant visual vignette of Hudson sitting entranced on the rounded crest of a down and watching the drift of thistledown through the air; large and small shapes draw his attention. The chapters are self-contained essays on flora and fauna, the shape of the topography, and the quality of village and town life; these are built into a comprehensive depiction of a region. His journeys across the downs brought Hudson into contact with shepherds who often became his confidants and valuable sources of information. Hudson also prepared himself in libraries and often cites earlier authorities on points of local history as he moves through the South and Southwest of England. He frequently and specifically refers to distinguished predecessors in the field of natural history, including Gilbert White and Richard Jefferies, and also to William Cobbett. There is genuine affinity here with Cobbett, for Hudson's essays characteristically move between the study of flora and fauna and Cobbett-like observations on the lives of countrymen and countrywomen he encounters.

Subsequent books indicate Hudson's progress through the English countryside. Each contains some choice essays on natural life. The careful study of a young cuckoo in a robin's nest, ejecting eggs and young, is the opening essay of *Hampshire Days* (1903) and shows Hudson at his best as a field naturalist; *The Land's End* (1908) contains a gripping account, in "The Great Frost," of the hardships endured by migratory birds. Toward the people of these districts he frequently adopts a historical and even anthropological approach. Interest in race brings Hudson into frequent discussion of physiological types. He often appears eager to refute the notion that "the Saxon" type dominates in southern England and to argue the survival of earlier peoples, such as "the Iberian" type with small frame, dark hair and eyes, and narrow skull, a physical type for which Hudson showed some fondness. He was himself long limbed, roundheaded, and dark eyed and thought himself a descendant of the neolithic "Beaker" people of the Southwest.

Ventures into the English countryside for material set up a pattern of journeying each spring and summer. Hudson, accompanied by his wife, went on foot along country roads and paths, seeking shelter in villages, where often they had to persuade cottagers to provide them with a bed. An account of their progress and its difficulties is given by Hudson in *Afoot in England* (1909). Later, Hudson took to the bicycle and was able to cover more ground. In "Rural Rides" (a title consciously taken from Cobbett), which first appeared as an article in the *Saturday Review,* he describes his pleasure, while looking for a night's shelter in Hurstbourne Tarrant, at coming upon the farmhouse where Cobbett had lodged in 1821; Hudson stays the night there and rides on "by serpentine roads through a beautiful, wooded, undulating country" to Silchester, some thirty kilometers away.

Evidently Hudson was on his way to the cottage of James Lawes on the edge of the common at Silchester. Lawes was a retired Wiltshire shepherd in his seventies in 1901 when Hudson first met him. Through conversations over the years of their acquaintance Lawes provided the memories of the nineteenth-century shepherd and his village that are the heart of Hudson's greatest study of English country life, *A Shepherd's Life*. The names of people and places are disguised, the Winterbourne Bishop of the book being modeled on the village of Martin on the bare South Wiltshire downs; Lawes appears in the book as "Caleb Bawcombe," his father as "Isaac." The book has a long historical reach because "Isaac" was born in 1800 and passed his memories on to his son. Hudson used a method of gathering material that makes the book a pioneer work of oral history. Direct questioning was unprofitable. While making his stops for a night's shelter at Lawes's cottage, Hudson learned to draw the old man out by telling of what he himself observed in the woods and fields that day; then the old shepherd would respond. Hudson found Lawes shared his tender regard for wild nature. Further, Lawes is himself described in terms of animal imagery: the beard is goatlike, the ears stand out from the head, the eyes display an "unhuman intelligence in them–fawnlike eyes that gazed steadily at you as one may gaze through the window." Despite such touches, which recall the images of Hudson's romances, *A Shepherd's Life* is solidly circumstantial and packed with factual detail. The key chapter, "Shepherd of the Downs," began life as an article in *Longman's Magazine* in 1902. The book's focus shifts, from modern impressions of Salisbury, the city on the plain, to episodes of

The happiest time of my boyhood was at that early period a little past the age of six, when I had my own pony to ride on & was allowed to stay on his back as long & go as far from home as I liked. I was like the young bird when on first quitting the nest it suddenly becomes conscious of its power to fly. My early flying days were however soon interrupted when my mother took me on my first visit to Buenos Ayres; that is to say, the first I remember since I must have been taken there once before as an infant in arms, since we lived too far from town for any missionary-clergyman to travel all that way to us just to baptise me. Buenos Ayres is now the wealthiest, most populous & Europeanized city in South America: what it was like then these glimpses into a far past will serve to show. Coming as a small boy of an exceptionally impressible mind, from that great green plain where people lived the simple life Every thing I saw in the great city (as it was considered then) impressed me deeply & the sights which impressed me the most are as vivid in my mind today as they ever were. I was a solitary little boy in my rambles about the streets, for though I had a younger brother who was my only playmate, he was not yet five & too small to keep me company in my walks. Nor did I mind having no one with me. Very, very early in my boyhood I had acquired the habits of going

Page from the manuscript for Far Away and Long Ago *(1918), Hudson's account of his boyhood on the Argentine pampas (auctioned by Sotheby's, sale 5998)*

deer and sheep stealing in the hungry times of the early nineteenth century, and to the varied life stories of Lawes's family. Hudson's achievement lies in the quiet, unforced organization of these impressions and memories into essaylike chapters that present a way of life now gone.

Far Away and Long Ago, which appeared in 1918, is also built on memories. Hudson says in the opening chapter that during a period of illness, while recollecting his early life, a clear and coherent vision came to his mind. "Over it all my eyes could range at will, choosing this or that point to dwell upon, to examine it in all its details." The foundation of many of Hudson's interests and preoccupations are found in this parade of impressions: the brilliant flocks of birds that first attracted him to nature study, the brutality of the cattle-ranching life, which appalled his tender heart, and the strange figures, grotesque wanderers of the plain, or enchanting beauties trapped in isolated ranches who fed his romantic imagination. The work is packed with brilliantly realized, colorful people and scenes and is also extraordinarily broad in range of tone. There are subjective reports of childhood terrors, factual recollections of bird-life discoveries, dramas of civil war, gently comic scenes of life in Buenos Aires, and speculation on the place of man in the animate universe. The sensibility of the author controls and orders the material, and it is finally the young Hudson, sensitive, grave, and a little withdrawn, who emerges as a subject equal to the rich content of the book. Hudson gives the impression that he wrote the book under the compulsion of inspiration during the six weeks of his confinement to bed. Perhaps he completed a first draft there, but he was always a laborious craftsman and evidently revised the work over the next two years, incorporating some material published earlier in periodicals. It was, in any event, complete in late 1917, when Hudson sent the manuscript to Edward Garnett, asking his opinion. Garnett replied that it was a masterpiece; reviewers agreed with him on publication and *Far Away and Long Ago* has continued to occupy a position, similar to Edmund Gosse's *Father and Son* (1907), in the front rank of autobiography in English.

Hudson has been praised as a stylist. But one gets no sense in Hudson of any surrender of the language to euphony. Galsworthy thought the secret of Hudson's style lay in its "indefinable freedom from any thought of after-benefit." The writing conveys the object seen, the emotion felt, and, at that instant, nothing else. Hudson's passionate interest suffices as justification. Reasons do not have to be found: if life is worth living it is worth describing. Hudson the writer may be viewed essentially as the field naturalist who steadily and patiently carries his habit of observing and describing into many corners of life.

Letters:
Letters from W. H. Hudson, 1901-1922, edited by Edward Garnett (New York: Dutton, 1923);
Men, Books and Birds, edited by Morley Roberts (London: Nash & Grayson, 1925);
W. H. Hudson's Letters to R. B. Cunninghame-Graham, edited by Richard Curle (London: Golden Cockerel, 1941);
Letters on the Ornithology of Buenos Ayres, edited by David R. Dewar (Ithaca, N.Y.: Cornell University Press, 1951).

Bibliographies:
G. F. Wilson, *A Bibliography of the Writings of W. H. Hudson* (London: Bookman's Journal, 1922);
John R. Payne, *W. H. Hudson: A Bibliography* (Folkestone, Kent & Hamden, Conn.: Dawson/Archon, 1977).

Biographies:
Morley Roberts, *W. H. Hudson: A Portrait* (London: Dutton, 1924);
Robert Hamilton, *W. H. Hudson: The Vision of Earth* (London: Dent, 1946);
Ruth Tomalin, *W. H. Hudson* (London: Witherby, 1954).

References:
Henry Seidel Canby, *Definitions* (New York: Harcourt, Brace, 1924);
John T. Frederick, *William Henry Hudson* (New York: Twayne, 1972);
H. J. Massingham, *Untrodden Ways* (New York: Dutton, 1933);
Forrest Reid, *Retrospective Adventures* (London: Faber & Faber, 1941);
Edward Thomas, *A Literary Pilgrim in England* (New York: Dodd, Mead, 1917).

Holbrook Jackson

(31 December 1874 - 16 June 1948)

D. E. Parker
University of Toronto
and
Robert Beum

BOOKS: *Edward Fitzgerald and Omar Khayyám, an Essay and a Bibliography* (London: Nutt, 1899);

The Eternal Now ... and Other Verses (London: Nutt, 1900);

Bernard Shaw (Philadelphia: Jacobs / London: Richards, 1907);

William Morris (London: Fifield, 1908; revised & enlarged edition, London: Cape, 1926);

Great English Novelists (London: Richards, 1908; Philadelphia: Jacobs, 1908);

Platitudes in the Making (New York: Kennerley, 1910; London: Rider, 1911);

Romance and Reality (London: Richards, 1911; New York: Kennerley, 1912);

All Manner of Folk (London: Richards, 1912; New York: Kennerley, 1912);

The Eighteen Nineties (London: Richards, 1913; New York: Kennerley, 1913);

Town: An Essay (Westminster: Stevens / Flying Fame, 1913);

Southward Ho! and Other Essays (London: Dent, 1914; New York: Dutton, 1914);

Occasions (London: Richards, 1922; New York: Scribners, 1923);

A Brief Survey of Printing, by Jackson and Stanley Morison (New York: Knopf, 1923);

Essays of To-Day and Yesterday (London: Harrap, 1927);

The Anatomy of Bibliomania, 2 volumes (London: Soncino, 1930, 1931; New York: Scribners, 1931);

The Fear of Books (London: Soncino / New York: Scribners, 1932);

William Caxton (London: Robinson, 1933);

The Printing of Books (London & Toronto: Cassell, 1938; New York: Scribners, 1939);

Oscar Wilde's Salome (London: Fanfare, 1938);

The Aesthetics of Printing (London: Strangeways, 1939; Berkeley Heights, N.J.: Oriole, 1954);

photograph by Alvin Langdon Coburn

Bookman's Holiday (London: Faber & Faber, 1945); republished as *Bookman's Pleasure* (New York: Farrar, Straus, 1947);

The Reading of Books (London: Faber & Faber, 1946; New York: Scribners, 1947);

Dreamers of Dreams: The Rise and Fall of 19th Century Idealism (London: Faber & Faber, 1948; New York: Farrar, Straus, 1949).

OTHER: *Everychild: A Book of Verses for Children*, edited by Jackson (Leeds: Bean, 1906).

Holbrook Jackson is known today mainly as a bibliophile and as the author of the agreeably written but also careful and well-balanced study *The Eighteen Nineties* (1913), a book that was the first and remains the best interpretive survey of the period's arts and letters. And Jackson's other essays, taken as a whole, are among the best of their era. They were well received when they appeared, but they never reached the wide public whose idols among essayists were men of thinner but more genteel and more optimistic stamp, such as E. V. Lucas and A. C. Benson. It may not overstate the case to say that Jackson is among the most rewarding of the many early-twentieth-century essayists whose work stands largely neglected at present. His essays, almost always clear and economical, range from the familiar to the expository and argumentative; sometimes they are as much narrative as essayistic; the subjects are diverse and seldom trivial; and the point of view is often quietly but intriguingly unconventional. Virtually all of Jackson's work is, in fact, charmingly substantive. A man of many interests who possessed both a practical imagination and a grasp of large cultural and philosophical issues, he wrote from an unusually well-stocked mind. It was also a balanced stock: he was about equally interested in the ancients and the moderns, and though he was something of an antiquarian he was also eminently capable in the business end of the book trade and up-to-date in advertising techniques, the color industry, and many branches of the decorative arts.

Jackson was relatively prolific. After the age of twenty-four, when he published his first book (1899)—an essay on Edward Fitzgerald's *Omar Khayyám* (1859)—he produced more than twenty books. He published no fiction and, after his early years, no poetry; unmistakably, however, the concreteness, particularism, and élan of his nonfiction are those of a creative, if self-effacing, artist.

Born in Liverpool on 31 December 1874, he attended local schools until he was fifteen, but his education came primarily through voracious and eclectic personal reading, and he began publishing articles as early as age sixteen, while he was a clerk in a commercial office. He attended no university. After his book on Fitzgerald he produced a collection of his own poems (*The Eternal Now*, 1900) and edited an anthology of verse for children (*Everychild*, 1906). Then he moved to London with his wife, Frances Jones Jackson, whom he had married in 1900, and their daughter, Gwendolen, to begin a career in journalism. For one thrilling year, in 1907, he was joint editor, with A. R. Orage, of the Guild Socialism journal, the *New Age*.

Jackson had many friends and was widely liked and respected, but he was also notably independent, not so much by determined choice as by circumstance. He joined no contemporary cults or literary movements and found no one to tout his talents; nor did anyone else's luster happen to rub off on him. He was busy, responsible, and other-directed: there was little time for cultivating associations potentially useful to his reputation as a writer. Since World War II, familiar essays have not been favored by either the public or the literary coteries: Jackson has suffered the same fate as most of the other essayists.

Busy with the *New Age*, Jackson nevertheless found time to do considerable free-lance writing as well as to produce the earliest biography of Bernard Shaw. What *Bernard Shaw* (1907) contributes to the literature on Shaw as person, Fabian, philosopher, and man of the theater is mostly enthusiasm. The book suffers greatly from its uncritical attitude and its lack of commentary on the plays themselves. However, the interest it shows in a writer's personality, ideas, and milieu rather than in analyses of specific literary techniques was to be characteristic of all Jackson's work. In 1908 he published *William Morris*, another biography. Again the attitude is essentially uncritical, and again he pays little attention to the literary aspects of Morris's career but discusses—in a lucid and vigorous style—the practical side of Morris's life, the magnetic personality of the man, and his views on the place of the beautiful in everyday affairs, and on the relation between art and labor and between the state and the individual. Jackson never lost his interest in Morris; in 1946 he produced an edition of Morris's essays on art and socialism. In 1908 Jackson also published *Great English Novelists*, a pleasant and highly readable handbook dealing with novelists from Daniel Defoe to George Meredith. This book, too, focuses on the biographical side of the writers but includes some critical commentary, most of it sound enough. The greatest virtue of the book is the way Jackson manages to set each writer in a vividly realized milieu: the individual portraits then emerge with such liveliness that the reader feels in touch with a human being whose reality is not lessened by being in the past.

It was his literary interests that recommended Jackson to Thomas Power O'Connor, M.P., and founder of *T. P.'s Weekly* (in 1902), a penny literary paper of more than ordinary merit. In 1911 O'Connor made Jackson acting editor. A few years later O'Connor launched a monthly journal he called *T. P.'s Magazine,* and because of Jackson's ability as an observer and chronicler of life in an easy, agreeable style, O'Connor found him the obvious candidate to edit it. Jackson kept this job for two years, then bought out *T. P.'s Weekly* from O'Connor and absorbed it into his own literary journal, *To-Day,* which he edited from 1917 to 1923. *To-Day* published established writers like Augustine Birrell but also some of the early work of T. S. Eliot, Ezra Pound, Richard Aldington, and other writers who would become well known later. In 1917 Jackson became editorial director of the National Trade Press, a position in which he developed expertise in the use of color in advertising; from 1933 to 1935 he was chairman of the British Colour Council. During these busy years, Jackson published several books, the most important of which are his cultural study *The Eighteen Nineties* and his four major collections of essays: *Romance and Reality* (1911), *All Manner of Folk* (1912), *Southward Ho! and Other Essays* (1914), and *Occasions* (1922).

The essays in *Romance and Reality* generally reverse the organization suggested by the title and start with "Reality." Jackson deliberately ignores philosophical fussing over the term: by the "real" he means simply the pragmatic world of here and now, from which he moves into the world of the imagination—or "Romance." His essay on H. G. Wells illustrates this method: "starting where Karl Marx did, [Wells] gradually increased the gap between the two hypothetical classes, ignoring the revolutionary possibilities of a class war, which a mere scientist could not afford to do, until in the illimitable future he gives us an amazing picture of a class segregation so complete as to have produced two distinct races. . . . [T]he journey into the future is described with an imaginative power unsurpassed in any of Wells' later works, and is an excellent example of his method of building an imaginative structure on a scientific basis." The first four sections of *Romance and Reality* consist of essays that discuss, informally but not superficially, various ways in which the imagination transfigures ordi-

nary things; the stronger pieces here include "Peter Panism," "Make Believe," and "Between Waking and Awake." The last section of the book is devoted to the respective claims of romance and reality in the lives and work of individual artists, including Maurice Maeterlinck, Anna Pavlova, and William Rothenstein.

Southward Ho! and Other Essays, a stronger and much more diversified book, comprises twenty-six essays. Most of them are fruitfully revised versions of pieces that had appeared in *Romance and Reality* and *All Manner of Folk.* All twenty-six are free from certain traits that plague many Edwardian and Georgian essays: finical gentility and the effete sentimentalizing that passes itself off as both sensitivity and piety. The texture of the writing is distinctly masculine; the scent on the pages is that mixed but bracing one of the world taken as a whole, where smoke and fumes as well as sachets and pomanders have their rightful, and in any event, their significant, place. On the other hand, awareness of the world as mostly a place of hap, and often of mishap, does not negate an essential romanticism in Jackson. But Jackson's is a romanticism of energy, fascination, and multiplicity of interest, not a Shelleyan or Wagnerian thirst for the infinite or—the other side of that—a withdrawal into melancholy and languor. In the title essay and in "Spring" and "April" there is a rhapsodic note, but the emotions are really felt, and both closeness of observation and intellectual penetration prevent any degeneration into vapid, platitudinous emoting. Practically all of these essays present Jackson as one who loves quietness and idleness. And he did; but the irony is that he was already an extremely occupied man whose many business and personal projects constantly demanded self-discipline, and one senses—in these essays as elsewhere—that he was a more balanced and richer human being, hence a more interesting writer, for all the demands made by business affairs and works of practical imagination on the one hand and by innate curiosity on the other. Essays such as "Here and Now" and "Going to Nowhere" are variations on Walt Whitman's theme, "I loaf and invite my soul," but even in them something intimates that if Jackson's circumstances had been less commercial his imagination would have been the poorer. In any case, wit—a subdued, not a showy wit—prevents any patch of prose from becoming purple.

In these brief essays the personal note is always strong (there are even autobiographical passages). There is often an arguable thesis, but the argumentation is informal and agreeable, never labored or pedantic. What they explore is the truth of personal experience. Though Jackson was definitely within the fold of guild socialism he was not doctrinaire, and in fact he was essentially apolitical. "Lords of Whim," one of the deeper and more original essays, reveals some of the foundations of Jackson's apolitical vision: "Political liberty is but one of the instruments of Freedom; it can never be anything more. Real Freedom begins deep down in the consciousness of the individual; it is the stuff of variation and growth, the fuel of life." Eschewing the rhetoric of exhortative or sentimental idealism, "Lords of Whim" presents Jackson as an ardent defender of individualism, originality, and freedom of choice.

The title essay is a seminarrative reminiscence of Jackson's youthful vision of the South Seas and a loving sketch of the point of embarkation, the port of Liverpool before its modernization. The essay is a tour de force in the modulation of tones; and for economy, particularity, and evocativeness in scene description, the quiet opening paragraph is as arresting as anything by Joseph Conrad or Henry Tomlinson: "Those who remember Liverpool before the multi-domed Dock Offices and the sky-scraper of the Royal Liver Insurance Company flaunted themselves on the pierhead, overtopping the tallest spars of the fleetest barques of the South Sea trade, and making even the colossal red funnels of the *Mauretania* look like toys, will remember also the St. George's Dock. And if they are further companioned by a sentimental regard for old familiar things, as which of us is not, they will no doubt resent somewhat the intrusion of those arrogant monsters of iron and stone, modern hybrids of building construction, half engineering and half architecture, usurping the place of that same old rectangular basin of muddy green water. For do they not stand precisely where it once stood? Are they not the monstrous gravestones of the cosiest dock in the whole world?" Nostalgic reminiscence, appreciation, community of spirit, well-mannered but still scornful judgment, and controlled mournfulness—the complete harmonizing of disparate tones rapidly succeeding one another in a passage at once expository and precisely descriptive is English prose at its unobtrusive finest. Later in the essay Jackson shows that if he had put his hand to the genre he might well have written fiction that would be at least vigorous: "Down the

Mersey we tacked on a high tide; and I watched with riotous glee the towers and domes of the great city fade behind us. The river tossed and tumbled, scattering spindrift like confetti of silver. Over towards the North Fort we sped, peeped into the mouths of the big guns, and with a fluttering of patched sails, tacked and scurried across towards the Perch Rock Battery, bidding adieu as it were to the watchdogs of Liverpool, and so out into the Channel; and I turned and saw old England dissolve itself into the nothing it had become for me. Rio first; then, in an heroic curve, we tacked down to the Plate, glimpsed into Buenos Ayres for water and fresh meat, and off round the Horn on swift mysterious wings." Here are verve, rapidity, and authenticity, if nothing more momentous.

Often conventional, the topics of *Southward Ho!* nevertheless yield unexpected and provocative turns of thought and relatively fresh if not absolutely original observations. "Lords of Whim," for example, laments—seemingly in classically Liberal fashion—"the despotism of custom" and the decline of true individuality, and Jackson hopes for a time when the trend will be reversed. But what, if anything, could bring about such a turnaround? The answer is unexpected, one that neither classical liberalism nor mainstream socialism would be expected to give: "the revolt will not be political, it will not be industrial, it will not be ethical. . . . It will . . . be brought about by fashion. Men and women one of these days will have the courage to be eccentric. They will do as they like—just as the great ones have always done."

"Deserts of Noise," conventional enough in its protest against the sheer noisiness of modern life, is enlivened by touches such as Jackson's characterization of the clangor as "the wailing of a lost multitude, of a people who have mislaid life's highway" and as "the tumult of a people who have forgotten the meaning of utility in their haste to buy and sell." Sometimes the memorable surprise is simply a point of observation metaphorically rendered, as in his tribute to Pavlova in "The Spirit of the Dance," where he remarks that "She is the first dancer I have seen whose face also dances." What comes across in every essay is the sense of the author's good nature. Much can be forgiven of such a tolerant, appreciative, and well-meaning human being—and there is relatively little in either the writing or the life that creates any need for forgiveness.

"Superman" is one of the most interesting and least shrill of all the commentaries on

Friedrich Nietzsche's *Ubermensch* concept (developed in the 1880s). Jackson exposes an important weakness in Nietzsche's concept–its vagueness–without undervaluing the philosopher's genius or sincerity. "Immortal Russia" (written in 1908) is an inspired and vivid account of an incident that brought Jackson a new insight into historical Russia. Jackson speaks more prophetically here than elsewhere, and events have borne him out.

As strong, some will say stronger, is the narrative essay "Hunger-Tameness." Here, stark description not only creates the mood but somehow does the work of exposition; the result is a powerful economy of technique. The conception itself is original and important. In a part of the Strand on a spring day of "vindictive," dust-driving wind Jackson gradually becomes aware of knots of the most ragged of London's rabble: filthy, mostly fetid "loiterers with a purpose . . . eager little groups of dejected men." (Again there is freshness in expression: "Their very eagerness was unclean.") A policeman "raised a hand aloft" and the tatterdemalions rush off to get their free soup. The whole situation invites both maudlinism and pious sociopoliticizing, but Jackson turns it into a compelling account. An epiphany, agonizing and overpowering, slowly takes shape, and the narration of it is as gripping as any in modern fiction. The throng of men was "long-suffering but tame . . . dirty and hungry, but patient. . . . I was not so much impressed by its squalor as by its tameness–the slow decay, the evil-smelling tameness of the thing, obsessed me. . . . I thought of certain animals and how hunger makes them fierce and brave. . . . Hungry savages peopled my brain, but none stood in queues awaiting soup. They were fierce. . . . That struck me as splendid. But these men starved patiently. There was food all about them . . . and they became tame, not fierce like the animals. . . . Nature had produced in them something new; she had produced patience with hunger, she had made it possible for beings to fester and decompose without resistance, to be acquiescent in a living death. She had created something lower than the brutes." This is not as superficial as the approach of Beatrice Webb or Henry George and considerably more readable.

In "The Fire" (1912), written during a coal shortage resulting from a miners' strike, Jackson composed a fine tribute to the gift of Prometheus and shows his affinities with D. H. Lawrence, who likewise scorned "progress" and

preferred flame to electricity. "Triumphant materialism is conquering the fire by giving us the comfort of mere warmth. . . . I believe in sitting by the fire much more than I believe in progress. . . . What have cheapness and cleanliness and convenience to do with so sacred a thing?" As Lawrence does, Jackson spontaneously mistrusts and dislikes modernity's rampant technicalizing, rationalizing, and specializing of experience, and it is interesting to see the Lawrentian vision–or at least large parts of it– arrived at, quite independently, by a man far more urbane and balanced (Lawrence's detractors have always been eager to prove that his radically antitechnological and antiprogressive views are nothing more than the idiosyncrasies of a quite abnormal, irrational personality). Jackson appears not to have known Lawrence's work as early as 1912, but even much of the language in "The Fire" has a Lawrentian ring; witness the passage just quoted, or this: "To do a thing that we really like doing, imperatively, instinctively like doing, links us with the whole of humanity." Lawrence had not come into his own similar phrasings until well after 1912. Jackson's personality is complex: his love of the natural, the primal, and the instinctual is neither learned nor a pose; his love of refinement and erudition is equally real.

"In the Shadows," titled after the immensely popular tune of the late Edwardian and early Georgian years, develops into an interesting study of the implications of modern people's preference for "trivial and unsatisfying art, which begins anywhere and goes nowhere." Jackson again anticipates a Lawrentian theme: tedium has become "the keynote of civilisation. . . . The average man of to-day is not a citizen of a kingdom, he is a citizen of boredom." "On a Certain Arrangement of Grey and Black" is a small but solid contribution to the literature on James Whistler. It will tell most readers something they do not already know about that artist and therefore about his famous painting of his mother. Seemingly without any conscious attempt to do so, Jackson also suggests the way in which Whistler's "Arrangement in Grey and Black" presents a locus classicus of the difference between an artist's conscious intention (or at least what he took to be his intention) and the actual result in the created objet d'art.

Social historians tend to view the Victorian age–up to 1880 or so, at least–as one of individual energy, gusto, and productivity. It is usually suggested, as well, that this prodigious individual-

TO·DAY

EDITED BY HOLBROOK JACKSON

VOL. I   MARCH 1917   No. 1

SPEAKING EDITORIALLY

THERE is room for many journals—even for those with large circulations—and if *To-day* deliberately appeals to the few who like to think their own thoughts and to read the work of writers who are among the best—but not necessarily among the "best sellers," —the editor is catholic enough in taste and, he hopes, tolerant enough to recognize the rights of the many, even if he does not cater for their needs. He is also optimist enough to believe that there are many more who are not definitely of "the many" than those who cater for the latter would credit.

◢ ◢ ◢

SO *To-day* makes its appearance in difficult and tragic times, confident that in my firm resolve to give only of the best in thought, imagination, and expression, I shall win sufficient support to enable me to provide a quiet corner, as it were, in a turbulent world, for the exercise of such fair judgments and delights as may be obtained only by the companionship of literature.

◢ ◢ ◢

THE chances of war are, however, only partially responsible for this new series of *To-day*. The idea embodied in this journal is an old one. A decade ago I imagined such a journal, and discussed it

A

with a friend who wished to join me in the enterprise, but who has since made an editorial reputation elsewhere. The project was postponed through unpropitious circumstances rather than lack of initiative, and further delayed by successive editorial appointments which left little time for the realization of so personal an experiment in journalism. Briefly my aim was, and is, the promotion of a small and companionable review of life and letters, giving only what is durable in prose and poetry, and, remembering our hurried days, to provide a medium for essays and lyric verse and those briefer forms of the art of letters, such as the aphorism, emblem, and character, which would express in concentrated form the wit and wisdom of our time. The stoppage of the weekly series of *To-day* provided me with the opportunity of realizing a long-deferred wish, and the beginning of that realization is now before the reader.

◢ ◢ ◢

The Yellow Pansy

("*There's pansies—that's for thoughts.*"—SHAKESPEARE)

By WILLIAM WATSON

Winter had swooped, a lean and hungry hawk ;
It seemed an age since Summer was entombed ;
Yet, in our garden, on its frozen stalk,
A yellow pansy bloomed.

'Twas Nature saying by trope and metaphor :
" Behold, when empire against empire strives,
Though all else perish, ground 'neath iron war,
The golden thought survives."

Jackson's editorial for the inaugural issue of the literary journal he edited until 1923

ism declined in Victoria's last decade and was accompanied by a lowered vitality in the arts. One of the great virtues of *The Eighteen Nineties* is its exposition of the period's tremendous and multifarious productivity and of the high quality it achieved in many areas of crafts, arts, and techniques. Indeed it is curious that a book so admirable and presumably so well known has not had a greater effect in countering the debatable but still widely accepted assertion that the end-of-the-century era was culturally retrograde and counterproductively despairing and perverse. Jackson is a more reliable, and far more tolerant and entertaining, guide through the period than most of the literary critics and other commentators who lay claim to an understanding of the 1890s. This achievement is all the more remarkable when one considers that Jackson deals with subjects as diverse as theater; pen-and-pencil drawing; the Celtic movement; modernism as a development from Romanticism; aestheticism and its critics; Shaw; Whistler; the contemporary influence of Henrik Ibsen and Nietzsche; and the revival of the art of printing. The ease with which he handles this diversity and at the same time avoids superficiality is something not indigenous to cultural histories by English writers. The performance seems even more impressive when one reflects that this mellow-toned but also vital, Balzacian mine of detailed information and relevant observation was almost completely written before Jackson had turned thirty-nine.

In explaining what brought about the beneficent revolution in the art of printing (and of book manufacture in general), Jackson takes up a theme–dear also to G. K. Chesterton–that not only makes sense in itself but also reveals that there was as much of the traditionalist as of the socialist in Jackson. Those who in the 1890s returned the craft of the printed book to its former (pre-eighteenth-century) glory "were moved by that vital form of atavism which, by throwing back to an earlier period, picks up the dropped thread of tradition, and so continues the process of evolution; their protest therefore became, in the best sense of the word, a revolution: a turning round to the period when craftsmanship, imagination and life were one and indivisible." *The Eighteen Nineties* elicited a major review from Paul Elmer More, then editor of the *Nation,* in which More, though he praised the book for the excellence of its survey and style, took Jackson to task for being an "apologist" for the excesses and weaknesses of the "naughty decade." To More the moral and volitional inadequacies of the decadents were simply that, and he accuses Jackson of sheer intellectual confusion when the latter "tries to moralize the facts." It may be that More's intense ethicalism and its concomitant revulsion at the spectacle of fin de siècle immoralism and moral iconoclasm prevent him from seeing any positive element in the Decadence. In any case, the point Jackson makes is provocative, and it is one that is still overlooked sometimes: "Every physical excess of the time went hand in hand with spiritual desire. The soul seemed to be trying the way of the flesh with calamitous desperation. Long years of Puritanism and rationalism had proved the folly of salvation by morality and salvation by reason, so in a fit of despair the unsatisfied spirit of the age sought respite in salvation by sin. The recognition of sin was the beginning of the revolt against rationalism and the beginning of the revival of mysticism. The latter revealed itself in the Theosophical movement, in the sudden popularity of Maurice Maeterlinck, and in numerous conversions to Rome, the first and last home of Christian mysticism."

The final sentences of *The Eighteen Nineties* are still worth pondering. They make one of the most important points that can be made–but is not always made–about the 1890s, and at the same time, as is customary with Jackson, they transcend the particular topic and rise to a large and life-affirming truth: "In the work of no single artist was a final interpretation of reality attained. The art of the time was perhaps too personal for that; just as it was too personal for work within prescribed conventions or formalities. The age favoured experiment and adventure, and it even looked not unkindly upon the various whims of the inquisitive, on the assumption, doubtless, that discovery was as often the result of accident as of design. In this large tolerance the spirit of renaissance worked through mind and imagination, inspiring artists with a new confidence in themselves and courage to take risks. The results were not always happy; but that does not make the spirit in which the risks were taken less admira-

ble, for those who make great effort contribute to life as well as those who achieve."

The essays collected in *Occasions* maintain the same high quality established in previous volumes. As usual, what interests Jackson most is not his own personality but the attempt to *discern,* and the delight in that attempt. Despite his defense of eccentricity he seems particularly interested in discovering and articulating what he takes to be the norms of human response. In this he sometimes reminds one of Samuel Johnson, and like Johnson he maintains this inquiry without "psychologizing," without anything resembling clinical or scientific pretension. Further reminiscent of Johnson is Jackson's mixture of prudence and idealism; and it is just as easy to overlook or underestimate Jackson's social and aesthetic idealism as it is to miss the religious depths and the sense of wonder beneath the impressive surface of Johnson's common sense and aggressively logical argumentation.

A tiny essay such as "The Advantage of Being Prejudiced" is characteristic. In conversational but still dignified, firmly structured language, Jackson sets out an idea that runs counter to twentieth-century clichés. But there is no self-congratulatory iconoclasm: wit and pithy example suffice to provide the slight shock necessary to stimulate the reader to think. The motive behind the essay is sensed to be legitimately corrective: the writer is only reminding one of truths half-forgotten and is not offering the reminder as evidence of his own moral or intellectual superiority. This particular essay is, if anything, more relevant today than it was in 1922: "In the newspapers, and in all common argument and opinion, there is perhaps no mental state so belittled and despised as that known as prejudice. To say 'he is prejudiced' is enough to condemn any man. I have known people with a prejudice against prejudice grown violent even in their denunciation of prejudiced persons. . . . It is a curious fact that people are always surprised at the existence of prejudice; they seem amazed that anyone should be so foolish as to be prejudiced. Nevertheless, the habit is so universal that if it had been fundamentally evil society and all its institutions ought to have been wrecked without the help of the Great War. . . . Some of the world's greatest men have been prejudiced about most things; We say that a man is prejudiced when he is not open to reason. And so he is. But is that wrong? When you jump into a river to save a drowning child, you do not reason about your action. If you did you would leave the child to its fate. . . . But you throw reason to the winds, and jump into the water because you are prejudiced in favour of saving life at any cost, even at the cost of your own. . . . [P]rejudice springs from those instincts which are at the source of life. It has the spontaneity of life."

The Anatomy of Bibliomania (1930, 1931) displays the lifetime of encyclopedic reading that, together with his earlier writing, Jackson regarded as his training, his apprenticeship for the writing of *The Anatomy*, which was to be the keystone of his career. Like its prototype, Robert Burton's *Anatomy of Melancholy* (1621), it stands as a monumental example of the essay of whimsical learning, long drawn out: "I [was] enamoured by my Burton as a writer, and finding my subject of bibliomania amenable to his method, with an affinity to its leisureliness and copious garrulity, I was (therefore) bold to imitate. . . . I found in the ample form and slow measure of his diction (which goes trippingly enough on occasion) a refuge, from the dire-track of civilisation safe in the hallowed quiet of the past." *The Anatomy* covers every possible aspect of book loving, buying, repairing, and preserving, with chapters on borrowers, biblioklepts, and bibliopegic dandies. The whimsical, discursive tone can be gauged from Jackson's comment on the polybiblius: "Andrew Lang reports that there was once a bibliophile who claimed that a man could only love one book at a time, and he used to carry the darling of the moment in a charming leather case. In support of this I may cite what Alexandre Dumas tells of the Marquis de Ganay, a roué of books, as amorous of them as any philanderer of the Regency is amorous of women; and his fidelity is as erratic as theirs. Whilst the book is a new toy he is the perfect knight; for a month none more faithful or so full of adoration. He carries it with him, introduces it to his friends, puts it under his pillow at night, and if he awakens before morning, he lights the candle and takes a peep at his treasure; but in a little while the affair ends, and he thinks of the favourite no more. But such kinds are abnormal, most bibliophiles love more than one book at the same time. Only in the East is man polygamous; nearly everywhere he is polybiblius—a creature of many books."

Two years after the appearance of *The Anatomy*, Jackson published *The Fear of Books* (1932), which surveyed various reasons why, in every historical period, certain books have been hated and suppressed. He examines the prejudices, dis-

honesties, and timidities that have led persons in political or moral authority to ban and destroy material that seemed to threaten their supremacy or challenge their doctrine. The book is filled with an immense amount of bookish information—scraps of gossip, knowledge, and history about books—which is stitched together into a series of essays on bibliophobia.

As a publisher Jackson's aim was to produce aesthetically satisfying books with good, readable print. In 1923 he was joint author of *A Brief Survey of Printing*, which ten years later led to a longer work on William Caxton. In a further extension of these interests, *The Printing of Books* (1938), Jackson narrowed his subject to the field of typography and produced an informal, nontechnical history of printing beginning with William Morris and the other Pre-Raphaelites, particularly emphasizing the ethics and aesthetics of printing. His preoccupation here is the art of printing from the point of view of readers and authors rather than from that of printers. The book begins with a plea for readability as opposed to "fine" printing, goes on to show the often unconscious influence of authors on their printers, and concludes with a collection of articles on the subject of printing collected from technical journals on typography.

In 1945 Jackson published *Bookman's Holiday* (known in North America as *Bookman's Pleasure*, 1947), a miscellany of literary anecdotes written with his usual charm, eloquence, and wit. In it he gives glimpses of authors from the sixteenth to twentieth centuries, what they looked like, where and how they lived, talked, played, quarreled, and died. The book was intended, of course, as a bedside companion, not as a scholar's reference tool.

In *The Reading of Books* (1946) Jackson discusses reading as a collaborative art. He sees reading at its most intense becoming "writing by proxy," the reader "becoming someone else for the time being." "When we read, we do not so much enter into the souls of others, we let them enter into us. We become Shakespeare or his characters." On this theme Jackson makes his leisurely but purposeful way through a host of writers starting with Horace and continuing to authors of the twentieth century. His analysis of the literary temperament and his discussion of the methods and results of literary productivity are rich with illustrative instances. He is most at home in the period at the end of the nineteenth century and the first decades of the twentieth century, where his knowledge is often firsthand or drawn from sources no longer readily available.

Dreamers of Dreams (1948), Jackson's last book, is an examination of the theme of transcendentalism in six nineteenth-century writers: Thomas Carlyle, John Ruskin, William Morris, Ralph Waldo Emerson, Henry David Thoreau, and Walt Whitman. All six are related to one another in sympathy and ideas. Jackson sees Carlyle as the most powerful and remarkable of the group and traces his influence, both direct and indirect, on all the others. "Through Emerson and Ruskin, he gave a new quality to the minds of the others by emphasizing the more obvious causes of nineteenth century discontents and the mystical element of his moral teaching had a wide if vague influence under the name of Transcendentalism." As in his earlier books, Jackson keeps formal criticism to a minimum. The aspects of these six literary figures that seem most important to him are those that create an environment for their ideas. What concerns him least is the writer's individual literary expression.

Experienced writers of "major" status have often told younger writers that their best hope is to acquire a mind well stocked with a close knowledge of the concrete—of objects, persons, places, and processes: Honoré de Balzac knew the Paris streets; Joseph Conrad, the structure of ships and the moods of sea and weather; Charles Dickens, the contortions possible to the human face and the false-dulcet tones of middle-class snob speech. The actuality-crammed mind sometimes fails to show itself when it comes to writing: in practical matters from carpentry to the medieval art of illumination, Morris knew almost everything, but his prose is often monochromatic and sometimes ghostly. Less original, less of a genius than Morris, Jackson is the more rewarding prose writer; his knowledge of arts and trades and of shops and theaters and quays in London and Paris gives his writing the "presence of reality." Jackson was preeminently an unbookish bookman who carried forward the great tradition of the familiar essay of the nineteenth century. One need not share the man's bibliomania to realize that more than a few of his essays are as rewarding as any produced in the Georgian era.

Letters:
XX Unpublished Letters of Holbrook Jackson to Joseph Ishill (Berkeley Heights, N.J.: Oriole, 1960).

Reference:
Paul Elmer More, "Decadent Wit," in *Shelburne Essays,* tenth series (Boston & New York: Houghton Mifflin, 1919).

Richard Jefferies

(6 November 1848 - 14 August 1887)

Keith Wilson
University of Ottawa

BOOKS: *Reporting, Editing, and Authorship, Practical Hints for Beginners in Literature* (London: Snow, 1873);

Jack Brass, Emperor of England (London: Pettit, 1873);

A Memoir of the Goddards of North Wilts, Compiled from Ancient Records, Registers and Family Papers (London: Privately printed by Simmons & Botten, 1873);

The Scarlet Shawl: A Novel (London: Tinsley, 1874);

Restless Human Hearts: A Novel, 3 volumes (London: Tinsley, 1875);

Suez-cide!! Or How Miss Britannia Bought a Dirty Puddle and Lost Her Sugarplums (London: Snow, 1876);

World's End: A Story in Three Books, 3 volumes (London: Tinsley, 1877);

The Gamekeeper at Home: Sketches of Natural History and Rural Life (London: Smith, Elder, 1878; Boston: Roberts, 1879);

Wild Life in a Southern County (London: Smith, Elder, 1879; Boston: Roberts, 1879); republished as *An English Village* (Boston: Little, Brown, 1903);

The Amateur Poacher (London: Smith, Elder, 1879; Boston: Roberts, 1879);

Greene Ferne Farm (London: Smith, Elder, 1880);

Hodge and His Masters, 2 volumes (London: Smith, Elder, 1880);

Round About a Great Estate (London: Smith, Elder, 1880; Boston: Roberts, 1880);

Wood Magic: A Fable, 2 volumes (London & New York: Cassell, Petter, Galpin, 1881);

Bevis: The Story of a Boy, 3 volumes (London: Low, Marston, Searle & Rivington, 1882);

Nature Near London (London: Chatto & Windus, 1883; New York: Crowell, 1907);

The Story of My Heart: My Autobiography (London: Longmans, Green, 1883; Boston: Roberts, 1883);

Red Deer (London: Longmans, Green, 1884; New York: Longmans, Green, 1892);

Richard Jefferies

The Life of the Fields (London: Chatto & Windus, 1884; New York: Crowell, 1907);

The Dewy Morn: A Novel, 2 volumes (London: Bentley, 1884; New York: Macmillan, 1900);

After London; or, Wild England (London & New York: Cassell, 1885);

The Open Air (London: Chatto & Windus, 1885; New York: Harper, 1886);

Amaryllis at the Fair: A Novel (London: Low, Marston, Searle & Rivington, 1887; New York: Harper, 1887);

Field and Hedgerow: Being the Last Essays of Richard Jefferies, Collected by His Widow (London & New York: Longmans, Green, 1889);

The Toilers of the Field (London & New York: Longmans, Green, 1892);

The Early Fiction of Richard Jefferies, edited by Grace Toplis (London: Simpkin, Marshall, Hamilton, Kent, 1896);

Jefferies' Land: A History of Swindon and Its Environs, edited by Toplis (London: Simpkin, Marshall, Hamilton, Kent, 1896);

T. T. T. (Wells: Young, 1896);

Nature and Eternity: With Other Uncollected Papers (Portland, Maine: Mosher, 1902);

The Hills and the Vale, introduction by Edward Thomas (London: Duckworth, 1909);

The Nature Diaries and Note-Books of Richard Jefferies, with an Essay, "A Tangle of Autumn," Now Printed for the First Time, edited by Samuel J. Looker (Billericay, Sussex: Grey Walls, 1948);

Beauty is Immortal ("Felise of The Dewy Morn") with Some Hitherto Uncollected Essays and Manuscripts, edited by Looker (Worthing: Aldridge, 1948);

The Old House at Coate, and Other Hitherto Unprinted Essays, edited by Looker (London: Lutterworth Press, 1948; Cambridge, Mass.: Harvard University Press, 1948);

Chronicles of the Hedges, and Other Essays, edited by Looker (London: Phoenix House, 1948);

Field and Farm: Essays Now First Collected, with Some from MSS, edited by Looker (London: Phoenix House, 1957);

Landscape and Labour. Essays and Letters Now First Collected with an Introduction, Notes and Bibliography by John Pearson (Bradford-on-Avon: Moonraker Press, 1979).

OTHER: *Society Novelettes*, by various authors, 2 volumes (London: Vizetelly, 1883)–includes two short stories by Jefferies: "Kiss and Try" (volume 1) and "Out of the Season" (volume 2);

Gilbert White, *The Natural History of Selborne*, introduction by Jefferies (London: Walter Scott, 1887).

The name of Richard Jefferies is one invoked most often by association, whether with predecessors such as William Cobbett or Gilbert White, with contemporaries such as Thomas Hardy or W. H. Hudson, or with successors such as Edward Thomas or Henry Williamson. His rep-utation is most assured as the author of two idylls of childhood, *Wood Magic: A Fable* (1881) and *Bevis: The Story of a Boy* (1882), the prophetic romance *After London; or, Wild England* (1885), and *Amaryllis at the Fair* (1887), the best of his largely forgettable novels. His nature essays, which range between the earlier journalistic and documentary pieces and the later, more mystical renderings of natural impression, form the numerically largest component of his published work. The most authoritative bibliography of his published essays, which appears in *Landscape and Labour* (1979), the most recent of eight posthumous collections (excluding anthologies) that began with *Field and Hedgerow: Being the Last Essays of Richard Jefferies, Collected by His Widow* (1889), includes more than 450 items. This excludes the country books serialized in the *Pall Mall Gazette* (*The Gamekeeper at Home: Sketches of Natural History and Rural Life* [1878], *Wild Life in a Southern County* [1879], *The Amateur Poacher* [1879], and *Round About a Great Estate* [1880]), and the articles published in the *Wilts and Gloucestershire Standard*, which became *Hodge and His Masters* (1880), as well as *Red Deer* (1884). All these books may tacitly declare cohesion in their thematic integrity and in the designation of their component parts as "Chapters," but they too are in essence essay collections. Three volumes of essays proper were published in Jefferies's lifetime: *Nature Near London* (1883), *The Life of the Fields* (1884), and *The Open Air* (1885). Thus the essay, whether always so designated or not, is the form to which Jefferies devoted most of his creative energy and short life. His achievement in it was such as to encourage Q. D. Leavis, an early defender of Jefferies's fading modern reputation, to describe him as "a many-sided and comprehensive genius . . . in the central and most important tradition of English prose style."

John Richard Jefferies was born on 6 November 1848 at Coate Farm, near Swindon, in North Wiltshire. He was the second child and oldest son of Elizabeth and James Luckett Jefferies, whose small farm of about forty acres was the residue of a larger property whose gradual loss attested both to the decline of the Jefferies stock and the periodic difficulties faced by the English agricultural interest. The fact that the farm was a freehold property placed James Jefferies on a firmer footing than that of the average tenant farmer, and his children enjoyed a comfortable if modest upbringing. Much of Richard Jefferies's childhood between the ages of four and nine was spent at the home of the Harrilds, an aunt and uncle on his mother's side, in the London suburb of Sydenham, and it was here that he received early education at a private school. His relationship with his aunt remained close throughout his life, a closeness reflected in the confiding letters that passed between them. The more general influence of London on his formative years was considerable. His uncle, Thomas Harrild, was a printer, as was another uncle, Robert Harrild; a third uncle, Frederick Gyde, was an accomplished engraver. These family connections opened on to a world very different from that of Coate farmhouse and would allow the growing child a perspective from which to translate rural experience into conscious art.

He returned to more consistent residence at Coate in his tenth year, and attended school in Swindon, walking the two and a half miles, like the young Thomas Hardy, along paths through fields. His schooling was erratic and ended by the time he was fifteen, being replaced by sporadic work on the farm and long solitary walks through the surrounding countryside, which gave him a local reputation as a strange and idle boy. His solitude was fed by arbitrarily found but inspiring books, including *Percy's Reliques*, *The Odyssey*, and *Don Quixote*. The last two works were perhaps not unconnected with an abortive adventure that took the sixteen-year-old Jefferies on a trip to France with his cousin, James Cox, from where they intended to walk to Moscow. Returning to England a week later, they attempted a trip to New York, which collapsed when they discovered that the price of a ticket did not include food.

These childhood and early adolescent freedoms, which Jefferies was to draw on for such good purpose in *Wood Magic*, *Bevis*, and *The Amateur Poacher*, ended with a position gained in March 1866, as a reporter on the *North Wilts Herald*. His employment was interrupted by illness during much of 1867, although this is the period during which Jefferies published his first substantial work: "History of Malmesbury" was published in the *North Wilts Herald* between April and September 1867 and "History of Swindon and Its Environs" in the *North Wilts Herald* between October 1867 and February 1868. By then a recovered Jefferies had become the Swindon correspondent for the *Wilts and Gloucestershire Standard*, for which he was to work intermittently until a growing reputation drew him toward London.

An important stage in that process came in November 1872 with the publication by the London *Times* of three letters by Jefferies about Wiltshire laborers. Their tone of condescension is in part a function of Jefferies's sympathy with the farmers' interests, in part of his calculation as to what was likely to be received favorably by a *Times* readership. The letters were the first of Jefferies's works to receive attention outside the Swindon area, but not necessarily more representative of his opinion than "A True Tale of the Wiltshire Labourer," written earlier for the *Wilts and Gloucestershire Standard* although unpublished until appearance in the posthumous collection *The Toilers of the Field* (1892). Together the letters and "A True Tale of the Wiltshire Labourers" reveal a young Jefferies both governed by the presuppositions of his own class and sensitive to the problems of those born beneath it.

If the *Times* letters were the first published items to bring Jefferies some genuine attention, this was not for lack of assiduous effort. A novel entitled "Fortune" had already gone the rounds of publishers, eventually to be accepted, but never published, by Smith, Elder. Several extremely poor short stories had appeared in the *North Wilts Herald*, and Jefferies had made attempts at both poetry and drama. Frustrated at trying to break into less ephemeral print, Jefferies, in 1873, paid for the publishing by John Snow of London of a pamphlet entitled *Reporting, Editing, and Authorship, Practical Hints for Beginners in Literature*–a somewhat grandiloquent title given the extent of his own publishing successes thus far. This was rapidly followed by a political pamphlet, *Jack Brass, Emperor of England* (1873), an attack on communism Carlylian in its minatory intensity if not in its rhetorical assurance. He was on safer but more parochial and derivative ground with the short, privately published book *A Memoir of the Goddards of North Wilts, Compiled from Ancient Records, Registers and Family Papers* (1873), in the costs of which he was assisted by a member of the Goddard family. A second political satire, inferior even to *Jack Brass* and laboring under the coyly declarative title *Suezcide!! Or How Miss Britannia Bought a Dirty Puddle and Lost Her Sugarplums*, appeared in 1876.

Despite these rather rash acts of desperation, Jefferies was about to achieve more palpable successes. In December 1873 *Fraser's Magazine* published the essay "The Future of Farming," following it with four more during 1874. In all Jefferies was to publish twelve articles in *Fraser's*, the last, "A Great Agricultural Problem," in March 1878. Five of the *Fraser's* articles—"The Farmer at Home," "The Labourer's Daily Life," "Field-Faring Women," "An English Homestead," and "John Smith's Shanty" (first part)—were republished in *The Toilers of the Field*. In 1874 Jefferies also published "The Power of the Farmers" in the June issue of *Fortnightly Review* and "The Size of Farms" in the October issue of *New Quarterly Magazine*. Thus within two years of the *Times* letters, Jefferies's work was receiving attention well beyond the boundaries of Wiltshire.

These early essays have much of the manner of Jefferies's first letter to the *Times*. Essentially informative rather than imaginative, they offer a journalist's description of the circumstances of rural living. "Such is a slight outline of the home-life and the faith of the farmer" ends "The Farmer at Home," a no-nonsense resolution echoed in that of "The Labourer's Daily Life": "These are some of the lights and shades of the labourer's daily life impartially presented." The impartiality is less characteristic than this son of a freehold farmer might claim, and judgmental generalizations abound: "It is this lack of poetical feeling that makes the English peasantry so uninteresting a study. They have no appreciation of beauty." But even the early pieces have an authority that derives from close observation and informed judgment. Some of the more ambitious essays, of which the best is "John Smith's Shanty," take the form of dramatized scenes. The fate of John Smith, imprisoned for a fortnight for wife-beating, becomes a moral exemplum that leads into a speculative projection into a future where education has improved dramatically the lots both of John Smiths and of their wives.

What must have seemed to Jefferies himself a more satisfying success was the publication in July 1874, the month of his marriage to Jessie Baden, a neighboring farmer's daughter, of *The Scarlet Shawl*, his first novel. Neither this nor the other two early novels, *Restless Human Hearts* (1875) and *World's End: A Story in Three Books* (1877), were commercial or critical successes, although *World's End*, unlike its predecessors, did not actually cost Jefferies a contribution to its publication expenses. All three novels were published by William Tinsley, who thus followed the pattern he had established with Thomas Hardy a few years earlier of losing a significant author after publishing his three earliest and financially least successful novels. All three novels reflect the almost sacramental view of nature and the in-

terest in the "soul-life" that are to distinguish Jefferies's later works, both fictional and nonfictional.

Shortly after their wedding, Jefferies and his wife moved from his parents' house at Coate to Swindon, where they would be based until early 1877 when they moved to the London suburb of Surbiton. Jefferies spent much of this period, particularly 1876, with the Harrilds in Sydenham, as it became increasingly obvious that, whatever his rural subject matter, his literary future lay within the immediate orbit of the London journals. Jefferies had placed nine articles in 1875: three with *Fraser's*, three with the *Graphic*, two with the *New Quarterly*, and one with the *Standard*. In addition a short story entitled "A Sin and A Shame" had appeared in *New Monthly Magazine*. In 1876, perhaps as a result of the long stay in Sydenham, he placed fourteen items in eight different journals: three with the *World*, three with *Cassell's Family Magazine*, two with *Fraser's*, two with the *Graphic*, one with the *New Quarterly*, one with the *Globe*, and two short stories, one with the *New Monthly*, and the other with *London Society*. With the birth of his first child in May 1875, the need to profit from his pen had become more urgent, and the essay's superiority to fiction in generating short-term rewards was becoming apparent.

Four of the 1875 articles—"Marlborough Forest" and "Village Churches" (*Graphic*), "The Story of Swindon," (*Fraser's Magazine*), and "Village Organization" (*New Quarterly*)—were included in the posthumous collection of Jefferies's essays entitled *The Hills and the Vale* (1909), which featured an introduction by Edward Thomas. Between them they demonstrate the two directions that Jefferies's nonfiction prose was to take. "The Story of Swindon" and "Village Organization" are journalistic exercises in social analysis, informed and opinionative. "Marlborough Forest" and "Village Churches" are impressionistic musings, acknowledged by Thomas as being, at this early stage, "as imperfect in their class as 'The Story of Swindon' is perfect in its own." The new voice is often strained, as in the opening of "Marlborough Forest" ("The great painter, Autumn, has just touched with the tip of his brush a branch of the beech-tree . . . ") or the close of "Village Churches" ("And where is there a place where springtime possesses such a tender yet melancholy interest to the heart as in a village churchyard, where the budding leaves and flowers in the grass may naturally be taken as symbolical of

Page from the notebook Jefferies kept in 1880-1881 (from Richard Jefferies: Man of the Fields, *by Samuel J. Looker and Crichton Porteous, 1965)*

a still more beautiful springtime yet in store for the soul?"). But behind the clichéd metaphor and tired cadences lies an attempt to evoke the visionary intensity of a subtle response to nature, the impulse that was to breathe life into Jefferies's more mature essays.

On 5 January 1877 the *Livestock Journal* published the first of what were to be regular weekly contributions from Jefferies on agricultural matters, many of which carried such unprepossessing titles as "The Neglected Pig" and "The Mystery of Offal." These unsigned articles became Jefferies's bread-and-butter work for much of the next two years, and the regular employment was probably responsible for the decision to move to Surbiton in February 1877. He was also enjoying a more literary success with the serialization of "The Rise of Maximin, Emperor of the Occident" (a romantic novel written in 1874) between October 1876 and July 1877 in the *New Monthly Magazine*. This undistinguished novel was never to be republished (its serial publication was not discovered until 1979), but its existence as the fourth novel published in little more than three years indicates where Jefferies's energies and real interests went in the time left to him from more

practical exercises in journalism.

It was a more developed form of the latter that was to bring Jefferies his first unequivocal success with a book-length work. During 1877, he contributed eleven articles to the *Pall Mall Gazette*, the first, entitled "Joint Stock Agriculture," published on 16 March. But by the end of the year, this sporadic work had developed into a regular series, *The Gamekeeper at Home*, which ran between 12 December 1877 and 24 April 1878. The series caught the attention of Smith, Elder and was published by them in book form in August 1878. It was to be followed by three more works that originated as series in the *Pall Mall Gazette: Wild Life in a Southern County* (serialized between May and December 1878 and published as a book in February 1879), *The Amateur Poacher* (serialized between March and July 1879 and also published in 1879), and *Round About a Great Estate* (serialized between January and April 1880 and published in 1880). To these may be added *Hodge and His Masters*, published also by Smith, Elder in 1880, which had originally run in the *Standard* as two serials, "Hodge at His Work" (November 1878 to February 1879) and "Hodge's Masters" (August

1879 to January 1880). Between them these four books established Jefferies as a major voice in the evocation of English country life. As Thomas was to write of *The Gamekeeper at Home*, "it is perhaps the first thoroughly rustic book in English, by a countryman and about the country, with no alien savours whatever."

The subtitle of *The Gamekeeper at Home—Sketches of Natural History and Rural Life*—might stand as a description of any of this group of country books. In each case the sketches are held together by associative links implied in the book's title. Thus in *The Gamekeeper at Home*, "the character of a particular Keeper has been used as a nucleus about which to arrange materials that would otherwise have lacked a connecting link." The original for the book's anonymous keeper was Haylock of Burderop Park, with whom the young Jefferies had spent many hours exploring the countryside around Coate. Nine chapters cover all aspects of a keeper's life, including his home and family, his estate, his daily and seasonal activities, and his enemies. By focusing on the keeper, Jefferies opens up a rich vein of homiletic musings, filled equally with rustic lore and proprietorial orthodoxy: "To make a good keeper it requires not only honesty and skill, but a considerable amount of 'backbone' in the character to resist temptation and to control subordinates ... the faithful and upright keeper is not only a valuable servant, but a protection to all kinds of property." The eye for detail possessed by the gamekeeper's companion is the book's greatest asset, producing the meticulous observation of passing phenomena that will be essential to the eliciting of nature's spiritual richness in the later essays.

The topography of Coate and Burderop provides the structural principle for *Wild Life in a Southern County*. Since the various examples of Wiltshire wildlife "are so closely connected, it is best, perhaps, to take the places they prefer for the convenience of division, and group them as far as possible in the districts they usually frequent." The twenty chapters therefore follow "the contour of the country," ranging over habitat both man-made and natural. The subject matter and organizational strategy necessitate closer attention to the animal and vegetable than to the human, with the result that certain passages lose descriptive energy and read like extracts from a naturalist's field notes. Nearly twice as long as *The Gamekeeper at Home*, the book has at times an embarrassment of detail: "On September 29 the

heaths and furze were white with the spiders' webs alluded to above. September 27, larks singing joyously. October 2, a few grasshoppers still calling in the grass—heard one or two three or four days later. October 4, the ivy in full flower. October 7, the thrushes singing again in the morning." But precision of eye and ear and the author's own enthusiasm carry a sympathetic reader over the inevitable longueurs, and the book proved sufficiently popular to warrant a second edition in 1879.

The same year saw the publication of the obvious companion volume to *The Gamekeeper at Home—The Amateur Poacher*. Jefferies's preface indicates that this time the various sketches will be structured temporally: "The following pages are arranged somewhat in the order of time, beginning with the first gun, and attempts at shooting. Then come the fields, the first hills, and woods explored, often without a gun, or any thought of destruction: and next the poachers, and other odd characters observed at their work." It is customarily regarded as the most successful of the group of country books, possessing a cohesion that results from its personal origins in Jefferies's memories of boyhood. Its unity as a work of fictionalized biography takes it further from the essay form than the other serialized works, but as W. J. Keith has suggested, it is perhaps "the great turning-point in Jefferies' career," bringing together what Keith identifies as four distinctive themes: the "Bevis" theme of childhood nostalgia, the country theme, the social theme, and the visionary theme.

The social theme receives its fullest nonfictional treatment in *Hodge and His Masters*. This two-volume, twenty-eight chapter collection devotes rather more time to his masters than to Hodge, concentrating as much on the country town as on the country. The subtleties of rural class relationship are conveyed in cameo presentations of free- and leasehold farmers, the squire, the country solicitor, the county-court judge, the banker, the newspaper editor, as well as the agricultural laborer. While Jefferies's sympathies are still very much with the farmers, the life of the laborer is treated with a compassion that contrasts sharply with the easy judgments of some of the earlier essays. As Hodge declines toward his inevitable end in the workhouse, he becomes an emblematic figure deprived of the strength possessed when he "Atlas-like supported upon his shoulders the agricultural world" but granted the ultimate benediction of incorporation into the cyclical mysteries that his life has served: "he ceased to exist by imperceptible degrees, like an oaktree.... The low mound will soon be level, and the place of his burial shall not be known."

Jefferies's growing reputation was signaled in the appearance of his name on the title page of *Hodge and His Masters*, and *Round About a Great Estate* displayed similar confidence in its drawing power. Again topography is used to pull the ten chapters together, with the "great house at Okebourne Chace" providing a center of convenience, and memories of Coate personalities providing originals for thinly drawn characters. The book celebrates an age already passing, a change in part due to improvements in rudimentary education, and Jefferies is anxious to record the past without mourning it: "In this book some notes have been made of the former state of things before it passes away entirely. But I would not have it therefore thought that I wish it to continue or return. My sympathies and hopes are with the light of the future, only I should like it to come from nature."

Jefferies's own future was now looking considerably more assured than could have been predicted on his move to London three years earlier. In addition to the popularity of the country books, he had a new novel, *Greene Ferne Farm*, published by Smith, Elder in 1880 after its serialization in *Time* between April 1879 and February 1880. *Wood Magic*, the first of the "Bevis" novels, was completed by late 1880, contributions continued to the *Pall Mall Gazette*, and the papers eventually collected in *Nature Near London* had begun to appear in the *Standard*. By the end of the following year, *Bevis* had been completed and Jefferies's spiritual autobiography, *The Story of My Heart*, begun.

Between them *Wood Magic* (1881), *Bevis* (1882), and *The Story of My Heart* (1883) move Jefferies's work unequivocally away from the early factually based and sociologically inclined articles to the more visionary essays of his final years. Much of the appeal of the two books of boyhood lies in their evocation of a child's education by nature and his growth into self-consciousness, frequently destructive self-consciousness. The younger Bevis is a seven-year-old who can converse with nature, the older Bevis a twelve-year-old who can deliberately destroy it. The extent to which both capacities combine to make the child the father of the man that Jefferies became is clear when one reads *The Story of My Heart* in association with the childhood idylls. The adolescent

visionary experience with which the autobiography begins is the fullest statement of the quasireligious apprehension of nature that inspires Jefferies's most distinctive work: "Touching the crumble of earth, the blade of grass, the thyme flower, breathing the earth-encircling air, thinking of the sea and the sky, holding out my hand for the sunbeams to touch it, prone on the sward in token of deep reverence, thus I prayed that I might touch to the unutterable existence infinitely higher than deity." Intense response to the natural becomes the means of recognizing a supernatural power that transcends both time and space: "I need no earth, or sea, or sun to think my thought. If my thought-part—the psyche—were entirely separated from the body, and from the earth, I should of myself desire the same. In itself my soul desires; my existence, my soulexistence is in itself my prayer, and so long as it exists so long will it pray that I may have the fullest soul-life."

This emphasis on "soul-life" as a capacity transcending the natural stimuli that provoke its recognition appears all the more poignant in the light of the fatal illness that made its initial presence felt in December 1881, when *Wood Magic* had just been published, *Bevis* just completed, and *The Story of My Heart* just begun. A tubercular fistula was diagnosed, which necessitated four operations during 1882 and the family's removal from Surbiton to Hove, on the Sussex coast, in the hope that sea air would aid Jefferies's condition. His remaining years would be increasingly peripatetic, with moves to Eltham, Surrey, in 1884, Rotherfield and Crowborough in Sussex in 1885, and Goring on the Sussex coast in 1886. All but one of the *Standard* essays had appeared before the illness struck, and *Nature Near London*, the resulting collection, was published in 1883, by Chatto and Windus, Jefferies's involvement with Smith, Elder having ceased with *Round About a Great Estate*.

Nature Near London comprises nineteen separate essays, held together only by the geographical association that the book's title announces. Most of the essays are structured around walks, the objects passed constantly surprising with their vibrant contingency: "Dark starlings, greenfinch, gilded fly, glistening beetle, blue butterfly, humble bee with scarf about his thick waist, add their moving dots of colour to the surface. There is no design, no balance, nothing like a pattern perfect on the right-hand side, and exactly equal on the left-hand. Even trees which have some semblance

Page from the manuscript for The Story of My Heart *(1883), about which Jefferies said, "it really is an autobiography, an actual record of thought" (from the 1947 edition of* The Story of My Heart, *edited by Samuel J. Looker)* of balance in form are not really so, and as you walk round them so their outline changes." Enjoyment of nature's rich multiplicity is premised upon acceptance of what chance offers (" 'Always get over a stile,' is the one rule that should ever be borne in mind by those who wish to see the land as it really is") and on active perception and the kind of sympathy that can take pleasure in the four-year survival of a trout in a stream a few yards distant from a fishing pond. No longer is a gun his inevitable companion, and the vibrancy of shared detail is all the greater now that it can appear gratuitous rather than an aspect of rural sociology. That there should be nature near London at all is conveyed as a gift, carrying with it no responsibilities other than silence and appreciation. The collection ends with three evocations of the Sussex Downs, culminating in "The Breeze on Beachy Head," an essay that points unmistakably in the direction of the visionary suggestiveness of the autobiography: "The sun sinks behind the summit of the Downs and slender streaks of purple are drawn along above them. A shadow comes forth from the cliff; a duskiness dwells on the water; something tempts the eye upwards, and near the zenith there is a star."

Jefferies's work for the *Pall Mall Gazette* had attracted the attention of the publisher, C. J. Longman, with whom he began a professional association when the three-part essay "Bits of Oak Bark" (collected in *The Life of the Fields*) appeared in *Longman's Magazine* in March 1883. Longman's published not only *The Story of My Heart* but also the last of the thematically-centered country books, *Red Deer* (1884). In June 1883 Jefferies was well enough to take a trip to Exmoor, where he began *Red Deer*, completing it in little more than a month. In manner it looks back to the earlier books, the natural history of the wild Exmoor deer sharing place with the lore of hunting them. Its sense of its subject is remarkable when one remembers that the terrain was unfamiliar to Jefferies, his visit brief, and his health erratic.

More representative of Jefferies's current work was *The Life of the Fields* (1884), culled mainly from contributions made to ten journals between February 1883 and April 1884, with one piece–the four-part "Country Literature"–dating back to the *Pall Mall Gazette* of October and November 1881. The twenty-three essays cover a broad range of subjects and settings, the latter including Sussex, Wiltshire, Somerset, London, and, in "The Plainest City in Europe," Paris.

Many of the essays show the intensity that *The Story of My Heart* had encouraged, felt at its most rhetorically ambitious in the opening study, "The Pageant of Summer" (published originally in *Longman's Magazine* in June 1883). This variegated evocation of the energizing principle inherent in summer shows Jefferies uniting phenomena, response, and moral significance in a way unique to these mature essays: "my hope becomes as broad as the horizon afar, reiterated by every leaf, sung on every bough, reflected in the gleam of every flower. There is so much for us yet to come, so much to be gathered, and enjoyed. Not for you and me, now, but for our race, who will ultimately use this magical secret for their happiness. Earth holds secrets enough to give them the life of the fabled Immortals." The lessons that Jefferies extracts from nature imply the possibility of escape from alienating self-consciousness and temporal inevitability: "The hours when the mind is absorbed by beauty are the only hours when we really live, so that the longer we can stay among these things so much the more is snatched from inevitable Time. . . . To be beautiful and to be calm, without mental fear, is the ideal of nature. If I cannot achieve it, at least I can think it." "Meadow Thoughts" becomes a paean to nature's prodigality, a glorious waste that in no way diminishes the power of the particular: "The gleaming rays on the water in my palm held me for a moment, the touch of the water gave me something from itself. A moment, and the gleam was gone, the water flowing away, but I had had them."

Behind the emotional incandescence of many of these essays lies the analytic detail that distinguished the earlier, more journalistic, articles: salad oil is the remedy when a dog's head swells to twice its usual size from a viper's bite ("By the Exe"), and a kestrel's hovering requires the balance of four distinct forces ("The Hovering of the Kestrel"). Two of the essays ("Nature and the Gamekeeper" and "The Sacrifice to Trout") are primarily concerned with the ecological effects of game preservation. And the urgency of the message often provokes the tone of the lecture hall: "Open your eyes and see those things which are around us at this hour" ("Venice in the East End"). But familiar as both subject matter and authorial personality are, a change has occurred whose roots are probably to be found both in the self-reflection that generated *The Story of My Heart* and in the illness that made life's ultimate mysteries much more immediate. When *The Life*

Page from the manuscript for one of the essays included in Field and Hedgerow, *published in 1889, two years after Jefferies's death (HM 11899; by permission of the Henry E. Huntington Library and Art Gallery) of the Fields* was published, Jefferies had only three more years left.

Jefferies's next two books were works of fiction, the novel *The Dewy Morn* (1884) and the futuristic romance *After London* (1885). There was to be one more volume of essays published in his lifetime, *The Open Air* (1885). This collection of twenty-one essays, most of them first published in journals since the summer of 1884, has a variety similar to that of *The Life of the Fields*. Its best-known essay, "One of the New Voters," had been published in the *Manchester Guardian* at the beginning of 1885 and looks back to the earlier essays of social analysis, such as "John Smith's Shanty." If nature is a constantly renewed gift to the thoughtful mind, the situation of the farm laborer–his body starved of food and poisoned by harvest beer, his mind deprived of recreation and conversation–is not matter for easy sentimentalizing: "There is so much in the wheat, there are books of meditation in it, it is dear to the heart. Behind these beautiful aspects comes the reality of human labour–hours upon hours of heat and strain; there comes the reality of a rude life, and in the end little enough of gain. The wheat is beautiful, but human life is labour." Some of the essays meld social homily and nature mysticism in ways very characteristic of Jefferies's later work. The effect is sometimes ponderous, nowhere more so than in "St. Guido," in which the Wheat lectures the child Guido on equitable food distribution and flower appreciation as a route to contentment. But when he avoids such arch contrivance, Jefferies writes with a sincerity fired by a sense of his own decaying powers: "Time changes the places that knew us, and if we go back in after years, still even then it is not the old spot; the gate swings differently, new thatch has been put on the old gables, the road has been widened, and the sward the driven sheep lingered on is gone. Who dares to think then? For faces fade as flowers, and there is no consolation" ("Wild Flowers").

Such truths were by 1885 almost unbearably manifest for the ailing Jefferies. In September his spine gave way, and there was no position in which he was able to write comfortably. Much of the final book to be published before his death, the melancholic novel *Amaryllis at the Fair* (1887), was dictated to his wife, as were the last essays. The opening essay of *Field and Hedgerow* (1889), the collection edited by his widow, is entitled "Hours of Spring" and is conventionally regarded as the last to come from Jefferies's own

pen. Its celebration of nature's generative power has an elegiac tone rendered all the more poignant by the circumstances of its production: "A thousand thousand buds and leaves and flowers and blades of grass, things to note day by day, increasing so rapidly that no pencil can put them down and no book hold them, not even to number them–and how to write the thoughts they give? All these without me–how can they manage without me?" The last piece in this volume of twenty-eight essays, thought to be Jefferies's final essay, dictated painfully to his wife, is "My Old Village." Its closing lines confront and ironically resolve the tension between the demystified nature apparent to the nonvisionary eye and the elusive wonder revealed to Jefferies's "soul-life" and articulated throughout his mature essays: "No-one else seems to have seen the sparkle on the brook, or heard the music at the hatch, or to have felt back through the centuries; and when I try to describe these things to them they look at me with stolid incredulity. No one seems to understand how I got food from the clouds, nor what there was in the night, nor why it is not so good to look at it out of a window. They turn their faces away from me, so that perhaps after all I was mistaken, and there never was any such place or any such meadows, and I was never there. And perhaps in course of time I shall find out also, when I pass away physically, that as a matter of fact there never was any earth."

While "Hours of Spring" and "My Old Village" have a particular force deriving from Jefferies's unflagging descriptive strength in the face of wasting mortality, it is fitting that this posthumous collection should reflect the range of his essays. Some, such as "House-Martins" and "Some April Insects," are little more than brief exercises in speculative nature study. Some, such as "Field Sports in Art" and "Nature in the Louvre," relate nature to its aesthetic imitation. But all display that immediacy of response distinctive of Jefferies's prose evocations, and encapsulated in the joyful integrity of the chaffinch, characteristically appropriated as "My Chaffinch," in the poem by Jefferies with which his widow closes the volume:

No note he took of what the swallows said
    About the firing of some evil gun,
Nor if the butterflies were blue or red,
    For all his feelings were intent in one.
The loving soul, a-thrill in all his nerves,
A life immortal as a man's deserves.

In continued pursuit of ease from his pain, Jefferies made a final move, in December 1886, from the cottage atop a windswept hill near Crowborough ("Forty miles that battering-ram wind had travelled without so much as a bough to check it till it struck the house on the hill") in which he had lived for almost eighteen months of unrelieved anxiety and illness. Despite his prodigious output in recent years, his family had little money, and the move was made possible only after a grant of a hundred pounds from the Royal Literary Fund, whose support Jefferies was initially unwilling to accept, and further support from a fund set up for Jefferies, again in the face of his reluctance, by C. J. Longman. By now, tuberculosis had severely affected the lungs, and the choice of residence–Sea View, Sea Lane, Goring–was dictated by the need for sea air. A temporary improvement did not disguise the desperateness of his condition: he died at his home on 14 August 1887 and was buried, like W. H. Hudson after him, at the Broadwater Cemetery in Worthing.

Because of the quantity of his essays and their distribution, often anonymously, among newspapers and journals, new collections of Jefferies's work have continued to appear since *Field and Hedgerow*. *The Toilers of the Field* (1892) comprises the early *Fraser's Magazine* articles, the letters to the *Times*, the previously unpublished "A True Tale of the Wiltshire Labourer," and five articles (four of them very slight) published in *Longman's Magazine* after his death. The next significant collection was *The Hills and the Vale* (1909), a compilation of eighteen essays, three of which were previously unpublished and the rest reprints of essays that had appeared in journals between 1875 and 1895. This valuable collection, like the later four collections made by Samuel J. Looker, inevitably has less temporal unity than those authorized by Jefferies himself, and in the Looker volumes titles are frequently the composition of the editor rather than the author. But despite the somewhat piecemeal process by which many of Jefferies's essays have eventually found a place between hard covers, all the posthumous compilations have produced a welcome enlargement of the Jefferies canon, even if they do not suggest the need for a radical rethinking of the shape of his career.

Jefferies's originality as an essayist still rests primarily on the later, less journalistic, meditative works, produced after *The Story of My Heart* had forced him to theorize about, as well as experi-

ence, his exceptionally acute response to nature. Perhaps its closest analogue is to be found in the hypersensitivity of his contemporary, Gerard Manley Hopkins, whose attempts to express his sense of nature's urgent mystery led him to new poetic language and prosody. The detailed renderings of natural phenomena in Hopkins's journals are disconcertingly reminiscent of sections of Jefferies's prose. For Jefferies that response never became something to be curbed for the sake of spiritual health but rather something to be celebrated for the same end. Behind the celebration, however, was the pragmatism of the born countryman, well aware of the rhythms of rural life in both social and transcendental manifestations. His achievement as a chronicler of the English countryside is unequaled, and more broadly he is probably what Richard Mabey, in his introduction to the most recent anthology of Jefferies's work, *Landscape with Figures* (1983), has called him–"the most imaginative observer of the natural world of his century."

Bibliographies:

Harold Joliffe, *A Catalogue of the Books in the Richard Jefferies Collection of the Swindon Public Libraries* (Swindon: The Libraries, Museum, Arts and Music Committee, 1948);

John G. Pearson, "Newly-Discovered Works Written by Richard Jefferies," *Victorian Periodicals Review*, 12 (Spring 1979): 33.

References:

Reginald Arkell, *Richard Jefferies* (London: Rich & Cowan, 1933); republished as *Richard Jefferies and His Countryside* (London: Jenkins, 1946);

Walter Besant, *The Eulogy of Richard Jefferies* (London: Chatto & Windus, 1888);

W. J. Keith, *Richard Jefferies: A Critical Study* (Toronto: University of Toronto Press / London: Oxford University Press, 1965);

Q. D. Leavis, "Lives and Works of Richard Jefferies," *Scrutiny*, 6 (March 1938): 435-446;

Samuel J. Looker, "Bibliographical Discoveries in the Work of Richard Jefferies," *Notes and Queries*, 12 February 1944, pp. 91-92;

Looker, ed., *Concerning Richard Jefferies, by Various Writers* (Worthing: Aldridge, 1944);

Looker, ed., *Richard Jefferies: A Tribute by Various Writers* (Worthing: Aldridge, 1946);

Looker, and Crichton Porteous, *Richard Jefferies: Man of the Fields* (London: John Baker, 1965);

Richard Mabey, Introduction to *Landscape with Figures* (Harmondsworth, U.K.: Penguin, 1983);

Edna Manning, *Richard Jefferies: A Modern Appraisal*, introduction by Cyril F. Wright (Windsor: Goldscheider, 1984);

C. J. Masseck, *Richard Jefferies: Etude d'une Personalité* (Paris: Emile Larose, 1913);

Irving Muntz, "Richard Jefferies as a Descriptive Writer," *Gentleman's Magazine*, 277 (November 1894): 514-532;

H. S. Salt, *Richard Jefferies: A Study* (London: Sonnenschein, 1894); republished, without

bibliography, as *Richard Jefferies: His Life and His Ideals* (London: Fifield, 1905);

Brian Taylor, *Richard Jefferies* (Boston: Twayne, 1982);

Edward Thomas, *Richard Jefferies: His Life and Work* (London: Hutchinson, 1909);

Henry Williamson, "Richard Jefferies," *Atlantic Monthly*, 159 (June 1937): 681-688;

Williamson, "Some Nature Writers and Civilisation," in *Essays by Divers Hands* (Transactions of the Royal Society of Literature), 30 (Oxford: Oxford University Press, 1960);

Williamson, "A Wiltshire Lad," *Fortnightly Review*, 162 (August 1937): 178-186.

Andrew Lang

(31 March 1844 - 20 July 1912)

Roger W. Calkins
Mount Allison University

BOOKS: *Ballads and Lyrics of Old France* (London: Longmans, Green, 1872; Portland, Me.: Mosher, 1896);

Oxford: Brief Historical and Descriptive Notes (London: Seeley, Jackson & Halliday, 1879; London: Seeley / New York: Macmillan, 1890);

XXII Ballades in Blue China (London: Kegan Paul, 1880);

The Library (London: Macmillan, 1881);

XXII and X: XXXII Ballades in Blue China (London: Kegan Paul, 1881);

Helen of Troy (London: Bell, 1882; New York: Scribners, 1882);

Custom and Myth (London: Longmans, Green, 1884; New York: Harper, 1885);

Much Darker Days, as A. Hugh Longway (London: Longmans, Green, 1884);

The Princess Nobody: A Tale of Fairy Land after the Drawings by Richard Doyle (London: Longmans, Green, 1884);

Rhymes à la Mode (London: Kegan Paul, Trench, Trübner, 1885; London & New York: Longmans, Green, 1907);

That Very Mab, by Lang and May Kendall (London: Longmans, Green, 1885);

Books and Bookmen (London: Longmans, Green 1886; New York: Coombes, 1886);

In the Wrong Paradise and Other Stories (London: Kegan Paul, Trench, 1886; New York: Harper, 1886);

Letters to Dead Authors (London: Longmans, Green, 1886; New York: Scribners, 1886);

The Mark of Cain (Bristol: Arrowsmith, 1886; New York: Scribners, 1886);

The Politics of Aristotle, Introductory Essays (London: Longmans, Green, 1886);

He, by Lang and Walter Herries Pollock as the "Author of 'It' ... " (London: Longmans, Green, 1887; New York: Munro, 1887);

King Solomon's Wives; or, the Phantom Mines, as Hyder Ragged (London: Vizetelly, 1887; New York: Munro, 1887);

Myth, Ritual, and Religion, 2 volumes (London: Longmans, Green, 1887; London & New York: Longmans, Green, 1889);

The Gold of Fairnilee (Bristol: Arrowsmith, 1888; New York: Longmans, Green, 1888);

Grass of Parnassus: Rhymes Old and New (London & New York: Longmans, Green, 1888);

Pictures at Play; or, Dialogues of the Galleries by Two Art Critics, by Lang and William Ernest Henley (London: Longmans, Green, 1888);

Letters on Literature (London & New York: Longmans, Green, 1889);

Lost Leaders (London: Kegan Paul, Trench, 1889; New York: Longmans, Green, 1889);

Prince Prigio (Bristol: Arrowsmith / London: Simpkin, Marshall, 1889; New York: Crowell, 1901);

How to Fall in Literature: A Lecture (London: Field & Tuer, 1890);

Life, Letters, and Diaries of Sir Stafford Northcote, First Earl of Iddesleigh, 2 volumes (Edinburgh & London: Blackwood, 1890);

Old Friends: Essays in Epistolary Parody (London & New York: Longmans, Green, 1890);

The World's Desire, by Lang and Henry Rider Haggard (London: Longmans, Green, 1890; New York: Harper, 1890);

Angling Sketches (London & New York: Longmans, Green, 1891);

Essays in Little (London: Henry, 1891; New York: Scribners, 1891);

Homer and the Epic (London & New York: Longmans, Green, 1893);

Prince Ricardo of Pantouflia (Bristol: Arrowsmith, 1893; Bristol: Arrowsmith / New York: Longmans, Green, 1893);

St. Andrews (London & New York: Longmans, Green, 1893);

Ban and Arrière Ban: A Rally of Fugitive Rhymes (London & New York: Longmans, Green, 1894);

Cock Lane and Common-Sense (London & New York: Longmans, Green, 1894);

A Monk of Fife: A Romance of the Days of Jeanne d'Arc (London & New York: Longmans, Green, 1895);

My Own Fairy Book (Bristol: Arrowsmith, 1895; New York: Longmans, Green, 1895);

The Book of Dreams and Ghosts (London, New York & Bombay: Longmans, Green, 1897);

The Life and Letters of John Gibson Lockhart, 2 volumes (London: Nimmo, 1897; London: Nimmo / New York: Scribners, 1897);

Modern Mythology (London, New York & Bombay: Longmans, Green, 1897);

Pickle the Spy; or, the Incognito of Prince Charles (London, New York & Bombay: Longmans, Green, 1897);

The Companions of Pickle (London & New York: Longmans, Green, 1898);

The Making of Religion (London & New York: Longmans, Green, 1898);

Parson Kelly, by Lang and Alfred Edward Woodley Mason (London & New York: Longmans, Green, 1899);

A History of Scotland from the Roman Occupation to the Suppressing of the Last Jacobite Rising, 4 volumes (Edinburgh & London: Blackwood, 1900-1907; New York: Dodd, Mead / Edinburgh & London: Blackwood, 1901-1907);

Prince Charles Edward (Paris & New York: Goupil / Manzi, Joyant, 1900; London: Goupil, 1900);

Alfred Tennyson (Edinburgh & London: Blackwood, 1901; New York: Dodd, Mead, 1901);

The Disentanglers (London & New York: Longmans, Green, 1901);

Magic and Religion (London, New York & Bombay: Longmans, Green, 1901);

The Mystery of Mary Stuart (London, New York & Bombay: Longmans, Green, 1901);

James VI and the Gowrie Mystery (London & New York: Longmans, Green, 1902);

Social Origins (London, New York & Bombay: Longmans, Green, 1903);

The Story of the Golden Fleece (London: Kelly, 1903; Philadelphia: Altemus, 1903);

The Valet's Tragedy and Other Studies (London & New York: Longmans, Green, 1903);

Historical Mysteries (London: Smith, Elder, 1904);

Adventures Among Books (London, New York & Bombay: Longmans, Green, 1905);

The Clyde Mystery: A Study in Forgery and Folklore (Glasgow: MacLehose, 1905);

John Knox and the Reformation (London, New York & Bombay: Longmans, Green, 1905);

New Collected Rhymes (London & New York: Longmans, Green, 1905);

The Puzzle of Dickens's Last Plot (London: Chapman & Hall, 1905);

The Secret of the Totem (London, New York & Bombay: Longmans, Green, 1905);

Homer and His Age (London & New York: Longmans, Green, 1906);

Portraits and Jewels of Mary Stuart (Glasgow: MacLehose, 1906);

Sir Walter Scott (London: Hodder & Stoughton, 1906; New York: Scribners, 1906);

The Story of Joan of Arc (London: T. C. & E. C. Jack, 1906; London: T. C. & E. C. Jack / New York: Dutton, 1906);

The King Over the Water, by Lang and Alice Shield (London, New York, Bombay & Calcutta: Longmans, Green, 1907);

Tales of Troy and Greece (London & New York: Longmans, Green, 1907);

The Maid of France: Being the Story of the Life and Death of Jeanne d'Arc (London & New York: Longmans, Green, 1908);

La Jeanne d'Arc de M. Anatole France (Paris: Perrin, 1909);

Sir George Mackenzie, King's Advocate of Rosehaugh: His Life and Times 1636(?)-1691 (London & New York: Longmans, Green, 1909);

Sir Walter Scott and the Border Minstrelsy (London & New York: Longmans, Green, 1910);

The World of Homer (London & New York: Longmans, Green, 1910);

Method in the Study of Totemism (Glasgow: MacLehose, 1911);

A Short History of Scotland (Edinburgh & London: Blackwood, 1911; New York: Dodd, Mead, 1911);

History of English Literature from "Beowulf" to Swinburne (London: Longmans, Green, 1912; New York: Longmans, Green, 1912);

Shakespeare, Bacon, and the Great Unknown (London & New York: Longmans, Green, 1912);

Highways and Byways in the Border, by Lang and John Lang (London: Macmillan, 1913).

OTHER: *The Blue Fairy Book* (1889), *The Red Fairy Book* (1890), *The Green Fairy Book* (1892), *The Yellow Fairy Book* (1894), *The Pink Fairy Book* (1897), *The Grey Fairy Book* (1900), *The Violet Fairy Book* (1901), *The Crimson Fairy Book* (1903), *The Brown Fairy Book* (1904), *The Orange Fairy Book* (1906), *The Olive Fairy Book* (1907), *The Lilac Fairy Book* (1910), edited by Lang (London & New York: Longmans, Green, 1889-1910).

TRANSLATIONS: Homer, *The Odyssey*, translated by Lang and Samuel Henry Butcher (London: Macmillan, 1879; New York: Macmillan, 1883);

Theocritus, Bion, and Moschus (London: Macmillan, 1880; New York: Macmillan, 1889);

Homer, *The Iliad*, translated by Lang, Walter Leaf, and Ernest Myers (London: Macmillan, 1883; New York: Alden, 1883);

Aucassin and Nicolete (London: Nutt, 1887; New Rochelle, N. Y.: Clarke Conwell, 1902);

Charles Deulin, *Johnny Nut and the Golden Goose* (London: Longmans, Green, 1887);

The Dead Leman and Other Tales from the French, translated by Lang and Paul Sylvester (London: Swan, Sonnenschein, 1889; New York: Scribner & Welford, 1889);

The Miracles of Madame Saint Katherine of Fierbois (Chicago: Way & Williams, 1897);

Homer, *The Homeric Hymns* (New York: Longmans, Green, 1899; London: Allen, 1899);

Victor Hugo, *Notre-Dame of Paris* (London: Heinemann, 1902).

For more than thirty-five years, from 1875 to 1912, Andrew Lang's essays, reviews, and editorial leaders shaped the opinions and influenced the tastes of the reading public of England and the United States. He was a prolific and facile writer who was always stimulating and often con-

Andrew Lang, 1885 (portrait by Sir W. B. Richmond; by permission of the Trustees of the National Galleries of Scotland)

troversial. His principal interest was the reviewing of literature, but he wrote with authority about anthropology, folklore, history, biography, and sports–particularly golf and angling. He had great technical facility as a poet, and he created delightful fairy tales; as a novelist he was better at parody than at serious fiction. He is best remembered as the editor of *The Blue Fairy Book* and its various colored successors in the twelve-volume series; they delight children today as they did when the first volume appeared in 1889.

The son of John and Jane Plenderleath Sellar Lang, Andrew Lang was born on 31 March 1844, in Selkirk, Scotland, and his Scots ancestry remained an influence upon his mind and speech all his life. His father was sheriff-clerk of Selkirkshire. Andrew taught himself to read when four years old, and a taste for fairy tales

and the novels of Sir Walter Scott that he acquired as a boy remained with him throughout his life. He entered Edinburgh Academy in 1854 and there discovered a new world of reading: Charles Dickens, William Makepeace Thackeray, Alexander Dumas, Edgar Allan Poe, George Gordon, Lord Byron, Alexander Pope, and Henry Wadsworth Longfellow. This imaginative occupation often distracted Lang from his academic studies, and he particularly resented the loss of time required by the study of Greek. However, when he was introduced to Homer's *Iliad* he was struck by the beauty of the poetry and became a devoted student of Homer thereafter. At about the same time he discovered the poetry of Alfred, Lord Tennyson. The musical quality, the metrical felicity, and especially the nostalgia for a lost world of romance in Tennyson's poetry touched a responsive chord in Lang.

Aucassin and Nicolete

Some Bibliographer who wants a narrow plot of ground may take up the subject of Aucassin and Nicolete. *A new translation of this pretty, curious, and unique romance in alternate prose and rhyme, by mr Laurence Housman; has just been published by mr murray. mr Housman and I differ in principle and practice as to translation, but that is not the question here.*

In the absence of books, I can only write from memory about this romance and its

First page from the manuscript for Lang's translation of Aucassin and Nicolete *(HM 11384; by permission of the Henry E. Huntington Library and Art Gallery)*

208

In 1861 he entered the University of St. Andrews and resided at St. Leonard's Hall. Although he remained at St. Andrews only two years, he had the happiest memories of his student life there, for he found students with interests similar to his own. He and a small group of friends began the *St. Leonard's Magazine*, a twelve-page weekly of arts and literature; Lang was editor and chief contributor. In later years Lang often spent his summers at St. Andrews, where he made use of the university library for his research. Of all the honors he was to receive, he thought most highly of the honorary doctorate awarded him by St. Andrews University.

Lang transferred to the University of Glasgow in 1864 in order to qualify as a candidate for the Snell exhibition, a major scholarship to Oxford. He won the competition and entered Balliol College, Oxford, in 1865. With Benjamin Jowett as his tutor, he took first class in two subjects in 1868 and was subsequently elected to an open fellowship at Merton College. However, what appeared to be the beginning of a brilliant academic career was interrupted by an acute lung infection in the autumn of 1872. Following the advice of his physician, he went to the French Riviera for two winters to recover his health. There he met Robert Louis Stevenson and began a lifelong friendship with him. When Lang returned to Oxford University he had become disillusioned with academic life, and in 1875 he vacated his Merton fellowship. On 17 April in the same year he married Leonora Blanche Alleyne, and they settled in Kensington, London, where Lang entered upon his career in journalism.

Lang had begun regular reviewing for the *Academy* in 1874 before leaving Oxford, and by 1875 he was publishing literary articles two or three times a week in the *Daily News* and once a week in the *Saturday Review*. Then occasional articles of his began to appear in other dailies and weeklies: the *Morning Post*, the *Athenæum*, the *Spectator*, *Cornhill Magazine*. American magazines such as *Harper's* and the *Nation* carried his articles as well. It may have been through the influence of a fellow student at Oxford, Frederick William Longman, that Lang first interested the old and distinguished publishing house of Longmans, Green, in his writing. He eventually became their chief adviser on literary matters, and they published the majority of his books. From the founding of *Longmans Magazine* in 1882 until its demise in 1905, Lang had a column in it, "At the sign of the ship," in which he wrote on any subject that in-

terested him. He found literary employment in other directions as well. Spencer Baynes employed him to write articles on a variety of subjects for the ninth edition of *The Encyclopædia Britannica*. The sheer volume of writing that issued from Lang's pen was the result of his unusual ability to write at any time or place.

Lang's popularity suggests that his temperament and style were perfectly in tune with the widest audience of his age. In his *A Story-Teller* (1923) novelist W. Pett Ridge commented, "We ... counted the day empty unless an article by Lang appeared." In *The Romantic 'Nineties* (1926) Richard Le Gallienne wrote, "His leaders in *The Daily News* read like fairy tales written by an erudite Puck. No other such combination of poet, scholar and journalist has been known in Fleet Street." It should be noted, however, that the newspapers for which Lang wrote had a different character than those of today. For example, English periodicals of the nineteenth century carried discussion and debate on controversial scholarly topics. Lang, whose knowledge of many subjects seems to have been encyclopedic, won a reputation for scholarly acumen and wisdom; he always wrote in a style that was limpid and witty, accessible to the least educated reader and interesting to the best. Arthur Quiller-Couch thought Lang's prose style the finest in England in his day, comparing it on points of conversational grace and urbanity to that of Thackeray in the previous age (*Pall Mall Magazine*, July 1897). G. K. Chesterton described Lang as universal, amusing, and lucid, and he added that these strengths led many pretentious and pedantic persons to despise Lang (*Illustrated London News*, 27 July 1912). Although Lang was a frequent subject of attack for his outspoken opinions and judgments of other writers, he had the advantage over his adversaries in that he never became upset or lost his temper. He was a master of ridicule and the witty put-down. Pretense and ignorance were always targets of his attack.

The love of fairy tale and romance which characterized Lang's earliest youthful readings and remained with him throughout his life reveals a side of Lang's personality different from that of the controversialist and parodist. This side may be seen in his literary reviews when he singles out works of romance and adventure for praise. R. L. Stevenson, H. Rider Haggard, Stanley Weyman, and S. R. Crockett are writers whose careers were launched or their popularity augmented by Lang's influential reviews. Treated

Lang on a fishing trip at Ingleborough, circa 1891

more critically in Lang's reviews were authors who are today considered more important: George Meredith, Fyodor Dostoyevski, Gustave Flaubert, Henry James, Joseph Conrad, Emile Zola, Thomas Hardy. Realism, naturalism, sociological or psychological studies of character–in short, the avant-garde of the late Victorian period–were of little interest to Lang, whose conservative love of Scott and Tennyson made him the spokesman of the complacent middle class of his time.

Early in his career Lang demonstrated a talent for writing poetry. His first book of poems, *Ballads and Lyrics of Old France* (1872), written while he was a student at Oxford, is academic in the sense that the poems are imitations of French Renaissance forms such as the rondeau and the triolet. The poems succeed through Lang's thorough knowledge of the French language and his

delicate ear for intricate rhymes and meter. This volume was followed in 1880 by *XXII Ballades in Blue China* and in 1881 by *XXII and X: XXXII Ballades in Blue China*, poems in imitation of the French ballade. What Lang hoped would be his first major work in poetry, *Helen of Troy*, an epic poem in six books, appeared in 1882. It received disappointing critical reviews and has been largely ignored since its publication. Lang's temperament was inappropriate for his subject. He eliminated the sensual elements from the story of Helen and adopted a tone of wistfulness. Although his lines flow gracefully, they fail to excite the imagination. Disappointed at the reception of his poem, Lang never again attempted a large subject in poetry. The books of poetry which he published afterward, *Rhymes à la Mode* (1885), *Grass of Parnassus* (1888), *Ban and Arrière Ban* (1894), and *New Collected Rhymes* (1905), include short poems that are often occasional in nature, usually witty, and quite successful as light verse.

Of greater importance to the world of letters were Lang's translations in prose from the Greek. He joined with S. H. Butcher in 1879 to produce a translation of Homer's *Odyssey* which was widely accepted as the standard translation for many years afterward. Lang's lifelong interest in tales of adventure and a past world of heroic action, and his admiration for the expressiveness of Homer's language, resulted in a translation with color, verve, and accuracy. He followed this book with his own translation of Theocritus, Bion, and Moschus in 1880. These authors are successfully rendered, but they lack the wide appeal of Homer. Then, with Walter Leaf and Ernest Myers, he published a translation of *The Iliad* in 1883. It failed to have the great success of *The Odyssey*, but it was highly competent and well accepted. Finally, after a pause during which he translated *Aucassin and Nicolete* (1887) and other tales from the French, he published his last Greek translation, *The Homeric Hymns*, in 1899. Lang was always in opposition to those scholars attempting to prove multiple authorship of Homer's works. Lang was convinced that the personality of Homer could be felt throughout his works, and he argued with wit and common sense for the unity of Homer. Along with several essays, he contributed three books to Homeric studies: *Homer and the Epic* (1893), *Homer and His Age* (1906), and *The World of Homer* (1910).

Lang's knowledge of mythology and anthropology was rare among the literary essayists of his period. His early interest in fairy tale, folktale, and the balladry of the Scottish border continued and widened during his university years and after to include examples from many national literatures. His first scholarly dispute in this field was with Max Müller of Oxford, the established authority on the anthropology of myth and folktale, who explained the existence of folktales as degenerate forms of higher literature. According to Müller's theory the variant forms of folktales in existence in primitive cultures were to be explained as linguistic mistakes in the transmission of the story from a sophisticated culture to a more primitive one. Lang's knowledge of many variants of individual myths and tales led him to the more reasonable conclusion that myths evolved spontaneously in primitive cultures as expressions of fundamental human needs and beliefs. Thus no linguistic connection need exist between variant myths and stories. Lang opened his attack with an article entitled "Mythology and Fairy Tales" in the *Fortnightly Review* of May 1873. In 1884 he gathered some of these articles into *Custom and Myth*, his first book on anthropological subjects. This collection was followed in 1887 by *Myth, Ritual, and Religion*, a book concerned largely with totemism in primitive societies. Lang began to find common elements in the religious beliefs of early societies, and these led him to think he might establish a new basis for belief in a divine creator. In *The Making of Religion* (1898) Lang attempted to show systematically that the religions of the world all sprang from common human needs, each religion being given its particular form and shape by a great leader such as Christ or Mohammud. Lang, who was a founding member of the Psychical Research Society and became its president in 1911, turned to psychical phenomena as a means of explaining miracles which are fundamental to much religious belief.

Lang's interest in myth and fairy tale led him to write and edit books of fairy stories which probably will outlast his more serious productions. His first effort in this direction, *The Princess Nobody: A Tale of Fairy Land* (1884), is a slight work and gives little hint of what was to follow. In *The Gold of Fairnilee* (1888) he turned to the valley of the Tweed and the Border country of his youth for inspiration, and this tale is his finest piece of prose fiction. A melancholy note indigenous to the romantic side of Lang's temperament sounds here, but there is neither sentimentality nor artifice. *Prince Prigio*, the production of the following year, is another kind of story altogether. An imitation of Thackeray's fairy tales, it is witty, Puckish, and thoroughly literary, not an attempt to recover the purity of primitive myth, but a lapse into play on the part of a serious literary man. In 1889 Lang edited *The Blue Fairy Book* for Longmans, Green, and every year thereafter the publisher brought out another book of children's stories with Lang's name on the cover. These included the twelve volumes of fairy tales, but interspersed among the fairy-tale volumes in various years were collections of romances, true stories, animal stories, stories of heroes, and children's poems, some forming separate color series. Although Lang wrote an introductory note for each volume and his name appeared on the cover as editor, the stories actually were rewritten and adapted for children by Lang's wife, Leonora, who had occasional help from May Kendall and Florence Sellar.

Andrew Lang, circa 1902

It was not until Lang was in his forties that he began publishing historical and biographical studies. In 1890 his biography of Sir Stafford Northcote made a useful contribution to parliamentary history, but he was less successful with his history of St. Andrews (1893), which he based on unauthenticated secondary sources. The criticism which followed the publication of this work taught Lang the necessity of using primary documents, a lesson he never forgot. An inquiry by Stevenson about a character in Scott's *Redgauntlet* (1824) who was a spy for the English with the code name "Pickle" (after Tobias Smollett's *Peregrine Pickle*, 1751) led Lang to research the affair. Lang came to the conclusion that Pickle was Alastair Ruadh MacDonell, son of the Laird of Glengary, and Lang's publication of his findings in 1897 in *Pickle the Spy; or, the Incognito of Prince Charles* signaled the beginning of his battles with the Scottish patriots. He settled that issue conclusively in the following year with *The Companions of Pickle*, in which he documented the activities of Pickle and other characters surrounding him. In spite of Lang's love of Scotland, he refused to bend the truth he found in historical documents to fit the legends of the Scottish heroes fostered by Scottish patriotism. His biography *Prince Charles Edward*, published in 1900, and his four-volume *A History of Scotland from the Roman Occupation to the Suppressing of the Last Jacobite Rising* (1900-1907) made it clear in the face of continued criticism that Lang's first loyalty was to historical truth. The work which aroused the greatest storm of criticism, however, was *John Knox and the Reformation* (1905). The main thrust of Lang's attack on Knox centered on Knox's *History of the Reformation* (1587), a piece of blatant propaganda in which Knox presented himself as the principal force behind the Scottish Reformation. Lang saw the narrow Calvinism resulting from Knox's influence as a curse upon Scotland for the next three centuries. Researches into Scottish history resulted in specialized studies as well, such as *The Mystery of Mary Stuart* (1901), *James VI and the Gowrie Mystery* (1902), and *Portraits and Jewels of Mary Stuart* (1906). He published *A Short History of Scotland* in one volume in 1911, the year before his death.

Closely allied to his historical studies are the biographies which he published during this period: *Alfred Tennyson* (1901), *Sir Walter Scott* (1906), and *Sir George Mackenzie* (1909). Worthy of special mention is *The Maid of France: Being the Story of the Life and Death of Jeanne d'Arc* (1908). The figure of Joan of Arc appealed to Lang because of her heroism, her moral strength, and the sheer romance of her rise and fall. When in 1904 Anatole France, in furtherance of his anticlerical campaign, attempted to portray Joan as merely a dupe of the Church, Lang refuted France's arguments by returning to the primary documents. As a Scotsman Lang was free of the English prejudice against Joan, and he easily avoided pitfalls to the understanding of this figure that stood in the way of the Catholic church on the one hand and Anatole France on the other. In the preface to his *Saint Joan* (1924) George Bernard Shaw faulted Lang for romanticizing Joan, but Lang was aware that he was not writing for impartial readers and that he had a balance of English ill-will to redress. A more serious criticism today is Lang's willingness to entertain occult phenomena such as extrasensory perception as explanation for the miraculous voices and visions that Joan received. Lang was deeply moved by the story of Joan of Arc. He conducted his research carefully and wrote with strong feeling. The book stands as a major success at the end of Lang's career.

During his lifetime Lang received honorary doctorates from St. Andrews and Oxford and was made an honorary fellow of Merton College. After his death the Andrew Lang Lecture was instituted at St. Andrews in his memory. From his entrance into journalism in 1875 until his death in 1912 no single individual exercised as much influence over the world of letters in England as did Lang. That his romanticism and nostalgia were backward looking and conservative is true, and this tendency in his work accounts in large measure for his present lapse into obscurity while the more innovative and radical writers of his period have continued to hold the interest of readers and scholars. But the large middle-class public to whom Lang addressed himself was well served by him. His argument was devoted to truth and was free of hypocrisy and cant. His taste in literature, though limited by his admiration for the noble and ideal, was worthy of imitation. His style was the perfection of urbane conversation. Although Lang hated to be called "versatile," he mastered many types of writing and excelled in them. Lang died on 20 July 1912, of angina pectoris, at Banchory, Aberdeenshire.

References:

Malcolm Elwin, "Andrew Lang and Other Critics," in his *Old Gods Falling* (London: Macmillan, 1939), pp. 182-217;

Roger Lancelyn Green, *Andrew Lang: A Critical Biography* (Leicester: Ward, 1946);

Eleanor De Selms Langstaff, *Andrew Lang* (Boston: Twayne, 1978);

George Saintsbury, "Andrew Lang in the 'Seventies—and After," in *The Eighteen-Seventies: Essays by Fellows of the Royal Society of Literature*, edited by Harley Granville-Barker (London: Macmillan, 1929), pp. 81-96;

Gardner B. Taplin, "Andrew Lang as a Student of the Traditional Narrative Ballad," *TSE: Tulane Studies in English*, 14 (1965): 57-73;

A. B. Webster, ed., *Concerning Andrew Lang: Being the Andrew Lang Lectures Delivered Before the University of St. Andrews, 1927-1937* (London: Oxford University Press, 1949);

Joseph Weintraub, "Andrew Lang: Critic of Romance," *English Literature in Transition 1880-1920*, 18 (1975): 5-15.

D. H. Lawrence

(11 September 1885 - 2 March 1930)

Michael S. Tait
University of Toronto

See also the Lawrence entries in *DLB 10: Modern British Dramatists, 1900-1945*; *DLB 19: British Poets 1880-1914*; and *DLB 36: British Novelists, 1890-1929: Modernists.*

BOOKS: *The White Peacock* (New York: Duffield, 1911; London: Heinemann, 1911);

The Trespasser (London: Duckworth, 1912; New York: Kennerley, 1912);

Love Poems and Others (London: Duckworth, 1913; New York: Kennerley, 1913);

Sons and Lovers (London: Duckworth, 1913; New York: Kennerley, 1913);

The Widowing of Mrs. Holroyd (New York: Kennerley, 1914; London: Duckworth, 1914);

The Prussian Officer and Other Stories (London: Duckworth, 1914; New York: Huebsch, 1916);

The Rainbow (London: Methuen, 1915; expurgated, New York: Huebsch, 1915);

Twilight in Italy (London: Duckworth, 1916; New York: Huebsch, 1916);

Amores (London: Duckworth, 1916; New York: Huebsch, 1916);

Look! We Have Come Through! (London: Chatto & Windus, 1917; New York: Huebsch, 1917);

New Poems (London: Secker, 1918; New York: Huebsch, 1920);

Bay: A Book of Poems (London: Beaumont Press, 1919);

Touch and Go (London: Daniel, 1920; New York: Seltzer, 1920);

Women in Love (New York: Privately printed for subscribers only, 1920; London: Secker, 1921);

The Lost Girl (London: Secker, 1920; New York: Seltzer, 1921);

Movements in European History, as Lawrence H. Davidson (London: Oxford University Press, 1921);

Psychoanalysis and the Unconscious (New York: Seltzer, 1921; London: Secker, 1923);

Tortoises (New York: Seltzer, 1921);

D. H. Lawrence, 1908 (by permission of the Nottingham Local History Library and George Roberts)

Sea and Sardinia (New York: Seltzer, 1921; London: Secker, 1923);

Aaron's Rod (New York: Seltzer, 1922; London: Secker, 1922);

Fantasia of the Unconscious (New York: Seltzer, 1922; London: Secker, 1923);

England, My England and Other Stories (New York: Seltzer, 1922; London: Secker, 1924);

The Ladybird, The Fox, The Captain's Doll (London: Secker, 1923); republished as *The Captain's Doll: Three Novelettes* (New York: Seltzer, 1923);

Studies in Classic American Literature (New York: Seltzer, 1923; London: Secker, 1924);

Kangaroo (London: Secker, 1923; New York: Seltzer, 1923);

Birds, Beasts and Flowers (New York: Seltzer, 1923; London: Secker, 1923);

The Boy in the Bush, by Lawrence and M. L. Skinner (London: Secker, 1924; New York: Seltzer, 1924);

St. Mawr: Together with The Princess (London: Secker, 1925);

St. Mawr (New York: Knopf, 1925);

Reflections on the Death of a Porcupine and Other Essays (Philadelphia: Centaur Press, 1925; London: Secker, 1934);

The Plumed Serpent (Quetzalcoatl) (London: Secker, 1926; New York: Knopf, 1926);

David (London: Secker, 1926; New York: Knopf, 1926);

Sun (expurgated, London: Archer, 1926; unexpurgated, Paris: Black Sun Press, 1928);

Glad Ghosts (London: Benn, 1926);

Mornings in Mexico (London: Secker, 1927; New York: Knopf, 1927);

Rawdon's Roof (London: Elkin Mathews & Marrot, 1928);

The Woman Who Rode Away and Other Stories (London: Secker, 1928; New York: Knopf, 1928);

Lady Chatterley's Lover (Florence: Privately printed, 1928; expurgated, London: Secker, 1932; New York: Knopf, 1932; unexpurgated, New York: Grove, 1959; Harmondsworth, U.K.: Penguin, 1960);

The Collected Poems of D. H. Lawrence, 2 volumes (London: Secker, 1928; New York: Cape & Smith, 1929);

The Paintings of D. H. Lawrence (London: Mandrake Press, 1929);

Pansies (London: Secker, 1929; New York: Knopf, 1929; definitive edition, London: Privately printed, 1929);

My Skirmish with Jolly Roger (New York: Random House, 1929); revised as *A Propos of Lady Chatterley's Lover* (London: Mandrake Press, 1930);

Pornography and Obscenity (London: Faber & Faber, 1929; New York: Knopf, 1930);

The Escaped Cock (Paris: Black Sun Press, 1929); republished as *The Man Who Died* (London: Secker, 1931; New York: Knopf, 1931);

Nettles (London: Faber & Faber, 1930);

Assorted Articles (London: Secker, 1930; New York: Knopf, 1930);

The Virgin and the Gipsy (Florence: Orioli, 1930; London: Secker, 1930; New York: Knopf, 1930);

Love Among the Haystacks & Other Pieces (London: Nonesuch Press, 1930; New York: Viking, 1933);

The Triumph of the Machine (London: Faber & Faber, 1930);

Apocalypse (Florence: Orioli, 1931; New York: Viking, 1931; London: Secker, 1932);

Etruscan Places (London: Secker, 1932; New York: Viking, 1932);

Last Poems, edited by Richard Aldington (Florence: Orioli, 1932; New York: Viking, 1933; London: Secker, 1933);

The Lovely Lady and Other Stories (London: Secker, 1933; New York: Viking, 1933);

A Collier's Friday Night (London: Secker, 1934);

A Modern Lover (London: Secker, 1934; New York: Viking, 1934);

Phoenix: The Posthumous Papers of D. H. Lawrence, edited by Edward D. McDonald (New York: Viking, 1936; London: Heinemann, 1936);

The First Lady Chatterley (New York: Dial, 1944);

The Complete Poems of D. H. Lawrence, 2 volumes, edited by Vivian de Sola Pinto and Warren Roberts (London: Heinemann, 1964; New York: Viking, 1964);

The Complete Plays of D. H. Lawrence (London: Heinemann, 1965; New York: Viking, 1966);

Phoenix II: Uncollected, Unpublished, and Other Prose Works, edited by Roberts and Harry T. Moore (New York: Viking, 1968; London: Heinemann, 1968);

John Thomas and Lady Jane (New York: Viking, 1972; London: Heinemann, 1972);

Mr. Noon, edited by Lindeth Vasey (London & New York: Cambridge University Press, 1984).

Collection: *The Cambridge Edition of the Letters and Works of D. H. Lawrence*, 34 volumes projected, general editors James T. Boulton and Warren Roberts (Cambridge, London, New York, New Rochelle, Melbourne & Sydney: Cambridge University Press, 1980-).

Lawrence at the home of poet Witter Bynner, in Santa Fe, New Mexico, early 1923 (photograph by Bynner; by permission of the University of Nottingham Library)

OTHER: M. M., *Memoirs of the Foreign Legion*, introduction by Lawrence (London: Secker, 1924).

David Herbert Lawrence was born 11 September 1885 in Eastwood, Nottinghamshire. His father, Arthur Lawrence, was a miner, his mother, Lydia Beardsall Lawrence, a former schoolmistress. After matriculating at Nottingham University College, he qualified himself as a teacher. During his employment at a school in Croyden, he met Ford Madox Hueffer, who recognized his unique gifts and introduced him to the London literary scene. By 1912 Lawrence had published two novels, *The White Peacock* and *The Trespasser*. His mother's death in 1910, a traumatic but liberating event, provided an important impetus for *Sons and Lovers* (1913), his first major work of fiction.

In March 1912 Lawrence met Frieda von Richthofen Weekley, wife of a Nottingham professor of languages. Two months later she left husband and children to join Lawrence on the continent. They were married on 13 July 1914. Their often stormy relationship endured to his death, and was central to his life and work. The war years marked a nadir in Lawrence's fortunes. In 1915 *The Rainbow* was suppressed for alleged obscenity, and subsequently, Lawrence had difficulty finding an English publisher for his greatest novel, *Women in Love*, which was printed for subscribers only in 1920. His literary notoriety, antiwar views, and German wife made him a target for severe harrassment.

After the war Lawrence and Frieda left England for a life of ceaseless global travel. At the invitation of Mabel Dodge Luhan, a rich literary amateur, they sailed to America, and for a time lived on a small ranch in the mountains around Taos, New Mexico. *The Plumed Serpent* (1926) and many of Lawrence's novellas, short stories, and essays reflect the impact of Mexico, Old and New, upon his imagination.

In 1925, mortally ill with tuberculosis, Lawrence returned to Italy where he completed *Lady Chatterley's Lover*, his last novel. Its appearance in 1928 sparked a notorious furor, exacerbated by an exhibition of his paintings in London the following year. The magnitude of his achievement, however, was recognized by many of his contemporaries at the time of his death in Vence, the south of France, on 2 March 1930.

Lawrence is the most variously prolific of modern English authors. The diversity of his output is complemented by its unity. Every aspect of his work, even apparent contradictions, expresses a rooted, uniquely potent vision of experience. His fiction and poetry are the center of his writing; the criticism, plays, and essays are, so to speak, sparks from the central forge, some more brilliant than others, a few simply bits of ash, all of interest because of their authorship.

Even in the comparatively restricted compass of the essays, most of which are collected in two posthumous volumes, *Phoenix* (1936) and *Phoenix II* (1968), the reader encounters an extraordinary variety of subject matter, form, style, and tone. Again, however, this body of miscellaneous discursive writing–sketches, introductions, reviews, religious and political tracts, commentaries on society, art, literature, education, psychology, and sex–composes, in a sense, one vast essay in which Lawrence seeks rationally to formulate and apply the complex intuitions that give rise to the great novels.

Relatively early in his career he attempted to define his philosophy in two extended essays, "Study of Thomas Hardy" (written in 1914) and "The Crown" (1915). The comments on Hardy are illuminating but incidental. The main body of the essay explores such ideas as the ultimate importance of individual fulfillment, which is undermined in modern culture by a worship of money and the machine; the discovery of man's full humanity in the sexual encounter; marriage, potentially a reconciliation between law and love, as the source of harmony not only between the sexes, but between the individual and society and the nations of the world. "The Crown," a six-part essay written for a fugitive periodical called *Signature* (4 October-1 November 1915), extends Lawrence's argument further into the realm of metaphysics. The central metaphor presents the lion and the unicorn locked in conflict beneath the crown. These creatures represent two eternal cosmic principles, eternally opposed; the lion darkness, passion, power; the unicorn light, virginity, love. The crown is not victory, which would result in the death of both elements, but a state of perfect equilibrium in which each retains its integrity. The relevance of this notion to Lawrence's view of the right relation of the sexes in *Women in Love* (1920) and elsewhere is evident.

Neither of these ambitious early treatises is altogether satisfactory. They are written in Lawrence's high, portentous style filled with cloudy symbolism and vehement assertions which, in the absence of a concrete context, fail to persuade. There is evidence that Lawrence was aware of the limitation of this sort of writing and of the reasons for it. In his foreword to *Fantasia of the Unconscious* (1922) he states: "This pseudo-philosophy of mine–'polyanalytics,' as one of my respected critics might say–is deduced from the novels and poems, not the reverse. The novels and poems come unwatched out of one's pen. And then the absolute need which one has for some sort of satisfactory mental attitude towards oneself and things in general makes one try to abstract some definite conclusions from one's experience as a writer and a man."

"The Reality of Peace" (*English Review*, May-August 1917), a shorter essay which presents some related themes, is more accessible. The symbolism is less esoteric, and Lawrence's ideas are grounded in the intensities of his inner experience. In part, the essay is a meditation on the relation between good and evil. One passage, typical of the dark eloquence of the argument, is reminis-

Frieda and D. H. Lawrence in Chapala, during their 1923 visit to Mexico (by permission of the
Harry Ransom Humanities Research Center, University of Texas at Austin)

cent of aspects of Carl Jung's thought. Lawrence invites the snake which dwells in the "natural marsh of my belly" to make itself known so he may embrace it: "Come then, brindled abhorrent one, you have your own being and your own righteousness, yes, and your own desirable beauty. Come then, lie down delicately in the sun of my mind, sleep on the bosom of my understanding; I shall know your living weight."

"Education of the People" (written in 1917), a series of twelve essays, is an assault on contemporary educational theory and practice. Its principal thesis is that a premature development of the child's conscious faculties at the expense of his instinctual responses does lasting damage to his psychic well-being. This treatise points forward to *Psychoanalysis and the Unconscious* (1921) and *Fantasia*

of the Unconscious, books in which, rejecting Sigmund Freud, Lawrence develops his own theory of the dynamics of the psyche. He posits the existence of "affective centres" in the body's nervous system, the most crucial of which is the solar plexus, the source of instinctual life. In contrast to the Hardy study and "The Crown," the education essays are abrasive in style as Lawrence takes parents and teachers harshly to task for methods of rearing and educating the young contrary to Lawrentian doctrine. The exasperated tone (never far from the surface in Lawrence's social criticism) reflects his private sense of betrayal by wrong-headed teachers and a high-minded mother: "Would to God a she-wolf had suckled me and stood over me with her paps, and kicked me back into a rocky corner when she'd had

*Lawrence sitting by the adobe oven at Kiowa Ranch, New Mexico, where the Lawrences stayed for five months in 1924
(by permission of the Harry Ransom Humanities Research Center, University of Texas at Austin)*

enough of me. It might have made a man of me." The acerbity of these writings also reflects the frustration of a prophet not only without honor in his own country, but one ostracized and reviled by it. This sense of isolation is particularly acute during the war years, from the 1915 banning of *The Rainbow* to Lawrence's departure from England in 1919.

Lawrence attempts to address the large social and political issues of his day in several other essays. For example, "Democracy" (composition date uncertain), inveighs against the concept of the average man and an abstract ideal of equality, and seeks to define the proper relation of individuals to each other and the state. It is well argued, but elsewhere Lawrence acknowledges that practical programs for change lie outside his province; In "The State of Funk" he says that "The great social change interests me and troubles me, but it is not my field. I know a change is coming—and I know we must have a more generous, more human system based on the life values not on the money values. That I know. But what steps to take I don't know. Other men know better."

It is a pleasure then to turn to essays more expressive of Lawrence's essential genius. He is always at his strongest when his ideas are formulated within a specific framework. Concepts which, abstractly stated, fail to convince may take

on profound imaginative and emotional resonance when communicated through images or when they arise, as is often the case, out of some immediate observation of the natural world. The subject of the brief "Whistling of Birds" (*Athenæum*, 11 April 1919) is the invitation to psychic renewal which spring, having banished winter, holds out to mankind. Lawrence articulates his theme through a detailed description of the first tentative bird songs he hears when the south wind is suddenly warm, although the ground is still littered with the corpses of birds killed by the frost. The essay is especially poignant in that its implied context is the conclusion of an appalling European war. "Flowery Tuscany" (*New Criterion*, October-December 1927) traces the changing seasons in this Italian region as narcissus gives way to aconite, and then in turn to crocus, hyacinth, tulip, and iris. Lawrence's visionary perspective is enhanced by the exactitude of his botanical observations. He writes of the grape hyacinth: "The upper buds are pure blue, shut tight. . . . As yet none of the lower bells has withered, to leave the greenish, separate sparseness of fruiting that spoils the grape hyacinth later on, and makes it seem naked and functional. All hyacinths are like that in the seeding. . . . If we were tiny as fairies, and lived only a summer, how lovely these great trees of bells would be to us, towers of night and dawn-blue globes. . . . we

Lawrence with his sister Ada, 1926 (from Ada Lawrence and G. Stuart Gelder,
Young Lorenzo: Early Life of D. H. Lawrence, *1931)*

should see a god in them." This essay is essentially a celebration of mutability in nature. In Mediterranean countries, in contrast to the frozen North, "change is the reality and permanence is artificial and a condition of imprisonment." Tuscany also proves that man having "moulded the earth to his necessity without violating it" can live in harmony with the landscape.

It is the absence of such harmony that Lawrence deplores in "Nottingham and the Mining Countryside" (*New Adelphi*, June-August 1930) and an earlier companion piece, "Return to Bestwood" (written in 1923). In this part of England nature has been despoiled by the engines of industry and the brutal ugliness of the mining towns: "The country is so lovely; the man-made England is so vile."

In the autumn of 1922 at the invitation of Mabel Dodge Luhan, Lawrence and Frieda arrived in California. Lawrence's encounter with the American Southwest and Mexico was, he makes clear, a religious experience. Its sources were first of all the majestic landscape, and then the fast-fading rituals of the native Indian population. One such ritual, presented for the diversion of an uncomprehending secular audience, is recalled in "Just Back from the Snake Dance–Tired Out" (*Laughing Horse*, September 1924). In "Indians and An Englishman" (*Dial*, February 1923) Lawrence pictures an ancient Apache shaman telling tribal tales to the beat of a drum. It is night and Lawrence stands at the edge of a fire-lit enclosure, at a frontier of his consciousness: "I know my derivation.... I have a dark-faced, bronze-voiced father far back in the resinous ages. My mother was no virgin. She lay in her hour with this dusky-lipped tribe-father.... he would like to deny me. But I stand on the far edge of their firelight, and am neither denied nor accepted. My way is my own, old red father: I can't cluster at the drum any more."

The most thematically complex of the American essays is "Reflections on the Death of a Porcupine" (1925). The argument proceeds from a statement of the uncomfortable necessity to kill a destructive rodent, to the right of each order of nature to devour or otherwise make use of an inferior order, to the idea that every created thing in its individual, essential being, in its relation to the cosmos, partakes of eternity. Once again the concepts grow out of immediate experience. The opening description of the porcupine is memorable: "The animal had raised all its hairs and bristles, so that by the light of the moon it seemed to have a tail, swaying, moonlit aureole arching its back as it went. That seemed curiously fearsome, as if the animal were emitting itself demon-like on the air."

Lawrence's essays are written with an authority which derives in a general way from his temperament and the depth of his convictions. But several are doubly persuasive in that they present what one might call an insider's perspective. Except for the circumstances of his genius, Lawrence, a miner's son, would have lived out his days in the dehumanizing environment he portrays in "Nottingham and the Mining Countryside." His literary criticism from the early essay on Thomas Mann (*Blue Review*, July 1913) to the brilliant *Studies in Classic American Literature* (1923) derives strength from the fact that the critic is as great a writer as any he evaluates. The practitioner's special insight also illuminates Lawrence's pronouncements on the art of the novel in several interrelated essays. In "Surgery for the Novel—or a Bomb" (*Literary Digest International Book Review*, April 1923) he rejects the restrictions of realism and urges a new fictional mode which will fuse religious, philosophic, and psychological intuitions without recourse to abstraction. "You can develop an instinct for life, if you will, instead of a theory of right and wrong, good and bad" he asserts in "Why the Novel Matters" (first published in *Phoenix*). Here he argues against the imposition of absolute moral standards on the stuff of fiction which, if authentic, reflects the totality of experience: "Being a novelist, I consider myself superior to the saint, the scientist, the philosopher, and the poet, who are all great masters of different bits of man alive, but never get the whole hog." For Lawrence an impersonal, hidden life-energy is the central presence in any great work of fiction. In "The Novel" (*Reflections on the Death of a Porcupine*, 1925) he says that "We have to choose between the quick and the dead. The quick is God-flame, in everything.... In this room where I write, there is a little table that is dead: it doesn't even weakly exist.... And there is a sleeping cat, very quick. And a glass lamp, alas, is dead.... And now we see the great, great merits of the novel. It can't exist without being 'quick.' "

Sexuality as a source of personal and social redemption or denied, of manifold disorders, is central to Lawrence's vision of life. His battle with the moral guardians of his day, the "censormorons" as he calls them, particularly after the publication of *Lady Chatterley's Lover* (1928) is all too familiar. The conflict resulted in two essays published as pamphlets, which are models of their kind. *Pornography and Obscenity* (1929) is an unanswerable indictment of mob attitudes in which the "grey disease of sex-hatred" is united with the "yellow disease of dirt-lust"; what Lawrence castigates is the demand for "purity" accompanied by an unspoken acknowledgment of the "dirty little secret." After a wide-ranging review of the manifestations and consequences of these attitudes, he concludes with the hope that one day the general public will distinguish the real moral threat—"the sneaking masturbation pornography of the press, the film, and present-day popular literature"—from "the creative portrayals of the sexual impulse ... which are necessary for the fulfillment of our consciousness." The banning of *Lady Chatterley's Lover* and the appearance of pirated editions presented Lawrence with the opportunity further to pursue these themes. "The mind has an old, grovelling fear of the body and the body's potencies," he writes in *A Propos of Lady Chatterley's Lover* (1930; first published as *My Skirmish with Jolly Roger*, 1929). In another essay ("Introduction to These Paintings," in *The Paintings of D. H. Lawrence*, 1929) he traces this psychological disorder to the collective trauma caused in sixteenth-century England by the advent of syphilis. In the *A Propos of Lady Chatterley's Lover* essay he identifies the source further back in history, in the teachings of three world-transforming ideal-

The Lawrences at Villa Mirenda, near Florence, in the Tuscan Hills, 1926 (photograph by Arthur Wilkinson)

ists: "Buddha, Plato, Jesus, they were all three utter pessimists as regards life, teaching that the only happiness lay in abstracting oneself from life, the daily, yearly, seasonal life of birth and death and fruition, and in living in the 'immutable' or eternal spirit."

Although diverse in subject and style, most of Lawrence's essays may be roughly categorized. One piece which defies classification is his introduction to *Memoirs of the Foreign Legion*, by M. M. (1924). The descriptions of Florence and the Monte Cassino monastery rival the best scenes from his travel writings (*Twilight in Italy*, 1916; *Sea and Sardinia*, 1921; *Mornings in Mexico*, 1927; *Etruscan Places*, 1932). In this essay, as so often in the travel volumes, the reader has the paradoxical sense that the objective truth of the thing described is in direct proportion to the subjectivity of Lawrence's perception of it. But the introduc-

tion is primarily a masterful character sketch of one Maurice Magnus (M. M.), social charmer, fraud, aristocrat, confidence man, suicide. It is also autobiography. It includes, finally, a profound meditation on historical change. From his window in the monastery Lawrence looks out on the modern Italian countryside; he divines within it the lineaments of a lost medieval order and is wracked with nostalgic anguish. Lawrence was right to consider this piece among his best.

After his death in 1930 Lawrence's reputation suffered a decline, and for more than two decades his work was widely dismissed. In the early 1950s, however, critics such as F. R. Leavis were responsible for a positive revaluation. At the present time, in spite of his errors, miscalculations, and extravagances, Lawrence's major stature as artist and prophet seems secure. In retrospect he appears to have had an uncanny awareness of the issues which would preoccupy Western society as the century drew to a close: the mutual distrust of the sexes, for instance; or the predicament of human beings in a progressively dehumanized, greed-driven world; or the destruction of nature through attitudes which reduce the earth to an object of commercial exploitation. All such problems have their origin for Lawrence in unresolved divisions in the individual psyche and in the collective experience of modern man. Many of these problems, Lawrence believes, have been exacerbated over the centuries by the debilitating values of a once vital but now moribund Christianity. Chief among these polarities are intellect and the senses, spirit and body, consciousness and the subconscious, the individual and the state, male and female, nature and human nature. In all he writes, Lawrence strives to define dichotomies and explore both the damage they do and the possibilities for a new integration of warring elements. Although these explorations find their most radical and subtle form in the fiction, the essays at their best provide a rich distillation of the ideas the great novels dramatize.

In the late essays in which the note of prophecy recurs, Lawrence develops a style perfectly adapted to his exalted matter. One of his last prose works, *Apocalypse* (1931), is an extended commentary on the Book of Revelation. At its conclusion he writes: "For man the vast marvel is to be alive. For man, as for flower and beast and bird, the supreme triumph is to be most vividly, most perfectly alive. . . . The dead may look after the afterwards. But the magnificent here and now of life in the flesh is ours, and ours alone, and ours only for a time. We ought to dance with rapture that we should be alive and part of the living incarnate cosmos. I am part of the sun as my eye is part of me. That I am part of the earth my feet know perfectly well, and my blood is a part of the sea." In this passage Lawrence affirms his vision of a sacramental universe in which the greatest of the divisions which afflict mankind, the alienation of the human consciousness from the totality of the cosmos, is healed and transcended.

Letters:
The Letters of D. H. Lawrence, 5 volumes, James T. Boulton (Cambridge: Cambridge University Press, 1979-1989).

References:
Philip Hobsbaum, *A Reader's Guide to D. H. Lawrence* (London: Thomas & Hudson, 1981);
Graham Hough, *The Dark Sun* (London: Duckworth, 1956);
F. R. Leavis, *D. H. Lawrence: Novelist* (London: Chatto & Windus, 1955);
Keith Sagar, *The Art of D. H. Lawrence* (Cambridge: Cambridge University Press, 1966).

Papers:
Collections of Lawrence's manuscripts include those at the University of California at Berkeley, the University of California at Los Angeles, the University of Tulsa, the University of Chicago, the Berg Collection at the New York Public Library, the University of Nottingham, the Humanities Research Center at the University of Texas at Austin, the Houghton Library at Harvard University, the Lockwood Memorial Library at the State University of New York at Buffalo, and the University of New Mexico.

E. V. Lucas
(11 June 1868 - 26 June 1938)

David Wright
University of Waterloo

BOOKS: *Sparks from a Flint: Odd Rhymes for Odd Times,* as E. V. L. (London: Howe, 1891);

Songs of the Bat (London: W. P. Griffith, 1892);

Bernard Barton and His Friends (London: E. Hicks, Jr., 1893);

The Flamp, The Ameliorator, and The Schoolboy's Apprentice (London: Richards, 1897);

All the World Over, drawings by Edith Farmiloe and verses by Lucas (London: Richards, 1898);

Willow and Leather: A Book of Praise (Bristol: Arrowsmith / London: Simpkin, Marshall, Hamilton, Kent, 1898);

The Book of Shops (London: Richards, 1899);

What Shall We Do Now? A Book of Suggestions for Children's Games and Enjoyment, by E. V. Lucas and Elizabeth Lucas (London: Richards, 1900; New York: Stokes, 1901);

Four and Twenty Toilers (London: Dalton, 1900);

Domesticities. A little book of household impressions (London: Smith, Elder, 1900);

The Visit to London (London: Methuen, 1902);

Wisdom While You Wait, by Lucas and Charles Larcom Graves (London: Privately printed, 1902; New York & London: Inside-Britt, 1903);

England Day by Day, by Lucas and Graves (London: Methuen, 1903);

Highways and Byways in Sussex (London & New York: Macmillan, 1904; revised, 1935); republished in 3 volumes as *West Sussex, Mid-Sussex,* and *East Sussex* (London: Macmillan, 1937);

The Life of Charles Lamb, 2 volumes (London: Methuen, 1905; New York & London: Putnam's, 1905; revised edition, London: Methuen, 1921);

A Wanderer in Holland (London: Methuen, 1905; New York: Macmillan, 1905);

Listener's Lure: An Oblique Narration (London: Methuen, 1906); republished as *Listener's Lure: A Kensington Comedy* (New York & London: Macmillan, 1906);

Change for a Halfpenny, by Lucas and Graves (London: Rivers, 1906);

A Wanderer in London (London: Methuen, 1906; New York: Macmillan / London: Methuen, 1906);

Signs of the Times, by Lucas and Graves (London: Rivers, 1906);

Fireside and Sunshine (London: Methuen, 1906; New York: Dutton, 1907);

Character and Comedy (London: Methuen, 1907; New York: Macmillan, 1907);

The Doll Doctor (London: G. Alleri, 1907);

A Swan and Her Friends (London: Methuen, 1907);

Hustled History, by Lucas and Graves (London: Pitman, 1908);

Over Bemerton's: An Easy-Going Chronicle (London: Methuen, 1908; New York: Macmillan, 1908);

Anne's Terrible Good Nature, and Other Stories for Children (London: Chatto & Windus, 1908; New York: Macmillan, 1908);

If: A Nightmare in the Conditional Mood, by Lucas and Graves (London: Pitman, 1908);

A Wanderer in Paris (London: Methuen, 1909; New York: Macmillan, 1909);

One Day and Another (London: Methuen, 1909; New York: Macmillan, 1909);

Farthest from the Truth, by Lucas and Graves (London: Pitman, 1909);

Mr. Ingleside (London: Methuen, 1910; New York: Macmillan, 1910);

The Slow Coach (London: Gardner, Darton, 1910; New York: Macmillan, 1910);

What a Life!, by Lucas and George Morrow (London: Methuen, 1911);

Old Lamps for New (London: Methuen, 1911; New York: Macmillan, 1911);

A Little of Everything (London: Methuen, 1912; New York: Macmillan, 1912);

London Lavender (London: Methuen, 1912; New York: Macmillan, 1912);

A Wanderer in Florence (London: Methuen, 1912; New York: Macmillan, 1912);

E. V. Lucas in his office, 1931 (photograph by Howard Coster)

The British School: An Anecdotal Guide to the British Painters and Paintings in the National Gallery (London: Methuen, 1913); republished as *British Pictures and Their Painters: An Anecdotal Guide to the British Section of the National Gallery* (New York: Macmillan, 1913);

Harvest Home (London: Methuen, 1913; New York: Macmillan, 1913);

Loiterer's Harvest (London: Methuen, 1913; New York: Macmillan, 1913);

All the Papers, by Lucas and Graves (London & New York: Pitman, 1914);

Landmarks (London: Methuen, 1914; New York: Macmillan, 1914);

A Wanderer in Venice (London: Methuen, 1914; New York: Macmillan, 1914);

Cloud and Silver (London: Methuen, 1916; New York: Doran, 1916);

Variety Lane (London: Methuen, 1916);

London Revisited (London: Methuen, 1916); republished as *More Wanderings in London* (New York: Doran, 1916);

The Vermilion Box (London: Methuen, 1916; New York: Doran, 1916);

Outposts of Mercy: The Record of a Visit in November and December, 1916, to the Various Units of the British Red Cross in Italy (London: Methuen, 1917);

A Boswell of Baghdad, with Diversions (London: Methuen, 1917; New York: Doran, 1917);

'Twixt Eagle and Dove (London: Methuen, 1918);

Quoth the Raven: An Unofficial History of the War, by Lucas and Morrow (London: Methuen, 1919);

Mixed Vintages, a blend of essays old and new (London: Methuen, 1919);

The Phantom Journal, and other essays and diversions (London: Methuen, 1919);

David Williams, Founder of the Royal Literary Fund (London: Murray, 1920);

Adventures and Enthusiasms (New York: Doran, 1920);

Specially Selected (London: Methuen, 1920);

Verena in the Midst (London: Methuen, 1920; New York: Doran, 1920);

Roving East and Roving West (London: Methuen, 1921; New York: Doran, 1921);

Rose and Rose (London: Methuen, 1921; New York: Doran, 1921);

Urbanities (London: Methuen, 1921);

Edwin Austin Abbey, Royal Academician: The Record of His Life and Work, 2 volumes (London: Methuen, 1921; London: Methuen / New York: Scribners, 1921);

Vermeer of Delft (London: Methuen, 1922);

Genevra's Money (London: Methuen, 1922; London: Doran, 1923);

Giving and Receiving. Essays and fantasies (London: Methuen, 1922; New York: Doran, 1922);

You Know What People Are (London: Methuen, 1922; New York: Doran, 1922);

Advisory Ben: A Story (London: Methuen, 1923; New York: Doran, 1924);

Luck of the Year. Essays, fantasies and stories (London: Methuen, 1923; New York: Doran, 1923);

Encounters and Diversions (London: Methuen, 1924);

The Same Star: A Comedy in Three Acts (London: Methuen, 1924);

A Wanderer among Pictures: A Companion to the Galleries of Europe (London: Methuen, 1924; New York: Doran, 1924);

Chardin and Vigée-Lebrun (London: Methuen, 1924; London: Methuen / New York: Doran, 1924);

John Constable, The Painter (London: Halton & Smith, 1924; London: Halton & Smith / New York: Minton, Balch, 1924);

Michael Angelo (London: Methuen, 1924; London: Methuen / New York: Doran, 1924);

Rembrandt (London: Methuen, 1924);

Introducing London (London: Methuen, 1925; London: Methuen / New York: Doran, 1925);

Zigzags in France, and various essays (London: Methuen, 1925);

Playtime & Company: A Book for Children (London: Methuen, 1925; New York: Doran, 1925);

Frans Hals (London: Methuen, 1926; London: Methuen / New York: Doran, 1926);

Giorgione (London: Methuen, 1926; London: Methuen / New York: Doran, 1926);

Leonardo da Vinci (London: Methuen, 1926; London: Methuen / New York: Doran, 1926);

Van Dyck (London: Methuen, 1926; London: Methuen / New York: Doran, 1926);

Velasquez (London: Methuen, 1926; London: Methuen / New York: Doran, 1926);

Selected Essays of E. V. Lucas, edited by E. A. Wodehouse (London: Methuen, 1926);

A Wanderer in Rome (London: Methuen, 1926; New York: Doran, 1926);

Events and Embroideries (London: Methuen, 1926; New York: Doran, 1927);

A Cat Book (London: Chatto & Windus, 1926; New York & London: Harper, 1927);

A Fronded Isle, and other essays (London: Methuen, 1927; Garden City, N.Y.: Doubleday, Doran, 1928);

The More I See of Men . . . Stray essays on dogs (London: Methuen, 1927);

Introducing Paris (London: Methuen, 1928);

Out of a Clear Sky. Essays and fantasies about birds (London: Methuen, 1928);

A Rover I Would Be. Essays and fantasies (London: Methuen, 1928; New York: Dutton, 1928);

The Colvins and Their Friends (London: Methuen, 1928; New York: Scribners, 1928);

Mr. Punch's County Songs (London: Methuen, 1928);

Vermeer the Magical (London: Methuen, 1929; Garden City, N.Y: Doubleday, Doran, 1929);

Windfall's Eve: An Entertainment (London: Methuen, 1929; Philadelphia: Lippincott, 1930);

Turning Things Over. Essays and fantasies (London: Methuen, 1929; New York: Dutton, 1929);

If Dogs Could Write: A Second Canine Miscellany (London: Methuen, 1929; Philadelphia: Lippincott, 1930);

Down the Sky: An Entertainment (London: Methuen, 1930; Philadelphia & London: Lippincott, 1930);

Traveller's Luck. Essays and fantasies (London: Methuen, 1930; Philadelphia: Lippincott, 1931);

"–And Such Small Deer" (London: Methuen, 1930; Philadelphia: Lippincott, 1931);

The Pekinese National Anthem (London: Methuen, 1930);

French Leaves (London: Methuen, 1931; Philadelphia: Lippincott, 1931);

Visibility Good. Essays and excursions (London: Methuen, 1931; Philadelphia: Lippincott, 1931);

The Barber's Clock: A Conversation Piece (London: Methuen, 1931; Philadelphia: Lippincott, 1932);

No-Nose at the Show (London: Methuen, 1931);

At the Sign of the Dove (London: Methuen, 1932);

Lemon Verbena, and other essays (London: Methuen, 1932; Philadelphia: Lippincott, 1932);

The Day of the Dog (London: Methuen, 1932);

Reading, Writing, and Remembering (London: Methuen, 1932; New York & London: Harper, 1932);

English Leaves (London: Methuen, 1933; Philadelphia: Lippincott, 1933);

Saunterer's Rewards (London: Methuen, 1933; Philadelphia: Lippincott, 1934);

At the Shrine of St. Charles: Stray Papers on Lamb Brought Together for the Centenary of His Death in 1834 (London: Methuen, 1934; New York: Dutton, 1934);

Pleasure Trove (London: Methuen, 1935; Philadelphia: Lippincott, 1935);

The Old Contemporaries (London: Methuen, 1935; New York: Harper, 1935);

Only the Other Day (London: Methuen, 1936; Philadelphia: Lippincott, 1937);

London Afresh (London: Methuen, 1936; Philadelphia & London: Lippincott, 1937);

All of a Piece. New essays (London: Methuen, 1937; Philadelphia & New York: Lippincott, 1937);

As the Bee Sucks, edited by Ernest H. Shepard (London: Methuen, 1937);

Adventures and Misgivings (London: Methuen, 1938);

Cricket all his Life, edited by Rupert Hart-Davis (London: Rupert Hart-Davis, 1950);

Selected Essays of E. V. Lucas, edited by H. N. Wethered (London: Methuen, 1954).

OTHER: *A Book of Verses for Children,* edited by Lucas (London: Richards, 1897);

Charles Lamb and the Lloyds, edited by Lucas (London: Smith, Elder, 1898; Philadelphia: Lippincott, 1899);

The Open Road: A Little Book for Wayfarers, edited by Lucas (London: Richards, 1899; New York: Holt, 1901);

Charles Lamb, *The Essays of Elia,* introduction by Lucas (London: Methuen, 1902);

The Works of Charles and Mary Lamb, 7 volumes, edited by Lucas (London: Methuen, 1903-1905; New York: Putnam's, 1903-1905);

The Friendly Town: A Little Book for the Urbane, edited by Lucas (London: Methuen, 1905; New York: Holt, 1906);

Another Book of Verses for Children, edited by Lucas (London: Gardner, Darton, 1907; New York: Macmillan, 1907);

The Gentlest Art: A Choice of Letters by Entertaining Hands, edited by Lucas (London: Methuen, 1907; New York: Macmillan, 1907);

The Hambledon Men, edited, with contributions, by Lucas (London: Frowde, 1907);

Her Infinite Variety: A Feminine Portrait Gallery, edited by Lucas (London: Methuen, 1908; re-published as *The Ladies' Pageant* (New York: Macmillan, 1908);

Runaways and Castaways, edited by Lucas (London: Gardner, Darton, 1908);

William Cowper's Letters: A Selection, edited by Lucas (London & New York: Frowde, 1908);

The Second Post: A Companion to The Gentlest Art, edited by Lucas (London: Methuen, 1910; New York: Macmillan, 1910);

Remember Louvain! A Little Book of Liberty and War, edited by Lucas (London: Methuen, 1914);

The Joy of Life: An Anthology of Lyrics Drawn Chiefly from the Works of Living Poets, edited by Lucas (London: Methuen, 1927);

Post-Bag Diversions, edited by Lucas (London: Methuen, 1934; New York & London: Harper, 1934);

The Letters of Charles Lamb, To Which Are Added Those of His Sister Mary Lamb, 3 volumes, edited by Lucas (London: Dent/Methuen, 1935; New Haven: Yale University Press, 1935).

E. V. Lucas was taught to swim by George Bernard Shaw, heard James Barrie reading *Peter Pan* while it was still in manuscript, and knew virtually everyone in the London literary and publishing worlds in the first third of the twentieth century. He was a prolific author, with more than a hundred works published, and Max Beerbohm once seriously estimated that in the course of his life Lucas probably wrote more words than he spoke. He wrote novels, biographies, art criticism, cricket history, humor and satire, books for children, books of verse, and travel books. He compiled several popular anthologies and, though his scholarship has since been largely superseded, was a recognized authority on Charles Lamb. Though he failed as a playwright, before and during the 1914-1918 war he wrote lyrics for successful London revues starring the celebrated music-hall comedian Harry Tate. It was as an essayist, however, that he was most admired. Few essay anthologies of the 1920s and 1930s omitted his work, and in *Essays by Modern Masters* (1926) E. V. Rieu, later the editor of *Penguin Classics,* ranked Lucas–along with Hilaire Belloc, G. K. Chesterton, Robert Lynd, and A. A. Milne–as one of the five "greatest living masters" of the essay form. Some years earlier the respected critic Edmund Gosse had already given his judgment that not since the death of Robert Louis Stevenson had there been a writer in English "so pro-

Audrey, Elizabeth, and E. V. Lucas, 1904

ficient in the pure art of the essayist as Mr. E. V. Lucas."

Edward Verrall Lucas was born on the southeast fringes of London, at Eltham in the county of Kent. The Edward was for a paternal grandfather, while Verrall had been the family name of a great-great-grandmother, but these names were virtually forgotten in later life, when he became known simply as "E. V." Lucas's ancestors for several generations had been farmers, millers, brewers, and country bankers. Almost without exception they had also been members of the Society of Friends, as were Lucas's father and mother. Yet Lucas himself carried no religious convictions into adult life, perhaps as a reaction against his father, Alfred, whom he came to regard as a

spoiled, selfish, and censorious man and whose "piety without works" he came to despise. Lucas nevertheless continued to attend meetings of the Friends until early adulthood, probably in order to please his very devout mother. Jane Drewett Lucas lived until her son was past fifty, and with her Lucas maintained a warm and loving relationship despite her reservations about his playing billiards on Sundays and his private conviction that her belief in the eventual physical resurrection of the body was "a macabre idea."

When Lucas was only a few months old his father's work as an insurance broker took the family to Brighton, in the county of Sussex, which became Lucas's home until he was twenty-three. He grew up thinking of himself as a Sussex man and throughout his life retained a special affection for the Sussex countryside, the South Downs in particular. Despite having three brothers and three sisters, he was a shy and even lonely child. Making friends at school was difficult, for his father continually withdrew him from one school to enroll him in another, usually as a result of a dispute about fees. In all he attended nine different schools in as many years, one of them as far away as Ackworth in Yorkshire. For consolation there was his reading, which was wide and voracious, ranging from R. M. Ballantyne, Capt. Frederick Marryat, and Harrison Ainsworth through Alexandre Dumas to Charles Dickens and William Makepeace Thackeray. In addition there were sudden enthusiasms, such as the one around the age of fourteen when he was "bitten by the Americans" and in turn devoured the works of Edgar Allan Poe, Bret Harte, Mark Twain, Max Adeler, and Artemus Ward. Lucas's father, while not sharing his son's passion for books, was evidently aware of it, and in the summer of 1884 the sixteen-year-old Lucas was apprenticed for a five-year term to a Brighton bookseller.

Though it gave him freedom of entry to a large circulating library containing many otherwise inaccessible books, Lucas was bored and frustrated by his work in the bookstore. He nevertheless completed his five years and, after a three-month vacation financed by a kindly uncle, joined the staff of the Brighton-based newspaper, the *Sussex Daily News.* For two years he reported local marriages, inquests, and funerals and covered such events as the visit to Brighton of Buffalo Bill's Wild West Show, as well as writing some book reviews and theater criticism. He also found a publisher for a short selection of his verses, though he later regretted having done so. Then came the turning point in his life. Another generous uncle gave him two hundred pounds to attend lectures at University College, and early in 1892 he left Brighton for London.

Lucas was not enrolled in a degree course, and, in the opinion of his later friend and editorial colleague E. V. Knox, he would remain throughout his life self-conscious about the incompleteness of his formal education. Nevertheless, once in London he quickly began to make the most of his new freedom and opportunities. He visited art galleries and museums. In summer he indulged one of his greatest passions by going to watch cricket at Lord's and the Oval, and he had some verses on the game privately printed. At Uni-

versity College he edited the college newspaper and became friends with the young professor of English literature W. P. Ker. Many evenings in his lodgings in Camden Town were spent translating Guy de Maupassant as an exercise in prose style. He contributed items to a leading evening newspaper, the *Globe,* and in the summer of 1893, with money running out, joined its staff and became joint author with Charles Graves, an uncle of Robert, of its celebrated "By the Way" column. In the same year the official publisher of the Society of Friends gave him his first commission for a book, a biography of Bernard Barton, the Quaker poet who became the father-in-law of Edward Fitzgerald and was Charles Lamb's "B. B." The result was *Bernard Barton and his Friends* (1893).

Over the next few years Lucas moved closer to the centers of the London literary and publishing worlds. By 1896 he had met H. G. Wells, Joseph Conrad, and Arnold Bennett. In that year he joined the staff of the *Academy,* the weekly review edited by Lewis Hind, which was then the most highly regarded literary journal in Britain. He also helped edit *Lika Joka,* Harry Furniss's short-lived rival to *Punch.* After Grant Richards, the publisher, had invited him to compile a selection of verse for children, he joined the firm as a reader and was soon editing a series of children's books. Secure enough financially to acquire a large cottage in the Kent countryside–at Froghole, near Crockham Hill, some fifteen miles south of London–in 1897 he married Elizabeth Griffin, the daughter of American parents living in London, and their own daughter, Audrey, was born in the following year.

Lucas's reputation for versatility was firmly established in the years between 1899 and 1906. In 1899 he published *The Open Road,* an anthology of prose and verse about the English countryside, which during his lifetime went through more than forty editions and sold some ninety thousand copies. His first volume of essays, which he called *Domesticities,* appeared in 1900, as did *What Shall We Do Now?,* a collection of suggested games for children, written jointly with Elizabeth. The first of his informal travel guides in the "Wanderer" series, *A Wanderer in Holland,* was published in 1905, and a year later came *Listener's Lure,* his first work of fiction. In addition he and Charles Graves had begun their series of works of "topical nonsense," the best known of which, *Wisdom While You Wait* (1902), a satire of

Lucas (right) and Charles Graves, his collaborator on works of "topical nonsense" such as Wisdom While You Wait, *a parody of advertisements for the* Encyclopædia Britannica

the marketing techniques of the *Encyclopædia Britannica,* sold fifty thousand copies.

The achievement of this very productive period which Lucas himself most valued was his work on Charles Lamb. He had followed up his study of Bernard Barton with *Charles Lamb and the Lloyds* (1898), based on newly discovered letters from Lamb to the Quaker banking family. This in turn led to a commission from Methuen for an introduction to *The Essays of Elia* (1902) and the preparation of a new edition of Lamb's works, together with a biography. Helped by men as different as W. J. Craig, the Shakespearean scholar, and Bertram Dobell, a poet and bibliophile with a bookstore in the Charing Cross

Road, Lucas assiduously tracked down Lamb manuscripts, though he was unable to go to see those already in the United States. After serious copyright difficulties were finally resolved, his seven-volume *Works of Charles and Mary Lamb* was published between 1903 and 1905 and his two-volume *Life of Charles Lamb* in 1905. Both works were well received, and together they established Lucas as a leading authority on Lamb.

The Lucases kept their Froghole home until 1908, and their child, Audrey, later remembered the life there as near idyllic. Elizabeth Lucas shared her husband's fine sense of irony, his liking for private ribaldry, and his palate for wine. She loved gardening, had remarkable flair as a cook, and made an apparently ideal hostess for the stream of literary figures who came to visit. One of them, Stephen Gwynn, later recalled Froghole as "the perfect household to stay in" (*Experiences of a Literary Man*, 1926). But Elizabeth Lucas was far more than an excellent hostess. Lady Cynthia Asquith found her "subtle, sympathetic and quickminded" (*Portrait of Barrie*, 1954). Arnold Bennett noted in his journal on 3 February 1910 that she was "like a nice Ibsen heroine." In a 24 December 1933 letter James Barrie called her "one of the happinesses of my life."

It was at Froghole that Barrie read to Lucas and Elizabeth the manuscript of *Peter Pan*. Barrie also brought Lucas into his team of literary cricketers. Known as the Allahakbarries, which allegedly meant "Heaven help us," the team in the early 1900s included Arthur Conan Doyle, E. W. Hornung, George Meredith's son Will, A. E. W. Mason, Augustine Birrell, Maurice Hewlett, Jerome K. Jerome, and–from *Punch*–Owen Seaman, Bernard Partridge, and P. G. Wodehouse. Some, such as Conan Doyle and Hornung, had genuine cricketing ability; others, like Barrie himself and Lucas, did not. Of Lucas it was said that he unfortunately tried to play with style. Nevertheless, inept though he was at the game, his knowledge of it was encyclopedic. When C. B. Fry, the well-known Oxford University and Sussex batsman who was still playing regularly for England, wanted a writer on cricket in 1904 for his new George Newnes publication, *C. B. Fry's Magazine*, he readily accepted Barrie's suggestion of Lucas. Lucas became a regular contributor, and several of his articles were included in his *The Hambledon Men* (1907), which Fry himself, writing more than thirty years later and after Lucas's death, assessed as "the best book ever written on cricket of olden times" (*Life Worth Living*, 1939).

By 1908, the year he turned forty, Lucas was known as a prolific writer whose range extended from serious scholarship to light satire. By that year too he had formed the two most important associations of his professional life–with the weekly humorous journal *Punch* and with the publishing house of Methuen–each of which was to last until his death. After leaving the *Globe* in 1900, he had renewed his partnership with Charles Graves, and the two of them became regular contributors to *Punch*. Following the success of *Wisdom While You Wait*, Lucas joined the editorial staff of *Punch* (known as the Table) in 1904. Among his fellow contributors to *Punch* in the early years of the century was P. G. Wodehouse;

other writers who later joined him at the Table included A. A. Milne, E. V. Knox, and A. P. Herbert. As early as 1906 Lucas began substituting regularly for the editor, Owen Seaman, whenever Seaman was on one of his frequent trips to Scotland or the French Riviera, but Lucas's obligations to Methuen prevented him from aspiring to the editorship himself.

Lucas's association with Methuen had grown close during his work on Lamb, and in 1908 he accepted a permanent position with the firm. His appointment was as "a reader and general utility man," he told the rival publishing house of Macmillan with some modesty, and Methuen was to have first refusal of his writing. He is generally agreed to have been an excellent publisher's reader, discerning and courageous. He had, as A. A. Milne recorded, a gift for praise, encouragement, and reassurance, and he was always prepared to give his support to works of quality which were not to his personal taste. In the opinion of Frank Swinnerton he was one of two publisher's readers–the other being Edward Garnett–who did more to encourage the growth of modern literature than any other men of their day. Algernon Methuen, the firm's founder, soon came to rely on his judgment, and Lucas's voice in the affairs of the firm was an influential one long before he formally took over as its chairman on Methuen's death in 1924.

In 1904 the Lucases had acquired a second home, a London house in Gordon Place, Kensington, where the Joseph Conrads were near neighbors and where Audrey became close friends with their elder son, Borys. Then in 1908 the family moved to Kingston Manor, near Lewes. In this substantial house in his beloved Sussex countryside Lucas was able to indulge his fantasy of being the local squire, and though he was normally away in London from Tuesday until Friday, there were frequent weekend house parties, the guests including Barrie, John Galsworthy, Arnold Bennett, Hugh Walpole, John Drinkwater, G. K. Chesterton, and A. A. Milne. But by 1914 the family, while remaining in Sussex, had moved again, this time to Tillington, near Petworth. The Lucases were to see very little of Tillington, however, since for most of the duration of World War I their home there was lent or let, either to relatives or to friends such as Sir Sidney and Lady Colvin, later the subjects of Lucas's respectful *The Colvins and their Friends* (1928).

Too old to fight, Lucas was nevertheless in France with Elizabeth in the spring of 1915.

Lucas with John and Ada Galsworthy at Froghole, the Lucases' cottage in Kent

James Barrie had provided an initial sum of two thousand pounds and asked Elizabeth to help administer it for the relief of French children displaced by the war. Lucas and Elizabeth went to Paris and, after discussing the project with the British ambassador and enlisting the support of the Friends' War Victims Relief Committee, managed to take over a large chateau at Bettancourt, near Révigny, outside Rheims, as a hospital and clearinghouse for children from the war zone. Lucas worked hard to help convert the chateau to its new function, becoming known as Papa Lucas to the first children there, and then returned to England. Elizabeth remained at Bettancourt, and for the rest of the war Audrey divided her time between her mother in France and her father in England. Lucas, meanwhile, did considerable work for the Red Cross, including his visit to the Austro-Italian front in late 1916, described in his *Outposts of Mercy* (1917), and his organization of the Red Cross's sale of donated books and manuscripts, held at Christie's in April 1918.

This unusual wartime separation, with the wife, not the husband, in the war zone, marked the effective end of the marriage. Henceforth,

though they retained many mutual friends, foremost among them Barrie, Lucas and Elizabeth lived separate lives. Elizabeth emerged in the mid 1920s as a writer of numerous articles on architecture, furniture, and antiques, an author of several books on cookery, and a translator from French to English. Audrey kept in touch with her father at intervals for a while, but the two then went many years without meeting and did not begin seeing each other again until 1931. Lucas, for his part, seems consciously to have written Elizabeth out of his life. In the closest he came to an autobiography, his *Reading, Writing, and Remembering* (1932), he avoided any mention of the wife with whom he had lived for some twenty years.

For his last twenty years Lucas was a man without domestic ties and framed his life accordingly. In London he lived in a book-lined apartment conveniently close to the Essex Street offices of Methuen and the nearby Bouverie Street offices of *Punch*; for weekends there was a country retreat where he kept Aberdeen terriers and Shetland ponies. Dining out in agreeable and stimulating company became a preoccupation, whether at a good restaurant, at regular functions such as those of the Literary Society, or at one of his many clubs. Max Beerbohm, in a drawing which Lucas relished, portrayed him as "The Six-Club Man," appearing successively in different and appropriate dress at the Garrick, the Athenæum, Savage's, Brooks's, the Burlington Fine Arts, and the National Sporting. Cricket remained a passion; a bemused American admirer, Robert E. Sherwood, editor of the American humor magazine *Life*, found him "childish and rapturous" on the subject. He rarely missed the opening game of the season at Lord's, and the staff at Methuen learned to anticipate his absence on test-match days. He traveled abroad more fre-^uently and at greater length than before. Late in 1919 he embarked on a journey around the world which included a long stopover in India and his first though not his last visit to the United States. Even after he became chairman of Methuen on the death of Sir Algernon Methuen in 1924, he still found time for frequent trips to France and Italy. In the 1930s he developed a special affection for Sweden, and one of his last summers saw him leisurely cruising the Gotha Canal between Gothenburg and Stockholm.

Despite these indications of a continuing zest for life, Lucas in his later years was often an unhappy man and at times perhaps even an embittered one. His foibles—such as his dread of sitting in a draft—became more exaggerated, his sleep more restless, and his tongue more caustic. Though he could be charming to his guests, especially if they were young and lacking in self-confidence, to waiters and servants he was frequently a bully. Audrey Lucas believed that he was "at times acutely aware of the emptiness of some part of his way of living." Writing just after Lucas's death, James Agate, in an assessment which Audrey Lucas praised for its "superb perception," suggested that "the severity of the writer was a mask hiding the torments of a man knowing as much about hell as any of Maupassant's characters, or even Maupassant himself." Possibly Lucas never surmounted his personal losses. His brother Percy, the only one of his brothers and sisters to whom he had been close, had died of pneumonia contracted on the Somme during World War I, and this death was followed by his separation from Elizabeth and the death of his beloved mother. According to Frank Swinnerton, however, "his unhappiness lay deep in temperament" and had less to do with his private life than with his doubts about his authenticity as a writer. Arguing that Lucas realized

only too well "that he lacked the genius to invent and the courage to be, in print, as pungent and terrible as he was in mordant reverie," Swinnerton concluded that he never forgave himself for this failure.

Lucas's published works, including his essays, do indeed stop well short of revealing the man himself. "Nobody could guess the realities of *his* character from *his* books," Arnold Bennett wrote to Hugh Walpole on 23 February 1918, and this remained true to the end. "Some albatross hung around his neck," wrote Christopher Morley after Lucas's death, "but no one ever inquired, and those who read his light and well-bred writings were unlikely to guess the savage quality of the spirit." It would certainly be difficult to find evidence of a savage, mordant, or tormented nature in Lucas's essays. Very occasionally there is a flash of anger, as when he contemplates the cheapness of life in war ("Of Plans for One More Spring," *Cloud and Silver*, 1916) or recounts his experiences of a bullfight ("Whenever I See a Grey Horse. . . ," *Giving and Receiving*, 1922). From time to time a mock-querulous note appears, as he affects disdain for such nuisances of modern life as the telephone, the automobile, and radio. (In fact he used the telephone frequently, employed a chauffeur, and gave talks for the B.B.C.) But generally his essays retained from first to last their characteristic qualities of urbanity, serenity, and geniality, giving no hint of any changes in the author's temperament or outlook. Thus it is usually impossible to distinguish the work of his early thirties from that of his late sixties, and any essay not containing an identifiably topical reference might as easily have come from his first published collection (*Domesticities*, 1900) as from his last (*Adventures and Misgivings*, 1938).

"No essayist of his quality," wrote A. A. Milne, "has had so little to say of the world within him, so much to say of the world around him" (*Times* [London], 30 June 1938). Lucas's essays, though concealing the nature of the man himself, abundantly reveal his enthusiasms: for his favorite authors, painters, and places, for cricket, for dogs, horses, and birds. They leave no doubt of the delight he took in the works of Charles Lamb, Ibn Khallikan, and Jean-Baptiste Corot, in London and Sussex, in *Wisden* (the annual reference book known as "the cricketer's Bible") and the *Dictionary of National Biography*. According to A. P. Herbert in his *Independent Member* (1950), Lucas had as a favorite maxim, "Nothing is

Participants in a 1913 cricket match at Downe House, Sussex: (first row) Percy Lucas, Audrey Lucas, T. Wrigley, Charles Tennyson, Willie Winter; (second row) A. A. Milne, Maurice Hewlett, J. M. Barrie, George Morrow, E. V. Lucas, Walter Frith; (third row) George Ll. Davies, T. L. Gilmour, Will Meredith, G. Meredith, Jr., Denis Mackail, Harry Graham, Dr. Goffe

wasted." Almost any thought crossing his mind could become the subject for an essay, as could almost any incident he took part in or witnessed. Some of his essays, especially those he referred to as "fantasies," take the form of imaginary conversations–between people, between animals, and even between items of furniture. Others, as Grant Overton, the fiction editor of *Collier's Weekly*, noted, "compose themselves perfectly as short stories." An example is "A London Thrill" (*'Twixt Eagle and Dove*, 1918), prompted by seeing a woman arrested for a breach of the peace in Gerrard Street. He wrote essays on monocles, on braces, on secret passages, and on one-legged men. "No. 344260" (*A Boswell of Baghdad*, 1917) is on the design of the first pound note to come into his possession. Twice he was challenged to write on the unlikeliest topic the challenger could conceive. He duly produced essays on "Custard" (*Visibility Good*, 1931) and on "Matches" (*Adventures and Misgivings*, 1938).

In his time Lucas was widely admired and frequently envied for the apparent facility of his writing. He could, declared A. St. John Adcock, "write a delightfully quaint, witty or wise essay on nothing at all." A. B. Walkley, admitting that he had never seen Lucas writing, was nevertheless "sure that he does it easily." Lucas evidently did

rely to some extent on well-tried techniques. One of these was the first-sentence generalization designed to intrigue by its seeming inconsequentiality. "After all, choosing a walking-stick is a serious business." ("Concerning Walks," *Domesticities*, 1900.) "My acquaintance among ferrymen is not extensive, but I can not remember any that were cheerful." ("Thoughts at the Ferry," *The Phantom Journal*, 1919.) "I would go so far as to maintain that it is impossible to find people without odd uncles." ("Parents' Brothers," *Turning Things Over*, 1929.) Yet he never became casual or mechanical in his writing. He remained punctilious about matching his words to his thoughts and constructing sentences with their words in the most effective order. Audrey Lucas recalled the detailed care he took with her writing style, as well as his own. His fastidiousness was always unobtrusive, however. As Desmond MacCarthy asserted, with emphasis, Lucas "wrote *inconspicuously* well" (*Sunday Times* [London], 3 July 1938).

Lucas's prolific output was as much the result of his ability to organize his time as of his fluent pen. He was a thoroughly professional writer. For the last fourteen years of his life, in addition to his other responsibilities, he contributed a regular weekly column to the London *Sunday Times* under the heading "A Wanderer's Notebook." W. W. Hadley, the paper's editor, later recalled Lucas as "the perfect contributor. The article was always on my desk on Tuesday morning. He received his proof on Wednesday morning and on Thursday it was back, shortened if it were too long, lengthened if it were too short, though usually it exactly fitted the column." Lucas was highly professional also in his ability to publish the same piece several times. Most of the essays in his published collections had already appeared in newspapers and magazines, often on both sides of the Atlantic. In addition he frequently included in his latest book essays taken from earlier volumes, so that many of his essays appear in at least two different collections. As early as 1913 this practice had drawn a rebuke from his friend and fellow man of letters Maurice Hewlett. "I don't at all approve of your anthologies of your own gems," Hewlett had written in a 12 October 1913 letter to Lucas. "Leave them to posterity to collect." Lucas, however, remained unrepentant.

A shrewd exploiter of his own talent, Lucas at the same time clearly reveled in the practice of his craft. In later life money can have been only a secondary motive for his writing, since, despite many years of extremely comfortable living, at his death he left an estate of more than twenty-four thousand pounds. Audrey Lucas was convinced that her father would have been lost without his work, and she pointed to an incident which occurred in the very last year of his life. Lucas had his fingers crushed in a car door. After a minute or two of silent agony, his first words were, "Thank God it was the *left* hand."

In 1932 Lucas was made a Companion of Honour, but, as often happens, this official recognition came when his reputation was starting to decline. His colleagues at *Punch* had already persuaded him to become the magazine's film critic, a tactful approach to the problem of reducing his other contributions. Lucas had become a devotee of the cinema–he particularly admired James Cagney and Spencer Tracy–but his film criticism was insipid and uninspired. Ironically, the popularity of the cinema, together with radio, helped reduce the market for his own brand of light essay, yet he continued to write in the way he assumed his public expected. Uncommitted and disengaged, without political or religious convictions, he appeared increasingly anachronistic, an Edwardian leftover in a world containing Mussolini, Hitler, and Franco. His last piece for *Punch*, "Budgies" (budgerigars), which appeared just

four days before his death, could have been written at any time in the previous forty years.

Lucas died in a London nursing home on 26 June 1938. His doctor had advised him for some time to give up alcohol, together with red meat. Characteristically, he wove an essay out of his experience of abstinence ("The Wagon," *Adventures and Misgivings*, 1938), and, characteristically also, he compromised by restricting himself to champagne. He died, in his daughter's words, "as autocratically as he lived," refusing to receive visitors. The Sunday on which he died was the rest day in the England-Australia cricket match, and he would undoubtedly have approved of where the next day's *Manchester Guardian* placed the report of his death. It appeared directly under an account of the game headed "Lord's Test Match: Record Crowd." Two days later he was cremated. There was no religious ceremony.

Lucas's reputation, already in decline at his death, has not recovered since, and it is unlikely that his essays will ever again be praised as highly as they were by Edmund Gosse. In the long run he paid the price for what H. N. Wethered has called "his addiction to ephemeral journalism," for, as R. G. G. Price has suggested, like Thomas de Quincey and G. K. Chesterton, he diluted his reputation by simply writing too much. John Ashbery, introducing a 1975 reprint of *What A Life!*, which Lucas and George Morrow first published in 1911, claimed that a small cult following existed for this innovative piece of proto-Dada, but he doubted that anyone was reading Lucas's other books. Such skepticism was premature. There is still a readership for Lucas's wide-ranging, urbane, and well-written essays which, as Claude A. Prance has rightly observed, "require no particular effort to enjoy their full flavour." But Lucas himself may well be headed for oblivion. Modern scholarship, while revising his work on Lamb, has for the most part treated him as merely a footnote in the lives of his more highly regarded contemporaries. Half a century after his death he still awaits a biographer.

References:

A. St. John Adcock, "E. V. Lucas," in his *The Glory That Was Grub Street* (London: Low, Marston, 1928; New York: Stokes, 1928), pp. 191-201;

James Agate, *Ego 3* (London: Harrap, 1938), pp. 388-389;

George Leonard Barnett, "A Critical Analysis of the Lucas Edition of Lamb's Letters," *Mod-*

ern Language Quarterly, 9 (September 1948): 303-314;

Arnold Bennett, "Chesterton and Lucas," in his *Books and Persons* (London: Chatto & Windus, 1917; New York: Doran, 1917), pp. 150-154;

Visranath Chatterjee, "E. V. Lucas: Prince of Essayists," *Calcutta Review,* new series, 3 (April-June 1972): 315-320;

John Farrar and others, *E. V. Lucas: Appreciations* (New York: Doran, 1925);

Edmund Gosse, "The Essays of Mr. Lucas," in his *Books on the Table* (London: Heinemann, 1921; New York: Scribners, 1921), pp. 103-110;

Rupert Hart-Davis, Introductory note to *Cricket All His Life,* edited by Hart-Davis (London: Rupert Hart-Davis, 1950);

Audrey Lucas, *E. V. Lucas: A Portrait* (London: Methuen, 1939);

Christopher Morley, "E. V. Lucas (1868-1938)," in his *The Ironing Board* (Garden City, N.Y.: Doubleday, 1949; London: Faber & Faber, 1950), pp. 166-167;

Grant Overton, "That Literary Wanderer, E. V. Lucas," in his *Cargoes for Crusoes* (New York: Appleton, 1924), pp. 212-231;

Claude A. Prance, "Edward Verrall Lucas," *Charles Lamb Bulletin,* new series 8 (October 1974): 157-162;

R. G. G. Price, *A History of Punch* (London: Collins, 1957);

F. H. Pritchard, Introduction to *Essays of Today,* edited by Pritchard (London: Harrap, 1923; Boston: Little, Brown, 1924);

Duane Schneider, "The Lucas Edition of Lamb's Letters: Corrections and Notes," *Notes and Queries,* 219 (May 1974), 171-174;

Frank Swinnerton, "E. V. Lucas," in his *Figures in the Foreground: Literary Reminiscences, 1917- 40* (London: Hutchinson, 1963; Garden City, N.Y.: Doubleday, 1964), pp. 82-88;

Swinnerton, "Literary Men," in his *The Georgian Scene: A Literary Panorama* (New York: Farrar & Rinehart, 1934), pp. 231-251;

A. B. Walkley, " 'E. V.' and Proust," in his *More Prejudice* (London: Heinemann, 1923; New York: Knopf, 1923), pp. 52-56;

Arthur Waugh, "Mr. E. V. Lucas," in his *Tradition and Change* (London: Chapman & Hall, 1919; New York: Dutton, 1919), pp. 292-298;

H. N. Wethered, Introduction to *Selected Essays of E. V. Lucas,* edited by Wethered (London: Methuen, 1954);

E. A. Wodehouse, Introduction to *Selected Essays of E. V. Lucas,* edited by Wodehouse (London: Methuen, 1926).

Papers:

The largest collection of Lucas manuscripts is in the Harry Ransom Humanities Research Center, University of Texas at Austin. Columbia University's Butler Library has Lucas manuscripts and letters, including his correspondence with Grant Richards and Arnold Bennett. His correspondence with the publishing house of Macmillan is in the British Library, London, and his correspondence with Bertram Dobell is in the Bodleian Library, Oxford. There are letters to John Galsworthy at the University of Birmingham. The Hereford and Worcester County Archives, Worcester, England, have letters from Lucas to Sir Edward Elgar. There is only routine correspondence in the archives at *Punch,* and there appear to be no archives at Methuen.

Robert Lynd

(20 April 1879 - 6 October 1949)

Alan Thomas
University of Toronto

BOOKS: *The Mantle of the Emperor,* by Lynd and Ladbroke D. Black (London: Griffiths, 1906);

Irish and English: Portraits and Impressions (London: Griffiths, 1908);

Home Life in Ireland (London: Mills & Boon, 1909; Chicago: McClurg, 1912);

Rambles in Ireland (London: Mills & Boon, 1912; Boston: Estes, 1912);

The Book of This and That (London: Mills & Boon, 1915);

If the Germans Conquered England, and Other Essays (Dublin & London: Maunsel, 1917);

Ireland a Nation (London: Richards, 1919; New York: Dodd, Mead, 1920);

Old and New Masters (London: Unwin, 1919; New York: Scribners, 1919);

The Art of Letters (London: Unwin, 1920; New York: Scribners, 1921; revised edition, London: Duckworth, 1928);

The Passion of Labour (London: Bell, 1920; New York: Scribners, 1921);

The Pleasures of Ignorance (London: Richards, 1921; New York: Scribners, 1921);

The Sporting Life and Other Trifles (London: Richards, 1922; New York: Scribners, 1922);

Books and Authors (London: Cobden-Sanderson, 1922; New York: Putnam's, 1923);

Solomon in All His Glory (London: Richards, 1922; New York: Putnam's, 1923);

Selected Essays Chosen by the Author (London: Dent, 1923; New York: Dutton, 1923);

The Blue Lion, and Other Essays (London: Methuen, 1923; New York: Appleton, 1923);

The Peal of Bells (London: Methuen, 1924; New York: Appleton, 1925);

The Money-Box (London: Methuen, 1925; New York: Appleton, 1926);

The Orange Tree (London: Methuen, 1926);

The Little Angel (London: Methuen, 1926);

The Goldfish (London: Methuen, 1927);

Dr. Johnson and Company (London: Hodder & Stoughton, 1927; Garden City, N.Y.: Doubleday, Doran, 1928);

The Green Man (London: Methuen, 1928);

It's a Fine World (London: Methuen, 1930);

Rain, Rain, Go to Spain (London: Methuen, 1931);

The Cockleshell (London: Methuen, 1933);

"Y. Y.": An Anthology of Essays by Robert Lynd, edited by Eileen Squire (London: Methuen, 1933);

Both Sides of the Road (London: Methuen, 1934);

I Tremble to Think (London: Dent, 1936);

In Defence of Pink (London: Dent, 1937);

Searchlights and Nightingales (London: Dent, 1939);

Life's Little Oddities (London: Dent, 1941);

Things One Hears (London: Dent, 1945);

Essays on Life and Literature (London: Dent / New York: Dutton, 1951);

Books and Writers (London: Dent, 1952).

OTHER: *The Silver Book of English Sonnets: A Selection of Lesser-Known Sonnets,* edited, with an introduction, by Lynd (London: Pleaid, 1927);

Collected Essays of Charles Lamb, edited, with an introduction, by Lynd, 2 volumes (London & Toronto: Dent, 1929; New York: Dutton, 1929);

Great Love Stories of All Nations, edited by Lynd (London: Harrap, 1932); republished as *Love throughout the Ages* (New York: Coward-McCann, 1932);

Modern Poetry, compiled by Lynd (London & New York: Nelson, 1939).

SELECTED PERIODICAL PUBLICATION–
UNCOLLECTED: "The Religious Background in Literature," *Transactions of the Royal Society of Literature,* third series, 8 (1928): 1-20.

Robert Lynd, an accomplished Irish literary and political essayist, was born in Belfast on 20 April 1879, the son of Robert John and Sarah Rentoul Lynd, and was educated at the Belfast Academical Institute and at Queen's College. His father was a Presbyterian minister and descendant of a line of ministers, and there were also divines on his mother's side. According to Desmond MacCarthy, his lifelong friend and fellow journalist, there was a family tradition that Lynd's great-grandfather emigrated from Scotland to Ireland because his congregation objected to the lavish display of silver buckle on his shoes. Lynd's father's family also farmed, and some of Lynd's more personal essays refer to boyhood days on the farm tending the livestock.

Given his Ulster-Presbyterian origins, Lynd's avowed, lifelong Irish nationalism indicates independence of mind. He was a supporter and apologist for the Sinn Fein movement, abhorrent to many Ulster Protestants, and also declared himself a socialist in a period in the province of Ulster when such alignments were generally regarded as anti-British. There is evidence that Lynd held his political views with firmness and defended them with spirit but with respect for others. Generally, he advocated the cause of Irish nationalism as the only reasonable and positive solution to the religious and political impasse found in the divided society of Ulster. Shortly before his death in 1949, he was honored by Queen's College (now University) with a doctorate, evidence of some local regard for Lynd, despite his nationalism.

Lynd's long career in daily and weekly journalism began in 1901, when he left Belfast for Manchester to work for the *Daily Dispatch*. After a few months he went on to London and lived there on the uncertain income of casual journalism. His first regular work was with the paper *Today*, edited by Ladbroke D. Black. In 1908 he joined the *Daily News* as assistant literary editor. This paper, of which Charles Dickens had been the first editor, had a long tradition of publishing literary essays (written for many years in the nineteenth century by Andrew Lang). Lynd's talents flowered under the twin demands of art and journalism; he found his touch as an essayist and remained with the *Daily News* and its successor, the *News Chronicle*, contributing a regular weekly essay until his death. For many years starting in 1913 he also wrote a weekly column for the *New Statesman*, using the initials "Y. Y."; and he contributed to the *Nation, John O'London's Weekly*, and other periodicals. As an essayist working amidst the clatter and rush of Fleet Street, he appears to have seen his task as providing a point of rest among the news columns. In reflective and humorous temper, he took up and examined features of the times, both trivial and momentous, in a

Robert Lynd

light manner and with refreshing freedom from the tyrannies of received opinion.

R. A. Scott-James, the literary editor of the *Daily News*, was later (in the *Dictionary of National Biography, 1941-50*) to recall Lynd as a romanticist in temperament and also in appearance, with "broad brow, waving hair, and lustrous dark eyes." (A portrait by Henry Lamb is in the National Portrait Gallery, London, and a bust in bronze is at Queen's University, Belfast.) Scott-James associated this romanticism with Lynd's devotion to Ireland. His first published books of any substance were on Ireland: *Irish and English* (1908); *Home Life in Ireland* (1909); and *Rambles in Ireland* (1912). These journalistic books range in approach from the sober assessment and description of living conditions to the personal and impressionistic recording of large general scenes. "Galway of the Races," an essay chosen by MacCarthy for his collection *Essays on Life and Literature* (1951), is of the latter type. Lynd, going to the races, observes, encounters, and talks–and from these fragments of experience builds up the large and varied scene, including its peculiarities of mass psychology, in a manner that recalls the best naturalistic novels. The capacity to write freely and vividly in this realistic mode is demonstrated again in the essay "Riots," which Lynd chose for his *Selected Essays* (1923). The locale for this piece is evidently Northern Ireland, but this is not explicitly stated. From the opening the reader is brought, with the observer, close to the action: "In the morning a girl on a white horse had led a tumultuous crowd out of a square near the middle of town. Behind her a long line of banners streamed, flagrant and green and golden-edged." Lynd takes up a position to observe the procession's return at a spot where "the Protestant boys" have been "gathering across the bogs and comforting themselves in companies with lively tunes." In such fluent lines, charged with allusion, Lynd leads into an account of the ensuing battle and its aftermath. As the parade, escorted by police, moves back into town, it passes detachments of soldiers "dangerous and prepared." Lynd concludes with a dark observation, lightly stated: "They were getting ready for the riots that they knew would begin in earnest after nightfall."

This is not so much essay writing as impressionistic reporting of a high order full of the color and vivacity that creates scenes and implies the psychology of participants. The observer's eye is the organizing point. Skill in handling the personal anecdote and personal impression of events, expressed with gifted fluency, was a marked feature of Lynd's early writing. "White Citizens" is an account of medical examinations for the Army (in *Essays on Life and Literature*), which is built on Lynd's own experience in 1916. The emphasis in the description of events is upon the ugliness of the examination hall, the mixture of tedium and military brusqueness of the procedure, and the vulnerability of the examinees, who, Lynd notes, are so many of them "wearing belts, bands and trusses . . . one felt at times as though one must be at a holy well among people awaiting miraculous cures rather than among young men in the prime of life about to be chosen as warriors in a great war." The swift shift here takes the reader from a detailed, eyewitness view of London lowlife (a genre George Orwell was also to employ in his social journalism) up to the sublime perspective of history.

The presence in Lynd's writing of the thinking man, able in a phrase to enlarge a perspective, justifies the term essayist rather than reporter. His openness and willingness to use himself and his experiences, and to think out loud, marks with a confident stamp Lynd's informal manner as an essayist. He appears thoroughly comfortable both in his person and his ideas, and from this platform can discuss the world. His ideas are in any event broadly tolerant, liberal, and humanistic. Richard Church commented in the foreword to the posthumous collection of literary essays *Books and Writers* (1952) that Lynd always wrote from a position "set firmly . . . in the centre of his own tolerance." One can see this tolerance in operation in the essays in which Lynd registers the views and practices of writers with whom, it is clear, he personally differs. The quality is also apparent in political essays, including those written in the exceptional circumstances of wartime. In the title essay for the collection *If the Germans Conquered England* (1917) Lynd explores the contending nations' values and succeeds in being patriotic, in a particularly dark period of war, without being jingoistic. His approach is indirect, and his stalking-horse is the imagined benefits resulting from a German victory: "One can imagine how she [Germany] would build technical schools, art schools and musical academies and opera houses. One can imagine how she would build the long-lost Shakespeare Memorial Theatre." Lynd maintains the carefully neutral tone as further advantages are rehearsed, of an economic kind, until the concluding paragraphs. Here a quick reversal of attitude occurs, expressed not through a list of counteradvantages but through literary quotation and historical allusion. For example, Lynd repeats lines from William Wordsworth's sonnet expressing the resentment behind the Spanish resistance to Napoleon: "He dares to speak / Of benefits and of a future day, / When our enlightened minds shall bless his sway." Lynd's control is often achieved through rhythm and balance of phrase; here he concludes with a rapid epigrammatic line: "No man with the slightest glimmer of patriotism would see his country made a nation of millionaires at the price of being a nation of slaves." The devil is given his due, but principle is reasserted, a principle, incidentally, that Lynd could equally advance in support of the cause of Irish independence.

Literary, historical, and cultural references and quotations are common features of several of his most celebrated essays and sometimes serve as titles–as in the case of "Thrice is he armed . . ." (*Essays on Life and Literature*). This essay on moral justice in war was written shortly after World War I, yet makes very few references to events of that war. The discussion is conducted through reference and allusion to those en-

Lynd in 1917

gaged in warfare and moral crusades through the ages, including Joan of Arc and the heroes of Thermopylae. The essay closes with more ringing lines from Wordsworth. Lynd was an educated man in the Western-humanist tradition, and these essays assume a shared culture and knowledge between author and reader. The manner is relaxed, the appeal is to common experience, not to special knowledge, and the tone is familiar. The reader is flattered and encouraged by such trust. In the best sense these essays are educational: they place living issues in the context of a broad range of historical and cultural reference.

Knowledgeable and informative, Lynd's collections of essays on writers and their works are unreservedly literary, of course, but not scholarly. The interest is largely placed on the writer as a person and a social being. This is especially true of *Dr. Johnson and Company* (1927). One would not learn precisely what Johnson wrote from this book, but one knows how he looked, how he ate, and above all, how he talked. Lynd was himself a man who enjoyed company. At their Hampstead home he and his wife, the poet Sylvia Dryhurst (whom he married in 1909), provided a center of

conviviality for literary people. Evidently in Johnson he recognized a fellow and master in this area of life and sincerely respected the quality in Johnson that made him seek to invigorate with conversation the lives of those around him. Johnson's interest in common life, rather than in the abstractions of history or philosophy, further appears to have been something Lynd could understand as a positive demonstration of the idea that the proper study of mankind is man. Indeed, Lynd asserts that Johnson was a man whose energies were fully and usefully employed when he was engaged in enlivening the scene at tavern or at tea table; by contrast, when at his desk, pen in hand, he was working only at half strength. *Dr. Johnson and Company* presents a variety of other figures in the literary world of the eighteenth century, and the book can still serve as a useful introduction to the life of the period. The occasion of its publication served as a harbinger of the modern revival of eighteenth-century studies, according to Scott-James, and though Lynd did not then have the advantage of the publication of James Boswell's diaries and papers, which came with later scholarly work, the chapter on Boswell provides a general reading of the character that accords with later revelations. Lynd appears to have well understood that group of intellectual men and women of another age who were morally serious and yet possessed of a relish for social life, as he was. Desmond MacCarthy was later to link that taste for social life (in his obituary of Lynd in the *Times,* 7 October 1949) with Lynd's function as an essayist who reminded his readers through his work "that living is not only a matter of arriving at right conclusions about politics, books, plays . . . but also something which . . . has to be enjoyed; and that response to its odd and often fascinating variety is necessary to living fully."

For many readers between the wars and into the 1940s, Lynd wore the guise of an entertainer. His popularity is demonstrated in the collections of his work that appeared virtually every year. He early had displayed a touch for the comic sketch, as in the delightful back-streets vignette "The Goldfish," which served as the title piece for his collected essays of 1927. The publishers of his annual collections dressed the humor to advantage in the late 1930s by employing illustrators whose work on the page and the endpapers conveyed a sense of light comedy. These essays were indeed light in manner, but Lynd demonstrates again and again his skill in using an indirect approach and a shifting perspective that allows the entry of ideas, and sometimes seriously grave ideas, into a piece apparently devoted to the trivial. An example is the title essay of the collection *In Defence of Pink* (1937), which takes as its starting point a remark by G. K. Chesterton in a recently published book of essays (*As I Was Saying*, 1936) that pink is a negative color, simply a dilution of red. Lynd toys with the instances of pink color in nature and in dress, steals up on the question of pinkness in politics, and suggests that pinkness equals moderation, what is sometimes seen as political "wobbling." From there, with terms established, he directs the argument rapidly and sharply at political targets: "I should trust Mussolini and Hitler more if they occasionally wobbled. It is their death-like rigidity that appalls me. Oh, for a few pink corpuscles flowing through their veins! How much better a time the Abyssinians and the Jews would have!"

The rhetorical manner of these essays brings writer and reader into a close relationship. The light essay can appear to be a form of elegant chatter. Scott-James evidently believed so in writing that Lynd "went on week after week, year after year, with little effort turning out essays on trifling everyday topics." Yet Lynd's essays usually have a serious point. Lightness of tone and apparent aimlessness of approach conceal that point until, with controlled ease, it emerges with the force of surprise. The essay, as a form, may be mistaken as static, but the movement of ideas actually possesses a dynamism analogous to the development of a story. It is a movement, moreover, in a direct relation to the speed of reading and assimilation: as Lynd writes or "talks," so the reader thinks. This immediacy of contact encourages the belief that it is the essayist himself that is the real subject before the reader. It is doubtless

for these reasons that the readers of the *New Statesman* and the *News Chronicle* came to regard Lynd with affection as well as admiration. He was a writer in a form that required the mind to display itself and called for the skill to make this procedure seem artless. This double capacity, exerted with unfaltering command through years of violent political stress and change, marked Lynd as one of the best practitioners of the informal essay in the early twentieth century.

At his death in 1949 colleagues and friends recognized that he was a writer who was more than a journalist but that his work, in view of its brief compass and ephemeral publication, might speedily be forgotten. MacCarthy in particular argued in his obituary notice in the *Times* that if Lynd had lived one hundred years earlier he would have been sure of "a modest little niche in English literature"; MacCarthy urged the publication of an Everyman's Library collection of the essays: "The work of Robert Lynd deserves to be remembered: posterity will lose something worth having if none of it is preserved." Dent published the suggested collection (*Essays on Life and Literature*) in 1951 and followed it with the more literary selection, *Books and Writers,* in 1952. There have been no further reissues of his work, and it appears that interest in Lynd as a writer has declined. However, since he wrote on a broad range of ordinary subjects, in the tradition of the English essay, and with attention to detail, it appears likely that social historians will come in time to find value in his material.

References:
Richard Church, Foreword to Lynd's *Books and Writers* (London: Dent, 1952);
Desmond MacCarthy, Introduction to Lynd's *Essays on Life and Literature* (London: Dent, 1951).

Alice Meynell

(11 October 1847 - 27 November 1922)

Frank M. Tierney
University of Ottawa

See also the Meynell entry in *DLB 19: British Poets, 1880-1914.*

BOOKS: *Preludes* (London: H. S. King, 1875);

The Poor Sisters of Nazareth (London & New York: Burns & Oates, 1889);

Poems (London: Elkin Mathews & John Lane, 1893; London: John Lane / Boston: Copeland & Day, 1896);

The Rhythm of Life And Other Essays (London: Elkin Mathews & John Lane, 1893; London: John Lane / Boston: Copeland & Day, 1893);

William Holman Hunt, His Life and Work, by Meynell and Frederick William Farrar (London: Art Journal Office, 1893);

Unto Us A Son Is Given (London, 1895);

Other Poems (London: Privately printed, 1896);

The Colour Of Life And Other Essays On Things Seen And Heard (London: John Lane, 1896; London: John Lane / Chicago: Way & Williams, 1896);

The Children (London & New York: John Lane, 1897);

London Impressions (London: Constable, 1898);

The Spirit Of Place And Other Essays (London & New York: John Lane, 1898);

John Ruskin (Edinburgh & London: Blackwood, 1900; New York: Dodd, Mead, 1900);

Later Poems (London & New York: John Lane, 1902); abridged as *The Shepherdess and Other Verses* (London: Burns & Oates, 1914);

Children of the Old Masters (Italian School) (London: Duckworth, 1903);

Ceres Runaway & Other Essays (London: Constable, 1909; New York: John Lane, 1910);

Mary, The Mother of Jesus: An Essay (London: Philip Luc Warner, 1912; London & Boston: Medici Society, 1923);

Poems, Collected Edition (London: Burns & Oates, 1913; New York: Scribners, 1913);

Childhood (London: Batsford, 1913; New York: Dutton, 1913);

Essays (London: Burns & Oates, 1914; New York: Scribners, 1914);

Poems on War, edited by Clement Shorter (London: Privately printed, 1915);

Ten Poems, edited by Francis Meynell (London: Romney Street Press, 1915);

A Father of Women and Other Poems (London: Burns & Oates, 1917);

Hearts of Controversy (London: Burns & Oates, 1917; New York: Scribners, 1918);

The Second Person Singular And Other Essays (London & New York: Oxford University Press, 1921);

The Last Poems of Alice Meynell (London: Burns, Oates & Washbourne, 1923);

The Poems of Alice Meynell, Complete Edition (London: Burns, Oates & Washbourne, 1923; New York: Scribners, 1923);

Essays of Today and Yesterday: Alice Meynell (London: Harrap, 1926);

Selected Poems And Prose, edited by Albert A. Cock (London: A. & C. Black, 1928);

Wayfaring, Selected Essays And Poems (London: Cape, 1929);

Selected Poems Of Alice Meynell (London: Nonesuch, 1930; New York: Scribners, 1931);

The Poems of Alice Meynell (London: Oxford University Press, 1940);

Alice Meynell: Prose and Poetry, edited by Frederick Page and others, with a biographical and critical introduction by V. Sackville-West (London: Cape, 1947);

Essays, edited by Sir Francis Meynell (Maryland: Newman Bookshop, 1947);

The Poems Of Alice Meynell, 1847-1923, edited by Sir Francis Meynell (London: Hollis & Carter, 1947);

The Wares Of Autolycus, edited by P. M. Fraser (London: Oxford University Press, 1965).

OTHER: Daniel Barbé, *Lourdes: Yesterday, To-Day, and To-Morrow,* translated by Meynell (London: Burns & Oates, 1894);

The Poems of Thomas Gordon Hake, edited, with a prefatory note, by Meynell (London: Elkin Mathews & John Lane, 1894);

Coventry Patmore, *The Poetry of Pathos and Delight*, edited by Meynell (London: Heinemann, 1896; New York: Putnam's, 1896);

Elizabeth Barrett Browning, *Prometheus Bound and Other Poems*, introduction by Meynell (London: Ward, Lock & Bowden, 1896);

The Flowers of the Mind: A Choice among the Best Poems, edited by Meynell (London: Richards, 1897);

Temple Scott, ed., *The Confessions of St. Augustine*, introduction by Meynell (London: Richards, 1900);

Adolfo Venturi, *The Madonna: A Pictorial Representation of the Life and Death of the Mother of Our Lord Jesus Christ by the Painters and Sculptors of Christendom*, translated, with an introduction, by Meynell (London: Burns & Oates, 1901);

William Wordsworth, *Poems*, introduction by Meynell (London: Blackie, 1903);

Alfred, Lord Tennyson, *Poems*, introduction by Meynell (London:. Blackie, 1903);

Elizabeth Barrett Browning, *Poems*, introduction by Meynell (London: Blackie, 1903);

Robert Browning, *Poems*, introduction by Meynell (London: Blackie, 1903);

Percy Bysshe Shelley, *Poems*, introduction by Meynell (London: Blackie, 1903);

John Keats, *Poems*, introduction by Meynell (London: Blackie, 1903);

Tennyson, *In Memoriam*, introduction by Meynell (London: Blackie, 1904);

Robert Herrick, *Poems*, introduction by Meynell (London: Blackie, 1905);

Samuel Taylor Coleridge, *Poems,* introduction by Meynell (London: Blackie, 1905);

William Cowper, *Poems,* introduction by Meynell (London: Blackie, 1905);

Coventry Patmore, *The Angel in the House, Together with The Victories of Love,* introduction by Meynell (London: Routledge, 1905);

Matthew Arnold, *Poems,* introduction by Meynell (London: Blackie, 1906);

Christina Rossetti, *Poems,* introduction by Meynell (London: Blackie, 1906);

Introduction to *The Taming of the Shrew,* volume 7 of *The Complete Works of William Shakespeare* (New York: Sproul, 1907; London: Harrap, 1907);

René Bazin, *The Nun,* translated by Meynell (London: Nash, 1908);

William Blake, *Poems,* introduction by Meynell (London: Blackie, 1911);

Elizabeth Barrett Browning, *The Art of Scansion,* introduction by Meynell (London: Privately printed by Clement Shorter, 1916);

The School of Poetry: An Anthology Chosen for Young Readers, edited by Meynell (London, Glasgow, Melbourne & Aukland: Collins, 1923).

Alice Meynell was a remarkable literary figure and personality of the latter half of the nineteenth century and first two decades of the twentieth. An independent woman for her era, Meynell was a leading essayist, an important poet—she was nominated for poet laureate to replace Alfred Austin–literary critic, editor, devoted wife, and loving mother of seven children. Her essays, written on a broad range of subjects, in smooth prose rhythms and confident mastery of form, were enthusiastically received by her contemporaries, and are still highly regarded. Her life and work were shaped by a refined spiritual life which found its roots and growth in Roman Catholicism. This commitment and her work in literature led her to form close friendships with Francis Thompson, Coventry Patmore, G. K. Chesterton, Aubrey de Vere, and Katherine Tynan, writers who had similar literary and religious sensibilities. She was admired as a literary figure and thought of affectionately by those who knew her personally. Meynell's importance rests in the quality and diversity of her work and the considerable size of her contribution: ten books of essays published during her lifetime and several editions of selected essays since her death, six full-length books of poetry (not including books of selected poems, or collections), religious books, a book on John Ruskin (1900), anthologies, translations, and many forewords, introductory notes, prefaces, and afterwords to books of poetry, religious works, an edition of *The Taming of the Shrew* (1907), and an essay on scansion by Elizabeth Barrett Browning (1916). Meynell edited books; assisted her husband with his work as editor of the *Weekly Register,* a Catholic periodical; contributed regularly to the *Spectator* and the *Saturday Review;* wrote a weekly column, "The Wares of Autolycus," for *Pall Mall Gazette,* where many of her essays first appeared; and lectured in the United States.

Alice Meynell was born Alice Christiana Gertrude Thompson on 11 October 1847 at Barnes, England, the younger daughter of Thomas and Christiana Thompson. Thomas's interesting background contributed to the shape of Alice's personality and character. Dr. Thomas Pepper Thompson of Liverpool, Alice's great-grandfather, had immigrated to Jamaica, where he acquired sugar plantations in the middle of the eighteenth century. He had an illegitimate son, James, who never married but had a mistress, Mary Edwards, a Creole woman, with whom he had a son (Thomas James, after his grandfather and father) and two daughters. Little is known of Mary except that she was related to Bryan Edwards, who became the chief justice of Jamaica in 1855. Mary no doubt had English blood, but the belief in the Meynell family is that she was of mixed parentage. James died in Jamaica, leaving his mistress and their three children; James's father returned to England with Mary and the children. Before he died in 1820 he named as his heir his grandson Thomas "the son of Mary Edwards of Rio Bueno in the parish of Trelawny and Island of Jamaica, and the reputed son of James Thompson, sometime since of Liverpool but lately of Maria Bueno Estate." Thomas received a fine private education, then attended Trinity College, Cambridge. He ran unsuccessfully for Parliament, then lived off the inheritance from his grandfather. After his first wife died in 1844, Thomas married Christiana Weller, a tender, passionate, and impractical woman from Liverpool, who had musical talent and hoped for a career as a pianist. The wedding was held in the parish church at Barnes on 21 October 1845, with Charles Dickens–a close friend of Thomas–as a witness.

Thomas and Christiana immediately began travels through Europe that characterized their restless married life. Elizabeth (called Mimi),

Elizabeth and Alice Thompson (from Viola Meynell, Alice Meynell: A Memoir, *1929)*

their first child, was born in 1846 at the Villa Claremont outside Lausanne. Alice was born the following year. Shortly afterward the family moved to Prestbury, near Cheltenham. By October 1848 Alice, at the age of one, was speaking both English and French. The children's education was erratic, however, because the family moved so often. The girls spent most of their childhood in Italy; Amélie, a Swiss nurse to the family for many years, was probably their chief caretaker. It was fortunate for the children, however, that their father was a man of culture, scholarship, and refined sensibility, who devoted himself to their education, which he began in the summer of 1852 with an emphasis on poetry, dialogues in French and Italian, and studies of history and the Sunday Collect. The children studied every morning and memorized every afternoon with only an occasional day off. Her father was the dominant influence on Alice's spirit, character, and literary sensibility; her essay "A Remembrance" (first published in the *Scots Observer,* 9 August 1890) is a loving portrait of this unusual man.

By the age of thirteen Alice was already writing and kept a notebook, "*First Endeavours* by A. C. T.," which contains jottings, poetry, and the fourth chapter of a romance, "The Beauty of Asytler Abbey." Her readings at this time were extensive and included Jane Austen, Charlotte Brontë, Charles Dickens, George Eliot, Nathaniel Hawthorne, Edward Bulwer-Lytton, Walter Scott, William Makepeace Thackeray, Anthony Trollope, and the major Romantic and Victorian poets. When Alice was eighteen and Elizabeth nineteen, the family moved to the Isle of Wight so that the girls would have a more settled and conventional life. Restless and still without a vocation, Alice was decided upon the importance and satisfaction of an intellectual life, and the disadvantage and frustration of being a woman. Here, by 1864, began her lifelong concern for women's emancipation. Elizabeth's studies at the South Kensington School of Art, and later at Florence and Rome, were followed by outstanding success: she exhibited at the Royal Academy in 1874, attracting the admiring attention of Queen Victoria, who bought *The Roll Call,* for which Elizabeth re-

Wilfrid Meynell

Ruskin, Alfred Tennyson, Coventry Patmore, and Aubrey de Vere.

In 1876 Wilfrid Meynell was invited to one of Mrs. Thompson's musical afternoons, where he met Alice. Wilfrid, the seventh of eight children of a colliery owner, had been born in Newcastle to a Quaker family, became a Catholic at eighteen, and soon after moved to London to become a journalist. Throughout 1876 Wilfrid visited Alice, corresponded with her, and sent her his own poems to critique. Alice and Wilfrid were engaged on New Year's Day 1877 and married on 16 April. Wilfrid, a kind, intelligent, good-humored man and a perceptive critic of art and literature, was devoted to his wife and completely supportive of her many activities. Their home was a meeting place for the British literary world. In 1881 Wilfrid became editor of the *Weekly Register,* a Catholic periodical, and Alice helped him with editing while contributing regularly to the *Spectator,* the *Saturday Review,* the *Art Journal,* and the *Scots Observer,* among other journals and periodicals. Wilfrid began the monthly magazine *Merry England* in 1883 with the publishers Burns and Oates; the following year he continued the magazine alone. In 1888 the Meynells began an association with Francis Thompson which continued for many years at much time and cost for Alice and Wilfrid. From 1878 to 1891 eight children (one of whom died in early infancy) were born to them.

Meynell's essay "The Rhythm of Life" was published on 16 March 1889, like much of her work, in the *Scots Observer,* which in late 1890 became the *National Observer.* The editor of the *Scots Observer,* poet W. E. Henley, called the essay "one of the best things it has so far been my privilege to print." Henley pressured Meynell for further contributions, which she produced according to the free time that she had from caring for her family, and while maintaining the high standard of prose that she demanded of herself. Henley was the first editor to awaken the public to Meynell's essays and to promote them for a collection, *The Rhythm of Life and Other Essays,* which the publisher John Lane accepted and released late in 1892 (along with *Poems,* which was well received), with 1893 on the title page. The *Pall Mall Gazette,* the *St. James' Gazette,* the *Literary World,* and many more journals and papers praised the essays heartily, but the ultimate accolade came from Coventry Patmore in the *Fortnightly Review* (December 1892), where he called Meynell "a woman of genius." The essays are writ-

ceived twelve hundred pounds copyright fee from the engraver. She was later proposed as the first woman R. A. though she did not actually receive the honor.

During these years Alice worked quietly at her writing and pursued her deep spiritual commitment, converting to Roman Catholicism on 20 July 1868. She was encouraged in her writing by a Jesuit priest, Augustus Dignam, who received her into the Church. An editor and an author, Dignam was a man of culture and high intelligence with refined taste in poetry and extensive reading in architecture and music. Alice's love for him grew until their relationship became uncomfortable and had to be curtailed; this situation produced her much-anthologized poem "Renouncement" and the lesser-known "After a Parting." She continued writing from 1868 to 1875 when her first book, *Preludes,* was published. Comprising some forty poems written between 1870 and 1875, the book received favorable reviews and particular praise from John ten in a tight, economic, precise style, particularly evident in her choice of words, that suggests considerable experience and maturation rather than a first book. The title essay discusses the metrical nature of life and the rule of "periodicity" over the mental experience of man. The volume includes the essay on her father, "A Remembrance," and critical essays on Patmore (*National Observer*, 25 July 1891), James Russell Lowell, and Oliver Wendall Holmes (*National Observer*, 26 March 1892). "Dormus Angusta" (*National Observer*, 28 November 1891) expresses the need for tolerance of those who are slow, stupid, or commonplace, pointing out that they must not be the object of ridicule or humor; it stresses the value of the precise word and right language, for our words serve not only to express our feelings but to refine and define our experience. She continues her discussion and analysis of language and words in "Composure" (*National Observer*, 9 May 1891) with particular reference to Samuel Johnson. Language has an "educative power" and "speech is a school"; language shapes the person in quality and temper and enforces a tradition. Her essay on Lowell continues this theme. In "Decivilised" (*National Observer*, 24 January 1891) she writes about man in his colonial and provincial exploits and attitudes, and in "The Sun" (*Scots Observer*, 1 November 1890) about the beauty of the landscape of Suffolk. This volume also includes her essay in praise of Coventry Patmore's odes, an essay that enhanced her friendship with him.

Aubrey de Vere had shown some of Meynell's poems to Patmore in 1873, thus initiating between Patmore and Meynell admiration for each other's work. Patmore would later say that Meynell's was the "greatest friendship of my life." Their literary association evolved into a warm friendship by 1892. Patmore, then sixty-nine years old and married to his third wife, was charming, handsome, and vigorous. He admired the brilliance and profound intellect of this completely feminine woman and was captivated by her beauty. She told Wilfrid that Patmore said, "in some respects it [his love for her] is more than he has ever felt for a woman before." But she could offer him no more than friendship, which lasted three years. Throughout this period, as throughout her marriage, Meynell constantly expressed her total love and devotion to Wilfrid. There is no doubt from Meynell's correspondence with Wilfrid that Patmore did, on occasion, press his attention too firmly and had to accept rebuke. His obsessiveness and jealousy of her friendships with other persons eventually ended their own friendship. The exact reason for the severance remains unknown because, after Patmore's death, Meynell destroyed all but a few of his letters to her; she explained to her son Francis that the letters might be misunderstood.

The second person who openly expressed his deep love for Alice Meynell was Francis Thompson. The Meynells' first knowledge of Thompson came when Wilfrid received a manuscript of poems from him in February 1887 for the *Merry England*. Wilfrid did not read the manuscript until six months later, and, recognizing Thompson's genius, wanted to publish an article and one of his poems. He tried to contact Thompson without success. In April 1888 Wilfrid printed "The Passion of Mary," hoping that Thompson would see it and contact him. Thompson arrived at Wilfrid's office destitute and ravaged by drugs. Wilfrid and Alice graciously took him into their home and assumed responsibility for him, paying for his lodging, clothes, and food for the rest of his life. Thompson returned their kindness with lasting affection for Wilfrid and love for Alice. He loved her at a distance, spiritually, intellectually, and hopelessly. He expressed his worship only in his poetry. Meynell admired his poetry and cared for him with the affection she gave to one of her children. Thompson accepted the situation without remorse.

Meynell's writing continued with publication of a single poem *Unto Us A Son Is Given* (1895), *Other Poems* (1896), and her second volume of essays, *The Colour Of Life And Other Essays On Things Seen And Heard* (1896). All but one of the essays in this collection were from the *Pall Mall Gazette*, to which she began to contribute in 1893 in her column "The Wares of Autolycus." The column appeared daily from May 1893 until the end of 1898. The topics were clearly defined subjects, especially women's clothes and fashions, foreign dishes, and, from 1895, studies of the role of women in society. The essays were written by female journalists, unsigned, with a different author each day. Meynell wrote on literary and other topics on Friday initially, then from April 1896, on Wednesdays. She continued to contribute to the *Pall Mall Gazette* following the cessation of the column in 1898.

The Rhythm of Life essays were carefully thought-out ideas, written at a time when Meynell was inexperienced but learning her craft

Alice Meynell (etching by Tristram Ellis, based on an 1877 watercolor by Adrian Stokes)

quickly. *The Colour of Life* essays were written to a weekly publication date and are easier reading, expressing original and delicate impressions as in "Cloud" (27 September 1895), "A Woman In Grey" (7 February 1896), and "Eyes" (22 November 1895). The title essay, "The Colour of Life" (28 June 1895), explains that red is the color not of life but of violence, that "The true colour of life is the colour of the body." Meynell gives an example of boys bathing in the evening having shed the "hues of dust and soot and fog," now closer to the colors of nature to which all must return. Among other essays, "Symmetry and Incident" (*Fortnightly Review*, November 1894) compares the art forms of Greece and Japan, and "Donkey Races" (4 October 1895) comments on English acting.

It was through her column that George Meredith came to know and admire Meynell. They first met in the spring of 1896 when he invited Meynell and Wilfrid to visit him at his home. For the next few years Meredith was their close and interesting friend. She admired his intellect and was stimulated by talking with him about literature. He was devoted to her from a distance and was pleased with whatever amount of friendship and time she could offer him. Throughout their years of friendship Meredith was in failing health yet maintained sharp interest in Meynell's work and wrote criticism in praise of her achievements.

In the year following publication of *The Colour of Life*, Meynell released her third book of essays, *The Children* (1897). This volume includes many of the essays written earlier on childhood and children, most of which had appeared in periodicals. These are exceptional achievements, offering a fine balance of humor and tenderness purified of sentimentality. She writes with immediacy and accuracy about what it is like to be a child, causing the reader to recall happenings and qualities from early life. The "Children in Mid-

Meynell circa 1895 (drawing by John Singer Sargent; by permission of the National Portrait Gallery, London)

Winter" expresses a loving openness for children, whom she describes as "flower-like" and "like the soft golden-pink roses that fill the barrows in Oxford Street." Her own children are subjects, as in "The Boy" about Everard and "The Child of Tumult" and "The Child of Subsiding Tumult" about Francis. This book, like her other works, was received with hearty approbation by the critics. It was at this time that she was invited to be president of the Society of Women Journalists.

A series of essays on the City of London, written for the *Pall Mall Gazette* during 1897, was published the following year in the volume *London Impressions*. Her next major collection was *The Spirit Of Place And Other Essays* (1898), which consisted largely of essays first published in her "Wares of

Autolycus" column of the *Pall Mall Gazette*. The title essay (23 March 1898) is exemplary of Meynell's powers of observation, sensitivity, and description. She writes of how "bells . . . of an unseen cathedral in France where one has arrived by night" express the personality and character of the people and landscape. In "Rain" (6 April 1898) she explores the swiftness of rain too fast for the eye; the flight of a bird and its shadow are described in "Shadows" (27 May 1896); the exquisite joy of "sleep shared between a woman and a child" is limned in "Solitude" (15 April 1896). There is an essay on the French poet Marceline Valmore (26 August 1896), who loved her child, and "Mrs. Dingley" (22 February 1895), an essay on a figure in Swift's life. The smooth prose rhythms of the earlier volumes are enhanced in this book's confident, masterful essays. The subjects are treated sensitively, delicately, and, as always, with the poet's eye.

Between *The Spirit of Place* and the sixth collection of essays, *Ceres Runaway & Other Essays* (1909), Meynell published her major work *John Ruskin* (1900), a book of poems (1902), and *Children of the Old Masters* (1903). Throughout these years–and throughout her married life–the household functioned happily but haphazardly. Routine chores were left to the domestic help. Austere in living habits, clothing, food, and general household management, Meynell was not skilled at nursing, sewing, or mending; she was a gay, gentle, and understanding mother who played games with the children when they were young and gave patient and wise counsel to them throughout their lives. Her family tried to protect her from household duties to allow time for her writing. She was a reserved person who kept part of herself aloof and accorded the children the privacy and independence she herself valued and guarded. She loved them dearly, however, and sought their praise even though she was indifferent to the praise of others. Paradoxically, she could be unobservant about her family while continuing to be loyal and loving. Their son Francis, a conscientious objector, was arrested and imprisoned during World War I because he refused noncombatant service, and he began a secret hunger strike in prison. Although they disagreed with his actions, Alice and Wilfrid accepted him upon his release.

Meynell was socially active from the 1880s until close to the end of her life. The personality and social habits that she acquired as a child continued throughout her life. Her passions were always controlled. Her personal discipline and her faith in the precepts and teachings of the Catholic church were the moral frame of reference implicit in everything she said, did, and wrote. Her obedience was voluntary, the antithesis of slavery to her passions. Her social behavior was admirable. She possessed exquisite thoughtfulness and courtesy, tolerance, and modesty. But she was often silent, having little patience with small talk, and she refused to laugh if she was not amused. She did not mind differences of opinion but would not abide atheism or moral turpitude. Throughout her productive years, indeed throughout her marriage, she relied on Wilfrid's critical support. Their marriage was a partnership. The sole physical problem that disturbed

Alice throughout her life was migraine headaches, which she called "wheels."

Wilfrid sold the *Weekly Register* in 1899 and became literary adviser to Burns and Oates. In the summer of 1900 Wilfrid and Alice spent a month in Italy, their first trip together and Alice's first since their marriage. In 1901 she was invited to visit America for about three months with her friend Agnes Tobin. They left England on 7 September. Meynell gave lectures in New York, Chicago, Los Angeles, Boston, Santa Barbara, Indianapolis, San Francisco, and elsewhere, and was well received. The visit was prolonged when Agnes became ill. They returned to England in April 1902. *Later Poems,* published that year, received positive reviews. From 1902 to 1905 Meynell wrote art reviews for the *Pall Mall Gazette,* but her journalism lessened from 1905 to 1914, allowing her time to travel abroad every year but one. Her time was also freer because the children were growing up and beginning to leave home. Monica was married in 1903, Madeline in 1907, and Everard in 1910. To the tenderness given to the children when they lived at home were added the care and courtesy given to greatly honored friends when the children came home to visit. This transition of growing to maturity and following new lives of their own began in the early years of the century. At this same time Meynell had difficult and trying experiences. She was displeased with the amount and quality of her writing. Francis Thompson died in 1907 and her own mother in 1910. Although Meynell held her reserve in the face of suffering and death, family and close friends were aware of the depth of her pain. These middle years of her life revealed little outward sign of change, but the energies of her youth began to diminish, and the frequency of her headaches increased.

When *Ceres Runaway & Other Essays* was released by Constable in 1909, eleven years had passed since her last volume of essays and seven years since *Later Poems.* No volume of Meynell's was received with greater acclaim. Essays focused on the pleasure of natural observation, the work of writers, the poets' muse, the use of language, the function of a theater audience, the delight of humor, and the joy of children. The title essay, "Ceres Runaway" (*Outlook,* 16 June 1906), expresses the refreshing force of green that crops up in forbidden places in towns. Other subjects include the joy of the Thames in "The Tow Path" (*Pall Mall Gazette,* 7 September 1898); the imaginative experience along the Thames in "The Teth-

Meynell in 1912 (photograph by Sherril Schell)

ered Constellations" (*Pall Mall Gazette*, 14 September 1898); the limitations of dialect in "The Little Language"; the impermanence of buildings in "Tithonus" (*Pall Mall Gazette*, 15 March 1899); the value of the theater audience as performers in "The Audience" (*Pall Mall Gazette*, 8 November 1895); and the experience of raising children (based on their son Francis) in "The Child of Tumult" and "The Child of Subsiding Tumult" (*Pall Mall Gazette*, 20 October 1897 and 6 July 1898). Meynell's precision, critical insights, elevated taste, and gentle charm continue throughout this volume.

Between *Ceres Runaway* and her seventh book of essays, *Childhood* (1913), Meynell wrote a book for the Medici Society, *Mary, The Mother of Jesus* (1912). Her acquaintanceship with G. K. Chesterton and his wife grew during these years

and continued for the rest of her life. She admired Chesterton's work, and he gave her critical approval. Meynell worked enthusiastically for woman suffrage; she marched in processions, wrote for suffrage papers, and served as president and vice-president of suffrage societies while remaining detached from militant activities. Family journalism continued with Wilfrid, Alice, Everard, and other members of the family contributing significantly. In 1911 Meynell wrote an article on Elizabeth Barrett Browning for the *Encyclopaedia Britannica;* the same year the family moved from London to a country home they had been longing for, their "eighty acres" at Greatham, Sussex.

Her little book of essays on children, *Childhood,* published by Batsford, was compiled mainly from her "Wares of Autolycus" column of 1897 and 1898 but also includes new essays, some of them inspired by her grandchildren. The work examines such topics as "Toys," "The Stranger's Children," "The Influential Child," and "Injustice." A collected edition of her poems was also published in 1913, the year she was suggested to replace Alfred Austin as poet laureate. Her appointment was advocated by many, including the *London Budget*, the *Daily Citizen*, the *Pall Mall Gazette*, and the *Daily Mail*. The matter was settled with the appointment of Robert Bridges.

Meynell's *Essays,* largely a collection of essays from earlier books, was published early in 1914 by Burns and Oates. The reviews were uniformly complimentary, including one in the *Liverpool Courier* in which Dixon Scott called her prose "absolutely the most perfect produced in our language for at least the last twenty years." Alfred Noyes wrote to Francis: "what a marvelous volume–far and away the most significant and beautiful collection of Essays in the English language!" The reviewer for the *Times Literary Supplement* wrote that her essays were independent of fashion and ways of thought and that "Their delicacy–of scrupulousness, balance, fineness, skill–is as rare in life and in art as ever it was." Most of the essays were from *The Rhythm of Life, The Colour Of Life, The Spirit Of Place, The Children,* and *Ceres Runaway,* but four essays from the *Pall Mall Gazette* had not previously been published in any book: "The Seventeenth Century" (25 January 1895), "Prue" (15 March 1895), "Mrs. Johnson" (22 March 1895), and "Madame Roland" (21 September 1898).

In November 1914 The Royal Society of Literature elected Meynell to their academic committee. In his address of reception, Sir Henry Newbolt said: "It would be impossible to overestimate the value of Mrs. Meynell's Essays to the general public." Of her poetry there is "a union of wit and religious emotion as rare now as it was characteristic of the seventeenth century in England."

Meynell's health began to fail in 1914. She became frail, slept badly, and felt the cold acutely. In spite of this she entered upon the last and greatest period of her creative life. Francis published his mother's *Ten Poems* (1915) at his Romney Street Press in a small quarto edition limited to fifty copies. These poems, with others added, were republished in 1917 under the title *A Father of Women and Other Poems.* Also published in 1915 was *Poems on War,* privately printed by Clement Shorter, and Meynell's second to last volume of essays, *Hearts of Controversy,* was published in 1917 by Burns and Oates. Reviewers were again uniformly impressed. The *Sphere* wrote that Meynell is "one of the finest living essayists, matchless in the grace of an incommunicable style, restrained, keenly analytical." The book comprises six literary studies reprinted, with revisions, from the periodicals in which they had originally appeared. Her essays on Tennyson (*Dublin Review,* January-March 1910), Dickens (*Atlantic Monthly,* January 1903), and Swinburne (*Dublin Review,* July-September 1909) are included.

In February 1918 Meynell suffered an illness that left her severely weakened. She continued writing poetry through 1918 and 1919. She was disturbed by Francis's support of the Russian revolution, his editorship of the *Communist,* his attempt to smuggle diamonds from Russia to support the *Daily Herald,* and the suit against him for his role as editor of the *Communist.*

During her final years Meynell generally withdrew from the social and literary gatherings of London: she wanted more time for her family, work, and correspondence. She continued to work in her garden at Greatham but with less energy. During this time she still edited, wrote poetry, and prepared her tenth and final book of essays, *The Second Person Singular,* published by Oxford University Press in 1921. She told Everard that "Ten of the twenty essays, as they stand, are up to my little high-water mark, and the other ten are not contemptible second-class." Some critics considered the volume her best work. *The Second Person Singular* is an excellent summary of her thought and style. The essays explore Italy, landscape, and her literary judgments. There are studies of Joanna Baillie (*Pall Mall Gazette,* 25 January 1899), Thomas Lovell Beddoes (*Pall Mall Gazette,* 2 February 1898), George Darley (*Pall Mall Gazette,* 16 February 1898), Sydney Dobell (*Pall Mall Gazette,* 5 January 1898), Edward Gibbon (*Pall Mall Gazette,* 10 January 1900), Robert Greene (*Pall Mall Gazette,* 15 September 1897), Meredith, and Patmore. The title essay (*Pall Mall Gazette,* 20 April 1898) points to the weakening of grammar and vocabulary as civilization advances.

Meynell's final months were spent preparing a poetry anthology for children and compiling a list of "lately-written" poems to be published posthumously "if occasion occurs." Early in October, while in London, she became gravely ill. On 27 November 1922, at dawn, while sleeping, she died. *Last Poems* was published in 1923.

Alice Meynell was a loving wife and mother, happy with her home and family, enthusiastic to assist her husband with his editing and writing, and pleased with her own achievements as a journalist and poet, as a supporter of woman suffrage, and as a lecturer. She was happy in her personal life because of her love for Wilfrid and their seven children, and because of the spiritual strength derived from her faith. Her poetry has endured. Her prose is elaborate yet delicately polished, precise yet warm and captivating, elegant yet intellectually profound. Her essay style is designed to carry the intricacies of a significant idea. Her force was not as a dynamic, vigorous, indignant molder of contemporary thought, but rather as a sensitive, gentle, quiet guide and leader toward a refined and charitable way of life. Her literary criticism was perceptive, brave, bold, and courteous. Mediocrity, to her, was intolerable. She stands as a major essayist of the late nineteenth and early twentieth centuries. Her writings had a major impact on her own time and deserve further critical evaluation in the present.

Bibliographies:

Anne Kimball Tuell, "Bibliographical Notes Upon the Work of Mrs. Meynell," in her *Mrs. Meynell and Her Literary Generation* (New York: Dutton, 1925), pp. 259-271;

C. A. and H. W. Stonehill, "Alice Meynell," in their *Bibliographies of Modern Authors (Second Series)* (London: Castle, 1925), pp. 79-125;

Alice Meynell, 1847-1922, Catalogue and Centenary Exhibition of Books, Manuscripts, Letters and Portraits, Foreword by Francis Meynell (London: National Book League, 1947);

Terence L. Connolly, "Alice Meynell: A Short-Title List of Poetry, Essays, Miscellaneous Works, Anthologies, Translations, Editings and Introductions with data on some of the volumes in the complete collection at Boston College," in *Alice Meynell Centenary Tribute*, edited by Connolly (Boston: Humphries, 1948), pp. 41-72.

Biographies:

Viola Meynell, *Alice Meynell: A Memoir* (London: Cape, 1929);

June Badeni, *The Slender Tree: A Life of Alice Meynell* (Padstow, Cornwall: Tabb House Press, 1981).

References:

Alice Meynell (London & Westminster: National Book League and the British Council, 1948);

Alice Meynell Centenary Tribute, edited by Terence L. Connolly (Boston: Humphries, 1948);

Anne K. Tuell, *Mrs. Meynell And Her Literary Generation* (New York: Dutton, 1925).

Papers:

Cambridge University Library, Boston College Library, the University of Leeds, and the Library of Congress have collections of letters and other material.

George Orwell
(Eric Arthur Blair)

(25 June 1903 - 21 January 1950)

Robert L. Calder
University of Saskatchewan

See also the Orwell entry in *DLB 15: British Novelists, 1930-1959.*

BOOKS: *Down and Out in Paris and London* (London: Gollancz, 1933; New York & London: Harper, 1933);

Burmese Days (New York: Harper, 1934; London: Gollancz, 1935);

A Clergyman's Daughter (London: Gollancz, 1935; New York: Harper, 1936);

Keep the Aspidistra Flying (London: Gollancz, 1936; New York: Harcourt, Brace, 1956);

The Road to Wigan Pier (London: Gollancz, 1937; New York: Harcourt, Brace, 1958);

Homage to Catalonia (London: Secker & Warburg, 1938; New York: Harcourt, Brace, 1952);

Coming Up for Air (London: Gollancz, 1939; New York: Harcourt, Brace, 1950);

Inside the Whale, and Other Essays (London: Gollancz, 1940);

The Lion and the Unicorn: Socialism and the English Genius (London: Secker & Warburg, 1941);

Animal Farm (London: Secker & Warburg, 1945; New York: Harcourt, Brace, 1946);

Critical Essays (London: Secker & Warburg, 1946); republished as *Dickens, Dali and Others* (New York: Reynal & Hitchcock, 1946);

Nineteen Eighty-Four (London: Secker & Warburg, 1949; New York: Harcourt, Brace, 1949);

Shooting an Elephant, and Other Essays (London: Secker & Warburg, 1950; New York: Harcourt, Brace, 1950);

England Your England and Other Essays (London: Secker & Warburg, 1953); republished as *Such, Such Were the Joys* (New York: Harcourt, Brace, 1953);

A Collection of Essays (Garden City, N.Y.: Doubleday, 1954);

The Orwell Reader: Fiction, Essays, and Reportage (New York: Harcourt, Brace, 1956);

The Collected Essays, Journalism, and Letters of George Orwell, edited by Sonia Orwell and

George Orwell (Collection of Mabel Fierz)

Ian Angus, 4 volumes (London: Secker & Warburg, 1968; New York: Harcourt, Brace & World, 1968);

Orwell, the War Broadcasts, edited by W. J. West (London: Duckworth / BBC, 1985).

OTHER: "Fascism and Democracy" and "Patriots and Revolutionaries," in *The Betrayal of the Left,* edited by Victor Gollancz (London: Gollancz, 1941).

George Orwell is most widely known today as the novelist who wrote *Animal Farm* (1945) and

Nineteen Eighty-Four (1949), but in the 1930s and 1940s readers of left-wing intellectual periodicals and weeklies knew him as a perceptive and rigorously honest essayist. Indeed, it can be argued that he was essentially a writer of essays who used fiction as a means of presenting an argument, even to the extent of weaving two lengthy essays–the character Goldstein's book and the appendix on "Newspeak"–into *Nineteen Eighty-Four*.

Orwell's life and career are marked by ambivalences. He hated British imperialism but was enraged by the natives who hindered his administration of it in Burma. In many ways an archetypal Englishman with a love of things English, he was sharply critical of many elements of British life, once calling England "a family with the wrong members in control." A dedicated socialist for all of his adult life, he repeatedly attacked left-wing intellectuals who ignored or manipulated the truth–whether it be about Stalinist communism, the Spanish Civil War, or English politics and economics. Possessing what Raymond Williams has called "a kind of conscious double vision," he signaled his rejection of his middle-class roots in 1934 when he changed his name from Eric Blair to George Orwell, taking his surname from a river in Suffolk.

Orwell was born in Motihari, Bengal, India in 1903 to what he later called "lower upper middle class" parents: Richard and Ida Limouzin Blair. His father, a minor official in Indian Customs, returned with the family to England a few years later, and the young boy received a conventional, privileged upbringing. After attending a fashionable preparatory school in southern England, he won a scholarship to Eton, but he did not follow the expected path to Cambridge. Instead, he spent five years from 1922 to 1927 in Burma with the Indian Imperial Police.

Feeling guilty about his part in British imperialism, Orwell left Burma in 1927 to immerse himself in subsistence living, first in Paris and then in London, writing evocatively of his experiences in *Down and Out in Paris and London* (1933). From 1929 to 1935 he worked variously as a tutor, teacher, and bookshop assistant, and he wrote three novels: *Burmese Days* (1934), *A Clergyman's Daughter* (1935), and *Keep the Aspidistra Flying* (1936). Early in 1936 he began writing *The Road to Wigan Pier* (published in 1937). Commissioned by Victor Gollancz for the Left Book Club, it is both a vivid description of life in one of the most depressed industrial areas of Britain and an essay attacking various British reactions to the problem: those of the Labour Party, the middle classes, and those workers who have risen in the system. It was published with a critical introduction by Gollancz.

In July 1936 Orwell and his new wife, Eileen née O'Shaughnessy, joined the thousands of intellectuals fighting for their political beliefs in the Spanish Civil War. While most leftists enlisted in the International Brigade, Orwell found his way into the P.O.U.M., a small Marxist group critical of Soviet-controlled communism. Before being invalided out of the war from a bullet in the throat, he witnessed the internal dissension within the communist forces and the ruthlessness with which the P.O.U.M. was denounced and purged. Orwell recorded his disillusionment first in *Homage to Catalonia* (1938), a book that brilliantly succeeds on two levels. A documentary of specific events observed by one man in the course of 115 days, it vividly describes the war as it was fought by the young soldiers–ill-armed, dirty, and cold. Beyond this, however, it presents a shrewd interpretation of the various political forces manipulating the combatants. As a result, *Homage to Catalonia* was an unpalatable book for both left-wing and right-wing readers and had sold only nine-hundred copies at the time of Orwell's death. It is now, however, regarded as one of the finest analyses of the Spanish Civil War.

"Looking Back on the Spanish War," an essay published in 1943, continued Orwell's attack on the distortion of truth. After several anecdotes that place the reader on the battlefield with a humane observer, he charges that Spanish history was being written not in terms of what actually occurred but according to the interests of various political groups. The left-wing intelligentsia, he said, had dropped its traditional belief that "war is hell" to embrace a "war is glorious" stance in the struggle against Francisco Franco. In both cases, it had no real understanding of the obscenity of the actual battlefield experience. The real issue–the struggle of the common people against the moneyed classes–was obscured by journalistic accounts bearing no relation to the facts. The long-term danger, Orwell argued in a line he would use with great effect in *Nineteen Eighty-Four*, was that in the future a leader or clique might control not only the future but the past and actually persuade followers that two plus two equals five.

In 1939 Orwell wrote and published another novel, *Coming Up for Air*, and during World

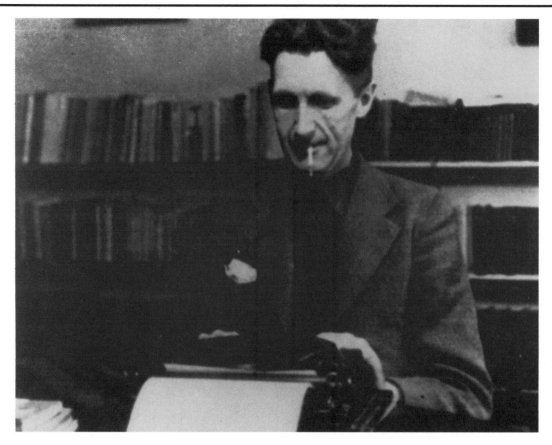

Orwell in his Islington flat, 1945 (photograph by Vernon Richards)

War II he served in the Home Guard and the Indian Overseas Service of the B.B.C. In 1945 he published *Animal Farm*, his brilliant Swiftian satire about the Russian revolution, after four publishers refused it on the grounds that it attacked an ally. Several years later, he wrote his most famous work, *Nineteen Eighty-Four*, a horrific vision of a world dominated by brutal totalitarianism. Though it may have been intended to be a satire on postwar European life, so many millions of readers interpreted it as a warning of future political enslavement that 1984 became a year-long measuring of the shape of the world against Orwell's imagination.

Two parts of *Nineteen Eighty-Four*, though not skillfully integrated into the fictional structure, are actually essays that provide both a theoretical foundation to the totalitarian dictatorship envisaged for the future and some Swiftian satire on politics in Orwell's own time. Supposedly a book written by the revolutionary Goldstein, "The Theory and Practice of Oligarchical Collectivism" describes an international political alignment remarkably similar to that which has evolved since the writing of the novel. The world

is divided into three superstates: Eurasia (Russia and eastern Europe), Oceania (the United States and the British Empire), and Eastasia (China and Southeast Asia). In some combination, the powers are continually at war, though always on a frontier and never in their heartland. In these limited struggles, borders shift but the essential balance of power never changes. The real purpose of the wars—and here Orwell misjudges their effects on a country's economy—is to use up consumer products and keep the large working populations at a subsistence level.

Through Goldstein's book, Orwell explains the development of the "mystique of the Party," through the "Thought Police," the mutability of history, and the reduction of individual freedom. Orwell also explained his concept of "doublethink" (intended as a satiric attack on myopic intellectuals of his day): "the power of holding two contradictory beliefs in one's mind simultaneously and accepting them both."

The other essay, attached to *Nineteen Eighty-Four* as an appendix, is "The Principles of Newspeak," one of Orwell's most effective arguments about the role of language in the control of

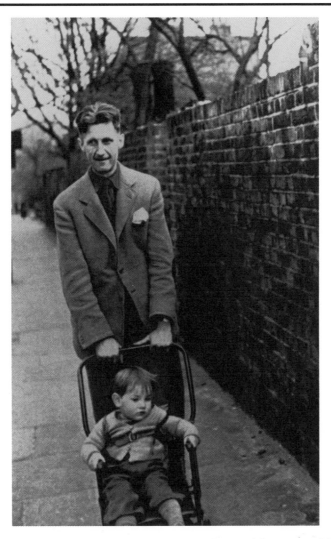

Orwell with Richard, his adopted son, in 1946 (photograph by Vernon Richards)

thought. Here he explains that, in the totalitarian nightmare of the novel, language had been reduced to a medium of expression and thought for properly conditioned devotees of the Party. Systematically, large amounts of vocabulary were eliminated and words stripped of any unorthodox connotations. The result was a diminishing of the range of thought possible so that all unconventional ideas were unthinkable.

Orwell had long suffered from tuberculosis, and *Nineteen Eighty-Four* was written in pain on the small island of Jura, where he had gone in 1947. He died on 21 January 1950.

Orwell's essays (in *The Collected Essays*, 1968) can generally be divided into five groups: autobiography, culture, sociology, politics, and literary criticism. The autobiographical articles include "Why I Write," "Confessions of a Book Reviewer," "How the Poor Die," "Marrakech," and

"Bookshop Memories," but two early pieces from his Burmese days are the most enduring. "A Hanging," a detached, controlled, yet vivid description of the execution of a native prisoner, is an eloquent demonstration of the wrongness of capital punishment. In "Shooting an Elephant," he recounts how he was required to dispose of an old rogue elephant who had destroyed property and killed a man. As he carried out his duties, Orwell points out, he realized that he was in fact a prisoner of the will of the natives who expected him to restore order. Thus, "when the white man turns tyrant it is his own freedom that he destroys." The posthumously published "Such, Such Were the Joys," a painful recollection of his school days at St. Cyprian's, is a contribution to the literature of the English educational system, showing how, according to Jeffrey Meyers, the system gave Orwell a permanent sense of poverty, fear, guilt, masochism, and sickness.

Among Orwell's cultural essays are "Raffles and Miss Blandish," "Decline of the English Murder," "Good Bad Books," and "Riding Down From Bangor." Two others in particular reveal both his affection for British popular culture and a pioneering semisociological approach to it. "The Art of Donald McGill" examines the phenomenon of vulgar seaside postcards, finding a healthy contempt for authority in the working class's exuberance for rudeness. In "Boys' Weeklies," Orwell surveys ten British two-penny papers on the grounds that popular literature is the most accurate gauge of the attitudes of the general public. Though he recognizes the usefulness of the weeklies in attracting youths to literature, he objects to their falsely glamorous picture of public-school life and to their ethos: snobbery, jingoism, conservatism, and what he calls "wealth-fantasy."

Of Orwell's more strictly sociological essays, two wartime pieces–"England Your England" and "The English People"–are notable. Here he identifies distinctly British virtues of gentleness and a sense of justice as opposed to the repressive goose-steps of the fascists, but he also attacks England as a class-ridden country rife with snobbery and privilege. It is at war, he argues, both because of the stupidity of the ruling class and its foreign policy and because of English left-wing intellectuals, who are equally out of touch and whose negativism has undermined the country's morale and image.

Orwell's fundamentally political nature is also revealed in his essays in literary criticism: "In Defence of P. G. Wodehouse," "Wells, Hitler and the World State," "Rudyard Kipling," "Politics vs. Literature: An Examination of *Gulliver's Travels*," "Arthur Koestler," "W. B. Yeats," and "Lear, Tolstoy and the Fool." His "Charles Dickens" is one of the earliest critical studies of the author, but it is equally a discussion of how far a novel should present political ideals. Dickens, in Orwell's view, was not a great stylist, was riddled with bourgeois snobbery, and was unable to create realistic working-class characters. He was thus not a champion of the poor or a revolutionary writer, but he was a nineteenth-century liberal, a free intelligence who vividly and memorably portrayed the essential decency of the common man. With an understanding of capitalism and a distrust of many social institutions, Dickens offered only the suggestion that "if men would behave decently the world would be decent."

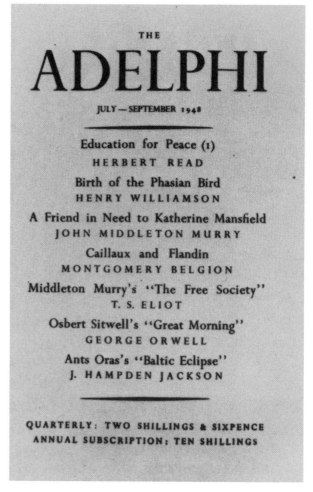

Cover for an issue of the journal that published many of Orwell's book reviews. Some of his poems, written as Eric Blair, also appeared in the Adelphi.

"Lear, Tolstoy and the Fool" is Orwell's reply to a scathing attack on William Shakespeare in a 1903 pamphlet by Leo Tolstoy, one of the most admired men of letters of his age. After demonstrating the inaccuracy of the assault, Orwell argues that the great Russian novelist's contempt was aroused by a remarkable similarity between Lear and himself. Both men made monumental and gratuitous acts of renunciation; both acted on misguided impulses and failed to get the results they wished; both were overly proud and poor judges of character; and both underwent a revulsion from sexuality. Having thus explained the underlying impetus for Tolstoy's pamphlet, Orwell argues that one cannot answer his criticism. One can only point out that Shakespeare has met the only true test of greatness: the common and enduring consent of millions of readers.

A recording session for the poetry magazine Voice: *(standing) Orwell, Nancy Barratt, William Empson; (sitting) Venu Chitale, J. M. Tambimuttu, T. S. Eliot, Una Marson, Mulk Raj Anand, C. Pemberton, and Narayana Menon (by permission of the BBC)*

"Inside the Whale" uses Henry Miller's novel *Tropic of Cancer* (1934) to discuss the political naïveté and irresponsibility of writers of the 1930s and to predict a totalitarian future in which freely created literature will be impossible. Thus, the only alternative will be Miller's passiveness to experience, going inside the whale to embrace "quietism–robbing reality of its terrors by simply submitting to it."

In 1948 in "Why I Write" Orwell observed that "every line of serious work that I have written since 1936 has been written, directly or indirectly, *against* totalitarianism and *for* democratic socialism, as I understand it." Clearly the impetus for *Animal Farm* and *Nineteen Eighty-Four*, it is equally the theme of a series of impressive political essays Orwell wrote in the mid 1940s. "Second Thoughts on James Burnham" tackles Burnham's particular worldview and observes that history is a cycle of mass revolts in which the populace is enslaved each time by new masters.

"The Prevention of Literature" argues for intellectual liberty, maintaining that there is a new and dangerous belief that intellectual honesty is a form of antisocial selfishness. There has been, Orwell writes, a poisonous effect of the Russian mythos on English thought, demanding of its adherents incredible leaps from pre-1939 antipathy to nazism, to the early World War II belief that Germany had been wronged, to a post-June 1941 conviction that nazism was a hideous evil. Totalitar-

ian regimes regard history as something to be created rather than learned, but in democracies, while the immediate enemies of truth are the press barons, the film magnates, and the bureaucrats, in the long run the most serious danger lies in the declining desire for freedom among intellectuals themselves. Anyone who does not recognize that the imagination atrophies in captivity, says Orwell, is demanding his own destruction and the end of serious literature.

In "Writers and Leviathan," Orwell continues his plea for intellectual integrity in an age when politics intrudes on the artistic life. Arguing that contemporary authors now write in dread of the opinion of their own group–in his time, the left–he suggests that one should write *about* politics but not *for* political orthodoxies. One cannot be politically neutral in such a critical period, but one must not be a propagandist.

Orwell's most famous essay, "Politics and the English Language," examines political conformity in terms of the abuse of language. Asserting that there is an intimate connection between words and thought, he argues that a clear and honest expression of clear thoughts is a necessary first step to political integrity. The use of clichés, euphemisms, jargon, and foreign expressions tends to prevent thought, leading to confused ideas or outright propaganda. "Politics and the English Language" continues to be widely taught as a prescription for effective writing, but its theory of the corruption of thought through the debasement of language informs a reading of *Nineteen Eighty-Four*. As print and electronic journalism have become increasingly sophisticated and influential, Orwell's thesis has become even more relevant. In general Orwell's essays remain interesting partly as insights into the history of political thought in the twentieth century but also because of the continuing value of his relentlessly honest exploration of the role of the intellectual artist in an often cynical world.

Bibliography:

Jeffrey and Valerie Meyers, *George Orwell: An Annotated Bibliography of Criticism* (New York: Garland, 1977).

Biographies:

Peter Stansky and William Abrahams, *The Unknown Orwell* (New York: Knopf, 1972);

Stansky and Abrahams, *Orwell: The Transformation* (New York: Knopf, 1980);

Bernard Crick, *George Orwell: A Life* (Boston: Little, Brown, 1980).

References:

Keith Alldritt, *The Making of George Orwell: A Literary History* (New York: St. Martin's, 1969);

John Atkins, *George Orwell: A Literary Study* (London: Calder, 1954);

Laurence Brander, *George Orwell* (London: Longmans, Green, 1954);

Jenni Calder, *Chronicles of Conscience: A Study of George Orwell and Arthur Koestler* (London: Secker & Warburg, 1968);

T. R. Fyvel, "George Orwell and Eric Blair: Glimpses of a Dual Life," *Encounter*, 13 (July 1959): 60-65;

Miriam Gross, ed., *The World of George Orwell* (New York: Simon & Schuster, 1971);

Harold J. Harris, "Orwell's Essays and 1984," *Twentieth Century Literature*, 4 (January 1959): 154-161;

Christopher Hollis, *A Study of George Orwell: The Man and His Works* (London: Hollis & Carter, 1956);

David L. Kubal, *Outside the Whale: George Orwell's Art and Politics* (Notre Dame: University of Notre Dame Press, 1972);

Q. D. Leavis, "The Literary Life Respectable," *Scrutiny*, 9 (September 1940): 173-176;

Jeffrey Meyers, *A Reader's Guide to George Orwell* (London: Thames & Hudson, 1975);

Meyers, ed., *George Orwell: The Critical Heritage* (London: Routledge & Kegan Paul, 1975);

Richard Rees, *George Orwell: Fugitive from the Camp of Victory* (London: Secker & Warburg, 1961);

Philip Rieff, "George Orwell and the Post-Liberal Imagination," *Kenyon Review*, 16 (Winter 1954): 49-70;

Alan Sandison, *The Last Man in Europe* (New York: Harper & Row, 1974);

Jerome Thale, "Orwell's Modest Proposal," *Critical Quarterly*, 9 (1962): 365-368;

Lionel Trilling, "George Orwell and the Politics of Truth," in his *The Opposing Self* (New York: Viking, 1955), pp. 151-172;

Anthony West, *Principles and Persuasions* (London: Eyre & Spottiswoode, 1958);

Raymond Williams, *Orwell* (London: Collins, 1971);

George Woodcock, *The Crystal Spirit: A Study of George Orwell* (Boston: Little, Brown, 1966).

Coventry Patmore

(23 July 1823 - 26 November 1896)

Paul J. Marcotte
University of Ottawa

See also the Patmore entry in *DLB 35: Victorian Poets After 1850*.

BOOKS: *Poems* (London: Moxon, 1844);

Tamerton Church-Tower and Other Poems (London: Pickering, 1853);

The Betrothal (London: Parker, 1854; Boston: Ticknor & Fields, 1856);

The Espousals (London: Parker, 1856; Boston: Ticknor & Fields, 1856);

The Angel in the House (London: Parker, 1858; New York: Dutton, 1876);

Faithful for Ever (London: Parker, 1860; Boston: Ticknor & Fields, 1861);

The Victories of Love (Boston: Burnham, 1862; London & Cambridge: Macmillan, 1863); revised and enlarged as *The Victories of Love, and Other Poems* (New York: Cassell, 1888);

Odes (London: Privately printed by Savill, Edwards, 1868);

The Unknown Eros and Other Odes . . . I-XXI, anonymous (London: Bell, 1877); revised, enlarged, and signed by Patmore as *The Unknown Eros: I-XLVI* (London: Bell, 1878);

Bryan Waller Procter (Barry Cornwall) (London: Bell, 1877);

Amelia (London: Privately printed, 1878); enlarged as *Amelia, Tamerton Church-Tower, etc.; with a Prefatory Study of English Metrical Law* (London: Bell, 1878);

Poems, 4 volumes (London: Bell, 1879);

How I Managed and Improved My Estate (London: Bell, 1886);

Hastings, Lewes, Rye and the Sussex Marshes (London: Bell, 1887);

Principle in Art (London: Bell, 1889; revised edition, 1898);

Religio Poetae (London: Bell, 1893; revised edition, 1898);

The Rod, the Root and the Flower (London: Bell, 1895);

Courage in Politics, and Other Essays, 1885-1896, edited by Frederick Page (London & New York: Oxford University Press, 1921);

Seven Unpublished Poems by Coventry Patmore to Alice Meynell (London: Privately printed, 1922).

Collections: *Poems, by Coventry Patmore*, edited by Basil Champneys (London: Bell, 1906);

The Poems of Coventry Patmore, edited by Frederick Page (London & New York: Oxford University Press, 1949).

OTHER: *The Children's Garland from the Best Poets*, edited by Patmore (London: Macmillan, 1862).

During the 1850s and 1860s Coventry Patmore was one of the most admired and influential of Victorian poets. *The Angel in the House* (1858) received critical acclaim, sold more than a quarter of a million copies, and actually challenged the popular supremacy of Alfred, Lord Tennyson's *Idylls of the King* (1859). It was Patmore who persuaded John Ruskin to defend the Pre-Raphaelite movement, and it was Patmore who invented the "motto of perfection" that the brotherhood eventually adopted: "It is the last rub which polishes the mirror." Indeed, it has been asserted that Patmore successfully competed with the talents of Tennyson, the Brownings, the Rossettis, and Matthew Arnold until he clearly grasped—what in a sense he had always suspected—that his inspiration was somehow essentially different from theirs. His mystical insights paralleled those of St. Bernard, St. Teresa, and St. John of the Cross; his conversion to Roman Catholicism was gradual, grudging, and carefully calculated; and his species of English patriotism was both traditional and unfashionable.

Patmore was born on 23 July 1823 in Woodford, Essex. Peter George Patmore, the poet's father, contributed enormously to the discovery and early development of his favorite son's literary proclivities. In effect, he made his eldest son Coventry his private pupil. A man who really loved and appreciated literature, who possessed a significant collection of books, and who hobnobbed with many of the leading writers of the period, Patmore's father was well qualified to perform what amounted to a labor of love. Although an affectionate father and a good husband, P. G. Patmore turned out to be a harbinger of the sociocultural mores that eventually eclipsed his son's literary reputation. Before his marriage to Eliza Robertson (a marriage that was opportunely arranged by Clarissa Patmore, the poet's grandmother), P. G. Patmore had been a dandy and an avowed agnostic. While the father took exclusive charge of his son's education, the grandmother—according to Edmund Gosse—inflated the boy's ego and self-esteem: "Coventry is a clever fellow" was the first sentence his grandmother taught him to speak. The poet's mother, a rigid Presbyterian with an outwardly cold and stern manner, was absolutely forbidden by her husband to give any religious instruction to their children; indeed, Gosse writes that Patmore often insisted "that his mother counted for nothing in his early training, except as a dark figure which it was always wise and generally easy to evade."

Nevertheless, it seems certain that it was she who found a way of covertly sowing the seeds of the Protestant religion in a son who possessed a vital predilection toward the supernatural.

Patmore was not a great traveler; his life, however, was profoundly influenced by things that happened to him when he was away from home. During a sojourn in France when he was sixteen, he fell in love with an attractive and sophisticated young lady who snubbed him unmercifully. In later years, Patmore attributed to this "tragic" experience the power "to discern sexual impurity and virginal purity, the one as the tangible blackness and horror of hell, and the other as the very bliss of heaven, and the flower and consummation of love between man and woman" (as quoted by Gosse). Three years after his experience in France, while visiting Edinburgh, Patmore was for the first time exposed to the practices and prejudices of his very pious Scottish relatives. Ironically it was their extreme antipathy toward Roman Catholicism that initially prompted Patmore to imagine, according to Gosse, "that the much abused Catholics might after all be possibly in the right." The idea of love and the influence of the Catholic church were the dominant forces that determined him "to sing the praises of nuptial love," the major theme of his art.

P. G. Patmore's actions continued to sculpt his son's life. Encouraged by the enthusiasm of literary confidants, the flattered father easily persuaded his protégé to publish *Poems* in 1844. The reviews varied from extreme admiration to absolute condemnation, reflecting the attitude of their respective authors toward Patmore's father more than their attitude toward his son's poetry. In any event the young Patmore soon came to regard his juvenilia as "trash" and "rubbish" hastily written and prematurely published to please his father. In the midst of the excitement occasioned by his son's initiation into the literary world, P. G. Patmore, accompanied by his wife, was forced to leave England in order to avoid the legal consequences of having speculated too optimistically in railway shares. For the first time in his life the young poet was forced to confront the exigencies of supporting himself. Having no other real alternative, Patmore eked out a living by writing for periodicals and translating. This hand-to-mouth existence was eventually terminated by the kindness of Monckton Milnes, who obtained an appointment for the clever but unfortunate young man as assistant librarian in the Brit-

Patmore in 1855 (drawing by John Brett)

ish Museum. Patmore retained this position from the end of 1846 to the beginning of 1866.

The librarianship and the publication of *Poems* proved to be seminal events in Patmore's life. *Poems* brought Patmore to the attention of a group of young artists who were in the process of forming the Pre-Raphaelite Brotherhood; it also persuaded Patmore of the need to embark upon a serious study of the principles of prosody. His employment financially enabled him to marry Emily Augusta Andrews on 11 September 1847. Although many scholars insist that Honoria, the heroine of *The Angel in the House*, is not a portrait of Emily, none deny that the character faithfully reflects the essential perfections that Patmore discovered in her; indeed, Patmore unequivocally declared that it was his first wife "by whom and for whom" he became a poet. Richard Garnett's celebrated description of Emily (as reported by Basil Champneys) appears to settle the matter: "This admirable lady . . . impressed me . . . as a Queen ruling by Love and Wisdom, 'A creature not too bright or good / For human nature's daily food,' wise, witty, frank, gracious, hospitable, without flaw or blemish that I could ever

discover, but perfectly at home in this terrestrial sphere."

Very few consequential poets have failed to write about the love of woman, but none approaches the subject as Patmore does. Gosse expresses the difference precisely: "Between Coventry Patmore . . . and almost all other poets of high distinction in the history of literature, there was to be this remarkable distinction, that while the rest have celebrated the liberty, the freshness and the delirium of love, whether in its physical or in its metaphysical sense, but always rather in the mood of anticipation than of possession, or, if in that of possession, at least in a spirit which feigns to ignore the bonds of custom, Patmore alone is eagerly pleased to hug and gild those bonds. He confesses himself not the poet of passion in the abstract, but of a love made willing captive by the marriage tie." It is evident that Patmore, long before his formal conversion to Roman Catholicism, regarded marriage as a sacrament and attributed many of the happy events that occur in *The Angel in the House* to its great efficacy; the transformation it imposes upon a wife (Jane) who appears ill suited to her husband (Frederick) illustrates most dramatically how much power Patmore attributed to the graces of matrimony.

Tragically, even as arrangements were being made in July 1862 to publish *The Victories of Love* (the fourth part of *The Angel in the House*) in *Macmillan's Magazine* (the sale of this work to a magazine suggests that Patmore was in immediate need of the hundred pounds *Macmillan's* paid for it), Emily Augusta Patmore died at Elm Cottage. She was only thirty-eight. Her departure devastated Patmore, and he withdrew from the literary world. Even his association with Tennyson, who had been his closest friend, suddenly ended. For a time things went from bad to worse. His dead wife's memory served far less satisfactorily as a source of artistic inspiration than her presence had done, even though she was not easy to forget. Indeed, nostalgia drove him to visit the scene of their honeymoon. Though he devoted himself to the upbringing of his six children, he soon learned that he was not suited to the task. His eldest daughter, Emily Honoria, did her best to help, but things did not go well: the conduct of his son, Milnes, disturbed him very much; his relationship with his second son, Tennyson, was severely strained by Patmore's intolerance and impatience; and he missed his three youngest children, who were boarded with different friends.

Harriet Robson, who became Patmore's third wife on 13 September 1881

He took little interest in the public's reception of *The Victories of Love*. His financial resources, which had been significantly depleted by his wife's long illness, continued to be a worry. As a result of all these factors, his health, never very robust, began to deteriorate. At the urging of Aubrey de Vere, he finally agreed to apply for a leave of absence from the British Museum and took a journey to Rome in February 1864.

A seeming exception to Patmore's temporary loss of interest in his literary career is evident in the chain of events that followed the publication, in 1862, of *The Children's Garland from the Best Poets* (edited by Patmore). After Emily's death and before Patmore's departure for Italy, "A. K. H. B." (Andrew Boyd), in an unfriendly review, accused him of having transcribed some of the *Garland* texts inaccurately. Other critics and the public generally were unhappy about the selec-

tion. Emily, though very ill, had assisted her husband with the work, and the Patmore children, particularly Emily Honoria, who was her father's favorite daughter and about eight years old, were pressed into service to test the selections. Because the endeavor was a family project, the last participated in by his wife, the grieving poet was deeply hurt and angered by the ungenerous reception it received. Indeed, almost twenty years later, in 1882, when the school board of London proposed that the *Garland* be given as a prize on condition that some other poem be substituted for "The Outlandish Knight," Patmore categorically refused to make the change. Only Patmore's memory of Emily's heroic contribution to the preparation of the *Garland* can account adequately for his persistent belligerence in connection with this book.

Patmore's wretchedness was not much dissipated by his journey to Rome. According to Gosse, however, when de Vere actually introduced Patmore into "the best Catholic society of the great centre of Catholic life," his spirits immediately brightened. He felt comfortable among his fellow expatriates and the distinguished Italians with whom they socialized. In such an atmosphere he soon realized why he had journeyed to Rome: he knew that the time had come to settle the question that had been plaguing him off and on for years. A Jesuit, Father Cardella, was chosen to be his spiritual adviser. Although his intellectual objections to Catholicism were soon rebutted, Patmore still procrastinated, perhaps troubled by Emily's prophetic words: "When I am gone, they [the Catholics] will get you; and then I shall see you no more." Eventually, however, the decision was made, and as Patmore himself confesses, no one helped him to make it nearly so much as Marianne Caroline Byles, the woman who was destined to become the second Mrs. Patmore: "I had never before beheld so beautiful a personality, and this beauty seemed to be the pure effulgence of Catholic sanctity" (quoted by Gosse). Patmore was converted to Roman Catholicism in May 1864.

The Jane Austen-like relationship between the impoverished poet and the ascetic heiress had prospered in spite of the vow never to marry that Cardinal Manning had encouraged Byles to make. A dispensation was easily obtained, and Byles accepted Patmore's proposal of marriage immediately after his conversion. But their troubles were not yet over: Patmore discovered that his fiancée was a very wealthy woman. The revelation persuaded Patmore to leave Rome and abandon her. His vigilant friends, however, soon convinced him to return to Rome and resume the relationship. Patmore and Marianne Byles were married on 18 July 1865 at Bayswater.

Not much is known about the quality of the emotion that bound the two together as husband and wife. Champneys's observation may explain why the poet had, relatively speaking, so little to say directly about the essence of his second marriage: "The extraordinary self-effacement and reticence which was characteristic of [Marianne] in life seems fated to attend her memory." She died suddenly on 12 April 1880. The considerable fortune she brought to the marriage had enabled Patmore to retire from the British Museum in 1866 and, later that same year, to purchase Heron's Ghyll in Sussex. The condition of the estate–Patmore had actually purchased two contiguous estates–was so poor that it enabled him to demonstrate his abilities as a man of business. Patmore had desired such an opportunity ever since a phrenologist had told him that he possessed a head for business as well as one for poetry. A complete account of his proceedings is given in a little book he published in 1886: *How I Managed and Improved My Estate*. The degree of success he enjoyed may be inferred from the fact that, when he sold Heron's Ghyll to the Duke of Norfolk for twenty-seven thousand pounds, he estimated his net profit to have been ninety-five hundred pounds. Patmore left Heron's Ghyll in 1874 and settled in Hastings the following year; extraordinarily enough, the house he came to occupy, known as the Mansion, was the very one he had fallen in love with as a child.

In 1877 *The Unknown Eros* was published, containing some of the same odes that had been privately printed in 1868; the book was selectively circulated and, generally speaking, unenthusiastically received. Patmore's disappointment, even two years later, was so great that he collected and burned all the copies he could find. Nevertheless, privately he remained convinced that he had "hit upon *the* finest metre that ever was invented, and *the* finest mine of wholly unworked material that ever fell to the lot of an English poet." The meter, according to Champneys, "seems to be founded on no theoretic principle, nor can it be explained by analysis. Neither length of line nor incidence of rhyme are subject to any formal law: both depend upon the ear alone." The "mine," according to Calvert Alexander, was "Catholic mystical theology, especially

Coventry Patmore (photograph by G. Bradshaw, 1886)

the idea, so dear to the mystics, of setting forth the intimate union of the soul of the individual with Christ in the language of the most exalted type of earthly union–the soul as the spouse of Christ." Patmore's use of sexuality in general and of sexual union in particular shocked and offended many people; and although Patmore thought of himself as a prophet who could sing, the music of his verse failed to please the ear of an age that was captivated by the music of Algernon Swinburne. *The Unknown Eros*, as it is usually printed today, is introduced by a "Proem" and is divided into two books: book 1 contains twenty-six odes and book 2, eighteen. These odes were never very well received by Patmore's contemporaries, but he regarded them as being among his best works and–as noted by Gosse–consoled himself with the conviction that they appeared before their time: "I have respected posterity, and, should there be a posterity which cares for letters, I dare to hope it will respect me."

The year he published *The Unknown Eros*, Patmore also published *Bryan Waller Procter*. The work was obviously a labor of obligation: as reported by Champneys, Patmore said, "Mrs. Procter insisted so strenuously upon my writing the life and editing the remains of her husband [who was better known as Barry Cornwall] that I could not refuse, though it was a task little suited to me." It was not so much Patmore's indifference toward Cornwall's poetry as it was his growing preoccupation with religion that principally accounts for the perfunctory quality of the book. This conclusion is supported by the fact that Patmore published the religious love poem *Amelia* in 1878. Shortly before his death Patmore singled it out as the best of his works. It certainly forms a link between the *Angel* and the *Odes*, inasmuch as it is a narrative love poem written in the meter of the odes.

The last twenty years of Patmore's life were comparatively uneventful. Except for revision, his poetical career was over after the publication of a complete edition of his poetry in 1879. More and more of his time was devoted to the study of mystical theology. He continued to read the texts of St. Bernard, St. John of the Cross, St. Teresa, and St. Thomas Aquinas. He made four pilgrimages to Lourdes (in 1877, 1878, 1881, and 1885). The laureate of wedded love had become, in a sense, "consecrated" during the writing of the odes. The Marian poet that emerged had consciously blended—not "mixed up," as even some of his closest friends feared—amorousness with religion.

Patmore married Harriet Robson, a longtime friend of the family, on 13 September 1881. The couple had a son, Francis Joseph Mary Epiphanius ("Piffie"), in January 1883. Before this marriage, perhaps even before the death of his second wife, Patmore had already embarked upon the third and final phase of his literary career. It is almost as if he had come to the conclusion that prose is a more appropriate medium than verse for the prophet who knows what he has to say before he says it; indeed, it is almost as if the meaning of "The relation of the soul to Christ *as his betrothed wife*," a meaning he discovered again and again in the poems he had made and in the mystical works he had meditated on, had finally become sufficiently intelligible to him that he could explain it to other people and offer

it as a solution for many of the grave problems that plagued his world.

Thus, absolutely convinced that the marriage of man and woman is the symbol of God's marriage with humanity and determined to enable his reader to understand "*the burning heart of the Universe*," Patmore composed a prose work titled "Sponsa Dei." Gosse supposes that the manuscript was completed in 1883 and reports that it was burned by its author on Christmas Day, 1887. According to Champneys, "in the 'Sponsa Dei' Patmore had carried this symbol into fuller detail than in any of his other works either in verse or prose." When Gerard Manley Hopkins read it, his comment, "that's telling secrets," instantly persuaded Patmore to destroy a work that Gosse regarded as perhaps "audacious" but certainly "a masterpiece": Patmore "had come to the conclusion that, although wholly orthodox, . . . the world was not ready for so mystical an interpretation of the significance of physical love in religion, and that some parts of the book were too daring to be safely placed in all hands." From the point of view of the literary critic, however, Gosse insists that "No existing specimen of Patmore's prose seems to me so delicate, or penetrated by quite so high a charm of style, as this lost book was."

"If the flower of Patmore's prose work was thus sacrificed to a scruple," as Champneys sums up the fate of the "Sponsa Dei," enough remains to guarantee Patmore a place among English essayists. In 1884, five years before his move from Hastings to Lymington, Patmore and Frederick Greenwood, who was at that time editor of the *St. James's Gazette*, formed a partnership that was largely responsible for the achievements of Patmore as a prose writer. Originally drawn together, as Champneys says, by their mutual opposition to William Gladstone's "attempt to dissociate reform of the franchise from redistribution of seats," the relationship between a gentle editor and an imprudent contributor soon blossomed into genuine friendship. For the most part Greenwood allowed Patmore to choose his own subjects and write about them as he pleased. From time to time, however, conciliatory notes had to be prefixed to Patmore's articles, and carefully worded advice had to be communicated to the "Pegasus" of Greenwood's stable of writers.

In such circumstances Patmore embarked with diligence and enthusiasm upon what was to be the final phase of his literary career. He was afforded the opportunity to do precisely what he

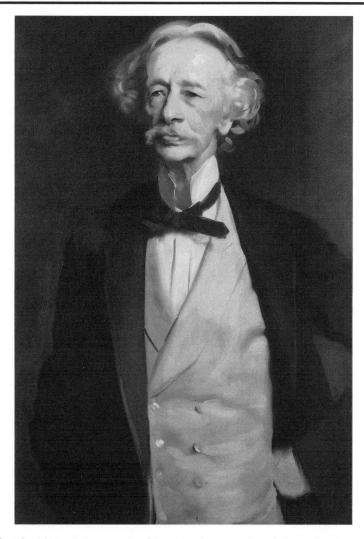

Portrait of Patmore by John Singer Sargent, painted in 1894 (by permission of the National Portrait Gallery, London)

wanted and precisely what his reading, meditation, and beliefs prepared and prompted him to attempt. Like his friends John Ruskin and Thomas Carlyle, he was an antizeitgeist Victorian whose patriotism could not compromise his conviction that England was in serious trouble. Patmore was an authoritarian advocate who regarded his enemies–social, political, and religious–as God's enemies, and to such enemies Patmore offered no quarter. Actually he lacked the prudence to modify his dogmatism and the will to adulterate the purity of his mysticism; notwithstanding such tendencies, he continued to publish articles in *St. James's* until 1891. In that year, Greenwood's editorship ended, and Greenwood devoted himself to the launching of a new review. Unfortunately, however, Patmore's relationship with Greenwood's *Anti-Jacobin* did not last very long: "I have been trying to write for Greenwood; but I feel that what

I do is out of keeping with his paper and with the world's sympathies generally. So I shall drop that" (in Champneys). He did, and, except for two articles, one on Francis Thompson and one on Alice Meynell, both of which appeared in the *Fortnightly Review*, he wrote nothing of importance for the press during his remaining years.

Between 1885 and 1891 Patmore had contributed more than a hundred articles to *St. James's*. They covered landed property, landscape, jewels, and market prices as well as religion, philosophy, and politics. In addition to those essays in *How I Managed and Improved My Estate*, Patmore published what he considered to be the best and most important of these articles (together with a few of earlier vintage) in three small volumes that almost entirely support his reputation as a prose writer: *Principle in Art* (1889), *Religio Poetae* (1893), and *The Rod, the Root and the Flower* (1895).

267

Principle in Art contains twenty-six essays. A few deal with criticism in general, a larger number with individual writers, and another few with special topics. In Patmore's view, "To criticise is to judge; to judge requires judicial qualification; and this is quite a different thing from a natural sensitiveness to beauty, however much that sensitiveness may have become heightened by converse with refined and beautiful objects of nature and works of art." The distinction he makes between "masculine" and "feminine" writers is surely his most characteristic principle: "masculine" writers are those in whom judgment predominates over visions and emotion; "feminine" writers are those in whom visions and emotion predominate over judgment. Samuel Taylor Coleridge is "masculine"; Percy Bysshe Shelley and John Keats are "feminine." "The point of rest in art," however, is the critical concept that has attracted the most attention. The idea was inspired by Coleridge's statement: "all harmony is founded on a relation to rest." In *King Lear*, for example, Kent is seen as "the point of rest," and all the emotions and intrigues represented in the play discover their true value in the relationship they bear to this character. Patmore's perspicaciousness as a critic is illustrated by his admiration for Thomas Hardy, an admiration avowed at a time when the novelist's reputation was far from established. Of course, as with most critics, Patmore's natural sensitiveness and judicial qualification sometimes deserted him: Is William Barnes, for example, actually as significant a writer as Patmore seemed to believe?

Religio Poetae is a collection of twenty-one essays; in each one, Patmore tends to relate the particular subject to religion. As if recapitulating his own evolution from poet to mystic, Patmore begins by talking about poetry and natural love; soon, however, it is obvious that human love is being scrutinized as a symbol. Divine love, the entity beyond the entity being discussed, conveys spiritual dignity to nuptial love without altering any of its natural aspects. "Dieu et Ma Dame," a phrase Patmore insists "is no irreverent or hyperbolic legend for his double but divided worship," is generally thought to explore the analogy (or identity) between natural (sexual) love and divine love in a manner close to the one employed in "Sponsa Dei." Perhaps it is for this reason that Champneys thought *Religio Poetae* showed Patmore the essayist at his best.

Others, however, believe that *The Rod, the Root and the Flower*, certainly a novelty even

among his books, is Patmore's prose masterpiece. Published the year before his death, it is divided into four sections, "Aurea Dicta," "Knowledge and Science," "Homo," and "Magna Moralia," and is entirely composed of aphorisms and "essayettes" (as Champneys calls them), which deal almost exclusively with religious subjects. The aphorisms can be as short as a single line; the short essays are never longer than a page and a half. Patmore, with good reason, identifies the contents of this book as "notes." As a boy he used to read books that had previously been read and marked by his father; there is good reason to believe that he sometimes read only the designated passages. Preferring the "untidyness" that is often occasioned by the juxtaposing of excerpts to the "barrenness" that is often encountered when books are read carefully from cover to cover, Patmore defended the mode he employed in *The Rod, the Root and the Flower* by contending that it is the only one by which "realities of a certain order can be approximately expressed." Herbert Read compares this book with Blaise Pascal's *Pensées* (1670). Of Patmore's style, Champneys says it is "specially direct, masculine, and free from artifice. It is the matter of which the reader is first made conscious, and it is mainly by the vivid impression produced, by realizing with what apparent ease thoughts hard to express are made clear, that he becomes aware of the excellence of the manner. . . . [T]he form is indissolubly wedded to the thought, and the union of the two displays that 'inevitable' quality which is one of the principal notes of first-rate art."

Patmore died on 26 November 1896 at Lymington, in the company of Harriet, his third wife. A short time before he passed away, as reported by Champneys, "He put his arms round her neck, and said 'I love you, dear, but the Lord is my Life and my Light.'" Five days after his death, robed in the habit of a tertiary of the Order of St. Francis, his body was laid to rest. Only a few friends gathered to bid him a quiet farewell. In a sense, he would have liked the world to believe that he had lived as peacefully as he died and was buried. His last years, though, punctuated by significant disappointments, were far from happy times: his quarrel with the Pious Society of Missions over their mortgaging of Saint Mary Star of the Sea, a church he had erected as a monument to the memory of his second wife, confirmed and aggravated a distrust he had long harbored toward the clergy; his unsuccessful candidacy for the laureateship, ignored by the vengeful Gladstone, confirmed and aggravated a disdain he had long held toward politicians; and, most devastating of all, the rejection of his deep and passionate love by Meynell confirmed and aggravated the impatience with which he had long awaited death.

While it has often been observed that Patmore has "not been accorded his just position" or "has not been accorded any position at all" in the history of English literature, Calvert Alexander's classification of Patmore, John Henry Newman, Aubrey de Vere, Robert S. Hawker, and Gerard Manley Hopkins as members of the "First Phase of the Catholic Literary Revival" is persuasive. Certainly every one of these writers–though each in his own way–was opposed to "Liberalism, the anti-intellectual Romantic aesthetic, [and] scientific naturalism." On the positive side each one–again, in his own way–made use of some religious doctrine as a means of expressing his solution to what he regarded as the Victorian social crisis. Patmore, who looked on himself as a "psychologist of love," was convinced that married love is a forerunner and image of divine love. J. C. Reid and others have pointed out that Patmore anchored this view on the following text: "But it is not the spiritual that comes first, but the physical, and then the spiritual" (I Corinthians 15:46); that "Patmore's views on love and marriage, while more profound and more metaphysical than those of his mid-Victorian contemporaries, were essentially those of orthodox Christianity"; and that as such opinions became increasingly unpopular, Patmore, the poet who constantly exalted the efficacy of marriage and its bonds, is more and more generally dismissed as a denominational apologist for an outdated social arrangement. Thus it seems certain that for the foreseeable future, Coventry Patmore's reputation will continue to reside "In the safe shadow of the world's contempt."

Letters:

Basil Champneys, *Memoirs and Correspondence of Coventry Patmore*, 2 volumes (London: Bell, 1900).

Biographies:

Edmund Gosse, *Coventry Patmore* (London: Hodder & Stoughton, 1905);

Augusto Guido, *Coventry Patmore* (Brescia, Italy: Morcelliana, 1946);

Derek Patmore, *The Life and Times of Coventry Patmore* (London: Constable, 1949);

E. J. Oliver, *Coventry Patmore* (New York: Sheed & Ward, 1956).

References:

Calvert Alexander, *The Catholic Literary Revival* (Milwaukee: Bruce, 1935);

Osbert Burdett, *The Idea of Coventry Patmore* (London: Oxford University Press, 1921);

Frederick Page, *Patmore–A Study in Poetry* (London: Oxford University Press, 1933);

Derek Patmore, *Portrait of My Family* (London: Constable, 1935);

Herbert Read, "Coventry Patmore," in *The Great Victorians*, edited by H. J. and Hugh Massingham (London: Ivor Nicholson & Watson, 1932), pp. 397-410;

J. C. Reid, *The Mind and Art of Coventry Patmore* (London: Routledge & Kegan Paul, 1957).

Papers:

There are major collections of Patmore's letters and miscellaneous papers in the Princeton University Library and the Boston College Library. The original manuscripts for *The Unknown Eros, The Rod, the Root and the Flower*, and *The Angel in the House* are held, respectively, at the British Library, Nottingham University, and the Grantham Library in Sussex. The National Library of Scotland contains letters of and to Patmore. Other papers, mainly correspondence, are contained in various institutions, including the Humanities Research Center Library of the University of Texas at Austin, the Knox College Archives (Galesburg, Illinois), the Salzmann Library of St. Francis Seminary (Milwaukee, Wisconsin), and the Gerard Manley Hopkins Collection at the College of Notre Dame Library, Baltimore.

Llewelyn Powys

(13 August 1884 - 2 December 1939)

Charles Lock
University of Toronto

BOOKS: *Confessions of Two Brothers*, with John Cowper Powys (Rochester, N.Y.: Manas, 1916; London: Browne, 1982);

Ebony and Ivory (New York: American Library Service, 1923; London: Richards, 1923);

Thirteen Worthies (New York: American Library Service, 1923; London: Richards, 1924);

Black Laughter (New York: Harcourt, Brace, 1924; London: Richards, 1925);

Honey and Gall (Girard, Kan.: Haldeman-Julius, 1924);

Cup-Bearers of Wine and Hellebore (Girard, Kan.: Haldeman-Julius, 1924);

Skin for Skin (New York: Harcourt, Brace, 1925; London: Cape, 1926);

The Verdict of Bridlegoose (New York: Harcourt, Brace, 1926; London: Cape, 1927);

Henry Hudson (London: Lane, 1927; New York: Harper, 1928);

The Cradle of God (New York: Harcourt, Brace, 1929; London: Cape, 1929);

The Pathetic Fallacy (London: Longmans, Green, 1930); republished as *An Hour on Christianity* (Philadelphia & London: Lippincott, 1930);

Apples Be Ripe (New York: Harcourt, Brace, 1930; London & New York: Longmans, Green, 1930);

A Pagan's Pilgrimage (New York: Harcourt, Brace, 1931; London: Longmans, Green, 1931);

Impassioned Clay (New York & London: Longmans, Green, 1931);

Now that the Gods Are Dead (New York: Equinox, 1932);

Glory of Life (London: Golden Cockerel, 1934; enlarged edition, London: Bodley Head, 1949);

Earth Memories (London: Lane, 1934; enlarged edition, New York: Norton, 1938);

Damnable Opinions (London: Watts, 1935);

Dorset Essays (London: Lane, 1935);

The Twelve Months (London: Lane, Bodley Head, 1936);

Somerset Essays (London: Lane, 1937);

Rats in the Sacristy (London: Watts, 1937);

Llewelyn Powys

Love and Death: An Imaginary Autobiography (London: Lane, Bodley Head, 1939; New York: Simon & Schuster, 1941);

A Baker's Dozen (Herrin, Ill.: Trovillion, 1939; London: Lane, 1941);

Swiss Essays (London: Lane, 1947);

Advice to a Young Poet (London: Bodley Head, 1949);

Two Essays by Llewelyn Powys (Guernsey, U.K.: Toucan, 1971).

Collections: *The Book of Days of Llewelyn Powys: Thoughts from His Philosophy*, compiled by

John Wallis (London: Golden Cockerel, 1937);

Llewelyn Powys: A Selection from His Writings, edited by Kenneth Hopkins (London: Macdonald, 1952).

SELECTED PERIODICAL PUBLICATIONS–
UNCOLLECTED: "Death," *New Age*, 10 April 1913;

"The Necrophilias," *Cerebralist*, December 1913;

"The Thirteenth Way" [on Wallace Stevens], *Dial*, 77 (July-December 1924): 45-50;

"Recollections of Thomas Hardy," *Virginia Quarterly Review*, 15 (1939): 425-434.

OTHER: Andrew Clark, *The Life and Times of Anthony à Wood*, edited and abridged by Powys (London: Wishart, 1932);

"A Voyage to the West Indies," *The Pleasure Ground*, edited by Malcolm Elwin (London: Macdonald, 1947), pp. 173-198.

Llewelyn Powys belonged to one of the most distinguished families in modern literature. Among his brothers were the novelists John Cowper Powys (1872-1963) and Theodore Francis Powys (1875-1953), and there is little question that Llewelyn is third in importance to these. While he is thus sometimes overshadowed, he also benefits from light reflected. The reviving and continuing interest in the work of his brothers has led to the reprinting in recent years of some of Llewelyn's books, although the books favored tend to be memoirs and autobiographical reminiscences, those that illuminate the brothers and the family background rather than those that do the most justice to Llewelyn. Even putting aside the particular problem of Llewelyn's context in his family, it is hard to gain a reliable impression of the entire body of his writing. As the author of essays (descriptive, literary, historical, and philosophical), a biography, a novel, travel books, works of popular philosophy and propaganda, autobiographical memoirs, and "an imaginary autobiography," Llewelyn Powys can be classified only as a "miscellaneous writer." The paucity of our equipment for evaluating nonfictional prose is a further obstacle to the appreciation of his work.

Powys was the fifth son and eighth of eleven children born to Rev. Charles Francis Powys and Mary Cowper Powys. One year after his birth, in Dorchester, Dorset (Thomas Hardy's "Casterbridge"), the family moved to the village of Montacute in Somerset, where C. F. Powys was to be rector for the next thirty-three years. In Llewelyn's childhood he absorbed the landscape of Montacute and its surroundings, and writing in later years, whether about Africa, Switzerland, or America, he constantly returned, as to a touchstone, to the Somerset countryside as a source of analogy and comparison. A conventional middle-class education at Sherborne, endured without distinction, and at Cambridge, from which Powys barely graduated in 1906, was followed by a series of unsatisfactory appointments as schoolteacher, private tutor, and for a short time, with his brother John's help, as lecturer in the United States. In 1909 occurred the event that was to condition and give shape to his life. Powys was twenty-five years old when he learned he had consumption; with death imminent the remaining thirty years of his life were to have an urgency and an energy that contrast sharply with the lax leisureliness of his youth. From the fall of 1909 to the spring of 1911 Powys was in a sanatorium at Davos in Switzerland. There his health improved, but his recovery was never to be more than provisional.

In 1914 it was thought that the altitude and climate of Kenya, where his brother William had a farm, would be beneficial to Powys's health. World War I broke out shortly after his arrival, and William was called up for military service, leaving Powys with the responsibility of running a farm of three hundred thousand acres and fourteen thousand sheep. This job Powys successfully discharged for the duration of the war; his tuberculosis was in abeyance, and one might wonder why he chose to leave Kenya in 1919. England still offered him no direction or vocation, and John Cowper once more arranged for Powys, after a period of depression, to move to America. This time he came not as a lecturer but as an aspiring writer.

In the ten years from 1909 to 1919 Llewelyn had undergone experiences and acquired materials that were a writer's gift. He had written some stories between 1912 and 1914 that were to be included in his first book, *Ebony and Ivory* (1923). Llewelyn's first publication in book form, however, was his part of *Confessions of Two Brothers*, written with John and published in 1916. The idea had been John's and it was meant to give help and encouragement to Powys. The latter, fully occupied with the farm in Kenya, did not have the time to take proper advantage of the opportunity. His eighty pages consist of dia-

The Powys family: front row, Llewelyn, William, and Lucy; middle row, Philippa, Littleton, Mary Cowper Powys, Margaret (Mrs. John Cowper Powys), and Gertrude; back row, Marion, Albert, Rev. Charles Francis Powys, John, and Theodore (Collection of the Powys family)

The Powys brothers, circa 1901: John, Littleton, Theodore, Albert, Llewelyn, and William (Collection of Isobel Powys Marks)

Powys as a student at Cambridge (Collection of E. E. Bissell)

ries and memoirs, hastily put together; they provide a chronological summary of his life so far, the raw material, as it were, of much of his later writings.

Between August 1920, when he moved to America, and May 1925, when he returned to England, Powys published six books. In addition he made uncounted contributions to many of the most distinguished newspapers and magazines in the United States and enjoyed literary success and fame that were the envy, and the humiliation, of his brothers. Powys's achievement is the more remarkable in that he had tried to publish essays and stories in British journals with scant success. Powys had to travel, not only for the experiences that would go into his books, but for the audience that would appreciate them.

Ebony and Ivory contrasts life in Europe with life in Africa. It combines some of the essays and stories written before he went to Kenya with what he had written about Kenya since 1919 that had already been well received in magazines. The title thus makes a thematic point of biographical contingency. Some structural cohesion is achieved through the uniformity of human behavior in Europe and Africa and through the contrast in philosophical outlooks. "Rubbish" is characteristic of the "Ebony" section and describes a white settler's attitude toward a dead, black, "human-shaped body." Powys's polemic against Christianity and all forms of metaphysical and spiritual faith is rhetorically grounded in his experience of Africa: "In our cities, in our country places, we have created a sweet and wistful atmosphere, heavy with intimations of immortality. . . . To look for a meaning, a purpose in life, out here in Africa . . . appears foolish." Then, in the "Ivory" section, set in England (and, in "Not Guilty," in Switzerland), the same harshness of human relations is presented. The most remarkable story, "Un Mufle," concerns the abuse of a deaf-mute; originally entitled "The Snouted Pig," it exemplifies, by repetitions and echoes from "Ebony," the bestiality of human motives in Europe as in Africa. Reviewers were quick to reach for comparisons with Joseph Conrad.

Powys's success can be somewhat measured by the names of well-known writers who wrote prefaces for him: *Ebony and Ivory* was introduced by Theodore Dreiser, and *Thirteen Worthies*, published a few months later in 1923, bears a preface by Van Wyck Brooks. The latter gathers thirteen essays on writers and "characters," mostly English, from Chaucer to Hardy. Biographical summaries and appreciations were the staple fare of such magazines as the *Freeman*, the *Forum*, and the *North American Review* in which Powys's thirteen essays were first published. What distinction the essays possess inheres as much in Powys's selection of subjects as in his style. Brooks directs the reader's attention to the essays on John Culpeper and Thomas Coryat with whom "most readers will make their first acquaintance in the savoury pages of this little book." Of the essays on Izaak Walton, John Bunyan, Christopher Marlowe, and others, Brooks makes only the fair and modest claim that they "are certain to revive in many a mind many an old affection." To a large extent Powys was providing the papers with the essays their readers wanted, and in this he was successful. One of the essays, however, that on Thomas Urquhart, had been printed in one of the most distinguished literary periodicals of the twentieth century. The issue of the *Dial* immediately following that in which the Urquhart essay appeared contains a now well-known poem by T. S. Eliot. Powys's essays on Michel de Montaigne, Urquhart, Coryat and others display something of

Powys in Africa, 1915

his partiality for the humanists of the Renaissance. From this book onward Powys's ideal is clarified as a blend of humanist sophistication and uninhibited sensual earthiness.

The year 1924 saw the publication of three books by Powys. The first was *Black Laughter*, a collection of further African essays, most of which had been printed in the *New York Evening Post* over the previous four years. Published in June 1924 and reprinted in July and September and frequently thereafter, *Black Laughter* was the book by which Powys was to be best known in the United States. Its twenty-six essays are arranged in narrative fashion and can be read as chapters of a story. Powys had begun *Ebony and Ivory* by remarking that "It is not given to managers of sheepfarms to understand the Universe: the sheepcounts, the labour-books, the mixing of Cooper's dip, are matters far too engrossing." Unlike *Ebony and Ivory*, *Black Laughter* is content to present incidents and observations without philosophical commentary. The tone has a quality of documentary detachment, and the book is valuable as a record of the settler's Africa. *Black Laughter* is also Powys's least personal book; its "I" tells the reader little about Powys's family, health, childhood, memories of England, or philosophy. Like the other farm managers he does not presume to understand the Universe; he is, rather, a representative settler, though not as harsh and insensitive as some.

The other two books of 1924, *Honey and Gall* and *Cup-Bearers of Wine and Hellebore*, barely deserve the title "book." Each consists of sixty-four staple-bound pages, in the Little Blue Book series issued by the Haldemann-Julius Company of Girard, Kansas. Both are collections of Powys's journalism, and *Honey and Gall* is full of platitudes on "The Blessings of Longevity," "The Sense of Smell," and other trite topics. By contrast, *Cup-Bearers*, subtitled "A Book of Intellectual Rowdies," contains six fine essays on François Rabelais, Jonathan Swift, Matthew Prior, William Prior, William Cowper, James Thomson, and Padraic Colum and is a considerable improvement on *Thirteen Worthies*. For the first time in Powys's writing one finds the confidence that can afford to indulge in self-reflective wit. The pretentious and the precious–constant stylistic dangers for Powys–had been avoided or mitigated by the impersonality of *Black Laughter*. They can be more creatively subdued or subverted by parody. This sentence from *Cup-Bearers* about Prior's "wenching" is self-parody in both style and attitudes: "However much one may regret in his poems the presence of a certain note of hard artificial and insensitive cynicism, one cannot but accede that he is able in his own facile way better almost than any other English poet to indicate the unwisdom of putting too high a value upon the ungenerous temptation of inordinate chastity." By the piling up of double negatives, the journalist (paid by the word) also mocks a common temptation of his profession. The essay on Prior had been published in the *Dial* in September 1923. With that magazine Powys had a relationship personal as well as professional. In October 1924 he married its managing editor, Alyse Gregory, whom he had known since 1921. Gregory was herself a fine novelist and essayist and had considerable influence and connections in New York literary circles. The stylistic assurance and confident wit of Powys's writings from *Cup-Bearers* onwards presumably owe something to his marriage. Powys was personally fulfilled, and his writing had the benefit of Gregory's constant help and encouragement.

In a few weeks in the winter of 1924-1925 Powys wrote what is widely regarded as his finest book, *Skin for Skin* (1925). The epigraph, from the book of Job, contains the title: "And Satan answered the Lord and said, 'Skin for skin, yea, all that a man hath will he give for his life'. . . . And the Lord said unto Satan, 'Behold he is in thine hand; but save his life.'" When tuberculosis had

Alyse Gregory, Powys's wife, on their wedding day (Collection of Miss Rosemary Manning)

Skin for Skin takes the reader from the Montacute vicarage to "A White Palace," the sanatorium at Clavadel near Davos. Powys's fellow patients are vividly described; it is an enclosed world not surprisingly similar to that of Thomas Mann's almost exactly contemporary novel, *The Magic Mountain* (1924; translated, 1927). A knowing, rather than coincidental, literary parallel shapes the chapter devoted to Powys's amorous affairs within the sanatorium. The title "Virginibus Puerisque" is descriptive, if somewhat coyly so, and it is the title of Robert Louis Stevenson's collection of essays written in Davos in the 1880s. When Powys was young, Stevenson had been one of his favorite writers; now, as essayist, consumptive, and traveler, Powys acknowledged his inspiration. That it was at Davos that *Treasure Island* (1883) was finished was always a challenge to Powys.

In March 1911 Powys had returned to England, and its familiar sights and people in the exceptionally hot summer that followed are described under the new light of sickness and survival. It was the summer of the coronation of George V and the beginnings of "Georgian Poetry." Not being a poet, Powys was never included in Edward Marsh's anthologies, but one of Marsh's strongest supporters, J. C. Squire, was almost the only editor to show interest in Powys's writings before 1914. Had Powys shown in 1911 the stylistic strength that in 1925 he brought to the description of that summer, he would surely have found a place and a role in English literature. The might-have-been of Powys as a Georgian is an impossibility precisely because his inspiration needed more than the English countryside alone: illness and exile were the conditions of his literary maturity. *Skin for Skin* signals that maturity and describes its progress by making tensile the distance between the time in 1910 when Llewelyn came to the philosophical awareness that death is final—that impermanence is the nature of being and that every moment is sacred for itself—and the present, 1925, when in illness and exile expression has been found.

Powys's developed style is intensely, even awkwardly, personal and intimate. Its humor is often for initiates, and the initiates are those who know all about Powys, his brothers, and his "circle." By 1925 John and Theodore Powys had barely begun to be famous—they were then far more obscure than Llewelyn—and yet "my brother John" and "my brother Theodore" are presented to the reader as people with inherently

first struck, Powys had hoped and in his pagan way prayed that he might live to thirty. In 1925 he was again spitting blood, but he was not depressed or frustrated; he kept in mind that he was a successful writer, happily married, and forty. *Skin for Skin* is a celebration, an expression of gratitude to whatever power it was that had saved his life.

For its theme the book reverts to the onset of Powys's illness and presents a narrative of the period from November 1909 to March 1912. The brief text, 112 pages, is not continuous but divided into fifteen chapters. Heedless of editorial demands and constraints—for this was his first book not made of previously printed materials—Llewelyn elected to compose in units of less than two thousand words. This pattern is repeated in most of his other book-length "free compositions": having begun as a "writer for the newspapers" he was inclined to value the training rather than to resent the yoke.

Powys in the Rockies, 1924 (Collection of E. E. Bissell)

interesting attitudes and ideas. This is partly due to Powys's own self-regard and self-absorption, but it is more significantly due to his admiration for William Hazlitt. What John Cowper Powys (in his *Autobiography*, 1967) called Hazlitt's "peculiar kind of self-conscious egoism" is akin to what Louis Marlow Wilkinson (in *Welsh Ambassadors*, 1936) called Llewelyn's "peculiar and excessive subjectivity." Wilkinson writes of his "inevitable tendency to feel and to think of any new place in terms of places already familiar to him, already, indeed, part of him," and he records John's coinage, on vacation with Llewelyn (known in the family as "Lulu") in Venice in 1912: "How he begins, at once, to Luluize Venice!" As with Hazlitt's circle, if in a lesser way, fame caught up with intimacy: to readers of Theodore's *Mr. Weston's Good Wine* (1927) and John's *Wolf Solent* (1929), talk of "my brothers" seems far from precious or tiresomely egocentric.

"Luluizing" is a feature not only of Powys's descriptive writing but also of his polemics, of which *Skin for Skin* contains a measure. Back in England Powys sometimes attended church, and was

tempted by conventional religious belief: "Why should not I, also, become as a little child and go to Heaven along with the Master of Corpus?" This is Luluizing at its most arcane: the Master of Corpus Christi College, Cambridge, was Edward Pearce, a prominent churchman who was to be consecrated bishop in 1927. Pearce was also John Cowper Powys's brother-in-law, and a loftily disapproving one. The success of Llewelyn's style lies in its avoidance of both the irritatingly inaccessible and mere phrase-making. "Luluizing" combines the authenticity of personal experience with a generality of notation. "Master of Corpus" is suggestive and representative, as are the names of Somerset villages richly scattered through Powys's prose. To the general reader such names cannot be denotative, but their connotation lies in their very particularity.

Shortly after the writing of *Skin for Skin*, Powys decided to return to England; this was hardly wise for his own career, and in following her husband Alyse Gregory forsook the only world she knew and one in which she was most successfully established. Their motives are not clear.

Powys's next book, *The Verdict of Bridlegoose* (1926), is a memoir of his life in America. The manner and style resemble those of *Skin for Skin*, yet *The Verdict of Bridlegoose* is generally found to be an unattractive book and was certainly not appreciated in the United States. Its problem is a lack of privacy. The people of whom Powys writes are, or were then, so famous that descriptions of meetings and friendships with, among others, Dreiser, F. Scott Fitzgerald, Frank Harris, Amy Lowell, H. L. Mencken, Jules Romains, Bertrand Russell, Alfred Stieglitz, Rebecca West, and Edmund Wilson smack somewhat of display. Unfortunately a book's usefulness may be inversely related to its charm; *The Verdict of Bridlegoose* remains a valuable and neglected record of Greenwich Village in its heyday.

Having expressed his opinion of America, Powys seems to have had nothing more to write; in England he had no familiar publishers, editors, or readers whose demands could be satisfied. The need for money virtually compelled him to accept an unlikely commission, to write a volume in "The Golden Hind" series of great explorers. Powys was assigned Henry Hudson, whom he must have found congenial, for he carried out far more research than was expected or necessary for such a series. He spent some six weeks of 1926 in the British Museum, and the preface acknowledges help from Kenneth Burke and other friends in New York. The result is a strikingly good biography, and one concurs with the judgment of Powys's biographer, Malcolm Elwin, that its failure to gain critical attention and esteem "undoubtedly lost to English literature more than one biographical masterpiece." *Henry Hudson* (1927) is extremely readable, and it gives a hint of the wide and indeed uncharted range of Powys's literary and scholarly competence.

Powys's third return to England was no more successful than previous homecomings; in terms of his career as a writer England was exile. Without a following among the reading public and without regular work for the newspapers he was more than happy to accept a prestigious offer luring him back to the United States. He was appointed for six months as "Visiting Critic" on the *New York Herald-Tribune*, and from November 1927 to April 1928 he wrote weekly reviews, which have never been collected or reprinted. Or so, from the Powys literature and scholarship, one should suppose. Yet a detail concerning Powys as a book reviewer epitomizes the extraordinary hermeticism of his reputation. In 1924

Powys with Gamel Woolsey (Collection of E. E. Bissell)

Powys had written an essay in the *Dial* on *Harmonium* (1923) by Wallace Stevens. This essay, "The Thirteenth Way," has been reprinted in full at least twice in standard academic works on Stevens's reputation. It is thus today probably the most widely known of all Powys's writings.

When his stint as "Visiting Critic" was finished, Powys decided yet again to renounce a successful life in America in favor of Europe. The summer of 1928 was spent in France, where he wrote his only novel, *Apples Be Ripe* (1930), which can safely be described as his most dismal failure. Oddly enough, for one so vocally Epicurean, Powys seems to have been motivated by guilt. In August 1928 he wrote to John, "I wanted to write a novel, but I cannot, I cannot do it. Theodore [Powys] told Louis [Wilkinson] that there was always something wrong about writers who could not write about anything but themselves and lately I have felt he was right." "Excessive subjectivity" will always provide ground for hostility to the writings of Powys; even as *Apples Be Ripe* succumbs to the mawkishly autobiographical it witnesses to Powys's conscientious effort to write about something not himself.

This period of aimless wandering, false starts, and failure as a professional writer was ended in the fall of 1928 when Powys went to Palestine. Hitherto, his most successful work commercially had been *Black Laughter*, and that fact may have formed part of his motivation in finding another foreign land to describe. This time, however, it was writing itself, rather than reasons of health or employment, that was the purpose of traveling, and this destination was laden with polemical potential. In the words of one of Powys's most eminent admirers, the late Philip Larkin, Powys "travelled to the Holy Land to make sure there was nothing there" (*Observer Review*, 27 March 1983). In a visit of four weeks Powys found nothing to shake his materialist philosophy, but he did find enough material to make three books: *The Cradle of God* (1929), *The Pathetic Fallacy* (1930; also published as *An Hour on Christianity*), and *A Pagan's Pilgrimage* (1931).

The Cradle of God combines a few elements of the travel book with what is essentially a retelling of the Bible. Powys's intimate knowledge of the Bible, especially of the Old Testament, is owed to his upbringing in an evangelical parsonage; the book's strong but unobtrusive autobiographical thread is derived from the reader's awareness of the discord between Powys's familiarity with the Bible and his rejection of Christianity. The book's title does not refer merely to geography. In telling of Solomon and the building of the temple, Llewelyn describes the Ark of the Covenant as "of the size of a child's coffin, of a size of a god's cradle," and such symbolic and allusive ambivalence runs through the book. Most polemically, the "cradle" of God is the human and specifically the Jewish imagination: "The long travail, the long labour, of the Jews had brought to birth their incarnation." By thus sustaining the figure of the cradle Powys holds together the book's diverse components to create what might be considered his most intricate and artful work.

The literary success of *The Cradle of God* is of stylistic interest. John Cowper Powys read the

manuscript with much enthusiasm and had only one serious matter to amend, as he said in a 4 March 1929 letter: "I don't altogether like the division into short chapters. Somehow I should like it to flow straight on like a tidal wave mounting and mounting." This advice was heeded, and the book as published has a multitude of spacings and no chapter divisions at all. The two hundred pages indeed have momentum, a momentum the more remarkable, as John noted, for the familiarity of the story's outline. The strong movement draws the reader on to the devious culmination of the New Testament—a cradle that is also a coffin. Never again, perhaps, would Llewelyn Powys so successfully reconcile his bent for the essay with the demands of a book.

After *The Cradle of God*, *The Pathetic Fallacy* seems rather straightforward, even abrasively unsubtle. In one respect it is a sequel to the previous book, taking the story through the New Testament and the origins of the Christian Church. Powys aims not only to continue the story but also to conclude it: his final chapter is entitled "The Passing of Christianity." Once more, the telling more than compensates for the familiarity of the story. *The Pathetic Fallacy* contains mockery, not always savage, and much celebration. The developing doctrines of Christianity are juxtaposed with the unchanging and undogmatic joy of life itself. Powys does not pretend to be a philosopher but he presumes unashamedly to be a stylist. The book's closing sentence is exemplary: "A wise man can do no better than to turn from the churches and look up through the airy majesty of the wayside trees with exultation, with resignation, at the unconquerable, unimplicated sun."

These two books, especially the latter, alienated Powys from many admirers of his descriptive and noncontroversial writings. Rejected by those as conservative in their religion as in their literary taste, Powys was quickly adopted by the humanist and rationalist lobby. The latter, however, appreciated only a part of Powys's work, for they were far from sympathetic to the whimsy, nostalgia, and antitechnological bias of his descriptive writings. The reputation of Powys became needlessly bifurcated, and has never since been made whole. There has always been space for discussion, for even the most hostile clerical reviewers of these two books were ready to concede their historical accuracy. And in his praise of *The Cradle of God* John (as quoted by Elwin) gave expression to the paradox that vitalizes Llewelyn's writings while confounding his reputation: "It is poetical,

Powys in 1934

it is blasphemous, it is more religious than the vulgar can understand."

The third book to come out of the Palestinian journey was a conventional travel book. *The Pagan's Pilgrimage*, despite its title, is almost entirely free of controversy. In the preface, as if to reassure his loyal readers, Powys apologizes for "meddling with theological matters" in his two previous books: "In the present volume I am once more back on safe and familiar ground." That it was the third of these books to be written, separated by over a year from the time of traveling, suggests a measure of reluctance: *A Pagan's Pilgrimage* is "safe" in a negative sense and "familiar" to readers not so much of Powys as of mediocre travelogues.

In the summer of 1930 Powys embarked upon the presentation of what might be termed his affirmative polemic. Uneasy with his new reputation as a destroyer and mocker, Powys set himself to wide and intense reading "for my most important book which is to be a positive 'constructive' trumpet call to youth" (*Letters*, 1943). Astronomy, geology, archaeology, mythology, and philosophy are all touched on, with sensitive purpose, in *Impassioned Clay* (1931). Powys's intention, epitomized by the title, is to place humanity entirely within the frame of nature. Humanity is not thereby deprived of value but rather manifests its true values. The expectation of immortality dulls us to the immediate; the acceptance that all beings are transient heightens our awareness, quickens our appreciation. Powys often spoke of *Impassioned Clay* as his best book, and many readers have found it to be the most satisfactory and comprehensive statement of Powys's philosophy.

It is worth noting that the book falls into two parts, and it is the first part that is memorable. The first seventy-six pages (in the first edition) were written at Powys's home in Dorset in

Powys at Chydyok, Chaldon Herring, England, circa 1936.
He is holding an ankh, the Egyptian symbol of enduring life.
(Collection of E. E. Bissell)

the summer of 1930, and they contain many refreshing observations and generalizations based on the wide reading specially undertaken. The remaining forty-five pages were written in upstate New York in the fall of 1930, Powys and his wife, Alyse, having precipitously crossed the Atlantic in August. These later pages are simply polemical, giving little evidence of the quickened apprehension and vital particularity that had earlier been so moderately and persuasively advocated.

The sudden removal to the United States had much to do with a complicated and long-running affair between Powys and a minor poet, Gamel Woolsey. Powys was in a condition of helpless infatuation, exhibiting extraordinary indecisiveness and wishful thinking. Probably realizing that he would never leave Alyse, Gamel, who had been left in England, married Gerald Brenan. Powys's response to this decisive and solving deed was to suggest a *ménage à quatre*. The entire episode, pathetic in itself and acutely hurtful to

Alyse, is worthy of attention because it illuminates Powys's adolescent character. Insensitive in dealing with the situation, and fantastic in his proposed solutions, Powys was exclusively self-aware and self-serving. The great charm he had for women may indeed be grounded in his incapacity to imagine the plight of a woman in love with him. That would explain his inability to write a novel, and it makes some sense of the particularly tasteless ending of *Apples Be Ripe*: the hero loves diverse girls at diverse times, but his corpse wins the devotion of all of them at once.

In February 1931, shortly after Gamel's marriage to Brenan, Alyse distracted Powys by taking him to the West Indies. From this vacation came the fine essay "A Voyage to the West Indies," which was not printed until 1947 (in Elwin's *Pleasure Ground*). Almost immediately on arrival back in New York, in March 1931, the couple returned to England and poverty. To Powys's bitter disappointment, *Impassioned Clay* was to sell fewer than three hundred copies in England. In the questing and confusion of his personal life he lacked the determination of a professional writer. And so, as in 1926, when he had had to accept the commission for the Hudson biography, now in 1931, five years and five books later, he was forced to take on the almost menial task of abridging into one volume Andrew Clark's five-volume *The Life and Times of Anthony à Wood* (1932). Along with fifty pounds the task brought Powys a quite unlooked-for kind of respectability–a leading article in the *Times* and an invitation to a commemorative lunch at Merton College, Oxford. The latter occasioned one of Powys's best satirical essays, "Merton Wood's Luncheon" (in *Earth Memories*, 1934).

The amply documented seventeenth-century "character" Anthony à Wood occupied Powys for a few months only; the period and the personality were congenial but the task of mere abridgement was not. Powys at once resumed the theme and style of *Impassioned Clay* for two essays commissioned in America for publication in book form, with fine printing and wood engravings. *Now that the Gods Are Dead* (1932) and *Glory of Life* (1934), essentially summaries of *Impassioned Clay*, were published as collectors' items, a radical betrayal of their hortatory style and popular aim. Since Powys's death the value of these essays as brief introductions to his thinking has caused them to be frequently reprinted, without illustrations or embellishments.

When Powys left the United States in March 1931 it was to be for the last time. Until December 1936 he lived in Dorset and in those five years traveled very little and never out of England. It was by far the most settled period of his entire adult life and one of the most productive. With the exception of one large project, Powys confined his ambition to essays and wrote sufficiently to fill five volumes. These reflect the division of his reputation even in their titles, for on the one side are *Earth Memories, Dorset Essays* (1935), and *Somerset Essays* (1937), on the other, *Damnable Opinions* (1935) and *Rats in the Sacristy* (1937).

The two latter collections were issued by Watts & Company, a controversial publisher of rationalist and atheist works. With their aggressive and rather uncharacteristic titles the books appealed to radicals, the disaffected, and the disenchanted. A sympathetic reviewer (quoted by Elwin) praised Powys by appropriating him: "To Rationalists everywhere he is a proud possession." Both volumes were a success in England, *Damnable Opinions* selling two thousand copies within weeks of publication; but neither volume found a publisher in the United States.

Damnable Opinions contains fifteen essays on topics mainly philosophical and religious, with Powys's own views being advanced in "The Epicurean Tradition." In this book more than in any other Powys addresses contemporary problems in contemporary terms, with citation of such modern thinkers as Friedrich Nietzsche, all tending toward Powys's conclusion that "the hope of the human race rests at present with science." Such fashionable shallowness is the product of Powys's unwilling confrontation of modern problems. In the intended application of Powys's ideas one sees their lamentable limitations. An essay called "The Aryan Way"—on a concept of which Powys fundamentally disapproved—finds nothing good to say of "the present politicians of Germany" *except* that they "intend to inaugurate a form of sterilization for imbeciles and syphilitics and other unfit persons." The madness of rationalism is forcefully, and quite unwittingly, expressed in the following: "Men of science should compete in devising plans for the eradication of wretchedness.... Under medical care painless infanticide should be legalized in every land. The populations of the earth should be controlled so that they coincide with the amount of food, clothing and shelter available.... It is barbarous and grossly ignorant to leave such matters to chance.

There should be enormous state departments full of calculating statisticians." Some wishes, alas, are fulfilled, and some opinions are more damnable than they know.

Rats in the Sacristy is a much more appealing and satisfying book. Its fourteen essays may represent the height of Powys's achievement in the biographical essay. His subjects range from Confucius and Lucretius to Rabelais and Thomas Hobbes; the book's quality may depend on its avoidance of anything of more immediacy and present relevance than the seventeenth century. The essays combine biographical summary with polemical interpretation, and the polemic remains fresh. Powys's defences of Julian the Apostate and of Machiavelli are noteworthy for their blend of provocation and good sense; throughout, the style contrives to be both quaint and whimsical, in the familiar manner, and sparklingly tendentious.

Simultaneously with the writing of the essays that fill these controversial volumes, Powys was turning out charming pieces for local and national newspapers, on country life and on the local lore and history of Somerset and Dorset. For these, among his best writings, Powys's old admirers were generally prepared to forgive him everything else. In "Out of the Past" and "On the Other Side of the Quantocks," from *Earth Memories*, Powys is most successful in contriving an essay out of an anecdote. *Dorset Essays* and *Somerset Essays* are, simply, among the best examples of local and rural writing in this century. Their distinction, that which often has them shelved in second-hand bookshops as literature rather than local history, lies as much in Powys's presented personality as in his style. One can speak of the division in Powys's readership and reputation; one hesitates to attribute any kind of deliberate strategy to Powys. His thoughts, however obliquely or subtly they may be presented, or even occluded, prevent the essays from being read in the mere indulgence of charm and nostalgia. From *Dorset Essays*, "Joseph Arch," "Dorchester Characters," and "A Rector of Durweston," and, from *Somerset Essays*, "Athelney," "Nancy Cooper," and "A Bronze Age Valley" are palpably more than merely descriptive or merely evocative.

This productive period, in which the bifurcation of Powys's reputation had been consolidated, ended in the autumn of 1936 with the relapse of his health. On 2 December he left England for the last time and returned to Davos, where he was to die exactly three years later. In those

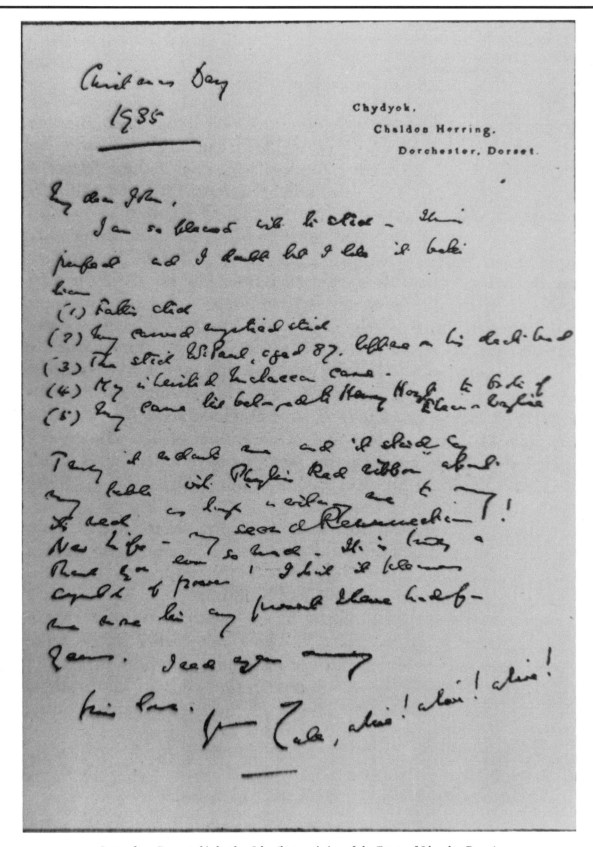

Letter from Powys to his brother John (by permission of the Estate of Llewelyn Powys)

Llewelyn Powys

fictionalized form, the story of a love affair of Powys in 1907, as remembered and recounted thirty years later. The heroine, Dittany Stone, is based at least as much on Gamel Woolsey as on any earlier lover, and it is part of the fiction to present the events of 1930 as those of 1907. It is easy to spot the inconsistencies. But *Love and Death* is not to be read as a roman à clef. As its themes, in addition to those indicated by the title, include memory and desire, the reader may take the shifting of dates, and indeed the very procedure of "fictionalizing" as not a hiding of the "facts" but a function of the text. To judge *Love and Death* poor as a novel is to miss the point; Powys knew from *Apples Be Ripe* how bad a novel he could write. *Love and Death* is, formally, a much more complicated and sophisticated book than has generally been recognized.

If, at the time of its publication, *Love and Death* gave entire satisfaction to neither side among Powys's following, the book can today epitomize the problem of his critical reputation. *Love and Death* is not a novel, nor a memoir, nor an autobiography, nor an essay. And if it were an essay, that might not be of any avail. The modern mode of criticism recognizes only the conventional genres and has neither the vocabulary nor the concepts for anything different. Criticism is impoverished as long as it has no power to speak of *Skin for Skin, The Cradle of God, Love and Death,* or the personal (and idiosyncratic) essay. Criticism is far more seriously impoverished by its silence concerning those "miscellaneous writers" of the sixteenth and seventeenth centuries who were Llewelyn Powys's abiding inspiration and enthusiasm.

Letters:

The Letters of Llewelyn Powys, edited by Louis Wilkinson (London: Lane, 1943);

So Wild a Thing: Letters to Gamel Woolsey, edited by Malcolm Elwin (Dulverton, Somerset: Ark, 1973).

Bibliography:

Malcolm Elwin, "List of Books by Llewelyn Powys," in his *The Life of Llewelyn Powys* (London: Lane, Bodley Head, 1946), pp. 282-283.

Biographies:

Louis Marlow [Wilkinson], *Welsh Ambassadors: Powys Lives and Letters* (London: Chapman & Hall, 1936);

three years he wrote the essays that were to be published posthumously as *Swiss Essays* (1947) and brought to completion *Love and Death* (1939), the "imaginary autobiography" on which he had been working since 1933. These two books display an extraordinary ease, almost a relaxation of style, an unhurried attention to the Swiss present and the English past, which is poignantly and explicitly juxtaposed with the imminence of death.

Love and Death was finally considered by Powys to be his best work; but it has most sharply divided his readers. It appears to tell, in

Malcolm Elwin, *The Life of Llewelyn Powys* (London: Lane, Bodley Head, 1946);

Kenneth Hopkins, *The Powys Brothers: A Biographical Appreciation* (London: Phoenix House, 1967);

Richard Perceval Graves, *The Brothers Powys* (London: Routledge & Kegan Paul, 1983).

References:

Gerald Brenan, *Personal Record 1920-1972* (London: Cape, 1974);

Peter Foss, "Llewelyn Powys: The Heart of Darkness," *Powys Review*, 9 (1982): 44-56;

Alyse Gregory, *The Cry of a Gull: Journals 1923-1948*, edited by Michael Adam (Dulverton, Somerset: Ark, 1973);

Kenneth Hopkins, *Llewelyn Powys* (London: Enitharmon, 1979);

Belinda Humfrey, ed., *Recollections of the Powys Brothers* (London: Owen, 1980);

Philip Larkin, Introduction to *Earth Memories* (Bristol: Redcliffe, 1983), pp. 1-6;

Larkin, "The Powys Pantomime," *Observer Review*, 27 March 1983, p. 32;

Charles Lock, "Confessions of Two Brothers," *Powys Review*, 12 (1983): 49-58;

Rosemary Manning, "Alyse Gregory: A Biographical Sketch Based on Her Published and Private Writings," *Powys Review*, 3 (1978): 80-98;

John Cowper Powys, *Autobiography* (London: Macdonald, 1967);

Powys, *Letters to His Brother Llewelyn*, edited by Malcolm Elwin, 2 volumes (London: Village, 1975);

Powys, *Letters to Louis Wilkinson 1935-56* (London: Macdonald, 1958);

Littleton Powys, *The Joy of It* (London: Chapman & Hall, 1937);

Richard Heron Ward, *The Powys Brothers* (London: Lane, Bodley Head, 1935);

Gamel Woolsey, "Letters to Alyse Gregory, 1930-1957," edited by Kenneth Hopkins, *Powys Review*, 8 (1981): 68-78;

Woolsey, *Letters to Llewelyn Powys, 1930-1939*, edited by Hopkins (North Walsham, Norfolk: Warren House, 1983).

Papers:

The largest collections of Powys's papers are in the Everett Needham Case Library, Colgate University, Hamilton, New York; and in the Humanities Research Center, University of Texas at Austin.

Dixon Scott
(July 1881 - 23 October 1915)

Peter Hinchcliffe
University of St. Jerome's College

BOOKS: *Liverpool* (London: Black, 1907);

Art and Democracy (London: Black, n.d.);

Stratford-on-Avon with Leamington and Warwick (London: Black, 1911);

Men of Letters, edited by A. St. John Adcock (London & New York: Hodder & Stoughton, 1916; enlarged edition, London: Hodder & Stoughton, 1923; New York: Doran, 1923);

A Number of Things, edited by Bertram Smith (London & Edinburgh: Foulis, 1917).

OTHER: "Colour Photography," in *Colour Photography and Other Recent Developments of the Art of the Camera*, edited by Charles Holme (London, Paris & New York: The Studio, 1908).

When one thinks of the effects of World War I upon English literary culture one recalls the young war poets, who were forced into a sudden flowering and then cut off in their prime. But there was another group of English writers, rather older, whose deaths in the war curtailed careers that had already begun to take shape— writers such as the novelist Saki (H. H. Munro) and the poet Edward Thomas. Among this group was the critic Dixon Scott, whose writing provides a lively record of literary opinion in the decade immediately preceding the war and whose best essays are truly prophetic of how later generations would judge the Edwardian and Georgian writers.

Walter Dixon Scott was born in a suburb of Liverpool in July 1881 (exact day unknown), the son of John Scott, a marine engineer with the Cunard Steamship Company, and Margaret (Dixon) Scott. (His father's family was connected with the famous novelist, hence the "Walter.") Scott was educated at local schools, took a commercial course at the Liverpool Institute, and at the age of sixteen became a clerk in the City and Midland Bank, a job he hated, though by all accounts he was good at it.

While still working in the bank, Scott began to contribute book reviews and short essays to the *Liverpool Courier*. At the end of 1906, when he was twenty-five, Scott determined to leave the bank and make his living by journalism. For the next eight years (except for 1908-1909, when he attended the University of Liverpool on a special scholarship arranged for him by Prof. Oliver Elton), Scott made a precarious living as a stringer for various newspapers and magazines: the *Liverpool Courier*, the *Manchester Guardian*, the *Bookman*, and *Country Life*. He also did a few short pieces on commission, such as the little books on Liverpool (1907) and Stratford (1911), and the 1908 articles on color photography. Unlike most aspiring British journalists who have been drawn to London, Scott believed that a provincial or rural perspective was necessary for his kind of writing, so he continued to live in Liverpool, or with his parents, who had retired to Marston Trussell, a village in Northamptonshire.

Throughout these years Scott suffered constant ill health that was probably psychosomatic in origin. His letters recount episodes of emotional depression and of chronic gastric problems that could not be relieved even by surgery. In ways that he half recognized, illness was related to his painful slowness in finding the direction that his talent should go. The years 1910 and 1911 seem to have been crucial to him. His illness reached its worst, and he decided to turn from the familiar essays with which he had begun to make a reputation to critical studies of living writers. From then on he devoted most of his effort to a series of brilliant review articles, mostly in the *Manchester Guardian* and the *Bookman*. Scott's work attracted the attention of editors and authors, Max Beerbohm and Henry James among them, and he seemed poised for a real breakthrough in his work when the war broke out.

By October 1914 he was commissioned into the 3rd West Lancashire Brigade of the Royal Field Artillery. Though only a lieutenant, he served as brigade quartermaster, arranging for all supplies and equipment. His depression lifted,

Dixon Scott (photograph by Gooch)

he became physically robust, and Scott's year in the army was probably the happiest of his life. In the fall of 1915 Scott's brigade was sent to Gallipoli to join the Dardanelles campaign. Not even his improved health was proof against that notoriously unhealthy region. Within a week of his arrival, Scott was stricken with dysentery, and two weeks later he was dead at the age of thirty-four.

After his death Scott's friends arranged to publish selections from his work. *Men of Letters*, nineteen literary studies, was published in 1916. (Six of them were revised by Scott before his death, for this was a book that he had planned.) *A Number of Things*, twenty familiar essays, all but one reprinted from newspapers or from *Country Life*, appeared the following year. Mary McCrossan, the British painter and one of Scott's oldest friends, edited a selection of his letters and notebooks in 1932.

Scott's writing is marked by extraordinary verve. A friend remarked that he had "a fine imagination, which made him see all the pinks scarlet and all the greys black." Alliteration, rising and

falling cadences, puns, paradoxes, and, above all, metaphors are heaped up in Scott's familiar essays. His essay on color photography escapes from technicalities by describing the autochrome process as the barb that tips the photographer's spear, and color picture taking itself becomes a battle to capture light. In his book on Liverpool, Scott compares civic architecture to an alphabet of different typefaces in which the city confesses different "types" of commercial and aesthetic interests. The influence of G. K. Chesterton, one of Scott's heroes, is obvious in his writing, and like Chesterton and Robert Louis Stevenson (another literary hero), Scott was concerned to create a sense of romance in twentieth-century life. Unlike those writers, however, Scott insisted upon the power and validity of purely modern experience, as his essay "A Fragment" (from *A Number of Things*) makes clear: "The village that offered you a spick-and-span picture-palace instead of the parapeted bridge of your dreams ought to have delighted you, not reduced you to disgust. It ought to have reminded you of the fact that you were seeing something R. L. S. never saw. . . . "

"I don't want to write English Essays," Scott said in one of his letters of 1911. One should not exaggerate the change that his writing underwent; the paradoxes and metaphors remain, but there is a more serious intent to the literary studies that he wrote during his last three years as a critic. Of the nineteen pieces collected in *Men of Letters*, eleven are reviews, often of minor books, such as would be sent out to a junior stringer–Arnold Bennett's *The Card* (1912), H. G. Wells's *Marriage* (1912), and Henry James's autobiographies. All the essays demonstrate an encyclopedic knowledge of the authors' work, so that each is a magisterial and enthusiastic survey of a literary career. Some of Scott's subjects, such as the playwright Stanley Houghton and the journalist Robertson Nicoll, are of interest mostly to literary historians, but those who turn to *Men of Letters* will find these figures placed in the context of their time and discussed with passionate interest.

Like all criticism of this period, the essays are "impressionistic," but Scott's impressions are incisive because he concentrates upon the prose style of each of his writers. No one has ever described the mechanical brilliance of Rudyard Kipling's prose in a sharper phrase than Scott: "a prodigious mental capacity . . . for stamping insubstantial dream-stuff into shapes as clear-cut and decisive as newly milled and minted metal discs."

Several of these essays advance a paradoxical argument, as their titles indicate: "The Innocence of Bernard Shaw," "The Meekness of Mr. Rudyard Kipling," "The Guilt of Mr. Chesterton," and so on. Sometimes Scott's approach is

merely whimsical. Arthur Waugh, reviewing *Men of Letters*, wrote, "He attacks themes already rather threadbare; and the natural temptation is to adopt a point of view that shall be startling at the outset." However, several of Scott's judgments make more sense now than they did seventy years ago. Biographies of Kipling have shown that he was indeed a shy man who hid his vulnerability behind a brazen mask, and Shaw's plays from *St. Joan* (1924) onward give credence to Scott's intuitive guess that their author was a romantic at the mercy of a sophisticated world. Incidental insights on Chesterton's narratives as pantomime and on James as a writer of ghost stories are still fresh and useful three generations later.

Beyond these specific virtues Dixon Scott offers the modern reader a generosity of intention that has rarely been matched by any journalist. Near the end of his essay on Granville Barker, Scott wrote, "I said, when we started out, that one of the chief joys of criticism was the joy of detection. There is only one other as great–that of indulging in praise. But when the first pleasure leads you at last imperatively to the second–what extraordinary happiness your craft brings you then!"

References:

Lascelles Abercrombie, Preface to *The Letters of W. Dixon Scott*, edited by Mary McCrossan (London: Joseph, 1932);

Max Beerbohm, Introduction to Scott's *Men of Letters* (London: Hodder & Stoughton, 1916);

Arthur Waugh, "Dixon Scott's Criticism," in his *Tradition and Change* (London: Chapman & Hall, 1919), pp. 253-260.

Logan Pearsall Smith

(18 October 1865 - 2 March 1946)

Kathryn Chittick
Trent University

BOOKS: *The Youth of Parnassus, and Other Stories* (London & New York: Macmillan, 1895);

Trivia (London: Chiswick, 1902; Garden City, N.Y.: Doubleday, Page, 1917);

The Life and Letters of Sir Henry Wotton, 2 volumes (Oxford: Clarendon, 1907);

Songs and Sonnets (London: Mathews, 1909);

The English Language (London: Williams & Norgate, 1912; New York: Holt, 1912);

Stories from the Old Testament. Retold by Logan P. Smith (Richmond, U.K.: Hogarth, 1920);

More Trivia (New York: Harcourt, Brace, 1921; London: Constable, 1922);

English Idioms (Oxford: Clarendon, 1923);

Four Words: Romantic, Originality, Creative, Genius (Oxford: Clarendon, 1924);

Words and Idioms (London: Constable, 1925; Boston: Houghton Mifflin, 1925);

The Prospects of Literature (London: Woolf, 1927);

Needed Words (Oxford: Clarendon, 1928);

Afterthoughts (London: Constable, 1931; New York: Harcourt, Brace, 1931);

Robert Bridges: Recollections (Oxford: Clarendon, 1931);

Last Words (London: Constable, 1933);

On Reading Shakespeare (London: Constable, 1933; New York: Harcourt, Brace, 1933);

Fine Writing (Oxford: Clarendon, 1936);

Reperusals and Re-collections (London: Constable, 1936; New York: Harcourt, Brace, 1937);

Unforgotten Years (Boston: Little, Brown, 1938; London: Constable, 1938);

Milton and His Modern Critics (London: Oxford University Press, 1940; Boston: Little, Brown, 1941);

Saved from Salvage (Edinburgh: Tragara, 1982).

Collection: *All Trivia* (London: Constable, 1933; New York: Harcourt, Brace, 1934)–comprises *Trivia, More Trivia, Afterthoughts*, and *Last Words.*

OTHER: *The Golden Urn*, edited by Smith and Bernard Berenson (Fiesole, Italy: Privately printed, 1897);

Logan Pearsall Smith, circa 1931 (Collection of Barbara Strachey)

Donne's Sermons: Selected Passages, edited, with an introduction, by Smith (Oxford: Clarendon, 1919);

A Treasury of English Prose, edited by Smith (London: Constable, 1919; Boston & New York: Houghton Mifflin, 1920);

Little Essays Drawn from the Writings of George Santayana, edited by Smith (New York: Scribners, 1920);

A Treasury of English Aphorisms, edited by Smith (London: Constable, 1928; Boston & New York: Houghton Mifflin, 1928);

The Golden Grove: Selected Passages from the Sermons and Writings of Jeremy Taylor, edited by Smith (Oxford: Clarendon, 1930);

Preface to *Words and Days: A Table-Book of Prose and Verse*, compiled by Bowyer Nichols (London: Oxford University Press, 1941);

A Religious Rebel: the Letters of "H. W. S." [Smith's mother], edited by Smith (London: Nisbet, 1949);

The Golden Shakespeare, compiled by Smith (New York: Macmillan, 1950).

Among the more arcane prose stylists of England in the twentieth century must be counted a naturalized American born in Millville, New Jersey, in 1865. Logan Pearsall Smith is most safely described as an essayist and critic, though his work is not easily classified. His best-known volume, *Trivia*, was published in 1902 and is made up of short, poemlike prose fragments. His work typically consists of epigrams: he was said to be the man who rediscovered the paragraph.

Smith's Edwardian aura of leisured amateurism may be explained partly by the fact that he never worked for his living as a writer. He subsisted on an independent though not lavish income inherited from his wealthy parents, Robert Pearsall Smith and Hannah Whitall Smith. In some ways Logan Pearsall Smith's reputation as a writer is slighter than that of his mother, who was a notable figure in the revival and temperance movements and who wrote such books as *The Christian's Secret of a Happy Life* (1875), *Everyday Religion* (1893), and *The Unselfishness of God* (1903). She and her husband, both from old Philadelphia Quaker families, eventually devoted themselves to evangelical pursuits, and this led them to England in 1873 and again in 1888, after which they stayed on permanently. Their circle of family and friends in America and England was a notable one. As a child in Philadelphia, Smith grew up in a home visited by such people as Walt Whitman and William James; he had a cousin who was president of Bryn Mawr, one sister who married Bernard Berenson, and another who was the first wife of Bertrand Russell. During the family's evangelical tours of England in the 1870s, they were welcomed as guests at Broadlands and other stately homes for months at a time.

Back in America as an adolescent, Smith attended Haverford College (a Quaker school) and Harvard before going to New York to work for a year in the family bottle-manufacturing firm.

Smith in 1874, age nine (Collection of Barbara Strachey)

Against his father's wishes, he then followed his family's example and, at the age of twenty-three, sailed to England, where he entered Balliol College, Oxford. He settled in England from this time and lived on a sum of twenty-five thousand dollars set aside for him by his father. At Oxford he studied under Benjamin Jowett but found his inspiration in Walter Pater. Smith seems to have been no more covetous of an academic reputation than he had been of a commercial one; instead he spent his time at Oxford shaping the modest life of letters that he was to lead thereafter. The example of Pater's life encouraged Smith in his authorial ambitions and in "the hope that somewhere, somehow, I might possibly create for myself the talent necessary for my purpose" (*Unforgotten Years*, 1938). Smith maintained that what Pater had was not genius but "perfected talent." The essential feature of Pater's work as Smith adopted it for his own purposes was the infinite pain taken with the craftsmanship of writing, and in particular, with prose.

In the perfecting of prose, Smith found his vocation and creed. Prose was not to be thought of as a mere workaday conveyance for ideas or a handmaiden to poetry: "to limit prose to mere lucidity was no more than a narrow and puritanical restriction. It was and could be . . . an instrument of many stops, musical, picturesque, intimate, and fervid; and thus conceived, it was the appropriate and most promising medium for the rendering of modern life" (*Unforgotten Years*).

Smith did not spurn poetry, though; Baudelaire, as much as Pater, provided inspiration at this time, and Smith's religiously articulated mission was to see the poetic possibilities of prose as it described modern life. It came to him that such prose should be written in verselike fragments, and his reading of Baudelaire led him to pursue suppleness as a shaping analogy for his own art: "it occurred to me that the separate page or paragraph of prose had not been adequately exploited. Every aspect of existence I believed could find its best expression in some special literary form. But in the experience of each of us were there not moods, brief impressions, and modern ways of feeling for which no exactly appropriate way of expression was at hand?" (*Unforgotten Years*).

This conception of prose goes back fundamentally to Smith's notion of "the oddity of existence." His prevailing literary and moral mood seems to be one of irony, for he is always sensitive to the gap between the individual and the cosmos, and to "the fact that, as Plato hinted, this universe is not one which should be taken too seriously, or that our personal affairs were not worthy of the care and anxiety that the ignominy of our existence forced us to bestow upon them" (*Unforgotten Years*). To catch glimpses of the universe's "grotesque" meaning and write these down as the quintessential expression of human life became the business of Smith's life. It may be that his perception of man's pathetic self-importance and the universe's grinning irony is simply a metaphysical characterization of the life he led at Oxford, the "dream-like quality of life, which grows as one spends one day after another by oneself" (*Unforgotten Years*). The keen responsiveness to the minutiae of existence when lived alone is reflected in the lyric quality of his prose aperçus. Smith was convinced that although solitude led to melancholy, "to taste life & its significance one must be alone" (*A Chime of Words: The Letters of Logan Pearsall Smith*, 1984).

This studentship of emotions continued for the rest of Smith's life. He received his B.A. in 1893, and an M.A. in 1906, but degrees seem to have been beside the point. The pattern of his life had been set. Like his friend and mentor Henry James, Smith never married, and found his tenderest companionship in the company of young men. In terms of so-called events, the recounting of his life will always seem dull; one must turn to his writing about the "trivial" life to feel what were dramatic modes of existence for him.

After Oxford, Smith went to Paris, quite self-consciously in the footsteps of James, and at age thirty produced a book of short stories, *The Youth of Parnassus, and Other Stories* (1895). The experience confirmed in him the taste for "the ecstasy and exasperation of the art of writing" and brought him appreciative words from Robert Bridges and Henry James. Other notables, such as Matthew Arnold, Edmund Gosse, Alfred North Whitehead, Gertrude Stein, and Edith Wharton, became his friends.

In 1902 he published *Trivia*. This he called in retrospect "the center and secret of my life." For all that Smith may have put in an apprenticeship after James's example, his own works were very far from being anything like the Richardsonian narratives of feeling that James had produced at the same age. *Trivia*'s discrete essays often take up less than a page in a very slight volume and are more properly called aphorisms. Smith seems to have had no special feeling for narrative, and a comparison of his writing to most imaginative prose would be misleading: in everything except line stops, it resembles verse. *Trivia* is to be dipped into rather than read straight through, and it sets the characteristic pattern for Smith's achievement as a writer.

Smith's work found its readers and reputation only gradually. Doubleday, Page waited fifteen years before publishing *Trivia* in America in 1917. Other volumes–*More Trivia* (1921), *Afterthoughts* (1931), and *Last Words* (1933)–followed; in 1933 they were published in one volume called *All Trivia*, and this was reprinted at least ten times during the last thirty years of Smith's long life.

His life, nonetheless, did not consist of a single book's work endlessly rewritten. Although he generally mocked scholarship as pedantry, he once wrote of its attractions, "There is pleasure in it like I imagine the pleasure of needlework–it fills the time, gives me a sense of work, and does

Smith as a young man (Collection of Barbara and Christopher Strachey)

not tax the brain". His labors in the library produced biography and criticism: *The Life and Letters of Sir Henry Wotton* (1907), *Songs and Sonnets* (1909), *The English Language* (1912), *Words and Idioms* (1925), *On Reading Shakespeare* (1933), and *Milton and His Modern Critics* (1940). These critical works give the impression more of an avid reader than of a scholar and have no more than the usual belletristic rigor of their age. They are a record of Smith's reading, while *Trivia* is a chart of his emotional life. He was fond of anthologies–one might say he had an anthologizing turn of mind–and published several. His first was *The Golden Urn* (1897), printed privately with the Berensons in Italy, containing a list of the "best" Italian pictures in galleries and collections, and the "best" lines from William Shakespeare, John Milton, and John Keats.

Smith's work seems to straddle the line between charm and pretension, and he was aware of the precariousness of this balance. He claimed no genius or originality, only devotion. When his reminiscences of his life appeared, first in the *At-*

lantic Monthly from July 1937 to August 1938, and then were expanded into the autobiography *Unforgotten Years*, they brought his earlier works to an attention they had not originally had. However, he maintained the graceful irony about himself that had supported his lean years: "To have written a best seller is a cloud on my declining years, but a cloud which has a silver, or rather a golden, lining which helps me bear the disgrace."

Smith enjoyed good health until old age, when he used to go underground Persephone-like, as he said, during the winter, only returning to an outdoor life when spring came. The bombing of London, where he remained during the blitz, caused him to become more bedridden in the last years of his life. An essential part of his oeuvre in his later years consists of his letters, especially to the young disciples who enjoyed his company in the 1920s and 1930s: Robert Gathorne-Hardy, John Russell, Desmond MacCarthy, R. C. Trevelyn, and Hugh Trevor-Roper. At his death in 1946 Smith left his dictionaries to Trevor-Roper.

The Smith family in 1894: (standing) Logan and his sister Alys; (seated) parents Robert and Hannah, sister Mary Costelloe, and her children, Karin and Ray (Collection of Barbara Strachey)

Smith could easily be seen as the prig he jokingly called himself. He was a prime mover of the Society for Pure English formed in 1913, and he used to judge his disciples by their attachment to its pamphlets and to good dictionaries. These young writers were exhorted to carry notebooks at all times. For all his charm, there is a good deal of the religious crank in Smith. He saw the pursuit of money as an encumbrance to the writing life and lamented those young writers who disappeared down the "sink of profitable publicity and shoddy writing". He did confess a weakness for society, not surprising in one for whom conversation was apparently one of the primal appetites: one of his obituaries called him a "Fellow in all common-rooms of the discerning mind" (*Observer*, 3 March 1946). But again and again Smith maintained that the greatest happiness was to have a vocation: "some disinterested job, say that of painting, or like mine, of polishing phrases, which one can work at all one's life and never

get tired for a moment." It is this idealism that finally saves Smith from priggishness. He is both urgent in its pursuit and forgiving of the inevitable human shortfall in attaining it: "The indefatigable pursuit of an unattainable Perfection–even though nothing more than the pounding of an old piano–is what alone gives a meaning to our life on this unavailing Star" (*Afterthoughts*). This almost anchorite worship of the Muse, while remaining content with an apprentice's share of fame, deservedly won Smith the love of young writers, who recognized in him someone whose devotion to aesthetic Bohemia was a lifelong affair.

Letters:

A Chime of Words: The Letters of Logan Pearsall Smith, edited by Edwin Tribble (New York: Ticknor & Fields, 1984).

Biographies:

Robert Gathorne-Hardy, *Recollections of Logan Pearsall Smith* (New York: Macmillan, 1950);

John Russell, *A Portrait of Logan Pearsall Smith* (London: Dropmore, 1950).

Papers:
Some Logan Pearsall Smith papers are in the Special Collections at Kent State University Library.

J. A. Spender

(23 December 1862 - 21 June 1942)

J. M. McEwen
Brock University

BOOKS: *The State and Pensions in Old Age* (London: Sonnenschein, 1892; New York: Scribners, 1900);

A Modern Journal, Being the Diary of Greville Minor for the Years of Agitation 1903-1904 (London: Methuen, 1904);

The Comments of Bagshot, first series (London: Constable, 1907; New York: Holt, 1908); second series (London: Constable, 1911; New York: Holt, 1912);

The Foundations of British Policy (London: Westminster Gazette, 1912);

The Indian Scene (London: Methuen, 1912);

The Life of the Right Hon. Sir Henry Campbell-Bannerman, G. C. B., 2 volumes (London: Hodder & Stoughton, 1923; Boston: Houghton Mifflin, 1924);

The Public Life, 2 volumes (London: Cassell, 1925; New York: Stokes, 1925);

The Changing East (London: Cassell, 1926; New York: Stokes, 1926; revised edition, London: Cassell, 1935);

Life, Journalism and Politics, 2 volumes (London: Cassell, 1927; New York: Stokes, 1927);

The America of To-day (London: Benn, 1928); republished as *Through English Eyes* (New York: Stokes, 1928);

Weetman Pearson, First Viscount Cowdray, 1856-1927 (London & Toronto: Cassell, 1930);

Sir Robert Hudson. A Memoir (London: Cassell, 1930);

Life of Herbert Henry Asquith, Lord Oxford and Asquith, by Spender and Cyril Asquith, 2 volumes (London: Hutchinson, 1932);

J. A. Spender (photography by Vandyk)

Fifty Years of Europe. A Study in Pre-War Documents (London: Cassell, 1933; New York: Stokes, 1933);

These Times (London: Cassell, 1934);

A Short History of Our Times (London & Toronto: Cassell, 1934);

Great Britain: Empire and Commonwealth, 1886-1935 (London: Cassell, 1936);

Men and Things (London: Cassell, 1937);

The Government of Mankind (London: Cassell, 1938);

New Lamps and Ancient Lights (London & Toronto: Cassell, 1940);

Between Two Wars (London & Toronto: Cassell, 1943);

Last Essays (London & Toronto: Cassell, 1944).

OTHER: *The Poems of William Watson,* edited, with an introduction by Spender (London & New York: Lane, 1905);

Charles Morley, *Travels in London,* with a memoir by Spender (London: Smith, Elder, 1916).

English journalism enjoyed a golden age in the quarter century preceding the advent of broadcasting in the 1920s. With mass as well as class readerships and with no other medium as a rival in shaping opinion or disseminating news, the press was in truth the fourth estate. Among many great newspapermen J. A. Spender stood out as a remarkable figure. The paper he edited for twenty-five years, the afternoon *Westminster Gazette,* became a staple in the reading diet of influential people, in London especially, and solely on account of the leading articles that flowed in a steady stream from the one powerful pen. His biographer Wilson Harris wrote how "day by day on that pea-green front page Spender preached a robust and reasoned Liberalism which sometimes left impetuous Radicals impatient but won high and constant commendation from such leaders as Rosebery, Campbell-Bannerman, Asquith, Haldane and Morley." It should be added that Spender was on terms of confidential friendship with all of them (three of whom were prime ministers) and with another equally important figure, Sir Edward Grey, for eleven years foreign secretary of Great Britain. If the outpouring of many thousands of political essays, for Spender's leading articles were such, constituted some kind of record in itself, his many other writings are a more lasting tribute to his life and work. Over a half century he produced more than twenty books, divided almost equally among histories, political biographies, and collections of essays on a great diversity of subjects. Together they form a useful mirror of the age.

John Alfred Spender was born in Bath on 23 December 1862, the third child but eldest son in a family of eight. Literary influences surrounded him from infancy, for the Spenders were close to writers such as Walter Savage Landor and Crabb Robinson. His father, Dr. J. Spender, was a physician, who was at least as interested in literary and theological subjects as in medicine, and his mother, Lily Spender, was a successful, if now forgotten, novelist whose earnings provided comfort for the family and a good education for the children. Spender's early education was at preparatory school and Bath College, whose headmaster, T. W. Dunn, impressed upon his apt pupil the importance of integrity, loyalty, and disinterestedness. A scholarship to Balliol College, Oxford, brought Spender under the influence of the legendary Benjamin Jowett, and among his contemporaries were Grey, Lord Curzon, and Cosmo Lang, later archbishop of Canterbury. Perhaps his clearest memory of Jowett was the somber warning: "Journalism is not a profession, not a profession, Mr. Spender."

Failure through illness to obtain the expected "first" forced Spender into the world with few means and no clear idea of a career, and it was almost by accident that he found himself editing the *Eastern Morning News* in the Yorkshire port of Hull. After five years of this invaluable apprenticeship he moved to London, where he took up residence at Toynbee Hall and became a freelance journalist. Necessity and inclination alike drove him to write more and more, and he produced his first book, *The State and Pensions in Old Age* (1892). Then came an unexpected stroke of good luck. As an occasional contributor to the *Pall Mall Gazette,* a leading quality paper, he had greatly impressed the editor, E. T. Cook, who offered him the position of assistant editor in 1892, financially enabling him to marry Mary Rawlinson in July of that year. But almost at once the paper changed hands and politics, which forced the editorial staff to resign. Again Spender was fortunate, for a wealthy Liberal, George Newnes, established a new paper to rival the *Pall Mall Gazette* and installed Cook and Spender in their old positions. This was the *Westminster Gazette,* and when Cook departed in 1896 Spender slipped effortlessly into the editor's chair, where he remained until 1921.

The names of many great journalists have been linked with a single paper, but in Spender's case it was something more. He became synonymous with the *Westminster Gazette.* The early years

Spender as an Oxford undergraduate

of his editorship explain why. His tireless efforts to prevent the Liberal party from tearing itself apart over the South African war won him the confidence of party leaders. This enabled him to play a key role in the negotiations surrounding the formation of the Liberal government in December 1905. Sometimes called "editorial king-maker" and "unofficial cabinet minister," over the next decade Spender had access to the workings of the government's mind, which enabled him to write with an authority no other journalist possessed. Being closely associated with Grey, Spender's paper was regarded abroad as the authoritative voice of the Liberal government, by Kaiser Wilhelm not least. Spender's political creed could be summed up in a few words: free trade and a strong navy. In the critical days before the declaration of war in 1914 his support of the government was invaluable, and it was to Spender that Grey uttered the historic words: "The lamps are going out all over Europe, and

we shall not see them lit again in our lifetime." With the fall of Asquith and Grey midway through the war, Spender's political influence waned rapidly, and in the Lloyd George era he was something of an anachronism.

So heavy were editorial demands during Spender's three decades at the *Westminster Gazette* that he had little time for other writing. His brief period of residence at Toynbee Hall, where he saw the deplorable living conditions in London's East End, had inspired *The State and Pensions in Old Age*. In some ways this was a forerunner of the great studies of English poverty produced by Charles Booth and Seebohm Rowntree a few years later. For his work Spender industriously compiled facts and figures about the elderly and collated information on pension schemes in other countries. He concluded that the only solution to the sorry plight of those who were impoverished and too old to work was a system of noncontributory pensions. Thereby he anticipated the Liberal legislation of 1908, when Asquith and Lloyd George carried the Old Age Pensions Bill, a very real step toward the welfare state. Spender's little book was thought worthy of praise by the veteran Radical, John Morley, who (as reported by Harris) commended it as "an admirable manual of the whole subject." Spender had made a promising beginning as a writer on social questions, but it ended there so far as books were concerned. When next he found time to write a full-length work, many years had passed, and other problems occupied his mind.

In the circumstances he did the next best thing, which was to publish in book form some of his writings from the *Westminster Gazette*. The first of these little volumes came out in 1904 as *A Modern Journal, Being the Diary of Greville Minor, for the Years of Agitation 1903-1904*. As this title suggests, the tone was light and the subjects of ephemeral interest. There followed in 1907 the first of two volumes entitled *The Comments of Bagshot*, another selection of articles from Spender's paper, consisting chiefly of aphorisms and reflections on various facets of life. While these tidbits were praised for their wit and pungency, such fare was better suited to the leisurely reading habits of Edwardian times than to ours, certainly more effective when served up in small helpings at weekly intervals rather than wholesale. Nonetheless some of Bagshot's wisdom may divert a modern reader. For example, on the subject of quick success: "It is silly to quarrel with the chamois because he did not come by the mule path"; or on political leadership: "A motto for Cabinets: Twenty wise men may easily add up into one fool." And one saying that seems peculiarly appropriate for the modern university is this: "Cleverness and stupidity are generally in the same boat against wisdom." A second volume of Bagshot's comments followed in 1911, which, like the first, came out in an American edition a year later. Perhaps better testimony to its success was the publication of a Wayfarer's Library edition in 1914. Bagshot, of course, was Spender thinly disguised, but this publication was in no sense an autobiography. That would come much later and with appropriate seriousness.

Two other little volumes from the prewar years can be passed over quickly. Like those attributed to Greville Minor and Bagshot, they, too, were collections of pieces from the *Westminster Gazette*, but about more consequential matters. *The Foundations of British Policy* (1912) bore testimony to Spender's deep interest in foreign affairs and his sense of Britain's essential interests. More substantial in size but more quickly dated was *The Indian Scene*, also published in 1912, which consisted of essays written after a lengthy visit to the Middle East and India. Britain's idea of how to govern India in the twentieth century was rapidly submerged by events, yet Spender was criticized for mildly suggesting that some Indians of long service and wide knowledge might be promoted to high executive positions. His penchant for aphorisms found an outlet even in these pages–for example: "To the traveller in India the surprising thing is, not that there should be unrest, but that there should ever be any rest." But these collections of essays scarcely hinted at Spender's potential as a writer of serious books. Not until after the war and subsequent to his departure from the editor's chair did his great knowledge and catholic interests become widely known. The habit of writing had become so strong that in the last twenty years of his life he turned out books with the same regularity as he once had produced leading articles. There were other similarities as well.

His next venture was biography, *The Life of the Right Hon. Sir Henry Campbell-Bannerman, G. C. B.*, published in two volumes in 1923. Spender's writing skills, coupled with his intimate knowledge of the Liberal party and its leaders, had convinced Campbell-Bannerman's literary executor, Lord Pentland, that he was the obvious man for the task. It was a wise choice. The result was a book both scholarly and readable, which provided a better understanding of the genial Scot

who had knit the Liberal party together and, from 1905 to 1908, had headed one of the most talented ministries in British history. Indeed half a century passed before the Spender biography had a rival, which supplemented rather than superseded the official life. Perhaps it was inevitable that his volume erred somewhat in providing overly much detailed narrative but insufficient critical analysis, for Spender was a product of his times and a Liberal always. On the whole the Campbell-Bannerman book received good reviews, and Spender's reputation as a biographer was established. About the same time he had to decline an offer to write the life of Earl Spencer, the famous "Red Earl" of Gladstonian days, but other opportunities would occur within a few years.

From biography he turned to something more reflective and discursive. In 1925 there appeared in two volumes *The Public Life*, which sets forth in clear language Spender's political philosophy and his view of the public life generally. The work is divided into seven parts, or "books," and there are thirty-one chapters in all. Such a plethora of headings make for a fragmented quality, as some critics pointed out. Even though the work is not a clearly organized whole, there are enough threads for a pattern to emerge. Spender was concerned for the future of British governmental institutions, for the quality of men and women elected to serve in them, and for the future of the press. Beginning with some historical chapters and drawing upon his own rich memories of leaders and events, he proceeded to make sage comments about the parliamentary system and what was needed to keep it healthy. Likewise he sensed that the press was in trouble as the number of newspapers diminished and control was in fewer hands, but he could only suggest vague palliatives. Though wisdom often shines through these pages, it is difficult not to feel that Spender is writing about a world that has passed away without his appreciating the fact. One can scarcely imagine such a book being written today.

The following year, 1926, he reverted to an earlier theme but a continuing love with the publication of *The Changing East*, which brought up to date his assessment of Egypt, Turkey, and India. Though Arnold Toynbee, as quoted by Harris, praised its "standard of excellence," it was primarily a book of travel, more descriptive than analytical. Comparisons with former visits yielded only moderately revised estimates of the political and social temper of these countries, and, it may be

The first issue of the paper with which Spender was associated for three decades; beginning as assistant editor in 1893, he became editor in 1896 added, brought neither Spender nor his readers much closer to sensing what would happen over the next few decades. As always he was the English Liberal whose faith in parliamentary institutions and organic growth limited his awareness of the potential of other political forces. Thus Gandhi's movement in India, for example, was seen as little more than a retreat to medievalism. Spender's comments on Egypt were more substantial, as he had been a member of the Milner Commission shortly after the war and knew that country well. Yet here, too, he did not guess that Egyptian nationalism would become a potent force before long, to the detriment of British influence. Turkey received the briefest treatment in this work, Spender's account of meeting Mustapha Kemal in Ankara throwing little fresh light on that regime. Of use to contemporaries *The Changing East* was a book for the moment.

By now Spender was in his mid sixties, and the inevitable autobiography could be delayed no longer. It was published in two volumes in 1927 as *Life, Journalism and Politics* and was well received in both Britain and the United States. Some of the ground here he had traversed already in *The Public Life*, so there were few surprises. In the earlier work he had looked at others, whereas now it was his own career and participation in events that pointed the moral. Unlike modern autobiographies, Spender's said virtually nothing about his private life, possibly because it was quite blameless. Such reticence was matched by his discretion about others, and posterity is the poorer. Doubtless he knew many interesting things about important people that would have been helpful in making historical judgments. Information he regarded as of value, such as the material on Campbell-Bannerman, Grey, and Rosebery, he set down without equivocation. At once the book was regarded as an essential companion piece to recently published works by and about Liberal statesmen he had known. In the words of the *Times Literary Supplement* reviewer, writing anonymously on 29 September 1927, "The secret of Mr. Spender's success as a publicist lay in his combination of acute judgment of men with deep appreciation of events; and his memoirs abound in examples of both." Possibly because of the author's restraint, sales were modest, yet many considered it his most significant book.

An unexpected opportunity came Spender's way in the autumn and winter of 1927-1928, and this led to another book along the lines of *The Changing East*. The English-Speaking Union had founded a memorial fellowship in honor of Walter Hines Page, American ambassador in London during the war, to enable a distinguished British journalist to travel, lecture, and study in the United States. Spender was an obvious choice as first holder of this award, and with his wife, the former Mary Rawlinson, whom he married in 1892, he spent three months traveling from coast to coast, visiting major cities and lesser centers alike. Afterwards he set down his impressions in a series of essays published in 1928–in Britain as *The America of To-day* and in the United States as *Through English Eyes*, titles equally appropriate. He began with the words, "This book can claim to be nothing more than a record of impressions at a particular moment and from a particular angle." It was unduly modest, for Spender had some worthwhile things to say on such subjects as prohibition, immigration, racial feeling, journalism, Anglo-American relations, and, of course, politics and politicians. Yet something was missing, as with his book on the East. Rarely is there a hint that within a short time great cracks would appear in the American structure or that a new era was about to begin.

With the demise of the *Westminster Gazette* in 1928, Spender's journalistic work dwindled, and he was forced to seek fresh sources of income. For the next few years he devoted much of his time to commissioned biographies. In one year, 1930, he published *Weetman Pearson, First Viscount Cowdray, 1856-1927* and *Sir Robert Hudson*. These books differed almost as much as their subjects. Cowdray had been a wealthy Liberal contractor and party benefactor who shored up the *Westminster Gazette* at a crucial moment and saved it from the clutches of Lloyd George's forces. Spender's editorial independence owed much to Cowdray's support, and it was only natural that Spender should write the official biography. The result was a competent survey of Cowdray's life and work, but the story of great contracting operations round the world hardly stirred Spender in the same way as writing of statesmen and events. The Hudson biography, by contrast, was only half the length, yet Hudson was a man about whom Spender could write with understanding and warmth. For nearly thirty years Hudson had been secretary of the National Liberal Federation, devoting his life to the Liberal cause. Between the two men there had been an affinity of outlook and interests, both political and literary, and as well they had had numerous friends in common. Harris commented of the result that it was "very near what an ideal short biography should be." The Cowdray and Hudson books were judged modest successes, but neither had provided the author with a large enough canvas for his talents.

A work of much greater substance and lasting value was the *Life of Herbert Henry Asquith, Lord Oxford and Asquith*, published in two volumes in 1932 and written in collaboration with Cyril Asquith, the subject's fourth son. To this end Spender contributed forty-three chapters by contrast to Asquith's fourteen, while two were written jointly. On the whole it was a successful literary partnership, each man's writing complementing the other's. Spender dealt with Asquith's public career, drawing upon his great knowledge of events as well as a friendship of thirty years to portray the Liberal leader in a favorable light. In the words of the *Times* reviewer, writing anonymously in October 1932, these two volumes were "massive and dignified, like the figure they commemorate." As this was official biography in the old style, it lacked the searching analysis and criticism that would come later, but for some years following publication, Asquith's reputation as a statesman rested on firmer ground. Even critics like Leonard Woolf were constrained to admit that they could not read these pages without a growing affection for the man. More recent studies have cast shadows over Asquith's private life as well as his premiership, which could hardly be guessed from his son's dutiful prose. Spender had enhanced his own reputation as a political biographer, but it was his last work of this kind, although he had assisted Lord Grey of Fallodon in preparing that stateman's autobiography, *Twenty-Five Years*.

He now turned to diplomatic history, putting to fresh use his knowledge of statesmen and nations. In light of events in Germany it was singularly appropriate that in the year 1933 he should have brought out *Fifty Years of Europe. A Study in Pre-War Documents*. Since the armistice in 1918 there had been an outpouring of works official and unofficial about the origins and background of World War I. Spender undertook to give some shape and order to this mass of evidence so that it would be comprehensible to an intelligent reader. He began the story with the visit of the German emperor to Emperor Franz Josef of Austria in 1871 and continued down to the Austrian ultimatum to Serbia in the summer of 1914. Drawing heavily from British, German, and Austrian documents, Spender showed himself a most com-

petent guide through the confusing maze of European diplomacy. The result was a lucid narrative that so wise a critic as J. L. Hammond praised as skillful, vivid, and dramatic. Inevitably reviewers also saw it as a textbook students would find indispensable, little guessing how soon it would be overtaken by events. It is ironic to read the *Times Literary Supplement* (5 October 1933) lauding Spender for making "an enormous contribution to that sane and balanced estimate of the causes of the war to which we must attain if we are to deal wisely with the conditions which the war left." Unhappily, sanity and balance were rapidly going out of fashion at that moment.

Perhaps this spurred Spender to try even harder, for in 1934 he published two books only four months apart, *These Times* and *A Short History of Our Times*. The titles notwithstanding, they were quite different, both in size and subject matter. The first, a slight work, consists of essays and notes that add up to a common-sense defense of classical English Liberalism. He warned against the perils inherent in revolutionary change, which must lead to the destruction of democracy and the loss of civilized values. Another danger he foresaw was a planned economy, and much that happened after 1945 would have been anathema to him. *A Short History of Our Times*, by contrast, was little more than a record of events in Britain during Spender's lifetime down to the 1920s. Mindful that history as then taught tailed off somewhere around the year 1870, he attempted to fill a very real gap. The result was only partly successful, as his predilection for the balanced view of events robbed the work of vitality. Some welcomed it as a useful guide, but there were others such as Raymond Mortimer in the *New Statesman and Nation* who dismissed it as a "nerveless chronicle, used chiefly as a cram-book for examinations."

Two years passed before the publication in 1936 of Spender's last large work of history, the massive (more than nine hundred pages) *Great Britain: Empire and Commonwealth, 1886-1935*. The deficiencies evident in *A Short History of Our Times* were remedied this time. Abandoning excessive detachment, he now wrote as an unapologetic Liberal, and the result was a far richer narrative. At the same time it was no mere partisan account of politics, of which he would have been incapable. In spite of the vast amount of material, Spender imposed a unity upon the whole, although the book had more than sixty chapters and most of them were subdivided. It spoke well

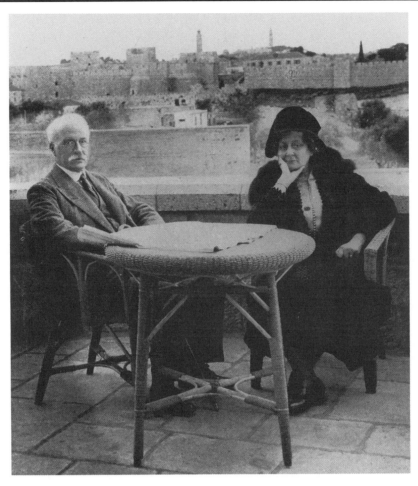

Spender with his wife, the former Mary Rawlinson, in Jerusalem, 1931

of the work that it continued to be a standard reference in university libraries for many years afterward. Of course, the empire and commonwealth Spender perceived have changed almost beyond recognition. The lasting value of his volume is not as a history but as a statement of the British philosophy of empire at a particular time.

Four of Spender's last five books were collections of essays, some of them pieces published earlier as newspaper articles. The other, which appeared in 1938, was called *The Government of Mankind*, and it must rank with *The Public Life* as one of his finest works. The idea came from a conversation with Lord Balfour several years earlier, which inspired Spender to reread the wisdom of sages and philosophers and to consider "how it looked in the light of modern experience." Partly historical and partly philosophical, the book ranges over the human story from ancient Egypt and Mesopotamia down to the "isms" of the twentieth century. At the end Spender remained convinced that there was a thread of purpose run-

ning throughout, that there was such a thing as the "ascent of man." Himself civilized, sensitive, and reasonable, ever the Liberal humanist, Spender remained unshaken in his conviction that government was an art. The *Times* reviewer wrote warmly on 4 November 1938 that this was "a remarkable book, rich in learning and the accumulated wisdom of a lifetime." It was also something of a cry for light in a darkening world.

The other four volumes need only brief mention. *Men and Things*, which came out in 1937, was a miscellany of thirty-five short papers under the headings of "Portraits," "Politics and History," "Things Seen," and "Side Issues." To old readers of Spender this was familiar stuff, and indeed it was a book that appealed to older people. Young extremists and simplistic solutions to complex problems were only two of his targets, and he took special pleasure in gently ridiculing modern poetry. In *New Lamps and Ancient Lights*, published in 1940, he continued to pour cool water on many of the current gods, Karl Marx and Sigmund Freud foremost. "Though we knew it or not," chided Spender, "we were engaged in an incessant dance of isms, ologies and categories, with the predetermined inevitable class conflict for its permanent background." And concerning Freud he wrote: "The idea of suppressed instincts is no doubt a clue to certain nervous disorders, but to jump from this to the conclusion that a suppressed sexualism is at the root of all human emotions is to fly in the teeth of common experience and probability." The final two works, *Between Two Wars* (1943) and *Last Essays* (1944), both published posthumously, added nothing to Spender's stature. His apology for the appeasement policy of Neville Chamberlain is no more attractive now than it was then. It is more pleasant to note his recollections of such figures as Matthew Arnold, Robert Browning, William Morris, and John Ruskin.

Spender's literary output of more than a score of books and some ten thousand newspaper articles places him among the most prolific of modern English writers. In addition his public services included membership on royal commissions and the presidency of the National Liberal Federation. To many he came to epitomize what seemed to be the best of another, perhaps more civilized, age. One anonymous reviewer of insight in the late 1930s called him "the finest specimen of the nineteenth-century Liberal now extant." This was true in both the best and the worst senses. Inevitably his mind and style became increasingly irritating to young writers and intellectuals of the interwar years who loved their Marcel Proust and W. H. Auden. Osbert Sitwell spoke of Spender as "clever, earnest, public-spirited, but with, enwrapping him, a spiritual aura of soft white wool that matched his hair" (quoted by Harris). The poet Stephen Spender felt a personal animus toward his uncle, which came out, according to Harris, in such remarks as, "He only saw a contemporary manner, never a contemporary vision," and "He was famous for his balanced point of view ... [but] it had become so balanced that the act of balancing seemed rather automatic." In the final analysis J. A. Spender will stand as a monument to failure, the failure of the Liberal ideal.

Biography:
Wilson Harris, *J. A. Spender* (London: Cassell, 1946).

Papers:
The papers of J. A. Spender are in the British Library, London.

Edward Thomas
(3 March 1878 - 9 April 1917)

Roy Scheele
Doane College

See also the Thomas entry in *DLB 19: British Poets, 1880-1914*.

BOOKS: *The Woodland Life* (Edinburgh & London: Blackwood, 1897);

Horae Solitariae (London: Duckworth, 1902; New York: Dutton, 1902);

Oxford (London: Black, 1903);

Rose Acre Papers (London: Brown, Langham, 1904);

Beautiful Wales (London: Black, 1905);

The Heart of England (London: Dent, 1906; London: Dent / New York: Dutton, 1906);

Richard Jefferies, His Life and Work (London: Hutchinson, 1909; Boston: Little, Brown, 1909);

The South Country (London: Dent, 1909; London: Dent / New York: Dutton, 1932);

Windsor Castle (London: Blackie, 1910);

Rest and Unrest (London: Duckworth, 1910; New York: Dutton, 1910);

Feminine Influence on the Poets (London: Secker, 1910; New York: John Lane, 1911);

Light and Twilight (London: Duckworth, 1911);

Maurice Maeterlinck (London: Methuen, 1911; New York: Dodd, Mead, 1911);

The Tenth Muse (London: Secker, 1911);

Celtic Stories (Oxford: Clarendon Press, 1911; Oxford & New York: Clarendon Press, 1913);

The Isle of Wight (London: Blackie, 1911);

Lafcadio Hearn (London: Constable, 1912; Boston & New York: Houghton Mifflin, 1912);

Norse Tales (Oxford: Clarendon Press, 1912);

Algernon Charles Swinburne, A Critical Study (London: Secker, 1912; New York: Kennerley, 1912);

George Borrow, The Man and His Books (London: Chapman & Hall, 1912; New York: Dutton, 1912);

The Country (London: Batsford, 1913);

The Icknield Way (London: Constable, 1913; New York: Dutton, 1913);

The Happy-Go-Lucky Morgans (London: Duckworth, 1913);

Walter Pater, A Critical Study (London: Secker, 1913; New York: Kennerley, 1913);

In Pursuit of Spring (London, Edinburgh, Dublin & New York: Nelson, 1914);

Four-and-Twenty Blackbirds (London: Duckworth, 1915);

The Life of The Duke of Marlborough (London: Chapman & Hall, 1915; New York: Brentano's, n.d.);

Keats (London: Jack, 1914 [i.e., 1916]; New York: Dodge, 1916?);

Six Poems, as Edward Eastaway (Flansham, U.K.: Pear Tree Press, 1916);

A Literary Pilgrim in England (London: Methuen, 1917; New York: Dodd, Mead, 1917);

Poems by Edward Thomas ("Edward Eastaway") (London: Selwyn & Blount, 1917; New York: Holt, 1917);

Last Poems (London: Selwyn & Blount, 1918);

Collected Poems (London: Selwyn & Blount, 1920; New York: Seltzer, 1921; enlarged edition, London: Ingpen & Grant, 1928);

Cloud Castle and Other Papers (London: Duckworth, 1922; New York: Dutton, 1923?);

Two Poems (London: Ingpen & Grant, 1927);

The Last Sheaf, Essays by Edward Thomas (London: Cape, 1928);

The Childhood of Edward Thomas: A Fragment of Autobiography (London: Faber & Faber, 1938);

The Prose of Edward Thomas, edited by Roland Gant (London: Falcon Press, 1948);

The Poems of Edward Thomas, edited by R. George Thomas (Oxford: Clarendon Press, 1978; New York: Oxford University Press, 1978);

The Chessplayer and Other Essays, introduction by R. George Thomas (Andoversford, U.K.: Whittington Press, 1981);

A Language Not to Be Betrayed: Selected Prose of Edward Thomas, edited by Edna Longley (Manchester, U.K.: Carcanet Press, 1981; New York: Persea Books, 1981).

OTHER: Richard Jefferies, *The Hills and the Vale,*

Thomas at age twenty (Collection of Myfanwy Thomas)

introduction by Thomas (London: Duckworth, 1909);

Isaac Taylor, *Words and Places in Illustration of History, Ethnology and Geography*, introduction by Thomas (London: Dent, 1911);

This England: An Anthology from Her Writers, edited by Thomas (London: Oxford University Press, 1915).

Although Edward Thomas's critical reputation is based on his achievement as a poet, that achievement represents a brief flowering at the end of a career as a writer of prose. For more than twenty years Thomas wrote prose of all sorts: essays, reviews, introductions to anthologies, travel books, critical and biographical studies, a fragmentary autobiography (*The Childhood of Edward Thomas*, 1938), a novel (*The Happy-Go-Lucky Morgans*, 1913), and an unfinished second novel (under the working title "Fiction"). It is a prodigious and uneven output, and the prodi-

giousness and unevenness have unfortunately led to a concensus that dismisses Thomas's prose as hackwork. Yet as Thomas's biographer R. George Thomas has remarked in his introduction to *Letters from Edward Thomas to Gordon Bottomley* (1968), "Read in conjunction with his books, these letters cast serious doubt on the use of the description 'hack-writing' that has slipped increasingly into much uninformed posthumous comment on his prose writings. . . . the letters at least demonstrate the patient care, the intensive scholarship, and the fastidious honesty with which he prepared himself for each successive publisher's assignment." The fact is that in spite of its unevenness, Thomas's prose, especially as it develops in his essays, forms a body of work that prepared him to write, in the last two-and-one-half years of his life, several of the finest poems of his generation.

Philip Edward Thomas was born in Lambeth on 3 March 1878. His parents were both Welsh, his father, Philip Henry Thomas, hailing from Tredegar and his mother, Elizabeth Town-

Helen Noble in February 1899, a few months before her marriage to Thomas (Collection of Myfanwy Thomas)

send Thomas, from Newport; they had been married in Wales and moved to London when Philip Henry Thomas went to work as a staff clerk for railways at the Board of Trade. Edward Thomas grew up in Battersea and from an early age spent many hours bird nesting and exploring on Wandsworth Common, fishing in local rivers and on farm ponds, and taking long walks in the country. He soon found confirmation of his interest in nature in the writings of Richard Jefferies, whose works he devoured along with those of other naturalists and travel writers and the standard English poets. By the time he left St. Paul's Public School in Hammersmith in 1895, Thomas had been writing essays "in an approach as near as possible to the style of Jefferies" for several years, and in 1897 some of these essays were published under the title *The Woodland Life*.

In terms both of his personal life and his career, 1895 was a pivotal year for Thomas. In April he was introduced to James Ashcroft Noble, a critic and journalist who encouraged Thomas's literary aspirations and helped to place several of his essays in *New Age*, the *Speaker*, and the *Globe*. Noble subsequently arranged with his own publishers, Blackwood, for the publication of *The Woodland Life*, though he died before the book appeared. In the Noble household Thomas also met and fell in love with Helen Noble, whom he would marry on 20 June 1899 while an undergraduate at Oxford. Thomas spent the summer of 1895 with relatives at Swindon in Wiltshire, and it was there, while fishing one day, that he met David "Dad" Uzzell, a reformed poacher who seemed to Thomas to have stepped out of the pages of Jefferies. Uzzell, whose minute knowledge of the countryside dwarfed Thomas's own, would later serve as the model for "Lob" and several other characters in Thomas's poetry and prose. It was also during this year that Thomas began to keep a diary of "Field Notes" which he later incorporated in *The Woodland Life*.

In 1900 Thomas took a second-class degree in history from Oxford and, with a wife and newly born son to support, went to editors for work as a reviewer. Thomas and his wife, Helen, were determined to live solely by his writing and to reside in the country, and, as he gained a reputation as a reviewer and commissions for books began to come to him, the Thomases moved to a succession of country cottages. Thomas rapidly became overworked, and in the years from 1900 to 1915 he produced more than a million words of reviews and twenty-seven books of prose. In spite of this prolific output, money was often scarce in the Thomas household. In his overworked state the bouts of depression from which he had suffered since adolescence became severe at times, and on several occasions he had nervous breakdowns. In letters to Gordon Bottomley and others during this period, Thomas often spoke deprecatingly of his worth as a writer. One such letter, written to Bottomley on 26 February 1908, suggests that much of Thomas's dissatisfaction with prose may have arisen from his wish to be writing poetry, which he saw as the more vital and organic art: "Poetry in verse is at one with the tides and the pulse; prose is chaos cut up into beds & borders & fountains & rusticwork like a garden."

The story of how Thomas eventually came to write poetry is well known and well attested. When he met Robert Frost in 1913 the two became good friends, having in common already a belief in what Frost called "the sound of sense," and in 1914 Thomas wrote the three most perceptive of the English reviews of Frost's *North of Boston*, a book which Thomas called "revolutionary." Frost was always grateful to Thomas for having championed his work, later remarking, "He gave me standing as a poet—he more than anyone else. . . ." For his part, Frost tried to persuade Thomas that he too should be writing poetry, pointing out passages in *Light and Twilight* (1911) and *In Pursuit of Spring* (1914) in order to encourage Thomas to turn his prose to the cadences of verse. Though others, including Walter de la Mare, had earlier offered much the same advice, Thomas was finally convinced by Frost and began writing poems in December 1914. It was a brief, halcyon period for Thomas, even though many of his poems were written (after he had enlisted in the Artists' Rifles in July 1915) under the seemingly unfavorable conditions of barracks life. In January 1917 Thomas was posted to France with the Royal Artillery; he was killed during a German barrage in the Arras offensive on Easter Monday of that year.

To consider Edward Thomas as an essayist it is necessary to recognize that in the essay, as in his prose generally, he was always searching for a form which would allow him to express the full range of his feelings and personality. Thomas gradually came to realize that his true subject was his own inner life, and his search for an appropriate form to express that life, which led eventually to the writing of poems, caused him to try his hand at everything from character sketches and fanciful essays to a novel based on childhood memories. As he wrote to Bottomley on 12 October 1909, "I am casting about for subjects which will compel me to depend simply on what I am—memory included but in a due subsidiary place." Thus, although much of his work in the genre does not fall within the confines of the essay proper, a reader ought not to allow this fact to obscure the real achievement of Thomas's more traditional essays.

The Woodland Life, published when Thomas was eighteen and dedicated to the memory of James Ashcroft Noble, marks the beginning of Thomas's career. It includes essays he had written when he was fifteen and sixteen; the chief literary model is Jefferies, but there are also touches of Walter Pater and echoes of the Romantic poets. The subject and setting is the natural world of Thomas's excursions, as can be seen from several of the titles ("A Wiltshire Molecatcher," "Winter in Richmond Park," "A Pine-Wood Near London," "A Surrey Woodland"). The essays are less remarkable individually than for the composite impression they give of Thomas's sharp eye for the detail and fecundity of the natural world. Again and again he individuates the different species of birds by their habits, songs, flight and feeding patterns, and flowers by the particulars of blossom and leaf. His style is ornate at times, but never excessively so, and Thomas shows already an ability to provide detail while sketching in the essentials of a scene: "The meadow-path, edged with a faint white line of daisies, whose unopened cups are crimson at the brim, runs with a twisting course athwart broad fields of grass, studded at their margins by the brilliant gold blossoms of celandine. Elms, misty-purple or rust-red with expanded buds, stand out in the midst of the grass, and near where the path leaves the roadway, seven vast trees are set in a circle—the pillars of a temple domed in summer by thick foliage penetrable only to the sunlight, and floored with level grass inlaid with

Thomas (standing) in late 1902 with his son, Merfyn; his paternal grandmother, Rachel Phillips Thomas; his father, Philip Henry Thomas; and his mother, Mary Elizabeth Townsend Thomas (Collection of Myfanwy Thomas)

pearly eyebright. Near a rude stile of unpeeled elm it skirts a tiny pond almost hidden by withered flags and the broad leaning trunk of a dead willow. The soft mud at the pool's margin is thickly marked with the broad-arrow prints of moorhens' feet; but in the course of an hour, when the winds of morning have risen, the rippling waters will erase all traces of the birds that fed around them in the dim light of dawn." Here, in the opening paragraph of "Lydiard Tregose," the comparison of the circle of trees to the pillars of a temple may seem overdrawn to a contemporary sensibility, but in the age of Pater it would hardly have seemed out of place. Especially in the concluding section of the volume, "A Diary in English Fields and Woods," based on Thomas's "Field Notes" (the entries range from 1 April 1895 to 30 March 1896), we can glimpse Thomas's mature style, and there is at times a wonderful freshness and precision of metaphor, as in the entry for 21 April:

> Blackthorn steeped in blossom now.
> Reeds piercing the ripple of the brook, with twin blades curved and meeting like calipers.

Thomas published three collections of essays in the period from 1902 to 1906, which together constitute his most sustained output in the genre. These collections are *Horae Solitariae* (1902), *Rose Acre Papers* (1904), and *The Heart of England* (1906). The first of these perhaps best illustrates the unevenness of Thomas's work in the essay. *Horae Solitariae* shows the young writer's natural tendency to try his hand at various subjects; however, some of the pieces have a sort of dream-narrative bent and are hardly essays at all in the traditional sense, revealing that even early on in his career Thomas was impatient of the confines of the form. Whether attempting to domesticate Greek mythology in an English setting, as in "The Passing of Pan" and "Caryatids," or returning to Arthurian legend, as in "Isoud with the White Hands," Thomas cannot be considered to have succeeded; the pieces simply do not carry the conviction of wholly realized art. What succeeds in the volume are the more traditional personal essays, such as "Epitaphs as a Form of English Literature," "Inns and Books," and "Digressions on Fish and Fishing," and the nature studies such as "Recollections of November," "Bro-

Thomas with his younger daughter, Myfanwy, and a neighbor's child, Tommy Dodd, 1914 (Collection of Myfanwy Thomas)

ken Memories," and "February in England." Thus the book is a kind of harbinger of the two sides of Thomas's development as an essayist: the dreamlike classical and legendary pieces that lead eventually to collections such as *Rest and Unrest* (1910), *Light and Twilight* (1911), and the posthumously published *Cloud Castle and Other Papers* (1922), and the personal and nature essays that prefigure the workmanlike norm and several masterpieces of *The Last Sheaf* (1928).

One element which is characteristic of all of Thomas's mature work strikes its first clear note in *Horae Solitariae*: his sense of humor. It is often a glancing, tongue-in-cheek humor, as in "Epitaphs as a Form of English Literature": "we should surely be the gainers by more practice of the art of epitaphs. . . . Style would certainly gain. Marble is no vulgar material, and cannot be wasted like foolscap; the author would be as much exalted by using marble as the goldsmith by using gold, and the richness of the medium would act as a check and corrective of matter and style. . . ." Or in this passage from "Digressions on Fish and Fishing": "Some fishermen are great readers out of doors, with a taste which ar-

gues (unless the result of gross insensibility) no mean judgment and knowledge of books. To know what will stand the fierce outdoor light that hopelessly demeans the average book is a literary achievement. In this way the sun is a true critic, and the only present test of immortality. Sir Thomas Browne wears well out of doors. So, strange to say, does Elia . . . though Hazlitt will have it that Lamb was the worst company on a walk." Such ironic humor is more than a mere stylistic flourish; it is always natural, always embedded in the tone and structure of the essay. In fact, Thomas's humor is pervasive enough throughout his writing to provide a caveat against taking the self-deprecation of his letters wholly at face value. When he signs one letter "Ever your hurried & harried prose man Edward Thomas," the play on "hurried" and "harried" cautions the reader not to feel too sorry for him.

With the publication of *The Heart of England*, Thomas began to come into his own as an essayist. Though he was contemptuous of the volume while it was being prepared for publication, calling it "pseudo-genial or purely rustic–Borrow and Jefferies sans testicles and guts," he softened his estimate when Bottomley praised parts of the book after reading it in proof. Focusing on the English countryside, the collection is divided into sections by topographical region, thereby suggesting a journey: "Leaving Town," "The Lowland," "The Upland," "The Mountains," "The Sea." Thomas would later modify and use this structure again in *The South Country* (1909) and, adapting it to reflect the stages of a tour, in the chapter headings of his two fine travel books *The Icknield Way* (1913) and *In Pursuit of Spring* (1914). At times mawkish and tediously literary, *The Heart of England* nevertheless reveals a writer in more confident possession of his material. In such essays as "Meadowland," "Poppies," "The Brook," "The Village," "A Winter Morning," and "The Inn," Thomas's use of description is more rounded and evocative than in his earlier books. In many cases the essays deal with scenes and subjects to which Thomas would later return in his poems. The nettles and deserted farmyard in "Poppies," for example, recur (far more forcefully) in Thomas's poem "Tall Nettles"; "The Metamorphosis," though hardly more than a sketch, provides a gloss of one section (lines 15-18) of his poem "After Rain." The collection also gives ample evidence of Thomas's ability to objectify his thoughts and feelings through the use of natural details: "A calm fell upon me such as I had sometimes found in June thunderstorms on lonely hills, or in midnights when I stepped for a moment after long foolish labours to my door, and heard the nightingales singing out from the Pleiades that overhung the wood, and saw the flower-faced owl sitting on the gate." One may suppose that the allusion to "long foolish labours" refers to Thomas's reviewing and early prose books. In any case the objectification of his inner life in the details of natural experience was very important to Thomas, who undoubtedly took the Wordsworthian norm of the restorative power of nature very seriously. For Thomas it afforded a way of maintaining mental equilibrium, of fighting back against his periodic bouts of melancholy.

Another way in which Thomas dealt with his depression was by writing dream narratives. These are primarily collected in *Rest and Unrest*, *Light and Twilight*, and *Cloud Castle*. In the preface to a posthumous edition of Thomas's *The Tenth Muse*, John Freeman says of *Rest and Unrest* (he is presumably thinking of the other two books as well): It "is a specimen of a few books in which reverie and imagination together have

woven a situation, a story, an air of sadness or beauty, of longing or ineffectuality–short character studies, passionate prose lyrics, sketches of nervous states edging upon morbidity." The difficulty of categorizing and describing such pieces points to their failure both as individual works and as collections. However, *Rest and Unrest* includes a narrative essay, "The Maiden's Wood," which succeeds very well. The essay carefully situates and describes the wood and then goes on to relate how it got its name: it was once the bower of a mentally unstable young woman who had been sent by her family to stay at the estate farm (almost as a substitute for an asylum) and whose five-year residence has passed into local legend, surviving only in a place name, as people and events often do in the country. "The Stile," from *Light and Twilight*, is a highly evocative but more or less conventional nature essay, chiefly important as a precursor of Thomas's late masterpiece, "This England." Two pieces from *Cloud Castle* also deserve attention. "Mike," a personal essay about a stray terrier that Thomas found and kept, is very effective and would be perfect of its kind were it not for a superfluous final paragraph. "The Moon" is a prose poem which wonderfully describes a sleepless night spent out of doors in a landscape magically transformed by full moonlight.

If one excepts the brief biographical-critical studies of *The Tenth Muse* (1911), *Rest and Unrest* and *Light and Twilight* were the last collections of Thomas's essays (or "papers," as he liked to call such irregular pieces) published in his lifetime. Thomas had yet to write his best essays, and these would not be gathered into a volume until eleven years after his death. However, he did soon publish (rather unwillingly, on assignment) a long essay on nature and nature writing. *The Country* (1913) is neither systematic nor primarily historical but rather discursive, and it is interesting for the light it throws by implication on Thomas's view of his own place within a long and distinguished tradition. While admitting the necessity of the classic pastoral contrast of country and city, Thomas warns against romanticizing nature and condemning the city per se; he is aware that all too often "The city becomes our scapegoat." Thomas makes clear in the essay his relish for the race of country speech, the salt and tang of its idioms and proverbs, and ultimately finds in the country a metaphor not of escape but of emergence into a timeless community: "Blake related the flower to Eternity. Calming us

Letter to C. F. Cazenove, Thomas's literary agent, written while Thomas was visiting Robert Frost in Gloustershire, about three months before the Frosts returned to the United States (from the Collection of Dr. Gordon N. Ray; by permission of the Pierpont Morgan Library) with its space and patience, the country relates us all to Eternity. We go to it as would-be poets, or as solitaries, vagabonds, lovers, to escape foul air, noise, hard hats, black uniforms, multitudes, confusion, incompleteness, elaborate means without clear ends,–to escape ourselves; and we do more than escape them. So vastly do we increase the circle of which we are the centre that we become as nothing. The larger the circle the less seems our distance from other men each at his separate centre; and at last that distance is nothing at all in the mighty circle, and all have but one circumference. And thus we truly find ourselves."

Long before writing *The Country*, Thomas had been agonizing over finding himself as a writer, and it is difficult not to see a reductive self-portrait in the passage quoted above. At this time Thomas saw himself as a would-be poet and viewed his voluminous prose as an "incompleteness," an exercise in "elaborate means without clear ends." One can see a clear progression in his work in the ten-year period from *The Woodland Life* to *The Heart of England*, but much of the best of this work is still decidedly literary. What Thomas wanted for his prose (and ultimately his verse) was the simplicity and immediacy of speech. On the basis of this standard his early admiration for Pater had turned to disdain, and in his *Walter Pater, A Critical Study* (1913) Thomas observes: "He has created a prose of such close pattern and rich material that almost any piece of it is an honest and beauteous sample.... It is, however, careful as a rule not to offend the ear, and thus is made a kind of lucid vacuum in which the forms and colours can appear as beyond the purest glass for display." Thomas's friendship with Frost was crucial to his finding himself, in terms of the confidence he lacked in his writing. Frost's commitment to "the sound of sense," the speech stresses and sentence tones that underlie all good writing, whether in verse or prose, confirmed the similar ideas that Thomas had arrived at on his own, as expressed time and again in his reviews of the poetry of his contemporaries. Frost was an influence on Thomas in this respect primarily as he sanctioned the rightness of Thomas's own observations, and additionally, perhaps, in his insistence that "the sound of sense" applied as much to prose as to verse. Thomas was now ready to enter a brief period of essay writing which, for its variety of subject and tone, descriptive immediacy, and fidelity to speech, is unparalleled in his prose work, and which led to the writing of his poems.

Many of these essays, published posthumously as *The Last Sheaf* (1928), were written between January 1913 and April 1915–the period immediately before and after Thomas wrote his first poems in December 1914. Three of the volume's nineteen essays ("England," "Tipperary," "It's a Long, Long Way") deal with Thomas's views of England and patriotism in time of war and appeared in the *English Review* in late 1914 and early 1915. A fourth, "This England," which relates this subject more personally to Thomas's feeling for the English countryside and his friendship with Robert Frost, was published in the *Nation* in November 1914. Several of the other essays have their equivalents or reflections in poems that Thomas wrote, for example, "Chalk Pits" ("The Chalk Pit") and "In the Crowd at Goodwood" ("The Gypsy"). Even as he began to write the *Last Sheaf* essays, Thomas was characteristically plagued by doubts. Referring to one in a letter to Bottomley of 7 July 1914, Thomas wrote: " 'Midsummer' was dreadful. Tracts of headily insincere words among better things & quite nice little islands ruined by their surroundings." This self-censure may seem harsh to a reader today. If one compares "Midsummer" with much of Thomas's earlier work in the essay, he is likely to be impressed by the supple mastery of tone and rhythm and the precision of image and metaphor in the later piece, and by the absence of discernible influence on the style. The new spareness and lyrical note anticipate the poems that Thomas was soon to write.

While the general level of *The Last Sheaf* is consistently high, three of the essays are masterpieces: "A Third-Class Carriage," "The First Cuckoo," and "This England." "A Third-Class Carriage" is an incisive study of English class structure. Its opening sentence is direct and powerful: "When the five silent travellers saw the colonel coming into their compartment, all but the little girl looked about in alarm to make sure that it was a mere third-class carriage." The description of activity in the compartment centers around the colonel and his smoking of a pipe, but an undercurrent of this concentration is the implied watchfulness of the other passengers and their unspoken suppositions as to why the colonel is traveling third class. When the little girl asks him to smell a bunch of roses she is holding, the colonel is unable to respond, except with "an indescribable joyless gesture designed to persuade the child that he was really delighted with the suggestion, although he said nothing, and did nothing

Second Lieutenant Edward Thomas, Royal Garrison Artillery, in December 1916, during his final leave before embarkation to France (Collection of Myfanwy Thomas)

else to prove it." The colonel's smug insistence on the barriers of class is pathetic, and Thomas makes us feel the truth of this unforgettably. The essay is on a par with George Orwell's best narrative essays, such as "Shooting an Elephant" and "A Hanging," and deserves a place alongside them in the anthologies.

"The First Cuckoo" is a remarkable nature essay, the summation of all that Thomas had learned about the form over many years of writing. It begins by discussing the power that physical impressions have on our feelings, as well as the ephemeral nature of most such impressions. Thomas then considers "recurring things of universal significance, like the appearance of the new moon, or of the faint Pleiades in early autumn.... But the first cry of the cuckoo in spring is more to us than the new moon.... It

has been accepted as the object upon which we concentrate whatever feeling we have towards the beginning of spring. It constitutes a natural, unmistakable festival. We wish to hear it, we are eager and anxious about it, we pause when it reaches us, as if perhaps it might be bringing more than it ever brought yet." The final half of the essay moves from the plane of universal human significance to the intensely personal as Thomas recounts his most recent first hearing of the cuckoo, while walking at sunset along a road between Laugharne and St. Clear's in Wales. The closing passage makes the reader participate in Thomas's uncertainty before he confirms the bird's far-off cry: "The road was deep in dust, but the marigolds in the ditch preserved their brightness and their coolness. Coming over the shoulder of the hill called Pwll y Pridd, by the farm Morfa Bach, where the primroses were so thick under the young emerald larches, I began to have a strong desire–almost amounting to a conviction–that I should hear the cuckoo. When I was down again at Goose's Bridge, by the brook that descends out of a furzy valley towards the Taf, I heard it, or thought I did. I stopped. Not a sound. I went on stealthily that I might stop as soon as I heard anything. Again I seemed to hear it; again it had gone by the time I was still. The third time I had no doubt. The cuckoo was singing over on the far side of the valley, perhaps three-quarters of a mile away, probably in a gorse bank just above the marsh. For half a minute he sang, changed his perch unseen and sang again, his notes as free from the dust and heat as the cups of the marigolds, and as soft as the pale white-blue sky, and as dim as the valley into whose twilight he was gathered, calling fainter and fainter, as I drew towards home."

A mixture of the personal and nature essay, "This England" is hauntingly beautiful and could stand, along with the poem "Words," as Thomas's own epitaph. Its subject is the country walks that Thomas and Robert Frost took when they were together near Ledington in August 1914, and the simple, direct, almost painterly description of the landscape makes the essay seem a distillation of Thomas's previous nature writing. The essay also records the evening walk with Frost (here referred to only as "a friend") that Thomas would later write about in the poem "The Sun Used to Shine." All this particularity is nestled under the rubric of a sentence of homage to the region, a sentence in which Thomas's abiding love of English place names, and the historical and literary roots of his feeling for the country, are encapsuled: "the name, Hereford, had somehow won in my mind a very distinctive meaning; it stood out among country names as the most delicately rustic of them all, with a touch of nobility given it long ago, I think, by Shakespeare's 'Harry of Hereford, Lancaster, and Derby.'" Nowhere in his work, perhaps, is Thomas's deep love of the English countryside more apparent; nowhere is his aptitude for friendship more clearly outlined. But love of the countryside and the delights of friendship coalesce at the end of the essay in Thomas's conviction that he must do something to protect these values with regard to the war in Europe. Looking at the new moon that evening, he writes, "I thought, like many other people, what things that same new moon sees eastward about the Meuse in Francee.... I was deluged,

in a second stroke, by another thought, or something that overpowered thought. All I can tell is, it seemed to me that either I had never loved England, or I had loved it foolishly, aesthetically, like a slave, not having realized that it was not mine unless I were willing and prepared to die rather than leave it as Belgian women and old men and children had left their country.... Something, I felt, had to be done before I could look again composedly at English landscape, at the elms and poplars about the houses, at the purple-headed wood-betony with two pairs of dark leaves on a stiff stem, who stood sentinel among the grasses or bracken by hedge-side or wood's-edge. What he stood sentinel for I did not know, any more than what I had got to do."

Within a year Thomas had worked out what he had to do: in July 1915 he enlisted in the infantry. Seven months earlier he had written his first poems and become "conscious of a possible perfection as I never was in prose." As decisive and irrevocable as his volunteering for the service, Thomas's writing of verse gave him the capacity to "look again composedly at English landscape." Many of his poems reflect that capacity, while others deal with his habitual doubts and fears. Several of the best of them ("The Owl," "The Gallows," "As the Team's Headbrass") powerfully record the psychological effects of the war on those who stayed at home. Thomas's poems, which bear eloquent witness to the England that he loved, are the final product of all he had learned in the long apprenticeship of his prose–an apprenticeship that ended, in a handful of essays, in mastery.

Letters:

Letters from Edward Thomas to Gordon Bottomley, edited by R. George Thomas (London, New York & Toronto: Oxford University Press, 1968).

Biographies:

Helen Thomas, *As It Was* (London: Heinemann, 1926);

Thomas, *World Without End* (London: Heinemann, 1931);

Robert P. Eckert, *Edward Thomas: A Biography and Bibliography* (London: Dent, 1937);

Eleanor Farjeon, *Edward Thomas: The Last Four Years* (London: Oxford University Press, 1958);

William Cooke, *Edward Thomas: A Critical Biography, 1878-1917* (London: Faber & Faber, 1970);

R. George Thomas, *Edward Thomas: A Portrait* (Oxford: Clarendon Press, 1985; New York: Oxford University Press, 1985).

References:

Neville Braybrook, "Edward Thomas, 1878-1917," *Queen's Quarterly*, 74 (Autumn 1976): 506-508;

H. Coombes, *Edward Thomas* (London: Chatto & Windus, 1956);

W. J. Keith, "Edward Thomas," in his *The Poetry of Nature: Rural Perspectives in Poetry from Wordsworth to the Present* (Toronto: University of Toronto Press, 1980), pp. 141-166;

Keith, "Edward Thomas," in his *The Rural Tradition: A Study of the Non-Fiction Prose Writers of the English Countryside* (Toronto: University of Toronto Press, 1974), pp. 191-211;

Jan Marsh, *Edward Thomas: A Poet for His Country* (London: Elek, 1978; New York: Harper & Row, 1978).

Papers:

Among the more important collections of Thomas's papers are those in the Bodleian Library, the British Museum, the University College Library, Cardiff, the Berg collection of the New York Public Library, and the Lockwood Memorial Library, Buffalo, New York.

Elizabeth Wordsworth

(22 June 1840 - 30 November 1932)

Nancy A. Barta-Smith
University of Iowa

BOOKS: *Ballads from English History* (London: The National Society, 1864);

Thoughts for the Chimney Corner (London: Hatchards, 1873);

Short Words for Long Evenings (London: Hatchards, 1875);

Thornwell Abbas, 2 volumes, as Grant Lloyd (London: Low, 1876);

In Doors and Out (London: Hatchards, 1881);

Ebb and Flow, 2 volumes, as Grant Lloyd (London: Smith, Elder, 1883);

Christopher Wordsworth: Bishop of Lincoln 1807-1885, by Wordsworth and John Henry Overton (London: Rivingtons, 1888);

Illustrations of the Creed (London: Rivingtons, 1889; New York: Dutton, 1890);

Saint Christopher and Other Poems (London: Longmans, Green, 1890);

William Wordsworth (London: Percival, 1891);

The Apple of Discord (Oxford: Printed by Bridge, 1892; revised edition, Oxford: Alden, 1902);

The decalogue (London & New York: Longmans, Green, 1893);

Belinda in the twentieth century (Oxford: Printed by Bridge, 1894);

First Principles in Women's Education (Oxford: James Parker, 1894);

Henry William Burrows, memorials (London: Kegan Paul, Trench, Trübner, 1894);

The snow garden, and other fairy tales for children (London: Longmans, Green, 1895);

The wonderful lamp (Oxford: Printed by Alden, 1895);

. . . One eye, two eyes, and three eyes (Oxford: Printed by Bridge, 1898);

Beauty and the beast (Oxford: Printed by Alden, Bocardo Press, 1899);

The Druid Stone (Oxford: Alden, 1903);

Only a Feather; or, Wayside Thoughts for Working People (Oxford: Wells Gardner, 1904);

Psalms for the Christian Festivals (London: Longmans, Green, 1906);

Elizabeth Wordsworth, 1900 (by permission of Lady Margaret Hall, Oxford)

Onward Steps, or, The incarnation and its practical teaching (London: Wells Gardner, Darton, 1911);

Glimpses of the Past (London & Oxford: A. R. Mowbray, 1912);

The Lord's Prayer in time of war (Oxford: Blackwell, 1916);

Essays Old and New (Oxford: Clarendon Press, 1919);

Poems and plays (London: Oxford University Press, 1931).

OTHER: Susan Mary Elizabeth, St. Helier, Lady Jeune, ed., *Ladies at Work: Papers on Paid Employments for Ladies*, includes an article by Wordsworth (London: Innes, 1893);

The life and adventures of Lady Anne, the little pedlar, by the author of the blue silk workbag, Harcourt family, etc. A new edition, introduction by Wordsworth (London: A. R.

Mowbray / Milwaukee: Young Churchman, 1913).

The intellectual gifts, personal warmth, and wit of Elizabeth Wordsworth were first exercised within the circle of her own family. It was not until she was nearly thirty that close personal friendships with Edward Benson, future Archbishop of Canterbury (then headmaster at Wellington), and with Charlotte Yonge, a popular novelist of the day, encouraged her to exercise these gifts more publicly. It was also Edward Benson, a family friend since Elizabeth's brother John had served under him as master at Wellington, who encouraged Elizabeth Wordsworth's father to accept elevation to the episcopate at Lincoln, thus physically removing her from the confines of the country parish at Stanford. These expansions of Elizabeth Wordsworth's sphere of experience helped to prepare her for the administrative role

314

she would play as the head of Lady Margaret Hall at Oxford. Much of what she has written followed inevitably from her position as educator of this second family and from her role as founder of St. Hughes, Oxford. Although Georgina Battiscombe's biography of Elizabeth Wordsworth, *Reluctant Pioneer*, focuses on what Battiscombe calls Wordsworth's presumably inadvertent support for the women's movement, Wordsworth's significance rests as well on her talent as essayist. Indeed, frequent differences in viewpoint between Elizabeth Wordsworth and her biographer illustrate concretely the dramatic re-visioning that was occurring during Wordsworth's lifetime. Her essays are both interesting and important for this reason.

At Elizabeth Wordsworth's birth, her father, the scholar and churchman Christopher Wordsworth, is said to have been unable to hide his disappointment. Somehow he had envisioned that his daughter would be able to communicate immediately. "I had rather thought," he is said to have commented, "it would be more like that" (pointing to a portrait of the Blessed Virgin and the already articulate Christ child). So as soon as possible he set himself the task of sharing with his eldest child his intellectual and, equally important, his moral gifts. In her memoir Elizabeth remarked that the atmosphere in the household was a "serious" one. Her father talked with his children as if they were adults, and at an early age his daughter Elizabeth learned to earn fruit for dessert by reciting a list of the sees and their respective bishops. The family's traditional values and her father's classical interest thus made her a spiritual inhabitant of an earlier age than the one in which she lived. This basically conservative background undoubtedly contributed to her less than radical stance on women's education as well. Battiscombe says that she affirmed to the end of her life a statement made in an article for the *Monthly Packet*: "In old days a real lady was educated by the atmosphere she habitually breathed. Many women go through the world without ever hearing as much good conversation as might be picked up at the breakfast table on a week's visit at some privileged house." As much as the modern reader may be unsettled by ideas of class or horrified to hear of education being "picked up," as it were, over morning tea, the association of education with everyday conversation and privilege is necessary if the reader is to understand Elizabeth Wordsworth's ideas and account for the enormity of the shift in worldview that has since occurred.

Modern studies had only recently earned respectability at Cambridge and Oxford; only recently had new colleges such as London College sprung up. Liberal education to Elizabeth Wordsworth's father and grandfather had meant an enrichment of intellectual and spiritual life that could only properly result in the development of character and virtuous action; it bore little resemblance to the imparting of information, and its fruition was seen in the goodness of one's life, not in professional accomplishments or scientific discoveries.

It was the force of Elizabeth Wordsworth's personality, molded in the classical and Anglo-Catholic tradition she imbibed at home, that was to endear her to the women she came to educate as principal of the first women's residence at Oxford, and that, indeed, was to remove reservations, at first widely held, regarding admission of women to degree examinations at Oxford and Cambridge. Her writings reflect the humanistic traditions she lived–a reverence for the deeply intellectual and spiritual heritage of Europe, grounded in the Greco-Roman and Christian legacy of a continent as yet unaffected by the materialistic values requisite to the practical exigencies of commerce or by the nihilism that Charles Darwin's evolutionary theories and resultant religious skepticism precipitated. If her unwavering belief in man's possibilities for virtuous action and in the meaningfulness of human experience seem naive to readers weaned on skepticism and angst, these beliefs can as well produce hope and ultimately joy in those willing to entertain the possibility that life has meaning after all. Even if Elizabeth Wordsworth herself did not actively join the cause of women's rights championed by such of her students as Kathleen Courtney and Maude Royden, surely the conferral upon her of the first M.A. degree (*honoris causa*) awarded by Oxford to a member of her sex testifies not just to recognition of her as symbol of "the Oxford woman" but to the fact that her work is worth recovering.

Elizabeth Wordsworth was born on 22 June 1840, the eldest child of Christopher Wordsworth, then headmaster of Harrow, and Susannah Hatley Frere Wordsworth. Her father had followed in the footsteps of her grandfather, another Christopher Wordsworth, distinguished master of Trinity College at Cambridge and brother of the poet William Wordsworth. In 1845, when she was four, Elizabeth moved with her family to Westminster after her father was

Christopher Wordsworth, Bishop of Lincoln (photograph by Elliott & Fry), and Susanna Hatley Wordsworth (portrait by E. U. Eddis), Elizabeth Wordsworth's parents, in 1883 (from Elizabeth Wordsworth, Glimpses of the Past, *1912)*

made canon there. This and subsequent moves related to her father's pastoral work had their effects on her intellectual and moral growth.

At Westminster the garden of the abbey, where she often spent hours sketching, and the old house at number 4 Little Cloister, its centuries of additions in evidence, must have nurtured both her religious faith and her respect for history and tradition. After 1851 eight months of the year were spent in the country because Canon Wordsworth also held the chapter living of Stanford-in-the-Vale, Berkshire. Life at the Vale of the White Horse at Stanford was in sharp contrast to the sublime experience of the abbey, but the walls were covered with prints. In the study, bookshelves filled every available space, and books lay about open–testament to the twenty-year task of Christopher Wordsworth's biblical commentary, a family project in which Elizabeth's help was to be indispensable. The commentary was pursued at Stanford in relative leisure. Elizabeth Wordsworth's imagination was stimulated not only by the wonders of the abbey at Westminster but by the natural beauty of the

countryside and the workings, and often hardships, of village life. Even though she belonged to a more-privileged group, she had a deep sympathy for the material and spiritual needs of the parishioners, who were always welcome at the vicarage, and from a young age, though scarcely older than her pupils, she participated in pastoral visits and the religious instruction of her father's flock.

But Elizabeth Wordsworth the educator was also pupil herself. Perhaps one of the reasons she has been described as lukewarm in her support of women's education is that she never experienced any particular disadvantage regarding her own. Indeed, she was better educated at home than she would have been in a school for girls, and her education there differed from that of her brothers far less than it would have elsewhere. Before he immersed himself in his biblical commentary her father wrote two scholarly books on Greece that went through several editions and transcribed the *Graffiti* of Pompeii, so it is not surprising that Elizabeth felt the incentive to learn Greek on her own with the help of the

Greek Testament. She learned Latin, French, and Italian as well. She traveled with her father in France, Italy, Germany, and Switzerland and studied English literature through free access to books. Naturally curious, she found books, not instructors, the key to education. Her mother's practice of having the girls read aloud developed her speaking voice; piano and singing fostered her love of music. Plain needlework was a concession to exclusively female occupations. Mathematics and science were left out of all of the children's education regardless of sex, though Elizabeth Wordsworth's talents as an artist led her to sketch much of the flora and fauna in the Vale.

In 1857 Elizabeth Wordsworth did have some formal education–a brief sojourn at a girls' school in Brighton. The Brighton experience did not further her religious education; her home occupation of copying portions of her father's commentary for the press, proofreading, and verifying references had assured her scholarship in this subject. (Theological questions had been mealtime conversation at home, and the Greek Testament was interpreted on Sunday evenings.) Her education at Brighton did contribute to her fluency in French, however, and it was there that she learned German and increased her appreciation of dancing and music. She was not enthusiastic about some subjects, though, describing the art education she received there as mechanical copying. At Brighton she began to develop an independent judgment about history and literature though her family's influence permanently marked her thoughts. The experience at Brighton also must have given her insight into all the vicissitudes of community living she would eventually deal with at Lady Margaret Hall. The long "crocodile" walks there, in particular, convinced her of the importance of physical health and games if the austerity of the family nursery with its cold baths had not already done so. She remained robust, continuing a regimen of cold baths and brisk daily walks until her death at ninety-two.

Elizabeth Wordsworth had begun writing before 1869, when her father became bishop of Lincoln and took a house for his family at Riseholme, but only one of her books appeared before this move: *Ballads from English History*, which was published anonymously in 1864 by The National Society. Twenty of the ballads have been ascribed to Elizabeth, two to her brother John, and one to their Aunt Anne, widow of Captain Frere. The preface was written by Canon Wordsworth.

From 1871 on Elizabeth Wordsworth sent her poems and stories to her friend Charlotte Yonge, some for publication in Yonge's children's magazine, the *Monthly Packet*. Wordsworth also wrote two pious tracts, *Thoughts for the Chimney Corner* (1873) and *Short Words for Long Evenings* (1875). Her novel *Thornwell Abbas*, published in 1876 under the pseudonym Grant Lloyd (the names of her two grandmothers), had been written almost a decade earlier. It is difficult to know whether the use of this pseudonym reflects the anxiety over authorship common among nineteenth-century women writers. Since she was to publish in other genres under her own name, the reason may have been the novel's autobiographical content. In it the surroundings of Westminster are much in evidence as is the similarity between Elizabeth Wordsworth's experiences and those of the principal characters of the novel, the daughter of a squire and the niece of a vicar who go to Oxford for Commemoration.

By the time *Thornwell Abbas* was published some important changes had occurred at Oxford. After 1872 fellows were allowed to marry, and other colleges followed suit. The young avantgarde women who became part of the university community contrasted with the more sedate wives of professors and heads of houses. Elizabeth Wordsworth's reputation as "excellent company" spread rapidly as well. The first lecture for women had been initiated in 1866 but was not continued in succeeding years. In 1873 John Ruskin came to Oxford to give public lectures on Italian art, and the young women turned out in good numbers, forming a committee under Louise Creighton to promote lectures and classes for women thereafter. Elizabeth Wordsworth attended at least two lectures by historian Robert Laing, receiving high praise for her essay on the Crusades. These lectures brought her into contact with other supporters of education for women at Oxford. During the 1870s her brothers and sisters were marrying while she continued to perform the social duties connected with her father's position and to write. In 1873 a completed novel was sent to Charlotte Yonge. It was not published until 1883, when it appeared as *Ebb and Flow*. There exists a manuscript for a blank-verse play, *The Shadow of the Sphinx* (dated July 1878), a fairy-tale version of Christ's Passion, set in Egypt with characters who speak Elizabethan English. Battiscombe judges the play unsuitable for production, and she credits Wordsworth with a remarkable gift for literary mimicry, citing

Family members at the wedding of Elizabeth Wordsworth's sister Dora to Rev. Edward Tucker Leeke, 8 April 1880: (standing) Rev. James John Trebeck, Rev. Edward Tucker Leeke, Mary Reeve Wordsworth, Rev. Christopher Wordsworth, Mary Wordsworth Trebeck, Percy Andrew Steedman, Priscilla Wordsworth Steedman, Susan Esther Coxe Wordsworth, and Rev. John Wordsworth; (seated) Susan Wordsworth, Dora Wordsworth Leeke, Susanna Wordsworth, Bishop Christopher Wordsworth, and Elizabeth Wordsworth (from Elizabeth Wordsworth, Glimpses of the Past, *1912)*

how closely she parodied Christina Rossetti's *Goblin Market* (1862) and William Wordsworth's *Prelude* (1850). Speaking of the relative merits of Elizabeth Wordsworth's addresses and publications, Battiscombe claims, "Whereas in speaking she was incisive and original, in writing she always fell back on borrowed tones and never found the use of her own voice"–too harsh a judgment in this reader's view.

During the 1870s supporters of women's education pressed for expansion of the opportunities for women begun at Oxford in 1867, when local examinations were opened to girls. Though reforms regarding examinations were coming gradually, the women in Oxford wanted halls of residence (which were already open at Cambridge) as well. There was some controversy among the women themselves. The Christ Church group was for church affiliation and tradition, while those at Balliol took a more avant-garde position. On 4 June 1878 the conservative

group under Edward Talbot decided to proceed with plans for a residence connected with the Church of England. Elizabeth was offered its headship in a letter dated 19 November 1878, and she suggested its name–Lady Margaret Hall, in memory of a benefactor of Oxford and Cambridge, Lady Margaret Beaufort, Countess of Richmond, mother of King Henry VII. Her status as principal doubtless created new opportunities for Elizabeth Wordsworth to write and increased the demands of her social life and perhaps the incentives for her to publish her work.

In 1881 *In Doors and Out*, a small book of poems, drew praise from the *Guardian*, a church weekly whose reviewer saw in the poems, despite their uneven quality, the spark of the same fire alive in another Wordsworth of greater repute. Battiscombe judges them better than any of Elizabeth Wordsworth's other poems. *Ebb and Flow* was finally published in 1883, under the same pseudonym Wordsworth used for her first novel. Her biographer finds charm in it and points out its similarity to Charlotte Yonge's work, though she does not call it parody. She says that both women chose to write about artists though "neither of them had any personal knowledge of the art world," a statement which seems to conflict with the evidence of Elizabeth Wordsworth's personal interest in sketching, her love of Westminster and of Ruskin (and her indebtedness to him for what she knows of art), and her frequent references to art in her essays.

On 4 March 1885 she published in the *Guardian* an article titled "The Watershed in George Eliot's Life," which reflects her customary critical standards. In Wordsworth's view Eliot's loss of faith led to a loss of morals, and she refuses to see Eliot's conduct as less reprehensible because Eliot was a person of genius. Also typically, her critical comments touch on contemporary life. She discusses how religion must meet the needs of intellect and points out the particular immediacy of this problem because of the ongoing expansion of intellectual opportunities for women.

This article was only one of many. During 1885-1886 Elizabeth Wordsworth prepared a series of addresses specifically designed to meet the religious needs of the new generation of women students at Oxford. They were published in 1889 as *Illustrations of the Creed*. She was aware of the dramatic social changes occurring around her and of the differences in life-style and educational needs of the educated or partially educated, especially in the middle class, from whom the traditions and sonorous language of Anglican High Church rhetoric might seem remote indeed and for whom the superficial quoting of scripture might have replaced understanding and living by it. *Illustrations of the Creed* is a series of homilies on the Anglican Creed examined phrase by phrase; the introduction in particular is an apologia not so much for religion but for Elizabeth Wordsworth's imaginative vision. As humanist, she is reconciler. The rhetoric of analysis and defense (the modern approach perhaps) is basically one that sets minds and therefore individuals at odds, negating similarities. It is therefore antagonistic to her imaginative vision of the human as shared possibility tending toward common ends. Though today's feminists may consider institutions to be the consolidation of power over others, Wordsworth sees them as monuments externalizing beliefs, as concrete projections of collective memory. An immaterial spiritual reality gives meaning to the ma-

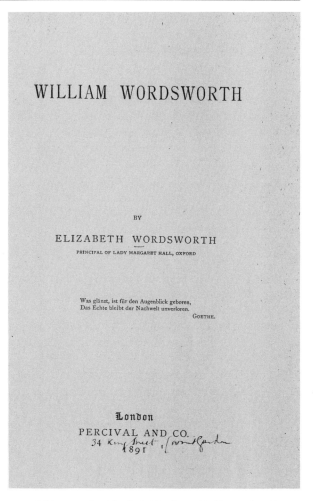

Title page for Elizabeth Wordsworth's biography of her granduncle

terial institution just as rites and sacraments are outward signs of inward grace. This perspective is perhaps the point most necessary to understanding her ideas. It recurs repeatedly in her essays. She does not set the immaterial and material at odds; she values things because they are continually infused with significance when man's imaginative powers, consciousness and memory, interpret daily experience. This interpretation is an *imputing* of meaning, however, not a *discovering* of it, because the humanist places on man and his unique faculties a special value. That men impute meaning naturally or *un*consciously is proof to Elizabeth Wordsworth that establishing institutions is likewise a *natural* human endeavor—"to deny this would be to fly in the face of the laws which govern humanity." The institution itself always follows the idea, however. Therefore, in her view, it can never be proof of the idea, only expression of it, just as in her biography of her father she says that what he cared about in art as in everything else was the idea that lay behind it. Thus her discussion of the Creed is not an argument but an explanation.

During the 1880s she wrote frequently for the *Guardian*, and for *Aunt Judy's Magazine* and Charlotte Yonge's *Monthly Packet*, two publications for children (the second specifically for girls). One article from the *Monthly Packet*, republished in a book called *Ladies at Work* (1893), edited by Lady Jeune, is an interesting statement of Elizabeth Wordsworth's views on the role of women intertwined with the philosophy that informs her other essays–the goal of education as development of person and character, not just mind.

Despite her conservative views and position at Lady Margaret Hall, Elizabeth Wordsworth's social life included more liberal thinkers, such as Mark Pattison and members of the Balliol camp of Somerville, the nondenominational hall, such as T. H. Green, Strachan-Davidson, Evelyn Abbot, and Benjamin Jowett. The social and administrative responsibilities incumbent on the principal of Lady Margaret Hall too often kept her away from her family during a difficult time, for in 1884 her mother died and was followed by her father in 1885. Less than a year passed before she and Canon John Overton of Lincoln began work on a biography of her father. *Christopher Wordsworth: Bishop of Lincoln 1807-1885*, published in 1888, was followed by *Saint Christopher and Other Poems* in 1890, and a biographical and critical study, *William Wordsworth*, in 1891. The first published play of those Elizabeth Wordsworth wrote for performance by Lady Margaret Hall students also dates from this period. *The Apple of Discord* (1892) is an entertaining short comic opera based on the classical story of Paris and the Golden Apple. The prize, characteristically, is not just beauty but learning, which until then "No woman's hand has plucked from mystic bough."

In 1886 an unexpected windfall of six hundred pounds allowed Elizabeth Wordsworth to found a second hall, St. Hughes, in her father's memory. It grew so rapidly that moves to new houses were required in both 1887 and 1888, and other expansions occurred subsequently. During the 1880s and 1890s these developments and a series of brilliant and outspoken students at Lady Margaret Hall–Janet Hogarth, Kathleen Courtney, Gertrude Bell, Eleanor Lodge, and Barbara Bradley among others–challenged Elizabeth Wordsworth's energies and values. She worked tirelessly for the granting of the B.A. degree to women and for the continued growth of Lady Margaret Hall. Between 1889 and 1896 it became a formally constituted college.

An accomplished speaker, Elizabeth Wordsworth was in constant demand during these years. Manuscripts for many addresses exist from this period, but most were never published. At a Church Congress in Exeter in October 1893 she delivered a talk, *First Principles in Women's Education*, which did appear as a pamphlet in 1894. She finds those first principles in Genesis and asserts a unique gender relationship between the sexes in the human species because humans differ from animals not just in degree but "in kind," as she later says in *Essays Old and New* (1919).

As Lady Margaret Hall grew, its family atmosphere changed, and Elizabeth Wordsworth's age, as well as the loss of personal contact inherent in the institution Lady Margaret Hall had become, perhaps precipitated her resignation from the headship on 8 October 1908. Thereafter she made her home in Oxford surrounded by her books and few comforts. She entertained, however, asking old students to lunch and tea, and occasionally housed new ones; she continued to write for magazines, to lecture from time to time, and to read voraciously. In 1912 she published *Glimpses of the Past*, as she said, to provide for the younger Wordsworth descendants a family record. This task, of course, was thoroughly consistent with her reverence for personal experience, especially as it is preserved in memory as raw material for the creative imagination. The Bible and classics sustained her during World War I when sorrow for the deaths at the front was compounded by those of many old friends. Her last major publication, *Essays Old and New*, a collection of articles and addresses, appeared in 1919.

This volume is undoubtedly Elizabeth Wordsworth's most important essay collection. Battiscombe holds the book rather in low esteem, calling all or nearly all of Wordsworth's published writings commonplace. She prefers the unpublished addresses, still extant in manuscript. The addresses are "real," Battiscombe judges, adding that Elizabeth Wordsworth herself declared in one of them, "reality is the answer to the commonplace." To this reader such a judgment seems to ignore the significant change in values and beliefs (and the critical standards those beliefs might engender) between the time in which Elizabeth Wordsworth lived and the time in

Elizabeth Wordsworth, 1909 (by permission of Lady Margaret Hall, Oxford)

which her biographer lived. One cannot discount the difficulty with which the modern, practical, bourgeois mind finds sympathy for Elizabeth Wordsworth's critical perspective; yet it is imperative that this difficulty be overcome if one is to appreciate and understand her thought. It is also essential to understand what the humanistic essay is and does.

Battiscombe prefers the addresses because every page reveals Wordsworth's "exceptional knowledge of the Bible." She cites as evidence the use of the original Greek and Hebrew, alternative readings from the Septuagint, meanings of obscure words and doubtful passages, matters of dating and authorship. In addition she applauds the seeds of religious skepticism she reads into Elizabeth Wordsworth's admission of the *possibility* of a base for the Bible in mythology in spite of Wordsworth's *belief* that the Bible's base lies in history. Similarly Battiscombe approves that Wordsworth's scholarship is not confined to the

Bible but runs as well to novels, but these are modernist preferences.

The more scholarly approach of the addresses is partly due to the fact that many were conceived for Bible studies delivered in conjunction with religious services at Lady Margaret Hall. Elizabeth Wordsworth's essays are distillations of insight and reflection on life and human nature rather than compendiums of information on any subject. Of course there is scholarship in the published essays. Classical education conferred a vast amount of knowledge, but its purpose was not to impart information but to foster a rich inner life and character. Elizabeth Wordsworth always worked within the humanistic framework. In *Essays Old and New* she writes a kind of cultural criticism in which man more than any text is central. A humanistic orientation does not simply imply treatment of subject matters traditionally called the humanities. When Elizabeth Wordsworth says that the real is the answer to

321

the commonplace, she affirms immaterial (moral and spiritual) realities. She considered not only the mundane aspect of daily life, but also the bare facts of intellectual investigation, commonplace unless infused with the meaning supplied by religion and belief in the possibility of man's moral goodness.

Thus she says in the first essay, "Dante and Goethe," "we all feel the change which has come over the world since Dante's time–an inner change far more important than all that science has done for our outward life." The points on which she contrasts Dante and Goethe are, not surprisingly, reality, moral earnestness, nature, and love. She says Dante was born in an age when skepticism was not yet widespread and when "moral responsibility," at least in theory, was fully recognized. She contrasts the books of the two authors "not only in the incidents they narrate, but in the relative pitch of their writers' minds." Goethe's early life was more full of objects "than of influences which could form the character." There were no heroes. In contrast, Dante loses himself in his subject. His thought is synthetic. He sees in phenomena parts of a "magnificent whole to which they, and all things else, are tending." He has the powers of idealizing "the common incidents of human life." Goethe is precisely Dante's inverse. He is "self-conscious, analytical, and irreverent." Like Mephistopheles, he despoils everything. To Dante it is a natural function of human imagination to look up to something outside itself. Goethe must settle for Mephistophelian theatrics instead, as a sort of pantomime of the sublime, since for him the sublime does not exist as antidote for human weakness. But even this statement obscures the issue because the meanings of words have changed. If reality for the modern is material reality, the most sublime moments may well be those spent in bed rather than those spent in church. Because of the disparity in these two beliefs regarding the existence of immaterial reality, Wordsworth sees Dante's idea of the devil as a traitor; Goethe's as a scoffer. Love for Goethe is earthy passion; for Dante "ennobling unselfish affection."

Not unexpectedly, Wordsworth ends her essay by asking the questions that are the focus of her critical perspective: What has Goethe taught? "What impulses has he awakened for good?" She believes that the two questions are always closely allied. When she concludes with a postscript written forty years after the original essay, she has not lost sight of her cultural and

moral emphasis. In the figure of Faust she sees the present leaders of a Germany losing its soul to war, and she asks whether Goethe's life and work are a reflection of national spirit or whether he himself bears responsibility for molding and producing that spirit.

This moral earnestness is only one way in which Elizabeth Wordsworth reflects a humanistic vision. If all things are truly pieces of one whole, then it is not just the variety of human experience that enriches life but also the continuity afforded by historical perspective. "At Stratford-on-Avon" includes one of the most delightful examples of her seemingly unconscious wit and humor: "The thought may perhaps have occurred to some of us, how much more Roman (after all) we are in a certain sense, at least, than the Romans, if we realize that Caesar had never read a single line of Horace or Virgil. . . ." Then, pushing the analogy further, she adds that poor Shakespeare "lived in a pre-Shakesperian world." Her point is a serious one, however, reflecting her early exposure to her father's serious conversation. The Romans, Shakespeare, and Elizabeth Wordsworth's readers are of a piece because "the great makers of human society seldom live in the society they have helped to mold–*they* labour, and other men enter into their labours."

That all men are responsible for molding society is never questioned. Elizabeth Wordsworth's insistent message cannot escape her readers. It is Stratford-on-Avon–its "flora and fauna"–that has set her thinking, but her point, like Dante's whole, is tending elsewhere. If Shakespeare's art is true, then "Shakespeare's people are *ourselves*." In her view contemporary writers of drama are unable to claim Shakespeare as forebear, evidence of a void in contemporary literature, and her parting hope is that this loss to art will not mold a generation of vacuous men in its image.

Wordsworth returns to the question of reality in the third essay in this collection, "Behind the Scenes," overlaying it with both her Shakespearean reference point and her ideas on continuity. Her discussion of the creative possibilities of the imagination bridges thought from Plato to Jacob Bronowski's "Reach of the Imagination." Turning Shakespeare's meaning askew, she says of later treatment of Macbeth's famous lines "Life's but a walking shadow, a poor player / that struts and frets his hour upon the stage, / And then is heard no more," that "the impression left on most of our minds is that what goes on behind the scenes is 'real,' while all that goes on

Elizabeth Wordsworth, Mrs. Johnson, and Mrs. Toynbee at a Lady Margaret Hall garden party, 16 June 1909 (photograph by Miss A. L. Hodson; from Elizabeth Wordsworth, Glimpses of the Past, *1912)*

upon the stage is what the children call 'pretense.' " She would rather affirm another reality: the play's the thing. "The greatness of the drama lies in this, that it testifies to, and helps to stimulate, the *growth* of human society." "A child is a born actor ... because he is always trying to work his way out of what he *is*, to what he wants to be." And "actors are most themselves when they are on the stage." The imagination, in her view, completes and perfects a human experience that is never fully realized in what the modern reader has learned to call the real, daily life. The San Sisto Madonna is not really smudges of paint on canvas; one does not know real men by reading biographies containing "all the foolish trifles that can be raked together about their pri-

vate lives." The celebration of plotless, trivial daily experience found in some contemporary fiction would never qualify as literature. Inadvertently exemplifying the idea of continuity she exposits elsewhere, Elizabeth Wordsworth links arms with modern linguistic theory when she laments those who "lose sight of the thing signified in the sign." To her the commonplace is not the real, but only a sign of an immaterial reality; in the modern view the real is unremittingly material. Carrying the point into the realm of education she adds: "And what manner of education is best for children? That in which they are kept constantly with their coevals, and never allowed even to dream of being grown-up; or that in which the shadows of their future selves are ever flung in front of them, in which a noble idea is ever before their eyes, and in which their very play things and daily furniture are metamorphosed by the wondrous light of Imagination, or by the still more potent ministry of Faith, into the theatre where they may rehearse what will some day be their *real* parts, and thus grow to a higher stature, and the measure of a perfected fullness?" "Portia and Antigone in their own degree are, to everyday life, what converse with grown-up people ought to be with children," she says.

If Wordsworth laments the state of contemporary drama, however, she finds in Jane Austen a writer in sympathy with her essentially conservative perspective: "the real strength of England lay in the quiet country homes such as Jane Austen depicts, where the religion, simple as it seems, was genuine, real, and absolutely without 'pose' or self-consciousness, where there was an unquestioning belief in the essentials of the Christian faith, and where, we may add, the boys were brought up to behave as gentlemen, and the girls as ladies, as a matter of course." That a woman so instrumental in obtaining higher education for women was so conservative regarding sexual roles is obviously a source of frustration for her biographer, but the term she uses, *reluctant* pioneer, is perhaps misleading. Elizabeth Wordsworth had immense enthusiasm for educating women–but not because of their "right" to such education and never because of the possibilities for employment it might afford. Intellectual growth develops imaginative capacity and character, makes men and women more human. Jane Austen's novels return in imagination to "the simple, dutiful, straightforward, and unpretending characters of those men and women . . . on whose 'reserves' of moral and spiritual, as well as of physical force we are living our own strenuous, over-excited, and, too often, superficial lives." Austen preserves imaginatively a style of life that was rapidly disappearing–life before "the days of railways, chloroform, and electricity," a life of comfort but more important, of civilization. Finally Wordsworth finds Austen's humor too little appreciated, a humor that she sees as essentially conservative: "The present writer has long cherished a theory that there is a kind of English humour which often, if not always, goes hand-in-hand with conversation. It seems to be the product of an orderly, comfortable state of society where a 'fierce indignation' is almost entirely lacking." Elizabeth Wordsworth, herself a "good talker," possessed the same kind of humor and was short on reasons for "fierce indignation."

Imaginative vision rooted in the necessary relationship between beauty and goodness, whether based in religious faith or not, constitutes Wordsworth's critical perspective and is explicitly the subject matter of her discussion of Browning's "Andrea Del Sarto." Andrea says of failed artists, "Ah, but a man's reach should exceed his grasp, / Or what's a Heaven for?" But the fault in some artists is not failure to achieve imaginative vision but failure to have it, or more precisely, to have the vision Wordsworth has. She sees in the pictures of Frans Snyders, Jan Baptist Weenix, David Teniers, and Paul Potter the many eighteenth-century British versifiers whose dullness "had its climax in the great yawn of the goddess in the *Dunciad*." The "low pitched aspirations" of such painters and writers are the more disturbing to her because she must make a connection between art and life. "A character of this type has an almost painful fascination for us, us English people of the present day, because we have an uneasy feeling that it is only too like ourselves." In her judgment the great value of Browning's poem is in "its aspirations after infinity, and its high conception of love." It is this upward intellectual and imaginative orientation, this affirmation of a uniquely human possibility, that distinguishes her essay as humanistic. Present-day feminists may question this transcendence of self as "patriarchal" value, but for Elizabeth Wordsworth it is human essence. Man is not a species of animal to which intellect is added. Such a view is once again based on a materialistic idea of what is real: "It seems a difference not in degree only but also in kind which exists between the animals and man, capable as he is, not only of these lower feelings, but of friendships from which they may be said to be entirely banished, and of love which transfigures and survives them." She shares Browning's insight into human nature here and says explicitly what was implied in *First Principles in Women's Education* when she claimed that the gender relationship between man and woman is not merely that between male and female.

Wordsworth's discussion of idealistic and realistic art in "Andrea del Sarto" next puts her readers in the presence of "a third characteristic of human nature, affecting rather the spectator than the artist." The unfinishedness or suggestiveness of a work attracts the human mind, which is never passive. The highest masterpieces combine

Elizabeth Wordsworth, 1922 (portrait by T. Binney-Gibbs; by permission of Lady Margaret Hall, Oxford)

suggestiveness with finish. Novels that reproduce "wearisome banalities," attempts to promote spiritual edification by biblical detail (precisely the kind of biblical detail admired by Battiscombe as scholarship), and any work that leaves no room for the play of the imagination all fall into the same category as realistic art.

Elizabeth Wordsworth's closing remarks do much to explain the unremitting pessimism, realism become materialism, of the modern view. Dante's Belacqua, at the entrance to Purgatory, has no choice but to wait there a period of time equal to what he wasted on earth. Artists such as Andrea del Sarto seem to have begun their wait prematurely, she says: "they prefer sitting with dejected heads and listless hands in their self-chosen gloom . . . forgetting that it is part of the highest will that man should exercise his own." In effect, contemporary men choose not to pass from doubt, gloom, and despair to happiness and freedom. Elizabeth Wordsworth would have found meaning or true liberation impossible in the existentialist's embracing of his fate.

The next essay in this collection is a sketch of both Ruskin's thoughts on art and her own. Her enthusiasm for Ruskin was both personal and ideological. In her memoir she describes his visit during the early days of Lady Margaret Hall at length–the charming conversation and his subsequent gift of his books to its incipient library. She credits him as well with what knowledge she has of art. In this essay she examines his claim that the two influences on his life were a lofty moral standard and a love of the beautiful in art. This association of goodness and beauty, of course, engendered Elizabeth Wordsworth's respect, though it is interesting that she calls the two antithetical. There are, as well, other reasons for similarity between Elizabeth Wordsworth's and Ruskin's views since the early influences on what she calls Ruskin's maturing mind were Sir Walter Scott, one of her favorite authors, and later Dante, in whom interest had been revived after Gabriele Rossetti's arrival in England in 1824. Added to these influences on Ruskin, she cites those of Thomas Carlyle, her great-uncle William Wordsworth, and the classical poets and thinkers–especially Homer and Plato–whom Ruskin studied at Oxford and whom she mastered at home.

In discussing Ruskin's early recognition of J. M. W. Turner's artistic talent she finds in Turner's love for the landscapes he painted the common ground on which "the antithesis" of art and beauty meets. When you love something, she says, it is ever present in the imagination. Her discussion of Ruskin thus reinforces again the essential role of imagination and will and the moral implications of her humanistic vision. "If Turner had only ten minutes to make a sketch he would put on paper the really important things; while a commonplace man would be only doing the balustrades in the foreground of the picture," she muses.

The next four essays–"A Venture of Faith," "Old Finery," "Flattery," and "A Plea for Fetish Worship"–are homiletic and are perhaps the cause for Battiscombe's judgment of the "uneven quality" of the collection. In the first one Wordsworth judges the life of Christopher Columbus. Although he died destitute and the twentieth-century mind might consider him a failure in terms of its idea of "success," she sees his achievement, as usual, in his imaginative vision. "Now, we have just seen there was a time when all those vast and rich and lovely territories in America, existed for the European world, merely in one man's brain." She finds in his enterprise an exercise of faith rather than the Marxist's discovery of power and greed. And to the reader she urges, where faith is concerned, strong probability is enough to engender fervent belief.

In "Old Finery" she gives things symbolic value as emblems of labor, kindness, and fidelity. Characteristically books, the study chair, the sewing machine, and old letters come off well because in them intellect and imagination hold sway. But Elizabeth Wordsworth, whom Battiscombe says had a particular love of color and attention to dress, cannot bring herself to disparage the ephemeral and the commonplace. "It is *now* that we have to live," she says. There is a great deal of "actuality" in Aristophanes and Shakespeare. She does insist that the delight in the commonplace things comes from their connection to meaningful human experience. Old finery

is treasured not for the profit margin available in selling antiques but because such finery "caught the light, it flowed in the warmth, it swayed and moved, animated by the vitality of its wearer."

The next essay, "Flattery," is more a demonstration of her astute understanding of psychology than anything else. She defends the flatterer against maligners such as Alexander Pope, admitting that most of us really like flattery and that in some cases it may well be true and hardly blameworthy. In addition, the English national character with its "grim sense of duty" may need encouragement. To the objection that only small minds need praise, she counters that it is small people who often overstate their own worth and great ones who are self-deprecatory because of their high standards: "It was Prospero, the great magician, when he was telling a very momentous story, who fancied he was boring Miranda. The *real* bore of the play, good old Gonzalo, never discovered he was one!"

Ironically, she indulges in a bit of flattery herself regarding women. Though twentieth-century women may disclaim their power over men as disdainful sexual manipulation born of economic dependency, she sees their influence more sympathetically as imaginative vision: "What are women for but to put men into good humour with themselves? A woman by doing so often makes a man what she tells him he is." In her view, the true criterion by which one judges the difference between compliment and flattery is motive: what "cold and selfish men call flattery" may only be "the natural . . . enthusiasm of some happy dispositions which really find material for admiration and approval where others would only criticise."

In "A Plea for Fetish Worship" she finds meaning in "the unreasoning passionate devotion which . . . men and women so frequently display." Though primitive fetishes may pale by comparison with venerable statues, these commonplace objects have habit, antiquity, and tradition to sanction and consecrate them. Once again she sees the commonplace as infused with meaning by men in whom that meaning becomes either obsession or great idea. Thus this essay reaffirms the individual's responsibility for his imaginative vision, which can become a bête noire or draw him outside himself. The essay is thereby related to her comments on the unfinished or suggestive characteristic of art. Her vision, as usual, is a moral and religious one. Self-interest, the piling up of human occupations, is not the end to which human life tends as a whole. One needs a force or influence that will "do justice to the countless claims of others."

Though Elizabeth Wordsworth's biographer sees the next essay, "The English Church and the English Character," as chauvinistic and its most interesting moments as its asides, it is infused with belief in aspirations for human progress (not just technological progress), and this belief informs Wordsworth's assessment of the English Church and character. She sees the former as representing the feminine element in human life, which leaves room for individual freedom and sympathy, yet she finds its moral claims manly, a judgment that surely must have perplexed her feminist biographer.

"The Lilac Bush," the final essay in this collection, is a fitting concluding piece, since it contains a reiteration of her ideas on imagination, using the lilac bush as a metaphor. The beauty of the bush during the fortnight every year when it blooms is guarded in the mind's eye year-round. All human experiences are harbored in this way and are in her view "the best part of our existence in this world." Since for her the spiritual is real and material things pass away, memory is a uniquely human gift. Thus things once again are valuable because of their human connection. A lost ring is never truly lost because thanks to human imagination it can be seen at will. More important still, the affection it symbolizes, its giver, cannot be lost either. This essay reaffirms the distance between Elizabeth Wordsworth and the modernists. The "real" always interferes—more or less—with the "ideal," she says. Apprehending the character of others—and by *character* she means all that those persons *can* be in the best sense of the word—especially the character of those one lives with, may be difficult. But for her such moments of apprehension are "like the blossoming

of the lilac or the crocus, as rare as they are wonderful." The metaphor must always remain a metaphor, however, for "a man is not a man" in the way flowers are flowers. Elizabeth Wordsworth had a deep reverence for "the gift of personality" (which includes will and therefore moral responsibility). In her view a gift so revered is surely too valuable to be destroyed by its maker. Whereas the modern mind sees in religion an anodyne for man's fear of death, Elizabeth Wordsworth is so filled with wonder at the mystery of human life that she must believe it lives forever.

Surely these thoughts contributed to the equanimity with which she lived out the last years of her life. She remained on the Lady Margaret Hall Council until 1922 after what must have been the deeply gratifying bestowal of the M.A. degree *honoris causa* in 1920. With her usual wit, she announced the news in a self-deprecatory way, noting that *honoris causa* meant without having to pay fees. After World War I her overseas travels were curtailed, but otherwise she spent the years much as she had since her retirement. She remained vigorous enough to participate in Lady Margaret Hall's golden anniversary in 1928. She continued to have friends to tea, to write letters, still quoting passages from the classics in the original, to walk, and to hold readings with her Bible class till the evening she collapsed. With her sister at her side she died quietly two days later, on 30 November 1932.

Biography:
Georgina Battiscombe, *Reluctant Pioneer: The Life of Elizabeth Wordsworth* (London: Constable, 1978).

Papers:
Elizabeth Wordsworth's papers, including manuscripts and letters, are held in the archives of Lady Margaret Hall, Oxford.

William Butler Yeats

(13 June 1865 - 28 January 1939)

Diane Tolomeo Edwards
University of Victoria

See also the Yeats entries in *DLB 10: Modern British Dramatists, 1900-1945* and *DLB 19: British Poets, 1880-1914.*

BOOKS: *Mosada: A Dramatic Poem* (Dublin: Printed by Sealy, Bryers & Walker, 1886);

The Wanderings of Oisin and Other Poems (London: Kegan Paul, Trench, 1889);

John Sherman and Dhoya, as Ganconagh (London: Unwin, 1891; New York: Cassell, 1891);

The Countess Kathleen and Various Legends and Lyrics (London: Unwin, 1892; Boston: Roberts / London: Unwin, 1892);

The Celtic Twilight (London: Lawrence & Bullen, 1893; New York & London: Macmillan, 1894; revised and enlarged edition, London: Bullen, 1902; New York: Macmillan, 1902);

The Land of Heart's Desire (London: Unwin, 1894; Chicago: Stone & Kimball, 1894; revised edition, Portland, Maine: Mosher, 1903);

Poems (London: Unwin, 1895; London: Unwin / Boston: Copeland & Day, 1895; revised edition, London: Unwin, 1899; revised again, 1901, 1912, 1927);

The Secret Rose (London: Lawrence & Bullen, 1897; New York: Dodd, Mead / London: Lawrence & Bullen, 1897);

The Tables of the Law; The Adoration of the Magi (London: Privately printed, 1897; London: Elkin Mathews, 1904);

The Wind Among the Reeds (London: Elkin Mathews, 1899; New York & London: John Lane / Bodley Head, 1902);

The Shadowy Waters (London: Hodder & Stoughton, 1900; New York: Dodd, Mead, 1901);

Is the Order of R. R. & A. C. [Rosae Rubeae et Aureae Crucis] to remain a Magical Order? (N.p., 1901);

Cathleen ni Houlihan (London: Bullen, 1902);

Where There Is Nothing (New York: John Lane, 1902; London: Bullen, 1903);

Ideas of Good and Evil (London: Bullen, 1903; New York: Macmillan, 1903);

William Butler Yeats, 1930

In the Seven Woods: Being Poems Chiefly of the Irish Heroic Age (Dundrum: Dun Emer Press, 1903; New York & London: Macmillan, 1903);

The Hour-Glass: A Morality (London: Heinemann, 1903);

The Hour-Glass and Other Plays (New York & London: Macmillan, 1904); republished as *The Hour-Glass, Cathleen ni Houlihan, The Pot of Broth* (London: Bullen, 1904);

The King's Threshold (New York: John Quinn, 1904);

The King's Threshold and On Baile's Strand (London: Bullen, 1904);

328

Stories of Red Hanrahan (Dundrum: Dun Emer Press, 1905);

Poems 1899-1905 (London: Bullen / Dublin: Maunsel, 1906);

The Poetical Works of William B. Yeats, 2 volumes (New York & London: Macmillan, 1906, 1907; revised, 1912);

Deirdre (London: Bullen / Dublin: Maunsel, 1907);

Discoveries; A Volume of Essays (Dundrum: Dun Emer Press, 1907);

The Unicorn from the Stars and Other Plays, by Yeats and Lady Gregory (New York: Macmillan, 1908);

The Golden Helmet (New York: John Quinn, 1908);

The Collected Works in Verse and Prose of William Butler Yeats, 8 volumes (Stratford-on-Avon: Shakespeare Head Press, 1908);

Poems: Second Series (London: & Stratford-on-Avon: Bullen, 1909);

The Green Helmet and Other Poems (Dundrum: Cuala Press, 1910; New York: Paget, 1911; enlarged edition, London: Macmillan, 1912);

Synge and the Ireland of His Time (Dundrum: Cuala Press, 1911);

The Countess Cathleen, revised edition (London: Unwin, 1912);

The Cutting of An Agate (New York: Macmillan, 1912; enlarged edition, London: Macmillan, 1919);

Stories of Red Hanrahan, The Secret Rose, Rosa Alchemica (London & Stratford-upon-Avon: Bullen, 1913; New York: Macmillan, 1914);

Poems Written in Discouragement 1912-1913 (Dundrum: Cuala Press, 1913);

Responsibilities: Poems and a Play (Dundrum: Cuala Press, 1914);

Reveries over Childhood and Youth (Dundrum: Cuala Press, 1915; New York: Macmillan, 1916; London: Macmillan, 1916);

Responsibilities and Other Poems (London: Macmillan, 1916; New York: Macmillan, 1916);

The Wild Swans at Coole (Dundrum: Cuala Press, 1917; enlarged edition, London: Macmillan, 1919; New York: Macmillan, 1919);

Per Amica Silentia Lunae (London: Macmillan, 1918; New York: Macmillan, 1918);

Two Plays for Dancers (Dundrum: Cuala Press, 1919);

Michael Robartes and the Dancer (Dundrum: Cuala Press, 1921);

Four Plays for Dancers (London: Macmillan, 1921; New York: Macmillan, 1921);

The Trembling of the Veil (London: Laurie, 1922);

Later Poems (London: Macmillan, 1922; New York: Macmillan, 1924);

Plays in Prose and Verse, Written for an Irish Theatre, by Yeats and Lady Gregory (London: Macmillan, 1922; New York: Macmillan, 1924);

The Player Queen (London: Macmillan, 1922);

Plays and Controversies (London: Macmillan, 1923; New York: Macmillan, 1924);

Essays (London: Macmillan, 1924; New York: Macmillan, 1924);

The Cat and the Moon (Dublin: Cuala Press, 1924);

The Bounty of Sweden (Dublin: Cuala Press, 1925);

Early Poems and Stories (London: Macmillan, 1925; New York: Macmillan, 1925);

A Vision: An Explanation of Life Founded upon the Writings of Giraldus and upon Certain Doctrines Attributed to Kusta Ben Luka (London: Laurie, 1925); substantially revised as *A Vision* (London: Macmillan, 1937; New York: Macmillan, 1938);

Autobiographies: Reveries Over Childhood and Youth and The Trembling of the Veil (London: Macmillan, 1926; New York: Macmillan, 1927);

October Blast (Dublin: Cuala Press, 1927);

Stories of Red Hanrahan and The Secret Rose (London: Macmillan, 1927);

The Tower (London: Macmillan, 1928; New York: Macmillan, 1928);

Sophocles' King Oedipus: A Version for the Modern Stage by W. B Yeats (London: Macmillan, 1928; New York: Macmillan, 1928);

The Death of Synge and Other Passages from an Old Diary (Dublin: Cuala Press, 1928);

A Packet for Ezra Pound (Dublin: Cuala Press, 1929);

The Winding Stair (New York: Fountain Press, 1929);

Stories of Michael Robartes and His Friends. An Extract from a Record made by his Pupils; and a play in prose (Dublin: Cuala Press, 1932);

Words for Music Perhaps and Other Poems (Dublin: Cuala Press, 1932);

The Winding Stair and Other Poems (London: Macmillan, 1933; New York: Macmillan, 1933);

The Collected Poems (New York: Macmillan, 1933; London: Macmillan, 1933);

Letters to the New Island, edited by Horace Reynolds (Cambridge, Mass.: Harvard University Press, 1934; London: Oxford University Press, 1970);

The Words Upon the Window Pane (Dublin: Cuala Press, 1934);

Yeats with Charles and Thea Rolleston, children of the writer T. W. Rolleston, in Dublin, 1894 (photograph by T. W. Rolleston; Collection of Lady Albery)

Wheels and Butterflies (London: Macmillan, 1934; New York: Macmillan, 1935);

The Collected Plays (London: Macmillan, 1934; New York: Macmillan, 1935);

The King of the Great Clock Tower (Dublin: Cuala Press, 1934; New York: Macmillan, 1935);

A Full Moon in March (London: Macmillan, 1935);

Dramatis Personæ (Dublin: Cuala Press, 1935);

Poems (Dublin: Cuala Press, 1935);

Dramatis Personae 1896-1902, Estrangement, The Death of Synge, The Bounty of Sweden (New York: Macmillan, 1936; London: Macmillan, 1936);

Nine One-Act Plays (London: Macmillan, 1937);

Essays, 1931 to 1936 (Dublin: Cuala Press, 1937);

The Herne's Egg: A Stage Play (London: Macmillan, 1938);

The Herne's Egg and Other Plays (New York: Macmillan, 1938);

New Poems (Dublin: Cuala Press, 1938);

The Autobiography of William Butler Yeats, Consisting of Reveries Over Childhood and Youth, The Trembling of the Veil and Dramatis Personae (New York: Macmillan, 1938); republished, with *Estrangement, The Death of Synge*, and *The*

Bounty of Sweden, as *Autobiographies* (London: Macmillan, 1955);

Last Poems and Two Plays (Dublin: Cuala Press, 1939);

On the Boiler (Dublin: Cuala Press, 1939);

Last Poems & Plays (London: Macmillan, 1940; New York: Macmillan, 1940);

If I Were Four-and-Twenty (Dublin: Cuala Press, 1940);

The Poems of W. B. Yeats, Definitive Edition, 2 volumes (London: Macmillan, 1949);

The Collected Plays of W. B. Yeats (London: Macmillan, 1952; New York: Macmillan, 1953);

The Variorum Edition of the Poems of W. B. Yeats, edited by Peter Allt and Russell K. Alspach (New York: Macmillan, 1957);

Mythologies (New York: Macmillan, 1959);

Senate Speeches, edited by Donald R. Pearce (Bloomington: Indiana University Press, 1960);

Essays and Introductions (New York: Macmillan, 1961)

Explorations (New York: Macmillan, 1962);

The Variorum Edition of the Plays of W. B. Yeats, edited by Russell K. Alspach, assisted by Catherine C. Alspach (London & New York: Macmillan, 1966);

Yeats in Boston during his 1903-1904 tour of the United States

Uncollected Prose, edited by John P. Frayne, 2 volumes (New York: Columbia University Press, 1970);

Memoirs: Autobiography, first draft, transcribed and edited by Denis Donoghue (London: Macmillan, 1972).

OTHER: *The Oxford Book of Modern Verse, 1892-1935*, edited, with an introduction, by Yeats (Oxford: Clarendon Press, 1936).

William Butler Yeats was born into an Irish-Protestant family on 13 June 1865, in Dublin, the oldest of the four children of the artist John Butler Yeats and Susan Pollexfen Yeats. While he was a young boy, Yeats's family moved to London, but he returned to Dublin when he was nineteen to attend the Metropolitan School of Art and then the Royal Hibernian Academy School. It was during this time (1884-1886) that Yeats realized his talent lay not in painting but in writing.

In London he was one of the organizers of the Rhymers' Club (1891), a group of literary figures who discussed poetry and art. He also became interested in esoteric religion, and joined the Hermetic Students of the Golden Dawn. His interest in folklore, symbol, and myth is evident from his earliest writings on, and his involvement in the Celtic Revival led to, among other things, his founding of the Irish National Theatre (1899). This was to become the Abbey Theatre, for which Yeats wrote his plays.

When he was fifty-two, Yeats married the much younger Georgiana Hyde-Lees, who encouraged his work in the occult. His famous *A Vision* (1925; revised, 1937) postulates a cyclical theory of history and a dense symbolic system that underlies much of his later writing.

Yeats received the Nobel Prize for Literature in 1923 and was made a senator of the Irish Free State (1922-1928), and his politics worked with his artistic concerns to produce some of his finest writing. Yeats died in France on 28 January 1939. His body was returned to Ireland in 1948.

Most readers think of Yeats as a poet; he himself, however, saw his work more as drama, wanting his verses "to be spoken on a stage or sung," writing for the ear rather than the eye. Besides his poems and plays he also produced a substantial body of prose works, including stories, autobiographies, introductions, letters, and critical essays, and a great deal of this work seems to be of permanent value. Near the end of his life, in an introduction written for a projected edition of his complete works, Yeats wrote of his critical prose that "much seems an evasion, a deliberate turning away." Yet what seemed evasion to Yeats seems to us more like synthesis: familiar writers and ideas about writing are shaken together and form patterns and connections hitherto not perceived. At the same time, Yeats resists the idiosyncratic in his essays, expressing the belief that "all that is personal soon rots; it must be packed in ice or salt" ("A General Introduction for My Work," written in 1937, posthumously published in *Essays and Introductions*, 1961).

This is not to suggest that Yeats's essays are coldly logical and impersonal, but rather that, when Yeats chooses to be autobiographical, he does so from artistic motives. His frequent use of the first-person pronoun led him to pronouncements on the mind of the artist and, frequently, on that mind within other artists. His essays are often hard to distinguish from his critical writings, not because he wrote essays about criticism, but because his method in both is essentially inductive, using incidents from his own life and memory to explore the creative process wherever it occurs. Added to this approach was his belief in the shifting borders of mind and memory, so that experiences and knowledge transcend an individual in the realm of symbol. To read Yeats's essays, then, is to explore the sources of symbols and images and the nature of the processes through which they become art.

The essays stand within the early tradition of the genre: they are "trials," irregular rough pieces rather than formally styled and structured arguments. Their roughness arises from a lack of preoccupation with self and an absence of rhetoric: "what moves natural men in the arts is what moves them in life, and that is, intensity of personal life, intonations that show them, in a book or a play, the strength, the essential moment of a man who would be exciting in the market or at the dispensary door" ("Prophet, Priest and King," first published in *Discoveries*, 1907). The essays frequently denounce rhetoric; Yeats attrib-

Etching of Yeats by Augustus John (by permission of the National Portrait Gallery, London)

uted his aversion to rhetoric partly to the influence of his father, John Butler Yeats, an artist and a skeptic who trusted emotions more than intellect. In *The Trembling of the Veil* (1922), the second of his *Autobiographies*, the younger Yeats recalled a dinner he attended in his twenties: he had been particularly loquacious, and on the way home his father had become angry with him for "talking for effect," leading Yeats to explain that his father "had always hated rhetoric and emphasis and had made me hate it." Traditional rhetorical devices are not in fact absent from the essays, but they are used as aids to clarity, not in the debater's manner. In the brief essay "The Musician and the Orator" (first published in *Discoveries*), Yeats encourages the writer or speaker to use "all means of persuasion–stories, laughter, tears, and but so much music as he can discover on the wings of words" over the "impersonal" sound of music itself.

Yeats's unusual prose style relies heavily on associative aspects of language and on symbolic images. Sometimes this mode takes the form of a striking simile, as when "makers of religions" are likened to "charioteers standing by deserted chariots and holding broken reins in their hands." At other times, metaphors are drawn from nature or the domestic arts: like a river, Friedrich Nietzsche's thought "flows always, though with an even more violent current, in the bed Blake's thought has worn"; Ireland's nationalism "had filled no roomy vessels with strong sweet wine, where we [artists] have filled our porcelain jars against the coming winter." Clearly the mind and ear of the poet are at work in such locutions, which gain attention without making effect an end in itself. The reader already knows about charioteers, river beds, and porcelain jars: everything is anchored in common experience. In a late essay, Yeats explained part of this method by announcing, "I am philosophical, not scientific, which means that observed facts do not mean much until I can make them part of my experience" ("Private Thoughts," in *On the Boiler*, 1939).

Another striking characteristic of Yeats's essays is his refusal to avoid generalizations which other writers might offer more cautiously. Offering them as observations rather than dogma, he presents his readers with statements such as "the arts have failed; fewer people are interested in them every generation"; or, "all art is a disengaging of a soul from place and history"; or again, "all folk literature, and all literature that keeps the folk tradition, delights in unbounded and immortal things." These are sweeping statements, and sometimes debatable ones, but they are made with the intention of enlightening readers rather than demanding belief. Richard Ellmann, in *The Identity of Yeats* (1954), has pointed out that, for Yeats, having a set of beliefs would necessitate the mind's subordination to them, whereas the mind is instead their vehicle of expression. Yeats preferred to call beliefs "ideas," and where these ideas originated remained a major preoccupation in his essays as well as in his poems.

Yeats indicated his sense of the importance of ideas in the title of his earliest collection of essays, *Ideas of Good and Evil* (1903), a title drawn from William Blake. Written between 1895 and 1903, these essays show in an early stage the stylistic and thematic range of Yeats's work. George Russell (Æ) wrote to Yeats that the book "will do more than anything you have yet written to bring the mystical interpretation of life into literature," though it might be more accurate to say that Yeats hoped for such an interpretation to penetrate all aspects of art, not only literature. To this

end, he writes on very diverse matters: Blake's illustrations to Dante; symbolism in painting, magic, and the theater; the poetry of Percy Bysshe Shelley, William Shakespeare, Blake, and William Morris.

One of the most important essays in the volume is "The Philosophy of Shelley's Poetry" (*Dome*, July 1900). It tells, as so many of Yeats's essays do, perhaps more about its author than about its subject. Fourteen years earlier, Yeats had written of the Anglo-Irish poet Sir Samuel Ferguson that his poetry went "deeper than knowledge or fancy, deeper than the intelligence which knows of difference–of the good and the evil, of the foolish and the wise, of this one and of that–to the universal emotions that have not heard of aristocracies" ("The Poetry of Sir Samuel Ferguson," *Irish Fireside*, 2 October 1886). When he came to write about Shelley, Yeats reinforced the idea of the supremacy of emotion or imagination over the intellect and saw in Shelley's concept of Intellectual Beauty a unity between living souls and "the happy dead," but suggested that Shelley's poetry may have suffered from lack of a systematic study of magic and symbol.

Yeats discusses Shelley's symbols in terms of "some great Memory that renews the world and men's thoughts age after age." Yet the idea of a "great Memory" as a source of symbols is not readily apparent in Shelley's poetry. Seizing the opportunity to expound his conviction of such a memory (a prototype of Carl Jung's idea of the collective unconscious and collective memory), Yeats insists that "our thoughts are not, as we suppose, the deep, but a little foam upon the deep." This is one of the central themes of these essays, that images and symbols derive not from an individual consciousness but from a collective mind and memory. Thus, Yeats argues, a symbol such as the tower might have grown in importance had Shelley lived longer, even as its appeal for Yeats grew so that in 1928 he published an entire volume of poems entitled *The Tower*. Such symbols were for Yeats open symbols because of their antiquity, having "numberless meanings besides the one or two the writer lays emphasis upon" so that his art "can escape from the barrenness and shallowness of a too conscious arrangement, into the abundance and depth of Nature."

In the opening essay (*Cornhill Magazine*, March 1902) of *Ideas of Good and Evil* Yeats addresses the question, "What is 'Popular Poetry'?" He indicates that it is precisely that poetry which

*Yeats, Compton Mackenzie, Augustus John, Sir Edward Lutyens (seated); G. K. Chesterton, James Stephens, and Lennox Robin-
son (standing) at the home of Oliver St. John Gogarty in 1923*

*Guests at the peacock dinner, held in honor of Wilfred Scawen Blunt at his home, Newbuildings Place, on 18 January 1914.
From left: Victor Plarr, Sturge Moore, Yeats, Blunt, Ezra Pound, Richard Aldington, and F. S. Flint (Fitzwilliam Museum)*

Yeats on the grounds of Thoor Ballylee, the tower dwelling (near Coole, Ireland) that he bought in 1916 (private collection; from Yeats, *by Frank Tuohy, 1976)*

refuses to take its place in the interrelatedness of past and present. "Popular" poetry does not then arise from the people at all, but from a single poet who does not require his readers to look anywhere else but at his poem in order to understand it. Into this category Yeats places, among others, Robert Burns and William Wadsworth Longfellow, who both used no words which "borrow their beauty from those that used them before." They lack, literally, a background, "a half-faded curtain embroidered with kings and queens . . . or else with holy letters and images." Ultimately, the true poetry of the people derives from an unwritten tradition going back to "the foundation of the world," but it has been obstructed by the values of the countinghouse, which interfere with heredity and religion, two channels that connect people to their past.

The essay on "Magic" (*Monthly Review*, September 1901) was written at about the same time. Its ideas overlap those already noted and raise a question which Yeats was to probe for the rest of his life: where does a story come from? At the beginning of "Magic" he announces the doctrines of shared minds, shared memories, and symbols which tap into both. The spiritual world thus precedes thought and becomes the source of visions and images. An artist or a peasant can invoke it and call forth its power in the physical realm: "imagination is always seeking to remake the world according to the impulses and the patterns in that Great Mind." This is how Yeats interprets much of what he calls magic: individuals can "enchant" others by casting their imaginations over the object of their enchantment, a situation experienced by anyone who has ever called someone only to discover that that person had just been thinking of the caller. This ability to influence the imagination of others has been significantly dulled by the migration of people to cities and by an educational process that has desensitized their souls; Yeats hoped to counteract this dullness with imagination and art.

Much of Yeats's attitude in these matters is linked to his early interests in Blake, theosophy, and the Order of the Golden Dawn, a hermetic society which he joined when he was twenty-five. Its members explored the origins and functions of visions and symbols such as the four elements, the rose, the sun, the moon, and geometric patterns. In a secret pamphlet written for them in 1901, Yeats reiterated that the power of Magic lies in the truth that "everything we formulate in the imagination, if we formulate it strongly enough, realises itself in the circumstances of life." This belief may partially explain why the essays have such appeal. As formulations of his imagination they held for Yeats the power to become incarnate in his generation or another. He writes from a conviction that an idea set loose by an artist may cause empires to rise or fall. By invoking a collective memory, he hopes to reconnect spiritual to concrete realities. Thus, the essays do not announce as much as explain the importance of the unseen for the seen. Though they are often personal and frequently conversational, they do not point to the one voice which utters them but to the pageant of antiquity from which they spring. Whether readers agree with Yeats or not, they feel the urgency of the arguments. Yeats, like C. S. Lewis and other modern Neoplatonists, insisted that, contrary to what the majority think, the unseen realm is more real than the material, and nature is but the "looking-glass" of art and the archetypal ideas to which art points. Yeats's poems illustrate this better than the essays, as in "Lapis Lazuli," in which life is seen to imitate art, or "Among School Children," in which the dancer and the dance are seen as one. Eventually, these ideas would lead Yeats to formulate his notion of "tragic joy" and the transfiguring power of art, but the germ of it exists in these early essays.

Two other essays in *Ideas of Good and Evil* deal with symbolism in painting and in poetry. In "Symbolism in Painting" (first published as part of the introduction to *A Book of Images*, 1898) Yeats argues for the supremacy of symbol over allegory because it is based on understanding something rather than simply knowing it, and "it entangles, in complex colours and forms, a part of the Divine Essence." He concludes by positing that the only debate worth pursuing is over that precise point: whether symbols are reflections of eternal realities "or a momentary dream." At stake is his entire life and career as an artist, and once again a reader notices the urgency of the argument, coming not from rhetorical cleverness but from the passionate core of Yeats's being.

In "The Symbolism of Poetry" (*Dome*, April 1900), Yeats underscores this attitude by claiming it is false to believe that, as some claim, artists have no "philosophy" about their work, for that is the very source of their inspiration, "calling into outer life some portion of the divine life, or of the buried reality." This is the meaning of symbol, a vehicle between inner and outer reality. Yeats repeats in a slightly different way the previous essay's idea that artists need not seek for something new: they need only "to understand and to copy" their inspiration for the outer world to see.

The essays in *Ideas of Good and Evil* indicate that what preoccupied Yeats in his mature poetry and drama was present, sometimes in simpler form but at times remarkably unchanged, in the thinking of his youth. The essays in the enlarged edition of *The Cutting of An Agate* (1919; first edition, 1912) are fewer but continue the themes of the earlier volume. Reviewing the book, T. S. Eliot said that "Mr. Yeats on any subject is a cause of bewilderment and distress" (*Athenæum*, 4 July 1919), yet found him praiseworthy despite or perhaps because of this peculiarity. In the essay titled "The Tragic Theatre" (*Mask*, October 1910) there is an instance which might represent Eliot's concern. Yeats argues for the purity of tragedy over comedy, partly because one has to bring something more to it if one wishes to find pleasure in it: tragedy "moves us by setting us to reverie, by alluring us almost to the intensity of trance," so that our minds expand, filled with images. Because tragedy is more dependent on emo-

tion and motivation than is comedy, Yeats asserts that only in comedy is character "continuously present." While one sees what Yeats is getting at, such an observation might indeed bewilder or even distress some who are not prepared to accept that Hamlet is best revealed to us in his moments of gaiety. Late in Yeats's life the concept still preoccupied and excited him. In a letter written in 1932, Yeats contrasted the choice of the saint with that of the hero: the former was comic, the latter, tragic, and he goes on to say, "live Tragically but be not deceived." The essays in this 1919 volume can sometimes, therefore, be read as blueprints, though not fixed ones, for his later poetic and dramatic structures.

Stylistically and thematically striking in this volume are the twenty-one short essays published as *Discoveries* in late 1907 (the composition date assigned them in *The Cutting of An Agate* is 1906). Some of them—for example, the short paragraph called "The Tresses of the Hair" (*Gentleman's Magazine*, November 1906) and the longer one, "A Guitar Player"—resemble parables. Some read like journal entries, others like preliminary sketches. The subjects are the arts; the treatment is exploratory—six of the pieces end with questions. Many of them are at once clearer and more lyrical than the longer essays: "she sang among people whose life had nothing it could share with an exquisite art, that should rise out of life as the blade out of the spear-shaft, a song out of the mood, the fountain from its pool, all art out of the body, laughter from a happy company." Or again, "if it be true that God is a circle whose centre is everywhere, the saint goes to the centre, the poet and artist to the ring where everything comes round again." In citing St. Bonaventure's analogy of the circle, Yeats clearly sides with the poet over the saint and prefigures his own geometric system of cycles and gyres.

In a subsequent essay in the volume, on the Irish playwright J. M. Synge, Yeats continues this idea that the artist shows us a reflection or reversed image so that we may see the familiar in a new way. The artist is not didactic, for, argues Yeats, "only that which does not condescend, which does not explain, is irresistible." Yeats sometimes violates this code in his essays, and not all of them can be called "irresistible," but most of them pass an important test: they can be read again and again with pleasure.

The volume ends with an essay on Edmund Spenser which is chronologically the earliest written (in 1902). Yeats's interest here lies mostly in

Yeats with his wife, Georgiana Hyde-Lees, and their children, Anne and Michael (private collection; from Yeats, *by Frank Tuohy, 1976)*

Spenser's use of allegory and in the ending of an age of the imagination and the beginning of the countinghouse outlook Yeats so deplored. The "sacredness of an earth" gave way to the ravishing of nature by commerce and a denial that this life is full of both physical and spiritual beauty. Clearly Yeats is speaking from his own conviction when he states that Spenser wanted men to live well "that they might live splendidly among men and be celebrated in many songs." Elsewhere Yeats elevates symbolism above allegory; here he admits both are means of communion with God, yet faults Spenser for using allegory in such a way that it often "interrupts" that communion. Nevertheless, Yeats was obviously attracted to Spenser's use of pageantry and procession, and pays him an indirect compliment by acknowledging that some of the processions "make one forget or forgive their allegory."

Many of Yeats's later essays reflect his interest in Oriental mysticism. Some are, more accurately, reviews or introductions of others' works, but all illuminate concerns which animated Yeats as much as his subjects. He had read Nietzsche's works by 1903 and had absorbed from them ideas of historical recurrence and cycles. In the introduction to *Gitanjali* (1912) by Rabindranath Tagore he brings these two strands of his thought together when he says of certain Indian writers that there is in their thought "a sense of visible beauty and meaning as though they held that doctrine of Nietzsche that we must not believe in the moral or intellectual beauty which does not sooner or later impress itself upon physical things." One sees here a repetition of Yeats's early sense of the effect that ideas have upon the material world.

In a relatively late essay on Æ, "My Friend's Book" (*Spectator*, 9 April 1932), Yeats summarized another central concept in a way that illuminates his own work since its beginnings. He is citing Æ's notion of a poet, but one can readily hear in it Yeats's own conviction about where art originates: "a poet, he contends, does not transmute into song what he has learned in experience. He reverses the order and says that the poet first imagines and that later the imagination attracts its affinities." That the imagination incarnates itself in art is at the core of Yeats's work as a poet and dramatist. The visionary, or poet, is primarily a listener and only a speaker as a result of what he has heard. Here is where poet and mystic fuse, and the effect is evident especially in the late essays of Yeats, in which one feels at times that one is eavesdropping on his private meditations: not everything is readily clear, nor does Yeats attempt to explain every point or allusion. But the result is fascinating because it draws one into intimacy with genius working out its expression. One contemporary critic rightly noted that "Mr. Yeats has a characteristic capacity for appearing to take us into his confidence. He allows us the privilege of hearing him think aloud." At times we encounter thinking that seems arbitrary or undemonstrated, such as: "though we speak of five senses there is only one, light," yet we are willing to accept them if not as truths, yet as pieces of a vision that will continue to unfold.

By 1910 Yeats had conceived his doctrine of "the Mask," formulating ideas about antitheses in the self and the world. The theory is complex, and it evolved over the rest of his life, fed by and contributing to his own work in the drama, much of which relies on the wearing of a mask or the assumption of a distinctly emblematic persona to portray its theme. In his *Autobiographies* (which are not, strictly speaking, essays, but which exhibit much of the essayist's style), Yeats calls the mask "an emotional antithesis" to the intellectual attempt to "sustain us in defeat" and concludes that "we begin to live when we have conceived life as tragedy." This is not a pessimistic view, for Yeats's sense of tragedy led to his notion of "tragic joy." Several times in his prose he wrote the same thought: "tragedy is a joy to the man who dies." Such convictions go directly against those middle-class attitudes Yeats decried so vehemently all of his life. They focus on the inner and imaginative life rather than on the material. The creation of an elaborate system which included masks, lunar phases, and historical cycles, as detailed in *A Vision* and the later poems, was his attempt at creating a mythology in which the poet and the artist rather than the scientist express a "Unity of Being." The system, he thought, allowed him greater access to the collective memory.

In *The Trembling of the Veil* (1922; enlarged, 1926) Yeats had attributed genius to knowledge which comes from beyond one's own mind, for "our images must be given to us, we cannot choose them deliberately." His essays, from the earliest to the last, seek to demonstrate this belief but do not always convince a reader that it is operational in their writing. Much of their thought appears quite deliberately organized, and some-

times the images look more and more inward instead of pointing beyond the self. Yeats himself wrote in "Private Thoughts" that he regarded statements about the world as so many "perforated Chinese ivory balls" which lie nested "one inside another, each complete." A single ivory ball might distract a reader from seeing that greater unity to which it belongs, and a single essay or poem might have the same effect. Unlike Ralph Waldo Emerson's essays, which can profitably be read singly, Yeats's essays need to be read together. Many ideas get repeated, and their cumulative effect helps one focus more clearly on ideas that may seem elusive in any given presentation.

Many of Yeats's essays were devoted to the current state of the arts in Ireland. His series known as "The Irish Dramatic Movement: 1901-1919" posthumously collected in its entirety in *Explorations* (1962), surveys the development and defends the actors and plays of the Abbey Theatre. He wrote on painting, music, and the works of other writers, but nothing he did was more controversial than his work as editor of *The Oxford Book of Modern Verse, 1892-1935* (1936). His unorthodox selection is preceded by an introduction which, if regarded as an essay, is probably his most brilliant. Yeats himself wrote that "a little of my favourite thoughts are there," and his wife concurred that "it is [the] best bit of prose I have written for years." In its thirty-five pages Yeats justifies his inclusions and omissions in the anthology and in doing so gives a clear indication of how his convictions about poetry and art had crystallized over his lifetime. He explains that the opening selection is a prose passage by Walter Pater which Yeats had rewritten as free verse to show "its revolutionary importance" in the movement against Victorianism. In discussing the shift to the poetry of the twentieth century, Yeats's prose, like his poetry, resists paraphrase. His strongest writing comes out in passages such as: "Nature, steel-bound or stone-built in the nineteenth century, became a flux where man drowned or swam; the moment had come for some poet to cry 'the flux is in my own mind.'" Again, writing about some of the more obscure modern poems, Yeats says it is "as though their words and rhythms remained gummed to one another instead of separating and falling into order." Yet he does not distance himself from these modern writers. What he does reject entirely are poems written in time of war, and this omission probably caused more criticism of the vol-

Yeats in 1936 at Casa Pastor, Palma-de-Mallorca

ume than anything else. Yeats's refusal to include war poems, however, was entirely consistent with his own ideas about the nature of poetry. He justifies his omissions because such poems were written about "passive suffering," which he declared was "not a theme for poetry." He reiterates his belief that "tragedy is a joy to the man who dies," a refrain which sounds throughout his essays, and insists that the suffering of war is not an occasion of tragic joy, only of blind suffering.

When it was published on 19 November 1936, the volume generated a controversy that assuredly contributed to its status as a best-seller (fifteen thousand copies sold in three months, according to a letter Yeats wrote in 1937). Yeats did not mind the criticisms directed against him, asserting in a letter to Dorothy Wellesley (13 August 1936) that "the more alive one is the more one is attacked," and that the vindictiveness of his critics was "a sure sign that I have some where got down to reality." The powerful voice of Yeats's introduction is full of authority and insight, regard-

less of whether one agrees with all his assertions. Stuart N. Hampshire, writing in *Oxford Magazine* (4 February 1937), went as far as to claim that the introduction more than the poems themselves was what made the anthology "magnificent and exciting"; John Hayward, however, called it "shapeless" and "unintegrated" in his review for the *Spectator* (20 November 1936). The latter comment is at least partially true of some of Yeats's earlier essays, but seems unfairly applied here, for Yeats is remarkably clear in his statements about the modern poets, sometimes even bordering on the humorous, a rare tone in Yeats's essays: "I read Gerard Hopkins with great difficulty, I cannot keep my attention fixed for more than a few minutes; I suspect a bias born when I began to think."

Yeats's last essays, in *On the Boiler* (1939), deal with, according to his preface, "whatever interests me at the moment." The title and introductory poem raise the question "why should not old men be mad?," and the book's thirty pages present a series of observations on aging men who were not possessed by imagination or energy, and their artistic counterparts. As a member of the Irish Senate for six years (1922-1928), Yeats had to deal with men whose "minds knew no play that my mind could play at," yet they and their descendants ruled the nation. In contrast he sets the "arrogance" of the Abbey Theatre playwrights, who offered not what the press demanded but what they wished to write. Yeats laments the diminishing numbers of the more intelligent and skilled families and the more rapid growth of the "unintelligent classes." He sketches his notion of a civilization's inverting itself, of opposites being everywhere, of a line's beginning with a dot, and of a new civilization's being born "not from a void, but of our own rich experience."

These writings are at once poignant and hopeful as they lament past and present errors and admonish future generations: "let schools teach what is too difficult for grown men, but is easy to the imitation or docility of childhood." By the end of his life Yeats seems to have achieved a unity of opposites within himself, an old man delighting still in the imaginative life of the child, able to see the connection and tension between public life and the artist's vision. His poem "A Prayer for Old Age" had asked God to keep him from thoughts existing "in the mind alone," to help him feel them in his bones as well. The petition of its final verse seems to have been answered in Yeats's old age. If the words are understood as Yeats meant them, they offer a vision of the old fool who is among the truly wise in this world. "I pray—for fashion's word is out / And prayer comes round again— / That I may seem, though I die old, / A foolish, passionate man."

Letters:

Letters on Poetry from W. B. Yeats to Dorothy Wellesley (London, New York & Toronto: Oxford University Press, 1940);

Some Letters from W. B. Yeats to John O'Leary and His Sister, edited by Allan Wade (New York: New York Public Library, 1953);

W. B. Yeats and T. Sturge Moore: Their Correspondence, 1901-1937, edited by Ursula Bridge (London: Routledge & Kegan Paul, 1953);

Letters of W. B. Yeats to Katharine Tynan, edited by Roger McHugh (Dublin: Clonmore & Reynolds, 1953; London: Burns, Oates & Washbourne, 1953; New York: Macmillan, 1953);

The Letters of W. B. Yeats, edited by Wade (London: Hart-Davis, 1954; New York: Macmillan, 1953);

Ah, Sweet Dancer: W. B. Yeats and Margot Ruddock, A Correspondence, edited by McHugh (London & New York: Macmillan, 1970);

The Correspondence of Robert Bridges and W. B. Yeats, edited by Richard J. Finneran (London: Macmillan, 1977);

The Collected Letters of W. B. Yeats, edited by John Kelly (Oxford: Clarendon Press, 1986).

Bibliographies:

Alphonse J. Symons, *A Bibliography of the First Editions of Books by William Butler Yeats* (London: First Edition Club, 1924);

Allan Wade, *A Bibliography of the Writings of W. B. Yeats*, third edition, revised and edited by Russell K. Alspach (London: Hart-Davis, 1968);

K. P. S. Jochum, *W. B. Yeats: A Classified Bibliography of Criticism, Including Additions to Allan Wade's Bibliography of the Writings of W. B. Yeats and a Section on the Irish Literary and Dramatic Revival* (Urbana, Ill., Chicago & London: University of Illinois Press, 1978).

Biographies:

Joseph M. Hone, *W. B. Yeats, 1865-1939* (London: Macmillan, 1942);

A. Norman Jeffares, *W. B. Yeats, Man and Poet* (New York: Barnes & Noble, 1966);

William M. Murphy, *The Yeats Family and the Pollexfens of Sligo* (Dublin: Dolmen, 1971);

Michael MacLiammoir, *W. B. Yeats and His World* (New York: Viking, 1972).

References:

Daniel Albright, *The Myth against Myth: A Study of Yeats' Imagination in Old Age* (London: Oxford University Press, 1972);

James L. Allen, *Yeats's Epitaph: A Key to Symbolic Unity in His Life and Work* (Washington: University Press of America, 1982);

Harold Bloom, *Yeats* (New York: Oxford University Press, 1970);

Denis Donoghue, *Yeats* (London: Fontana / Collins, 1971; New York: Viking, 1971);

Donoghue and J. R. Mulryne, eds., *An Honoured Guest: New Essays on W. B. Yeats* (London: Arnold, 1965);

Richard Ellmann, *The Identity of Yeats* (London: Macmillan, 1954);

Ellmann, *Yeats: The Man and the Masks* (London: Macmillan, 1949);

Edward Engelberg, *The Vast Design: Patterns in W. B. Yeats's Aesthetic* (Toronto: University of Toronto Press, 1964);

Richard Fallis, " 'I Seek an Image': The Method of Yeats's Criticism," *Modern Language Quarterly*, 37 (March 1976): 68-81;

James Hall, *The Permanence of Yeats* (New York: Collier, 1961);

A. Norman Jeffares, *The Circus Animals* (London: Macmillan, 1970);

Jeffares, *W. B. Yeats, Man and Poet* (London: Routledge, 1949; New Haven: Yale University Press, 1949);

Jeffares, ed., *W. B. Yeats: The Critical Heritage* (London: Routledge & Kegan Paul, 1977);

Jeffares and K. G. W. Cross, eds., *In Excited Reverie: A Centenary Tribute to W. B. Yeats, 1865-1939* (London: Macmillan, 1965; New York: St. Martin's, 1965);

Elizabeth Bergmann Loizeaux, *Yeats and the Visual Arts* (New Brunswick, N.J., & London: Rutgers University Press, 1986);

Balachandra Rajan, *W. B. Yeats: A Critical Introduction* (London: Hutchinson University Library, 1965);

Vinod Sena, *The Poet as Critic: W. B. Yeats on Poetry, Drama, and Tradition* (Delhi: Macmillan India, 1980); republished as *W. B. Yeats: The Poet as Critic* (London: Macmillan, 1981);

Lionel Trilling, "Yeats as Critic," in his *Speaking of Literature and Society*, edited by Diana Trilling (New York: Harcourt Brace Jovanovich, 1980);

F. A. Wilson, *Yeats's Iconography* (London: Gollancz, 1960);

John Butler Yeats, *Letters to His Son W. B. Yeats and Others, 1869-1922* (New York: Dutton, 1946).

Papers:

The National Library of Ireland in Dublin houses the largest collection of Yeats papers. Copies of its papers are at the State University of New York at Stony Brook, which also has a copy of the collection of Michael B. Yeats in Dalkey. Other collections are housed in the Berg Collection of the New York Public Library, and at Cornell University, Harvard University, the University of Chicago, and the Huntington Library.

Checklist of Further Readings

Agate, James. *Agate's Folly*. London: Chapman & Hall, 1925.

Agate. *Fantasies and Impromptus*. London: Collins, 1923.

Agate. *White Horse and Red Lion*. London: Collins, 1924.

Barron, Oswald. *Day In and Day Out*. London & New York: Cassell, 1924.

Bensusan, S. L. *Fireside Papers*. London: Epworth Press, 1946.

Bowen, Elizabeth. *Collected Impressions*. London & New York: Longmans, Green, 1950.

Bowen, Marjorie (Gabrielle Margaret Vere Campbell). *World's Wonder and Other Essays*. London: Hutchinson, 1938.

Brown, Ivor. *Masques and Phases*. London: Cobden-Sanderson, 1926.

Butchart, Isabel. *Other People's Fires*. London: Sidgwick & Jackson, 1924.

Church, Richard. *Calling for a Spade*. London: Dent, 1939.

Church. *Calm October*. London: Heinemann, 1961.

Church. *A Country Window*. London: Heinemann, 1958.

Collins, V. H., ed. *Three Centuries of English Essays*. Freeport, N.Y.: Books for Libraries Press, 1967; London: Oxford University Press, 1981.

Darwin, Sir Francis. *Springtime and Other Essays*. London: John Murray, 1920.

Davidson, John. *The Man Forbid, and Other Essays*. Boston: Ball, 1910.

Delafield, E. M. (Edmee Elizabeth Monica De La Pasture). *General Impressions*. London: Macmillan, 1933.

De La Mare, Walter. *Pleasures and Speculations*. London: Faber & Faber, 1940.

Dent, J. C., ed. *Ten Modern Essays*. London: Heinemann, 1930.

English Essays of Today. London & New York: Published for The English Association by Oxford University Press, 1936.

Feldberg, Katherine, ed. *Of Men and Manners: The Englishman and His World*. Miami: University of Miami Press, 1970.

Fleming, Peter ("Moth"). *Variety: Essays, Sketches and Stories*. London & Toronto: Cape, 1933.

Freeman, John. *English Portraits and Essays.* London: Hodder & Stoughton, 1924.

Gardiner, A. G. ("Alpha of the Plough"). *Selected Essays.* London & Toronto: Dent, 1920; New York: Dutton, 1920.

Gardiner. *Many Furrows.* London & Toronto: Dent, 1924; New York: Dutton, 1924.

Garvin, Viola Taylor ("V"). *As You See It.* London: Methuen, 1922.

Gosse, Edmund. "Essay," entry in *Encyclopædia Britannica*, eleventh edition. New York: Encyclopædia Britannica Co., 1910.

Gould, Gerald. *Refuge from Nightmare and Other Essays.* London: Methuen, 1933.

Gregory, Alyse. *Wheels on Gravel.* London: John Lane, 1938.

Hamilton, Hamish, ed. *Majority, 1931-1952.* London: Hamish Hamilton, 1952.

Harrison, Frederic. *Memories and Thoughts.* London & New York: Macmillan, 1906.

Hastings, William Thomson, ed. *Contemporary Essays.* Boston & New York: Houghton Mifflin, 1928.

Hewlett, Maurice. *In a Green Shade.* London: Bell, 1920.

Hewlett. *Last Essays.* London: Heinemann, 1924; New York: Scribners, 1924.

Hewlett. *Wiltshire Essays.* London & New York: Oxford University Press, 1921.

Inge, W. R. *Labels & Libels.* New York & London: Harper, 1929.

Inge. *A Rustic Moralist.* London: Putnam's, 1937.

Inge, ed. *The Post Victorians.* London: Ivor Nicholson & Watson, 1933.

Jepson, R. W., ed. *Essays by Modern Writers.* London & New York: Longmans, Green, 1935.

Joad, C. E. M. *Opinions.* London: Westhouse, 1945.

Joad. *More Opinions.* London: Westhouse, 1946.

Koestler, Arthur. *Drinkers of Infinity: Essays, 1955-1967.* London: Hutchinson, 1968.

Macaulay, Rose. *A Casual Commentary.* London: Methuen, 1925; New York: Boni & Liveright, 1926.

Macaulay. *Personal Pleasures.* London: Gollancz, 1935; New York: Macmillan, 1936.

Machen, Arthur. *Dog and Duck.* New York: Knopf, 1924.

Marriott, J. W., ed. *Modern Essays and Sketches.* London, Edinburgh & New York: Thomas Nelson & Sons, 1935.

Massingham, H. J. *Untrodden Ways.* London: Unwin, 1923.

McDowall, Arthur. *A Detached Observer*, edited by Mary McDowall. London: Oxford University Press, 1934.

McDowall. *Ruminations*. London: Heinemann, 1925; Boston & New York: Houghton Mifflin, 1925.

Middleton, Richard. *Monologues*. London: Unwin, 1913.

Milne, James. *A London Book Window*. London: John Lane, 1924; Freeport, N.Y.: Books for Libraries Press, 1968.

Montague, C. E. *The Right Place*. London: Chatto & Windus, 1924.

Murray, D. L. *Scenes & Silhouettes*. London: Cape, 1926.

Nevinson, H. W. *Words and Deeds*. Harmondsworth & New York: Penguin, 1942.

Norman, Sylva, ed. *Contemporary Essays 1933*. London: E. Mathews & Marrot, 1933.

Norwood, Gilbert. *Spoken in Jest*. Toronto: Macmillan, 1938.

Partridge, Eric. *Journey to the Edge of Morning*. London: Muller, 1946.

Ponsonby, Arthur. *Casual Observations*. London: Allen & Unwin, 1930.

Priestley, J. B., ed. *Essayists Past and Present*. New York: Dial, 1925; London: Herbert Jenkins, 1925.

Pritchard, F. H., ed. *Essays of To-Day*. London: Harrap, 1923; Boston: Little, Brown, 1924.

Pritchard, ed. *Essays of To-Day and Yesterday*. London: Harrap, 1926.

Pritchard, ed. *More Essays of To-Day*. London: Harrap, 1928.

Read, Herbert. *A Coat of Many Colours*. London: Routledge & Kegan Paul, 1956.

Rhondda, Margaret Haig (Thomas) Mackworth, Second Viscountess. *Notes on the Way*. London: Macmillan, 1937; Freeport, N.Y.: Books for Libraries Press, 1968.

Rhys, E., ed. *Modern English Essays*, 5 volumes. London & Toronto: Dent, 1922; New York: Dutton, 1922.

Rhys, and Vaughan, Lloyd, eds. *A Century of English Essays*. London: Everyman's Library, 1913; New York: Dutton, 1913.

Runciman, James. *Side Lights*, edited by John F. Runciman. London: Unwin, 1893.

Saintsbury, George. *The Collected Essays and Papers of George Saintsbury*, 4 volumes. London & Toronto: Dent / New York: Dutton, 1923-1924.

Sharp, William ("Fiona MacLeod"). *At the Turn of the Year*. Edinburgh: Turnbull & Spears, 1913.

Sharp. *Where the Forest Murmurs*. New York: Scribners, 1906.

Spectator Harvest, with a foreword by Wilson Harris. London: Hamish Hamilton, 1952.

Squire, J. C. *Essays at Large, by Solomon Eagle.* London & New York: Hodder & Stoughton, 1922.

Squire. *Life and Letters; Essays by J. C. Squire.* New York: Doran, 1921.

Street, G. S. *A Book of Essays.* Westminster: Constable, 1902; New York: Dutton, 1903.

Street. *People and Questions.* London: Secker, 1910.

Swinnerton, Frank. *The Georgian Scene: A Literary Panorama.* New York: Farrar & Rinehart, 1934. Republished as *The Georgian Literary Scene: A Panorama.* London & Toronto: Heinemann, 1935.

Tanner, W. M. and D. Barrett, eds. *Modern Familiar Essays.* Boston: Little, Brown, 1930.

Thomas, Gilbert Oliver. *Calm Weather.* London: Chapman & Hall, 1930.

Walker, Hugh. *The English Essay and Essayist.* London & Toronto: Dent / New York: Dutton, 1915.

Waugh, Evelyn. *A Little Order,* edited by Donat Gallagher. London: Eyre Methuen, 1977; Boston: Little, Brown, 1981.

West, Rebecca. *The Strange Necessity: Essays and Reviews.* London: Cape, 1928; Garden City, N.Y.: Doubleday, Doran, 1928.

Woolf, Leonard S. and Virginia, eds. *The Hogarth Essays.* Freeport, N.Y.: Books for Libraries Press, 1970.

Contributors

Nancy A. Barta-Smith .... *University of Iowa*
Robert Beum .... *Saskatoon, Saskatchewan*
G. K. Blank .... *University of Victoria*
Robert L. Calder .... *University of Saskatchewan*
Roger W. Calkins .... *Mount Allison University*
Kathryn Chittick .... *Trent University*
Diane Tolomeo Edwards .... *University of Victoria*
Averil Gardner .... *Memorial University of Newfoundland*
Philip Gardner .... *Memorial University of Newfoundland*
James Hepburn .... *Sussex, England*
Peter Hinchcliffe .... *University of St. Jerome's College*
Peter Hunt .... *Springwood, New South Wales, Australia*
Christopher Kent .... *University of Saskatchewan*
Edward Krickel .... *University of Georgia*
Thomas A. Kuhlman .... *Creighton University*
Charles Lock .... *University of Toronto*
Rita Malenczyk .... *New York University*
Paul J. Marcotte .... *University of Ottawa*
J. M. McEwen .... *Brock University*
D. E. Parker .... *University of Toronto*
David Rampton .... *University of Ottawa*
Carl Rapp .... *University of Georgia*
Roy Scheele .... *Doane College*
Donald E. Stanford .... *Louisiana State University*
J. H. Stape .... *Université de Limoges*
Warren Stevenson .... *University of British Columbia*
Michael S. Tait .... *University of Toronto*
Frank M. Tierney .... *University of Ottawa*
Alan Thomas .... *University of Toronto*
Keith Wilson .... *University of Ottawa*
David Wright .... *University of Waterloo*

Cumulative Index

Dictionary of Literary Biography, Volumes 1-98
Dictionary of Literary Biography Yearbook, 1980-1989
Dictionary of Literary Biography Documentary Series, Volumes 1-7

Cumulative Index

DLB before number: *Dictionary of Literary Biography,* Volumes 1-98
Y before number: *Dictionary of Literary Biography Yearbook,* 1980-1989
DS before number: *Dictionary of Literary Biography Documentary Series,* Volumes 1-7

A

B

C

Cumulative Index

D

E

L

Cumulative Index

Q

R

S

W

Y

Z

(Continued from front endsheets)

71: *American Literary Critics and Scholars, 1880-1900*, edited by John W. Rathbun and Monica M. Grecu (1988)

72: *French Novelists, 1930-1960*, edited by Catharine Savage Brosman (1988)

73: *American Magazine Journalists, 1741-1850*, edited by Sam G. Riley (1988)

74: *American Short-Story Writers Before 1880*, edited by Bobby Ellen Kimbel, with the assistance of William E. Grant (1988)

75: *Contemporary German Fiction Writers*, Second Series, edited by Wolfgang D. Elfe and James Hardin (1988)

76: *Afro-American Writers, 1940-1955*, edited by Trudier Harris (1988)

77: *British Mystery Writers, 1920-1939*, edited by Bernard Benstock and Thomas F. Staley (1988)

78: *American Short-Story Writers, 1880-1910*, edited by Bobby Ellen Kimbel, with the assistance of William E. Grant (1988)

79: *American Magazine Journalists, 1850-1900*, edited by Sam G. Riley (1988)

80: *Restoration and Eighteenth-Century Dramatists*, First Series, edited by Paula R. Backscheider (1989)

81: *Austrian Fiction Writers, 1875-1913*, edited by James Hardin and Donald G. Daviau (1989)

82: *Chicano Writers*, First Series, edited by Francisco A. Lomelí and Carl R. Shirley (1989)

83: *French Novelists Since 1960*, edited by Catharine Savage Brosman (1989)

84: *Restoration and Eighteenth-Century Dramatists*, Second Series, edited by Paula R. Backscheider (1989)

85: *Austrian Fiction Writers After 1914*, edited by James Hardin and Donald G. Daviau (1989)

86: *American Short-Story Writers, 1910-1945*, First Series, edited by Bobby Ellen Kimbel (1989)

87: *British Mystery and Thriller Writers Since 1940*, First Series, edited by Bernard Benstock and Thomas F. Staley (1989)

88: *Canadian Writers, 1920-1959*, Second Series, edited by W. H. New (1989)

89: *Restoration and Eighteenth-Century Dramatists*, Third Series, edited by Paula R. Backscheider (1989)

90: *German Writers in the Age of Goethe, 1789-1832*, edited by James Hardin and Christoph E. Schweitzer (1989)

91: *American Magazine Journalists, 1900-1960*, First Series, edited by Sam G. Riley (1990)

92: *Canadian Writers, 1890-1920*, edited by W. H. New (1990)

93: *British Romantic Poets, 1789-1832*, First Series, edited by John R. Greenfield (1990)

94: *German Writers in the Age of Goethe: Sturm und Drang to Classicism*, edited by James Hardin and Christoph E. Schweitzer (1990)

95: *Eighteenth-Century British Poets*, First Series, edited by John Sitter (1990)

96: *British Romantic Poets, 1789-1832*, Second Series, edited by John R. Greenfield (1990)

97: *German Writers from the Enlightenment to Sturm und Drang, 1720-1764*, edited by James Hardin and Christoph E. Schweitzer (1990)

98: *Modern British Essayists*, First Series, edited by Robert Beum (1990)

Documentary Series

1: *Sherwood Anderson, Willa Cather, John Dos Passos, Theodore Dreiser, F. Scott Fitzgerald, Ernest Hemingway, Sinclair Lewis*, edited by Margaret A. Van Antwerp (1982)